The role of ecosystems in disaster risk red

**UNITED NATIONS
UNIVERSITY**

UNU-EHS

Institute for Environment
and Human Security

PEDRR
Ecosystems for Adaptation
and Disaster Risk Reduction

The role of ecosystems in disaster risk reduction

Edited by Fabrice G. Renaud, Karen Sudmeier-Rieux and Marisol Estrella

United Nations
University Press

TOKYO · NEW YORK · PARIS

© United Nations University, 2013

The views expressed in this publication are those of the authors and do not necessarily reflect the views of the United Nations University.

United Nations University Press
United Nations University, 53-70, Jingumae 5-chome,
Shibuya-ku, Tokyo 150-8925, Japan
Tel: +81-3-5467-1212   Fax: +81-3-3406-7345
E-mail: sales@unu.edu   General enquiries: press@unu.edu
http://www.unu.edu

United Nations University Office at the United Nations, New York
2 United Nations Plaza, Room DC2-2062, New York, NY 10017, USA
Tel: +1-212-963-6387   Fax: +1-212-371-9454
E-mail: unuony@unu.edu

United Nations University Press is the publishing division of the United Nations University.

Cover design by Maria Paul
Cover photograph by Michael Crozier

Printed in the United States of America for the Americas and Asia
Printed in the United Kingdom for Europe, Africa and the Middle East

ISBN 978-92-808-1221-3
e-ISBN 978-92-808-7190-6

Library of Congress Cataloging-in-Publication Data

The role of ecosystems in disaster risk reduction / edited by Fabrice G. Renaud, Karen Sudmeier-Rieux and Marisol Estrella.
    pages   cm
 Includes bibliographical references and index.
 ISBN 978-9280812213 (pbk.)
 1. Hazardous geographic environments. 2. Natural disasters – Environmental aspects. 3. Ecosystem management. 4. Emergency management. 5. Ecological disturbances. I. Renaud, Fabrice G. II. Sudmeier-Rieux, Karen. III. Estrella, Marisol.
 GF85.R65   2013
 363.34'72 — dc23   2013002399

Endorsements

"The application of disaster risk reduction has saved millions of lives and helped communities globally. But the ecosystems on which communities depend upon for their protection, economic well-being and recovery have, until now, been largely ignored in disaster risk reduction. Incorporating ecosystems into disaster risk reduction can save lives, aid recovery and help build a more resilient and secure planet for all. This timely book is an essential tool for policymakers, scientists, economists, sociologists, and practitioners on why and how to integrate ecosystems into disaster risk reduction. Scientific studies have repeatedly confirmed the role of healthy ecosystems in providing resilience against disasters; and they have demonstrated how environmental degradation contributes to more severe disasters including droughts, floods, and storm surges. A key challenge is how to integrate this knowledge into policy and planning. Multidisciplinary approaches that combine ecology and engineering, science with sociology and economics have to be implemented. This book provides a sobering evaluation of the consequences of ignoring ecosystems in disaster risk reduction. But it also offers a range of well-considered and practical solutions which could be used in many existing regulations, policies and risk reduction activities."

Deborah Brosnan, Environment and Policy Scientist, University of California, Davis, One Health Institute

"In 2004, the earth shook, the waters rose, and the Indian Ocean tsunami changed the world. Almost a quarter of a million coastal dwellers died that day. Several years later, the earth shook again, this time in Haiti, and a disturbingly similar number of people lost their lives. In both cases, sustainable, healthy ecosystems could have substantially mitigated these disasters.

Recent disasters in Japan, the US East Coast, and several in SE Asia including Thailand and the Philippines, have led to a simple yet unsolvable question: How can the world's most vulnerable populations reduce the risk posed by natural hazards?

The Role of Ecosystems in Disaster Risk Reduction brings together the world's experts on how the natural environment has evolved tools to buffer against natural hazards in real, sustainable and cost effective ways. From coastal ecosystems that buffer large waves while providing valuable services to Indian Ocean communities to protective services that forests provide in the Swiss Alps, this book is a valuable contribution showing how environmentally and economically sustainable solutions can provide real benefits to exposed populations and resources."

Brian G. McAdoo, College Rector, Professor of Science, Yale-NUS College

"Why do ecosystems matter in disaster risk reduction? This book meets an urgent need. Intuitively we understand that working with and not against nature will help in protecting us from impacts of extreme natural events, but evidence has been lacking regarding the effectiveness and efficiency of such measures, particularly as alternatives to or in combination with engineered solutions. This rich collection of research findings and tested practices takes us around the globe, from coasts to forests, from agricultural landscapes to protected areas, from cities to mountains. It addresses conflicts between socio-economic development and environmental concerns, taken to its extreme in Cape Town where policymakers and planners have had to overcome the legacy of apartheid to find a sustainable trajectory. And it gives readers an array of methods and instruments to help overcome the sector and disciplinary stovepipes that often stand in the way of the holistic approaches needed to meet and reconcile multiple objectives: protecting vulnerable people and assets, halting the erosion of biodiversity and making sustainable use of our natural resource base. Those looking for the state of the art in ecosystem-based disaster risk reduction now know where to go."

Johan Schaar, Co-Director, Vulnerability and Adaptation Initiative, World Resources Institute

"With the human and economic losses of disaster events projected to grow, and with two-thirds of global disaster losses being caused by hydro-meteorological events, this is a very timely compilation of the evidence needed to link up ecosystem management with disaster risk management as mutually reinforcing initiatives. It comes at a time when the post-2015 development paradigm and framework for disaster risk management are on the drawing boards. It will surely go a long way in informing the convergence of policies and benchmarks for ecosystem management as an integral aspect of climate and disaster risk management, to ensure near-term development gains and long-term climate and disaster resilience.

An extremely timely and comprehensive publication, a game-changer in the approach to natural resource management for sustainable development – and for climate and disaster resilience."

Prashant Singh, Team Leader, Partnerships and Governance, Global Facility for Disaster Reduction and Recovery (GFDRR) at The World Bank

"How do ecosystems relate to disasters? How do ecosystems contribute to disaster risk reduction (DRR)? This book gives us answers to these questions.

It is timely to address DRR-related coastal issues and water resources management, which are inevitable to countries being prone to water-related disasters such as storm surges and tsunamis as well as floods, droughts and erosion. Forestry and vegetation cover are also dealt with in relation to land management and landslides. These are serious problems which many parts of the world are facing in the twenty-first century under the pressure of sustainable development and survivable societies. Future perspectives are also given in concluding chapters.

This book will be of interest to disaster managers and policymakers, eco-hydrologists, coastal and water resources planners, engineers and managers, research scientists and students, international donor agencies, and many professionals from NGOs and the media."

Kaoru Takara, Disaster Prevention Research Institute, Kyoto University, Japan

Contents

Figures

Tables

Boxes

Contributors

Chris Baker is head of the Wetlands and Water Resources Management programme at Wetlands International.

Srimal Bandara is a graduate of the University of Moratuwa, Sri Lanka, and presently employed by the Sri Lanka Ports Authority.

Michael W. Beck is lead scientist for the Global Marine Team of The Nature Conservancy and an adjunct faculty member at the University of California, Santa Cruz, USA. He has been a visiting Pew Marine Fellow at the United Nations University Institute for Environment and Human Security.

Kirsten Carey is a Master's student on the Programme in Globalization, Environment and Social Change, Department of Human Geography, Stockholm University, Sweden.

Alvin Chandra is an Environment Officer at the Environment Protection Authority, Tasmania, Australia, and Vice-President of the Erasmus Mundus Students and Alumni Association, Oceania Regional Chapter. He also co-leads the Disaster Risk Reduction Group for the Commission on Ecosystem Management of the International Union for Conservation of Nature.

Bruno Chatenoux is a civil engineer and geologist involved as a geographic information system expert with the Global Change and Vulnerability Unit at the United Nations Environment Programme, GRID-Geneva.

Darryl Colenbrander obtained an MSc in Integrated Coastal Management through the Oceanographic Research Institute and the University of KwaZulu-Natal, South Africa. Since 2008 he has been employed by the City of Cape Town as the Environmental Resource Management Department's Coastal

Coordinator, where his current focal point is the development of city-wide strategic coastal planning and regulatory mechanisms.

James Dalton is the Coordinator of Global Initiatives in the Water Programme of the International Union for Conservation of Nature (IUCN). He is based at the IUCN headquarters in Gland, Switzerland.

Yaella Depietri is a PhD student at the Institut de Ciència i Tecnologia Ambientals, Universitat Autònoma de Barcelona, Spain, and at the United Nations University Institute for Environment and Human Security (UNU-EHS) in Bonn, Germany.

Marc-Henri Derron is a lecturer at the Centre for Research on Terrestrial Environment at the University of Lausanne, Switzerland. He holds a PhD in environmental geology and has worked for six years in the Geohazards group of the Geological Survey of Norway. His present research focuses on active remote sensing for geohazards assessment, landslide investigation, monitoring and early warning.

Luuk Dorren specializes in natural hazards and protection forests. He has a PhD in physical geography. Since 2008, he has been working for the Swiss Federal Office for the Environment, co-leading the hazard and risk assessment of the national road network. In addition, he teaches mountain risk engineering at the University of Natural Resources and Life Sciences, Vienna, Austria.

Nigel Dudley is Industry Fellow, School of Geography, Planning and Environmental Management at the

University of Queensland, Australia, and works with Equilibrium Research in the UK. His work focuses principally on the integration of protected areas into wider environmental management strategies.

Marisol Estrella is Programme Coordinator for the Disaster Risk Reduction Unit of the United Nations Environment Programme Post-Conflict and Disaster Management Branch based in Geneva, Switzerland.

Zach Ferdaña is the Senior Marine Conservation Planner for the Global Marine Team of The Nature Conservancy.

Harindra J.S. Fernando is currently the Wayne and Diana Murdy Endowed Professor of Engineering and Geosciences at the University of Notre Dame, USA. During 1984–2009, he was affiliated with the Department of Mechanical and Aerospace Engineering at Arizona State University, USA. In 1994 he was appointed the founding Director of the Center for Environmental Fluid Dynamics at Arizona State University, a position he held till 2009 while holding a co-appointment with the School of Sustainability, Arizona State University.

Madeleine Fogde is Senior Programme Manager for the Swedish International Agricultural Network Initiative and the Integrated Sustainable Sanitation Programme at Stockholm Environment Institute, Sweden.

Urbano Fra Paleo is Associate Professor of Human Geography at the University of Santiago de Compostela, Spain, and a Visiting Professor at the University for Peace, Costa Rica. He is a member of the Scientific Committee of the Integrated Risk Governance Project and has been a Research Associate at the University of Denver, USA, and a Fellow of the American Geographical Society Library. He is editor of *Building Safer Communities: Governance, Spatial Planning and Responses to Natural Hazards* (IOS Press, 2009).

Daniel A. Friess is an Assistant Professor in the Department of Geography, National University of Singapore. His research interests concern physical-ecological linkages in mangrove forests and how they influence ecosystem stability in the face of threats such as sea level rise.

Romana Gaspirc is a Technical Officer within the Wetlands and Water Resources Management programme at Wetlands International.

Ben Gilmer is a geographer for the Global Marine Team of The Nature Conservancy.

Thomas Glade is leading the Working Group on Geomorphic Systems and Risk Research and Head of the Department of Geography and Regional Research at the University of Vienna, Austria. His research interests cover geomorphic processes, human impacts on the environment, and natural hazard and risk analysis, including studies on vulnerability.

Lorenzo Guadagno is a Knowledge Management Officer at the Ecosystems and Livelihoods Adaptation Network, Gland,

Switzerland. He has been working with the Secretariat of the International Strategy for Disaster Reduction and the International Union for Conservation of Nature and is a member of its Commission on Ecosystem Management.

Anil Kumar Gupta is Associate Professor at the Government of India's National Institute of Disaster Management and Director of the Indo-German Programme on Environmental Knowledge for Disaster Risk Management. His areas include legal and policy framework, risk and vulnerability analysis, environmental impact assessment, human resource planning and mainstreaming disaster risk reduction.

Sam S.L. Hettiarachchi is Professor of Civil Engineering of the University of Moratuwa, Sri Lanka, and serves as Chairman of the Working Group on Risk Assessment and Reduction of the UNESCO/Intergovernmental Oceanographic Commission Intergovernmental Coordination Group for the establishment of the Indian Ocean Tsunami Warning System.

Mark Hoover is currently a Research Associate at Yale University, USA. His contributions to this book were undertaken while he was a Research Associate at the Center for Land Use Education and Research at the University of Connecticut, USA.

Michel Jaboyedoff is a geologist with degrees in physics and a PhD degree in clay mineralogy. Since 2005, he has been a full professor at the University of Lausanne, Switzerland, focusing his research on natural hazards and related risks. He is involved in several risk management projects around the world (Argentina, Canada, Nepal, Norway, Switzerland) and is part of several European FP7 Projects and Swiss National Science Foundation Projects.

Stéphanie Jaquet has a Master's degree from the University of Lausanne, Switzerland, in environmental geosciences, with a focus on the analysis, monitoring and representation of natural hazards during which she specialized in landslide risk management and community forestry in Nepal. Currently she is a Project Officer at the Global Risk Forum in Davos, Switzerland.

Ilan Kelman is a Senior Research Fellow at the Center for International Climate and Environmental Research – Oslo, Norway. His main research interests are island sustainability and disaster diplomacy.

Ritesh Kumar is a Conservation Programme Manager at Wetlands International South Asia and a member of the Scientific and Technical Review Panel of the Ramsar Convention.

Carmen Lacambra is the Director of Environmental Services at Grupo Laera, a ThinkTank Consultancy Team based in Bogotá, Colombia, and with projects in Central and South America. Most of the projects Carmen has been involved in focus on climate change adaptation strategies and disaster management plans for several cities in the region

and for different sectors of the economy, as well as the incorporation of natural ecosystems in planning, adaptation and disaster risk management initiatives.

Luis Macario has an MSc in rural development from Eduardo Mondlane University, Mozambique. He is currently working as a water and sanitation specialist for the Water and Sanitation Program of the World Bank in Mozambique.

Kathy MacKinnon is a Vice-Chair of the World Commission on Protected Areas of the International Union for Conservation of Nature, with responsibility for the Convention on Biological Diversity and Climate Change. Previously she was Lead Biodiversity Specialist at the World Bank, where she worked on biodiversity conservation and ecosystem-based approaches to climate change.

Stavros Mavrogenis is a researcher at the European Centre for Environmental Research and Training, Panteion University of Athens, Greece. His main field of interest is climate change adaptation law and policy for Small Island Developing States (SIDS), disaster risk reduction in the Global South and disaster diplomacy.

Imen Meliane is the International Marine Policy Director for The Nature Conservancy.

Iris Möller is Deputy Director, Cambridge Coastal Research Unit, Department of Geography, and College Lecturer in Physical Geography, Fitzwilliam College, University of Cambridge, UK. Her research focuses on quantifying the coastal landform dynamics and the sea defence service provided by coastal environments over a range of time-scales and in varying environmental settings.

Radhika Murti is the Programme Coordinator for Disaster Risk Reduction at the International Union for Conservation of Nature. Her work focuses on the development and implementation of global initiatives on ecosystem-based disaster risk reduction.

Sreeja S. Nair is Assistant Professor at the Government of India's National Institute of Disaster Management (NIDM) and Coordinator of the Indo-German Programme on Environmental Knowledge for Disaster Risk Management. She is in charge of the Geoinformatics facility at NIDM. She coordinates research projects on risk and vulnerability analysis, disaster databases, and climate change.

N.A. Kithsiri Nandasena is a graduate of the University of Mortauwa, Sri Lanka, and currently reading for a PhD degree at the University of Saitama, Japan.

Sarah Newkirk is California Coastal Program Director for The Nature Conservancy and previously was the New York Coastal Program Director.

Gregg Oelofse is the Head of Environmental Policy and Strategy at the City of Cape Town, South Africa. He has a Master's degree in Conservation Biology and has been working as an environmental professional for 18 years. His interests include integrated coastal management, ecosystem services,

adaptation, urban biodiversity conservation and environmental fiscal reform mechanisms.

Maria Papathoma-Koehle is a postdoctoral researcher in the Department of Geography and Regional Research at the University of Vienna, Austria. Her research focuses on physical vulnerability to alpine hazards.

Pascal Peduzzi is an environmental scientist. He is head of the Global Change and Vulnerability Unit at the United Nations Environment Programme, GRID-Geneva.

Penny Price is Climate Adaptation lead for the Western Cape Government, South Africa, Chair of the Provincial Strategic Outcome 7 Working Group on Climate Adaptation, and a member of South Africa's National Climate Adaptation Technical Group.

George T. Raber is an Associate Professor in the Department of Geography and Geology at the University of Southern Mississippi, USA.

A. Harsha R. Ratnasooriya is a Senior Lecturer in Civil Engineering at the University of Moratuwa, Sri Lanka. He has been engaged in research into bioshields against coastal hazards.

Fabrice G. Renaud is Head of the Environmental Vulnerability and Ecosystem Services section of the United Nations University Institute for Environment and Human Security (UNU-EHS), Bonn, Germany. He is responsible for carrying out research and developing concepts and projects dealing with the environmental dimension of vulnerability, with the resilience of social-ecological systems to external shocks, with water pollution, and with land degradation processes, particularly in the context of climate change.

Nina Saalismaa is an independent environmental consultant specializing in ecosystem-based disaster risk reduction.

Saman P. Samarawickrama is Professor of Civil Engineering at the University of Moratuwa, Sri Lanka. His research covers a wide portfolio in coastal and harbour engineering.

Christine C. Shepard is a marine scientist with the Global Marine Team of The Nature Conservancy.

Tom Spencer is Director, Cambridge Coastal Research Unit, Department of Geography, and Reader in Coastal Ecology and Geomorphology, University of Cambridge, UK. He is author (with H.A. Viles) of *Coastal Problems: Geomorphology, Ecology and Society at the Coast* (Edward Arnold, 1995) and (with O. Slaymaker) of *Physical Geography and Global Environmental Change* (Longman, 1998). In 2005 he edited (with C.A. Fletcher) *Flooding and Environmental Challenges for Venice and Its Lagoon: State of Knowledge* (Cambridge University Press).

Sue Stolton is a partner in Equilibrium Research, UK, and a member of the World Commission on Protected Areas of the International Union for Conservation of Nature. Her work focuses on protected areas and broad-scale approaches to conservation.

Jeffrey D. Stone is a project manager and senior geospatial analyst for the Science Services Program at the Association of State Floodplain Managers.

Karen Sudmeier-Rieux holds a PhD from the Center for Research on Terrestrial Environment at the University of Lausanne, Switzerland, where she is currently a researcher and a consultant on issues related to the environment and disaster risk reduction. She is thematic lead on disaster risk reduction for the International Union for Conservation of Nature (IUCN) Commission on Ecosystem Management and has published a number of IUCN publications and articles on ecosystems, livelihoods and disaster risk reduction.

Sakhile Tsotsobe is Coastal Coordinator in the City of Cape Town's Sport, Recreation and Amenities Department, responsible for developing and managing coastal management programmes related to the use of beach amenities. He is part of a team that develops adaptation strategies for climate change and sea level rise risk. He previously worked as a biological oceanographer at South Africa's Department of Environmental Affairs.

Pieter van Eijk is a Senior Technical Officer within the Wetlands and Livelihoods programme at Wetlands International.

Adonis Velegrakis is Professor in the Department of Marine Sciences, School of Environment, University of the Aegean, Greece. He has an MSc and a PhD in Oceanography and an LLM in Environmental Law and Law of the Sea. His areas of expertise include beach erosion and vulnerability to climatic changes and extreme events, marine and coastal environmental impact assessments and coastal morphodynamics.

André Wehrli is an expert in protection forests and natural hazards. He holds a PhD in natural sciences from the Swiss Federal Institute of Technology in Zurich and has been working for the Swiss Federal Office for the Environment since 2005. In addition, he works as a freelance consultant on disaster risk reduction for Swiss Humanitarian Aid.

Adam W. Whelchel is Director of Science for the Connecticut Chapter of The Nature Conservancy. He is project manager for the New York and Connecticut Coastal Resilience Program.

Foreword: Why do ecosystems matter in disaster reduction?

Margareta Wahlström, Special Representative of the Secretary-General for Disaster Risk Reduction and Head of the UN Office for Disaster Risk Reduction

The current global framework for disaster risk reduction, the Hyogo Framework for Action, was agreed in Kobe, Japan, in January 2005 as the world struggled to come to terms with the loss of life and devastation caused by the Asian tsunami of a few weeks earlier. Sustainable ecosystems and environmental management were placed top of the list under the Hyogo Framework's Priority for Action No. 4 on reducing underlying risk factors, and a few months later Hurricane Katrina engulfed New Orleans in a disaster that was both predictable and predicted. As is often the case following major disaster events, there was much focus on what should have been done to strengthen the city's physical infrastructure, such as improving the levee and drainage systems or building protection walls.

There is, of course, a very important but less appreciated "resilience gap" that faced New Orleans and the many small towns and villages that bore the brunt of the Asian tsunami, and that was the deterioration of their natural defences. In other words, there was a general failure to appreciate why ecosystems matter in disaster risk reduction and how they help to build a community's resilience to disaster events. In the case of New Orleans, economic development prior to Katrina had taken place at the expense of losing 4,800 km^2 of wetlands in the Mississippi Delta, which took thousands of years to accumulate and helped to dissipate the energy of storm surges in centuries past.

If one considers that floods disrupt the lives of over 100 million people every year, then it seems obvious that ecosystems have a role to play in limiting the impacts on our built environment and that we cannot simply pretend we can avoid harm by constructing more dykes, dams, spillways and other built structures. The proper use and preservation of natural and constructed wetlands not only help withstand storm surges but also reduce the volumes of rainwater runoff in urban areas. A key benefit of wetlands and environmental buffers is to act as flood retention basins and reduce flooding in built-up areas. One statistic worth pondering in relation to the value of well-managed ecosystems is that 1.3 million trees can catch 7 billion m^3 of rainwater per year, which amounts to a major reduction in stormwater drainage.

This is a welcome and timely publication that will make a major contribution towards shaping the successor to the Hyogo Framework for Action, which expires in 2015. It is also a forceful and eloquent reminder that environmental management is an essential part of best practice in disaster risk reduction.

Acknowledgements

We are extremely grateful to the following experts who have volunteered their time and knowledge to peer-review the chapters in this book. Alphabetically, our sincere thanks go to Sálvano Briceño (Science Committee, Integrated Research on Disaster Risk, Switzerland), George Buoma (Environmental Policy Advisor, USA), Jane Gibbs (Coast and Flood Policy, New South Wales Government, Australia), Bruce Glavovic (Resource & Environmental Planning Programme, Massey University, New Zealand), Frank Graf (Institute for Snow and Avalanche Research – WSL/SLF, Switzerland), Dennis Hamro-Drotz (UNEP Post-conflict and Disaster Management Branch, Switzerland), Marcus Kaplan (German Development Institute, Germany), Brian G. McAdoo (Department of Earth Science and Geography, Vassar College, USA, and Yale-NUS College, Singapore), Jeffrey A. McNeely (Cornell University, USA), Padma Narsey Lal (Ecosystem Sciences, Commonwealth Scientific and Industrial Research Organisation, Australia), Hassan Partow (UNEP Post-conflict and Disaster Management Branch, Switzerland), Jyotiraj Patra (Risk, Resources, Resilience and Global Sustainability – R3GS, India), Jonathan Randall (Environmental and Social Performance, Millennium Challenge Corporation, USA), Torsten Schlurmann (Franzius-Institute for Hydraulic, Waterways and Coastal Engineering, Leibniz Universität Hannover, Germany), Rajib Shaw (Graduate School of Global Environmental Studies, Kyoto University, Japan), David C. Smith (Institute of Sustainable Development, University of the West Indies, Jamaica), Keshar Man Sthapit (HELVETAS Swiss Intercooperation, Afghanistan), Alexia

Stokes (Institut National de Recherche Agronomique, France), Joerg Szarzynski (United Nations University Institute for Environment and Human Security, Germany), Paul Venton (International Development Consultant: Disasters, Climate Change and Environment, USA), Torsten Welle (United Nations University Institute for Environment and Human Security, Germany) and Bettina Wolfgramm (Centre for Development and Environment, University of Bern, Switzerland, and University of Central Asia, Bishkek, Kyrgyzstan). We are also grateful to Philipp Koch and Hannes Etter from the United Nations University Institute for Environment and Human Security for their support during the preparation of this book.

Abbreviations

ADV	Acoustic Doppler Velocity
AsgiSA	Accelerated and Shared Growth Initiative for South Africa
CAMP	coastal area management plan
CARICOM	Caribbean Community
CbA	community-based adaptation
CBA	cost–benefit analysis
CBD	Convention on Biological Diversity
CCA	climate change adaptation
CCSR	Center for Climate Systems Research
CCT	City of Cape Town
CDB	Caribbean Development Bank
CEA	country environmental analysis
CENOE	Centro Nacional Operativo de Emergência [National Emergency Operations Centre], Mozambique
CF	community forest
CFUG	Community Forest User Group
CRED	Centre for Research on the Epidemiology of Disasters
CRiSTAL	Community-based Risk Screening Tool – Adaptation and Livelihoods
Defra	Department for Environment, Food and Rural Affairs, UK
DIA	disaster impact assessment
DMP	Disaster Management Plan
DoF	Department of Forests, Nepal
DRM	disaster risk management
DRR	disaster risk reduction
EbA	ecosystem-based adaptation

Eco-DRR	ecosystem-based disaster risk reduction
EIA	environmental impact assessment
EM-DAT	Emergency Events Database
FECOFUN	Federation of Community Forest Users, Nepal
FEMA	Federal Emergency Management Agency, USA
GCM	Global Circulation Model
GDP	gross domestic product
GIS	Geographic Information System
GRRT	Green Recovery and Reconstruction Toolkit
HAZUS-MH	Hazards U.S. – Multi-Hazards tool
HFA	Hyogo Framework for Action
ICZM	integrated coastal zone management
INGC	Instituto Nacional de Gestão das Calamidades [National Disaster Management Institute], Mozambique
IPCC	Intergovernmental Panel on Climate Change
ISDR	International Strategy for Disaster Reduction
IUCN	International Union for Conservation of Nature
IWRM	integrated water resources management
LiDAR	Light Detection and Ranging
MEOW	Maximum Envelopes of Water
MERET	Managing Environmental Resources to Enable Transitions to More Sustainable Livelihoods
MESCAL	Mangrove Ecosystems for Climate Change Adaptation and Livelihoods
MSL	mean sea level
MSV	Many Strong Voices
NDMA	National Disaster Management Authority, Pakistan
NEP	National Estuary Program, USA
NGO	non-governmental organization
NOAA-CSC	National Oceanic and Atmospheric Administration's Coastal Services Center
NWP	Nairobi Work Programme
OECD	Organisation for Economic Co-operation and Development
PAARSS	Projecto de Abastecimento de Água Rural e Saneamento em Sofala [Programme for Rural Water Supply and Sanitation]
PARPA	Plano de Acção para a Redução da Pobreza Absoluta [National Poverty Reduction Strategy]
PEDRR	Partnership for Environment and Disaster Risk Reduction
PIOJ	Planning Institute of Jamaica
PROFOR	Programa de Repoblamiento Forestal
REA	rapid environmental impact assessment
RiVAMP	Risk and Vulnerability Assessment Methodology Development Project
SBSTA	Subsidiary Body for Scientific and Technological Advice
SEA	strategic environmental assessment
SIDS	Small Island Developing States
SLOSH	Sea, Lake and Overland Surges from Hurricanes

SLR	sea level rise
SLRTF	Sea Level Rise Task Force
SOVI	Social Vulnerability Index
SREX	Special Report on Managing the Risks of Extreme Events and Disasters
TEEB	The Economics of Ecosystems and Biodiversity
UDDT	urine-diverting dry toilet
UNDP	United Nations Development Programme
UNEP	United Nations Environment Programme
UNESCO	United Nations Educational, Scientific and Cultural Organization
UNFCCC	United Nations Framework Convention on Climate Change
UNISDR	United Nations International Strategy for Disaster Reduction
UNU-EHS	United Nations University Institute for Environment and Human Security
UWI	University of the West Indies
VDC	Village Development Committee
WFP	World Food Programme
WSSD	World Summit on Sustainable Development

Part I

Why do ecosystems matter in disaster risk reduction?

1

The relevance of ecosystems for disaster risk reduction

Fabrice G. Renaud, Karen Sudmeier-Rieux and Marisol Estrella

Introduction

Each year we witness strikingly similar images of loss and destruction caused by disasters.[1] Disasters linked to recurring and extreme hazard events – namely floods, droughts, heat waves, tropical cyclones, volcanic eruptions and earthquakes – repeatedly undermine local and national development efforts to support livelihoods, promote economic growth and achieve overall human well-being. A closer look at disasters reveals that they are induced by a complex mix of drivers, such as people living in dangerous places, poor governance, environmental degradation, inadequate early warning, and lack of preparedness by the public and the authorities, all interlinked with challenges of development. Given the current global economic downturn and shrinking financial resources, the importance of pursuing integrated, "win–win" solutions to disaster reduction and sustainable development is more critical than ever. Ecosystem management, or the sound management of natural resources, is a well-tested solution to sustainable development that is being revisited because of its inherent "win–win" and "no-regrets" appeal to address rising disaster and climate change issues (IPCC, 2012; UNISDR, 2009a, 2011a).

Worldwide, disasters are increasingly affecting people and communities, although the number of disasters, of people affected and of casualties and the extent of economic losses can vary considerably from year to year. For example, in 2010, 373 disaster events[2] were recorded (compared with 387 events on average for the period 2000–2009), resulting in about

The role of ecosystems in disaster risk reduction, Renaud, Sudmeier-Rieux and Estrella (eds), United Nations University Press, 2013, ISBN 978-92-808-1221-3

300,000 casualties (about 80,000 on average for 2000–2009), 207 million people affected[3] (227 million on average for 2000–2009) and US$109 billion in damages (US$99 billion average for 2000–2009) (CRED, 2011). The type of hazard generating the most important impacts varies annually (see Table 1.1). Given these fluctuations, an analysis of trends is more informative and, according to the Emergency Events Database (EM-DAT, 2012), the number of disasters reported worldwide has increased rapidly since the 1960s, peaked in the early 2000s, and subsequently reached a plateau. At the same time, although casualties since the 1960s have declined (particularly when considering weather-related hazards; UNISDR, 2011a), the number of people reported as affected has increased and estimated economic losses have increased considerably (Adikari and Yoshitani, 2009). Hydro-meteorological events (floods, droughts and windstorms) typically represent the majority of reported disasters (Guha-Sapir et al., 2011; Rodriguez et al., 2009; Scheuren et al., 2008).

The increasing trends in reported disasters, people affected and economic losses are linked to increased exposure of populations and triggered by demographic factors (such as natural population growth), rapid urbanization and the concentration of populations and economic assets

Table 1.1 Deadliest events worldwide for the period 1980–2011

Hazard	Countries affected	Casualties	Date
Earthquake	Haiti	222,570	12 January 2010
Earthquake, tsunami	Sri Lanka, Indonesia, Thailand, India, Bangladesh, Myanmar, Maldives, Malaysia	220,000	26 December 2004
Cyclone Nargis, storm surge	Myanmar	140,000	2–5 May 2008
Tropical cyclone, storm surge	Bangladesh	139,000	29–30 April 1991
Earthquake	Pakistan, India, Afghanistan	88,000	8 October 2005
Earthquake	China	84,000	12 May 2008
Heat wave, drought	France, Germany, Italy, Portugal, Romania, Spain, United Kingdom	70,000	July–August 2003
Heat wave	Russian Federation	56,000	July–September 2010
Earthquake	Iran	40,000	26 June 1990
Earthquake	Iran: Bam	26,200	26 December 2003

Source: NatCatSERVICE (2012).

in specific geographical regions, such as floodplains and coastal areas that are regularly affected by hazard events (IPCC, 2012; UNISDR, 2011a). Improved information technology also contributes to explaining these trends because disasters are reported more effectively now than in the 1960s. Furthermore, a multitude of human-induced factors can explain catastrophic events, including an over-reliance on engineered structures to protect populations from specific hazards, which are often under-designed and can provide a false sense of security. Examples include flooding following Hurricane Katrina in New Orleans, flooding following Atlantic storm Xynthia in western France and tsunami impacts in the context of the Great East Japan Earthquake.

Given the prevalence of hydro-meteorological disasters globally, it is anticipated that climate change impacts will exacerbate disaster risks. The Fourth Assessment Report of the Intergovernmental Panel on Climate Change (IPCC) in 2007 had already noted that several categories of hazards, such as heat waves, changes in precipitation patterns (with an increase in intense rainfall events), droughts, tropical cyclone activity and sea level rise, would increase in intensity and/or frequency in the future as a consequence of climate change (IPCC, 2007b). For some hazards, this was confirmed by the recently released IPCC Special Report on Managing the Risks of Extreme Events and Disasters to Advance Climate Change Adaptation (SREX), particularly with respect to increases in the frequency and magnitude of warm daily temperatures and increases in the frequency of heavy precipitation, whereas confidence levels linked to droughts and fluvial floods were lower (IPCC, 2012). These links and their impacts will vary from region to region. For example, droughts are most likely to intensify in the Mediterranean region, central Europe, central North America, Central America and Mexico, north-east Brazil and southern Africa (IPCC, 2012). It is further likely that the mean intensity of tropical cyclones will increase under climate change, although not necessarily in all ocean basins, while their frequency could slightly decrease or remain constant (IPCC, 2012; Peduzzi et al., 2012).

While the scientific community continues to address knowledge gaps related to climate change impacts and weather extremes, scientists have also highlighted current drivers of risk, namely human-created exposure and vulnerability owing to poor land-use planning, poverty, urbanization and ecosystem degradation (IPCC, 2012; UNISDR, 2011a). The Millennium Ecosystem Assessment showed that many of our essential ecosystems are being used unsustainably, limiting their capacities to regulate the climate, to provide protection with respect to hazards, and to sustain livelihoods (Millennium Ecosystem Assessment, 2005). The IPCC also concluded that climate change affects natural systems worldwide (IPCC, 2007a, 2012).

In many regions of the world, underlying risk factors, including the degradation of ecosystems, are not necessarily addressed by relevant authorities (UNISDR, 2011a). Additionally, the role of ecosystems in the context of disasters is perhaps the most overlooked component in disaster risk reduction (DRR) and development planning. Whereas ecosystem management is still perceived by many as having conservation value only (for example, maintaining biodiversity), its role in the context of DRR in terms of providing hazard protection, livelihood recovery and sustainability, and resilient development is often ignored. Yet, in some cases, ecosystem-based solutions to DRR are in greater demand by governments, tax payers and low-income countries where there may be little choice but to invest in ecosystems as the most readily available and effective solution to reducing underlying risk factors. Even then, hard engineered solutions for risk reduction, such as the construction of dykes to protect against flooding or of sea walls in areas prone to tsunamis and storm surges, often remain the more favoured intervention approach in DRR.

To fill this gap in opportunities presented by ecosystems for DRR, we revisit and present in this chapter and throughout this book examples where ecosystem-based or ecosystem-inclusive solutions can be applied successfully as part of a more systemic approach to DRR. We also highlight the opportunities for combined or hybrid ecosystem–engineering solutions as well as the limitations of ecosystem-based approaches in particular contexts.

Paradigm shifts in DRR and emerging opportunities (and challenges) for applying ecosystem-based approaches

That ecosystems offer protection against the vagaries of nature is well known by communities around the world, such as the centuries-old protection forests in Switzerland, and has been documented by scientists for decades (Bender, 1995; Burby, 1998; Daily, 1997; Prugh et al., 1999; Chapter 13 in this volume). Yet it is only over the last decade that the role of ecosystems for DRR has been considered seriously within the DRR community – and also within the environmental conservation community – as potentially contributing to hazard mitigation, livelihood security and resilience to disasters (Dudley et al., 2010; FAO, 2011; March, 2012; Sudmeier-Rieux et al., 2006, 2009; UNEP, 2009; UNISDR, 2005; WWF, 2008).

The Indian Ocean tsunami in 2004 served as a key turning point in shifting international attention towards disaster prevention and risk reduction in general and ecosystem-based approaches in particular. The event spurred the establishment of the "Hyogo Framework for Action

(2005–2015): Building the Resilience of Nations and Communities to Disasters", which emanated from the World Conference on Disaster Reduction held in 2005 in Kobe, Hyogo, Japan and which was subsequently adopted by the General Assembly of the United Nations (A/RES/60/1952) in January 2006. The Indian Ocean tsunami also focused global attention on the environmental impacts of the disaster (including from post-disaster response and reconstruction operations) and highlighted the potential role of coastal ecosystems in providing hazard protection and mitigation. It was during this period that global environmental initiatives such as Mangroves for the Future were launched.

The role of ecosystems in DRR is now well acknowledged in the International Strategy for Disaster Reduction (ISDR), which involves the international community in promoting global DRR through implementation of the Hyogo Framework for Action (HFA). The HFA has five priorities for action with respect to building resilience to disasters (UNISDR, 2005). One of these priorities for action, entitled "Reduce the underlying risk factors", recommends two key activities that have a direct link to ecosystems and ecosystem management (UNISDR, 2005: 10–11):

1. *Environmental and natural resource management* with components that include:
   a. sustainable use and management of ecosystems;
   b. implementation of integrated environmental and natural resource management approaches that incorporate disaster risk reduction;
   c. linking disaster risk reduction with existing climate variability and future climate change.
2. *Land-use planning and other technical measures* with a component on incorporating disaster risk assessment into rural development planning and management.

The ISDR Global Assessment Reports on Disaster Risk Reduction in 2009 and 2011 (UNISDR, 2009b, 2011) as well as the Chair Summaries of both the 2009 and 2011 Global Platforms for Disaster Risk Reduction have highlighted the importance of integrating ecosystem management as a key component in DRR strategies. The recent IPCC Special Report (2012) has subsequently echoed this message in stressing the value of investing in ecosystems as part of climate change adaptation (CCA) strategies, and ecosystem-based adaptation (EbA) has been formally endorsed by the Subsidiary Body for Scientific and Technological Advice, under the auspices of the Nairobi Work Programme of the United Nations Framework Convention on Climate Change (discussed further below). Moreover, outcomes from "Rio+20 – The Future We Want" now clearly recognize DRR as a critical component of sustainable development. At a UN General Assembly Thematic Debate on Disaster Risk Reduction in April 2012 in New York, organized in preparation for the Rio+20 conference, the President's Summary recognized that ecosystem management provides integrated solutions for DRR and CCA.

Despite the international recognition of the role of ecosystems in DRR, there is limited progress in applying ecosystem-based DRR approaches in policy and practice at the country level. Many experiences of ecosystem-based DRR are generally implemented only at project or pilot demonstration levels, and few cases achieve the necessary scale to demonstrate tangible impacts for DRR. This is partly reflected in the uneven progress of HFA implementation in general. The *Mid-Term Review* of the HFA showed that least progress was recorded under "Priority for Action 4: Reduce the underlying risk factors", which includes the need to address ecosystem degradation (UNISDR, 2011b: 27).

There are, however, some regions where progress is being made. For example, the European Union's Water Framework Directive enacted in 2000 is one of most progressive policy directives to date globally on integrating ecosystem management with DRR (European Commission, 2000). Implemented through the member states of the European Union, the Directive supports an integrated approach to water risk management and aims to balance the ecological requirements of river flows with the need for water supply and flood defence structures (Defra, 2008). The European Union's Flood Directive (European Commission, 2007) spawned a number of country-level programmes, namely "Making Space for Water" in the United Kingdom, "Room for the River" in the Netherlands, "Living Rivers" in the United Kingdom and France and "Environmental Enhancement of Rivers" in Ireland, which promote the use of the natural capacity of wetlands, peat bogs and other natural spaces to store excess water (Arnaud-Fassetta and Fort, 2008; Defra, 2008; Deltacommissie, 2008; Gilligan, 2008). A combination of environmental and economic arguments, together with legislation on ecosystem-based flood management, has led to a powerful force for change in river management practices in recent years and ushered in an array of alternative, "softer" approaches (Wharton and Gilvear, 2006), such as more natural river designs, river restoration and more strategic integrated approaches that link ecosystem and DRR goals. Within the European Union, there is growing acceptance that "rivers are meant to flood and must have room to move" (Gilvear et al., 1995, cited in Wharton and Gilvear, 2006: 2) and that rivers are dynamic and linked to their surrounding floodplain (Wharton and Gilvear, 2006).

There are several reasons to explain the general lack of uptake of ecosystem considerations in DRR. The first is that ecosystem management is rarely considered as part of the portfolio of solutions to DRR. Implementing ecosystem management approaches for DRR requires a combined set of technical expertise from the environmental and disaster management communities, which traditionally work independently of each other. Enhancing national and local capacities to apply integrated ecosystem and DRR solutions is thus necessary to replicate and scale up such efforts.

Secondly, DRR and disaster risk management in general are still not considered within broader development sectoral planning processes with appropriate budget allocations. As a result, DRR, and especially ecosystem management, are often sidelined or viewed in direct competition with other development priorities. Applying ecosystem-based approaches may require much longer temporal scales to implement and yield tangible disaster reduction outcomes. On the other hand, policy-makers and decision-makers are under pressure to show immediate results from their efforts to protect the public against hazards, which the choice of engineered structures provides, together with the fact that engineered solutions also generate financial profits for some stakeholders.

A third challenge is the poor science–policy interactions on ecosystem-based DRR, which have led to unclear and sometimes contradictory scientific information on the role of ecosystems for DRR. Scientifically quantifying ecosystem services for DRR (for example in terms of hazard mitigation or vulnerability reduction) and building a strong economic case for ecosystem-based approaches remain a challenge and thus a constraint to informed decision-making on all possible cost-effective DRR options. Nonetheless, there is now a growing body of knowledge and evidence base (from science fields and practitioners on the ground) that ecosystems and their services are effective for DRR. This book is a reflection of this emerging trend in ecosystem-based DRR.

Examining the role of ecosystems in disaster risk reduction

Examples of what works

Disaster risk is generally calculated based on three main variables: the frequency and magnitude of hazard events, the exposure (of people and their assets) to hazards, and the underlying vulnerabilities (for example, ranging from poor building construction to poverty and lack of preparedness). Sustainable ecosystem management has the potential to influence all three elements of the disaster risk equation – in terms of regulating and mitigating hazards, controlling exposure and reducing vulnerability.

Many experiences and scientific studies from around the world point to these three main benefits of ecosystems for DRR. Some are discussed in greater detail in this book. First, healthy and well-managed ecosystems can serve as natural infrastructure to prevent hazards or buffer hazard impacts. For example, in many mountain areas, vegetation cover and root structures protect against erosion and increase slope stability by binding soil together, preventing many types of landslides (Dolidon et al., 2009; Peduzzi, 2010; Chapters 12 and 14 in this volume). Well-managed protection forests can be effective in protecting against rock fall and reducing the risk of avalanches (Bebi et al., 2009; Chapter 13 in this volume). Along coastlines, wetlands, tidal flats, deltas and estuaries absorb water from upland areas, storm surges and tidal waves (Batker et al., 2010; Costanza et al., 2008; Gedan et al., 2011; Ramsar Convention on Wetlands, 2010; Zhao et al., 2005; Chapters 3, 4 and 9 in this volume). Coral reefs, sea grasses, sand dunes and coastal vegetation such as mangroves and saltmarshes can effectively reduce wave heights and reduce erosion from storms and high tides, while buffering against saltwater intrusion and trapping sediment and organic matter (Campbell et al., 2009; IOC, 2009; Krysanova et al., 2008; Chapters 3, 4 and 5 in this volume). Healthy peatlands, wet grasslands and other wetlands can contribute to controlling floods in coastal areas, inland river basins and mountain areas subject to glacial melt by storing water and releasing it slowly, reducing the speed and volume of runoff after heavy rainfall or snowmelt (Campbell et al., 2009; Chapters 10, 15 and 16 in this volume).

Secondly, healthy and well-managed ecosystems also can help reduce the exposure of people and their productive assets to hazards. Floodplains, in their natural state, are meant to absorb flood waters and allow rivers to be dynamic, providing the space needed to reduce flood risk (Gilvear et al., 1995; Chapter 9 in this volume). In drylands, maintaining vegetation cover and agricultural practices such as use of shadow crops, nutrient-enriching plants and vegetation litter increase resilience to drought by conserving soil and retaining moisture. Shelterbelts, greenbelts and other types of living fences act as barriers against wind erosion and sand storms (Campbell et al., 2009; Krysanova et al., 2008).

Thirdly, ecosystems sustain human livelihoods and provide for basic needs, such as food, shelter and water – before, during and after hazard events (for example, Ingram et al., 2012; Chapters 5, 8 and 11 in this volume). In this regard, well-managed, healthy ecosystems can reduce vulnerabilities to disasters by supporting livelihoods that are sustainable and resilient to disasters. In Lebanon, the International Union for Conservation of Nature (IUCN) worked with the government and farming communities to re-establish forests planted with mixed tree species–utilizing both native, fire-tolerant trees and pine trees – in order to better manage fire hazards and sustain livelihoods from selling pine nuts (Murti et al., 2010).

In Burkina Faso and Niger, local farmers restored degraded drylands by applying traditional agricultural and agroforestry techniques, such as on-farm tree planting and planting in shallow pits, to improve soil and water retention. Three decades later, hundreds of thousands of farmers have replicated, adapted and benefited from these techniques, significantly increasing local resilience to droughts. In Burkina Faso, more than 200,000 hectares of drylands have been rehabilitated, now producing an additional 80,000 tons of food per year. In Niger, more than 200 million on-farm trees have been regenerated, providing 500,000 additional tons of food per year. Women have particularly benefited from the improved supply of water, fuelwood and other tree products (Reij et al., 2012).

In Ethiopia, since the 1980s the government and local communities, together with the World Food Programme (WFP), have been implementing a sustainable land management and rain catchment programme known as MERET (Managing Environmental Resources to Enable Transitions to More Sustainable Livelihoods), which has vastly increased food production and mitigated the impacts of drought and floods. The programme has increased the food security of MERET households by 50 per cent, reduced the average annual food gap from 6 to 3 months, rehabilitated 1 million hectares of land, and reforested 600,000 hectares (WFP, 2010). A programme evaluation in 2005 found that the return on investment averaged more than 12 per cent for the main activities implemented through the programme.

Finally, well-managed, healthy ecosystems are better able to support the post-disaster recovery needs of communities, such as accessing safe drinking water, as illustrated in the case of Negril, Jamaica (Chapter 5 in this volume).

That sustainable ecosystem management provides multiple social, economic and environmental benefits – regardless of whether a disaster occurs – is what we regard as a "no-regret" investment. Aside from hazard mitigation and enhancing local resilience to disasters, ecosystems contribute to national gross domestic product, poverty reduction, food security, biodiversity and carbon sequestration. Chapter 2 elaborates further on these issues.

Gaps that need addressing

At times, there is contradictory or misperceived evidence on the role of ecosystems in DRR. For example, the role of vegetation in protecting coastal areas against erosion or the impacts of storm surges is well established. However, evidence of the role of coastal vegetation in buffering against extreme events such as cyclones or tsunamis is much sparser. Following the 2004 Indian Ocean tsunami, peer-reviewed journal articles contradicted each other with respect to the effect of coastal vegetation in reducing the impacts of tsunami waves (see, for example, a discussion based on an original paper by Kathiresan and Rajendran in 2005 that was subsequently debated by Kathiresan and Rajendran, 2006; Kerr et al., 2006; Vermaat and Thampanya, 2006, 2007; as well as further results and discussions by Cochard et al., 2008; Danielsen et al., 2005; Kaplan et al., 2009; Kerr and Baird, 2007; Renaud 2013; Chapters 3 and 4 in this volume). Nonetheless, in the interval between the Indian Ocean tsunami disaster and the systematic and scientific collection of evidence on the role of coastal vegetation in protecting populations against tsunami waves, millions of dollars were spent in replanting mangroves in various affected countries, sometimes with disappointing results (see Cochard, 2011). Even in areas where mangroves were successfully established, further research is required to ascertain whether populations are more protected from tsunami waves.

Another example where further scientific analysis is required relates to determining linkages between vegetation/forest cover and flooding. It is often perceived that the greater the forest cover the less the likelihood of floods. However, this is a subject that is still scientifically debated (Bradshaw et al., 2007; van Dijk et al., 2009; WWF, 2008). For example, the Food and Agriculture Organization and the Center for International Forestry Research (FAO and CIFOR, 2005) showed that the cause–effect relationship will vary depending on the scale of the flood-generating weather event and of the catchment considered. This was confirmed further by Bathurst et al. (2011a, 2011b) through rigorous empirical and modelling catchment-scale studies in Latin America.

The two examples above point to areas where more research is required to establish the role of ecosystems in DRR. As mentioned in the previous section, there are, however, many examples where greater certainties exist and where ecosystems have been integrated in risk prevention actions. In order for the role of ecosystems to be considered seriously by decision-makers at various governance scales, research gaps need to be addressed by the science community and implementation experiences upscaled and better communicated by practitioners in terms of what works and what does not work (see Chapter 18 in this volume).

Another potential pitfall is to overemphasize the role of ecosystems in DRR. That ecosystems and society are intertwined goes without saying but, in order to reduce future disaster risks, we need to analyse complex vulnerability, risk and environmental factors in a more systematic manner. As an example we can consider the situation on the island of Hispaniola, which is divided between Haiti and the Dominican Republic. In 2004 both countries were affected by intense rainfall brought about by a low pressure system, which generated flooding in the south-central, cross-border region of the island on 24–25 May (Gubbels and Brakenridge, 2004), and by Hurricane/Tropical Storm Jeanne, which affected the island

Table 1.2 Casualties linked to two major meteorological events over the island of Hispaniola in 2004

	Casualties in:		
Storm system	Haiti	Dominican Republic	Date
Intense rainfall	2,665	688	24–25 May
Tropical Storm Jeanne	2,754	<20[a]	16–17 September

Sources: Data on casualties from Centre for Research on the Epidemiology of Disasters, "EM-DAT: The OFDA/CRED International Disaster Database", <http://www.emdat.be> – Université catholique de Louvain – Brussels – Belgium (accessed 2 October 2012).
Note:
[a] Numbers vary from source to source.

in mid-September (Lawrence and Cobb, 2005). For both events, the damage and number of casualties were higher on the Haiti side of the island when compared with the Dominican Republic side (Table 1.2).

The different impacts between the two countries were often principally attributed to an environmental factor: Haiti has experienced massive deforestation, with forest cover representing 3.8 per cent of the land area in 2004 in contrast to 40.8 per cent in the Dominican Republic at the same period (Table 1.3), thus generating more devastating floods in Haiti. It is highly likely that deforestation played an important role in generating the disasters that affected Haiti. However, other factors explaining the underlying vulnerability of the exposed communities also need to be taken into account when considering DRR interventions (see also Jäger et al., 2007). Haiti is a much poorer country than the Dominican Republic and many social, economic and governance indicators help explain these different levels of overexploitation of environmental resources, vulnerability and possibly of flood impact (Table 1.3).

Reforestation alone would not solve the flood-related problems in Haiti, and it is possible that other DRR interventions would still be required and be more efficient in saving lives (for example, effective early warning systems, improved preparedness). This example highlights the need to address the complexity of human–environment systems (also referred to as social-ecological systems) when dealing with DRR questions. Attitudes that dismiss the role of ecosystems in the context of DRR or overemphasize it are equally counterproductive when trying to reduce the impacts of hazards on people and societies. Taking a scientific, systems and analytical approach is important in order to avoid investing in the wrong measures and wasting limited resources. Therefore, science has a particularly important role to play in the context of DRR, sustainable

Table 1.3 Social, economic and governance indicators for Haiti and the Dominican Republic

Indicator	Haiti	Dominican Republic	Year
GDP per capita (PPP US$)[1]	1,892	7,449	2004
Life expectancy at birth (years)[1]	52	67.5	2004
Proportion of undernourished (per cent)[1]	47	27	2001–3
Under 5 mortality (per '000 live births)[1]	117	32	2004
Human development index rank[1]	154	94	2004
Population with sustainable access to improved water sources (per cent)[1]	54	95	2004
Population with sustainable access to improved sanitation (per cent)[1]	30	78	2004
Life expectancy index[1]	0.45	0.71	2004
Human poverty index (per cent)[1]	39.4	11.9	2004
Population below national poverty line (per cent)[1]	65.0	28.6	1990–2003
Land area ('000 ha)[2]	2,756	4,832	2004
Permanent crop land[2]	280,000 ha = 10.2 per cent	450,000 ha = 9.3 per cent	2004
Forest cover[2]	105,800 ha = 3.8 per cent	1,972,000 ha = 40.8 per cent	2004
Degraded land[3]	None: 0 per cent, light: 0 per cent, moderate: 1 per cent, severe: 1 per cent, very severe: 98 per cent	None: 0 per cent, light: 0 per cent, moderate: 59 per cent, severe: 40 per cent, very severe: 1 per cent	2005
Population density (people per km²)[4]	334	189	2004
Electrification rate (per cent)[5]	36.0	92.5	2005

Table 1.3 (cont.)

Indicator	Haiti	Dominican Republic	Year
Control of corruption (percentile rank among all countries)[6]	2	41	2004

Sources: [1] UNDP (2006); [2] <http://faostat.fao.org/DesktopDefault.aspx?PageID= 377&lang=en#ancor>;   [3] <ftp://ftp.fao.org/agl/agll/docs/wsr.pdf>;   [4] <http://data. worldbank.org/indicator/EN.POP.DNST?page=1>;   [5] IEA   (2006);   [6] <http://info. worldbank.org/governance/wgi/sc_country.asp> (the lower the number, the lower the control of corruption).
Note: Indicator values were selected for time periods close to Tropical Storm Jeanne to reflect the situation then.

development and CCA, the last two being discussed intensively in the context of Rio+20 and the Climate Adaptation Fund.

Moving towards integration of ecosystems, disaster risk reduction and climate change adaptation

Concepts of risk and vulnerability are addressed by various communities: disaster risk reduction, climate change adaptation and sustainability science, to name only the most prominent ones. Concepts and definitions used by these communities vary greatly (for example, Renaud and Perez, 2010). Because sustainable development, climate change adaptation and disaster risk reduction are intimately linked, attempts are being made by researchers and experts to find common understanding on key concepts and definitions. For example, Birkmann and von Teichman (2010), who reviewed the status of integration between DRR and CCA, showed that major differences between the two are linked to different spatial and temporal scales of analysis, different knowledge bases and different norms, and they propose various evaluation and quality criteria to link the two more effectively. Costa and Kropp (2012) further showed the differences and commonalities with respect to the concept of vulnerability between the CCA and DRR communities, which paves the way for greater understanding in the future. More recently, the IPCC Special Report on extreme events (2012) applied definitions of disaster risk that are closely related to those used in the ISDR system.

International and intergovernmental forums have recently started to push for better integration between DRR and CCA. In the Bali Action Plan, the Parties to the United Nations Framework Convention on Climate Change (UNFCCC) recognized the links between DRR and climate change (UNFCCC, 2008). In 2010, the UNFCCC Cancun Adaptation Framework formally recognized DRR as an essential element of CCA and encouraged governments to consider linking adaptation measures to the Hyogo Framework for Action (UNFCCC, 2011a: paragraph 14(e); Llosa and Zodrow, 2011).

The profile of ecosystem-based approaches to adaptation has risen within the UNFCCC process and is featured prominently in particular within the discussions on the Nairobi Work Programme (NWP) on impacts, vulnerability and adaptation to climate change. At the UNFCCC negotiations held in Durban, South Africa, in November–December 2011, the 35th session of the Subsidiary Body for Scientific and Technological Advice (SBSTA) under the NWP presented a report that synthesized the state of knowledge on EbA (UNFCCC, 2011b). Noteworthy is the report's emphasis on the "vital role healthy ecosystems can play in maintaining and increasing resilience to climate change and in reducing climate-related risk and vulnerability" (UNFCCC, 2011b: para. 5). Examples of EbA measures include "flood defence through the maintenance and/or restoration of wetlands and the conservation of agricultural biodiversity in order to support crop and livestock adaptation to climate change" (UNFCCC, 2011b: para. 5). Although the theoretical concept of EbA is relatively new, the report acknowledges that practical approaches of EbA have long been applied by communities locally in response to the effects of climate variability and/or long-term climate change.

Adopting a broader perspective towards sustainable ecosystem management, therefore, helps tackle the challenges of DRR and CCA in a much more integrated manner. Especially in the context of climate change and the scale of solutions needed to adapt to weather extremes, human-built infrastructure – such as dams, dykes and seawalls – alone may not be feasible, owing to their high costs and technology requirements. Ecosystems and the services they provide are often more locally accessible especially to poor and rural communities and less expensive to maintain than human-built infrastructure (UNFCCC, 2011b: para. 10), although engineered and ecosystem-based measures can be combined in a complementary way and are not necessarily mutually exclusive (Chapters 9 and 10 in this volume).

Ecosystem-based DRR approaches can be readily applied in the context of adaptation and bring together knowledge, expertise, experience and resources from three distinct communities: environment, disaster management and climate change adaptation. In this regard, ecosystem-based DRR can potentially deliver on multiple development priorities across different sectors, producing cost-effective, "win–win" solutions (discussed further in Chapter 2 in this volume).

Objectives of the book

In September 2010, the Partnership for Environment and Disaster Risk Reduction (PEDRR) organized a workshop in Bonn, Germany, on Ecosystems, Livelihoods and Disaster Risk Reduction that was attended by international scientists and experts.[4] The objectives of the workshop were to:

- take stock of the latest scientific developments on the linkages between ecosystems and their role in DRR, with a focus on reducing threats and vulnerabilities and increasing the resilience of social-ecological systems;
- take stock of good practices on ecosystem-based approaches for DRR; and
- enhance the dialogue between the scientific and practitioner communities in order to improve knowledge and practice.

A conclusion of the workshop was to bring together several of the presented papers and to invite additional contributions to illustrate the scientific and knowledge basis of the role of ecosystems and DRR. The aim of this book is to provide an overview of knowledge and practice in this multidisciplinary field of ecosystem management and DRR. It was intentional to invite contributions from both scientists and the practitioner community in order to capture their respective perspectives on the topic. This book does not claim to provide an exhaustive review or representation of this continually evolving field. Many hazards are not addressed here, such as earthquakes, wildfires and volcanic eruptions. There are knowledge gaps, for instance related to quantifying the cost-effectiveness of ecosystem-based DRR approaches (vis-à-vis engineered measures), which the PEDRR network and contributing authors have been unable to address adequately (see also Chapter 9). Rather, this book is a starting point for what we hope will be a continuing dialogue between scientists, practitioners and, ultimately, policy-makers and development planners.

Definitions of some key terms used throughout the book

There are many different definitions of key terms linked to risk assessment, depending on the scientific and expertise domain and the context within which risk assessment is performed. Contributors to this book come from a diversity of backgrounds and it was decided at the outset not to prescribe specific definitions for key terms but to let the authors of the chapters provide the reader with their own definition of the terms. Box 1.1 provides some definitions typically used.

Box 1.1 Use of terms

As editors, we have, for the most part, adopted the ISDR terminology for key terms, unless otherwise specified:

A *hazard* is a dangerous phenomenon of environmental origin that may cause loss of life, injury or other health impacts, property damage, loss of livelihoods and services, social and economic disruption, or environmental damage (adapted from UNISDR, 2009a).

A *disaster* constitutes a serious disruption of the functioning of a community or a society involving widespread human, material, economic or environmental losses and impacts, which exceeds the ability of the affected community or society to cope using its own resources (UNISDR, 2009a).

Vulnerability is the intrinsic and dynamic feature of an element at risk (community, region, state, infrastructure, environment, etc.) that determines the expected damage/harm resulting from a given hazardous event and is often even affected by the harmful event itself. Vulnerability changes continuously over time and is driven by physical, social, economic and environmental factors (Thywissen, 2006).

Resilience is the ability of a system and its component parts to anticipate, absorb, accommodate or recover from the effects of a hazardous event in a timely and efficient manner, including through ensuring the preservation, restoration or improvement of its essential basic structures and functions (IPCC, 2012).

Risk is the probability of harmful consequences – or loss in lives, health status, livelihoods, assets and services – resulting from interactions between natural or human-induced hazards and vulnerable conditions (adapted from UNISDR, 2009a). Risk is conventionally expressed by the equation: Risk = Hazard × Vulnerability × Exposure (UNDP, 2004), although, for some, exposure is integrated in the vulnerability component.

Finally, *adaptation* is an adjustment in natural or human systems in response to actual or expected climatic stimuli or their effects that moderates harm or exploits beneficial opportunities (IPCC, 2007b).

Structure of the book

The book is divided into five main sections. Part I, entitled "Why do ecosystems matter in disaster risk reduction?", comprises this introductory chapter and a literature review by Estrella and Saalismaa (Chapter 2).

Part II, "Ecosystems and coastal disaster risk reduction", has six contributions. The first two chapters address the role of coastal vegetation and other ecosystem features in buffering against coastal hazards. Hettiarachchi et al. (Chapter 3) present results of flume simulations of coastal features dissipating the energy of tsunami waves, while Lacambra et al. (Chapter 4) provide a comprehensive review of the role of coastal vegetation in terms of hazard mitigation and livelihood maintenance. Peduzzi et al. (Chapter 5) present an example of how ecosystem and risk assessments were integrated in Jamaica through the RiVAMP methodology developed by the United Nations Environment Programme (UNEP). Beck et al. (Chapter 6) present the "Coastal Resilience" programme, which aims to support decision-making to reduce socioeconomic and ecological vulnerability to coastal hazards, and they provide an example of its application in New York and Connecticut in the United States of America. This chapter is followed by Colenbrander et al. (Chapter 7), who describe the risk reduction strategies put in place for coastal areas by the City of Cape Town in South Africa. The last chapter in this section by Mavrogenis and Kelman (Chapter 8) describes lessons learned from the challenges and local initiatives on ecosystem-based climate work in Tonga.

Part III, "Water resources management for disaster risk reduction", has three chapters. Van Eijk et al. (Chapter 9) describe the regulating role of wetlands for maintaining dynamic river basins for flood management and community resilience; Dalton et al. (Chapter 10) discuss Integrated Water Resources Management for reducing water-induced disasters; and Fogde et al. (Chapter 11) present a case study in Mozambique looking into sanitation initiatives during major floods.

Part IV, "Sustainable land management for disaster risk reduction", has contributions from: Papathoma-Koehle and Glade on the role of vegetation cover change for landslide hazard and risk (Chapter 12); Wehrli and Dorren on protection forests as a key factor in integrated land and risk management in the Alps (Chapter 13); and Jaquet et al., who describe initial results on the role of community forests in terms of landslide risk reduction in Nepal (Chapter 14).

The last section, entitled "Policy, planning and future perspectives", addresses the role of protected areas in mitigating disasters (Dudley et al., Chapter 15); the role of ecosystems in the context of urban risks (Guadagno et al., Chapter 16); and the role of environmental impact assessments and strategic environmental assessments in disaster management (Gupta and Nair, Chapter 17). Estrella et al. (Chapter 18) provide a conclusion and way forward in terms of addressing, scientifically and politically, the integration of ecosystems, their services, livelihoods and disaster risk reduction.

Notes

1. In this book, we will refer to disasters caused by environmental hazards as a result of either geological or hydro-meteorological events that may have been aggravated by human activities (e.g. land-use change) or induced climate change. We therefore exclude technology-related disasters, although it is sometimes impossible to distinguish between a cascading chain of events such as occurred when the Tōhoku earthquake generated tsunami waves leading to a nuclear meltdown in Japan in 2011.
2. For EM-DAT (2012) a hazard event is considered a disaster when 10 or more people are reported killed; or 100 or more people are reported affected; or a declaration of a state of emergency is issued; or a call for international assistance is made.
3. According to EM-DAT (2012), "people affected" implies "people requiring immediate assistance during a period of emergency; it can also include displaced or evacuated people".
4. See <http://www.pedrr.net/> for more information on the partnership.

REFERENCES

Adikari, Y. and J. Yoshitani (2009) *Global Trends in Water-related Disasters: An Insight for Policymakers*. Paris: UNESCO. Available at <http://unesdoc.unesco.org/images/0018/001817/181793e.pdf> (accessed 9 October 2012).

Arnaud-Fassetta, G. and M. Fort (2008) "The Integration of Functional Space in Fluvial Geomorphology, as a Tool for Mitigating Flood Risk. Application to the Left-Bank Tributaries of the Aude River, Mediterranean France". In B. Gumiero, M. Rinaldi and B. Fokkens (eds), *Proceedings of the 4th ECRR International Conference on River Restoration, Venice, 16–21 June 2008*. Venice: Centro Italiano per la Riqualificazione Fluviale, IGV, pp. 313–322.

Bathurst, J.C. et al. (2011a) "Forest Impact on Floods Due to Extreme Rainfall and Snowmelt in Four Latin American Environments 1: Field Data Analysis". *Journal of Hydrology* 400: 281–291.

Bathurst, J.C. et al. (2011b) "Forest Impact on Floods Due to Extreme Rainfall and Snowmelt in Four Latin American Environments 2: Model Analysis". *Journal of Hydrology* 400: 292–304.

Batker, D.P., I. de la Torre, R. Costanza, P. Swedeen, J.W. Day, R. Boumans and K. Bagstad (2010) *Gaining Ground – Wetlands, Hurricanes and the Economy: The Value of Restoring the Mississippi River Delta*. Tacoma, WA: Earth Economics.

Bebi, P., D. Kulakowski and R. Christian (2009) "Snow Avalanche Disturbances in Forest Ecosystems – State of Research and Implications for Management". *Forest Ecology and Management* 257: 1883–1892.

Bender, S. (1995) "Protected Areas as Protection Against Natural Hazards". In J.A. McNeely (ed.), *Expanding Partnerships in Conservation*. Washington, DC: Island Press.

Birkmann, J. and K. von Teichman (2010) "Integrating Disaster Risk Reduction and Climate Change Adaptation: Key Challenges – Scales, Knowledge, and Norms. *Sustainability Science* 5: 171–184.

Bradshaw, C.J.A., N.S. Sodhi, K.S.-H. Peh and B.W. Brook (2007) "Global Evidence That Deforestation Amplifies Flood Risk and Severity in the Developing World". *Global Change Biology* 13: 2379–2395.

Burby, R. (ed.) (1998) *Cooperating with Nature: Confronting Natural Hazards with Land Use Planning for Sustainable Communities.* Washington, DC: Joseph Henry Press.

Campbell, A., V. Kapos, J.P.W. Scharlemann, P. Bubb, A. Chenery, L. Coad, B. Dickson, N. Doswald, M.S.I. Khan, F. Kershaw and M. Rashid (2009) *Review of the Literature on the Links between Biodiversity and Climate Change: Impacts, Adaptation and Mitigation.* Secretariat of the Convention on Biological Diversity, Technical series 42.

Cochard, R. (2011) "The 2004 Tsunami in Aceh and Southern Thailand: Coastal Ecosystem Services, Damages and Resilience". In N.-A. Mörner (ed.), *The Tsunami Threat – Research and Technology.* Vienna: InTech, pp. 179–216.

Cochard, R. et al. (2008) "The 2004 Tsunami in Aceh and Southern Thailand: A Review on Coastal Ecosystems, Wave Hazards and Vulnerability". *Perspectives in Plant Ecology* 10: 3–40.

Costa, L. and J.P. Kropp (2012) "Linking Components of Vulnerability in Theoretic Frameworks and Case Studies". *Sustainability Science* (online first).

Costanza, R., O.M. Pérez-Maqueo, M.L. Martínez, P. Sutton, S.J. Anderson and K. Mulder (2008) "The Value of Coastal Wetlands for Hurricane Protection". *Ambio* 37: 241–248.

CRED [Centre for Research on the Epidemiology of Disasters] (2011) "Disaster Data: A Balanced Perspective". CRED Crunch No. 23, February. Available at <http://reliefweb.int/sites/reliefweb.int/files/resources/F7E6E30438715736C125784C004D2F49-Full_Report.pdf> (accessed 9 October 2012).

Daily, G.C. (ed.) (1997) *Nature's Services: Societal Dependence on Natural Ecosystems.* Washington, DC: Island Press.

Danielsen, F., M.K. Sorensen, M.F. Olwig, V. Selvam, F. Parish, N.D. Burgess, T. Hiraishi, V.M. Karunagaran, M.S. Rasmussen, L.B. Hansen, A. Quarto and N. Suryadiputra (2005) "The Asian Tsunami: A Protective Role for Coastal Vegetation". *Science* 310: 643.

Defra [Department for Environment, Food and Rural Affairs] (2008) "Making Space for Water Urban Flood Risk and Integrated Drainage – Pilots: Upper Rea Catchment including Longbridge, Northfield and Rubery Districts of Birmingham. Volume Seven –Environment". Birmingham City Council, UK. Available at <http://archive.defra.gov.uk/environment/flooding/documents/manage/surfacewater/upreavol7.pdf> (accessed 8 October 2012).

Deltacommissie (2008) *Working Together with Water: A Living Land Builds for Its Future. Findings of the Deltacommissie 2008 – Summary and Conclusions.* Available at <http://www.deltacommissie.com/doc/deltareport_summary.pdf> (accessed 9 October 2012).

Dolidon, N., T. Hofer, L. Jansky and R. Sidle (2009) "Watershed and Forest Management for Landslide Risk Reduction". In K. Sassa and P. Canuti (eds) *Landslides: Disaster Risk Reduction.* Berlin: Springer, pp. 633–646.

Dudley, N. et al. (2010) *Natural Solutions: Protected Areas Helping People Cope with Climate Change*. Gland, Switzerland, Washington DC, and New York: IUCN-WCPA, TNC, UNDP, WCS, World Bank, WWF.

EM-DAT (2012) "Natural Disasters Trends", <http://www.emdat.be/natural-disasters-trends> (accessed May 2012).

European Commission (2000) "Directive 2000/60/EC of the European Parliament and of the Council of 23 October 2000 Establishing a Framework for Community Action in the Field of Water Policy". Brussels: European Commission.

European Commission (2007) "Directive 2007/60/EC of the European Parliament and of the Council of 23 October 2007 on the assessment and management of flood risks". Brussels: European Commission.

FAO [Food and Agriculture Organization] (2011) *Resilient Livelihoods. Disaster Risk Reduction for Food and Nutrition Security*. Rome: Food and Agriculture Organization of the United Nations.

FAO and CIFOR [Center for International Forestry Research] (2005) *Forests and Floods: Drowning in Fiction or Thriving on Facts?* RAP Publication 2005/03, Forest Perspective 2. Rome: Food and Agriculture Organization of the United Nations.

Gedan, K.B., M.L. Kirwan, E. Wolanski, E.B. Barbier and B.R. Silliman (2011) "The Present and Future Role of Coastal Wetland Vegetation in Protecting Shorelines: Answering Recent Challenges to the Paradigm". *Climatic Change* 106: 7–29.

Gilligan, N. (2008) "Hydromorphology and River Enhancement for Flood Risk Management in Ireland". In *Proceedings from 4th ECRR Conference on River Restoration. Italy, Venice S. Servolo Island, 16–21 June 2008*, pp. 323–328.

Gilvear, D. et al. (1995) *Wild Rivers*. Report to WWF (Scotland).

Gubbels, T. and R. Brakenridge (2004) "Flood Disaster Hits Hispaniola". *Earth Observatory*, June, <http://earthobservatory.nasa.gov/Features/Haiti2004/> (accessed 9 October 2012).

Guha-Sapir, D., F. Vos, R. Below and S. Ponserre (2011) "Annual Disaster Statistical Review 2010. The Numbers and Trends". CRED, Brussels.

IEA [International Energy Agency] (2006) *World Energy Outlook 2006*. Paris: IEA Publications. Available at <http://www.iea.org/publications/freepublications/publication/name,3650,en.html> (accessed 9 October 2012).

Ingram, J.C., F. DeClerck and C. Rumbaitis del Rion (eds) (2012) *Integrating Ecology and Poverty Reduction*. New York: Springer.

IOC [Intergovernmental Oceanographic Commission] (2009) *Tsunami Risk Assessment and Mitigation for the Indian Ocean. Knowing Your Tsunami Risk – and What to Do about It*. Intergovernmental Oceanographic Commission Manuals and Guides 52. Paris: UNESCO.

IPCC [Intergovernmental Panel on Climate Change] (2007a) *Climate Change 2007: Synthesis Report*. Geneva: Intergovernmental Panel on Climate Change.

IPCC (2007b) *Climate Change 2007: Impacts, Adaptation and Vulnerability. Contribution of Working Group II to the Fourth Assessment Report of the Intergovernmental Panel on Climate Change* [M.L. Parry, O.F. Canziani, J.P. Palutikof, P.J. van der Linden and C.E. Hanson, eds]. Cambridge: Cambridge University Press.

IPCC (2012) *Managing the Risks of Extreme Events and Disasters to Advance Climate Change Adaptation.* A Special Report of Working Groups I and II of the Intergovernmental Panel on Climate Change [Field, C.B., V. Barros, T.F. Stocker, D. Qin, D.J. Dokken, K.L. Ebi, M.D. Mastrandrea, K.J. Mach, G.-K. Plattner, S.K. Allen, M. Tignor, and P.M. Midgley (eds.)]. Cambridge and New York: Cambridge University Press.

Jäger, J. et al. (2007) "Vulnerability of People and the Environment: Challenges and Opportunities". In United Nations Environment Programme, *Global Environment Outlook (GEO-4): Environment for Development.* Nairobi: United Nations Environment Programme, pp. 301–394.

Kaplan, M., F.G. Renaud and G. Lüchters (2009) "Vulnerability Assessment and Protective Effects of Coastal Vegetation during the 2004 Tsunami in Sri Lanka". *Natural Hazards and Earth System Sciences* 9: 1479–1494.

Kathiresan, K. and N. Rajendran (2005) "Coastal Mangrove Forests Mitigated Tsunami". *Estuarine, Coastal and Shelf Science* 65: 601–606.

Kathiresan, K. and N. Rajendran (2006) "Reply to Comments of Kerr et al. 'Coastal Mangrove Forests Mitigated Tsunami'". *Estuarine, Coastal and Shelf Science* 67: 542.

Kerr, A.M. and A.H. Baird (2007) "Natural Barriers to Natural Disasters". *BioScience* 57: 102–103.

Kerr, A.M., A.H. Baird and S.J. Campbell (2006) "Comments on 'Coastal Mangrove Forests Mitigated Tsunami' by K. Kathiresan and N. Rajendran". *Estuarine, Coastal and Shelf Science* 67: 539–541.

Krysanova, V., H. Buiteveld, D. Haase, F.F. Hattermann, K. van Niekerk, K. Roest, P. Martinez-Santos and M Schlüter (2008) "Practices and Lessons Learned in Coping with Climatic Hazards at the River-basin Scale: Floods and Drought". *Ecology and Society* 13: 32.

Lawrence, M.B. and H.D. Cobb (2005) "Tropical Cyclone Report: Hurricane Jeanne, 13–28 September 2004". NOAA, National Hurricane Center, <http://www.nhc.noaa.gov/2004jeanne.shtml> (accessed 9 October 2012).

Llosa, S. and I. Zodrow (2011) "Disaster Risk Reduction Legislation as a Basis for Effective Adaptation". Background paper to the *2011 Global Assessment Report on Disaster Risk Reduction.* Geneva: UNISDR.

March, J.A. (2012) "Integrating Natural Resource Management into Disaster Response and Mitigation". In J.C. Ingram, F. DeClerck and C. Rumbaitis del Rio (eds), *Integrating Ecology and Poverty Reduction: Ecological Dimensions.* New York: Springer, 393–406.

Millennium Ecosystem Assessment (2005) *Ecosystems and Human Well-being: Synthesis.* Washington, DC: Island Press.

Murti, R., M. Valderrabano and P. Regato (2010) "Reducing Fire Disasters through Ecosystem Management in Lebanon". Case study prepared for the PEDRR Background Paper "Demonstrating the Role of Ecosystems-based Management for Disaster Risk Reduction" submitted to the *2011 Global Assessment Report on Disaster Risk Reduction.* Geneva: UNISDR. Available at <http//www.preventionweb.net/english/hyogo/gar/2011/en/bgdocs/PEDRR_2010.pdf> (accessed 9 October 2012).

NatCatSERVICE (2012) "Significant Natural Catastrophes 1980–2011", as at March 2012, http://www.munichre.com/app_pages/www/@res/pdf/NatCatService/ significant_natural_catastrophes/2011/NatCatSERVICE_significant_dth_en. pdf> (accessed 9 October 2012).

Peduzzi, P. (2010) "Landslides and Vegetation Cover in the 2005 North Pakistan Earthquake". *Natural Hazards and Earth System Science* 10: 623–640.

Peduzzi, P., B. Chatenoux, H. Dao, A. de Bono, C. Herold, J. Kossin, F. Mouton and O. Nordbeck (2012) "Global Trends in Tropical Cyclone Risk". *Nature Climate Change* 2: 289–294.

Prugh, T., R. Costanza, J.H. Cumberland, H. Daly, R. Goodland and R.B. Norgaard (1999) *Natural Capital and Human Economic Survival*. Solomons, MD: International Society for Ecological Economics.

Ramsar Convention on Wetlands (2010) "Flood Control". Wetland ecosystem services, Factsheet 1. Ramsar Convention Secretariat, Gland, Switzerland. Available at <http://www.ramsar.org/pdf/info/services_01_e.pdf> (accessed 8 October 2012).

Reij, C., G. Tappan and M. Smale (2010) "Resilience to Drought through Agroecological Restoration of Drylands, Burkina Faso and Niger". Case study prepared for the PEDRR Background Paper to the *2011 Global Assessment Report on Disaster Risk Reduction*. Geneva: UNISDR.

Renaud, F. (2013) "Environmental Components of Vulnerability". In J. Birkmann (ed.), *Measuring Vulnerability to Natural Hazards: Toward Disaster Resilient Societies*, 2nd edn. Tokyo: United Nations University Press.

Renaud, F. and R. Perez (2010) "Climate Change Vulnerability and Adaptation Assessments". *Sustainability Science* 5: 155–157.

Rodriguez, J., F. Vos, R. Below and D. Guha-Sapir (2009) "Annual Disaster Statistical Review 2008. The Numbers and Trends". CRED, Brussels.

Scheuren, J.-M., O. Le Polain de Waroux, R. Below, D. Guha-Sapir and S. Ponserre (2008) "Annual Disaster Statistical Review. The Numbers and Trends 2007". CRED, Brussels.

Sudmeier-Rieux, K., H. Masundire, A. Rizvi and S. Rietbergen (eds) (2006) *Ecosystems, Livelihoods and Disasters. An Integrated Approach to Disaster Risk Management*. Ecosystem Management Series No. 4. Gland, Switzerland: International Union for Conservation of Nature.

Sudmeier-Rieux, K., N. Ash and I. Kelman (2009) "Keeping Safe in Perilous Times: Protection Against Natural Hazards". In J. McNeely, R. A. Mittmeier, T. M. Brooks and N. Ash (eds), *The Wealth of Nature: Ecosystem Services, Biodiversity and Human Well-Being*. Arlington: CEMEX, pp. 101–112.

Thywissen, K. (2006) "Components of Risk: A Comparative Glossary". SOURCE No. 2, UNU-EHS, Bonn, Germany.

UNDP [United Nations Development Programme] (2004) *Reducing Disaster Risk: A Challenge for Development. A Global Report*. New York: United Nations Development Programme, Bureau for Crisis Prevention and Recovery.

UNDP (2006) *Human Development Report 2006*. New York: Palgrave Macmillan. Available at <http://hdr.undp.org/en/media/HDR06-complete.pdf> (accessed 9 October 2012).

UNEP [United Nations Environment Programme] (2009) *Environment and Disaster Risk: Emerging Perspectives*. Prepared on behalf of the UNISDR Working

Group on Environment and Disaster. Nairobi: UNEP. Available at: <http://postconflict.unep.ch/publications/env_vulnerability.pdf> (accessed 9 October 2012).

UNFCCC [United Nations Framework Convention on Climate Change] (2008) *Report of the Conference of the Parties on Its Thirteenth Session, Held in Bali from 3 to 15 December 2007.* FCCC/CP/2007/6, 14 March. Geneva: United Nations.

UNFCCC (2011a) *Report of the Conference of the Parties on Its Sixteenth Session, Held in Cancun from 29 November to 10 December 2010.* FCCC/CP/2010/7, 15 March. Geneva: United Nations.

UNFCCC (2011b) *Ecosystem-based Approaches to Adaptation: Compilation of Information.* Report presented at the 35th session of the Subsidiary Body for Scientific and Technological Advice, Durban, South Africa, 28 November – 3 December 2011. FCCC/SBSTA/2011/INF.8. Available at <http://unfccc.int/resource/docs/2011/sbsta/eng/inf08.pdf> (accessed 9 October 2012).

UNISDR [United Nations International Strategy for Disaster Reduction] (2005) "Hyogo Framework for Action 2005–2015: Building the Resilience of Nations and Communities to Disasters". United Nations International Strategy for Disaster Reduction, Geneva.

UNISDR (2009a) "2009 UNISDR Terminology on Disaster Risk Reduction". United Nations, Geneva. Available at <http://www.unisdr.org/files/7817_UNISDRTerminologyEnglish.pdf> (accessed 9 October 2012).

UNISDR (2009b) *2009 Global Assessment Report on Disaster Risk Reduction.* Geneva: United Nations.

UNISDR (2011a) *2011 Global Assessment Report on Disaster Risk Reduction: Revealing Risk, Redefining Development.* Geneva: United Nations.

UNISDR (2011b) *Hyogo Framework for Action 2005–2015. Building the Resilience of Nations and Communities to Disasters. Mid-Term Review 2010–2011.* Geneva: United Nations.

Van Dijk, A.I.J.M., M. van Noordwijk, I.R. Calder, S.L.A. Bruijnzeel, J. Schellekens and N.A. Chappell (2009) "Forest–Flood Relation Still Tenuous – Comment on 'Global Evidence That Deforestation Amplifies Flood Risk and Severity in the Developing World'". *Global Change Biology* 15: 110–115.

Vermaat, J.E. and U. Thampanya (2006) "Mangroves Mitigate Tsunami Damage: A Further Response". *Estuarine, Coastal and Shelf Science* 69: 1–3.

Vermaat, J.E. and U. Thampanya (2007) "Erratum to 'Mangroves Mitigate Tsunami Damage: A Further Response'". *Estuarine, Coastal and Shelf Science* 75: 564.

WFP [World Food Programme] (2010) "Climate Change: Enabling People to Adapt for the Future". Office for Climate Change and Disaster Risk Reduction. Available at <http://www.wfp.org/content/climate-change-enabling-people-adapt-future-0> (accessed 9 October 2012).

Wharton, G. and D. Gilvear (2006) "River Restoration in the UK: Meeting the Dual Needs of the European Union Water Framework Directive and Flood Defence?" *International Journal of River Basin Management* 4: 1–12.

WWF (2008) *Natural Security. Protected Areas and Hazard Mitigation.* The Arguments for Protection Series, World Wide Fund for Nature.

Zhao, B. et al. (2005) "Estimation of Ecological Service Values of Wetlands in Shanghai, China". *Chinese Geographical Science* 15: 151–156.

2

Ecosystem-based disaster risk reduction (Eco-DRR): An overview

Marisol Estrella and Nina Saalismaa

What is a disaster?

A disaster is generally defined as a serious disruption of the functioning of a community or society that results in widespread damage and losses and that exceeds the ability of the affected community or society to cope using its own resources (UNISDR, 2009a). Disasters occur when three main conditions are present: one or more hazard events, vulnerability and exposure to physical hazards.

It is important to distinguish between a hazard event and a disaster. Physical hazards such as cyclones, flooding or landslides do not by themselves cause disasters. A disaster takes place when the effects of a hazard event overwhelm a community's or society's ability to cope with the damages incurred. The impacts from a hazard are determined by the degree of people's and society's *vulnerabilities* and exposure to the hazard event. Put simply, disasters are not natural and adverse impacts may be prevented, mitigated and/or anticipated through human efforts that analyse and reduce the causal factors of vulnerability and exposure. Although physical hazards such as earthquakes and cyclones cannot be prevented, the likelihood of potential damage or risks can be limited or managed more effectively. Therefore, disaster risk reduction (DRR) is essentially about minimizing the impact of hazard events by enhancing capacities to better manage and recover from the effects of hazards.

Exposure is expressed as the number of people, the amount of infrastructure or other elements of value that are present in a hazard zone

The role of ecosystems in disaster risk reduction, Renaud, Sudmeier-Rieux and Estrella (eds), United Nations University Press, 2013, ISBN 978-92-808-1221-3

and therefore subject to losses. As more and more people and their assets (livelihoods, property, infrastructure, etc.) become concentrated in hazard-prone zones, they increase their exposure; thus, their risk of potential losses increases. Managing exposure is therefore about improving land-use planning and zoning and, when needed, evacuating people from a hazard zone.

Vulnerability, on the other hand, is quite a complex concept that is considered independent from exposure by the United Nations International Strategy for Disaster Reduction (UNISDR, 2009a) but embedded with exposure by many social science researchers and within the climate change community. Interestingly, many of the definitions of the Intergovernmental Panel on Climate Change have recently changed to become more aligned with those of UNISDR, notably its definition of vulnerability, which is now given as "the propensity or predisposition to be adversely affected" (IPCC, 2012: 3). In all cases, the question of vulnerability is critical for understanding disasters and making choices about how to intervene (Twigg, 2004). Although there are multiple, varying definitions of vulnerability (see Birkmann, 2006), on the whole it is used to describe a range of factors – physical, social, economic, environmental, cultural, political/institutional, and even psychological – that shape how hazards affect communities. Vulnerability reveals structural economic and social reasons why people choose – or are obliged – to live the way they do and reside in hazardous locations (Wisner et al., 2004). Often a whole chain of causal factors is involved, with environmental drivers as an important component of vulnerability. In this regard, vulnerability is inversely related to an enhanced capacity to prepare and plan for, cope with and recover from hazard impacts. Mortality risk associated with weather-related hazards is now declining globally as a result of strengthened risk governance capacities, but economic loss risk continues to increase across all regions, especially threatening the economies of low-income countries (UNISDR, 2011).

With disaster risk increasing globally and compounded by the potential impacts of climate change, traditional approaches to disaster management, which focused heavily on disaster response capacities or engineered infrastructure as physical defences, may no longer be sufficient. There is need to think and act differently about the risks we face, the vulnerabilities that drive risk, and the available forms of capital or resources that could be harnessed for reducing risk.

Ecosystem management provides important and readily accessible solutions to DRR by enhancing a system's and a community's overall resilience, or its ability to effect positive change or "bounce forward" (Manyena et al., 2011). Ecosystem-based approaches to DRR offer a good alternative and/or complement because they are often already part of livelihood and hazard mitigation strategies of local communities.

Box 2.1 Definition of ecosystem

Ecosystem = dynamic complex of plants, animals and other living communities and the non-living environment interacting as a functional unit. Humans are an integral part of ecosystems.

Source: Millennium Ecosystem Assessment (2005: v).

This chapter provides an overview of the important linkages between environment and disasters and the role of ecosystems in DRR. It discusses a range of available ecosystem management approaches that have been applied for DRR, drawing on case studies and examples from around the world. Finally, it elaborates on key challenges to implementing ecosystem-based disaster risk reduction (Eco-DRR) and proposed ways forward.

Understanding linkages between the environment, disasters and development

That the environment, development and disasters are linked is now widely accepted. What is less understood is the multidimensional role of the environment in the context of disasters, and how environment–disaster linkages in turn are affected by development processes that create or perpetuate vulnerabilities (Sudmeier-Rieux and Ash, 2009; UNEP and UNISDR, 2008).

Disasters can have adverse consequences on the environment and on ecosystems in particular, which could have immediate to long-term effects on the populations whose life, health, livelihoods and well-being depend on ecosystems and the natural resources they provide. Environmental impacts may include: (i) direct damage to natural resources and infrastructure, affecting ecosystem functions, (ii) acute emergencies from the uncontrolled, unplanned or accidental release of hazardous substances, especially from industries, and (iii) indirect damage as a result of post-disaster relief and recovery operations that fail to take their potential environmental impacts into account (see Figure 2.1). As a result, existing vulnerabilities may be exacerbated or, worse, new vulnerabilities and risk patterns may emerge, especially in circumstances where there are cumulative impacts due to recurring natural hazards (UNEP and UNISDR, 2008).

On the other hand, environmental degradation itself is a major driver of disaster risk (UNISDR, 2009b). Degraded ecosystems can aggravate

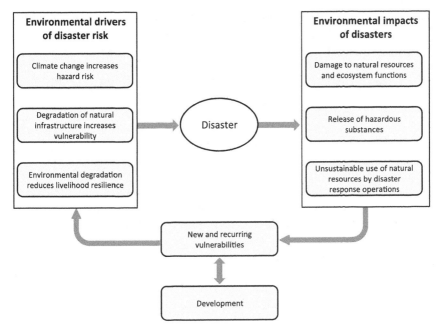

Figure 2.1 Environmental causes and consequences of disasters
Source: Adapted from UNEP and UNISDR (2008).

the impact of natural hazards, for instance by altering physical processes that affect the magnitude, frequency and timing of these hazards. This has been evidenced in areas such as Haiti and Pakistan, where very high rates of deforestation have led to increased susceptibility to floods and landslides during hurricanes and heavy rainfall events (Peduzzi, 2010; Sudmeier-Rieux et al., 2011).[1] In the United States, the devastation caused by Hurricane Katrina in 2005 was exacerbated as a result of canalization and drainage of the Mississippi floodplains, a decrease in delta sedimentation owing to dams and levees, and degradation of barrier islands (Batker et al., 2010; Day et al., 2007; see also World Bank, 2010).

Environmental degradation also contributes to risk by increasing socioeconomic vulnerability to hazard impacts as the capacity of degraded ecosystems to meet people's needs for food and other services is reduced (UNISDR, 2009a). This was the case in Myanmar, where existing degradation of coastal vegetation limited livelihood recovery efforts following the devastating impacts of Cyclone Nargis in 2005 (UNEP, 2009). Poor communities are particularly affected because their livelihoods depend heavily on natural resources and ecosystem services (Millennium Ecosystem Assessment, 2005). Climate change is expected to further increase vulnerabilities, with unpredictable precipitation patterns and other extreme weather events, as well as the adverse impacts on ecosystems' structures and functions that weaken their natural resilience against hazards (Campbell et al., 2009; IPCC, 2012; Sudmeier-Rieux and Ash, 2009; World Bank, 2010).

However, it is important to keep in mind the multiple causal factors of vulnerability and drivers of risk, with the natural environment and environmental degradation as only one factor. A more in-depth analysis, for instance, of differences between Haiti and the Dominican Republic with respect to hazard impacts shows that, in addition to environmental degradation, higher vulnerability in Haiti is linked to extent of land area, population density and gross domestic product per capita, amongst other factors (see Chapter 1 in this volume).

Environment–disaster linkages should be examined in the broader context of development. Linkages between poverty, environmental degradation and disaster risk are now better documented; the poor often occupy fragile and marginal spaces, suffer the highest casualties and generally have the least capacity to recover from disasters (TEEB, 2010; UNISDR, 2009b). Nonetheless, vulnerability extends beyond poverty, as development policies and economic activities may also create unsafe conditions. For instance, urbanization and agricultural intensification have resulted in significant land-cover and land-use changes as well as natural resource overexploitation, increasing human exposure to hazards.

What is ecosystem-based disaster risk reduction?

Ecosystem-based disaster risk reduction (Eco-DRR) is the sustainable management, conservation and restoration of ecosystems to reduce disaster risk, with the aim of achieving sustainable and resilient development. People derive indispensable benefits from nature, also known as ecosystem services (see Box 2.2), which can be harnessed for hazard mitigation, disaster recovery, climate change mitigation and adaptation, livelihoods development and poverty reduction (Figure 2.2). In contrast to conventional engineering solutions such as floodwalls or dykes, Eco-DRR provides multiple benefits for human well-being regardless of a disaster event, and involves relatively low-cost construction and maintenance where ecosystems are healthy and well managed. In this regard, Eco-DRR is considered to be a cost-effective, no-regret investment (PEDRR, 2010; TEEB, 2010).

Box 2.2 Definition of ecosystem services

Ecosystem services = the direct and indirect benefits people obtain from nature

Examples:

Provisioning services: food, raw materials, freshwater, medicinal resources

Regulating services: natural hazard control, erosion control, air quality regulation, climate regulation, water purification, disease and pest regulation, pollination

Cultural services: recreation, tourism, spiritual fulfilment, aesthetic and cultural inspiration

Supporting services: soil formation, nutrient cycling

Source: Millennium Ecosystem Assessment (2005: 40).

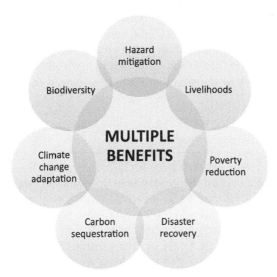

Figure 2.2 Multiple benefits of ecosystems
Source: Authors' figure, presented at the PEDRR training course.

Linking ecosystems to disaster risk reduction

Ecosystems contribute to reducing disaster risk in two important ways. If healthy and appropriately managed, ecosystems can provide natural protection (that is, reduced hazard exposure) and can enhance the livelihood resilience of hazard-prone communities (Sudmeier-Rieux and Ash, 2009).

Sustainable or healthy ecosystems imply that the functional integrity of ecosystems is largely intact and that human demand for ecosystem services does not impinge upon the capacity of ecosystems to maintain future generations (Sudmeier-Rieux and Ash, 2009).

Providing natural protection

Ecosystems can reduce physical exposure to common natural hazards, namely landslides, flooding, avalanches, storm surges, wildfires and drought, by serving as natural protective barriers or buffers (ProAct Network, 2008; Sudmeier-Rieux and Ash, 2009; World Bank, 2010). For example, in the European Alps, mountain forests have a long history of being managed for protection against avalanches and rock fall (Chapter 13 in this volume).[2] In Switzerland, national guidelines for protection forest management have been developed collaboratively with local forest managers and scientists, and the state provides financial incentives to manage forests for hazard protection (Brang et al., 2006).

Several countries in Europe – such as Germany, the Netherlands, the United Kingdom, East European countries bordering the Danube River (WWF, 2008) and Switzerland (Département du Territoire, 2009)[3] – aim to mitigate floods through "Making Space for Water" initiatives that remove built infrastructure (such as concrete river channels) and restore wetlands and rivers to improve their water retention capacity (Box 2.3).[4]

Box 2.3 "Making Space for Water": A government strategy for flood and coastal erosion risk management in the UK

In 2005 the UK's Department for Environment, Food and Rural Affairs (Defra) launched the government programme "Making Space for Water", which developed an innovative country strategy for flood and coastal erosion risk management. This initiative was triggered by severe flooding events in 2005, 2000 and 1998. Various projects are taking place throughout the UK to assess how natural resources and processes can help to protect against floods, improve urban drainage and reduce coastal erosion. In the past, there was heavy reliance on rigid, man-made structures for flood risk management along the UK's riverbanks and coastlines, which required constant repair and costly upgrades. The new approach to risk management adopts the use of natural infrastructure and processes for hazard mitigation. This programme aims to address future development pressures, address rising coastal hazards as a result of climate change, and reduce hazard mitigation costs.

Source: Defra (2005).

Box 2.4   Community-based forest rehabilitation for slope stability, Bolivia

"The PROFOR reforestation project (*Programa de Repoblamiento Forestal*), supported by the Swiss Development Cooperation [*sic*], was implemented for 15 years in rural areas of the Bolivian Altiplano. PROFOR used a community forestry approach for slope stabilisation and income generation. 80 hectares of forest plantations were established in one of the project areas, Khuluyo Village, where environmental degradation had increased the risk of landslides from surrounding hillsides. In 2003, PROFOR results in Khuluyo were assessed through community consultations and social mapping. Results indicated that PROFOR project activities had diversified livelihoods and improved both slope stability and the condition of watersheds. This in turn, increased community resilience to climatic risks, including resilience to extended dry periods and landslides. The case suggests that addressing climate change adaptation within development cooperation should include sustainable management of natural resources as a strategy to improve resilience in rural livelihoods."

Source: Robledo et al. (2004: Abstract).

In Argentina, extensive areas of natural forest are protected to provide services for flood control, which is seen as a low-cost alternative to costly infrastructure, with added biodiversity benefits (World Bank, 2010). In Bolivia, community-based forest rehabilitation is being used for slope stabilization (Box 2.4).

Following the 2004 Indian Ocean tsunami, numerous coastal reforestation projects were initiated in Asia to restore affected areas and to provide protection against coastal hazards. For example, Indonesia announced plans to reforest 600,000 hectares of depleted mangrove forest in five years, and the governments of Sri Lanka and Thailand launched large programmes to rehabilitate mangrove areas for coastal protection (Harakunarak and Aksornkoae, 2005). Multi-partner initiatives, such as Green Coasts and Mangroves for the Future,[5] have supported sustainable post-tsunami coastal development and resilience-building with respect to hazards in the main tsunami-affected countries. However, there remains considerable scientific debate regarding the tsunami mitigation potential of coastal ecosystems (see Chatenoux and Peduzzi, 2007; Iverson and Prasad, 2008; Kerr et al., 2009; Olwig et al., 2007; Osti et al., 2009). Their hazard-mitigating effects against lower-magnitude, *non-tsunami* coastal hazards, such as tropical storms, are better acknowledged (FAO, 2007a; IOC, 2009; see also Table 2.1).

Table 2.1 Hazard mitigation functions of ecosystems

Ecosystem	Hazard mitigation
Mountain forests, vegetation on hillsides	• Vegetation cover and root structures protect against erosion and increase slope stability by binding soil together, preventing landslides (Dolidon et al., 2009; Norris et al., 2008; Peduzzi, 2010). • Forests protect against rock fall and stabilize snow, reducing the risk of avalanches (Bebi et al., 2009; Dorren et al., 2004). • Catchment forests, especially primary forests, reduce risk of floods by increasing infiltration of rainfall and delaying peak floodwater flows, except when soils are fully saturated (Krysanova et al., 2008). • Forests on watersheds are important for water recharge and purification, drought mitigation and safeguarding drinking water supply (see World Bank, 2010). • See Chapters 12, 13 and 14 in this volume.
Wetlands, floodplains	• Wetlands and floodplains control floods in coastal areas, inland river basins and mountain areas subject to glacial melt (Campbell et al., 2009). • Peatlands, wet grasslands and other wetlands store water and release it slowly, reducing the speed and volume of runoff after heavy rainfall or snowmelt in springtime. • Marshes, lakes and floodplains release wet season flows slowly during drought periods. • See Chapters 3 and 10 in this volume.
Coastal ecosystems (mangroves, saltmarshes, coral reefs, barrier islands, sand dunes)	• Coastal wetlands, tidal flats, deltas and estuaries reduce the height and speed of storm surges and tidal waves. • Coastal ecosystems protect against hurricanes, storm surges, flooding and other coastal hazards – combined protection by coral reefs, seagrass beds and sand dunes/coastal wetlands/coastal forests is particularly effective (see, for example, Badola and Hussain, 2005; Batker et al., 2010; Granek and Ruttenberg, 2007). • Coral reefs and coastal wetlands such as mangroves and saltmarshes absorb (low-magnitude) wave energy, reduce wave heights and reduce erosion from storms and high tides (Mazda et al., 1997; Möller, 2006; Vo-Luong and Massel, 2008). • Coastal wetlands buffer against saltwater intrusion and adapt to (slow) sea level rise by trapping sediment and organic matter (Campbell et al., 2009). • Non-porous natural barriers such as sand dunes (with associated plant communities) and barrier islands dissipate wave energy and act as barriers against waves, currents, storm surges and tsunamis (IOC, 2009; UNEP-WCMC, 2006). • See Chapters 3, 4, 5, 6 and 7 in this volume.

Table 2.1 (cont.)

Ecosystem	Hazard mitigation
Drylands	• Natural vegetation management and restoration in drylands contributes to ameliorate the effects of drought and control desertification, as trees, grasses and shrubs conserve soil and retain moisture. • Shelterbelts, greenbelts and other types of living fences act as barriers against wind erosion and sand storms. • Maintaining vegetation cover in dryland areas and agricultural practices such as use of shadow crops, nutrient-enriching plants and vegetation litter increase resilience to drought (Campbell et al., 2009; Krysanova et al., 2008). • Prescribed burning and creation of physical firebreaks in dry landscapes reduce fuel loads and the risk of unwanted large-scale fires.

Source: Based on PEDRR (2010: Table 2.2).

It is suggested that the regulating services of ecosystems may form the largest portion of the total economic value of ecosystem services, although they are also, along with cultural services, the most difficult to measure in economic terms (TEEB, 2010). Unfortunately, up to 70 per cent of ecosystem-regulating services are being degraded or used unsustainably (Millennium Ecosystem Assessment, 2005).

Some examples of the economic values of ecosystems' hazard mitigation functions are presented in Table 2.2, although it is important to note that ecosystem service values are often very context specific. For example, the role of coastal vegetation in protecting against extreme weather events can be vital or marginal, depending on the location of a community. In consequence, the value of a service measured in one location can be extrapolated to similar sites and contexts only if suitable adjustments are made (TEEB, 2010). In addition, it is often difficult to assess the full economic value of a given ecosystem, especially non-use values, although even approximate estimates can be useful to guide resource management decisions. Information on monetized hazard mitigation values of ecosystems is still scarce, but through The Economics of Ecosystems and Biodiversity (TEEB) programme as well as similar initiatives by the World Bank to incorporate the value of natural capital into national accounting systems,[6] amongst others, considerable attention and efforts are now under way to better address the economic valuation of ecosystem services, including hazard mitigation values, and their subsequent incorporation into national planning.

Table 2.2 Examples of the estimated economic value of ecosystem services for natural hazard mitigation

Ecosystem	Hazard	Hazard mitigation value (US$)	Sources
Coral reefs (global)	Coastal	189,000/hectare/year	TEEB (2010)
Coral reefs (Caribbean)	Coastal	700,000–2.2 billion per year (total value)	Conservation International (2008)
Coastal wetlands (United States)	Hurricane	8,240/hectare/year	Costanza et al. (2008)
Coastal wetlands (United States)	Storms	23.2 billion/year (total value)	Costanza et al. (2008)
Luzňice floodplain (Czech Republic)	Floods	11,788/hectare/year	ProAct Network (2008)
Muthurajawela marsh (Sri Lanka)	Flood	5 million/year (total value); 1,750/ hectare/year	Emerton and Bos (2004); see also Emerton and Kekulandala (2003)
Coastal ecosystems (Catalonia, Spain)	Disturbance protection, including storms	77,420/hectare/year	Brenner et al. (2010)
Protection forests along mountain roads (Switzerland)	Avalanche	1,000/hectare/year (total value) or a replacement value of 18,000–53,000 per hectare	Dorren and Berger (2012)

Source: Based on PEDRR (2010: Table 2.1).

Enhancing livelihood resilience

Ecosystems also reduce disaster risk by reducing social and economic vulnerability and by enhancing livelihood resilience. Ecosystems sustain human livelihoods and provide essential goods such as food, fibres, medicines and construction materials, which are important for strengthening local resilience against disasters. For example, in addition to providing coastal hazard protection, mangroves, coral reefs and seagrass beds support fishing and tourism activities on which local livelihoods are heavily reliant (Campbell et al., 2009). In China, wetlands are being restored for flood mitigation while providing other social and economic benefits that can reduce vulnerability to hazard impacts (see Box 2.5). In Mexico, the World Bank is undertaking a large-scale coastal wetland and mangrove swamp restoration project for coastal protection as well as for community water supply and food production (World Bank, 2010).

Box 2.5 Restoring wetlands for flood mitigation and local development, China

"In Hubei Province, a wetland restoration programme by WWF and partners reconnected lakes to Yangtze River and rehabilitated 448 km² of wetlands with a capacity to store up to 285 million m³ of flood-waters. The local government subsequently reconnected further eight lakes covering 350 km². Sluice gates at lakes have been seasonally re-opened, and illegal aquaculture facilities have been removed or modi-fied. Local administration has designated lake and marshland areas as nature reserves. In addition to contributing to flood prevention, restored lakes and floodplains have enhanced biodiversity, increased income from fisheries by 20–30% and improved water quality to drink-able levels. While central government was principally concerned to re-duce flood risk, local communities and governments were motivated by better access to clean water and increased incomes. Working in partnership with government agencies has ensured that new practices are mainstreamed in daily operations, and similar measures are adopted in other areas."

Source: PEDRR (2010: 15, based on WWF, 2008).

Moreover, in post-disaster contexts, disaster-affected communities, es-pecially in poor rural areas, often turn to their surrounding environment to meet immediate needs (food, water, shelter). Ecosystems and the re-sources they provide thus form an essential part of local coping and re-covery strategies, reducing people's vulnerability to hazards. For instance, in Negril, Jamaica, following a major storm, a local fishing community re-lies heavily on groundwater springs when floodwaters cut off their pota-ble drinking water supply; maintaining the water quality of springs would protect people against waterborne diseases associated with floods (UNEP, 2010). This important role of ecosystems in supporting local recovery is often poorly acknowledged in post-disaster interventions as well as in long-term prevention strategies.

Linking Eco-DRR to climate change adaptation

Climate change is expected to increase disaster risk in two ways. It will result in precipitation and temperature changes and alter the intensity and frequency of some extreme weather events, and it will thus amplify vulnerabilities of communities to natural hazards, particularly through ac-celerated ecosystem degradation, water and food variability and scarcity, and changes in livelihoods (for further discussion, see Christensen et al., 2007; IPCC, 2012; UNISDR, 2009b, 2011). Climate change, however, is primarily regarded as an *added* risk factor, aggravating already existing conditions of vulnerability and exposure that cause disasters (UNISDR, 2009b). Effective climate risk management addresses the projected impacts of climate change by seeking to reduce vulnerability associated with climate risks and, at the same time, anticipating the potential climate change impacts across sectors, including on critical ecosystems and the services they provide.

Ecosystems yield important benefits for climate change mitigation through carbon sequestration (for example, forests and peatlands) and for climate change adaptation by buffering against extreme weather events and sea level rise and by securing the natural assets needed to make livelihoods resilient to climate change impacts (see Campbell et al., 2009; Colls et al., 2009; World Bank, 2010). Ecosystem management is recognized as a key strategy for adapting to climate change (UNFCCC, 2011). This is also known as ecosystem-based adaptation (EbA), which integrates the use of biodiversity and ecosystem services into a strategy that reduces vulnerability and increases resilience by helping people adapt to the adverse impacts of climate change. EbA is closely related to Eco-DRR. Both approaches recognize the role of healthy and well-managed ecosystems in enabling communities to prevent, prepare for, cope with and recover from climate-related disasters and extreme events. The main differences between the two approaches relate to temporal and spatial scales: EbA often also addresses long-term climate change impacts and ecosystem changes, whereas Eco-DRR focuses especially on specific hazard events, often within specified time periods and locations, that may or may not be linked to climate change or climate variability.

Linking Eco-DRR to sustainable development

Eco-DRR is essentially about promoting sustainable development in hazard-prone areas. Ecosystem management not only helps mitigate natural hazard impacts and increase human resilience against hazards but also generates a range of other social, economic and environmental benefits for multiple stakeholders, which in turn feed back into reduced risk. In order to be effective, Eco-DRR should be implemented as an integrated approach to address disaster and climate change risks in the context of national and local development planning and within the framework of overall disaster management strategies.

Eco-DRR combines disaster risk reduction, climate change adaptation and sound ecosystem management for overall sustainable development gains (Figure 2.3). Despite the obvious linkages, these three working

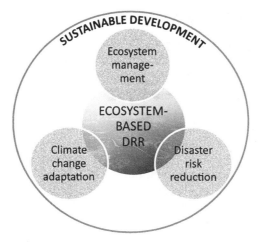

Figure 2.3 Eco-DRR in the framework of sustainable development
Source: Adapted from Sudmeier-Rieux and Ash (2009).

spheres are usually dealt with by different sets of institutional actors and are regulated by different sets of legal and regulatory frameworks, at both national and global policy levels. However, the linkages between ecosystems, disasters, climate change and development need to be acknowledged and steps taken to maximize collaboration, knowledge and resources for increased cost-effectiveness and overall development gains.

Applications of Eco-DRR

Implementing Eco-DRR can build on existing ecosystem management principles, strategies and approaches and include a range of instruments, such as: environmental assessment tools, integrated water resources management, coastal zone management, integrated fire management, sustainable dryland management and protected area management (for a full discussion, see PEDRR, 2010).

Environmental assessments

Environmental impact assessments (EIAs) and strategic environmental assessments (SEAs) are the best-known tools for assessing the potential environmental impacts of proposed policies, programmes or projects. EIAs and SEAs are being adapted to incorporate analysis of disaster risk-related information, such as natural hazard profiles and hazard scenarios as well as vulnerability indicators, which can potentially adversely impact or may be affected by proposed projects, programmes, plans or policies.

Efforts to mainstream DRR in EIAs have been spearheaded by the Caribbean Development Bank (CDB) and the Caribbean Community (CARICOM).[7] Together they have produced a sourcebook for integrating natural hazard concerns, including potential climate change impacts, into the application of EIAs in countries such as Grenada and Trinidad (CDB and CARICOM, 2004). SEAs also provide an opportunity to ensure that disaster risk is considered in weighing alternative development options (OECD, 2008).[8] In Sri Lanka, the government in collaboration with the United Nations Development Programme (UNDP) and the United Nations Environment Programme (UNEP) carried out an integrated SEA process as part of a post-conflict development initiative. This process takes into account major hazards in assessing potential vulnerabilities with respect to future development in the Northern Province, especially along the coast (UNDP and Government of Sri Lanka, 2011). Despite these emerging practices, applications of EIAs and especially SEAs for disaster risk reduction remain very limited and still need to be mainstreamed as part of development planning processes.[9]

Integrated water resources management

Integrated water resources management (IWRM) is a governance and development process to manage water, land and related resources in order to maximize economic and social welfare in an equitable manner without compromising the sustainability of ecosystems (Global Water Partnership, 2000, 2009). IWRM provides a framework for negotiating between different water users and ensures a balance between economic efficiency (allocating scarce water resources to different sectors), social equity (access to and benefiting from water use) and environmental sustainability (protecting aquatic ecosystems and the water resource base) (Global Water Partnership, 2000, 2009).

IWRM has the potential for minimizing and managing land–water-related disaster risks, for instance with respect to excess water (that is, flood and landslide mitigation) and water scarcity (that is, drought management). Good IWRM means better policies for improved catchment or watershed management, which result in multiple benefits including secure water supplies, reduced pollution and sedimentation, and reduced hazards. IWRM can help build a strong flood or drought mitigation strategy through the restoration of wetlands, forest and river basins combined with sustainable land-use planning (see also Chapter 3 in this volume). It may be applied in a number of contexts, including for managing transboundary river basins,[10] as well as for addressing urban disaster risks (PEDRR, 2011).

Integrated coastal zone management

Coastal areas are exposed to multiple hazards and often have high concentrations of human populations and economic assets. Integrated coastal zone management (ICZM) provides a multi-stakeholder, multi-sectoral framework for the sustainable management of coastal zones to ensure their continued functions and services. It presents an opportunity for addressing coastal risks in an integrated manner, by adopting a combination of ecosystem-based measures (for example, greenbelts, coastal forests, coastal wetlands, sand dunes, coral reefs), engineered measures (for example, dykes) and non-structural measures (for example, regulatory frameworks, awareness-raising).

Numerous country-level experiences draw on ICZM for reducing vulnerability to coastal hazards and developing the coastal zone. For example, since the 1960s, Bangladesh has implemented ICZM and invested in mangrove coastal afforestation or greenbelts, with the aim of reducing the impacts of storm surges as well as providing multiple benefits to local communities, including timber, fodder and fuelwood production, stabilizing newly accreted mud flats, and sustaining group-based forestry activities for additional income (Iftekhar and Islam, 2004). In the United States, following the devastating impacts of Hurricane Katrina in 2005, the restoration of coastal wetlands and barrier islands has been adopted to complement the levee system in the states of Louisiana and Mississippi (see Box 2.6), as part of a comprehensive ICZM strategy (Louisiana-Mississippi Gulf Coast Ecosystem Restoration Working Group, 2010).[11] (See also Chapters 6 and 7 in this volume for other examples of coastal planning.)

Box 2.6 Preserving wetlands for flood protection, New Orleans, USA

> "Following the disastrous failure of flood defence structures during Hurricane Katrina in 2005, the State of Louisiana and the City of New Orleans have undertaken steps to increase their resilience to sea-level rise, hurricanes and river flooding. An approach using several lines of defence has been adopted. One of the key protection measures is the conservation and restoration of wetlands as a buffer zone between the sea and the city. Detailed actions promoting wetlands as green infrastructure are included in the New Orleans Masterplan" (Kazmierczak and Carter, 2010: v). This signals a significant change, from an emphasis on levees and floodgates to the incorporation of more natural solutions in flood defence.

Integrated fire management

Integrated fire management aims to balance the beneficial and negative effects of fire in a given area and reduce the risk of wildfire disasters threatening human life and ecosystem functions.[12] In South Africa, integrated fire management has become an important employment opportunity for marginal community members, while effectively reducing the risk of unwanted fires through prescribed burning and community sensitization (PEDRR, 2010).[13] Several countries in Europe also use prescribed burning both for decreasing wildfire hazards and for biodiversity and forest management objectives, and there is growing interest in the better use and integration of traditional fire use and management (Goldammer, 2010; Rego et al., 2010).

Sustainable dryland management

Sustainable dryland management is an approach that attempts to manage arid, semi-arid and sub-humid lands for food production and other human needs without compromising the long-term sustainability of the fragile natural resource base (water, soil) and ecosystem functions. The approach involves traditional and innovative techniques that enhance land, soil and water conservation.

Restoring and maintaining the provision of dryland ecosystems' goods and services are key to enhancing the economic and social well-being of dryland communities and strengthening their capacity to manage rainfall scarcity and uncertainty (see Box 2.7). Most drought mitigation strategies traditionally practised in drylands are ecosystem based. Well-known examples are mobile livestock herding to avoid climatic risks and the collection and consumption of wild fruits and roots as a major coping strategy during drought periods (Okori et al., 2009). Agricultural practices such as agroforestry (that is, intercropping food crops with trees), mulching, rainwater harvesting and use of shelterbelts contribute to conserve water and soils, reduce wind erosion and restore fertility, which improves community resilience during dry conditions (Campbell et al., 2009).

Protected area management

Although protected area management is commonly associated with nature conservation and tourism, history shows that human societies have long practised principles of protected area management for their multiple benefits, such as for hunting, cultivation and grazing, as well as for their buffering effects against natural hazards. For instance, Japan introduced

Box 2.7 Resilience to drought through agro-ecological restoration of drylands, Burkina Faso and Niger

Two different, but almost simultaneous, agro-ecological restoration processes started 30 years ago in the Sahel area of Africa to increase water availability, restore soil fertility and improve agricultural yields in degraded drylands. These initiatives were led by poor farmers from southern Niger and the Central Plateau of Burkina Faso whose livelihoods had been increasingly affected by drought and land degradation. With very little external support, local farmers experimented with low-cost adaptations of traditional agricultural and agroforestry techniques to solve local problems and exchanged knowledge with others. Three decades later, hundreds of thousands of farmers have replicated, adapted and benefited from these techniques and have transformed the once barren landscape at an unprecedented geographical and temporal scale. In Burkina Faso, more than 200,000 hectares of dryland have been rehabilitated, now producing an additional 80,000 tons of food per year. In Niger, more than 200 million on-farm trees have been regenerated, providing 500,000 additional tons of food per year, as well as many other goods and services. Women have particularly benefited from improved supply of water, fuelwood and other tree products. By supporting poverty reduction and increasing the coping and adaptive capacities of local populations, the initiatives have significantly reduced the risks and vulnerabilities associated with frequent droughts in the region.

Sources: Reij et al. (2009a, 2009b).

forest protection in the fifteenth and sixteenth centuries as a counter-measure against landslides, and today it has 17 designated uses of protection forests, 13 of which are related to mitigating or preventing hazard events (Stolton et al., 2008). In Switzerland, protection forests have been recognized over the last century for their role in mitigating impacts from avalanches, rock falls and landslides (Chapter 13 in this volume). The Whangamarino Ramsar site in New Zealand contains protected wetlands and swamps that serve as natural reservoirs against floods by containing excess rain and runoff and thus reducing flood peaks (Ming et al., 2007). In eastern Madagascar, the Mantadia National Park protects upland forests and watersheds, which reduce flooding damage to lowland agrarian communities (Kramer et al., 1997).

Protected areas and community conservation areas cover almost 20 per cent of the Earth[14] and encompass terrestrial, coastal and marine

environments, making them a significant form of land and water management. Because of their legal status and relatively well-resourced management and governance institutions, they ensure effective long-term
management, facilitating investments in resilient ecosystems, their regular
monitoring, and development of appropriate responses to threats and
vulnerabilities (Dudley et al., 2010; see also Chapter 15 in this volume).

Recognizing the limits of ecosystems for DRR

Investing in ecosystems should not be viewed as a single solution to risk
reduction. Ecosystem-based measures should be part of a larger disaster
risk management strategy and should always be complementary to other
essential risk management measures, such as early warning systems and
evacuation plans. Eco-DRR, like all DRR activities, reduces risk but does
not remove risk. It is important to recognize that ecosystems also have
limits in providing protection against hazards.

Ecosystem composition (size, density, species) and health status, the
type and intensity of the hazard event, and other physical features related to the specific location of ecosystems (for example, topography,
soils) all affect ecosystems' effectiveness in hazard regulation (Campbell
et al., 2009; PEDRR, 2010; Chapter 3 in this volume). Healthy ecosystems
are considered more resilient to the impacts of extreme events and are
able to recover more effectively than degraded ecosystems (Sudmeier-
Rieux and Ash, 2009). Using forests to stabilize avalanche-prone slopes
reduces the frequency of avalanches but not the fact that avalanches will
still occur under specific conditions. Forests do not seem to protect
against severe events such as large-scale flooding or tsunamis (Campbell
et al., 2009; FAO, 2007a; FAO and CIFOR, 2005; Feagin et al., 2010). The
force of tsunamis may, in many cases, be too strong for coastal vegetation
– just like for most seawalls (FAO, 2007b; Chapter 4 in this volume).

Sometimes a "hybrid" approach combining both natural and hard engineering defences may be most effective. For example, mangrove forests
are rehabilitated and maintained to protect against storm surges and
complement constructed sea dykes, increasing the effectiveness and
lifespan of the dykes, as demonstrated in Viet Nam (Powell et al., 2011).
It is important to weigh the value-added of applying or mixing various
alternatives. Especially in the context of extreme events and adapting to
climate change, human-built infrastructure may often not be feasible due
to its high costs and technology requirements. Conventional engineering
solutions may also generate adverse environmental impacts or provide a
false sense of security, and may still fail dramatically, amplifying disaster

damage (Batker et al., 2010; Campbell et al., 2009; Ramsar Convention on Wetlands, 2010).

Maintaining and restoring ecosystems as natural infrastructure can offer high benefit–cost ratios compared with engineered infrastructure, when taking into account the full range of benefits provided by ecosystems (TEEB, 2010; World Bank, 2010). In some cases, however, natural buffers are not feasible because of biological limitations, space constraints, incompatibility with priority land uses or prohibitive costs; therefore, engineered infrastructure may be required to provide the necessary protection.

Finally, Eco-DRR requires reliable data on hazards and vulnerabilities and needs to be grounded in a good understanding of the local ecological context, such as the geological and hydrological conditions of a given area as well as the plant–wildlife–human interactions that take place. Just as conventional human-built DRR structures such as floodwalls and storm channels require engineering expertise, Eco-DRR requires environmental specialists to work in collaboration with structural engineers, land-use planners, disaster managers and local stakeholders.

Key issues

In applying Eco-DRR, it is important to stress the combination of "hardware" and "software" measures, for instance implementing eco-engineering solutions that utilize appropriate technical expertise, which are in turn supported by policies and are integrated into development planning and decision-making processes. Effective implementation also requires the involvement of different actors (public and private sectors, civil society, communities, academia, etc.) and multiple sectors, as well as the appropriate institutional structures and mechanisms to create successful partnerships. This chapter concludes by outlining some of the key issues and next steps to facilitate the implementation and scaling-up of Eco-DRR practice, many of which are further elaborated throughout the book.

Policies and legal frameworks to support Eco-DRR practice

Establishing integrated national policies and legislation that promote ecosystems and natural infrastructure for risk reduction is an important enabling factor for effective Eco-DRR implementation, as demonstrated by the supportive policies in countries such as the Netherlands, the United Kingdom, Sri Lanka and Switzerland. Such innovative policies are still, however, more exceptions than common practice. Integrated policies can both minimize implementation costs and improve the flow of services (TEEB, 2010; World Bank, 2010). In many cases, however, appropriate policies and legislation may be in place but the main problem lies in their enforcement and the lack of political will.

As discussed in the section "What is ecosystem-based disaster risk reduction?", cross-sectoral collaboration is key in order to facilitate implementation of Eco-DRR. It is particularly important to develop multidisciplinary teams and platforms and involve people with different technical expertise and knowledge, for instance city engineers and land developers working together with ecologists and disaster management experts. This should apply at both national and subnational levels.

Develop national and local capacities for Eco-DRR

Although there are now a significant number of DRR trainings being delivered around the world, very few of them address environment–disaster linkages and focus on ecosystem management tools for DRR. Training materials with an environment-DRR thematic coverage have only recently been developed.[15]

Capacity development should enhance awareness and capacities at the country level to apply environmental tools for DRR and mainstream these into national and local development planning. This involves increasing awareness among policy-makers and decision-makers in government and building the capacities of practitioners and technical staff involved in programme and project implementation. Capacity development should target land-use planners, city planners, disaster managers and staff in key sectoral agencies (for example, forestry, agriculture, tourism). Environment-DRR training should also be integrated into already existing national training programmes in order to ensure that they are mainstreamed in governance and institutional practice. The Partnership for Environment and Disaster Risk Reduction (PEDRR) has developed a training course on Eco-DRR, targeting national and local governments in particular.[16]

Knowledge and research on ecosystem resilience thresholds

Finally, a key challenge remains in measuring ecosystem resilience thresholds to various hazards, that is, how much impact or change inflicted by a certain hazard an ecosystem can absorb. Only limited information exists on the performance thresholds of different ecosystems and levels of ecosystem resilience against environmental change and different hazards (that is, hazard type, intensity and frequency). There are clear knowledge gaps in assessing ecosystem capacity to maintain services over time, especially in the context of changing environmental conditions and disturbances (TEEB, 2010). Further scientific research on ecosystem services is therefore needed, including long-term monitoring and evaluation of ecosystem functions and performance before and after disaster events.

Another critical area for further study is the economic valuation of ecosystem services for hazard mitigation, which was discussed earlier in this chapter. Given the challenges of fully monetizing ecosystem services, there should also be further research and development of evidence-based valuation methodologies that aim to quantify the role of ecosystems for DRR.

Next steps

In recent years, several international reports have concluded that ecosystem-based approaches are beneficial and should be integrated in the portfolio of actions in addressing disaster risks (see IPCC, 2012; TEEB, 2010; UNISDR, 2009b, 2011; World Bank, 2010). It is now the task of policy-makers and practitioners to take up this message, seek appropriate technical expertise and scale up the Eco-DRR practice.

Notes

1. Susceptible = open, subject or unresistant to some stimulus, influence or agency (<http://www.merriam-webster.com/dictionary/susceptible>). For example, a landslide susceptibility map ranks the slope stability of an area into categories from stable to unstable.
2. See, for example, the Protocol on the Implementation of the Alpine Convention Relating to Mountain Forests, <http://www.alpconv.org/en/convention/protocols/Documents/protokoll_bergwaldGB.pdf> (accessed 10 October 2012).
3. See also <http://etat.geneve.ch/dt/eau/renaturation-878-5114.html>.
4. Defra (2005), Deltacommissie (2008), Parliamentary Office of Science and Technology (2009). See also <http://www.deltacommissie.com/en/advies>.
5. See <http://www.wetlands.org/Whatwedo/Ouractions/GreenCoastscommunitybasedrestoration/tabid/436/Default.aspx> and <http://www.mangrovesforthefuture.org> (accessed 10 October 2012).
6. In October 2010, at the Convention on Biological Diversity meeting in Nagoya, Japan, the World Bank announced a new Global Partnership for Ecosystems and Ecosystem Services Valuation and Wealth Accounting, now known as Wealth Accounting and the Valuation of Ecosystem Services (WAVES). For further information, see <http://www.wavespartnership.org/waves/> (accessed 10 October 2012).
7. CARICOM is an intergovernmental entity comprising 15 Caribbean countries.
8. The Organisation for Economic Co-operation and Development (OECD) has also developed a guidance note on linking SEAs with adaptation to climate change, with clear linkages to DRR.
9. See also Chapter 17 in this volume.

10. See also Zukunft Alpenrhein at <http://www.alpenrhein.net/> (accessed 10 October 2012).
11. See also CLEAR (Coastal Louisiana Ecosystem Assessment & Restoration) at <http://www.clear.lsu.edu/needs_in_louisiana> (accessed 10 October 2012).
12. See Global Fire Management Control at <http://www.gfmc.org>; Fire Paradox at http://www.fireparadox.org>; the WAMIS portal at <http://www.wamis.co.za/> (accessed 10 October 2012).
13. See also Working on Fire at <http://www.workingonfire.org/> (accessed 10 October 2012).
14. See the World Database on Protected Areas at <http://www.wdpa.org> (accessed 10 October 2012).
15. The Asian Disaster Preparedness Center has developed a regional training manual on DRR for coastal zone managers. UNEP together with local partners developed and delivered integrated DRR-coastal zone management trainings in Sri Lanka, India and Indonesia. The International Union for Conservation of Nature (IUCN) has undertaken extensive work and capacity-building on integrated watershed management. The Global Fire Monitoring Center has developed ecosystem-based wildfire management trainings. WWF-US/American Red Cross launched its Green Recovery and Reconstruction Toolkit in 2010, which has a specific module on "greening" DRR.
16. For further information on the training course, visit the PEDRR website at <http://www.pedrr.net> (accessed 10 October 2012).

REFERENCES

Badola, R. and S.A. Hussain (2005) "Valuing Ecosystem Functions: An Empirical Study on the Storm Protection Function of Bhitarkanika Mangrove Ecosystem, India". *Environmental Conservation* 32: 85–92.

Batker, D.P. et al. (2010) "Gaining Ground: Wetlands, Hurricanes and the Economy: The Value of Restoring the Mississippi River Delta". Earth Economics, Tacoma.

Bebi, P., D. Kulakowski and R. Christian (2009) "Snow Avalanche Disturbances in Forest Ecosystems – State of Research and Implications for Management". *Forest Ecology and Management* 257: 1883–1892.

Birkmann, J. (2006) "Measuring Vulnerability to Promote Disaster-Resilient Societies: Conceptual Frameworks and Definitions". In J. Birkmann (ed.), *Measuring Vulnerability to Natural Hazards: Toward Disaster Resilient Societies*. Tokyo: United Nations University Press, pp. 9–54.

Brang, P. et al. (2006) "Management of Protection Forests in the European Alps: An Overview". *Forest, Snow and Landscape Research* 80: 23–44.

Brenner, J. et al. (2010) "An Assessment of the Non-market Value of the Ecosystem Services Provided by the Catalan Coastal Zone, Spain". *Ocean & Coastal Management* 53: 27–38.

Campbell, A. et al. (2009) *Review of the Literature on the Links between Biodiversity and Climate Change: Impacts, Adaptation and Mitigation*. CBD Technical Series No. 42. Montreal: Secretariat of the Convention on Biological Diversity.

CDB [Caribbean Development Bank] and CARICOM Secretariat (2004) *Sourcebook on the Integration of Natural Hazards into Environmental Impact Assess-*

ment (EIA): NHIA-EIA Sourcebook. Bridgetown, Barbados: Caribbean Development Bank.

Chatenoux, B. and P. Peduzzi (2007) "Impacts from the 2004 Indian Ocean Tsunami: Analysing the Potential Protecting Role of Environmental Features". *Natural Hazards* 40: 289–304.

Christensen J.H. et al. (2007) "Regional Climate Projections". In IPCC, *Climate Change 2007: The Physical Science Basis*. Contribution of Working Group I to the Fourth Assessment Report of the Intergovernmental Panel on Climate Change [Solomon, S., et al. (eds)]. Cambridge, UK, and New York, USA: Cambridge University Press, pp. 847–940.

Colls, A., N. Ash and N. Ikkala (2009) *Ecosystem-based Adaptation: A Natural Response to Climate Change*. Gland, Switzerland: International Union for Conservation of Nature.

Conservation International (2008) *Economic Values of Coral Reefs, Mangroves, and Seagrasses: A Global Compilation*. Arlington, VA: Conservation International.

Costanza, R. et al. (2008) "The Value of Coastal Wetlands for Hurricane Protection". *Ambio* 37: 241–248.

Day, J.W. et al. (2007) "Restoration of the Mississippi Delta: Lessons from Hurricanes Katrina and Rita". *Science* 315 (5819): 1679–1684.

Defra [Department for Environment, Food and Rural Affairs] (2005) *Making Space for Water: Taking Forward a New Government Strategy for Flood and Coastal Erosion Risk Management in England*. London: Defra. Available at <http://archive.defra.gov.uk/environment/flooding/documents/policy/strategy/strategy-response1.pdf> (accessed 10 October 2012).

Deltacommissie (2008) *Working Together with Water: A Living Land Builds for Its Future. Findings of the Deltacommissie 2008 – Summary and Conclusions*. Available at <http://www.deltacommissie.com/doc/deltareport_summary.pdf> (accessed 9 October 2012).

Département du Territoire (2009) *Renaturation des cours d'eau du canton de Genève. Bilan de 10 ans d'actions*. Geneva: Republique et canton de Genève. Available at <http://etat.geneve.ch/dt/eau/a_votre_service-publications_bilan_ans_renaturation_cours_eau_1998_2008_disponible_ligne-1868.html> (accessed 10 October 2012).

Dolidon, N. et al. (2009) "Watershed and Forest Management for Landslide Risk Reduction". In K. Sassa and P. Canuti (eds), *Landslides. Disaster Risk Reduction*. Berlin: Springer, pp. 633–646.

Dorren, L.K.A. and F. Berger (2012) "Integrating Forests in the Analysis and Management of Rockfall Risks: Experiences from Research and Practice in the Alps". In E. Eberhardt et al. (eds), *Landslides and Engineered Slopes: Protecting Society through Improved Understanding*. London: Taylor and Francis Group, pp. 117–127.

Dorren, L. et al. (2004) "Integrity, Stability and Management of Protection Forests in the European Alps". *Forest Ecology and Management* 195: 165–176.

Dudley, N. et al. (2010) *Natural Solutions: Protected Areas Helping People Cope with Climate Change*. Gland, Switzerland, Washington, DC, and New York: IUCN-WCPA, TNC, UNDP, WCS, World Bank and WWF.

Emerton, L. and E. Bos (2004) *Value: Counting Ecosystems as an Economic Part of Water Infrastructure*. Water and Nature Initiative. Gland, Switzerland, and Cambridge, UK: IUCN.

Emerton, L. and L.D.C.B. Kekulandala (2003) *Assessment of the Economic Value of Muthurajawela Wetland*. Occasional Papers of IUCN Sri Lanka No. 4.

FAO [Food and Agriculture Organization] (2007a) "Coastal Protection in the Aftermath of the Indian Ocean Tsunami: What Role for Forests and Trees?" *Proceedings of the Regional Technical Workshop, Khao Lak, Thailand, 28–31 August 2006*. RAP Publication 2007/7. Available at <http://www.fao.org/docrep/010/ag127e/ag127e00.htm> (accessed 10 October 2012).

FAO (2007b) *The Role of Coastal Forests in the Mitigation of Tsunami Impacts*. RAP Publication 2007/1.

FAO [Food and Agriculture Organization] and CIFOR [Center for International Forestry Research] (2005) *Forests and Floods: Drowning in Fiction or Thriving on Facts?* RAP Publication 2005/03. Forest Perspectives 2. Bangkok: FAO & CIFOR.

Feagin, R.A. et al. (2010) "Shelter from the Storm? Use and Misuse of Coastal Vegetation Bioshields for Managing Natural Disasters". *Conservation Letters* 3: 1–11.

Global Water Partnership (2000) *Integrated Water Resources Management*. TAC Background Papers No. 4. Stockholm: Global Water Partnership.

Global Water Partnership (2009) "Lessons from Integrated Water Resources Management in Practice". Policy Brief 9. Available at <http://www.gwptoolbox.org/images/stories/gwplibrary/policy/pb_9_english.pdf> (accessed 10 October 2012).

Goldammer, J.G. (2010) *Use of Prescribed Fire in Land Management, Nature Conservation and Forestry in Temperate-Boreal Eurasia*. Results and Recommendations of the Symposium on Fire Management in Cultural and Natural Landscapes, Nature Conservation and Forestry in Temperate-Boreal Eurasia and members of the Eurasian Fire in Nature Conservation Network (EFNCN), Freiburg, Germany, 25–27 January 2008. Fire Ecology Research Group / Global Fire Monitoring Center. Available at <http://www.fire.uni-freiburg.de/programmes/natcon/EFNCN-White-Paper-2010.pdf> (accessed 10 October 2012).

Granek, E.F. and B.I. Ruttenberg (2007) "Protective Capacity of Mangroves during Tropical Storms: A Case Study from 'Wilma' and 'Gamma' in Belize". *Marine Ecology Progress Series* 343: 101–105.

Harakunarak, A. and S. Aksornkoae (2005) "Life-saving Belts: Post-Tsunami Reassessment of Mangrove Ecosystem Values and Management in Thailand". *Tropical Coasts* 12(1): 48–55.

Iftekhar, M.S. and M.R. Islam (2004) "Managing Mangroves in Bangladesh: A Strategy Analysis". *Journal of Coastal Conservation* 10: 139–146.

IOC [Intergovernmental Oceanographic Commission] (2009) *Tsunami Risk Assessment and Mitigation for the Indian Ocean. Knowing Your Tsunami Risk – and What to Do about It*. Intergovernmental Oceanographic Commission Manuals and Guides 52. Paris: UNESCO.

IPCC [Intergovernmental Panel on Climate Change] (2012) "Summary for Policymakers". In *Managing the Risks of Extreme Events and Disasters to Advance*

Climate Change Adaptation [Field, C.B., V. Barros, T.F. Stocker, D. Qin, D.J. Dokken, K.L. Ebi, M.D. Mastrandrea, K.J. Mach, G.-K. Plattner, S.K. Allen, M. Tignor, and P.M. Midgley (eds.)]. A Special Report of Working Groups I and II of the Intergovernmental Panel on Climate Change. Cambridge University Press, Cambridge, UK, and New York, NY, USA, pp. 1–19. Available at <http://www.ipcc-wg2.gov/SREX/> (accessed 10 October 2012).

Iverson, L.R. and A.M. Prasad (2008) "Modeling Tsunami Damage in Aceh: A Reply". *Landscape Ecology* 23: 7–10.

Kazmierczak A. and J. Carter (2010) *Adaptation to Climate Change Using Green and Blue Infrastructure: A Database of Case Studies*. Manchester: University of Manchester.

Kerr, A.M. et al. (2009) "Reply to 'Using Remote Sensing to Assess the Protective Role of Coastal Woody Vegetation against Tsunami Waves'". *International Journal of Remote Sensing* 30(14): 3817–3820.

Kramer, R.A. et al. (1997) "Ecological and Economic Analysis of Watershed Protection in Eastern Madagascar". *Journal of Environmental Management* 49(3): 277–295.

Krysanova, V. et al. (2008) "Practices and Lessons Learned in Coping with Climatic Hazards at the River-Basin Scale: Floods and Drought". *Ecology and Society* 13: 32.

Louisiana-Mississippi Gulf Coast Ecosystem Restoration Working Group (2010) "Roadmap for Restoring Ecosystem Resiliency and Sustainability". Council on Environmental Quality, March. Available at <http://www.whitehouse.gov/administration/eop/ceq/initiatives/gulfcoast/roadmap> (accessed 10 October 2012).

Manyena, S.B., G. O'Brien, P. O'Keefe and J. Rose (2011) "Disaster Resilience: A Bounce Back or Bounce Forward Ability?" *Local Environment* 16(5): 417–424.

Mazda, Y. et al. (1997) "Mangroves as a Coastal Protection from Waves in the Tong Kong Delta, Vietnam". *Mangroves and Salt Marshes* 1: 127–135.

Millennium Ecosystem Assessment (2005) *Ecosystems and Human Well-being: Current State and Trends: Findings of the Condition and Trends Working Group*. Washington, DC: Island Press.

Ming J. et al. (2007) "Flood Mitigation Benefit of Wetland Soil – A Case Study in Momoge National Nature Reserve in China". *Ecological Economics* 61(2–3): 217–223.

Möller, I. (2006) "Quantifying Saltmarsh Vegetation and Its Effect on Wave Height Dissipation: Results from a UK East Coast Saltmarsh". *Estuarine, Coastal and Shelf Science* 69(3–4): 337–351.

Norris, J.E. et al. (eds) (2008) *Slope Stability and Erosion Control: Ecotechnological Solutions*. Dordrecht: Springer.

OECD [Organisation for Economic Co-operation and Development] (2008) "Strategic Environmental Assessment (SEA) and Disaster Risk Reduction (DRR)". DAC Network on Environment and Development Co-operation (ENVIRONET). Available at <http://www.oecd.org/dac/environmentanddevelopment/42201482.pdf> (accessed 10 October 2012).

Okori, W., J. Obua and V. Baryamureeb (2009) "Famine Disaster Causes and Management Based on Local Community's Perception in Northern Uganda". *Research Journal of Social Sciences* 4: 21–32.

Olwig, M.F. et al. (2007) "Using Remote Sensing to Assess the Protective Role of Coastal Woody Vegetation against Tsunami Waves". *International Journal of Remote Sensing* 28(13/14): 3153–3169.

Osti, R., S. Tanaka and T. Tokioka (2009) "The Importance of Mangrove Forest in Tsunami Disaster Mitigation". *Disasters* 33(2): 203–213.

Parliamentary Office of Science and Technology (2009) "Coastal Management". POSTnote 342, October, London. Available at <http://www.parliament.uk/business/publications/research/briefing-papers/POST-PN-342/> (accessed 10 October 2012).

PEDRR [Partnership for Environment and Disaster Risk Reduction] (2010) "Demonstrating the Role of Ecosystems-based Management for Disaster Risk Reduction". Background paper to the *2011 Global Assessment Report on Disaster Risk Reduction*. Available at <http://www.preventionweb.net/english/hyogo/gar/2011/en/bgdocs/PEDRR_2010.pdf> (accessed 10 October 2012).

PEDRR (2011) "Managing Watersheds for Urban Resilience". Policy Brief presented at the Global Platform for Disaster Risk Reduction Roundtable "Managing Watersheds for Urban Resilience", Geneva, Switzerland, 12 May. Available at <http://pedrr.net/portals/0/PEDRR_policy_brief.pdf> (accessed 10 October 2012).

Peduzzi, P. (2010) "Landslides and Vegetation Cover in the 2005 North Pakistan Earthquake: A GIS and Statistical Quantitative Approach". *Natural Hazards and Earth System Sciences* 10: 623–640.

Powell, N. et al. (2011) "World Resources Report Case Study. Mangrove Restoration and Rehabilitation for Climate Change Adaptation in Vietnam". World Resources Report, Washington DC. Available at <http://www.worldresourcesreport.org/case-studies/vietnam-mangrove-restoration-and-rehabilitation> (accessed 10 October 2012).

ProAct Network (2008) *The Role of Environmental Management and Eco-engineering in Disaster Risk Reduction and Climate Change Adaptation.* Tannay: ProAct Network.

Ramsar Convention on Wetlands (2010) "Flood Control". Wetland ecosystem services, Factsheet 1. Ramsar Convention Secretariat, Gland, Switzerland. Available at <http://www.ramsar.org/pdf/info/services_01_e.pdf> (accessed 10 October 2012).

Rego, F. et al. (2010) *Towards Integrated Fire Management.* EFI Policy Brief 4. European Forest Institute.

Reij, C., G. Tappan and M. Smale (2009a) *Agroenvironmental Transformation in the Sahel: Another Kind of "Green Revolution".* IFPRI Discussion Paper 00914. Washington, DC: International Food Policy Research Institute.

Reij, C., G. Tappan and M. Smale (2009b) "Re-greening the Sahel: Farmer-led Innovation in Burkina Faso and Niger". In D.J. Spielman and R. Pandya-Lorch (eds), *Millions Fed: Proven Successes in Agricultural Development.* Washington, DC: International Food Policy Research Institute, pp. 53–58.

Robledo, C., M. Fischler and A. Patiño (2004) "Increasing the Resilience of Hillside Communities in Bolivia – Has Vulnerability to Climate Change Been Reduced as a Result of Previous Sustainable Development Cooperation?" *Mountain Research and Development* 24(1): 14–18.

Stolton, S., N. Dudley and J. Randall (2008) *Natural Security: Protected Areas and Hazard Mitigation*. Gland, Switzerland: WWF and Equilibrium.

Sudmeier-Rieux, K. and N. Ash (2009) *Environmental Guidance Note for Disaster Risk Reduction: Healthy Ecosystems for Human Security*. Ecosystem Management Series No. 8, Commission on Ecosystem Management, revised edition. Gland, Switzerland: IUCN.

Sudmeier-Rieux, K. et al. (2011) "The 2005 Pakistan Earthquake Revisited: Methods for Integrated Landslide Assessment". *Mountain Research and Development* 31(2): 112–121.

TEEB (2010) *The Economics of Ecosystems and Biodiversity: Ecological and Economic Foundations*. London: Earthscan. Available at <http://www.TEEBweb.org/EcologicalandEconomicFoundations/tabid/1018/Default.aspx> (accessed 10 October 2012).

Twigg, J. (2004) *Disaster Risk Reduction. Mitigation and Preparedness in Development and Emergency Planning*. Good Practice Review, March, Number 9. London: Humanitarian Practice Network, Overseas Development Institute.

UNDP [United Nations Development Programme] and Government of Sri Lanka (2011) *Integrated Strategic Environmental Assessment of the Northern Province: Supporting Development and Sustaining Peace* (Draft report). Colombo: UNDP Sri Lanka.

UNEP [United Nations Environment Programme] (2009) *Learning from Cyclone Nargis. Investing in the Environment for Livelihoods and Disaster Risk Reduction. A Case Study*. Geneva: UNEP Post-Conflict and Disaster Management Branch.

UNEP (2010) *Linking Ecosystems to Risk and Vulnerability Reduction: The Case of Jamaica. Risk and Vulnerability Assessment Methodology Development Project (RiVAMP) Pilot Assessment Report*, 2nd edn. Geneva: UNEP Post-Conflict and Disaster Management Branch.

UNEP and UNISDR [United Nations International Strategy for Disaster Reduction] (2008) *Environment and Disaster Risk: Emerging Perspectives*, 2nd edn. Geneva: UNISDR Secretariat.

UNEP-WCMC [United Nations Environment Programme World Conservation Monitoring Centre] (2006) *In the Front Line: Shoreline Protection and Other Ecosystem Services from Mangroves and Coral Reefs*. Cambridge: UNEP-WCMC.

UNFCCC [United Nations Framework Convention on Climate Change] (2011) *Ecosystem-based Approaches to Adaptation: Compilation of Information*. Report presented at the 35th session of the Subsidiary Body for Scientific and Technological Advice, Durban, South Africa, 28 November – 3 December 2011. FCCC/SBSTA/2011/INF.8, 16 November Available at <http://unfccc.int/resource/docs/2011/sbsta/eng/inf08.pdf> (accessed 9 October 2012).

UNISDR [United Nations International Strategy for Disaster Reduction] (2009a) "2009 UNISDR Terminology on Disaster Risk Reduction". United Nations, Geneva. Available at <http://unisdr.org/files/7817_UNISDRTerminologyEnglish.pdf> (accessed 9 October 2012).

UNISDR (2009b) *2009 Global Assessment Report on Disaster Risk Reduction*. Geneva: United Nations.

UNISDR (2011) *2011 Global Assessment Report on Disaster Risk Reduction*. Geneva: United Nations.

Vo-Luong, P. and S. Massel (2008) "Energy Dissipation in Non-uniform Mangrove Forests of Arbitrary Depth". *Journal of Marine Systems* 74: 603–622.

Wisner, B. et al. (2004) *At Risk: Natural Hazards, People's Vulnerability and Disasters*, 2nd edn. London and New York: Routledge.

World Bank (2010) *Convenient Solutions to an Inconvenient Truth: Ecosystem-based Approaches to Climate Change*. Washington, DC: World Bank.

WWF (2008) "Water for Life: Lessons for Climate Change Adaptation from Better Management of Rivers for People and Nature". WWF International, Gland, Switzerland.

Part II

Ecosystems and coastal disaster risk reduction

3

Investigating the performance of coastal ecosystems for hazard mitigation

Sam S.L. Hettiarachchi, Saman P. Samarawickrama, Harindra J.S. Fernando, A. Harsha R. Ratnasooriya, N.A. Kithsiri Nandasena and Srimal Bandara

Approach to mitigation of coastal hazards

The Indian Ocean coastal zone, which comprises coastal communities, the built environment and ecosystems, is exposed to a wide range of hazards both episodic and chronic arising from natural phenomena and human-induced activities (US IOTWS Program, 2007). Episodic hazards include storms, earthquakes, tsunamis and oil spills, most of which have limited predictability and may result in major disasters. Chronic conditions include shoreline erosion, flooding, sedimentation, sea level rise, natural resource degradation and environmental pollution. These conditions, which may result from or increase owing to episodic hazards, can be measured and monitored continuously over time. Unplanned or poorly designed engineering interventions in the coastal zone also contribute to the increase in chronic conditions.

There are many mitigation measures that could be adopted in the context of coastal zone management when planning for coastal hazards in order to reduce waves of high amplitude, heavy inundation and extreme impacts. These range from pure hazard mitigation to vulnerability reduction and improving the capacity and preparedness of populations. In combination, they reduce disaster risk and contribute to the development of disaster-resilient communities. These measures can be broadly classified into three categories, and the classification recognizes the overlap between exposure and vulnerability:

The role of ecosystems in disaster risk reduction, Renaud, Sudmeier-Rieux and Estrella (eds), United Nations University Press, 2013, ISBN 978-92-808-1221-3

- measures that mitigate the impact of the hazard
- measures that mitigate exposure and vulnerability to the hazard
- measures that promote successful evacuation from hazard zones

For existing and projected scenarios of coastal zone activities, the preparation of mitigation measures for multiple hazards requires a deep understanding of physical processes over a wider coastal region. It is important that mitigation measures against coastal hazards be developed within a multiple hazard coastal risk assessment framework, which should be an integral component of an overall coastal area management plan (CAMP). This will ensure a rational, balanced utilization of resources and, where possible, restore and enhance the stability and environmental quality of the coastal zone.

Within an overall CAMP, measures that mitigate the impact of the hazard represent a coherent set of interventions, specified in time and space, to achieve a certain expected level of protection against existing or anticipated damage from single or multiple hazards. On many occasions, these measures are proactive in leading to shoreline restoration and stability.

Measures that mitigate the impact of the hazard

Classification of measures

Although coastal hazards generate a wide range of impacts, coastal erosion, flooding and environmental pollution have apparent and immediate consequences for society and are therefore often the principal concerns in the administration of coastal districts.

It is recognized that, irrespective of the source of the hazard, the underlying principles of protection against flooding and erosion are similar. However, depending on the magnitude of the hazard and its impacts, and based on overall risk assessment, larger and robust measures have to be adopted. Furthermore, the impact of episodic hazards may contribute to long-term changes in sedimentation and coastal erosion. Coast and flood protection schemes can be broadly divided into direct and indirect measures (Fleming, 1992).

Direct measures or physical interventions (for example, protective structures) confront the hazard and they prevent or alleviate the immediate effects of the problem. These measures may be part of a wider coastal zone management plan, which will provide protection against erosion and flooding but cannot necessarily reduce or eliminate the cause of problems (for example, coastal erosion). However, they can contribute positively to reducing negative effects and on many occasions lead to efficient recovery via beach development. It is recognized that poorly designed direct measures have the capacity to seriously undermine beach stability and increase erosion.

Indirect measures (corrective measures) focus on the causes of the problem, to reduce or eliminate them altogether. For example, the prevention of sand mining and modifications to poorly designed structures will check coastal erosion and will achieve the desired stable dynamic equilibrium of the coastline. In addition, maintenance of drainage paths without obstructions will allow floods to discharge efficiently without causing excessive inundation.

Direct measures that mitigate the impact of the hazards may be achieved not only by engineered methods but also by harnessing the full potential of natural coastal ecosystems. Such measures can therefore be classified into:

(a) the implementation of engineered measures for protection, including offshore breakwaters, dykes and revetments;
(b) the effective use of natural coastal ecosystems, including coral reefs, sand dunes and coastal vegetation.

Natural episodic hazards such as extreme wind waves, storm surges and tsunamis cause coastal erosion, flooding, damage to infrastructure and ecosystems, and environmental pollution and may seriously affect human lives and livelihoods. Flooding caused by tsunamis is different from that of wind waves and storm surges. In the case of tsunamis, severe overtopping of long waves of high amplitude is accompanied by massive inundation and flooding. The heights of the waves propagating inland and the mass flow of water may be much higher than those observed for extreme wind waves and storm surges. These extreme events also contribute to changes in the bottom bathymetry of near-shore regions, leading to long-term changes in coastal erosion trends.

Engineered and ecosystem-based measures used to mitigate the impacts of hazards associated with very high amplitude waves can be classified into three types depending on their function and location in protecting the coast (IOC, 2009):

1. reduce the impacts of waves prior to reaching the shoreline (partial barrier located in coastal waters);
2. protect the coastal zone by preventing the inland movement of waves (full barrier at the shoreline);
3. mitigate the severe impacts of waves on entry to the shoreline (partial barrier at the shoreline).

Mitigation measures against a given hazard cannot be developed in isolation for a particular location. It is important to recognize that measures adopted at a given location or region will require the mitigation of multiple hazards of different origins, potential impacts of varying intensities and spatial distribution and a wide range of frequency of occurrence while sustaining multiple uses of the coastal zone. Therefore, there is a strong need to understand the dynamic hydraulic behaviour of the existing coastline over a broader region, the impact of the hazard under consideration, the impacts of other potential applicable hazards and other critical interactions leading to the stability of the coastline.

It is extremely difficult to take materials out of the natural transport mechanism without contributing to new or increased erosion problems elsewhere. Therefore, attention must be focused on potential impacts on neighbouring regions by analysing the sediment budget via coastal cells. In the absence of this approach, the problem is most likely to be transferred to a neighbouring region, or the mitigation measure adopted may be undermined by the new hydraulic regime leading to overall instability. It is good practice to harness the full potential of natural defences and to incorporate them in coastal protection designs, which is why it is necessary to understand the behavioural cycle of ecosystems.

It is equally important to note that mitigation can be achieved by either adopting a single measure or developing a well-integrated hybrid solution comprising a number of measures that could satisfy environmental concerns. Hybrid methods therefore refer to combinations of engineered methods or a combination of natural methods, as well as the joint application of engineered and natural methods. They represent efficient mitigation systems and effective resource utilization, which can effectively reduce the impact of various coastal hazards.

Engineered methods

A number of coastal engineering methods are used against coastal erosion and flooding (IOC, 2009). Armoured sloping revetments and concrete seawalls having medium and high crest levels are used to protect land and infrastructure from the effects of coastal flooding. These structures can withstand severe wave- and flood-induced loading and provide sufficient protection at an acceptable level of risk. They are also used as a frontline defence against coastal erosion in order to protect valuable assets located along the coastline. However, these structures do not aid beach development or stability and therefore have to be used together with appropriate beach restoration schemes. If protective structures are used on their own, adequate protection has to be provided against toe instability arising from high wave reflection. Beach restoration schemes include fields of groynes, offshore breakwaters, artificial headlands and beach nourishment. The aim of these schemes is to ensure the development of a healthy beach as a way of solving the problem of erosion. They perform a number of different functions with varying engineering lifespans as well as different capital and maintenance costs. Depending on the situation, it may also become necessary to adopt a hybrid solution for improved performance and efficiency.

In adopting engineered methods, it is necessary to ensure that multiple uses of the existing natural environment continue to be sustained. From an engineering point of view, the design must be robust, reliable and functional. From an economic perspective, the design should be afford-able and cost-effective. Due consideration must be given to convenient maintenance and effective operation. Equally it is important to minimize negative impacts on socioeconomic, livelihood and environmental issues.

Natural features

Coastlines offer varying natural defences against wave action, currents and flooding arising from storms. These include offshore seabeds, sand-banks, coral reefs and beaches on which waves break, sand dunes, which act as barriers against overtopping and as a natural supply of sand, and coastal vegetation, which provides resistance against flows. Natural de-fences play a vital role in mitigating the impact of coastal hazards, in coastal protection and in conservation. A comprehensive overview of coastal vegetation is presented in Chapter 4 in this volume. However, when-ever these natural defences are in danger of degradation, it is important to conserve and strengthen them at every possible opportunity, because conservation enhances their capacity to protect coastal populations.

Field investigations conducted in Indian Ocean states after the Indian Ocean tsunami of December 2004 highlighted the performance of coastal ecosystems, including reefs, dunes and vegetation, and their ability to mit-igate the impact of the tsunami (Kerr and Baird, 2007; Marris, 2005, 2006; and UNEP-WCMC, 2006). Depending on the height and other character-istics of the incoming waves, there were many examples that provided evidence of the efficient wave energy absorption of ecosystems and ve-getation. Some ecosystems performed well while others failed owing to threshold resilience characteristics being exceeded (FAO, 2007; JWRC, 2008). For hazards having extreme impacts and where the frequency of occurrence is low, natural ecosystems can provide cost-effective and envir-onmentally friendly solutions.

Coral reefs

Coral reefs provide partial barriers and have the ability to dissipate inci-dent wave energy when waves break over them. Therefore, coral reefs act as natural submerged breakwaters for the dissipation of wave energy. The length of the reef in the direction of wave propagation, the submerged depth of flow (water depth above the reef system) and the geometry of

the reef (porosity, tortuosity, surface roughness and the overall void matrix) are important characteristics that are related to energy dissipation.
Energy dissipation certainly reduces the velocity regime of the incident
wave system. This aspect was clearly observed when the waves from the
Indian Ocean tsunami reached the Kenyan coastline. Waves reached the
coastline under low-tide conditions when the reefs were exposed. Energy
dissipation was high and there was minimum inundation of the coast
(GEUS, 2007).

It is also recognized that, arising from the energy dissipation process,
beaches behind reef systems have been developed to resist waves of reduced energy levels (see Chapter 5 in this volume). Illegal coral mining
not only reduces the effectiveness of the coral reef system in dissipating
energy but also increases the local velocity, depending on the type of
damage caused by the mining process (see, for example, Chatenoux and
Peduzzi, 2007). Furthermore, fishermen destroy coral reefs with explo-
sives in order to create gaps for manoeuvring fishing vessels. These actions change the hydraulic regime, leading to coastal erosion.

Illegal coral mining and destruction by fishermen create defenceless
"low-resistance paths" that allow focused water jetting during extreme
events and increase the erosion and destruction of the coast, which is
usually protected by the reefs. It was observed in Sri Lanka that tsunami-
related damage was high in some areas where excessive coral mining had
taken place (Fernando et al., 2005).

Sand dunes

Sand dunes act as full barriers against extreme waves, thus preventing the
inland movement of waves and thereby flooding. Their effectiveness was
proved in many countries during the Indian Ocean tsunami (FAO, 2007;
University of Moratuwa, 2005). Dunes on which coastal vegetation have
grown perform more efficiently, ensuring stability, greater energy dissipation and resistance to erosion.

The presence of a healthy dune system provides an environmentally
important natural defence mechanism that has the ability to mitigate a
wide range of hazards. Dunes represent the final line of defence on the
beach. They restrict or prevent the intrusion of waves, reduce the impact
of wind and salt spray and also control the movement of sand behind
them. The dual role of a dune system to perform as a barrier against
wave impact and flooding and as a reserve supplier of sand to the beaches
at critical times of storms is a unique aspect that has to be understood in
dune management. Of equal importance is the fact that beach and dune
build-up takes place during calm weather conditions. It is in this context
that the annual cycle of dune building and erosion can be understood

fully on a scientific basis by recognizing the human pressure and impacts of extreme weather-related events on the coastal zone.

Dunes are subjected to the wind and wave attacks that take place within the annual cycle of weather patterns. They are also subjected to extreme wind attacks in the presence of cyclonic conditions and to extreme waves during severe storms, storm surges and tsunami conditions. Extreme hazardous events can cause extensive erosion of the dune systems and will restrict their ability to act as barriers and providers of sand. On some occasions, recovery after extreme hazard events may take a long time. Therefore the conservation and strengthening of natural systems are of great importance. This requires regular monitoring, particularly after extreme events, and, if necessary, methods for environmental recovery should be undertaken as a priority.

When dunes are overtopped they fail progressively owing to erosion, but the presence of coastal vegetation provides for increased stability. Post-disaster field studies have demonstrated that sand dunes perform extremely well against coastal flooding (FAO, 2007; University of Moratuwa, 2005). Even when overtopped, dunes with coastal vegetation on the surface have shown greater stability in resisting failure. It is therefore strongly recommended to adopt sand dunes in combination with coastal vegetation to enhance the stability and performance of dune systems.

Coastal revetments separate the sand dunes of the back beach from the active foreshore, thus interrupting the active interaction between two important sections of the dune system. Once the seasonal interaction is affected, the natural forces that build the dunes are no longer active. Although the revetment will fix the defence line, it does not in any way aid beach stabilization. The reflective slopes or vertical faces of the revetments generate high velocities arising from the interaction of the incident and reflective waves, thus leading to beach scour. There have been several instances where the revetments themselves have induced large-scale erosion in the toe region, leading to premature collapse. Hence, great care should be exercised in constructing coastal revetments/seawalls in areas where dunes are present. The dynamics of the dune system with respect to seasonal variation and the natural forces that come into play in the build-up of dunes have to be clearly understood. If revetments/seawalls have to be constructed as a final option, such works must be supported with beach development mechanisms, for example the use of a field of groynes. Regular nourishment may also have to be undertaken to maintain the sediment budget to avoid coastal erosion.

On many occasions, engineered protective measures (that is, coastal revetments/seawalls) are constructed to arrest long-term recession even in front of dune systems. Such interventions are made when there is a strong need to protect human settlements and infrastructure from frequently occurring excessive wave conditions. In many instances, coastal erosion has resulted from human interventions or hazard events far upstream of the area affected by erosion. The imbalance of the sediment budget generated at an upstream location may have severe impacts for downstream areas. Hence, even if sound dune management is being practised at a given site, such sites may still be prone to severe erosion owing to the impacts of events taking place upstream of the erosion-affected site.

Coastal vegetation

As mentioned above, coastal vegetation on its own and vegetation growing on dunes are effective barriers against hazards (FAO, 2007; JWRC, 2008; UNEP, 2005; University of Moratuwa, 2005; see Chapter 4 in this volume for a detailed literature review).

A wide variety of vegetation is observed along coastlines and on the banks of estuaries and lagoons. Vegetation on sandy beaches and on dunes can be broadly classified into three categories: primary species, secondary species and tertiary species. As with all natural species, some of this vegetation exhibits the characteristics of two different groups, leading to overlaps. Primary species, which are essentially grasses and creepers, grow on the incipient and frontal dunes and perform effectively as windbreakers. Behind the frontal dune crest, the sand on the dunes is more stable and the impact of wind and waves in particular is reduced. In this region there is greater diversity of plant species and larger shrubs become more dominant. Further back, large trees are observed among a variety of species. The shelter and soil characteristics assist the growth of trees. Mangrove forests are observed along estuaries and lagoons and on coastlines with a fair proportion of mud/silt type of soils.

Coastal vegetation acts as a partial barrier on the coastline and can be used effectively to dissipate part of the incoming wave energy. The energy dissipation is dependent on the density of vegetation, its overall porosity and the tortuous characteristics of the porous matrix of the vegetation. It is important that the vegetation itself is resilient against the wave propagation and the accompanying imposed loads and that it has a root structure to resist the high-velocity regime at the floor bed.

Vegetation will restrict wave propagation up to a specific water level, beyond which overtopping will take place. Once the threshold values for stability (velocity and force regimes) are exceeded, the vegetation itself will erode rapidly and be destroyed even at moderate water depth. In this respect, the stability of the vegetation in relation to the overall hydraulic regime and issues relating to inland drainage from overtopping have to be given due consideration. It is essential to have a good understanding of the threshold resilience characteristics of such natural systems (see below).

Investigating the performance of coastal ecosystems

The hydraulic performance of coral reefs, coastal vegetation and dunes can be investigated by adopting physical modelling and mathematical modelling. In view of the widely varying characteristics of such systems, physical modelling using a large flume facility provides the best option in that a large-scale ratio can be used for the simulation of the ecosystem. This enables experiments to be conducted at near prototype scale, thus minimizing scale effects. However, such facilities where waves of high amplitude can be generated are not freely available, and hence it is necessary to use smaller flumes. When using small flumes every effort must be made to generate high-amplitude waves where possible or to adopt similar techniques. For example, when generating tsunami waves one can use solitary waves. On the other hand, techniques can be adopted to generate a large wave by either using the dam break problem or creating a wave by moving a vertical plate in front of the experimental structure. The purpose of these investigations is to identify the dissipation characteristics and velocity profiles as the waves propagate through or over the structure. Even steady flow permeability tests using high-velocity regimes (non-Darcy flow) provide useful information about dissipation characteristics, particularly for the simulation of tsunami waves.

Mathematical modelling is a useful tool, but such models have to be calibrated and verified using experimental results from flume tests. Once this process has been successfully achieved the model can be used for specific ecosystem configurations.

Case study: Investigating the impact of coral reefs on tsunami wave propagation

Impacts arising from the mining and destruction of coral reefs

Post-tsunami field investigations carried out on the south-western coast of Sri Lanka indicated sharp variation in inundation and destruction over a comparatively small scale of spatial variation along the coastline (Goff et al., 2006; Liu et al., 2005). For example, the town of Peraliya, just north of Hikkaduwa, where a passenger train was destroyed, had an inundation distance of the order of 1.5 km, whereas a location just south of the town had an inundation of less than 0.5 km. Along the eastern and southern coasts and the south-western coast up to the city of Galle, variation in inundation was very much related to local geomorphologic features such as headlands, embayments and river/estuarine inlets, whereas for the stretch of coastline from Galle to Ambalangoda inundation could not be related to such coastline features. It was observed that, within this stretch, the area north of Hikkaduwa up to Akurala, where extensive coral mining had taken place over the past few decades, was severely damaged by tsunami waves. It is possible that the concentration of wave energy resulting from complex wave processes along the south-western coast may have contributed to this significantly high local damage. However, the removal of coral was also considered to be a major contributor to the phenomenon (Fernando et al., 2005, 2007a; the subsection on coral reefs above).

In the light of the tsunami damage in areas where coral mining and destruction have occurred, it was considered relevant to examine these aspects via physical modelling to obtain a better understanding of the influence of coral reefs in their normal and damaged states.

The results presented in this chapter represent the first attempt to understand the hydraulic performance of reefs, simulated by vertical cylindrical members (Fernando et al., 2007b). The voids matrix investigated is therefore well defined. In the following stages, more complex configurations having very close similarity to reef systems would be examined.

Experimental set-up

The experiment was carried out in a 0.8 m (W) × 1.8 m (D) × 32 m (L) wave tank with a programmable paddle wave generator. The waves propagate first on a horizontal (flat) topography and then on a 1/24 sloping uniform topography. Leading elevation waves of height 20, 30 and 40 cm with a frequency (ω) of 0.4 Hz were used to represent solitary waves. Typical waveforms as measured approximately at the middle of the tank are shown in the Figure 3.1.

On the sloping surface, placed at a mean water depth of 30 cm, were porous strips of vertical cylinders attached to a bottom plate (Figures 3.2 and 3.3). In some cases, the obstruction covered the entire width, whereas in others the rods were removed in the middle to create a least-resistance path. The rods were of diameter 1.25 cm and height 20 cm. Two types of rod packing densities (porosities) of 20 per cent and 50 per cent were used. In the case of non-uniform packing channel width, $w = 6.5$ cm was used, which was intended to simulate the removal of corals in a reef.

Acoustic Doppler Velocity (ADV) meter measurements were carried out to map the velocity field, covering several locations (as shown in Figure 3.2), at locations behind and within the structures. Figure 3.2 illustrates the schematic diagram of the experimental set-up indicating the

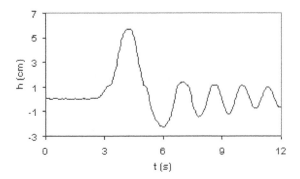

Figure 3.1 Wave profiles in the central part of the tank
Notes: Wave height = 20 cm, ω = 0.4 Hz.

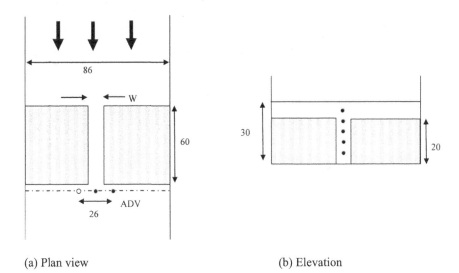

(a) Plan view   (b) Elevation

Figure 3.2 Schematic diagram of the experimental set-up
Note: All values are in cm.

locations of ADV measurements. Figure 3.3 illustrates the simulation of coral reefs for two-dimensional physical modelling, showing the structure under construction and a completed structure with a narrow opening. Figure 3.4 gives the representation of high-density (20 per cent porosity) and low-density (50 per cent porosity) structures in two-dimensional physical modelling. Fernando et al. (2007b) describe the details of the experimental programme.

Figure 3.3 Simulation of coral reefs in two-dimensional physical modelling

Figure 3.4 Representation of high-density (20 per cent porosity) and low-density (50 per cent porosity) structures

Results

Figures 3.5, 3.6 and 3.7 give the normalized velocity in the X direction as a function of normalized height for low-density (50 per cent porosity) and high-density (20 per cent porosity) structures for waves of amplitude 10, 20 and 30 cm respectively. Velocities in the Y and Z directions are not included here because the changes in magnitudes were very small.

The figures include the normalized velocities for the conditions of: (i) no structure, (ii) a structure without an opening and (iii) a structure with a narrow opening. Normalized velocity is taken as $U/U_{surface}$, where $U_{surface}$ is the surface velocity for the base case (no structure). Normalized height is taken as Z/H_0, where H_0 is the height of the obstructions (in this case, the rods).

With the introduction of the structure there is a considerable reduction in velocities in the water column, except for surface velocities. This could

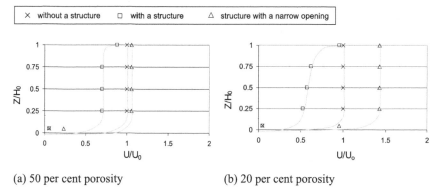

(a) 50 per cent porosity   (b) 20 per cent porosity

Figure 3.5 Normalized velocity as a function of normalized height = 10 cm, $\omega = 0.4$ Hz

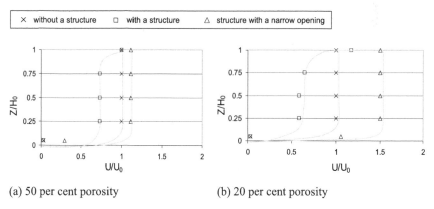

(a) 50 per cent porosity   (b) 20 per cent porosity

Figure 3.6 Normalized velocity as a function of normalized height = 20 cm, $\omega = 0.4$ Hz

be seen for all the wave conditions tested, with the greater impact being for the high-density structure. The low-density structure provides a 30 per cent reduction in the maximum velocity for waves of height (2η) 10 cm and 20 cm and a 20 per cent reduction for waves of height 30 cm. The high-density structure provides around a 40 per cent reduction in the maximum velocity for all three wave conditions.

A gap in the structure induces a significant increase in velocity for all conditions tested. In the case of the low-density structure, the percentage increases in maximum velocity are 7.5 per cent, 10 per cent and 15 per cent for the waves of height 10, 20 and 30 cm, respectively. For the high-density structure, the corresponding values are 43 per cent, 50 per

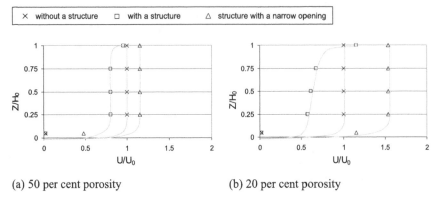

(a) 50 per cent porosity   (b) 20 per cent porosity

Figure 3.7 Normalized velocity as a function of normalized height = 30 cm, $\omega = 0.4$ Hz

cent and 54 per cent, respectively. There is no clear variation with wave height.

Figure 3.8 illustrates the variation of change in velocity with the porosity of the structure. The low-density structure provides around a 25 per cent reduction in velocity behind the structure and around a 10 per cent increase in velocity through the gap created to simulate the removal of corals. This is in the order of a 45 per cent increase in maximum velocity from behind the structure to the gap in the structure. The high-density structure provides around a 40 per cent reduction in velocity behind the

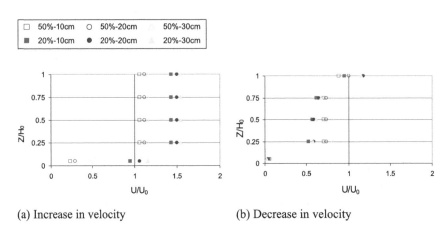

(a) Increase in velocity   (b) Decrease in velocity

Figure 3.8 Variation of normalized velocity with the porosity of the structure for solitary waves

structure and around a 50 per cent increase in velocity in the gap of the structure. This is in the order of a 150 per cent increase in maximum velocity from behind the structure to the gap in the structure.

As stated earlier, this experimental set-up represented realistic values for wave height, water depth and coral dimensions, although only solitary waves were used in the study. Therefore, the results are only indicative but they certainly provide a clear understanding of the wave–structure interaction.

It can be concluded that the coral reefs, which act as submerged break-waters, dissipate part of the wave energy and reduce the wave velocity. The porosity of the reef system has a significant influence on the dissipation process. In the case of a dense structure, the effectiveness of the reef in dissipating energy is high. However, when there is a gap in a coral reef there could be a significant increase in wave velocity and this increase is high for dense structures. Illegal coral mining and destruction create defenceless "low-resistance paths" that encourage focused water jetting. The experiments clearly illustrate the impact of increased water velocities through such openings and the influence of the overall porosity of the reef system. The high-velocity regime through openings can certainly contribute to intensified destruction.

Case study: Investigating the impact of a tsunami wave passing through coastal vegetation in a waterlogged condition

Response of coastal vegetation to tsunami hazard

The Indian Ocean tsunami of 26 December 2004 caused widespread damage in coastal regions of Sri Lanka. More than two-thirds of the coastline in the northern, eastern and southern areas, as well as the relatively sheltered western area, was subjected to inundation. The inundation depth and distance and the associated damage caused by the tsunami varied significantly with the local near-shore wave height, topography and hydraulic resistance to the overland flow. The ground surface resistance and the resistance offered by vegetation and fabricated features in the coastal zone are among the factors contributing to hydraulic resistance. Following post-tsunami surveys, considerable attention was focused on the resistance offered by coastal vegetation to the overland flow and its effectiveness as a tsunami damage mitigation measure. This was mainly because there were many examples from Sri Lanka, Indonesia and other affected countries that showed that coastal vegetation had resisted the wave-induced hazard and had been effective in dissipating wave energy, thus protecting infrastructure located behind. It was also realized that use of vegetation for this purpose would have the dual advantages of being environmentally friendly and cost-effective (FAO, 2007; University of Moratuwa, 2005).

Coastal vegetation in Sri Lanka varies with climatic zones. Based on the annual rainfall, Sri Lanka is divided into two climatic zones: a wet zone and a dry zone. The western and southern coastal areas fall mainly within the wet zone and the entire eastern and northern coastal areas are in the dry zone; hence the type of vegetation varies significantly along the tsunami-affected coastline. The presence of a large number of coastal wetlands, estuaries and lagoons has also contributed to the variety of coastal vegetation.

The hydraulic resistance offered by vegetation is dependent on the size and shape of plants, the standing structure of trees, the density and pattern of vegetation, drag characteristics and the ability of plants to resist the overland flow without being damaged or destroyed. These are the resistance characteristics of plant species. Maturity in terms of breaking strength and root–soil interaction is of particular importance in withstanding the impacts of coastal hazards (University of Moratuwa, 2005). In addition, other local factors such as topography and the distance from the vegetation belt to the shore are important features relative to the characteristics of the incoming wave. Whereas some plant species were unaffected, others were uprooted and/or broken owing to the hydraulic impact or destroyed by the salinity of sea water. It seems that, provided the threshold values of resilience are not exceeded, vegetation has the ability to resist wave-induced hazards and this property can be fully harnessed by adopting planned vegetation along the coastline, where appropriate.

Field investigations and physical modelling have been conducted to understand the significance of coastal vegetation in dissipating tsunami wave energy. Among these, Kathiresan and Rajendran (2005; although their findings were subsequently contested by Kerr et al., 2006), Mascarenhas and Jayakumar (2008) and Tanaka et al. (2007) provided useful insights with respect to field investigations, and Ratnasooriya et al. (2008) and Nandasena et al. (2009) referred to early physical modelling studies on a small scale relating to the conditions of the South Asia region.

Experimental set-up

Factors influencing the design of the experimental set-up

Large-scale experiments were conducted to assess the energy dissipation of tsunami waves passing through the coastal vegetation in order to study the energy dissipation characteristics of such systems. It is impossible to study the influence of varying characteristics of species, incident waves and location of vegetation with respect to the shoreline in a single series of experiments. Therefore it was necessary to prioritize the specific areas to be investigated in detail.

The primary focus was to study the dissipation characteristics of tsunami waves propagating through coastal vegetation located on a sloping beach head. However, the wave characteristics and in particular the wave-breaking process will depend on the mean water level and the incident wave characteristics. This demanded the accommodation of varying incident conditions and mean water levels (Bandara, 2008).

The second area of focus was to ensure variety with respect to vegetation and in this context to simulate at least two types of coastal vegetation. The two types are illustrated in Figure 3.11. The difference between the two types selected for the study refers to stem height and branch and leaf configuration. Type I plants are taller than Type II plants. Therefore the resistance of branches and leaves of Type II plants is applicable when waves are propagating over a greater mean water level as well as for larger wave heights.

The third area of focus was the impact of water that has not been discharged after the arrival of the first wave, which may not necessarily be the largest wave in the tsunami wave train. Owing to poor drainage conditions and inland topography, a fair proportion of water is retained inland and has not completely receded prior to the arrival of the second wave. In effect the incoming wave will now be propagating over the existing water, which has not receded. This aspect can be studied by conducting experiments on waterlogged conditions or in practice with a lower and higher water level.

The experiments were carried out in a 20 m (L) × 0.8 m (W) × 2 m (D) flume equipped with a programmable wave generator at Lanka Hydraulic Institute in Sri Lanka. The model scale was taken as 1:12.5, which was sufficiently large for proper simulation of the propagation of tsunami waves through vegetation and to reduce scale effects. Two types of vegetation that are found in the Sri Lankan coastal belt were modelled. Of the many types of wave forms that could be generated under laboratory conditions, large-scale solitary waves represent a reasonably good simulation of tsunami waves for physical modelling. Such waves can model many of the characteristics of a tsunami (Chang and Hwung, 2006).

The governing equations of a solitary wave propagating in space and time, as well as its velocity, are given by Chang and Hwung (2006) (see Figure 3.9).

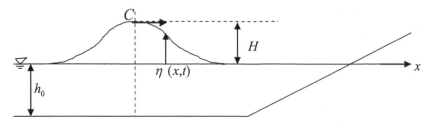

Figure 3.9 Detailed sketch of a solitary wave

Notes: h_0 = still water depth in front of the slope, $\eta(x,t)$ = free surface of solitary wave profile, x = distance, t = time, C = wave propagation velocity, and H = maximum wave height.

Details of the experimental set-up

Figure 3.10 shows a sketch of the experimental set-up in the flume, which was carried out at the same location as the experiment previously described.

The model scale was 1:12.5. Eight wave gauges were deployed to record water surface elevations: gauges 1 and 2 were to check the reliability of solitary wave generation and propagation, gauges 3, 4 and 5 were to observe energy dissipation through the vegetation model and the remaining gauges were to check the behaviour of the solitary profile deformed by the vegetation model as shown in Figure 3.10. The data were collected at a frequency of 100 Hz. Table 3.1 shows the solitary wave heights to the wave generator software (the second tsunami wave) and the measured maximum wave heights at gauge 1 at different water depths (inundation by the first tsunami wave). Two cases were studied: water

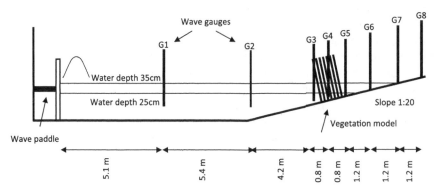

Figure 3.10 Experimental set-up

Table 3.1 Test conditions

Water depth (Wd)	Solitary wave height					
	Wave height to wave synthesizer (Hs)			Measured at gauge 1		
25 cm	9.6 cm	11.2 cm	12.8 cm	6.4 cm	7.5 cm	8.5 cm
35 cm	9.6 cm	11.2 cm	12.8 cm	7.2 cm	8.6 cm	9.7 cm

depths resulting from inundation by the first tsunami were 6 cm and 1 cm in front of and behind the vegetation model, formed by a water depth of 25 cm in front of the wave paddle; water depths were 16 cm and 11 cm, formed by a water depth of 35 cm in the model, as given in Table 3.1.

Type I vegetation was modelled by a PVC pipe of diameter 2 cm, as shown in Figure 3.11(b). The differences between Types I and II relate to stem height and the configuration of branches and leaves. Type I vegetation is taller than Type II. Therefore, for higher mean water levels, branches and leaves of Type II offer resistance. Even though an accurate scaling of Type II vegetation was rather difficult, for the simulation small tree branches from actual trees were used. They were carefully fixed to the PVC pipe. The bottom diameter of the Type II vegetation model was thus maintained at 2 cm, as in the case of Type I. The spacing between trees was 14.5 cm in a rectangular arrangement and the width of the vegetation model in the wave direction was 1.2 m. Figure 3.11(c) shows photographs of Type I (for example, *Cocos nucifera* and *Casuarina equisetifolia*) and Type II (for example, *Anacardium occidentale* and *Terminalia catappa*) vegetation species.

Type I Type II	Type I Type II	Type I Type II
(a) Sketch: Inundation at lower mean water levels	(b) In model	(c) In prototype – not at same scale

Figure 3.11 The two types of vegetation found in the Sri Lankan coastal belt

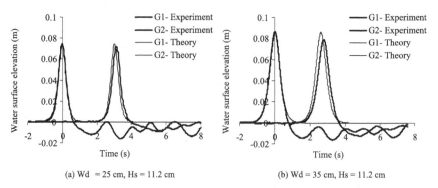

(a) Wd = 25 cm, Hs = 11.2 cm   (b) Wd = 35 cm, Hs = 11.2 cm

Figure 3.12 Comparison of experimental wave profile with theoretical wave

Results

The experimental data from gauges 1 and 2 were compared with the theoretical values for the solitary wave. Figure 3.12 depicts the solitary wave
profile observed at gauges 1 and 2 and the theoretical profile in water
depths (Wd) of, respectively, 25 cm and 35 cm for a wave height of
11.2 cm to the wave generator (Hs).

There exists a slight phase difference in time of the upper part of the
solitary profile at gauge 2, as shown in Figure 3.12, and a slight reduction
in the solitary peak can also be observed. This may be attributed to energy dissipation through the friction of the side walls of the flume and
limitations in generating a perfect profile. Using the travel time of the
solitary wave between gauges 1 and 2, and the distance between gauges 1
and 2, the average solitary wave velocity was calculated. Good agreement
between experimental and theoretical values was observed for the velocity of the solitary peak for the constant water depth between gauges 1
and 2.

Figure 3.13 shows the spatial evolution of the surface elevation for
the condition without vegetation: (a) wave height to wave generator
11.2 cm and water depth 25 cm and (b) wave height to wave generator
11.2 cm and water depth 35 cm. It can be observed that the solitary wave
gradually deforms from its initial shape as it travels along the slope. The
surface elevation at gauges 3 and 4 in Figure 3.13(a) and the surface elevation at gauges 5 and 6 in Figure 3.13(b) illustrate the bore-front. This
form of wave front is commonly observed as a characteristic of the tsunami wave when it reaches shallow water depths. Even though there is a
slight decay of the solitary peak during its travel, clear wave-breaking occurs between gauges 4 and 5 for water depth 25 cm and between gauges
6 and 7 for water depth 35 cm, respectively. This implies that the higher

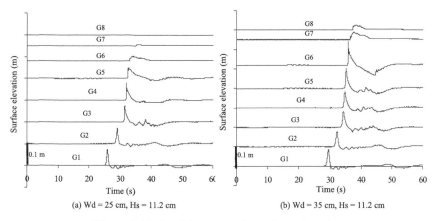

(a) Wd = 25 cm, Hs = 11.2 cm   (b) Wd = 35 cm, Hs = 11.2 cm

Figure 3.13 Spatial progress in surface elevation

water level facilitates the travel of the tsunami wave further inland. In practical terms, water retained after inundation by the first tsunami wave would assist the second wave to travel further inland and, if this is of greater height, would lead to large-scale inundation on land. The right tail of the solitary wave contains undulations that may be caused by reflections from the wave paddle. However, these fluctuations are reasonably less compared with the main solitary wave profile.

Figure 3.14 shows the maximum water surface elevation recorded at wave gauges with vegetation models of Type I (marked S) and Type II (marked S+B) and without vegetation (marked WV) for water depths of 25 cm and 35 cm for different solitary wave heights. It is observed that the dominant breaking of the solitary wave occurred between gauges 4 and 5 for input wave heights of 9.6 cm and 11.2 cm for a water level of 25 cm in the case without vegetation. In contrast, the dominant wave-breaking for a water level of 35 cm happened between gauges 6 and 7 for similar wave conditions.

The observations indicate that the inundation caused by the first tsunami wave could result in a larger amount of the energy of the second wave being transferred over a greater distance compared with the first tsunami wave. Figures 3.14(a), (b) and (c) indicate that, for a mean water level of 25 cm, the dominant wave-breaking of the solitary wave occurred inside the vegetation model. A considerable part of the energy is dissipated by the wave-breaking process itself. The energy-dissipating impact of the vegetation may not be that effective because of the more dominant process of wave energy dissipation by wave-breaking within the vegetation. In practical terms, the resilience of the vegetation must be very high, otherwise the vegetation may be destroyed by this process. In

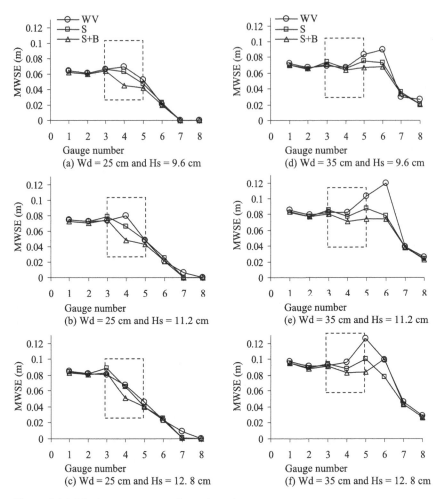

Figure 3.14 Maximum water surface elevation
Notes: MWSE = maximum water surface elevation, WV = without vegetation model, S = stem only (Type I) and S+B = stem, branches and leaves (Type II). The vegetation model is shown by the dotted box.

contrast, Figures 3.14(d), (e) and (f) indicate that, for a mean water level of 35 cm, dominant wave-breaking occurred just after the wave had propagated through the vegetation model. In this respect, the vegetation has a greater opportunity of dissipating energy before the wave-breaking process. Irrespective of the wave input and the location of the dominant wave-breaking, when the water depth was just below the height of branches and leaves, the model of branches together with leaves (Type II) dissipated more wave energy than the model comprising stems (Type I).

It can be concluded that the experimental programme provided a clear insight into the energy dissipation process in which two types of vegetation were examined for two mean water depths and varying incident wave conditions. It is evident that coastal vegetation has the potential to dissipate energy, and it was the mean water depth that determined the wave-breaking characteristics as well as the extent to which various components of vegetation come into play. Type II vegetation was effective in energy dissipation when waves had a strong interaction with the branches. In these circumstances, the waves travel through a porous medium with the desired porosity and tortuosity for energy dissipation. Provided the waves do not impose loads that exceed the threshold values of the plant species, a high degree of energy dissipation could be achieved. Field investigations after the Indian Ocean tsunami of December 2004 confirmed that damage to infrastructure behind coastal vegetation that was able to withstand the tsunami waves without being destroyed was considerably less than in areas where there was no vegetation or vegetation had been destroyed (FAO, 2007; University of Moratuwa, 2005).

Conclusion

This chapter has focused on the importance of the performance of coastal ecosystems for coastal hazard mitigation. It is evident that natural defence systems play a vital role in coast conservation and that they are able to withstand the impacts of severe coastal hazards with high-amplitude waves and currents provided their threshold values of stability are not exceeded. Therefore, if natural systems are to be fully harnessed for hazard mitigation, it is important to understand their performance against the expected hazards. This leads to the identification of appropriate natural defence systems for specific regions, taking into consideration the expected hazards, their frequency of occurrence and the magnitude of the impacts. All mitigation measures should be undertaken within a coastal zone management framework for multiple hazards, and there is high potential for the use of hybrid methods. Depending on the vulnerability of the coastline, it may even become necessary to adopt a combination of engineered and natural barriers.

Physical modelling investigations into simulated coral reef systems and vegetation have highlighted important information on the performance of natural defence systems. These investigations have led to a clearer understanding of several observations from post-tsunami surveys and have underscored the high potential for the use of coastal ecosystems for hazard mitigation. In comparison with the use of engineered methods, natural defence methods have wider application in areas where the occurrence of episodic hazardous events is infrequent and they can very effectively be used as part of hybrid systems for coast protection and conservation.

REFERENCES

Bandara, R.P.S.S. (2008) "Tsunami Impact Mitigation by Coastal Vegetation". MSc thesis, Department of Civil Engineering, University of Moratuwa, Sri Lanka.

Chang, Y.H. and H.H. Hwung (2006) "Experiments on the Run-up of Solitary Waves over Sloping Bottoms". Third Chinese–German Joint Symposium on Coastal and Ocean Engineering, National Cheng Kung University, Taiwan.

Chatenoux, B and P. Peduzzi (2007) "Impacts from the 2004 Indian Ocean Tsunami: Analysing the Potential Protecting Role of Environmental Features". *Natural Hazards* 40: 289–304.

FAO [Food and Agriculture Organization] (2007) "Coastal Protection in the Aftermath of the Indian Ocean Tsunami: What Role for Forests and Trees?" In *Proceedings of the Regional Technical Workshop, Bangkok, August 2006.* RAP Publication 2007/07.

Fernando, H.J.S. et al. (2005) "Coral Poaching Worsens Tsunami Destruction". *Eos* 86(33).

Fernando, H.J.S. et al. (2007a) "Tsunamis: A Journey through Their Manifestation and Aftermath". In M. Gad-el-Hak (ed.), *Large-Scale Disasters: Prediction, Control and Mitigation.* Cambridge: Cambridge University Press.

Fernando, H.J.S. et al. (2007b) "Effects of Porous Barriers such as Coral Reefs on Coastal Wave Propagation". *Journal of Hydro Environmental Research* 1: 187–194.

Fleming, C. (1992) "The Development of Coastal Engineering". In M.G. Barrett (ed.), *Coastal Zone Planning and Management: Proceedings of the Conference Coastal Management '92.* London: Thomas Telford.

GEUS [Geological Survey of Denmark and Greenland] (2007) "Tsunami Damage Projection for the Coastal Area of Kenya". Unpublished report, Geological Survey of Denmark and Greenland, Copenhagen.

Goff, J. et al. (2006) "Sri Lanka Field Survey after the December 2004 Indian Ocean Tsunami". *Earthquake Spectra* 22(S3): 155–172.

IOC [Intergovernmental Oceanographic Commission] (2009) *Hazard Awareness and Risk Mitigation in Integrated Coastal Area Management (ICAM).* IOC Manuals and Guides No. 50, ICAM Dossier No. 5. Paris: UNESCO.

JWRC [Japan Wildlife Research Centre] (2008) "Assessment of the Tsunami Mitigation Function of Coastal Forests/Trees and Proposal for Appropriate Forest Management". Seminar organized by Japan Wildlife Research Centre, Colombo, Sri Lanka, March.

Kathiresan, K. and N. Rajendran (2005) "Coastal Mangrove Forests Mitigated Tsunami, Short Note". *Estuarine, Coastal and Shelf Science* 65: 601–606.

Kerr, A.M. and A.H. Baird (2007) "Natural Barriers to Natural Disasters". *Bio Science* 57(2): 102–103.

Kerr A.M. et al. (2006) "Comments on 'Coastal Mangrove Forests Mitigated Tsunami' by K. Kathiresan and N. Rajendran". *Estuarine, Coastal and Shelf Science* 67: 539–541.

Liu, P.L.F. et al. (2005) "Observations by the International Tsunami Survey Team in Sri Lanka". *Science* 308: 1595.

Marris, E. (2005) "Tsunami Damage Was Enhanced by Coral Theft". *Nature* 436: 1072.

Marris, E. (2006) "Sri Lankan Signs Warn Coral Thieves of Nature's Wrath". *Nature* 440: 981.

Mascarenhas, A. and S. Jayakumar (2008) "An Environmental Perspective of the Post-tsunami Scenario along the Coast of Tamil Nadu, India: Role of Sand Dunes and Forests". *Environmental Management* 89(1): 24–34.

Nandasena, N.A.K. et al. (2009) "Investigations on Tsunami Inundation and Coastal Vegetation Characteristics". In *Proceedings of Third International Conference in Ocean Engineering* (ICOE 2009): 1118–1128.

Ratnasooriya, A.H.R. et al. (2008) "Mitigation of Tsunami Inundation by Coastal Vegetation". *"Engineer". Journal of the Institution of Engineers, Sri Lanka*, October.

Tanaka, N. et al. (2007) "Coastal Vegetation Structures and Their Functions in Tsunami Protection: Experience of the Recent Indian Ocean Tsunami". *Landscape and Ecological Engineering* 3: 33–45.

UNEP [United Nations Environment Programme] (2005) "Sri Lanka Post Tsunami Environmental Assessment". UNEP, Asian Tsunami Disaster Task Force and Ministry of Environment and Natural Resources, Sri Lanka.

UNEP-WCMC [United Nations Environment Programme World Conservation Monitoring Centre] (2006) *In the Front Line: Shoreline Protection and Other Ecosystem Services from Mangroves and Coral Reefs.* UNEP-WCMC Biodiversity Series No. 24. Cambridge: UNEP-WCMC.

University of Moratuwa (2005) "Brown Assessment: Post Tsunami Rapid Environmental Assessment". University of Moratuwa, Sri Lanka.

US IOTWS [Indian Ocean Tsunami Warning System] Program (2007) "How Resilient Is Your Coastal Community? A Guide for Evaluating Coastal Community Resilience to Tsunamis and Other Hazards". U.S. IOTWS Document No. 27-IOTWS-07. U.S. Indian Ocean Tsunami Warning System Program supported by the United States Agency for International Development and partners, Bangkok, Thailand.

4

Bioshields: Mangrove ecosystems as resilient natural coastal defences

Carmen Lacambra, Daniel A. Friess, Tom Spencer and Iris Möller

Introduction

Coastal areas are dynamic: tides can change the intertidal landscape within a matter of hours, and low-frequency, high-magnitude events such as storms, tsunamis and floods can change the coastal landscape dramatically. A number of ecosystems inhabit the dynamic intertidal zone in the tropics, including seagrass beds, coral reefs, saltmarshes and mangrove forests. The ecosystem function of these coastal habitats varies across a range of time-scales: thus, in mangroves, physiological changes take place over minutes to days, tree growth varies over months to years, and large-scale changes in forest communities occur over decades to centuries, unless extreme events suddenly affect forest structure (Spencer and Möller, 2012). Changes in habitat communities in turn have an impact on the broad socioeconomic and ecosystem services provided by these systems. Coastal habitats provide a range of ecosystem services and help support adjoining ecosystems and local livelihoods. For example, mangroves support offshore fisheries owing to nutrient export across the food chain, provide nursery grounds for juvenile fish and shellfish, assimilate pollutants, supply local timber products (Silvestri and Kershaw, 2010) and reduce coastal vulnerability as a result of hydrodynamic energy (wave and current) attenuation, up to a certain energy threshold (Figure 4.1).

The following sections present a case for mangroves as bioshields – "natural coastal defences" for communities vulnerable to natural disturbances and coastal hazards. Although information is available on the role

The role of ecosystems in disaster risk reduction, Renaud, Sudmeier-Rieux and Estrella (eds), United Nations University Press, 2013, ISBN 978-92-808-1221-3

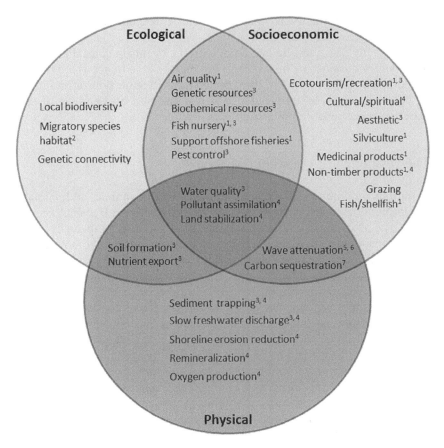

Figure 4.1 The interconnected ecosystem services provided by mangroves
Sources: [1] Walters et al. (2008); [2] Gilbert and Janssen (1998); [3] Silvestri and Kershaw (2010); [4] Moberg and Rönnbäck (2003); [5] Mazda et al. (2006); [6] Quartel et al. (2007); [7] Donato et al. (2011).

of mangroves in coastal protection and disaster vulnerability reduction, this information has focused on particular regions (specifically Southeast Asia) and on specific events. Furthermore, some baseline information on the dynamics of waves during disturbance conditions and normal conditions is contradictory, whereas their services for sustainable fisheries and wood production are more widely known.

Despite the importance of mangrove forests, it is estimated that 50 per cent globally have already been lost (Feller et al., 2010) at a rate of 1–2 per cent per year (Duke et al., 2007), though much uncertainty is inherent in large-scale ecosystem statistics (Friess and Webb, 2011). Large areas of remaining forest are experiencing varying levels of degradation, affecting their resilience to coastal change. This chapter introduces the concept of ecosystem resilience, with its application to mangrove forests. It then briefly discusses the impact of extreme events in coastal areas globally, before considering how mangroves may be able to act as a bioshield to reduce the vulnerability of local populations to natural hazards. Finally, we recognize that coastal protection is just one of a broad range of ecosystem services afforded by mangroves.

The resilience of coastal ecosystems

Variations in geological, geomorphologic, hydrodynamic and climatic conditions influence the past and current distribution of coastal ecosystems. The distribution of tropical intertidal habitats (especially mangroves, marshes and seagrass beds) is constrained by the inundation regime and hydrodynamic forcing, such that these habitats are generally found in low-energy environments that allow sediment deposition and subsequent vegetation establishment. Natural disturbances may be seen as an influential but low-frequency secondary factor (with the daily or seasonal rhythms of tidal inundation, sediment and nutrient transfers as the primary control) over human time-scales. Over geological time-scales, however, disturbance can be considered a quasi-continuous force (Woodley, 1992). The impact of natural disturbance is part of an ecosystem's life history and dynamics (Bengtsson et al., 2000; Elmqvist et al., 2003). A resilient ecosystem, as defined by Holling (1973), moves from an equilibrium state to a disturbance and recovery state. However, the thresholds that determine whether an ecosystem returns to a given stability landscape or not remain difficult to quantify and depend on ecosystem type, health and location and disturbance type. The need to use and review existing methodologies for the recognition of such thresholds or system switches has been identified by Andersen et al. (2009). A single event can alter the distribution and abundance of species and organisms and set conditions different from those prior to the event, thus promoting adaptive, and perhaps evolutionary, processes. It must be recognized, however, that, even in the absence of disturbances or where there are long return periods between disturbances, other processes (such as competition between species) can equally result in alternative end-states (Salazar-Vallejo, 2002).

Natural disturbances can alter the balance of complex ecosystem processes and affect ecosystem resilience. Reduced resilience may result in ecosystem fragility and sensitivity to further disruption (Peterson et al., 1997). The term "ecosystem resilience" has been expanded to include human activities (biodiversity loss, land-use change, hydrological and biogeochemical cycle alteration, climate change) as part of ecosystem change rather than as external to the ecosystem (Gunderson and Folke, 2005). Therefore, ecological resilience – for many social, ecological and engineer practitioners – incorporates all agents affected within a system in order to understand ecosystem responses to a disturbance as well as the inter-relations among those agents (Carpenter et al., 2001; Gunderson, 2000; Folke et al., 2002; Gunderson and Folke, 2005; Holling, 2001). It is impor-tant to clarify that, although the term "resilience" is commonly used in the context of socio-ecological resilience in relation to natural hazards, this contribution focuses solely on ecological resilience as an important attribute of coastal ecosystems that can reduce the vulnerability of coastal areas (including settlements, economic activities, livelihoods and natural ecosystems) to natural hazards.

Ecosystem resilience is essential to the sustained and long-term provi-sion of ecosystem services in complex systems faced with future uncer-tainty and "surprise" (Elmqvist et al., 2003; Gunderson and Holling, 2002), such as mangroves and other coastal ecosystems. In general, much research effort is focused towards identifying potential species distribu-tion changes and abundance in response to disturbances, whereas less is known about natural temporal patterns (regionally or globally), or func-tional attributes that allow a species to respond to disturbances (Hughes et al., 2003). There is also an express need to understand the linkages be-tween ecosystems, social systems and community interaction with the natural environment. The literature that integrates these three areas is, currently, generally descriptive (Lacambra et al., 2008a; Lacambra, 2009).

Uncertainty exists over the potential response of coastal habitats to disturbances promoted by climate change. Over long time-scales (dec-ades or centuries), coastal ecosystems such as mangroves may be able to keep pace vertically with sea level rise and/or migrate inland if not im-peded by either natural or fabricated barriers and if space is available to them (Fitzgerald et al., 2008). However, such capabilities are limited by the degree to which the ecosystem has been degraded and by its capacity to cope with other multiple stressors (for example, temperature rise and ocean acidification for coral reefs). An adaptive ecosystem management approach could improve ecosystem and societal resilience to both sudden disturbance events and gradual forcing and thus reduce the community's vulnerability to natural hazards. Despite increasing efforts to achieve this goal, originating particularly from climate change adaptation initiatives (see Andrade et al., 2010, for more detail), there is a need for further re-search on this topic because most current analyses and recommenda-tions are targeting communities and social conditions, and very few have focused on ecosystem management, impacts or responses (Lacambra et al., 2008b; Lacambra, 2009; Tomkins and Adger, 2003).

"Extreme events" at the coast

Before discussing evidence for the impact of extreme events on mangrove ecosystems and the impact of the existence of the latter on the societal and economic consequences of the former, it is necessary to reflect on what constitutes an "extreme event". From a socioeconomic perspective, an "extreme event" might be expected to be linked to the occurrence of a "natural disaster". The United Nations Department of Humanitarian Affairs and the International Decade for Natural Disasters Reduction (1990–2000) define a disaster as "a serious disruption of the functioning of a society, causing widespread human, material or environmental losses which exceed the ability of affected society to cope using only its own resources" (UNDHA-IDNDR, 1992). Statistics relating to disaster frequency and magnitude may not always represent the full impacts and consequences of each event and are often dependent upon accurate reporting. However, such data do give a broad overview of trends in the type, frequency and human impact of "extreme events". The figures summarized in Table 4.1 were compiled by EM-DAT[1] to analyse patterns at the global scale, in time and space, and according to the type of event, both coastal and non-coastal. The main findings include:

- The number of countries reporting natural disasters has almost tripled during the past 50 years, from 72 countries in the 1950s to 200 in the 2000s, with larger countries reporting more natural disasters.
- Flooding events consistently affect the greatest number of people. After floods, earthquakes are the events that impact most people, but most of these devastating events have not occurred directly in coastal areas.

In particular for coastal areas, the consequences of events[2] represented by casualties, people affected and damages can be summarized as follows:

- Storms are the deadliest events in tropical coastal areas, followed by earthquakes and floods, and 9 of the 10 most deadly events have affected coastal zones.
- Of the most deadly reported events since the 1900s, 50 per cent have affected coastal areas (for example, the Haiti 2010 earthquake, the Bangladesh cyclones of 1970 and 1991, the Southeast Asia tsunami in 2004, and Tropical Cyclone Nargis in Myanmar in 2008).
- Of the top 10 events (according to numbers of people affected) in the tropics, 50 per cent occurred in coastal areas, and, of those, 4 were tropical storms (Bangladesh 1965 and 1991, and India 1977 and 1999).
- Similarly, 73 per cent of the top 10 most damaging events have occurred in coastal areas (earthquakes and tropical storms being the most damaging events reported). This is in part owing to the geographical distribution of many high-magnitude disaster events (tsunamis, for

example, cause a high death toll and are restricted to the coastal zone). However, population location and social structures increase exposure to hazards in coastal areas. Population density is disproportionately greater in the coastal zone. The Intergovernmental Panel on Climate Change estimates that, by the 2080s, up to 561 million people may be at risk of a 1:1000 year coastal flooding event alone, assuming linear population growth and a conservative sea level rise of 0.34 metres maximum (Nicholls et al., 2007). McGranahan et al. (2007) estimate that 10 per cent of the global population and 13 per cent of the urban population, in only 2 per cent of the world's area, are located at or below 10 metres above sea level.

• Despite the frequency, magnitude and impacts of natural hazards in the tropics, economic damage has been severely underreported for all types of events, including in coastal areas. There are only 12 reports of damage in tropical countries, none of which seems to be a direct consequence of coastal marine hazards. Furthermore, and surprisingly, taking into account that the costs of recent natural disasters such as Hurricane Katrina in New Orleans (2005) have not been fully assessed (Grossi and Muir-Wood, 2006, in Nicholls et al., 2011), the situation for assessing disaster impacts in developing countries and Small Island Developing States (SIDS) could be very difficult – particularly in Asia (and excluding the SIDS), where it has been estimated that 13 per cent of the population live less than 10 metres above sea level (55 per cent in Viet Nam, 46 per cent in Bangladesh, 26 per cent in Thailand, 20 per cent in Indonesia) (McGranahan et al., 2007).

Although there is some uncertainty surrounding these figures, they give a broad indication of the types of events and impacts affecting tropical coastal populations and their geographical occurrence. Coastal disasters in the tropics are a major threat to coastal communities, especially in developing nations where vulnerability is likely to be higher owing to potentially lower preparedness and lower response and recovery capacity (McGranahan et al., 2007). However, even these figures may be an underestimate. The consequences of many devastating events in coastal areas in the tropics have not been adequately recorded, despite the efforts of many national and international agencies (although in recent years reporting mechanisms have improved). It is also difficult to address the economic impact of natural disasters, because the economic impacts may be both direct (damage to industry, infrastructure and services) and indirect (for example, damage to livelihoods, which may be hard to measure owing to the informality of societies, the transient status of some people and other inner conflicts independent of the disturbance itself). This may be the case especially with regard to events that result in fewer casualties and that may be overlooked.

Table 4.1 Summary of the disaster statistics presented in the text

	1950s	1960s	1970s	1980s	1990s	2000s
Number of events	293	582	903	1,824	2,971	4,437
Number of countries reporting events	72	121	137	168	200	200
Storms per decade	120	212	291	559	899	1,054
Floods per decade	81	155	263	524	865	1,728
Death toll per decade	2,000,033	1,564,651	332,442	27,030	172,008	815,855
Per cent of casualties in tropical coastal areas	0	3.7	98.8	0	80.7	64.55

Source: Based on data from EM-DAT's International Disaster Database.
Notes: Emphasis has been placed on floods and storms because they are the most frequent events. The last two rows refer to coastal areas; the rest of the figures are global (including coastal areas).

The above discussion highlights that a clear definition of what constitutes an "extreme event" is impossible because definitions are context dependent. It also illustrates, however, that the vulnerability of coastal areas to natural hazards is a useful way to conceptualize the importance of extreme events at particular locations. The role of ecosystems in diminishing such vulnerability and in increasing a region's capacity to respond to change and to cope with changing environmental conditions is thus potentially critical but is, at present, little understood.

The role of mangroves in extreme coastal events

Prior to the 2004 Asian tsunami, mangrove ecosystems were traditionally protected and restored for socioeconomic benefit (fisheries, timber and non-timber products). As a consequence of recent events, their potential role in coastal protection has received much more attention. This section describes the importance of mangroves in mediating the impact of extreme events. Specifically, it examines (i) how such events affect the ecosystem, and (ii) how the ecosystems could mitigate the impacts of those events on coastal populations (that is, the protective role of mangroves). Both sets of processes are related to ecosystem resilience. On the one hand, it is assumed that the impacts of disturbances have been constant over time and ecosystems have developed strategies that allow a response to such disturbances and a recovery to an equilibrium state (for example, adaptation strategies that allow improved larval or propagule dispersion after an event). On the other hand, despite the damage sustained by mangroves during high-magnitude events, the characteristics that mitigate the force of an event are also those that protect the ecosystem as a whole, and hence are useful in coastal protection.

The impacts of disturbances on mangroves

Tsunamis, storms, hurricanes/cyclones/typhoons, lightning strikes and freshwater discharges are common disturbances to mangrove ecosystems. Their impact on mangrove forests depends on the intensity, frequency and magnitude of the disturbance and on the geographical setting of the area (Alongi, 2008; Lugo, 2000; Piou et al., 2006). The mechanisms that affect forests as a consequence of natural disturbances are: winds, waves, sediment burial, water levels and subsidence (Badola and Hussain, 2005; Cahoon and Hensel, 2002; Hensel and Proffitt, 2002; Pimm et al., 1994). These five mechanisms can have a direct impact on mangrove forests by causing coastal flooding, sediment erosion and deposition, and tree damage (defoliation, breakage and uprooting). Indirectly, coastal disasters can also change flooding regimes and freshwater inputs over the short and medium term. The consequences of hurricanes and tsunamis for coastal ecosystems have been discussed in greater detail by, amongst others, Cahoon and Hensel (2002), Gedan et al. (2010), Hensel and Proffitt (2002), Lacambra et al. (2008a), Lacambra (2009), Milbrandt et al. (2006) and Pimm et al. (1994).

Spencer et al. (2009) have summarized the non-linearities associated with storm impacts. Whereas hurricanes with typical wind speeds of 120–150 km/hour result in a patchwork of affected and unaffected areas, severe storms (with wind speeds in excess of 200 km/hour) may overcome the structural resistance of the mangrove forest as a whole, reducing the canopy, creating environments unsuitable for plant re-establishment, and restricting the development of mangrove forest cover for up to 50 years. Slow-moving hurricanes produce prolonged coastal wave impacts and beach scouring. These systems can cover large areas and can be accompanied by high rainfall and extensive flooding. By comparison, compact, fast-moving and intense hurricanes (such as Hurricane Andrew in 1992) generate less wave scour but produce brief and extremely strong, short-term unidirectional currents and onshore surges. Such storms leave beaches and coastal barriers relatively intact but do great damage to subtidal seagrass meadows (Smith et al., 2009; Tedesco et al., 1995).

Spencer et al. (2009) also show that hurricanes are often only the trigger for ongoing system responses. Thus Knowlton et al. (1981) document ongoing coral mortality following Hurricane Allen (1980), at an order of magnitude more severe than the impact of the storm itself; and, more than two years after Hurricane Donna (1960), storm-damaged mangroves were still experiencing mortality in the Florida Keys (Craighead and Gilbert, 1962). Disturbance damage can change ecosystem structure and composition by altering age and size distribution, forest composition and biomass, species diversity, succession processes, nutrient cycling, and plant and animal interactions (Sherman et al., 2001). These changes are related to direct disturbance and to post-disturbance conditions such as gap creation, delayed mortality and the capacity for recolonization by vegetative growth of existing species or seed dispersal into the mangrove (Lugo, 2000). Sherman et al. (2001) state that the ability of a species to colonize a canopy gap is important in determining final species composition, regardless of the nature and strength of the disturbances. Piou et al. (2006) show, through the long-term assessment of mangrove recovery in Belize, that the pattern of surviving remnant mangrove vegetation can have a strong influence on the course of post-storm recovery. For *Rhizophora*, which has little ability to regenerate from fallen roots or coppice from broken trunks, the presence of a high density of surviving seedlings becomes critical; where there are few remaining seedlings, forest replacement by genera with pioneer traits, such as *Avicennia* and *Laguncularia*, which can coppice, is likely (Friess et al., 2012; Proffitt et al., 2006; Tomlinson, 1986).

There is a second, indirect cause of species composition change after disturbance. Cahoon et al. (2003) measured up to a 9–10 mm/year decrease in surface elevation over a 1.5–3-year period after Hurricane Mitch (1998) in Honduras. Tree death led to root collapse, and eventually to the loss of peat integrity. Defoliated and dead trees did not add new organic matter inputs from leaf fall, and seedlings were unable to reestablish once inundation frequencies increased with surface elevation collapse.

Tree height and species composition are the mangrove characteristics most commonly reported to be affected by disturbance. The former is related to physical resistance to wind and waves and the second to different species life traits and strategies to cope with disturbances and change (Cahoon and Hensel, 2002; Hensel and Proffitt, 2002; Lacambra et al., 2008a; Milbrandt et al., 2006; Pimm et al., 1994; Roth, 1992; Sherman et al., 2001). Larger trees are more likely to suffer stem breakage or toppling in the path of a hurricane (Roth, 1992; McCoy et al., 1996). Conversely, Milbrandt et al. (2006) and Smith et al. (1994) show mortality rates of 20 per cent and 10 per cent, respectively, for mangrove trees with breast height diameters of less than 5 cm affected by Hurricanes Charley and Andrew.

The main force driving tsunamis is long-period waves. Wave characteristics at mangrove margins are determined by the process base of the tsunami (tectonic movement, submarine landslide or volcanic eruption), the shoreline position in relation to the location of generation, and regional bathymetry and topography. Damage from the 2004 Asian tsunami reported in a number of publications (Alongi, 2008; Cochard et al., 2008; Dahdouh-Guebas et al., 2006; EJF, 2006; FAO, 2008) includes defoliation, breakage, bending of trunks and branches, uprooting, suffocation of roots and tree mortality. These impacts have been related to direct wave attack, prolonged inundation and burial by eroded sediments. Geographical position is an important influence on damage levels – the closer the trees are to the frontline, the greater the likelihood of damage – but impacts are also species specific. Furthermore, as with storms, smaller trees typically suffer more damage than bigger trees of the same species (Cochard et al. 2008; FAO, 2008). Wood density, flexibility and volume of tree crowns and foliage are other characteristics that influence the degree of breakage and bending under tsunami wave impacts.

The role of mangroves in disaster risk reduction

Intertidal wetlands perform an important role in disaster risk reduction by attenuating hydrodynamic energy up to a certain water level and wave height threshold. Vegetation structures decrease the velocity of incoming water by friction and drag around their stems and the bed surface (Möller, 2006). Importantly, wave attenuation by vegetation is spatially non-linear (Koch et al., 2009), because much hydrodynamic energy is absorbed by vegetation at the seaward edge. Interactions between hydrodynamic forcing and intertidal vegetation have been best studied in temperate saltmarshes (for example, Möller et al., 1999; Möller, 2006). Less direct research into interactions between hydrodynamics and vegetation has been conducted for tropical mangrove systems (some examples include Mazda et al., 2006; Vo-Luong and Massel, 2008). There are many mangrove characteristics that reduce incoming hydrodynamic energy (see Table 4.2). At the single plant scale, hydrodynamic energy is attenuated by (i) bottom friction from the mud surface; (ii) drag forces owing to complex mangrove root morphology (and foliage at higher water levels); and (iii) eddy viscosity owing to turbulent water motion through root gaps (Brinkman et al., 1997; Massel et al., 1999; Mazda et al., 2006). As in saltmarshes, the effectiveness of hydrodynamic attenuation by mangroves is dependent on the species and on stem density (Mazda et al., 1997, 2006; Vo-Luong and Massel, 2008). According to hierarchy theory (where behaviour at one scale results from lower-order processes at smaller temporal and spatial scales), single plant interactions contribute to hydrodynamic attenuation at the ecosystem scale (higher order), where attenuation is governed by characteristics such as the width of the mangrove forest.

Wave energy reduction of 50 per cent has been reported over a distance of 150 metres in a *Rhizophora* forest by Brinkman et al. (1997) and over a distance of 100 metres in a *Sonneratia* forest by Mazda et al. (2006). As has been reported for saltmarshes (Möller et al., 1999), wave dissipation through mangroves is also spatially non-linear, such that, for short-period (2–3 seconds) storm waves in the Can Gio mangrove biosphere reserve, South Viet Nam, 35 per cent of incident wave energy was reported to be typically dissipated at the outer edge, but this figure increased to 100 per cent at a distance of 40–50 metres within the forest (Vo-Luong and Massel, 2008). The effect of mangrove vegetation on wind waves is thus complex, being dependent on vegetation species and density, making generalizations difficult.

In addition to considerations of species type, cover and density at the small scale, at the meso-scale of several hundreds of square metres, geomorphological features such as creek channels also act as roughness elements that cannot be ignored with respect to their impact on tidal flow and wave propagation across the mangrove surface.

Although the 2004 Asian tsunami focused the discussion on the effectiveness of mangroves in protecting communities (for more detail, see Alongi, 2008; Kaplan et al., 2009), it must be remembered that the impact of tsunami waves results from a fundamentally very different physical process from that involved in a series of wind-generated storm waves. The role of mangroves in protecting against low-frequency, high-magnitude events such as tsunamis, where wave length, wave height and velocity characteristics are markedly different from short-period storm waves (Alongi, 2008), is not fully understood. Some studies suggest that communities living behind mangrove forests suffered less during the 2004 Asian tsunami compared with communities with no fronting mangrove (Dahdouh-Guebas et al., 2006; Danielsen et al., 2005; EJF, 2006; Kathiresan and Rajendran, 2005; Tanaka et al., 2007; Vermaat and Thampanya, 2006). There is also a strong perception within the local population that mangroves play a significant role in tsunami impact reduction; Venkatachalam et al. (2009) report that 94 per cent of fishers interviewed in their study thought that mangroves protected communities from further deaths and housing damage in Sri Lanka during the 2004 Asian tsunami. Other studies of this event inferred the protection benefit of mangroves by mere statistical correlation, visual interpretation on the ground or remote sensing. Because there are co-varying controls on tsunami impact (for example, near-shore and offshore bathymetry and the angle of approach

Table 4.2 Characteristics of mangroves reported to increase their effectiveness in coastal protection

Characteristic	Comment
Width	Greater width leads to less damage to human communities behind the forest
Density	Greater density creates greater energy dissipation
Species	Different species create different drag forces
Forest structure	Species composition and distribution, specimen age and size, and general structure of the system can influence the system's resilience and capacity to cope
Height	Although from root to canopy the resistance to wave energy varies with the tree structure and characteristics, taller trees seem to play a greater role in wave dissipation during storm conditions
Age	Age is related to tree size but also to diameter and root networks, which tend to be more solid in mature trees
Stiffness of plant	Depending on their stiffness, the trees can resist more or less energy
Orientation and geometry of the plantation	It has been assumed that this relates to the location of the forest and the way the waves and wind reach it
Continuity and uniformity	Fragments can channel the energy and increase it. The less fragmented the ecosystem, the greater its attenuation capacity
Health	This relates to the resistance and resilience of ecosystems
Root system	This stabilizes the substrate where the trees are, but in addition the robust network of roots acts as a brake on the wave energy
Length	This relates to the area and width of the ecosystem and its role as a coastal defence

Sources: For a more complete list of sources please see Alongi (2008) and Lacambra et al. (2008a). The table has been built including all sources, but the ones listed here are the primary sources of information in published scientific papers: Othman (1994); Mazda et al. (1997); Tri et al. (1998); Massel et al. (1999); Sathirathai and Barbier (2001); Hadi et al. (2003); Hiraishi and Harada (2003); Danielsen et al. (2005); Siripong et al. (2005); Braatz et al. (2007); Fritz and Blount (2007); Latief and Hadi (2008); Olwig et al. (2007); Quartel et al. (2007); Barbier et al. (2008); Lacambra et al. (2008a); Tanaka (2009); Yanagisawa et al. (2010); Gedan et al. (2010).

of the tsunami wave), such statistical/visual relationships do not necessarily imply a causal link between mangrove presence or characteristics and tsunami impact reduction. The mechanisms by which mangroves offer potential tsunami protection (for example, vegetation-induced roughness, habitat width or intertidal slope) are thus still largely unknown (Alongi, 2008; Feagin, 2008; Feagin et al., 2010; Kerr et al., 2006).

Knowledge gaps regarding wave attenuation in mangroves

Despite efforts to understand the protective role of mangroves (especially since the 2004 Asian tsunami), many assumptions are still made and knowledge gaps exist. Much of the information regarding the effectiveness of mangroves in coastal protection is based on models with few variables. The information sources in our section on "extreme events", together with other sources, were classified in order to understand the focus of research involving mangroves and coastal protection for all kinds of waves. For this purpose, 37 documents were reviewed, including books, peer-reviewed articles and technical discussions, with the aim of finding scientific evidence that could help determine the characteristics of mangroves that make them suitable as coastal defences.[3] Only those sources were used that include models or figures of wave dissipation within the forests. Documents were divided into nine categories: documents that did not state the origin of the figures; literature reviews; regulation and legislation documents; numerical models and computer-based models; *in situ* measurements; technical discussions; direct observation; models based on *in situ* measurement and observation; and cost–benefit analyses. Of these papers, 11 per cent did not state how the information was derived, 13.5 per cent were models based on *in situ* measurements and observation and 24 per cent were based on numerical modelling. Fewer than 50 per cent of the models clearly stated that they had been validated. Nearly two-thirds of these documents were published after the 2004 Asian tsunami, and one-third were directly related to the characteristics of the 2004 Asian tsunami.

In general, one of the most common characteristics thought to attenuate hydrodynamic energy (of both wind-generated waves and tsunami waves) is mangrove forest width, though there are also many other variables that contribute to attenuation (see Table 4.2; also Chapter 2 in this volume). Ecosystem width is evidently important in the attenuation of wave (wind-generated and tsunami) energy; however, other ecosystem characteristics, such as the relative density of the exposed root systems versus that of the tree canopy, are likely to play a significant role in wind wave attenuation in certain circumstances. Water depth, for example, dictates whether wave dissipation is achieved by the tree canopy or by the root layer (Gedan et al., 2010). Such secondary controls, however, seem to have been less researched.

The ecosystem's capacity to absorb the impact of natural hazards has been acknowledged, but a mangrove's physical resistance and resilience in relation to such impacts have not been fully researched. Furthermore, little is known about the threshold(s) beyond which the ecosystem changes to a different state. For mangrove forests in particular, research on resilience is not common. Lacambra (2009) has argued that proxy indicators can be used to assess an ecosystem's resilience when directly recorded information is not available. Particularly for mangroves, these indicators relate to (i) the intrinsic defence capacity of the system; (ii) its health; and (iii) the pressures placed upon the system. Within these three categories, the proxy parameters can include: ecosystem width, length, area, density and fragmentation, seaward margin distance to the shore, vegetation height, biodiversity, ecosystem uses, human activities within and surrounding the ecosystem, freshwater input, pollution, domestic and industrial discharges to or nearby the system, the dominant land use, characteristics and density of the human population, the presence and type of infrastructure and channelization.

Nevertheless, ecosystem resilience is only one of the conditions that must be understood before the potential for sustainable coastal protection by mangroves can be adequately assessed. Mangrove ecosystems are subject to continuous changes, and these changes result from a range of different drivers. Similarly, the mechanisms by which mangroves act as coastal protection can be explained at different scales, from the processes generated by the presence of a single tree to the protective role of an entire mangrove forest landscape. Hence, independently of the mangrove as a physical barrier attenuating the force of waves (under normal or under disturbance conditions), it is important to understand other characteristics that allow the system to respond to and cope with change, including ecological and geological factors. There is a clear need for studies that aim to improve this understanding.

Despite the increasing knowledge regarding the protective role of mangroves during average and extreme inundation/wave events, and despite the evidence base on the impact of extreme inundation/wave disturbances, there still seems to be a lack of understanding of the interlinkages between the biological and the geomorphological processes, including factors that determine the ecosystem's resilience. There is thus an urgent need to create methods that provide sound information to fill this knowledge gap.

Mangroves: More than just a coastal defence

Understanding mangrove ecosystem resilience is essential for the sustained production of the natural resources and ecosystem services they offer. In addition to coastal protection, ecosystem services provided by mangroves include the provision, support, regulation and creation of sociocultural services, which have also been the subject of an increasing number of studies over recent years. Das and Vincent observed in 2009 that, independent of their coastal protection value, mangroves are worth conserving because of the many benefits they provide to coastal communities. However, Aburto-Oropeza et al. (2007) identify a lack of understanding with regard to the linkages between the ecological functions of these systems and their social benefits; hence, greater knowledge of the process interactions will ultimately enable more effective ecosystem-based adaptation plans to be efficiently implemented.

The value of ecosystem services provided by mangroves

Barbier et al. (2008) and Silvestri and Kershaw (2010) clearly identify many of the ecosystem services that mangrove forests provide and have highlighted their links to the well-being of coastal communities (Figure 4.1). Although qualitatively describing such ecosystem services may be straightforward, it is often difficult to assign an economic value to them (Aburto-Oropeza et al., 2007; Barbier et al., 2008; Koch et al., 2009; Walters et al., 2008). This is because mangrove systems include a number of variables and interactions that may be non-linear temporally and/or spatially, and (potentially unknown) thresholds may exist beyond which a service provides a negative benefit. For example, intertidal wetlands may become a source (rather than a sink) of carbon if hydroperiod or erosion increases beyond a certain threshold (Chmura et al., 2003). It is also difficult to put a price on "well-being". Despite the difficulties inherent in the quantification of ecosystem services, attempts have been based on a benefit transfer approach. For example, one study estimates that 1 hectare of restored mangrove may be worth as much as US$4,290 per year (TEEB, 2009). This is low compared with estimates for coral reefs (US$129,200) but higher than estimates for woodlands/shrublands (US$1,571). It should, however, be kept in mind that The Economics of Ecosystems and Biodiversity (TEEB) database and value analysis were still under development when those figures were published.

Mangroves provide multiple services to increase livelihoods

Research throughout the tropics has highlighted the many benefits that mangroves provide to coastal communities (though it is important to note that not all perceived benefits have a proven causal relationship with mangrove extent, or have been rigorously tested – Manson et al., 2005). Such livelihood benefits may include:
• *Silviculture*. Mangroves are commonly utilized for construction timber and charcoal (Walters et al., 2008). In Cameroon, communities on the Wouri estuary depend on mangrove exploitation for wood, timber, fur-

niture and fuelwood (Figure 4.2(a), (b)), at both the household and industrial scale (Atheull et al., 2009). The Matang Mangrove Forest Reserve in Perak, Peninsular Malaysia, covers 40,800 hectares, large parts of which are sustainably harvested on a 30-year rotation (Ong, 1995). Many felled *Rhizophora* trunks are converted into charcoal in the local area (for example, Figure 4.2(b)) and exported to international markets.

- *Non-timber forest products.* Many non-timber products can be extracted from mangrove bark, leaves and fruits. Mangroves are an important source of tannins and dyes (Walters et al., 2008). Mangroves and associated halophytic plants have been used in traditional medicine in India for centuries (Agoramoorthy et al., 2008). Although non-timber forest products are of less commercial value than timber and fuel, non-governmental organizations involved in mangrove restoration are trying to encourage the harvesting of such products to alleviate the pressure on wood resources and to provide an alternative income for local populations (F. Garnier, Planete Urgence, Sumatra, personal communication, 2011).

- *Fisheries.* Mangroves support fisheries by (i) providing habitat for fish nurseries (Barletta et al., 2010); and (ii) exporting nutrients to offshore fisheries (Christensen et al., 2008) (Figure 4.2(c)). Mangroves are also important fishing grounds for artisanal fishers; there are examples from Mexico, Brazil, Indonesia and the Philippines – in fact from almost every country where mangroves are present. However, as Barletta et al. (2010) highlight, much remains unknown about this ecosystem service in specific regions, despite this being one of the first services attributed to mangroves. Rönnbäck (1999) estimates the global annual market value of capture fisheries supported by mangroves to be between US$750 and US$16,750 per hectare. Aburto-Oropeza et al. (2007) calculate the annual value of fisheries associated with mangroves in the Gulf of California to be US$37,500 per hectare of mangrove fringe, more than double Rönnbäck's estimation. However, the former is a global assessment and the latter a local assessment.

- *Biodiversity.* Mangroves not only are important for the life history of several fish species but also provide food and shelter to several species of crabs, sponges, insects and other invertebrates as well as birds, mammals, reptiles and amphibian species (for example, Figure 4.2(d)).

- *Carbon sequestration.* Mangroves have recently been viewed as one of the tropical ecosystems with the highest potential for carbon sequestration. They may play a disproportionate role in carbon sequestration, despite their limited distribution (Donato et al., 2011). At the time of writing, carbon-rich wetlands such as mangroves and peat swamps are being more seriously considered in conservation policies that incentivize ecosystem protection for carbon benefits, such as REDD+ (Reducing Emissions from Deforestation and Degradation).

- *Sediment trapping/land stabilization.* Mangroves play an important role in sediment binding and shoreline accretion (Gilman et al., 2007; Krauss et al., 2003; McKee et al., 2007). Sedimentation is enhanced and re-suspension reduced as a result of water velocity reduction by mangrove vegetation, and this process is intricately related to vegetation characteristics such as stem density and plant structure, similar to the link between vegetation characteristics and hydrodynamic attenuation. The relationship between sediment trapping/accretion and stem

Figure 4.2 Examples of ecosystem services provided by mangroves
(a) Harvested *Rhizophora* poles, Pontian, Malaysia; (b) Charcoal kiln, Sumatra, Indonesia; (c) Tiger prawn, Sumatra, Indonesia; (d) Wild boar in *Rhizophora*-dominated mangrove, Pulau Kukup Ramsar site, Malaysia.
Photos: D.A. Friess and A. Wee (National University of Singapore).

density has been shown for *Avicennia* (Young and Harvey, 1996) and for *Rhizophora*. In the case of the latter, aerial root density of 300 stems per m^2 has been shown to significantly increase sediment deposition by more than six times the deposition measured on an adjacent bare intertidal surface (D.A. Friess, unpublished data). Krauss et al. (2003) showed during field experiments that the efficiency of sediment trapping is species specific, with larger *Rhizophora* aerial roots trapping proportionally more sediment than *Avicennia* and *Bruguiera* pneumatophores. It must be noted, however, that species-specific increases in surficial sediment deposition may be offset by other species-specific subsurface processes, such as subsidence (Krauss et al., 2003).

The above list gives only a few key examples of the interaction between humans and mangroves. Many more examples exist and form the basis of entire programmes dedicated to restoring livelihoods and mangroves.[4] Pressures on mangroves worldwide include loss (land filling, land conversion, overexploitation), degradation (owing for example to overexploitation, pollution or coastal squeeze), lack of awareness about their importance, lack of management capacity or political will (poor territorial planning, poor governance, inefficient management of the natural resources) and population growth (Agoramoorthy et al., 2008; Barletta et al., 2010; Zhou and Cai, 2010).

Conclusions

With increasing population growth, increasing sea level rise and limited resource availability over the next century, coastal populations in developing nations are likely to be ever more vulnerable to natural hazards. It is important to understand how past events have affected coastal populations and their livelihoods and the potential impacts of other disturbances in order to plan for adaptation and disaster risk reduction, regardless of whether the need for such adaptation or risk management arises from climate change or from the continued environmental changes occurring "naturally" in coastal areas.

Considering the many different interests (often conflicting) in coastal areas, the increasing population and the dynamic physical environment here create a particular need for integrated approaches to coastal zone management and vulnerability assessment. It is important not only to adopt such approaches but to ensure that these approaches are in tune with each area's ecological, social and geophysical conditions and dynamics, and, most importantly, that they incorporate disaster research and management into land-use planning.

Despite the research undertaken on interactions between hydrodynamics and vegetation since the 1990s, and research into mangroves' role in disaster reduction during the 2004 Asian tsunami, there is still much to learn regarding the biophysical performance of mangroves during natural disturbances and other factors that may reduce the vulnerability of coastal populations. Although wetlands are effective shoreline buffers (Gedan et al., 2010), during extreme events mangroves alone cannot fully protect coastal communities (Kaplan et al., 2009; Lacambra, 2009; Osti et al., 2009; Venkatachalam et al., 2009). The 2004 tsunami stimulated a major research effort into the assessment of mangrove buffering capacity (see, for example, Chapter 2 in this volume). Tsunamis are a low-frequency disturbance and there are other extreme events, such as hurricanes, storm surges and high tides, that are more frequent; emphasis in future research needs to be placed on the role of mangroves in attenuating a broader range of physical impacts.

Understanding the interaction between physical processes and the characteristics of mangroves that could enhance or attenuate wave energy during a disturbance event is a major challenge. Coastal authorities promoting bioshields or alternative ways to protect coasts from or adapt them to environmental changes and disturbances (including sea level rise as a consequence of climate change) should be aware of the pros and cons of their use and those factors that may threaten their continued existence. Detailed local assessments must thus be conducted before embarking on mangrove reforestation programmes, bioshield programmes or hard engineering options. Coastal managers should consider not only the economic benefits of each option but also the long-term feasibility of protecting coastal communities and the need to create awareness among such communities of the risks that they are facing. In addition, these processes should involve participation by local populations and local stakeholders in order to promote the inclusion of these initiatives in local land-use planning strategies.

Considering the many anthropogenic pressures that mangroves face globally (including the needs of industry and local coastal communities), it remains a challenge to calculate the amount and characteristics of mangroves that can sustainably provide multiple ecosystem services, while improving livelihoods and reducing vulnerability to hazards. In some areas the pressure for urbanization will be greater than the need for sustainable fisheries, whereas in other locations local authorities may place greater value on sustainably managing their mangrove resources. It is crucial that robust information (on variables such as the role of mangroves in wave attenuation) is available, so that coastal management options are chosen in full knowledge of the potential consequences of those actions.

Acknowledgements

C.L. Lacambra gratefully acknowledges the support of the Gates Cambridge Trust. D.A. Friess gratefully acknowledges the Singapore-Delft Water Alliance (SDWA). This work was carried out as part of the "Relating Ecosystem Functioning and Ecosystem Services by Mangroves" research programme (R-303-001-024-272/414). The authors also wish to express thanks for the comments received at the Ecosystems, Livelihoods and Disaster Risk Reduction Workshop (Bonn, 2010), PEDRR's invitation to participate in this project and the comments from the reviewers of this chapter.

Notes

1. The International Disaster Database, <http://www.emdat.be/database> (accessed 11 October 2012).
2. Events included in these figures are earthquakes, floods, mass movements, storms, extreme temperatures, volcanoes and wildfires. Events that have been excluded are epidemics and droughts.
3. There is plenty of information on the Internet about the protective role of mangroves. The documents presented here are those that were widely accessible through academic search engines and that were written in English.
4. See Conservation International (<http://www.conservation.org/FMG/Articles/Pages/mangroves_in_aceh_after_the_disaster.aspx>); Wetlands International (<http://www.wetlands.org/LinkClick.aspx?fileticket=jkrE9dNpgpg%3D&tabid=56>); the World Rain Forest Movement (<http://www.wrm.org.uy/deforestation/mangroves/book.html>); the Mangrove Action Project (<http://69.90.183.227/lifeweb/eoi/map%20concept%20paper%20for%20danone%20group.pdf>); Alternatives to Mangrove Destruction for Women's Livelihoods in Central Africa (<http://www.afdb.org/en/projects-and-operations/project-portfolio/project/p-z1-c00-007/>); International Union for Conservation of Nature, Securing Coastal Livelihoods (<http://www.iucn.org/about/work/programmes/marine/marine_our_work/livelihoods/>).

REFERENCES

Aburto-Oropeza, O. et al. (2007) "Mangroves in the Gulf of California Increase Fishery Yields". *Proceedings of the National Academy of Sciences* 105: 10456–10459.

Agoramoorthy, G. et al. (2008) "Threat of Heavy Metal Pollution in Halophytic and Mangrove Plants of Tamil Nadu, India". *Environmental Pollution* 155: 320–326.

Alongi, D.M. (2008) "Mangrove Forests: Resilience, Protection from Tsunamis, and Responses to Global Climate Change". *Estuarine, Coastal and Shelf Science* 76: 11–13.

Andersen, T. et al. (2009) "Ecological Thresholds and Regime Shifts: Approaches to Identification". *Trends in Ecology and Evolution* 24: 49–57.

Andrade Pérez, A. et al. (eds) (2010) *Building Resilience to Climate Change: Ecosystem-based Adaptation and Lessons from the Field*. Gland, Switzerland: International Union for Conservation of Nature.

Atheull, A.N. et al. (2009) "Commercial Activities and Subsistence Utilization of Mangrove Forests around the Wouri Estuary and the Douala-Edea Reserve (Cameroon)". *Journal of Ethnobiology and Ethnomedicine* 5: 35.

Badola, R. and S.A. Hussain (2005) "Valuing Ecosystem Functions: An Empirical Study on the Storm Protection Function of Bhitarkanika Mangrove Ecosystem, India". *Environmental Conservation* 32: 85–92.

Barbier, E.B. et al. (2008) "Coastal Ecosystem-Based Management with Non-linear Ecological Functions and Values". *Science* 319: 321–323.

Barletta, M. et al. (2010) "Fish and Aquatic Habitat Conservation in South America: A Continental Overview with Emphasis on Neotropical Systems". *Journal of Fish Biology* 76: 2118–2176.

Bengtsson J. et al. (2000) "Biodiversity, Disturbances, Ecosystem Function and Management of European Forests". *Forest Ecology and Management* 132: 39–50.

Braatz, S. et al. (2007) *Coastal Protection in the Aftermath of the Indian Ocean Tsunami: What Role for Forests and Trees?* Proceedings of the Regional Technical Workshop, Khao Lak, Thailand, 28–31 August 2006. Bangkok: FAO.

Brinkman R.M. et al. (1997) "Surface Wave Attenuation in Mangrove Forests". *Proceedings of the 13th Australasian Coastal and Ocean Engineering Conference* 2: 909–914.

Cahoon, D.R. and P. Hensel (2002) "Hurricane Mitch: A Regional Perspective on Mangrove Damage, Recovery and Sustainability". USGS Open-File Report 03-183, U.S. Geological Survey.

Cahoon, D.R. et al. (2003) "Mass Tree Mortality Leads to Mangrove Peat Collapse at Bay Islands, Honduras after Hurricane Mitch". *Journal of Ecology* 91: 1093–1105.

Carpenter, S. et al. (2001) "From Metaphor to Measurement: Resilience of What to What?" *Ecosystems* 4: 765–781.

Chmura, G.L. et al. (2003) "Global Carbon Sequestration in Tidal, Saline Wetland Soils". *Global Biogeochemical Cycles* 17(4): 1–12.

Christensen, S.M. et al. (2008) "Mangrove Forest Management Planning in Coastal Buffer and Conservation Zones, Vietnam: A Multimethodological Approach Incorporating Multiple Stakeholders". *Ocean & Coastal Management* 51: 712–726.

Cochard, R., S.L. Ranamukhaarachchi, G.P. Shivakoti, O.V. Shipin, P.J. Edwards and K.T. Seeland (2008) "The 2004 Tsunami in Aceh and Southern Thailand: A Review on Coastal Ecosystems, Wave Hazards and Vulnerability". *Perspectives in Plant Ecology, Evolution and Systematics* 10: 3–40.

Craighead, F.C. and V.C. Gilbert (1962) "The Effects of Hurricane Donna on the Vegetation of Southern Florida". *Quarterly Journal of the Florida Academy of Sciences* 25: 1–28.

Dahdouh-Guebas, F. et al. (2006) "How Effective Were Mangroves as a Defence against the Recent Tsunami?" *Current Biology* 15: 443–447.

Danielsen, F. et al. (2005) "The Asian Tsunami: A Protective Role for Coastal Vegetation". *Science* 310: 643.

Das, S. and J.R. Vincent (2009) "Mangroves Protected Villages and Reduced Death Toll during Indian Super Cyclone". *Proceedings of the National Academy of Sciences* 106: 7357–7360.

Donato D.C. et al. (2011) "Mangroves among the Most Carbon-Rich Forests in the Tropics". *Nature Geoscience* 4: 293–397.

Duke, N.C. et al. (2007) "A World without Mangroves?" *Science* 317: 41–42.

EJF [Environmental Justice Foundation] (2006) "Mangroves: Nature's Defence against Tsunamis: A Report on the Impact of Mangrove Loss and Shrimp Farm Development on Coastal Defences". Environmental Justice Foundation, London.

Elmqvist T. et al. (2003) "Response Diversity, Ecosystem Change, and Resilience". *Frontiers in Ecology and the Environment* 1: 488–494.

FAO [Food and Agriculture Organization] (2008) *The Role of Coastal Forests in the Mitigation of Tsunami Impacts*. Food and Agriculture Organization of the United Nations.

Feagin, R.A. (2008) "Vegetation's Role in Coastal Protection". *Science* 320: 176–177.

Feagin, R.A. et al. (2010) "Shelter from the Storm? Use and Misuse of Coastal Vegetation Bioshields for Managing Natural Disasters". *Conservation Letters* 3: 1–11.

Feller, I.C. et al. (2010) "Biocomplexity in Mangrove Ecosystems". *Annual Review of Marine Science* 2: 27–49.

Fitzgerald, D.M. et al. (2008) "Coastal Impacts Due to Sea-level Rise". *Annual Review of Earth and Planetary Sciences* 36: 601–647.

Folke, C. et al. (2002) "Resilience and Sustainable Development: Building Adaptive Capacity in a World of Transformation". Scientific Background Paper on Resilience for the process of the World Summit on Sustainable Development on behalf of the Environmental Advisory Council to the Swedish Government. Stockholm.

Friess, D.A. and E.L. Webb (2011) "Bad Data Equals Bad Policy: How to Trust Estimates of Ecosystem Loss When There Is So Much Uncertainty?" *Environmental Conservation* 38(1): 1–5.

Friess, D.A. et al. (2012) "Are All Intertidal Wetlands Naturally Created Equal? Bottlenecks, Thresholds and Knowledge Gaps to Mangrove and Saltmarsh Ecosystems". *Biological Reviews* 87(2): 346–366.

Fritz, H.M. and C. Blount (2007) "Role of Forests and Trees in Protecting Coastal Areas against Cyclones". In S. Braatz et al. (eds), *Coastal Protection in the Aftermath of the Indian Ocean Tsunami: What Role for Forests and Trees?* Proceedings of the Regional Technical Workshop, Khao Lak, Thailand, 28–31 August 2006. Bangkok: FAO.

Gedan, K.B. et al. (2010) "The Present and Future Role of Coastal Wetland Vegetation in Protecting Shorelines: Answering Recent Challenges to the Paradigm". *Climatic Change* 106: 7–29.

Gilbert, A. and R. Janssen (1998) "Use of Environmental Functions to Communicate the Value of a Mangrove Ecosystem under Different Management Regimes". *Ecological Economics* 25: 323–346.

Gilman, E. et al. (2007) "Assessment of Mangrove Response to Projected Relative Sea-level Rise and Recent Historical Reconstruction of Shoreline Position". *Environmental Monitoring and Assessment* 124: 105–130.

Grossi, P. and R. Muir-Wood (2006) "Flood Risk in New Orleans: Implications for Future Management and Insurability". Risk Management Solutions, London.

Gunderson, L.H. (2000) "Ecological Resilience – in Theory and Application". *Annual Review of Ecology and Systematics* 31: 425–439.

Gunderson, L. and C. Folke (2005) "Resilience – Now More Than Ever". *Ecology and Society* 10(2): 22.

Gunderson, L.H. and C.S. Holling (2002) *Panarchy: Understanding Transformations in Human and Natural Systems.* Washington, DC: Island Press.

Hadi S. et al. (2003) "Analysis of Surface Wave Attenuation in Mangrove Forests". *Proceedings ITB Engineering Science* 35(2): 89–108.

Hensel, P. and C.E. Proffitt (2002). *Hurricane Mitch: Acute Impacts on Mangrove Forest Structure and an Evaluation of Recovery Trajectories: Executive Summary.* USGS Open-File Report 03-182, U.S. Geological Survey.

Hiraishi, T. and K. Harada (2003) "Greenbelt Tsunami Prevention in South-Pacific Region". *Report of the Port and Airport Research Institute* 42(2), June.

Holling, C.S. (1973) "Resilience and Stability of Ecological Systems". *Annual Review of Ecology and Systematics* 4: 1–23.

Holling, C.S. (2001) "Understanding the Complexity of Economic, Ecological, and Social Systems". *Ecosystems* 4: 390–405.

Hughes T. et al. (2003) "Climate Change, Human Impacts, and the Resilience of Coral Reefs". *Science* 301: 929–933.

Kaplan, M. et al. (2009) "Vulnerability Assessment and Protective Effects of Coastal Vegetation during the 2004 Tsunami in Sri Lanka". *Natural Hazards and Earth System Sciences* 9: 1479–1494.

Kathiresan, K. and N. Rajendran (2005) "Coastal Mangrove Forests Mitigated Tsunami". *Estuarine, Coastal and Shelf Science* 65: 601–606.

Kerr A.M. et al. (2006) "Comments on 'Coastal Mangrove Forests Mitigated Tsunami' by K. Kathiresan and N. Rajendran". *Estuarine, Coastal and Shelf Science* 67: 539–541.

Knowlton, N. et al. (1981) "Evidence for Delayed Mortality in Hurricane-damaged Jamaican Staghorn Corals". *Nature* 294: 251–252.

Koch, W.E. et al. (2009) "Non-linearity in Ecosystem Services: Temporal and Spatial Variability in Coastal Protection". *Frontiers in Ecology and the Environment* 7(1): 29–37.

Krauss, K.W. et al. (2003) "Differential Rates of Vertical Accretion and Elevation Change among Aerial Root Types in Micronesian Mangrove Forests". *Estuarine, Coastal and Shelf Science* 56: 251–259.

Lacambra, C. (2009) "Ecosystem-Inclusive Coastal Vulnerability Assessment in the Neotropics". PhD thesis.

Lacambra, C. et al. (2008a) "Tropical Coastal Ecosystems as Coastal Defences". In *The Role of Environmental Management and Eco-engineering in Disaster Risk Reduction and Climate Change Adaptation*. Tannay, Switzerland: ProAct Network.

Lacambra, C. et al. (2008b) "The Need for an Ecosystem-Inclusive Vulnerability Index for Coastal Areas in Colombia". *SOURCE* 10: 82–98.

Latief, H. and S. Hadi (2008) "The Role of Forests and Trees in Protecting Coastal Areas against Tsunamis". In S. Braatz et al. (eds), *Coastal Protection in the Aftermath of the Indian Ocean Tsunami: What Role for Forests and Trees?* Proceedings of the Regional Technical Workshop, Khao Lak, Thailand, 28–31 August 2006. Bangkok: FAO.

Lugo, A. (2000) "Effects and Outcomes of Caribbean Hurricanes in a Climate Change Scenario". *The Science of the Total Environment* 262: 243–251.

McCoy, E.D. et al. (1996) "Mangrove Damage Caused by Hurricane Andrew on the Southwestern Coast of Florida". *Bulletin of Marine Science* 59: 1–8.

McGranahan, G. et al. (2007) "The Rising Tide: Assessing the Risks of Climate Change and Human Settlements in Low Elevation Coastal Zones". *Environment and Urbanization* 19(1): 17–37.

McKee, K.L. et al. (2007) "Caribbean Mangroves Adjust to Rising Sea Level through Biotic Controls on Change in Soil Elevation". *Global Ecology and Biogeography* 16(5): 545–556.

Manson, F.J. et al. (2005) "An Evaluation of the Evidence for Linkages between Mangroves and Fisheries: A Synthesis of the Literature and Identification of Research Directions". *Oceanography and Marine Biology: An Annual Review* 43: 483–513.

Massel, S.R. et al. (1999) "Surface Wave Propagation in Mangrove Forests". *Fluid Dynamics Research* 24: 219–249.

Mazda, Y. et al. (1997) "Mangroves as a Coastal Protection from Waves in the Tong King Delta, Vietnam". *Mangroves and Salt Marshes* 1: 127–135.

Mazda, Y. et al. (2006) "Wave Reduction in a Mangrove Forest Dominated by *Sonneratia sp.*". *Wetlands Ecology and Management* 14: 365–378.

Milbrandt, E.C. et al. (2006) "Impact and Response of Southwest Florida Mangroves to the 2004 Hurricane Season". *Estuaries and Coasts* 29: 979–984.

Moberg, F. and P. Rönnbäck (2003) "Ecosystem Services of the Tropical Seascape: Interactions, Substitutions and Restoration". *Ocean and Coastal Management* 46: 27–46.

Möller, I. (2006) "Quantifying Saltmarsh Vegetation and Its Effect on Wave Height Dissipation: Results from a UK East Coast Saltmarsh". *Estuarine, Coastal and Shelf Science* 69: 337–351.

Möller, I. et al. (1999) "Wave Transformation over Salt Marshes: A Field and Numerical Modelling Study from North Norfolk, England". *Estuarine, Coastal and Shelf Science* 49: 411–426.

Nicholls, R.J. et al. (2007) "Coastal Systems and Low-lying Areas". In M.L. Parry, O.F. Canziani, J.P. Palutikof, P.J. van der Linden and C.E. Hanson (eds), *Climate Change 2007: Impacts, Adaptation and Vulnerability*. Contribution of Working Group II to the Fourth Assessment Report of the Intergovernmental

Panel on Climate Change. Cambridge: Cambridge University Press, pp. 315–56.

Nicholls, R.J. et al. (2011) "Sea-level Rise and Its Possible Impacts Given a 'Beyond 4 Degrees C World' in the Twenty-first Century". *Philosophical Transactions of the Royal Society of London* A369: 161–181.

Olwig, M.F. et al. (2007) "Using Remote Sensing to Assess the Protective Role of Coastal Woody Vegetation against Tsunami Waves". *International Journal of Remote Sensing* 28(13): 3153–3169.

Ong, J.-E. (1995) "The Ecology of Mangrove Conservation and Management". *Hydrobiologia* 295: 343–351.

Osti, R. et al. (2009) "The Importance of Mangrove Forest in Tsunami Disaster Mitigation". *Disasters* 33(2): 203–213.

Othman, M.A. (1994) "Value of Mangroves in Coastal Protection". *Hydrobiologia* 285: 277–282.

Peterson, G. et al. (1997) "Uncertainty, Climate Change, and Adaptive Management". *Conservation Ecology* [online] 1(2): 4.

Pimm, S.L. et al. (1994) "Hurricane Andrew". *BioScience* 44: 224–229.

Piou, C. et al. (2006) "Zonation Patterns of Belizean Offshore Mangrove Forests 41 Years After a Catastrophic Hurricane". *Biotropica* 38: 365–374.

Proffitt, C.E. et al. (2006) "Red Mangrove (*Rhizophora mangle*) Reproduction and Seedling Colonization after Hurricane Charley: Comparisons of Charlotte Harbor and Tampa Bay". *Estuaries and Coasts* 29: 972–978.

Quartel, S. et al. (2007) "Wave Attenuation in Coastal Mangroves in the Red River Delta, Vietnam". *Journal of Asian Earth Sciences* 29: 576–584.

Rönnbäck, P. (1999) "The Ecological Basis for Economic Value of Seafood Production Supported by Mangrove Ecosystems". *Ecological Economics* 29: 235–252.

Roth, L.C. (1992) "Hurricanes and Mangrove Regeneration: Effects of Hurricane Joan, October 1988, on the Vegetation of Isla del Venado, Bluefields, Nicaragua". *Biotropica* 24(3): 375–384.

Salazar-Vallejo, S.I. (2002) "Huracanes y Biodiversidad Costera Tropical". *Revista de Biologia Tropical* 50(2): 415–428.

Sathirathai, S. and E.B. Barbier (2001) "Valuing Mangrove Conservation in Southern Thailand". *Contemporary Economic Policy* 19: 109–122.

Sherman, R.E. et al. (2001) "Hurricane Impacts on a Mangrove Ecosystem in the Dominican Republic: Damage Patterns and Early Recovery". *Biotropica* 33: 393–408.

Silvestri, S. and F. Kershaw (eds) (2010) *Framing the Flow: Innovative Approaches to Understand, Protect and Value Ecosystem Services across Linked Habitats.* Cambridge: UNEP World Conservation Monitoring Centre.

Siripong, A. et al. (2005) "The 26 December 2004 Tsunami: Impacts on Mangroves along Some Thai Coasts". In *The Importance of Mangrove and Other Coastal Ecosystems in Mitigating Tsunami Disasters. Symposium held in Kuala Lumpur, Malaysia, 23 August 2005.*

Smith, T.J. III et al. (1994) "Mangroves, Hurricanes, and Lightning Strikes". *Bioscience* 44: 256–262.

Smith, T.J. et al. (2009) "Cumulative Impacts of Hurricanes on Florida Mangrove Ecosystems: Sediment Deposition, Storm Surges and Vegetation". *Wetlands* 29: 24–34.

Spencer, T. and I. Möller (2012) "Mangrove Systems". In D.J. Sherman (ed.), *Coastal Geomorphology*. Treatise in Geomorphology, Vol. 10. Amsterdam: Elsevier.

Spencer, T. et al. (2009) "Landscape, Landscape-scale Processes and Global Environmental Change: Synthesis and New Agendas for the Twenty-first Century". In O. Slaymaker, T. Spencer and C. Embleton-Hamann (eds), *Geomorphology and Global Environmental Change*. Cambridge: Cambridge University Press, pp. 403–423.

Tanaka, N. (2009) "Vegetation Bioshields for Tsunami Mitigation: Review of Effectiveness, Limitations, Construction, and Sustainable Management". *Landscape and Ecological Engineering* 5(1): 71–79.

Tanaka, N., Y. Sasaki, M.I.M. Mowjood, K.B.S.N. Jinadasa and S. Homchuen (2007) "Coastal Vegetation Structures and Their Functions in Tsunami Protection: Experience of the Recent Indian Ocean Tsunami". *Landscape and Ecological Engineering* 3: 33–45.

Tedesco, L.P. et al. (1995) "Impact of Hurricane Andrew on South Florida's Sandy Coastline". *Journal of Coastal Research, Special Issue* 18: 59–82.

TEEB [The Economics of Ecosystems and Biodiversity] (2009) "TEEB Climate Issues Update". September. Available at <http://www.unep.ch/etb/ebulletin/pdf/TEEB-ClimateIssuesUpdate-Sep2009.pdf> (accessed 12 October 2012).

Tomkins, E.L. and W.N. Adger (2003) "Building Resilience to Climate Change through Adaptive Management of Natural Resources". Tyndall Centre for Climate Change Research Working Paper 27, Norwich.

Tomlinson, P.B. (1986) *The Botany of Mangroves*. Cambridge: Cambridge University Press.

Tri, N.H. et al. (1998) "Natural Resource Management in Mitigating Climate Impacts: The Example of Mangrove Restoration in Vietnam". *Global Environmental Change* 8(1): 49–61.

UNDHA [United Nations Department of Humanitarian Affairs] and IDNDR [International Decade for Natural Disasters Reduction] (1992) *Glossary: Internationally Agreed Glossary of Basic Terms Related to Disaster Management*. Geneva: United Nations.

Venkatachalam, A.J. et al. (2009) "Risk Factors in Relation to Human Deaths and Other Tsunami (2004) Impacts in Sri Lanka: The Fishers'-Eye View". *Aquatic Conservation: Marine and Freshwater Ecosystems* 19: 57–66.

Vermaat, J.E. and U. Thampanya (2006) "Mangroves Mitigate Tsunami Damage: A Further Response". *Estuarine, Coastal and Shelf Science* 69: 1–3.

Vo-Luong, P. and S. Massel (2008) "Energy Dissipation in Non-uniform Mangrove Forests of Arbitrary Depth". *Journal of Marine Systems* 74: 603–622.

Walters, B.B. et al. (2008) "Ethnobiology, Socio-economics and Management of Mangrove Forests: A Review". *Aquatic Botany* 89: 220–236.

Woodley, J.D. (1992) "The Incidence of Hurricanes on the North Coast of Jamaica since 1870: Are the Classic Reef Descriptions Atypical?" *Hydrobiologia* 247: 133–138.

Yanagisawa, H. et al. (2010) "Tsunami Damage Reduction Performance of a Mangrove Forest in Banda Aceh, Indonesia Inferred from Field Data and a Numerical Model". *Journal of Geophysical Research* 115 (C06032), doi:10.1029/2009JC005587.

Young, B.M. and L.E. Harvey (1996) "A Spatial Analysis of the Relationship between Mangrove (*Avicennia marina* var. Australasica) Physiognomy and Sediment Accretion in the Hauraki Plains, New Zealand". *Estuarine, Coastal and Shelf Sciences* 42: 231–246.

Zhou, X. and L. Cai (2010) "Coastal and Marine Environmental Issues in the Pearl River Delta Region, China". *International Journal of Environmental Studies* 67(2): 137–145.

5

Integrating the role of ecosystems in disaster risk and vulnerability assessments: Lessons from the Risk and Vulnerability Assessment Methodology Development Project (RiVAMP) in Negril, Jamaica

Pascal Peduzzi, Adonis Velegrakis, Marisol Estrella and Bruno Chatenoux

Introduction

The role of ecosystems in disaster risk reduction has gained international recognition over the past decade, with mounting evidence to suggest that robust ecosystems may reduce disaster risks whereas degraded ecosystems may induce or increase risks. For example, vegetation coverage has been found to reduce susceptibility to landslides (see, for example, Peduzzi, 2010; Vanacker et al., 2003; Chapter 12 in this volume), and deforestation may lead to more frequent/severe drought conditions (Hasler et al., 2009) and related forest fires (Van der Werf et al., 2008). With regard to coastal ecosystems, these have been long considered as natural coastal buffers that can reduce the risk of erosion and inundation (for example, IFRC, 2002; Pethick and Burd, 1993; see also Chapters 3 and 4 in this volume), although their effectiveness has been shown to vary considerably depending on the hydrodynamic or wave regime (see, for example, Chatenoux and Peduzzi, 2007; Cochard et al., 2008).

The significance of coastal ecosystems for coastal risk reduction is gaining recognition. Coastal wetlands have the potential to attenuate storm waves/surges (for example, Feagin et al., 2011; Neumeier and Amos, 2006; Wamsley et al., 2010); their degradation/loss, which is predicted to be substantial by the end of the century (for example, McFadden et al., 2007), may result in an increased risk of storm-induced coastal inundation

The role of ecosystems in disaster risk reduction, Renaud, Sudmeier-Rieux and Estrella (eds), United Nations University Press, 2013, ISBN 978-92-808-1221-3

(Loder et al., 2009). Similarly, coral reefs and seagrass meadows have a significant potential to dissipate wave energy (for example, Fernando et al., 2008; Paul and Amos, 2011). Moreover, the results of a study on 27 Pacific atolls showed great resilience of coastal ecosystems to mean sea level rise through ecosystem dynamic response (Webb and Kench, 2010).

However, coastal ecosystems are usually heavily affected by coastal degradation during high-energy storm events (for example, Knudby et al., 2010; Lugo-Fernandez and Gravois, 2010; Witt et al., 2011). This degradation, if frequently repeated and/or augmented by other unfavourable natural or human-induced changes in environmental conditions (for example, Roder et al., 2009; Sheppard and Rioja-Nieto, 2005), can result in a significant decrease in the coastal protection potential of these ecosystems (for example, Sheppard et al., 2005). In turn, coastal ecosystem degradation could increase beach erosion and induce significant losses to coastal communities in terms of coastal protection and livelihoods (for example, Wielgus et al., 2010).

There have been relatively few studies related to the dynamic relationship between changing ecosystem conditions and risk[1] and vulnerability.[2] As a consequence, risk assessments often underestimate the potential role of ecosystems in reducing disaster risks and/or in climate change adaptation.

Disaster risk management encompasses a wide portfolio of activities and measures that aim to reduce the exposure and vulnerabilities of people and assets to natural hazardous events. These include, amongst others, early warning systems, emergency preparedness, public training and awareness, and land-use planning. Nevertheless, efforts to reduce natural hazard impacts should also be based on the best possible risk information in order to assess potential hazards efficiently, identify vulnerabilities that may amplify impacts and losses, and make informed decisions on how best to reduce and manage disaster risks. This chapter reflects on the efforts by the United Nations Environment Programme (UNEP), in collaboration with the Government of Jamaica, to integrate ecosystem considerations into disaster risk and vulnerability assessments. It focuses on a pilot study by UNEP's Risk and Vulnerability Assessment Methodology Development Project (RiVAMP), which takes into consideration the role of coastal ecosystems in assessing coastal risks and quantifying their coastal protection services.

The Risk and Vulnerability Assessment Methodology Development Project

Risk assessments of natural hazards require varied information, including on the hazards, exposure to hazards and underlying vulnerabilities. Current thinking and practice have moved away from a predominantly hazard-oriented analysis towards more integrated approaches (for example, Turner et al., 2003) that take into account the complex interactions between events and vulnerabilities and consider the physical/environmental, social, economic, institutional and/or political features of a given community that may influence susceptibility to hazards (Peduzzi et al., 2009). Hence, there has been a greater focus on understanding vulnerability in the context of disaster risk reduction,[3] and a paradigm shift appears to have been taking place over the last few years towards the development of more holistic concepts of vulnerability (Birkmann, 2006; Thywissen, 2006).

Vulnerability assessments have traditionally focused on social and economic indicators or cultural factors (for example, local/traditional attitudes) that might influence risk, with much less emphasis on the environmental dimensions of vulnerability and/or the effectiveness of ecosystem services in disaster risk reduction. Conceptual frameworks and practical guidelines regarding the integration of ecosystem dynamics in vulnerability assessments have only recently emerged, and still require further field testing.

RiVAMP was conceived by UNEP as a methodology that considers the role of ecosystems in the analysis of disaster risk and vulnerability, utilizing varied scientific and social research methods. RiVAMP aims to demonstrate the role of ecosystems in disaster risk reduction, including adaptation to risks related to climate change, and, thus, to enable policymakers to make investment and land-use decisions that support improved ecosystem management and, ultimately, sustainable development. The targeted end-users of RiVAMP are national and local government decision-makers, especially land-use and spatial development planners, as well as key actors in natural resource management and disaster management.

In the present contribution, RiVAMP methodology refers to a pilot study that was intended for application in the coastal areas of Small Island Developing States (SIDS), with the main hazard focus on tropical cyclone effects (for example, coastal storm surges and flooding) as well as the effects of global climate change (for example, mean sea level rise) in the context of coastal degradation. The methodology builds on previous experiences, namely modelling the potential protective role of coastal ecosystems elsewhere (Chatenoux and Peduzzi, 2007), methodologies developed for risk assessments in high-altitude areas (Peduzzi et al., 2010) and studying the role of deforestation in landslide vulnerability (Peduzzi, 2010). RiVAMP's long-term objective is to develop methodologies that could be applied in river basins and low-lying coastal plains (which would include beaches) in order to develop an integrated assessment method that considers the entire catchment area.

Negril, Jamaica, as the study area

Jamaica is highly exposed to tropical cyclones, and the government has prioritized hazard mitigation and climate change adaptation in its *Vision 2030 Jamaica: National Development Plan* (Government of Jamaica, 2009). At the same time, the country is renowned for its diverse coastal ecosystems, which support a coastal tourism industry that accounts for a large portion of total employment (32 per cent) and of the country's gross domestic product (36 per cent) (for example, Edwards, 2009). Nonetheless, Jamaica's coastal ecosystems are under pressure from both internal and external drivers, including tourist and urban development, agricultural practices and climate change impacts. The Planning Institute of Jamaica (PIOJ), a national government agency, and the Institute of Sustainable Development at the University of the West Indies (UWI) have been direct implementing partners of the study.

The coastal area of Negril, located on the western coast of Jamaica (Figure 5.1), was chosen by the Government of Jamaica as the study area for the RiVAMP pilot assessment. In this area there are two beaches, Long Bay to the south (length of about 7 km) and Bloody Bay (length of about 2 km) to the north; these are fronted by a narrow (up to 4 km width) and shallow shelf, exhibiting both fringing and shallow (patch) coral reefs and seagrass meadows. The two beaches comprise a sand barrier system that fronts the Great Morass, a low-lying back-barrier environment (elevation <3 metres) that extends approximately 4 km inland and is underlain, for the most part, by peat of varying thickness (Bjork, 1984). The two beaches are bounded by limestone promontories and characterized by the presence of low beach ridges – rarely exceeding 2 metres (m) in height – and a lack of a developed backshore dune system (UWI, 2002).

A two-lane highway has been constructed along the sand barrier, with Negril Town and numerous tourism establishments built along its sides. To the south lies West End (or "The Cliffs"), built on the steep limestone escarpment bordering the southern margin of Long Bay, where the splash from partially reflected storm waves can reach up to 8 m, often damaging cliff property (UNEP, 2010).

The coastal sediments consist almost entirely of moderately to poorly sorted sand (UWI, 2002). The onshore sediments are generally coarser than those found in the shallow near-shore waters and mostly show median grain diameters (D50) of between 0.2 and 0.3 mm (SWI, 2007). Sediments are composed of either bioclastic material or amorphous/recrystallized grains formed through its geochemical alteration (UWI, 2002). Coral fragments form only a minor fraction of the beach sediments and the main sediment source appears to be biogenic material generated

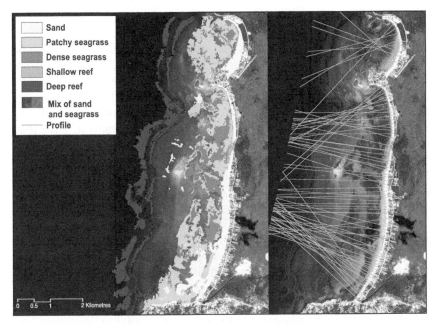

Figure 5.1 Distribution of the coastal ecosystems of Negril, Jamaica, and locations of the 74 beach profiles used in the study
Sources: Key ecosystem features derived from analysis of a QuickBird high-resolution satellite image (0.6 m, multispectral) obtained on 16 January 2008; beach profiles collated from SWI (2007).
Note: The fringing reef is found at about 20–25 metres depth (UNEP, 2010).

Please see page 479 for a colour version of this figure.

in the near-shore seagrass meadows that also include some *Halimeda* patches. However, sediment production rates are considered to be low, not exceeding 5,000 cubic metres per year (m³/yr) (SWI, 2007), and the changes in the composition of the beach biogenic material observed in recent decades might indicate a decrease in the spatial coverage of the seagrass meadows and/or pollution stress (UWI, 2002). It appears that the supply side of beach sediments is both limited and diminishing, suggesting increased beach vulnerability to erosion (see, for example, Veleg-rakis et al., 2008).

The area is characterized by a generally moderate hydrodynamic regime. Tidal ranges are small, not exceeding 0.6 m and 0.2 m on springs and neaps, respectively; tidal currents show a predominant north-east–south-west orientation, with magnitudes of up to 0.2 metres per second (m/s) (SWI, 2007). The Negril coast is also affected by meteorological and wave-induced currents that can dominate or even reverse the weak tidal flow. The wind and swell waves impinging onto the Negril beaches come mainly from the north-west and west, and the beaches may also be affected by energetic waves and storm surges induced by tropical storms. Wave modelling (SWI, 2007) has predicted (exceedance probability of 99 per cent) that the 10-year event will be associated with an offshore significant wave height of 6.4 m and an increase in the offshore sea level of up to 0.65 m above the mean sea level (MSL), if combined with high tides and the projected long-term sea level rise. Offshore significant wave heights of 9.2 m and (combined) sea levels 0.93 m above the present MSL are likely (exceedance probability of 63 per cent) for the 50-year event. In comparison, the coastal sea level increase for the 10-year (return period) event will be up to 0.6 m, and the 50-year wave event could increase coastal sea levels in excess of 1.5 m above the MSL in some sections of the Negril coast (SWI, 2007; UNEP, 2010).

With a permanent population of approximately 3,000, Negril is the third-largest tourist resort destination in Jamaica, after Ocho Rios and Montego Bay. Over the last 40 years, despite its status as an Environmental Protection Area and Marine Park, Negril has experienced a rapid growth in tourism, which has led to accelerated coastal development and population increase. At the same time, Negril has been experiencing rapid and significant beach retreat (that is, reduction in beach width), estimated to be on average 0.5 m/yr and 1.0 m/yr in Bloody Bay and Long Bay, respectively, for the period 1968–2006 (SWI, 2007).

Local and expert consultations revealed that beach erosion is attributed to various factors. In addition to the MSL rise and worsening storms, these include anthropogenic influences: increasing development coupled with unsustainable fishing practices and seagrass removal (for the comfort of the tourists); the degradation of coral reefs owing to, for example, the establishment in the area of invasive species (such as the red lionfish *Pterois volitans*), which has negatively affected populations of the indigenous herbivorous fauna that controlled algae coverage of the coral reefs; and the partial conversion of the Great Morass into crop land, which has increased particulate and nutrient concentrations in coastal waters and, thus, might have placed an additional stress on coastal ecosystems (coral reefs and seagrasses) (see, for example, SWI, 2007; UNEP, 2010; UWI, 2002).

In this context, it appears that the Negril tourist industry, which largely depends on the condition of Negril beaches and contributes substantially to the country's gross domestic product, is under considerable pressure. Therefore, the Government of Jamaica specifically requested UNEP to examine the problem of beach erosion and the potential mitigating role of the coastal ecosystems.

Box 5.1 Main activities of RiVAMP

---

1. *Scientific assessment* to identify the beach erosion drivers, estimate associated hazards (e.g. storm surge-induced flooding) and assess the effectiveness of shallow coastal ecosystems (coral reefs and sea-grasses):

- Remote sensing techniques using satellite imagery and aerial photographs to construct a coastal bathymetric map as well as to differentiate the key environmental features and ecosystems (coral reefs and seagrasses) near-shore.
- Modelling exposure to 10- and 50-year return period storms, using GIS analysis, based on a digital elevation model with 6 m resolution and inundation levels estimated through modelling.
- Application of 2-D and 1-D numerical wave modelling to assess beach morphodynamics and the significance of coral reefs and seagrasses.
- Application of statistical and multiple regression analysis to determine the mitigating role of coral reefs and seagrasses against beach erosion.

2. *Stakeholder consultations* to identify the main drivers of ecosystem degradation, assess awareness of environment and disaster linkages, and assess the environmental dimensions of vulnerability and exposure to hazards:

- National consultations in Kingston, involving a cross-section of government agencies and academe in Kingston.
- Parish-level consultations (Westmoreland and Hanover parishes) in Negril, involving government agencies, the private sector (hotel and restaurant sector, engineering consulting firms) and non-governmental organizations.
- Community consultations in Whitehall and Little Bay.

The RiVAMP methodology

A unique aspect of the RiVAMP methodology is the combination of coastal science and stakeholder consultation approaches, which allows the technical analysis to be balanced and qualified by local knowledge/experience. Box 5.1 summarizes the main activities in pilot testing the RiVAMP methodology.

Scientific assessment: Data gathering

The scientific assessment, designed and carried out by UNEP/GRID-Geneva, focused on identification of beach erosion drivers, estimation of

Table 5.1 Main geo-environmental information used/converted in GIS

Environmental characteristics	Information
Occurrence/extent of coral reefs, seagrass meadows and sediment type (2008 shoreline)	Derived from QuickBird satellite image (16 January 2008) with 0.6 m resolution – 4 bands (blue, green, red and near infra-red)
Digital elevation model	6 m resolution (collated)
Near-shore bathymetry	2 m resolution, generated from bathymetric data (2006) provided by Smith Warner International
1968, 1980, 1991, 2003 and 2006 shorelines	Collated from aerial photographs and previous field observations – corrected for tidal effects
Beach morphology (2006)	74 beach profiles (2006) – collated from SWI (2007)

associated hazards (for example, storm surge-induced inundation) and assessment of the effectiveness of shallow coastal ecosystems (coral reefs and seagrasses) in providing beach protection. The assessment entailed the application of remote sensing techniques on satellite imagery and aerial photographs, Geographic Information System (GIS) mapping and analysis, and modelling of the buffering effects of coastal ecosystems on the coastline.

Shoreline (beach) retreat was estimated by revisiting already available information and analysing newly acquired satellite information (see Table 5.1). The collated information consisted of the historical shorelines in 1968, 1980, 1991, 2003 and 2006 obtained from remotely sensed information (for example, aerial photographs and satellite images) and field surveys and a comprehensive set of 74 beach profiles along Bloody Bay and Long Bay acquired in November 2006 by Smith Warner International (SWI, 2007). The coastal bathymetric map was constructed using bathymetric information obtained by Smith Warner International in 2006 (see Table 5.1); this information was also used to extend the 74 beach profiles offshore to a distance of about 3 km from the shoreline. The occurrence and extent of key environmental features and ecosystems (such as coral reefs and seagrass meadows) offshore of the Negril shoreline (Figure 5.1) were obtained from a QuickBird high-resolution satellite image (0.6 m, multispectral, obtained on 16 January 2008), and the segmentation functions extracted using Definiens software. All this information was then analysed spatially and integrated using GIS tools.

Scientific assessment: Analysis

In order to evaluate the significance of coastal ecosystems to the beach morphodynamics of Negril, two different approaches were used. First, ecosystem control on the coastal dynamics was studied using both 2-D and 1-D numerical wave modelling. Secondly, multiple regression analysis was performed on matrices containing the various environmental characteristics of the Negril coastal environment (beach slopes, extent of fronting coral reefs and seagrasses, waves, etc.) and the observed beach retreat at different (74) beach locations, in order to identify/model crucial parameters controlling beach erosion.

Numerical modelling

In order to study the near-shore hydrodynamics under different wave conditions, a 2-D wave propagation model (for example, Vousdoukas et al., 2009) was used to estimate near-shore wave-induced currents.[4] It must be noted that the main purpose of the 2-D modelling was to obtain a broad picture of the near-shore wave dynamics and not to model in detail the influence of the coral reefs and seagrass meadows on coastal dynamics; therefore, dissipation effects owing to reef roughness/vegetation and the seagrass meadows (see, for example, Chen et al., 2007, 2011; Massel and Gourlay, 2000; Nelson, 1996; Sheppard et al., 2005; Vousdoukas et al., 2011; Vousdoukas et al., in press) were not included. However, in order to gain some further insight into the influence of the near-shore coastal ecosystems on near-shore dynamics, the cross-shore distribution of the wave energy or bed shear stress (that is, bed wave force per unit area), which are the principal drivers of beach sediment erosion/transport (Paphitis et al., 2001), were simulated using the 1-D (one-line) cross-shore model Sbeach (Larson and Kraus, 1989). In this modelling, seabed-type controls were included in the simulation of the bed shear stress, according to Sheppard et al. (2005) for coral reefs and Chen et al. (2007) for seagrasses.

The offshore bathymetry survey used for model initialization was complemented with the 74 beach profiles obtained at the same time (see Table 5.1). With regard to model forcing, several experiments were conducted using different offshore wave regimes, such as wind waves, swell waves and extreme storm conditions.

Finally, in order to assess the range of shoreline retreat (that is, reduction of beach width) of the Negril beaches under various rates of MSL rise and storm surges, an ensemble of five beach morphodynamic models – those of Bruun (1988), Edelman (1972), Larson and Kraus (1989), Dean (1991) and Leont'yev (1996) – were used (for example, Velegrakis et al., 2009). Previous experiments (Monioudi, 2011) have shown that, although the Bruun (1988) and Dean (1991) models are mainly used to predict beach response to long-term sea level rise and the other models (that is, Edelman, 1972; Larson and Kraus, 1989; and Leont'yev, 1996) are used in relation to short-term sea level rise (owing to storm surges, for example), there were relatively small differences between the predictions of these two groups, if used as ensembles; thus, and for the purpose of the RiVAMP study, the two model groups were combined.

Experiments were carried out for different morphological (beach slope), hydrodynamic (wave) and sedimentary (grain size) characteristics. Regarding beach morphology, linear beach profiles were used (beach slopes of 1/10, 1/15, 1/20, 1/25 and 1/30), because experiments showed relatively small differences (maximum deviation <25 per cent) between model predictions using natural (non-linear) profiles and predictions using equivalent linear profiles, particularly at low sea level rise rates (Figure 5.2). The models were run using varying wave conditions[5] and 14 sea level rise rates (0.04 to 3.00 m). This approach allows for a broad application, because it can provide predictions for a wide range of environmental conditions. If the envelope of the rates of retreat predicted (under all tested conditions) by the models of the ensemble is used, then the

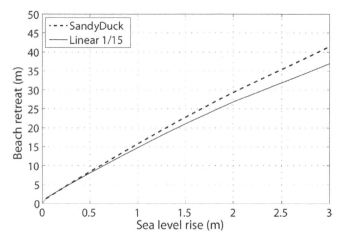

Figure 5.2 Comparison between model predictions using natural profiles and predictions using equivalent linear profiles, under the same wave and sedimentary conditions

Sources: Model predictions from the Leont'yev (1996) model (see also Monioudi et al., 2012).

Notes: The "mean" beach profile (first spatial EOF mode) of the 1997 Sandy-Duck experiment (US Army Corps of Engineers, <http://www.frf.usace.army.mil/dksrv/sd97dir.html>, accessed 23 October 2012) is used as the natural profile. Of all the models of the ensemble, the Leont'yev model showed the highest deviation (up to 25 per cent for very high rates of level rise) between model predictions for natural profiles and equivalent linear profiles, i.e. profiles having beach slopes equal to the mean slopes (at the swash zone) of the natural profiles.

potential exposure of a large range of beaches where little field informa-tion may be available can be assessed (see, for example, Velegrakis et al., 2009). Consequently, although this approach cannot replace morpho-dynamic modelling on the basis of detailed field information, it can, nevertheless, be used for a rapid assessment of future beach retreat at island and/or basin scale (see, for example, Monioudi et al., 2012).

Beach spatial characteristics and storm surge inundation

Although comparison of the historical shorelines can help in assessing historical changes and beach erosion rates of the Negril beaches, it should also be noted that such analyses have limitations, owing to: (a) the ab-sence of validation by simultaneous ground-truthing; (b) tidal effects; and (c) a lack of information across different seasons and without control for the effects of the seasonal and/or random erosion and accretion patterns (see also UNEP, 2010). In order to acquire a more realistic (and conserv-ative) estimation of beach erosion rates, historical shorelines were trans-formed using the following procedure. The horizontal displacement of the shoreline as the result of tidal effects was estimated for the 2006 and 2008 data sets (for which acquiring times are available), on the basis of the local tidal curves and the 2006 beach profiles, and for the remainder of the data sets the shorelines (at the 74 profiles) were displaced land-ward using the maximum horizontal landward displacement that could be driven by a 0.3 m tidal rise above the MSL.

In order to quantify the role of the different environmental and bathy-metric features in influencing beach erosion rates, multiple regression analysis was used to identify parameters that could best explain the ob-served beach erosion rates and, thus, assess the potential role of the coastal ecosystems (coral reefs and seagrasses) in beach erosion mitiga-tion. Hence, rates of beach erosion at the 74 Negril beach profiles (SWI, 2007) were estimated by comparing previous (corrected) shoreline posi-tions (see above) and the 2008 shoreline position (obtained from the QuickBird satellite image). Then the cross-shore widths of the shallow (patch) coral reefs and seagrass meadows (at the 74 extended beach pro-files) were considered in relation to beach erosion rates and other para-meters, such as beach slopes and the wave regime.

The assessment also entailed the estimation of exposure to storm surge inundation owing to tropical cyclones. This was carried out on the basis of a digital elevation model with 6 m resolution that was provided by PIOJ and inundation levels estimated through modelling. Using GIS, the exposure of the population and of assets (infrastructure) was assessed for different storm return periods (that is, 10-year and 50-year return peri-ods). It must be noted that population exposure refers mainly to the resi-dent population, because tourist populations could not be accounted for owing to a lack of information regarding hotel room capacities; therefore, human exposure is likely to be significantly underestimated. In addition, because future trends of population growth and infrastructure construction were not available, future (10- and 50-year) exposure is related to the present population; this may also significantly underestimate potential exposure to tropical cyclones and associated effects (storm surges and flooding).

Stakeholder consultations

Stakeholder consultation workshops took place at the national and parish (subnational) levels and involved national and local government authorities, the private sector (for example, hoteliers, private consulting firms, restaurant owners), academics and civil society organizations. The workshops mainly aimed to (a) raise awareness about the interplay between environmental conditions and natural hazards, (b) identify drivers of ecosystem degradation and (c) assess perceptions regarding vulnerability and exposure to hazard impacts. Consultations also took place in two Negril communities, namely Whitehall (an inland semi-urban community) and Little Bay (a coastal fishing village).

Focus group discussions took place during the workshops, and their results were reported in plenary sessions. During the community consultations, additional group exercises involving standard participatory appraisal techniques were used. These techniques included community mapping exercises, community transect walks, livelihood calendars and simple ranking exercises.

In the workshops, relevant ecosystems were identified and prioritized using a simple ranking method, which provided the participants with the opportunity to identify and prioritize the three ecosystems they considered to be the most critical. Participants were then divided into three groups to discuss each of the prioritized ecosystems. Key ecosystem-derived benefits (that is, goods and services), as well as the main threats and causes of ecosystem degradation, were discussed, with the participants sharing their perceptions on the links between ecosystem degradation, hazard impacts and disaster vulnerability. The final session in all workshops involved identification of proposed solutions to manage ecosystem degradation and disaster vulnerability.

The governance issue is considered an important RiVAMP component, given that the project aims to provide information that may be used in development planning decisions, which are likely to have policy implications. In national and parish-level workshops, a preliminary assessment of environmental governance and its tangible and potential links to disaster risk reduction and management was carried out. This analysis focused

Table 5.2 Community-level indicators used in the workshop discussions

Indicator	Description
Indicator 1	Ecosystems, their current status, types of services provided and changes over time
Indicator 2	Identification of services provided by each major type of ecosystem, particularly protection/mitigation services with regard to erosion/inundation
Indicator 3	Major causes of ecosystem degradation over time
Indicator 4	Assessment of exposure to hazards (storm surges, floods, landslides) over time. Evaluation and comparison of the role of natural triggers (e.g. tropical cyclones) versus human triggers (e.g. changes in land use) (links to Indicator 3)
Indicator 5	Types of nature-based livelihoods and natural resource management practices at the household/community level
Indicator 6	Local coping strategies that enable households/communities to absorb losses and recover from hazard impacts and/or reduce future risks
Indicator 7	Presence of formal, community-based mechanisms and structures (e.g. teams or committees) for dealing with potentially damaging phenomena, risk reduction and natural resource management

mainly on assessing whether or not integrated planning involving environment, disaster risk reduction and climate change adaptation issues is taking place. Moreover, the institutional structures and mechanisms in place to support cross-sectoral integration and the constraints on challenges to integrated planning were discussed through group exercises, including the use of scenarios, institutional self-assessments and institutional mapping. In community workshops, further analysis was undertaken with regard to local livelihoods and their linkages with ecosystems and vulnerability to hazards. Table 5.2 presents the indicators assessed during community consultations.

To complement discussions on governance in the national- and parish-level workshops, efforts were made to understand the community-level decision-making process (both formal and informal) and mechanisms to address the risk from disasters and other potentially damaging phenomena. It was also important to understand individual and community coping strategies that enable people to live with and recover from hazard impacts, and whether or not these strategies were associated with local ecosystems.

Finally, community consultations yielded critical information on the extent of flooding from storm surges, which was not available in public records. Revealed locations and heights of past flooding events were recorded through GPS measurements obtained by the UNEP team and community representatives during transect walks in Little Bay and in the wider Negril area. These measurements, combined with the available digital elevation model (see Table 5.1), provided further information for the assessment and helped to validate results in relation to the potential exposure to flooding.

Results

Key findings of the scientific assessment

The hydrodynamic modelling showed that the shallow coastal (patch) coral reefs (Figure 5.1) dissipate near-shore wave energy and, thus, have beach erosion mitigation effects. Several experiments were conducted, using different offshore wave regimes (including the 10-year and 50-year extremes). In all cases, the results showed significant effects of the reefs on wave propagation patterns (see also SWI, 2007) and wave-induced current fields. The reefs appear to create "shadows" in their lee that are associated with wave height and energy decreases as well as eddy flows (Figure 5.3), which may induce offshore beach sediment transport. It must also be noted that the Negril fringing reef also dissipates wave energy, with benefits for most of the Negril coast, particularly under high-energy wave conditions (see Figures 5.1 and 5.3).

The 1-D modelling experiments also demonstrated the sheltering effects of the shallow reefs. In all examined cases (with different offshore wave conditions and sea levels), the cross-shore distributions of both wave heights and wave-induced bed shear stresses (that is, of the force per bed unit area) were affected by the presence of the reefs. Wave heights have been shown to decrease substantially (Figure 5.4), owing mostly to the steep reef geometry. Shear stresses were also shown to be considerably affected by the presence of the reef (Figure 5.4). Numerical experiments showed that the changes were mostly due to geometry and not the differential bed roughness, which had a small impact on the shear stress distribution. However, it must be noted that, because the reef morphology depends upon its condition, degradation of the reef is likely to result also in geometry changes (and, probably, bed lowering), which could then decrease the reef's beach protection potential (Sheppard et al., 2005).

Similarly, experiments involving the presence of seagrass along the extended beach profiles have shown that seagrass can dissipate wave energy, providing protection to the beach in its lee (see also Peduzzi et al., in prep.). The modelling also showed that bed shear stresses are affected significantly by the presence of seagrasses, with the effects being more pronounced in the case of denser meadows (Figure 5.5). As previous re-

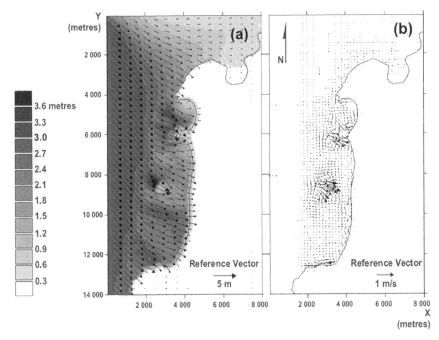

Figure 5.3 Numerical model results for (a) wave heights and (b) wave-induced currents at Negril
Notes: Note the diminishing wave heights behind both the fringing and the shallow reefs and the changed flow patterns in the lee of the shallow reefs. Wave conditions: offshore wave height = 2.8 m, wave period T = 8.7 s; wave approach from the north-west.

search has suggested, wave dissipation may be controlled not only by the extent, shoot density and canopy height of the meadows but also by the magnitude of the forcing and biomechanical characteristics of the seagrasses (see also, for example, Bradley and Houser, 2009; Paul and Amos, 2011). As Negril's seagrass meadows were found to be quite variable in their spatial and mechanical characteristics, more work is required in order to quantify (that is, parameterize) seagrass effects on the Negril beaches. Nevertheless, the present modelling provides evidence for a substantial potential for beach protection from seagrasses.

With regard to the assessment of the range of retreat forced by various rates of sea level rise, the applied models displayed differential behaviour for almost all the tested conditions. Model results showed significant ranges (Figure 5.6), since varying initial conditions and forcings (that is, morphology, sedimentology, hydrodynamics and sea level rise) were used. Most of the models (with the exception of the Bruun model) appear to

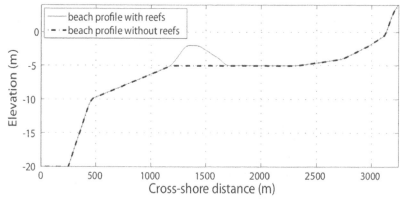

(a) Seabed profile from the Negril (40th profile from the south, see Figure 5.1), showing the presence of a narrow, steep reef. The bed profile "without reefs" was constructed by interpolation between the elevations at the edges of the reef, considering also neighbouring profiles. A wave friction factor of 0.12 (e.g. Sheppard et al., 2005) was applied in the modelling for the crest of the steep reef.

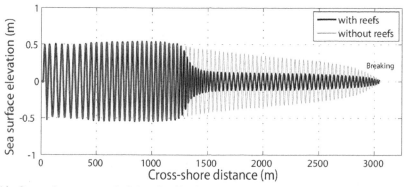

(b) Cross-shore wave height distribution under waves with an offshore wave height of 1 m and a wave period (T) of 6 s. Note the very significant decrease in the wave height in the lee of the reef.

Figure 5.4 Numerical model predictions for cross-shore wave height and bed shear stress distributions in the presence of shallow coral reefs
Note: The numerical model used is the Sbeach model (Larson and Kraus, 1989).

be sensitive to wave conditions, with a positive relationship between wave height and beach retreat. The effects of the sediment texture, however, were not always clear, although a weak trend could be discerned showing a decrease in beach retreat with sediment size (median diameter) increase. The means of the lower and upper limits of all model predictions were estimated, with the low prediction mean of the ensemble

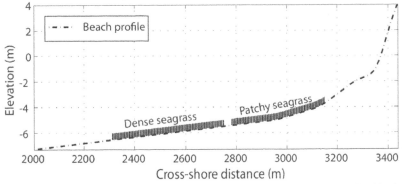

(a) Nearshore sea bed profile (Profile 21 – UNEP, 2010) showing the distribution of the seagrass meadows.

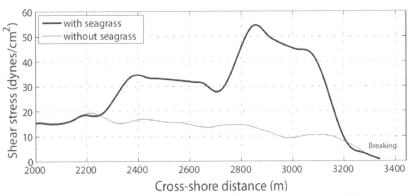

(b) Nearshore bed shear stress distribution (2000–3400 m) for offshore waves with height 1 m and period 6 s. Different wave friction (fw) factors were used for the sand bed and the dense (fw ≈ 0.102) and patchy (fw ≈ 0.052) seagrasses, according to Chen et al. (2007). Note the very significant increase in the bed shear stress over the seagrasses, which suggests significant wave energy dissipation. Sea-bed characteristics: median sediment size (D50), 0.28 mm; for dense seagrasses, number of shoots = 400/m², canopy height = 0.20 m and grass diameter = 0.01 m, and for patchy seagrasses the figures are 200/m², 0.20 m and 0.01 m, respectively.

Figure 5.5 Numerical model predictions for cross-shore bed shear stress distribution in the presence of patchy and dense seagrasses
Note: The numerical model used is the Sbeach model (Larson and Kraus, 1989)

(that is, the best fit of the lowest predictions from all models) given by $S = 0.33\alpha^2 + 7.4\alpha - 0.14$ ($R^2 = .98$) and the high prediction mean by $S = 0.74\alpha^2 + 28.9\alpha + 4.9$ ($R^2 = .97$), where S is the beach retreat and α the sea level rise (Figure 5.6).

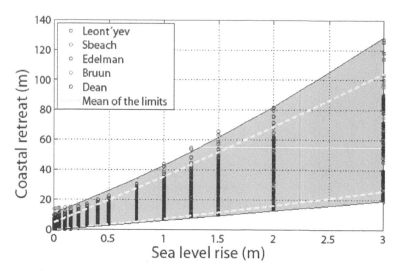

Figure 5.6 The means of the lower and upper limits of the beach retreats estimated by the ensemble models

Please see page 480 for a colour version of this figure.

Beach retreat predictions on the basis of the models of the ensemble
(Figure 5.6) showed a very significant beach erosion and inundation risk
in Negril. If the beach retreat predictions are compared with current onshore beach widths (from the 74 beach profiles), even under the most favourable projections of long-term sea level rise for 2060 (combined high
tidal level and long-term sea level rise increase of 0.52 m), an extreme
storm surge event (due to the 50-year return storm) may result in minimum beach retreats that exceed the current onshore beach width along
35 per cent of the Negril beaches (on the basis of the 74 beach profiles),
and an additional 50 per cent of the beach may be associated with a loss
of approximately 50 per cent of its present width (UNEP, 2010). These
predictions suggest that long-term sea level rise, if combined with extreme storm surges (and diminished biogenic sand supply and beach protection owing to coastal ecosystem degradation), will exert a very high
toll on Negril's beaches and associated economic activities (see also Wielgus et al., 2010).

   The results of the analysis of the historical shorelines (anchored on the
74 beach profiles – see Figure 5.1 and Table 5.1) confirmed that the Negril
beaches have been under severe erosion in the last 40 years, with some
sites experiencing shoreline retreats of more than 55 m (Figure 5.7).
These erosion rates are comparable with the beach erosion rates (average 0.5 m/yr) observed in other Caribbean islands (Anguilla, Barbuda,

Antigua, St Kitts, Nevis, Montserrat, Dominica and Grenada) during the last part of the twentieth century (Cambers, 2009).

Erosion has been both temporally and spatially variable, with Bloody Bay associated with lower erosion rates than Long Bay. Erosion rates showed a large spatial variability along the Long Bay shoreline (Figure 5.7). The beach sections at either side of the shallow coral reef "shadow" (see Figure 5.3) showed higher rates of erosion (see also SWI, 2007),

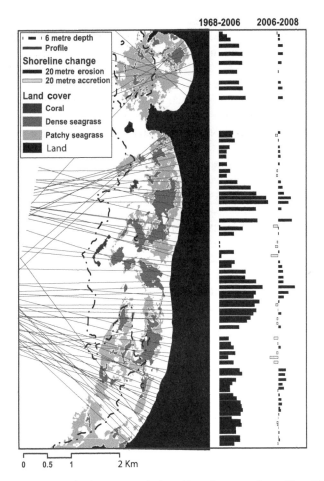

Figure 5.7 Near-shore bed cover and shoreline changes along Negril's beaches, also showing the location of the 74 beach profiles used

Note: Note the decreased rates of erosion at the beach sections fronted by either the shallow coral reef and/or extensive seagrass meadows.

Please see page 481 for a colour version of this figure.

whereas beach sections fronted by coral reefs and/or wide areas with sea-grass meadows showed generally lower areas of erosion. Erosion rates appear to have increased during recent years, with the 2006–2008 rates being significantly greater than the long-term average (Figure 5.7). Several factors may be responsible for the observed trends, for example the long-term sea level rise, the intensification of extreme events, diminishing sand production/supply from the seagrass meadows (UWI, 2002), increasing coastal development (UNEP, 2010) and, possibly, coastal ecosystem degradation.

Scatter plots of the beach erosion rate against the cross-shore widths of the fronting coral reefs and/or seagrass meadows (at the 74 beach profiles) provide further evidence of the mitigating role of these ecosystems in beach erosion (Figure 5.8). Multiple regression analysis further confirmed that both coral reefs and seagrass meadows are the main features that have a mitigating role in beach erosion (Peduzzi et al., in prep.).

The results of the analysis showed that the presence of coral reefs and seagrasses can significantly mitigate beach erosion, which is also controlled by beach slope and wave steepness. Areas with steep profiles and/or less steep waves result in milder beach erosion.

In conclusion, the observed beach erosion was found to be negatively correlated with the cross-shore widths of coral reefs and seagrass meadows. This also suggests that coral reefs and dense seagrasses provide shelter to the beach sections they front, confirming the findings from the numerical modelling (see also Sheppard et al., 2005). Therefore, degradation of the shallow coral reef and seagrass meadows is likely to result in an increased risk of beach retreat/erosion, particularly if the important role of seagrasses in biogenic sediment production (SWI, 2007; UNEP, 2010; UWI, 2002) is taken into consideration.

With regard to inundation of the low-lying back-barrier areas driven by storm surges, predictions for the 10-year and 50-year events under spring tides that also take into consideration the long-term sea level rise, as well as wave run-up effects (UNEP, 2010), suggest increased inundation risks. In such cases, the low ridges of the Negril beaches are likely to be breached and sea waters are predicted to flood considerable parts of the low-lying Great Morass, as well as the other neighbouring low-lying coastal areas (Figure 5.9). It must be noted that predictions do not take into account precipitation-induced flooding, which is also likely to accompany flooding driven by storm surges.

On the basis of the inundation map and maps of population and asset distribution (in GIS), approximately 2,500 people (representing more than 80 per cent of the present resident population) were found to be exposed to flooding during the 50-year return storm event. In comparison, the 10-year storm event would affect 16 per cent of the present

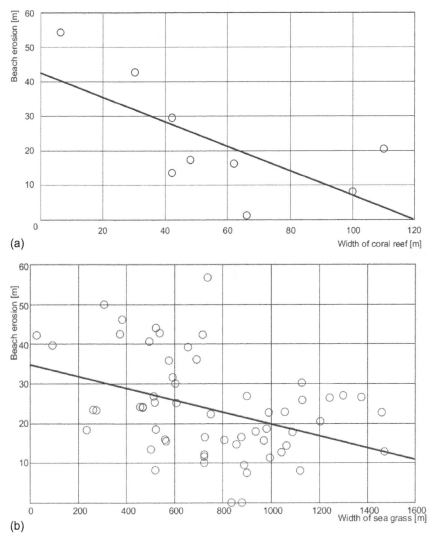

Figure 5.8 Scatter plots of beach retreat rates against the cross-shore widths of (a) the shallow coral reefs and (b) the seagrass meadows, showing an inverse relationship

resident population (500 people), because flooding will be confined close to the shoreline, affecting infrastructure and assets located mainly in Long Bay and in some low-lying areas to the south-east of Negril (for example, Homers Cove in the Little Bay area) (UNEP, 2010).

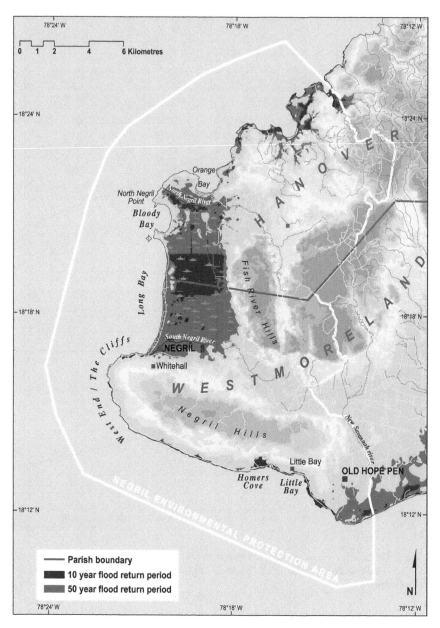

Figure 5.9. Flooding in the wider Negril area on the basis of a simplified inundation model and digital elevation models

Note: The inundation risk at the West End cliffs is based on information provided by people from local communities, who suggested that previous storm events have affected assets and infrastructure located 7.5 m above the MSL, mainly as a result of waves crashing against the cliffs (UNEP, 2010).

130

Key findings of stakeholder consultations

Stakeholder consultations provided an important supplement as well as some validation of the scientific assessment. Local ecosystems – namely coral reefs, seagrasses, mangroves and peatlands, as well as forests – were considered to be vital components, fuelling Jamaica's social and economic development. These were considered to support major activities such as fishing, farming and tourism (directly or indirectly) and to provide for basic needs (food, water, fuel, building materials, etc.). Ecosystems were also found to be valued in terms of their contribution to biodiversity, to climate change mitigation (particularly with respect to the Great Morass) and to Jamaica's social and cultural heritage. In the final sessions of all workshops, solutions were proposed for managing ecosystem degradation and disaster vulnerability; these were categorized into three main areas: (a) education and awareness, (b) environmental governance, and (c) technological investments (see UNEP, 2010).

Two major roles of ecosystems in disaster risk reduction could be discerned from the stakeholder consultations. First, coral reefs, in particular, were universally regarded as important natural buffers against coastal storm surges, providing shoreline protection. Fishers, in particular, stated that they seek refuge and dock their boats in the lee of coral reefs during tropical storms for protection. In national- and parish-level workshops (but not during community consultations), stakeholders also recognized the important function of the Great Morass in relation to flood control and its filtering properties (in terms of freshwater runoff and inland saltwater intrusion).

Secondly, community workshops revealed that ecosystems may contribute towards increasing local resilience by helping residents to cope with and recover from hazard impacts. Depending on the degree of destruction caused by tropical storms, which may cut off road access and electricity and other public services for several days or weeks, local residents (particularly in Little Bay to the south-east of Negril – see Figure 5.9) revealed that they have occasionally been forced to rely on unprotected groundwater systems for drinking and on local forests (including mangroves) for fuel and building materials for repairs. Given that groundwater quality is generally considered fit for drinking[6] and that wood sources remain easily accessible in the Negril area, this coping strategy has generally worked well in the past. Local reliance on natural resources for basic needs, particularly in the aftermath of extreme events, highlights the significance of local ecosystems (especially of those related to groundwater) in supporting local recovery.

However, with ecosystems in overall decline in Negril and throughout Jamaica, stakeholder consultations revealed that ecosystem degradation is contributing to increased local vulnerability and exposure to flooding and storm surges, validating the findings of the scientific assessment. In Whitehall, for instance, rapid urbanization, deforestation of the hillsides and increased impervious cover (for example, roads and cemented areas) have made certain parts of the community prone to flooding. Community mapping exercises revealed that flooding became a problem in the late 1980s, coinciding with the acceleration of urban and housing development. In Little Bay, beach erosion, which has also been linked to illegal sand mining, has resulted in more frequent and intense flooding over the past two decades; this information supports the findings of the flood exposure modelling undertaken in this study. It was also stated that storm-induced flooding has been exacerbated by coral reef degradation and removal of coastal vegetation (including mangroves) over the past 20–30 years.

Given that local livelihoods are dependent on natural resources and given the increasing frequency and intensity of tropical storms and hurricanes in the region (UNEP, 2010), the limited options in economic development may result in increased local vulnerability. Consultations in Little Bay and Whitehall communities revealed that traditional livelihoods, such as fishing and farming, no longer provide sufficient incomes, forcing many households to rely on alternative occupations in the tourist industry, which, however, is also vulnerable to adverse environmental conditions. For instance, declining fish stocks in Little Bay over the past decade have forced many women out of the fishing sector, contributing to their unemployment/underemployment and, consequently, to a reduction in household incomes. Those forced out of the fishing sector (both men and women) have supplemented incomes by tourism-related activities (for example as hotel clerks and cleaners, glass bottom boat operators or snorkelling guides) or, even, by illicit activities. Other available employment options, such as in retail and public transport or taxi services, are normally out of reach for the majority of the local population, because they often require either financial capital or specific skills.

An important knowledge gap was identified with regard to the significance of the seagrass meadows. Despite scientific studies that identify Negril's seagrasses as the most important source of beach material (for example, SWI, 2007; UWI, 2002) in Negril,[7] this was not commonly known amongst stakeholders at different levels. Residents in Little Bay expressed surprise on learning that seagrass meadows may also mitigate the effects of storm waves and, thus, protect their beaches. In Negril, seagrasses are generally regarded as a nuisance by hotel and beach operators, who regularly rake them up to provide white sand beds to foreign tourists. In addition, local residents discussed the widespread practice of harvesting seagrasses to prepare traditional drinks.

Policy implications

Beach erosion, ecosystem degradation and the increasing destructiveness of tropical storms and hurricanes (see, for example, Emanuel, 2005) may over time significantly undermine resource-dependent livelihoods, namely fishing and farming, as well as tourism, which are vital to the local and national economy (for example, Edwards, 2009). Given the importance of ecosystems with regard to both beach protection and livelihoods, a "business as usual" approach is no longer viewed as a viable option. Significant corrective measures are required to avert further decline of coastal ecosystems, as well as to protect lives and critical infrastructure. Based on the RiVAMP results, UNEP recommended a forward-looking "no-regret" strategy, which advocates the protection and restoration of ecosystems as a key component of Negril's disaster risk reduction, climate change adaptation and overall development strategies.

It appears that there is a clear need to integrate disaster risk and long-term climate change impacts into an integrated coastal zone development strategy, which at present is absent in Negril. This strategy calls for a multi-stakeholder approach, involving the private sector (that is, hoteliers and restaurant owners) and local communities, and a cross-sectoral mechanism or platform that engages disaster management agencies, coastal development planners and environmental protection agencies. Given the formal protection status of Negril, there is great opportunity to bring the relevant actors together at both the national and parish levels. The challenge remains in convincing policy-makers of the urgency of taking corrective action.

Lessons learned

In March 2010, the results of the RiVAMP pilot were presented formally in Kingston and Negril by UNEP. This received national coverage in print media and radio. The Kingston event was well attended, drawing a broad spectrum of government agencies, international development partners, the private sector, academics and civil society. As a follow-up activity, UNEP delivered a national training course on the RiVAMP methodology in December 2011, to transfer know-how and skills (in GIS mapping/ modelling and beach morphodynamic modelling) that would enable the Government of Jamaica to replicate this assessment in other coastal areas of the country.

One key factor that facilitated the RiVAMP pilot study was the support offered by key government agencies, such as the Planning Institute of Jamaica, the National Environment and Planning Agency, the National

Spatial Data Management Division under the Office of the Prime Minister and the Office of Disaster Preparedness and Emergency Management, amongst others. Strong local support and ownership of the project stemmed from involving national agencies in project design from the outset. UNEP adjusted initial plans when government agencies requested that the pilot study specifically address the problem of beach erosion in Negril. Therefore, flexibility proved to be critical. Another success factor was the very high level of technical capacity and data available at the national level. In addition, previous technical studies on Negril (SWI, 2007; UWI, 2002) offered important baseline data that facilitated undertaking additional modelling and statistical analyses. Such information may be less readily available in other SIDS, and low-cost and readily applicable methods will need to be developed. Nevertheless, several components of the assessment methodology that were employed (for example, near-shore ecosystem mapping from satellite imagery, predictions of coastal retreat under long- and short-term sea level rise using model ensembles) can be readily used in other SIDS, where very little field information is available.

RiVAMP also faced several challenges. Because of time constraints and limited resources, the assessment was not able to develop an economic valuation of ecosystem services for the study area, which posed a major limitation in communicating RiVAMP findings to policy-makers. Follow-up work on the methodology will need to include such valuations, particularly in relation to disaster risk reduction.

Finally, the lack of post-hazard impact assessments in the study area represented a major data gap for the risk assessment,[8] which was critical in order to "ground-truth" or test the tropical cyclone exposure model used in the study. As a result, it was not possible to verify RiVAMP's model of storm surge impact and to estimate risk more precisely on the basis of past exposure to hazard events.

Conclusions

The major findings of the study may be summarized as follows. Negril beaches show significant rates of erosion (0.5 to 1.0 m/yr during the last 40 years), which are comparable to the erosion rates recorded on other Caribbean beaches. The observed beach erosion was found to be negatively correlated with the cross-shore widths of coral reefs and seagrass meadows, suggesting that these ecosystems provide shelter to the beach sections they front, confirming the findings from 2-D and 1-D numerical modelling. Beach retreat predictions on the basis of a morphodynamic model ensemble suggest that Negril beaches are going to pay a very heavy toll under long- and short-term sea level rise because, even under the most favourable projections of long-term sea level rise for 2060, an extreme storm surge event (that is, due to the 50-year return storm) may result in (minimum) beach retreats that exceed the present beach width along 35 per cent of the Negril beaches, and an additional 50 per cent of the beach may be associated with a loss of approximately 50 per cent of its present width. Inundation maps constructed on the basis of flood heights driven by storm surges, digital elevation and population/assets distribution maps showed that 80 per cent and 16 per cent of the present resident population may be affected during a 50-year and 10-year storm surge, respectively, together with valuable assets/infrastructure.

Stakeholder consultations provided an important supplement to the assessment process and validated some of the scientific results. Stakeholders at all levels had a strong appreciation of the benefits provided by local ecosystems (for example, coral reefs, seagrasses, mangroves and peatlands), although in general most had limited knowledge of the important function of seagrasses in coastal protection. Consultations also revealed that stakeholders consider that the observed ecosystem degradation contributes towards increased local vulnerability/exposure to flooding and storm surges, which should be managed through increased education and awareness, appropriate environmental governance, and technological investment.

The RiVAMP pilot exercise demonstrated that a more integrated methodology for risk and vulnerability assessments can factor in ecosystem and climate change concerns, based on an evidence-based approach that utilizes both applied science approaches and local knowledge and experiences. The methodology and results of the pilot assessment are applicable to other coastal tourism-dependent areas, both in Jamaica and in other Caribbean islands. In addition, by involving local stakeholders in the process, RiVAMP can potentially influence development policies and help establish a more risk-conscious and environmentally sustainable development course for the coastal communities.

Notes

1. "The term risk refers to the expected losses from a given hazard to a given element at risk, over a specified future time period" (Office of United Nations Disaster Relief Coordinator, 1979, in Coburn et al., 1994: 10).
2. Vulnerability is "the degree to which a system acts adversely to the occurrence of a hazardous event of a given intensity" (Timmerman, 1981: 21).
3. A review by Birkmann (2006) found at least 25 different definitions.
4. The 2-D wave propagation model is based on the directional energy balance equation and a simple backward finite difference scheme (Booij et al., 1999) that incorporates

diffraction effects (Holthuijsen et al., 2003) and uses derived radiation stresses in conjunction with a depth- and short wave-averaged 2DH continuity and momentum equation solver.

5. Offshore wave heights of 0.5, 1.0, 1.5, 2.0, 3.0, 4.0, 5.0 and 6.0 metres and periods of 3–14 seconds were considered. For each set of wave conditions, experiments were carried out for seven different sediment grain sizes (median grain diameter D50 of 0.20, 0.33, 0.50, 0.80, 1.00, 2.00 and 5.00 mm).

6. However, although relevant local medical records were not available for this study, occasional gastrointestinal infections related to drinking from unprotected groundwater springs (especially after major storms) were reported during the consultations.

7. According to the UWI (2002) study, there has been a significant decline in the fraction of bioclastic (carbonate) beach material from the benthic foraminifera communities of the seagrasses, which used to contribute almost half of the identifiable beach material in Long Bay; this decline has been attributed to anthropogenic removal of seagrasses and/ or pollution stress.

8. Post-hazard impact assessments (for example for floods and storm surges) were not readily available in government records. It is possible that local insurance companies might have some information, but it could not be accessed by UNEP.

REFERENCES

Birkmann, J. (2006) "Measuring Vulnerability to Promote Disaster-Resilient Societies: Conceptual Frameworks and Definitions". In J. Birkmann (ed.), *Measuring Vulnerability to Natural Hazards – Towards Disaster Resilient Societies*. Tokyo: United Nations University Press, pp. 9–54.

Bjork, S. (1984) "Optimum Utilization Study of the Negril and Black River Lower Morasses". Lund/Petroleum Corporation of Jamaica. Kingston.

Booij, N., R.C. Ris and L.H. Holthuijsen (1999) "A Third-generation Model for Coastal Regions 1. Model Description and Validation". *Journal of Geophysical Research* 104(C4): 7649–7666.

Bradley, K. and C. Houser (2009) "Relative Velocity of Seagrass Blades: Implications for Wave Attenuation in Low-energy Environments". *Journal of Geophysical Research* 114: 1–13.

Bruun, P. (1988) "The Bruun Rule of Erosion by Sea Level Rise: A Discussion on Large-scale Two- and Three-dimensional Usages". *Journal of Coastal Research* 4(4): 622–648.

Cambers, G. (2009) "Caribbean Beach Changes and Climate Change Adaptation.". *Aquatic Ecosystem Health & Management* 12: 168–176.

Chatenoux, B. and P. Peduzzi (2007) "Impacts from the 2004 Indian Ocean Tsunami: Analysing the Potential Protecting Role of Environmental Features". *Natural Hazards* 40: 289–304.

Chen, S.-C., Y.-M. Kuo and Y.-H. Li (2011) "Flow Characteristics within Different Configurations of Submerged Flexible Vegetation". *Journal of Hydrology* 398(1–2): 124–134.

Chen, S.N. et al. (2007) "A Nearshore Model to Investigate the Effects of Seagrass Bed Geometry on Wave Attenuation and Suspended Sediment Transport". *Estuaries and Coasts* 30: 296–310.

Coburn, A.W., R.J.S. Spence and A. Pomonis (1994) *Vulnerability and Risk Assessment*, 2nd edn. Disaster Management Training Programme, UNDP and DHA.

Cochard R. et al. (2008) "The 2004 Tsunami in Aceh and Southern Thailand: A Review on Coastal Ecosystems, Wave Hazards and Vulnerability". *Perspectives in Plant Ecology, Evolution and Systematics* 10: 3–40.

Dean, R.G. (1991) "Equilibrium Beach Profiles: Characteristics and Applications". *Journal of Coastal Research* 7(1): 53–84.

Edelman, T. (1972) "Dune Erosion during Storm Conditions". In *Proceedings of the 13th International Conference on Coastal Engineering*. New York: ASCE, pp. 1305–1312.

Edwards, P.E.T. (2009) "Sustainable Financing for Ocean and Coastal Management in Jamaica: The Potential for Revenues from Tourist User Fees". *Marine Policy* 33: 376–385.

Emanuel, K. (2005) "Increasing Destructiveness of Tropical Cyclones over the Past 30 Years". *Nature* 436: 686–688.

Feagin R.A. et al. (2011) "Short Communication: Engineering Properties of Wetland Plants with Application to Wave Attenuation". *Coastal Engineering* 58: 251–255.

Fernando, H.J.S. et al. (2008) "Effects of Porous Barriers Such as Coral Reefs on Coastal Wave Propagation". *Journal of Hydro-environment Research* 1: 187–194.

Government of Jamaica (2009) *Vision 2030 Jamaica: National Development Plan*. Kingston, Jamaica: Planning Institute of Jamaica.

Hasler N., D. Werth and R. Avissar (2009) "Effects of Tropical Deforestation on Global Hydroclimate: A Multimodel Ensemble Analysis". *Journal of Climate* 22: 1124–1141.

Holthuijsen, L.H., A. Hemran and N. Booij (2003) "Phase-decoupled Refraction–Diffraction for Spectral Wave Models". *Coastal Engineering* 49: 291–305.

IFRC [International Federation of Red Cross and Red Crescent Societies] (2002) "Mangrove Planting Saves Lives and Money in Vietnam". *World Disaster Report 2002*, International Federation of Red Cross and Red Crescent Societies.

Knudby, A., C. Newman, Y. Shaghude and C. Muhando (2010) "Simple and Effective Monitoring of Historic Changes in Nearshore Environments Using the Free Archive of Landsat Imagery". *International Journal of Applied Earth Observation and Geoinformation* 12: 116–122.

Larson, M. and N.C. Kraus (1989) *SBEACH: Numerical Model to Simulate Storm-induced Beach Change*. Technical Report, U.S. Army Corps of Engineers, CERC.

Leont'yev, I.O. (1996) "Numerical Modeling of Beach Erosion during Storm Events". *Coastal Engineering* 29: 187–200.

Loder N.M. et al. (2009) "Sensitivity of Hurricane Surge to Morphological Parameters of Coastal Wetlands". *Estuarine, Coastal and Shelf Science* 84: 625–636.

Lugo-Fernandez, A. and M. Gravois (2010) "Understanding Impacts of Tropical Storms and Hurricanes on Submerged Bank Reefs and Coral Communities in the Northwestern Gulf of Mexico". *Continental Shelf Research* 30: 1226–1240.

McFadden, L., T. Spencer and R.J. Nicholls (2007) "Broad-scale Modelling of Coastal Wetlands: What Is Required?" *Hydrobiologia* 577: 5–15.

Massel, S.R. and M.R. Gourlay (2000) "On the Modelling of Wave Breaking and Set-up on Coral Reefs". *Coastal Engineering* 39: 1–27.

Monioudi, I. (2011) "Predictions of Beach Retreat under Sea Level Rise". PhD dissertation, Department of Marine Sciences, School of Environment, University of the Aegean (in Greek with English abstract).

Monioudi, I. et al. (2012) "Beach Erosion Predictions for Aegean Islands Due to Sea Level Rise". *Mediterranean Marine Science* (under revision).

Nelson, R.C. (1996) "Hydraulic Roughness of Coral Reef Platforms". *Applied Ocean Research* 18: 265–274.

Neumeier, U. and C.L. Amos (2006) "The Influence of Vegetation on Turbulence and Flow Velocities in European Salt-marshes". *Sedimentology* 53: 259–277.

Paphitis, D. et al. (2001) "Laboratory Investigations into the Threshold of Movement of Natural Sand-sized Sediments, under Unidirectional, Oscillatory and Combined Flows". *Sedimentology* 48: 645–659.

Paul, M. and C.L. Amos (2011) "Spatial and Seasonal Variation in Wave Attenuation over *Zostera noltii*". *Journal of Geophysical Research* 116: C08019.

Peduzzi, P. (2010) "Landslides and Vegetation Cover in the 2005 North Pakistan Earthquake: A GIS and Statistical Quantitative Approach". *Natural Hazards Earth System Science* 10: 623–640.

Peduzzi, P. et al. (2009) "Global Disaster Risk: Patterns, Trends and Drivers". In UNISDR, *2009 Global Assessment Report on Disaster Risk Reduction*. Geneva: United Nations International Strategy for Disaster Reduction, pp. 17–57.

Peduzzi, P., C. Herold and W. Silverio (2010) "Assessing High Altitude Glacier Thickness, Volume and Area Changes Using Field, GIS and Remote Sensing Techniques: The Case of Nevado Coropuna (Peru)". *The Cryosphere* 4: 313–323.

Peduzzi, P. et al (in prep.) "Beach Erosion in the Context of Ecosystem and Climate Change: The Case of Negril Beaches". Jamaica.

Pethick, J. and F. Burd (1993) "Coastal Defence and the Environment: A Guide to Good Practice". Ministry of Agriculture, Fisheries and Food, London.

Roder, C. et al. (2009) "Riverine Input of Particulate Material and Inorganic Nutrients to a Coastal Reef Ecosystem at the Caribbean Coast of Costa Rica". *Marine Pollution Bulletin* 58: 1937–1943.

Sheppard, C. and R. Rioja-Nieto (2005) "Sea Surface Temperature 1871–2099 in 38 Cells in the Caribbean Region". *Marine Environmental Research* 60: 389–396.

Sheppard, C. et al. (2005) "Coral Mortality Increases Wave Energy Reaching Shores Protected by Reef Flats: Examples from the Seychelles". *Estuarine, Coastal and Shelf Science* 64: 223–234.

SWI [Smith Warner International] (2007) *Preliminary Engineering Report Commissioned by the Negril Coral Reef Preservation Society (NCRPS)*. Kingston, Jamaica: Smith Warner International Ltd.

Thywissen, K. (2006) "Core Terminology of Disaster Reduction: A Comparative Glossary", In J. Birkmann (ed.), *Measuring Vulnerability to Natural Hazards: Towards Disaster Resilient Societies*. Tokyo: United Nations University Press, pp. 448–496.

Timmerman, P. (1981) "Vulnerability, Resilience and the Collapse of Society: A Review of Models and Possible Climatic Applications". Institute for Environmental Studies, University of Toronto, Toronto.

Turner, B.L. et al. (2003) "A Framework for Vulnerability Analysis in Sustainability Science". *Proceedings of the National Academy of Sciences* 100(14): 8074–8079.

UNEP [United Nations Environment Programme] (2010) *Linking Ecosystems to Risk and Vulnerability Reduction: The Case of Jamaica. Risk and Vulnerability Assessment Methodology Development Project (RiVAMP) Pilot Assessment Report.* Geneva: United Nations Environment Programme, UNEP Post-Conflict and Disaster Management Branch/GRID-Europe, 2nd edition.

UWI [University of the West Indies] (2002) *Beach Sands Resource Assessment, Negril, Jamaica.* Technical Report, Department of Geology and Geography, University of the West Indies, Mona, Jamaica.

Van der Werf, G.R. et al. (2008) "Climate Regulation of Fire Emissions and Deforestation in Equatorial Asia". *Proceedings of the National Academy of Sciences USA* 105: 20350–20355.

Vanacker, V. et al. (2003) "Linking Hydrological, Infinite Slope Stability and Land-use Change Models through GIS for Assessing the Impact of Deforestation on Slope Stability in High Andean Watersheds". *Geomorphology* 52: 299–315.

Velegrakis, A.F. et al. (2008) "Impacts of Dams on Their Downstream Beaches: A Case Study from Eresos Coastal Basin, Island of Lesvos, Greece". *Marine Georesources and Geotechnology* 26: 350–371.

Velegrakis, A.F. et al. (2009) "Beach Erosion Prediction for the Black Sea Coast, Due to Sea Level Rise". *Proceedings of the 9th MEDCOAST Conf., Sochi, Russia, 10–14 November, 2009*, pp. 776–787.

Vousdoukas, M., A.F. Velegrakis and T. Karambas (2009) "Morphology and Sedimentology of a Beach with Beachrocks: Vatera Beach, Lesbos, Greece". *Continental Shelf Research* 29: 1937–1947.

Vousdoukas, M.I. et al. (2011) "Plants, Hydraulics and Sediment Dynamics". In M.F. Johnson, S.P. Rice and R.E. Thomas (eds), *Critical Review of Ecohydraulic Experiments.* HYDRALAB-IV Project, EC contract no. 261520, pp. 25–69.

Vousdoukas, M.I., A.F. Velegrakisb, M. Paula, C. Dimitriadisb, E. Makrykostac and D. Koutsoubas (in press) "Field Observations and Modeling of Wave Attenuation over Colonized Beachrocks". *Continental Shelf Research.*

Wamsley, T.V. et al. (2010) "The Potential of Wetlands in Reducing Storm Surge". *Ocean Engineering* 37: 59–68.

Webb, A.P and P.S. Kench (2010) "The Dynamic Response of Reef Islands to Sea-level Rise: Evidence from Multi-decadal Analysis of Island Change in the Central Pacific". *Global and Planetary Change* 72(3): 234–246.

Wielgus, J., E. Cooper, R. Torres and L. Burke (2010) *Coastal Capital: Dominican Republic. Case Studies on the Economic Value of Coastal Ecosystems in the Dominican Republic.* Working Paper. Washington, DC: World Resources Institute. Available at <http://pdf.wri.org/working_papers/coastal_capital_dominican_republic.pdf> (accessed 15 October 2012).

Witt, D.D.L., Y.L. Young and S.C. Yim (2011) "Field Investigation of Tsunami Impact on Coral Reefs and Coastal Sandy Slopes". *Marine Geology* 289: 159–163.

6

Increasing the resilience of human and natural communities to coastal hazards: Supporting decisions in New York and Connecticut

Michael W. Beck, Ben Gilmer, Zach Ferdaña, George T. Raber, Christine C. Shepard, Imen Meliane, Jeffrey D. Stone, Adam W. Whelchel, Mark Hoover and Sarah Newkirk

Introduction

Coastal communities are increasingly vulnerable to coastal hazards, including storms and sea level rise (SLR) (Bender et al., 2010; IPCC, 2007; Karl et al., 2009; Weiss et al., 2011). These increasing hazards threaten not only the human-built infrastructure and coastal communities but also natural habitats and ecosystems and the many services they support. The exposure and vulnerability of human and natural communities are increasing as development and urbanization continue and natural buffers, such as coastal wetlands and dunes, are degraded or lost (Jha et al., 2011).

Despite awareness of growing coastal hazards, local decision-makers often have only limited access to the critical information necessary to support choices for managing the current and future vulnerability of human and natural communities (Climate Change Science Program, 2009; NRC, 2009). Local decision-makers often lack the tools to visualize current and future scenarios and identify alternatives for effective management (Frazier et al., 2010a, 2010b; Gesch, 2009). As a consequence, they are unable to comprehensively integrate coastal hazard risk and SLR into their decision-making to reduce vulnerability and increase the resilience of human and natural communities. To make matters more challenging, land-use planning in the United States and many other countries has historically focused on facilitating residential development and private business, with far less regard for community resilience to natural hazards (Burby, 1998). By resilience, we mean both the ability to absorb

The role of ecosystems in disaster risk reduction, Renaud, Sudmeier-Rieux and Estrella (eds), *United Nations University Press, 2013, ISBN 978-92-808-1221-3*

perturbations before communities change states and the ability to bounce back or return to similar states after perturbations (for example, Adger, 2000; Folke, 2006). In this case study, we look primarily at the perturbations from coastal hazards created by flooding and inundation from storm surge and SLR.

Mitigation of coastal hazards has traditionally been undertaken using shoreline hardening and engineered defences. These are expensive and in some instances have had mixed success (Khazai et al., 2007). It has been estimated that current "business as usual" planning and regulatory policies in the United States will promote continued development and shoreline hardening (Climate Change Science Program, 2009) in the face of increasing coastal hazards. This hardening in turn will cause further habitat loss because it prevents the inland migration of coastal ecosystems that get caught in the squeeze between the rising sea and bulkheads (Climate Change Science Program, 2009; Nicholls, 2011).

With the increase in economic impacts of coastal hazards, local, state and federal planners in the United States are starting to see land-use planning as a tool for risk reduction (Burby, 2006). They are also increasingly aware of the need to integrate future change considerations, but the use of climate change scenarios including SLR is in its infancy (Frazier et al., 2010b). The relationship between strategies of adaptation to climate change and development policies is also an emerging research issue (Kok and Metz, 2008; Markandya and Halsnaes, 2002; Smith et al., 2003; Tanner and Mitchell, 2008).

Alternative approaches to built infrastructure using ecosystem-based solutions or green infrastructure are nascent yet increasingly recognized among hazard and climate planners and managers. A growing body of evidence indicates the values of coastal ecosystems in wave attenuation, wave deflection and erosion reduction (Beck et al., 2011; Costanza et al., 2008; Dudley et al., 2010; Gedan et al., 2011; Hale et al., 2011; Shepard et al., 2011; Sheppard et al., 2005). Indeed, coastal ecosystems provide many additional benefits that are highly valued by society, often referred to as ecosystem services (Costanza et al., 1997, 2006, 2008; Hale et al., 2009).

Here we present a case study addressing vulnerability to storm hazards and climate change around Long Island Sound (Connecticut and New York) in the United States (Figure 6.1). We use a programme of work, Coastal Resilience, to understand social, economic and ecological vulnerability to coastal hazards and identify integrated solutions to address them. The work was designed to help local stakeholders understand the impacts of coastal hazards, including future SLR, and to inform their planning, land-use, acquisition, investment and permitting decisions. To assist decision-makers and stakeholders, the project also included an Internet-based mapping application designed to provide interactive

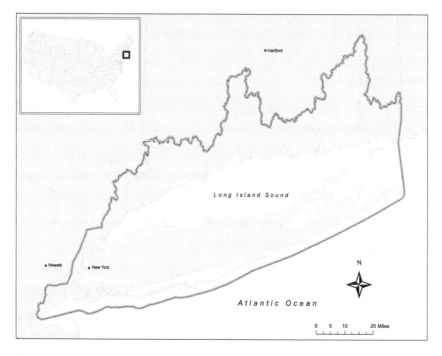

Figure 6.1 Study area along the shores of New York and Connecticut including
Long Island Sound and the Atlantic Ocean coasts
Source: See <http://lis.coastalresilience.org/lis.html> (accessed 16 October 2012).

decision support and alternative scenarios for coastal hazard mitigation
and conservation.[1]

Methods

Coastal Resilience provides a framework and tools to better inform local
decision-making about current and future coastal hazard risks and
choices for addressing them (Box 6.1). The project partners include The
Nature Conservancy, the Center for Climate Systems Research (CCSR)
at Columbia University, the National Aeronautics and Space Administration's Goddard Institute for Space Studies, the Association of State
Floodplain Managers, the Pace Land Use Law Center, the National
Oceanic and Atmospheric Administration's Coastal Services Center
(NOAA-CSC) and the Department of Geography and Geology at the
University of Southern Mississippi. We examine current ecological, bio-
logical, socioeconomic and management information alongside locally

Box 6.1 Coastal Resilience: Conceptual framework

Coastal Resilience provides a framework that supports decisions to reduce the ecological and socio-economic risks of coastal hazards

The framework includes 4 critical elements:
- **Raise Awareness**: Develop integrated databases on social, economic and ecological resources critical to communities and provide mapping and visualization tools;
- **Assess Risk**: Assess risk and vulnerability to coastal hazards including alternative scenarios for current and future storms and sea level rise with community input;
- **Identify Choices**: Identify choices for reducing vulnerability focusing on joint solutions across social, economic and ecological systems. Provide decision support including web based guidance and scenarios to assess options;
- **Take Action**: Help communities to develop and implement solutions.

(*Source*: <http://coastalresilience.org/>, accessed 16 October 2012)

These resources are provided to communities and practitioners through a variety of products, including a website that explains the approach, methods, decision support tools and strategies for addressing coastal hazards. Community engagement is critical at every point in this framework.

relevant, downscaled coastal flooding and inundation scenarios developed from widely accepted climate and hazard models (Ferdaña et al., 2010).

New York and Connecticut

The shores around Long Island Sound are densely populated and heavily developed. Current development places considerable pressure on natural habitats through nutrient loading, polluted surface and stormwater run-off, and habitat conversion and degradation. Despite this, the coastlines of Connecticut and New York support a diverse array of marine and coastal organisms and habitats. The area is home to significant island and fringing saltmarshes and near-shore eelgrass beds. A number of beach-dependent birds come to these shores to breed and feed during spring and summer months (for example, Seavey et al., 2010). These shores also support populations of shellfish and finfish that are important recreational and commercial resources, in addition to being important to overall ecosystem dynamics and water quality (Schimmel et al., 1999).

Large storm events such as tropical storms and hurricanes and extra-tropical storms (particularly winter storms from the north-east known as nor'easters) have driven the formation and continued development of the shorelines in Connecticut and New York. During the past 75 years, hurricanes and nor'easters have caused rapid beach erosion, dune displacement, wetland loss and coastal flooding. The most significant was the Great Hurricane of 1938 (21 September), also known as "The Long Island Express". The storm produced winds that reached over 300 kilometres per hour, generated 5-metre-high breakers, overwashed approximately one-half of Long Island, NY, and created 12 new inlets (Donnelly et al., 2001). The "Ash Wednesday" storm of 6 March 1962 was a major nor'easter that resulted in more than 50 washovers. With SLR, the baseline sea level on which storm surge operates will be higher, resulting in increased shoreward extent of flooding and severity of impact.

New York and Connecticut's coastal communities have a long history of trying to maintain their shorelines using a variety of structural mechanisms, including jetties, groynes, beachfill and construction of bulkheads. This extensive shoreline armouring increases the pressure on natural resources by modifying the required sediment transport and deposition.

Data collection, analysis and interpretation

The collection and analysis of Geographic Information System (GIS) data were a core component of this project, allowing visualization, exploration and analysis of multi-layered issues influencing coastal resilience.

Coastal flooding and inundation

A critical step in assessing coastal hazards risk is mapping coastal elevation data.[2] The elevation data used for mapping these SLR and storm surge scenarios came from LiDAR-based digital elevation models.[3]

To predict storm surge events we used the National Hurricane Center's Sea, Lake and Overland Surges from Hurricanes model (SLOSH), which estimates storm surge heights and winds resulting from historical, hypothetical or predicted hurricanes by taking into account pressure, size, forward speed, track and winds. From the model's outputs, we used the Maximum Envelopes of Water (MEOWs) result from the SLOSH model to portray what could happen when a specific storm makes landfall. MEOW Category 2 and 3 hurricanes, corresponding to storm surges with estimated 40- and 70-year return periods, respectively, were mapped.

The Columbia University CCSR members of the project team developed future SLR scenarios for three different emission scenarios using downscaled outputs from seven of the Global Circulation Models (GCMs) used for the 2007 report by the Intergovernmental Panel on Climate Change (IPCC). The methods are described in detail in Horton et al. (2010). We modelled probability distributions of SLR in decadal periods from the 2020s through the 2080s. The three emission scenarios were IPCC scenarios A1b, A2 and A2 + added meltwater. The IPCC methodology (A1b and A2 scenarios) incorporates two global factors – thermal expansion and ice melt – and two local factors – local ocean water density changes and local uplift or subsidence. We then developed a modified scenario (A2 + added meltwater) assuming a more rapid ice melt, using paleoclimatic analogues. The latter scenario was undertaken because the IPCC GCMs for the Fourth Assessment Report (IPCC, 2007) were not set up to model dynamic ice-sheet changes that could result in increased ice melt; such an increase is now thought to be a real possibility. This approach gives a significantly higher set of SLR scenarios than the existing IPCC (2007) method.

We used a bathtub fill approach to model inundation from SLR (see Poulter and Halpin, 2008). The bathtub fill approach fills low-lying elevation points with water; that is, we identified the new height of water based on SLR and "filled in" the coastal land with water to this elevation. This method can on occasion create erroneous inundated areas that are not connected to the ocean (that is, islands of water). An alternative approach forces coastal inundation to occur only where low-lying elevation is hydrologically connected to the ocean (Gesch, 2009), but that approach was beyond the scope of the current project.

Ecological analyses

We incorporated data on and analyses of critical coastal ecosystems that were important ecologically, were especially vulnerable to coastal hazards or provided critical ecosystem services. We focused in particular on coastal wetlands and marshes, as well as on the piping plover, barrier island habitats and submerged aquatic vegetation.

Intertidal habitats, including wetlands, require adjacent non-developed space to migrate over time in order to keep pace with rising sea levels. The project team modelled potential marsh advancement zones with SLR based on variables of accretion, erosion, land use/cover, elevation and projected sea level (Hoover et al., 2010).

Social vulnerability

We compiled and analysed socioeconomic information in order to better evaluate the consequences of SLR and storm surge hazards for human populations and infrastructure. A characterization of vulnerable communities provided managers with information to explore opportunities to minimize risk. We used socioeconomic data from the US Census Bureau

(2000) to depict these distributions and to create various indices at the census block group level based on demographic attributes such as age, income and access to critical facilities such as hospitals.

The analyses presented here were based on published vulnerability assessment methodologies and primarily on the Social Vulnerability Index (SOVI) (Cutter et al., 2003). We also provided additional analyses based on the Community Vulnerability Assessment Tool and the Australian Geological Survey Organisation's Cities Project (Granger, 2003).

SOVI and these other indices are based primarily on census-derived variables, including, for example, population density; housing unit density; median income; households below poverty; those requiring public assistance; those that rent, live in houses seasonally, live in mobile homes; and those without an automobile. These variables were mapped at the census block group scale, which is the smallest geographical unit for which the census provides detailed demographic data.

Economic exposure

Demographic data at the census block level were combined with economic data to forecast the potential economic damage of future SLR and floods based on the present-day economic landscape. We examined economic exposure and losses from flooding for infrastructure, including housing, transportation and commercial structures. Economic loss represents the full replacement value of commercial and residential structures. Loss calculations were the result of geographical analysis using the Hazards U.S. – Multi-Hazards (HAZUS-MH) tool developed by the Federal Emergency Management Agency (FEMA). HAZUS-MH uses GIS software to estimate potential economic losses from earthquakes, hurricanes and floods. To further understand infrastructure exposure, we added data on hardened shoreline structures, land use and locations of critical facilities (hospitals, fire stations).

Results

Coastal Resilience provides spatial databases and combined indices that characterize ecological, social and economic resources and their vulnerability to current and future coastal hazards. We illustrate some of the types of data and decision support in Figures 6.2–6.6.[4]

First we examined exposure to current and future impacts using a variety of different and realistic scenarios based on past storms and likely future SLR. Among those scenarios, we illustrate the potential storm surge flooding from a Category 2 hurricane based on current sea levels and the increased future flooding based on the same storm with sea levels

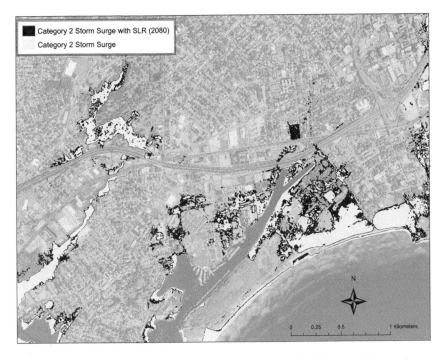

Figure 6.2 Visualizing storm surge and sea level rise in Bridgeport, Connecticut
Source: See <http://lis.coastalresilience.org/lis.html> (accessed 16 October 2012).
Notes: The storm surge is the predicted maximum surge from a Category 2 hurricane based on current sea levels. SLR is based on the IPCC A2 scenario for the year 2080.

predicted from an A2 IPCC emissions scenario for the year 2080 (Figure 6.2).

We provide significant data on current wetlands and other biological resources (see, for example, Figure 6.3).

The SOVI summarized the communities most vulnerable to coastal hazards on a relative scale throughout the project area in New York and Connecticut (Figure 6.4). We examined numerous economic resources at risk from coastal hazards, including, for example, the geographical distribution of potential building losses (replacement costs) across the region (Figure 6.5).

All of these types of data (ecological, social and economic) have been used individually by others for planning. The real benefit is to be able to combine these data sets to better assess the present and future distributions of coastal ecosystems with data characterizing infrastructure and social vulnerability to identify choices that could conserve ecological

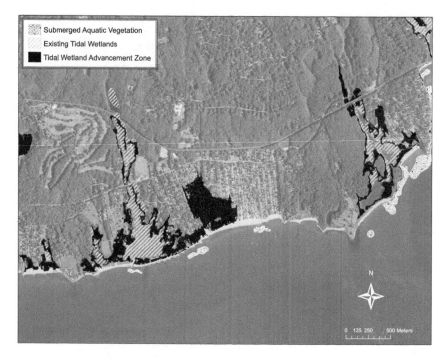

Figure 6.3 Ecological systems around Old Lyme, Connecticut
Source: See <http://lis.coastalresilience.org/lis.html> (accessed 16 October 2012).
Notes: The future advancement zones are areas in which marshes may migrate based on considerations of current elevation, land cover, accretion and erosion and future sea levels in 2080 based on IPCC A2 emissions scenarios (see Hoover et al., 2010).

resources while mitigating coastal hazards. Figure 6.6 illustrates one example of these types of integrated analyses. It shows "advancement zones" in vacant parcels for conservation, into which marshes could potentially migrate or advance under future SLR scenarios. One way that land-use planners use this integrated analysis is to identify areas that should remain undeveloped to allow for the landward advancement of tidal wetlands in order to maintain the continued protection of some of the most vulnerable low-lying human communities.

Discussion

Mutually beneficial solutions for improving the resilience of human and natural communities lie in examining relationships between coastal

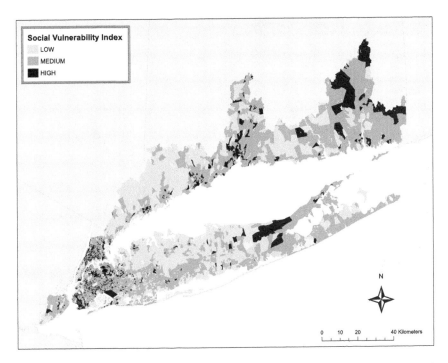

Figure 6.4 Social vulnerability: Low, medium and high social vulnerability of census block groups throughout the study area in New York and Connecticut
Source: See <http://lis.coastalresilience.org/lis.html> (accessed 16 October 2012).
Notes: Vulnerability is based on SOVI and provides a prediction of those most vulnerable to coastal hazards.

hazard mitigation and biodiversity conservation to preserve lives, infra-structure and livelihoods while protecting nature. Decision-makers will address people's needs first, but it is possible to reduce coastal losses to both people and nature. Ecosystem-based solutions can present a common ground to achieve both objectives. Processes such as urbanization, environmental degradation and climate change shape and configure hazards, which means it is becoming increasingly difficult to disentangle their natural and human attributes (UNISDR, 2011).

There has been an increased interest by the hazard management community in coastal protection options that are environmentally friendly, driven by increasing evidence of (i) the role of ecosystems in coastal protection, (ii) their cost-effectiveness in both initial costs and added benefits, and (iii) the opportunity in some areas to create sustainable livelihood alternatives. Evidence increasingly demonstrates that conservation and management of coastal ecosystems can play a key role in reducing coastal

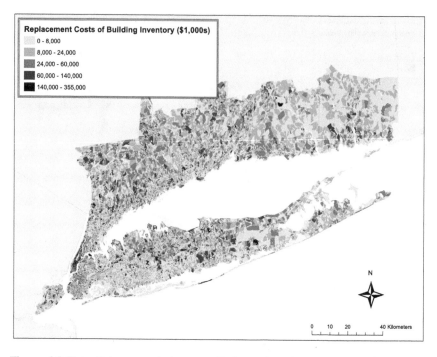

Figure 6.5 Potential economic impacts: Estimated replacement costs (i.e. potential economic losses) of built infrastructure from across the study area based on the HAZUS model
Source: See <http://lis.coastalresilience.org/lis.html> (accessed 16 October 2012).

hazards (Beck et al., 2011; Dudley et al., 2010; Costanza et al., 2008; Gedan et al., 2011; Hale et al., 2011; Sheppard et al., 2005) and thus the vulnerability of communities. For example, Shepard et al. (2011) examined the protective role that marshes can play in providing coastal protection services by doing a meta-analysis combining results from field studies that compared these coastal protection benefits with and without marshes (Figure 6.7).

The second major factor driving interest in green infrastructure solutions is the increasing evidence that they can be a cost-effective part of hazard mitigation and climate adaptation solutions (Campbell et al., 2009; Entergy Corporation, 2010; McKinsey & Co., 2009; World Bank, 2009; World Bank and United Nations, 2010). Further, ecosystem-based approaches can address multiple coastal management objectives, including natural resource protection with which local officials are charged. An ecosystem-based approach of protecting and restoring "green infrastructure" such as healthy coastal wetlands could be a more cost-effective, lower-maintenance means of protecting large coastal areas (Moberg and Rönnbäck, 2003). Strategies that aim to enhance the resilience of eco-

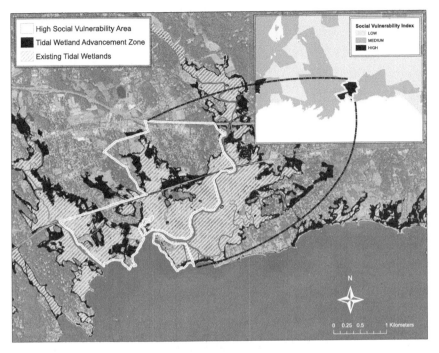

Figure 6.6 Integrating socioeconomic and ecological data to support land-use planning decisions to meet hazard mitigation and conservation objectives
Source: See <http://lis.coastalresilience.org/lis.html> (accessed 16 October 2012).
Notes: This figure shows the present-day distribution of tidal wetlands (grey hatched), the low elevation areas where marshes are predicted to advance between now and 2080 (black polygon), the communities of highest social vulnerability in the area based on SOVI (white polygon), and residential and commercial developments directly adjacent to tidal wetland advancement zones (aerial photography), Guilford, CT.

systems to enable the continued provision of goods and services can be particularly important for vulnerable communities that depend upon natural resources.

In fact, the incorporation of these approaches is imperative given the very high costs to society of engineered solutions. In many places, putting up enough artificial defences is impractical, too expensive, maladaptive and often with ongoing debt service and maintenance costs. One of the areas where there are real opportunities for identifying better joint solutions for human and natural communities is in building approaches that combine hazard mitigation and biodiversity conservation in coastal zones to preserve infrastructure while protecting human communities. In some of the most highly developed areas (for example, major urban cities), ecosystem-based options alone will rarely be viable alternatives. However,

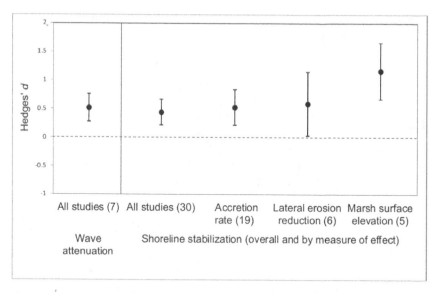

Figure 6.7 Average effect size of marsh vegetation (Hedges' d) on (a) wave attenuation and (b) shoreline stabilization as measured by increases in accretion/ marsh surface elevation change or decreases in lateral erosion
Notes: The results are based on a meta-analysis of multiple studies that compared attenuation and stabilization in areas with (treatment) and without marshes (control). The numbers of separate studies are in parentheses next to the services. Positive values of d indicate that, overall, treatments (marsh) attenuated waves and stabilized shorelines. The error bars are 95% confidence intervals. Because they do not overlap 0, the positive effects of treatments are significant. See Shepard et al. (2011) for further information.

we are finding that, even just outside of one of the largest urban areas, there are viable nature-based solutions. Changing approaches (and mindsets) to include green infrastructure is not simple, and there are strong vested interests that support only engineered approaches. Nonetheless, in a time of shrinking budgets, most municipalities are looking for cost-effective infrastructure approaches (because these works are almost all taxpayer supported).

To advance ecosystem-based approaches for risk reduction and adaptation, we need to integrate hazard and climate science with local decision-making processes. This work is just beginning; the present case is one of the first to attempt this integrated approach. This experience illustrates how the management of saltmarshes can be integrated into coastal zone hazard mitigation and climate change adaptation policies. There are, however, significant considerations and challenges in jointly informing decisions about hazard mitigation and conservation.

Access to relevant information and data

Providing communities and key decision-makers (for example, local planning agencies and natural resource managers) with easy access to information is critical to assist in coastal planning and management decisions regarding resources at risk from coastal hazards. One of the criteria that has increased use of Coastal Resilience is that it does not promote a specific outcome. Rather, it enables easy access to targeted information in one location for planners, elected officials, managers and citizens so that they can visualize the vulnerability and risks that communities face from coastal hazards and work within the given context of their specific communities or regions.

Mapping predictions of SLR and storm surges is best done with high-resolution bathymetric, topographic and airborne gravimetric data. These data can be expensive to acquire but costs are coming down and the data are becoming more available in many regions. These data are needed to provide a description of elevation characteristics throughout the coastline. When lower resolution data are all that is available (such as the global elevation data sets), it is still possible and necessary to plan for the future. However, a more precautionary stance in development planning is justified with lower-resolution elevation data because confidence in the flooding and inundation predictions (that is, where surges and sea level will reach) is lower.

Improvements in the quantification of ecosystem services will further their integration in risk management frameworks. Indeed, most studies on the role of ecosystems in coastal protection are often descriptive or limited to a singular experience, but new and better efforts in field experiments, models and global reviews are becoming available, such as Gedan et al. (2011); Scyphers et al. (2011); Shepard et al. (2011, Figure 6.7 above); see also Chapter 5 in this volume.

The importance of a flexible framework

Public management of risks is a multidisciplinary and multi-sector field often entrusted to a variety of institutions that operate at different spatial and temporal scales. The differing scales and responsibilities of these institutions present coordination challenges. Flexible decision support is critical for incorporating new information into development planning accessible by multiple partners, agencies and institutions.

With Coastal Resilience, we have endeavoured to create a framework that provides information to local communities, but it is also relevant at state and national scales. By focusing first on local decision-makers, we address the needs of stakeholders within their communities while providing a robust framework for identifying place-based ecological, social and economic relationships and appropriate solutions for hazard mitigation. Coastal Resilience accommodates adaptive planning; centralizes and provides decision support online; advances structured community dialogue; and is transferable to other geographies.

Coastal Resilience is being used in Connecticut and New York by local agencies to inform decision-making regarding natural resources and community land-use/policy planning. At the municipal level, communities such as Guilford, Old Saybrook and Westbrook (CT) are incorporating the SLR and storm surge projections from Coastal Resilience into their Natural Hazard Mitigation Plans, along with specific identification and prioritization of "at risk" neighbourhoods and infrastructure. Figures from Coastal Resilience have been incorporated in the Plan of Conservation and Development for Waterford, CT. Town planners and emergency managers across the coast of Connecticut are using the storm surge projections to reconsider evacuation routes and refuge locations in the face of increased storm activity. Ten communities in Connecticut reported using Coastal Resilience for preparedness and response before Tropical Storm Irene. This information is also being used by the Greater Bridgeport Regional Council for transportation (bus and rail) assessments and contingency planning in densely populated portions of the project area. In addition, the information is being used for detailed vulnerability assessments in Stamford, CT, and reconsideration of zoning restrictions elsewhere on future growth in future flood and inundation areas. The Town of Easthampton, NY, is using the decision support to evaluate revetment applications.

At the state level, the New York State Sea Level Rise Task Force (SLRTF) uses Coastal Resilience for vulnerability mapping in coastal New York. Just recently, figures from Coastal Resilience provided a primary motivation in Connecticut for the development and senate approval of a shoreline preservation task force in that state. A primary aim of the task forces is to develop new policies to address the unique needs of shoreline and waterfront residents and businesses with respect to shoreline erosion, rising sea levels and future storm planning.[5]

In New York, the SLRTF found that coastal wetlands provide a cost-effective approach to reducing the vulnerability of people and property. It recommends that New York "support increased reliance on non-structural measures and natural protective features to reduce impacts from coastal hazards ... and prevent further loss of natural systems that reduce risk of coastal flooding" (NYSSLRTF, 2010). It is evaluating state and local wetlands regulations in the face of SLR and identifying where retreat-oriented policies can be effective (that is, identifying where marshes can and should be allowed to migrate upslope).

Our aim is to increase the robustness of analyses for integrating assessments of ecological and social vulnerability and in the identification of options for reducing them. Figure 6.6 identifies one of the ways in which we have approached this problem systematically. We identify where communities are socially vulnerable and where marshes are at risk, as well as where development and conservation priorities could align to ensure that future vulnerabilities do not increase.

State and federal agencies are using the "advancement zone" analyses as a guide to rebalance management objectives directed at the acquisition, restoration and habitat conversion of saltmarshes for private preserves and national wildlife refuges and management areas to meet conservation and hazard mitigation management objectives. We are working with several National Estuary Programs (NEPs) towards providing decision support to communities in the Environmental Protection Agency's Peconic Estuary Program and the Long Island Sound NEP. Coastal Resilience is a part of NOAA-CSC's Digital Coast efforts to inform communities about the risks posed by coastal inundation.[6]

Community engagement

Planning for hazard mitigation and adaptation can be challenging when there is much uncertainty and disagreement about the best management practices to minimize risks. Nonetheless, there is a need to take anticipatory adaptive action. Extensive community engagement is essential for accessing information, understanding issues and building support for actions. It has been a key principle in the development of Coastal Resilience. During the development of Coastal Resilience we conducted extensive interviews and hosted multiple stakeholder workshops (in New York and Connecticut) to better understand community awareness and readiness; the resources at risk; and the planning support required to address existing and future impacts (see Table 6.1). At each workshop we asked for critical feedback on the issues being assessed and the tools being developed. In the subsequent workshops we identified how we responded to the feedback. Since the primary development period (two years), we have been deeply engaged with several municipalities in using the decision support tool. Stakeholders who have been engaged in the process included town planners, environmentalists, scientists, local elected officials and agency staff (county, state and federal representing environment, transportation and hazard management, among others). Engagement of stakeholders provides opportunities for coastal communities to employ local knowledge and for direct participation in developing and applying solutions. Structured dialogues with our pilot communities

Table 6.1 Stakeholders participating in the process

Towns/cities	Town of Guilford, CT
	Town of Old Saybrook, CT
	Town of Southold, NY
	Town of Stonington, CT
	Town of Waterford, CT
	Town of East Lyme, CT
	Town of Old Lyme, CT
	Town of Westbrook, CT
	City of Bridgeport, CT
	City of New Haven, CT
Regional planning organizations	Connecticut River Estuary Regional Planning Agency
	Southeastern Connecticut Council of Governments
	South Central Regional Council of Governments
	Greater Bridgeport Regional Council
Key working partners	Clean Air – Cool Planet
	Regional Planning Association
	Association of State Floodplain Managers
	NOAA Coastal Services Center
Academic partners	Columbia University
	Yale University
	University of Connecticut
	Clark University
	Pace University
Participating fields	Emergency management
	Public health
	Engineering
	Planning and zoning
	Conservation/environmental management
	Transportation/infrastructure
	Elected officials
	Citizen groups
	Land-use planning
	Marine and coastal science

(Guilford and Old Saybrook, CT, and Southold, NY) have resulted in initiatives to rewrite master planning documents.

Many local elected officials do not fully appreciate the threat posed by SLR, or they see the issues as occurring too far in the future to be a major consideration in current planning and capital expenditures. The outreach efforts for this project focused initially on increasing the receptivity to and importance of this issue with and between local and state regulatory agencies. Ongoing community engagement that provides a forum to comprehensively receive and consider common and conflicting interests is a central focus of Coastal Resilience.

Bringing together mismatching mandates

In theory, better integration of hazard mitigation, adaptation and conservation objectives could be developed through comprehensive adaptation plans. In practice, they are more likely to be components of pre-existing planning processes such as master plans; hazard mitigation plans; capital expenditure and economic development plans; wetlands management plans; and other resource management plans.

One major issue in planning for coastal hazards and climate change is that many local and state managers have divergent and sometimes conflicting mandates and timelines for addressing coastal hazards. In the United States, the state agency participants have purview to promote planning for SLR through existing federal coastal zone management acts and state statutes, but, since most land-use planning is undertaken by local governments, state agencies generally are in a regulatory review position for consistency. State-level agencies should be more proactive in asserting their responsibilities and helping local governments with their long-term planning requirements.

More important in terms of conflicting timelines and mandates are the differences between emergency and infrastructure decision-makers. Both types of decision-makers are charged with dealing with hazard management. The former principally address short-term crises (hour by hour) and the latter long-term development planning (decade by decade). It is increasingly recognized however that some of the most significant development planning decisions are made in the weeks following crises, and that effective long-term planning could reduce some, and possibly many, of the losses associated with crises.

As the hazard management community moves further towards predisaster planning to reduce risk and potential loss, it should broaden participation from sectoral and spatial planning, including natural resource management agencies, and plan at a longer time-scale. The dividing lines between sectoral and spatial planning, civil protection and natural resource management are often rigid, making it difficult sometimes to secure communication and coordination between these communities. This often leads to a fragmented response–preparedness–prevention–remediation chain, reproducing situations where the information, knowledge and policy actions run in parallel without any linkages, feedback and mutual interactions (Sapountzaki et al., 2011). The increased awareness of the need to integrate future climate change impacts in hazard and development planning is a critical opportunity that will improve communication and coordination amongst these actors, resulting in more resilient communities. As noted above, the local leaders with whom we have worked have realized and embraced the requirement that coastal climate change is not a stand-alone issue and needs to be incorporated comprehensively across the sectors and functions of their communities. This recognition provides the platform from which multiple objectives and inherently conflicting interests can be balanced and directed towards the ultimate outcome: more resilient communities able to accommodate coastal change.

Recommendations

Coastal towns and villages around Long Island Sound and other coastal portions of New York are willing to explore different approaches for addressing coastal hazards and climate change, including nature-based solutions. Few have addressed these challenges head-on; New York City stands out in this regard (Rosenzweig and Solecki, 2010).

The achievement of more integrated strategies for hazard mitigation, adaptation and conservation will require substantial changes in the present shoreline management paradigm. There are six key recommendations to enable progress in the design and implementation of ecosystem-based solutions in the Northeastern United States and beyond.

1. *Enhance data and decision support to inform community choices.* We have found that the keys to effective engagement are robust and reasonable scenarios of impacts and alternatives. We do not believe that the further development of support should slow decision-making processes, but we have consistently found that robust scenarios are critical for handling difficult decisions and conflicting interests.

2. *Amend and pass key legislation.* Most shoreline management regulations and laws currently do not account for growing coastal hazards. Amendments to the Coastal Zone Management Act, the National Flood Insurance Program and FEMA Natural Hazard Mitigation Plans would increase the ability to both plan for and fund ecosystem-based approaches at the regional, state and local levels.

3. *Promote voluntary land acquisition.* The passage and/or amendment of progressive legislation at the federal and state level should provide financial incentives to local governments to enable the voluntary acquisition of coastal property as a means to protect human life and adjoining property and permit natural, sustaining processes to occur in the coastal zone.

4. *Relocate vulnerable infrastructure and development.* In some cases where risk to human communities is extremely high, moving vulnerable infrastructure may be advised and even necessary.

5. *Engage in comprehensive, pre-storm planning and post-storm redevelopment.* Adoption of suitable future development and redevelopment

programmes at the local level should be considered as an opportunity to minimize future additional risk and remedy previous land-use decisions that did not address current and longer-term risks and costs. The recognition of and need for linking pre-storm planning and post-storm redevelopment strategies should be reinforced and enabled through the federal programmes mentioned above.

6. *Restore and protect natural resources.* Central to the advancement of ecosystem-based approaches is the need to invest in habitat restoration and protection. A continued and sustained investment in natural resources will provide a highly leveraged return of important ecosystem services and increased nature-based solutions for shoreline protection and erosion control.

Acknowledgements

The authors would like to thank and acknowledge the entire Coastal Resilience project team, including David Major, Richie Goldberg, Will McClintock, Colin Ebert, William Brooks, Tashya Allen, Jessica Bacher, Alex Felson, Matt Goldstein, Chris Starkey, Vera Agostini, Nicole Maher, Anton Benson, Nathan Frohling and Randy Parsons. We would also like to thank the following organizations that generously provide funds for this work: the David & Lucile Packard Foundation, the Roslyn Savings Foundation and Arrow Electronics. Michael W. Beck was supported in part by a Pew Marine Fellowship.

Notes

1. See <http://www.coastalresilience.org> (accessed 16 October 2012).
2. There is limited agreement on the basic definitions of risk and vulnerability even among the disaster risk reduction and climate change adaptation communities (Renaud and Perez, 2010). Following Shepard et al. (2012), we characterize vulnerability, hazard and risk as follows: "vulnerability" is the susceptibility of both biophysical and social systems to a "hazard", which is an event or occurrence that has the potential to cause harm to people and/or property; "risk" is the likelihood or probability of such harm.
3. LiDAR stands for Light Detection and Ranging.
4. Much more information is available online through the web mapping application at <http://lis.coastalresilience.org/> (accessed 16 October 2012).
5. *Connecticut Mirror*, 9 January 2012 and "Speaker Donovan Announces Shoreline Preservation Task Force", 6 February 2012, <http://www.housedems.ct.gov/Donovan/2012/pr084_2012-02-06.html> (accessed 16 October 2012).
6. See NOAA-CSC, "Coastal Inundation Toolkit", <http://www.csc.noaa.gov/digitalcoast/inundation/longisland.html> (accessed 16 October 2012).

REFERENCES

Adger, W.N. (2000) "Social and Ecological Resilience: Are They Related?" *Progress in Human Geography* 24: 347–364.

Beck, M.W. et al. (2011) "Oyster Reefs at Risk and Recommendations for Conservation, Restoration, and Management". *Bioscience* 61: 107–116.

Bender, M.A. et al. (2010) "Modeled Impact of Anthropogenic Warming on the Frequency of Intense Atlantic Hurricanes". *Science* 327: 454–458.

Burby, R.J. (1998) *Cooperating with Nature: Confronting Natural Hazards with Land-use Planning for Sustainable Communities.* Washington, DC: Joseph Henry Press.

Burby, R.J. (2006) "Hurricane Katrina and the Paradoxes of Government Disaster Policy: Bringing about Wise Governmental Decisions for Hazardous Areas". *Annals of the American Academy of Political and Social Sciences* 604: 171–191.

Campbell, A. et al. (2009) *The Linkages between Biodiversity and Climate Change Mitigation.* UNEP World Conservation Monitoring Centre. Available at <http://www.cbd.int/doc/meetings/cc/ahteg-bdcc-02-02/other/ahteg-bdcc-02-02-unep-wcmc-en.pdf> (accessed 26 October 2012).

Climate Change Science Program (2009) *Coastal Sensitivity to Sea-level Rise: A Focus on the Mid-Atlantic Region. A Report by the U.S. Climate Change Science Program and the Subcommittee on Global Change Research.* Washington, DC: US Environmental Protection Agency.

Costanza, R. et al. (1997) "The Value of the World's Ecosystem Services and Natural Capital". *Nature* 387: 253–260.

Costanza, R., W.J. Mitsch and J.W. Day Jr (2006) "A New Vision for New Orleans and the Mississippi Delta: Applying Ecological Economics and Ecological Engineering". *Frontiers in Ecology and the Environment* 4: 465–472.

Costanza, R. et al. (2008) "The Value of Coastal Wetlands for Hurricane Protection". *Ambio* 37: 241–248.

Cutter, S.L., B.J. Boruff and W.L. Shirley (2003) "Social Vulnerability to Environmental Hazards". *Social Science Quarterly* 84: 242–261.

Donnelly, J. et al. (2001) "700 Year Sedimentary Record of Intense Hurricane Landfalls in Southern New England". *Geological Society of America Bulletin* 113: 714–727.

Dudley, N. et al. (2010) *Natural Solutions: Protected Areas Helping People Cope with Climate Change.* Gland, Switzerland: IUCN.

Entergy Corporation (2010) "Building a Resilient Energy Gulf Coast: Executive Report". Entergy Corporation, New Orleans. Available at <http://www.entergy.com/content/our_community/environment/GulfCoastAdaptation/Building_a_Resilient_Gulf_Coast.pdf> (accessed 16 October 2012).

Ferdaña, Z. et al. (2010) "Adapting to Climate Change: Building Interactive Decision Support to Meet Management Objectives for Coastal Conservation and Hazard Mitigation on Long Island, New York, USA". In A. Andrade, B. Herrera and R. Cazzolla (eds), *Building Resilience to Climate Change: Ecosystem-based Adaptation and Lessons from the Field.* Gland, Switzerland: IUCN, pp. 73–87.

Folke, C. (2006) "Resilience: The Emergence of a Perspective for Social–Ecological Systems Analyses". *Global Environmental Change* 16: 253–267.

Frazier, T.G., N. Wood and B. Yarnal (2010a) "Stakeholder Perspectives on Land-use Strategies for Adapting to Climate-Change-Enhanced Coastal Hazards: Sarasota, Florida". *Applied Geography* 30: 506–517.

Frazier, T.G., N. Wood, B. Yarnal and D.H. Bauer (2010b) "Influence of Potential Sea Level Rise on Societal Vulnerability to Hurricane Storm-Surge Hazards, Sarasota County, Florida". *Applied Geography* 30: 490–505.

Gedan, K.B. et al. (2011) "The Present and Future Role of Coastal Wetland Vegetation in Protecting Shorelines: Answering Recent Challenges to the Paradigm". *Climatic Change* 106: 7–29.

Gesch, D.B. (2009) "Analysis of Lidar Elevation Data for Improved Identification and Delineation of Lands Vulnerable to Sea-level Rise". *Journal of Coastal Research* 53: 49–58.

Granger, K. (2003) "Quantifying Storm Tide Risk in Cairns". *Natural Hazards* 30: 165–185.

Hale, L. et al. (2009) "Ecosystem-based Adaptation in Marine and Coastal Ecosystems". *Renewable Resources Journal* 25: 21–28.

Hale, L.Z., S. Newkirk and M.W. Beck (2011) "Helping Coastal Communities Adapt to Climate Change". *Solutions* 1: 84–85.

Hoover, M., D.L. Civco and A.W. Whelchel (2010) "The Development of a Salt Marsh Migration Tool and Its Application in Long Island Sound". *American Society of Photogrammetry and Remote Sensing Conference Proceedings, San Diego, California, 26–30 April*. Available at <http://clear.uconn.edu/publications/research/tech_papers/Hoover_et_al_ASPRS2010.pdf> (accessed 16 October 2012).

Horton, R. et al. (2010) "Climate Risk Information". In C. Rosenzweig and W. Solecki (eds), *New York City Panel on Climate Change. Climate Change Adaptation in New York City: Building a Risk Management Response. Annals of the New York Academy of Sciences* 1187, Appendix A.

IPCC [Intergovernmental Panel on Climate Change] (2007) *Climate Change 2007: The Physical Science Basis. Contribution of Working Group I to the Fourth Assessment Report of the Intergovernmental Panel on Climate Change*. Cambridge: Cambridge University Press.

Jha, A. et al. (2011) "Five Feet High and Rising: Cities and Flooding in the 21st Century". World Bank Policy Research Working Paper Series, Washington, DC.

Karl, T.R., J.M. Melillo and T.C. Peterson (eds) (2009) *Global Climate Change Impacts in the United States*. Cambridge: Cambridge University Press.

Khazai, B., J. Ingram and D. Saah (2007) "The Protective Role of Natural and Engineered Defense Systems in Coastal Hazards". Kaulunani Urban and Community Forestry Program of the Department of Land and Natural Resources, Hawaii.

Kok, M. and B. Metz (2008) "Development Policy as a Way to Manage Climate Change Risks". *Climate Policy* 8: 99–118.

McKinsey & Co. (2009) *Shaping Climate-resilient Development: A Framework for Decision Making*. New York: McKinsey.

Markandya, A. and K. Halsnaes (eds) (2002) *Climate Change and Sustainable Development*. London: Earthscan.

Moberg, F. and P. Rönnbäck (2003) "Ecosystem Services of the Tropical Seascape: Interactions, Substitutions and Restoration". *Ocean & Coastal Management* 46: 27–46.

Nicholls, R.J. (2011) "Planning for the Impacts of Sea Level Rise". *Oceanography* 24: 144–157.

NRC [National Research Council] (2009) *Informing Decisions in a Changing Climate*. Washington, DC: National Academies Press.

NYSSLRTF [New York State Sea Level Rise Task Force] (2010) *Report to the Legislature*. Albany, NY. Available at <http://www.dec.ny.gov/docs/administration_pdf/slrtffinalrep.pdf> (accessed 16 October 2012).

Poulter, B. and P.N. Halpin (2008) "Raster Modeling of Coastal Flooding from Sea-level Rise". *International Journal of Geographical Information Science* 22: 167–182.

Renaud, F. and R. Perez (2010) "Climate Change Vulnerability and Adaptation Assessments". *Sustainability Science* 5: 155–157.

Rosenzweig, C. and W. Solecki (2010) "Introduction to Climate Change Adaptation in New York City: Building a Risk Management Response". *Annals of the New York Academy of Sciences* 1196: 13–18.

Sapountzaki, K. et al. (2011) "Disconnected Policies and Actors and the Missing Role of Spatial Planning throughout the Risk Management Cycle". *Natural Hazards* 59(3): 1445–1474.

Schimmel, S.C., S.J. Benyl and C.J. Strobel (1999) "An Assessment of the Ecological Condition of Long Island Sound, 1990–1993". *Environmental Monitoring and Assessment* 56: 27–49.

Scyphers, S.B. et al. (2011) "Oyster Reefs as Natural Breakwaters Mitigate Shoreline Loss and Facilitate Fisheries". *PLoS ONE* 6(8): e22396.

Seavey, J.R., B. Gilmer and K. McGarigal (2010) "Effect of Sea-level Rise on Piping Plover (*Charadrius melodus*) Breeding Habitat". *Biological Conservation* 144: 393–401.

Shepard, C., C. Crain and M.W. Beck (2011) "The Protective Role of Coastal Marshes: A Systematic Review and Metaanalysis". *PLoS ONE* 6(11): e27374.

Shepard, C. et al. (2012) "Assessing Future Risk: Quantifying the Effects of Sea Level Rise on Storm Surge Risk for the Southern Shores of Long Island, New York". *Natural Hazards* 60(2): 727–745.

Sheppard, C. et al. (2005) "Coral Mortality Increases Wave Energy Reaching Shores Protected by Reef Flats in the Seychelles". *Estuarine, Coastal and Shelf Science* 64: 223–234.

Smith, J., R. Klein and S. Huq (eds) (2003) *Climate Change Adaptive Capacity and Development*. London: Imperial College Press.

Tanner, T.M. and T. Mitchell (eds) (2008) *Poverty in a Changing Climate*. Institute of Development Studies, University of Sussex, UK.

UNISDR [United Nations International Strategy for Disaster Reduction] (2011) *2011 Global Assessment Report on Disaster Risk Reduction: Revealing Risk, Redefining Development*. New York: United Nations.

US Census Bureau (2000) "American FactFinder", <http://factfinder2.census.gov/faces/nav/jsf/pages/index.xhtml> (accessed 26 October 2012).

Weiss, J.L., J.T. Overpeck and B. Strauss (2011) "Implications of Recent Sea Level Rise Science for Low-elevation Areas in Coastal Cities of the Conterminous USA". *Climatic Change* 105: 635–645.

World Bank (2009) *Convenient Solutions to an Inconvenient Truth: Ecosystem-based Approaches to Climate Change*. Washington, DC: World Bank.

World Bank and United Nations (2010) *Natural Hazards, UnNatural Disasters: The Economics of Effective Prevention*. Washington, DC: World Bank.

7

A coastal adaptation strategy for the City of Cape Town: An ecosystem-based management approach towards risk reduction

Darryl Colenbrander, Penny Price, Gregg Oelofse and Sakhile Tsotsobe

Introduction

The coastal City of Cape Town (CCT) is located on the south-western tip of Africa in the Western Province of South Africa. It is home to approximately 3.8 million people, which constitutes about 65 per cent of the province's population, making it the major urban centre of the province. Population densities vary according to income group, with high-income areas (for example, Fish Hoek, Camps Bay, Durbanville) having relatively low densities, ranging from 0 to 50 persons/hectare (Figure 7.1), compared with low-income areas (for example, Khayelitsha, Nyanga, Imizamo Yethu), which have high densities ranging from 100 to 500 persons/hectare (Turok et al., 2010).[1]

The Cape Town metropolis constitutes the second-largest economy in South Africa in terms of gross domestic product (GDP), contributing 11.1 per cent to national GDP (CCT, 2009). In 2005, unemployment in the CCT was at 20.7 per cent, with many of the unemployed living in informal settlements (Rodriques et al., 2006). This spatial concentration of poverty (Figure 7.2), largely a result of apartheid, provides a spatial dimension to socioeconomic vulnerability in Cape Town.[2] Although headway has been made towards a unified non-racial society, South Africa still bears the spatial legacy of its racially divided past. The variance in population density is indicative of the ongoing challenge of a dual economy characterized by pervasive income inequality in South Africa as a whole. If

The role of ecosystems in disaster risk reduction, Renaud, Sudmeier-Rieux and Estrella (eds), United Nations University Press, 2013, ISBN 978-92-808-1221-3

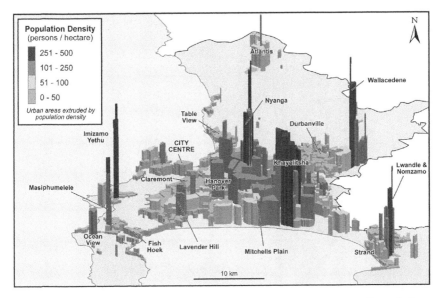

Figure 7.1 The distribution of the resident population across the City of Cape Town, 2001
Source: Turok et al. (2010).

examined within Blaikie's Pressure and Release model, the legacy of these racially driven structures, although shifting, remains one of the root causes of socioeconomic vulnerability in South Africa (Blaikie et al., 1994).

The city's economy is heavily reliant on a tertiary sector dominated by finance and business services, trade, tourism, etc. This reliance on the tertiary sector highlights an economic vulnerability implicit in an economy lacking diversity. This compounds the need to protect and develop alternative economies that focus on existing opportunities such as scenic beauty, lifestyle opportunities, a range of outdoor activities, and a "sense of place" that largely constitute Cape Town's global attractiveness, both as a tourist destination and as a place to live. The city's coast[3] provides a variety of goods and services, which include tourism and recreation (for example, water sports), economic and employment opportunities, desirable residential areas, discharge of stormwater and the assimilation of pollutants originating from land-based activities, filming and events, etc. It is the potential that the coast holds and its centrality to Cape Town's economy that necessitate proactive interventions to protect the coast and to further harness its potential as a means to

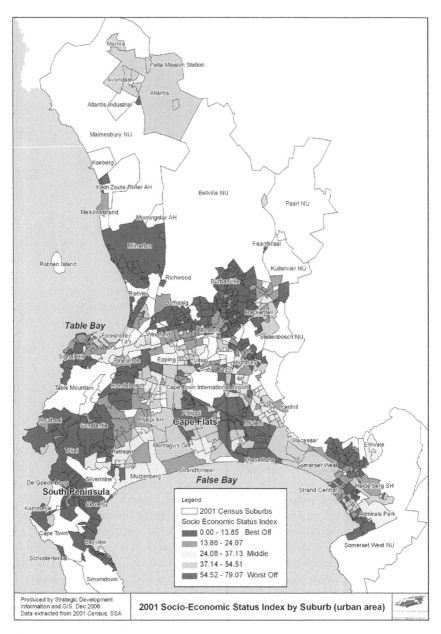

Figure 7.2 Map of Cape Town illustrating the spatial legacy of apartheid planning still evident in post-apartheid South African cities
Source: Map extracted from CCT (2005); data extracted from the 2001 census, Statistics South Africa.

improve the livelihoods of previously disadvantaged communities into the future.

The city's coastline spans 307 km in total, 240 km of which is managed by the municipality, with the remainder being managed by the iconic Table Mountain National Park (CCT, 2010a). The coastline of Cape Town is arguably one of its greatest socioeconomic and environmental assets and has the potential, if managed optimally, to play a significant role in the economic development and prosperity of the city. Paradoxically, however, such an extensive coastline, the interface between a complex socioeconomic built environment and a highly dynamic, storm-prone marine environment, poses a significant risk to the city.[4] A lack of proactive ecosystem-based risk reduction efforts against the projected impacts of climate change,[5] such as sea level rise, shifts in the duration and intensity of predominant wind regimes and subsequent erosion, may lead to reactive and unplanned "crisis management" measures. Although in the short term these crisis management measures may reduce the risk from storm surges and coastal erosion, there is real concern that such measures may have negative and irreversible socioeconomic and environmental impacts into the future.

The ability of coastal ecosystems to provide regulatory, provisional and cultural services is being reduced owing to a number of factors and pressures in addition to impacts related to climate change. The most prominent of these factors are the fragmentation and loss of natural areas, degradation of terrestrial ecosystems owing to unregulated recreational activities and inappropriate development, erosion and damage to sensitive coastal dune systems, inappropriately located buildings and infrastructure, and strip development (see Figure 7.3), which has also resulted in the privatization of sections of the coast.[6] Gaining access to the coast and the beach (as a public right) has become difficult in some areas as a consequence.

Although these are significant pressures, they are symptomatic of a lack of a strategic city-wide coastal planning and decision support framework and the subsequent ad hoc decision-making surrounding coastal planning and development. To address this, the CCT is in the process of developing a coastal set-back line. This is in effect a spatial planning mechanism that intends to guide and inform decisions relating to coastal development more effectively. The CCT is developing this as a key coastal adaptation strategy that focuses on harnessing ecosystems services as a means to minimize risk to the city from coastal hazards. Because this strategy is largely dependent upon functioning ecosystems, it becomes critical to manage the development pressures surrounding these coastal ecosystems.

Figure 7.3 Strip development of residential properties along the coast
Source: Colenbrander (2009).

Addressing the legacy of apartheid through coastal development

The current expansion rate of approximately 12 km² per annum of the physical urban footprint (primarily driven by in-migration and population growth rates) requires that the CCT plans for approximately 25,000 additional low-income households each year. With a housing backlog of approximately 330,000 units, demand is increasingly outstripping supply, resulting in a burgeoning informal settlement growth rate of 13 per cent per annum (CCT, 2005, 2009). The growth of informal settlements predominantly in the south-east of the city, combined with the concentration of new housing projects in this part of the city, places increasing pressures on undeveloped coastal land (CCT, 2005). This south-east quadrant of the city is bounded on one side by False Bay (Figure 7.2), a large (over 1,000 km²) relatively shallow bay (80 metres maximum depth) with a coastline characterized by long stretches of beach divided by rocky headlands (Du Plessis and Glass, 1991). This area constitutes the southern end of an extensive low-lying flat plain of deep sand referred to as

Figure 7.4 Informal settlement in the Cape Flats, Cape Town
Photo: City of Cape Town, 2007.

the Cape Flats, which connects Table Bay in the north and False Bay in the south.

Exposed to south-easterly wind-driven sand in the summer, the Cape Flats was historically characterized by partially vegetated and shifting dune systems. When the Group Areas Act (Act no. 41 of 1950) came into force under the National Party's apartheid laws, thousands of non-white Cape Town residents were relocated out of the city centre to the Cape Flats – the windswept sandy outskirts of town – in what was regarded as "environmental apartheid". Low-income housing and informal settlements increasingly characterized this area throughout the apartheid years. The spatial legacy of the apartheid era remains largely intact today (Figure 7.4). Then as now, few of these areas extend to the coastline, leaving a large swathe of undeveloped open land consisting largely of partially vegetated dunes (Figure 7.5). Such areas are characterized by harsh environmental conditions.

Today, owing to pressure for land to address the burgeoning housing backlog within the city boundaries, this coastal land is seen as an attractive area to meet these demands. These remaining dune systems, however, function as an important biodiversity corridor as well as acting as a

Figure 7.5 Open swathes of undeveloped land in the Cape Flats area
Photo: City of Cape Town, 2008.

natural buffer against storm surges, thereby providing a valuable regulatory service to the city. The value of this service is set to increase in the
future considering sea level rise and predicted increases in the intensity
and frequency of storm surges (Brundrit, 2008). Debates on the future of
this highly contested land, although diverse, are underpinned by the need
to redress the inequalities of the past through livelihood improvement
while simultaneously reducing vulnerability to coastal hazards.

If examined through vulnerability theory, the vulnerabilities being addressed by the arguments cannot be captured in one framework, but
rather span a number of vulnerability frameworks. For example, open
spaces are often hotspots for crime. Retaining open spaces through an
ecosystem-based approach has at times been perceived by local communities as indirectly contributing to crime because such open and unlit
spaces tend to harbour criminal activities. In surrounding communities,
there is a perception that, in removing open "green" spaces through developing these spaces, crime is reduced. In this sense, crime-related activities on this open land can be seen as a "dynamic pressure" in Blaikie's
Progression of Vulnerability. The need to promote direct access to the
coast in an attempt to redress the apartheid planning legacy aligns in some
respects with Amartya Sen's Entitlement Approach, whereas in Blaikie's
model this is seen as a root cause. The desirability of retaining the dunes

Figure 7.6 Camps Bay, a typical example of a highly developed and affluent coastal area in the South Peninsula
Photo: City of Cape Town, 2005.

as a natural buffer against storm surges and projected sea level rise in turn fits under an ecosystem-based approach to reducing vulnerability (Blaikie et al., 1994; Sen, 1986). These socioeconomic dimensions and their linkages to ecosystem-based management are discussed in more detail in the section on "Key challenges".

In stark contrast to the Cape Flats is the South Peninsula (Figure 7.6), which is characterized by a chain of mountains with a narrow strip of largely developed land situated between the mountains and the sea. Unlike the Cape Flats, most of this area was historically designated for "white residential" use under the racially dividing Group Areas Act. This area is generally more sheltered from the elements and in many instances elevated, affording excellent views. The sea views from the beachfront and convenient access to the extensive beaches on both sides of the mountain chain of the South Peninsula resulted in many historical developments being built very close to the beach. In some cases these developments have been built on reclaimed land. These areas are expected to become more vulnerable to storm surges and sea level rise. In contrast to the False Bay coastline, where the focus is on entitlement, access and historical redress, the focus in the South Peninsula is directed towards maintaining the status quo – the lifestyle and the "sense of place" associated with it.

Although both areas are vulnerable to storm surges and sea level rise, the socioeconomic vulnerabilities underpinning the two areas differ greatly. The residents of the Cape Flats, having experienced decades of racial oppression, have reduced access to the coastline and a strong sense of entitlement has been generated. This limited access in some respects reduces their vulnerability to the projected increases in sea level rise, storm surges and other dynamic coastal processes such as wind-driven dune migration. If hazard exposure were the same, however, the historical oppression and related poverty would reduce their capacity to cope in the face of disaster. The wealthier residents of the South Peninsula, on the other hand, potentially have a greater coping capacity owing to their socioeconomic advantages, such as having the choice of where to live and access to insurance. However, these socioeconomic "benefits" have, in some respects, resulted in their increased physical vulnerability by choosing to live in highly desirable but high-risk locations.

Both these examples of the Cape Flats and the South Peninsula give a clear indication that disaster risks need to be proactively managed. These examples also reflect the differing spectrum of interests that need to be considered in the process of managing risk at a local government level. Accommodating these vastly differing interests within the same risk reduction strategy is key to the success of such a strategy. Equally important is that, in this process of developing a risk reduction strategy, the CCT makes decisions that are in the interests of the broader community rather than a select few. Before developing a risk reduction strategy, it is important to develop an understanding of the concept of vulnerability and the city's risk profile.

Current risk and vulnerability

The previous section has highlighted the growing strategic importance and value of the coast from a socioeconomic perspective. This section has also described how Cape Town's socioeconomic and biophysical attributes have increased the city's vulnerability, often compounded by the historical legacy of apartheid's racially determined urban planning. The term "vulnerability" in itself is subjective and requires careful consideration, along with the other key concepts used to describe and frame vulnerability. In seeking to gain a better understanding of the vulnerabilities underpinning the city's risk profile from the perspective of storm surges and sea level rise, the CCT has undertaken a Sea-Level Rise Risk Assessment. Not only has this assessment improved the understanding of risk and vulnerability specific to the Cape Town context, but it has investigated approaches towards managing this risk. Key to this is the ecosystem-based management approach. This section will investigate this approach in more detail as the city's primary and most sustainable option towards adapting to climate change and reducing the city's risk profile.

Understanding vulnerability and risk

Understanding vulnerability is fundamental to the process of effectively adapting to impacts induced by climate change. As such, a key requirement of the Sea-Level Rise Risk Assessment was to generate information and knowledge and transform this knowledge into practical applications, in order to effectively manage risk and promote sustainable coastal development. In understanding the different dimensions of vulnerability within the context of a complex urban setting such as Cape Town, and with a view to converting this knowledge into practical outcomes, it was critical that the city adopt a multidisciplinary approach in conducting this assessment and developing adaptation responses.

As a starting point to understanding risk from sea level rise and storm surges, a Geographic Information System (GIS) was used to develop a risk model. This model spatially demarcates areas that may be physically affected by, and therefore vulnerable to, storm surges and sea level rise. This model has determined three inundation scenarios (Figure 7.7), which are based on the modelling of storm surges in conjunction with incremental sea level rise over the next 25 years.[7] When this model is overlaid

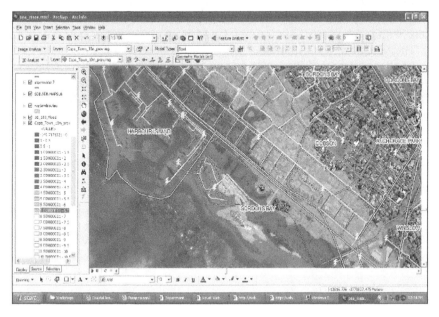

Figure 7.7 A screen-shot of the GIS Inundation Model depicting three temporary inundation scenarios, overlaid with the city's service infrastructure
Source: City of Cape Town (Environmental Resource Management Department).

Please see page 482 for a colour version of this figure.

Table 7.1 Quantifying the risk

25 years	Inundation level 1	Inundation level 2	Inundation level 3
Sea level	2.5 m	4.5 m	6.5 m
Probability in next 25 years	95 per cent	85 per cent	20 per cent
Threatened value	R5.2 billion (US$500 million)	R23.8 billion (US$2.3 billion)	R54.8 billion (US$5.4 billion)
Value at risk	R4.9 billion (US$490 million)	R20.2 billion (US$2 billion)	R11.0 billion (US$1.1 billion)

Source: Phase 3 of the Sea-Level Rise Risk Assessment (Cartwright, 2008).

with aerial imagery as well as critical city infrastructure, the city can begin to identify locations and infrastructure that are physically exposed and therefore vulnerable to damage and flooding from storm surges, as well as determine the degrees of this vulnerability.

Based on the spatial demarcation of these three inundation scenarios, the model estimates that an area covering approximately 25 km² is highly vulnerable to inundation from storm surges within the next 25 years. The value of exposed infrastructure within this area is estimated at R5 billion (Table 7.1) (Cartwright, 2008). Since completion of this risk assessment in 2010, the city has already experienced pockets of damage to infrastructure within this zone (inundation level 1) from storm surge events.

The values at risk in Table 7.1 have been derived via a formula that multiplies the probability of the respective inundation scenarios by the sum of the damage inflicted by the respective events.[8] This damage is captured by three proxy variables, namely the sum of private property loss, the loss of tourism revenue and the loss of public infrastructure. This formula is shown as:

$$\mathbf{R_e} = f_e \Sigma(\text{loss of private property value} + \text{loss of tourism revenue} + \text{loss of public infrastructure}),$$

where f_e represents the probability of a sea level rise event e, where "e" is a sea level rise event as described in scenarios 1–3 (Cartwright, 2008).

The figures in Table 7.1 represent the cumulative cost over a 25-year period for the entire area covered by the three inundation scenarios. It must be noted that the city will not be exposed to the full extent of the inundation scenarios across the entire coastline based on a single event. This is because the degree of inundation from storms is dependent upon a number of biophysical factors, which are localized.

The model is based on the assumption that the coast of Cape Town is a homogeneous environment and thus has applied a "blanket"

Figure 7.8 Examples of highly vulnerable areas in Cape Town
Source: City of Cape Town (Environmental Resource Management Department).

Please see page 483 for a colour version of this figure.

methodology to determine inundation scenarios. There are, however, local biophysical factors that have an impact on the "fetch" of storm surges, which affects the physical vulnerability of various locations. It is therefore important to understand these factors in managing this risk. These factors include aspects such as bathymetry, swell shadow, presence of kelp forests, wave focusing and swell refraction (Brundrit, 2009). In recognition of these influences and to disaggregate risk per location through "fine-tuning" the model, Phase 5 of the Risk Assessment was undertaken (Brundrit, 2009). Based on the fine-scale investigation of local biophysical factors, the CCT has identified a number of highly vulnerable areas along the coastline (Figure 7.8).

Managing existing vulnerability and risk

The identification of areas of high vulnerability to storm surges and sea level rise requires that the CCT actively manages these areas in the future. A key challenge, however, is the management of infrastructure and property currently at risk from storm surges and coastal erosion. There are

Figure 7.9 Private property in Milnerton at risk from storm surge events and coastal erosion
Photo: City of Cape Town, 2008.

numerous locations in Cape Town where privately owned properties are at risk but cannot simply be relocated (Figure 7.9).[9]

Under South African legislation, no organ of state[10] is responsible for protecting private property against coastal erosion and storm surges, unless that organ of state was or is directly responsible for the erosion and increased exposure to storm surges (Department of Environmental Affairs, 2008). As with several cases along the city's coastline, private property owners simply do not have the financial means to invest in hard-engineered sea defence mechanisms.[11] The end result is unregulated and ad hoc interventions by private property owners to protect their property that greatly increase the scope for maladaptation (see Figure 7.10).[12] This phenomenon is not limited to private property owners; the CCT has also been responsible for such ad hoc responses in the past. In an attempt to address this issue and to promote a strategic and consistent approach towards managing property at risk from storm surges and coastal erosion at a city-wide scale, a multi-criteria assessment tool is in the process of being developed. This tool is intended to more effectively assist in the decision-making process through creating an enabling platform to deter-

Figure 7.10 Ad hoc and unregulated approaches to coastal erosion and storm surge defence
Photo: City of Cape Town, 2008.

mine a consensus on the most appropriate way forward (Brundrit, 2009; Cartwright, 2009).[13]

Managing risk into the future: An ecosystem-based approach

A key factor aggravating physical vulnerability in many locations (such as Neptune's Isle and Milnerton) along Cape Town's Atlantic coastline is the extent to which the coastline is becoming more and more altered and "fixed" through artificial surfaces.[14] This has two primary impacts. First, by encroaching into the space in which coastal dynamic processes take place, the built environment of the city is exposed to increasing hazards; that is, the potential for damage to coastal infrastructure from coastal erosion is increased. Secondly, by reducing the spatial scale of these open and dynamic areas through encroachment, the critical threshold that ecosystems require to remain functional is lost.[15] Encroachment into sand dune systems along Cape Town's coast helps to illustrate these points (see Figure 7.11).

Figure 7.11 Dune cordons in Table View indicating the narrow belt into which they have been restricted (historically, these dunes extended hundreds of metres inland)
Source: City of Cape Town (Environmental Resource Management Department).

Sand dunes provide a critical buffer against storm surge events (see Chapter 2 in this volume). The functionality of these systems is dependent upon a critical mass in terms of the spatial scale of these systems. Because these dunes have been restricted to a narrow coastal belt (Figure 7.11), embryo and primary dunes are "cut off" from much larger systems. As a result of the cross-scale dependence of such systems, frontal dune cordons in heavily developed areas can no longer achieve a state of dynamic equilibrium as they would naturally do. They have therefore become artificial systems requiring management interventions, such as irrigation, to "hold" them in place. The end result is the reduced effectiveness of dunes in buffering city infrastructure against storm surges as well as increased expenditure by the city to maintain these dunes by artificial means (CSIR, 1989; Illenberger, 2008). The degradation of dune systems reflects the broader problem of hard infrastructure encroaching into the space of sensitive and dynamic coastal ecosystems.

This section has highlighted several examples showing the impacts of dynamic coastal processes on city infrastructure. The environmental coastal system in itself, however, is not responsible for increasing the city's risk profile. It is rather the interaction of dynamic coastal processes, climate change pressures, the location of infrastructure along the coast and, most critically, the decisions that are taken with regard to the location of infrastructure that creates this vulnerability (Colenbrander et al., 2012). The CCT realizes it must be proactive in preventing the number of exposed locations[16] such as Neptune's Isle and Milnerton from increasing into the future. This requires that the city develop a mechanism that more effectively shapes and informs decisions relating to coastal development at a city-wide scale.

Finding the balance: Promoting an ecosystem-based management approach while addressing socioeconomic imperatives

A critical ecosystem service within the context of managing coastal risk is the ability of dune ecosystems and coastal wetlands to provide an effective buffer against storm surges. These remaining open spaces as functional ecosystems are located within rural and, to a lesser extent, peri-urban areas in Cape Town, including parts of the False Bay coastline of the Cape Flats. Such areas, however, are becoming subject to increasing pressures from development and require some form of protection if the coast is to be retained as an asset to the city.

Retaining open spaces and harnessing ecosystem services to promote a risk-averse approach to urban development is only one step in the broader process of building a resilient coastal city. Another factor is remaining sensitive to the combined historical legacy and current socioeconomic complexities that characterize Cape Town and taking these into account in the decision-making process of balancing development with coastal ecosystem protection. Short- to medium-term economic imperatives are primarily driving the nature and priority of government strategies. Not only are development and growth required to sustain an increasing population, but South Africa has recently emerged from an unequal and difficult history (Glavovic, 2006). The national government is using development as a tool to address the inequalities of the past and to generate socioeconomic upliftment. The approach of using development to promote economic development is formally represented by the Accelerated and Shared Growth Initiative for South Africa (AsgiSA).[17] Owing to the perception that coastal frontage property equates to economic wealth and gain, with the strategic benefits (notably transport) of being located close to the coast, coastal areas are being targeted as key growth points.[18]

There is a perception that, by connecting previously disadvantaged communities to the coast via development, not only will the livelihoods of coastal communities be improved but the status and desirability of such areas will also be increased (Colenbrander et al., 2011). Using coastal development as a means to address socioeconomic issues is, however, contributing to the existing and longer-term pressures along the coast. This will both increase the vulnerability of newly established coastal developments and dependable communities, through the loss of ecosystems and their services, and also ultimately lock the city into an economic burden through having to protect and maintain such developments from the impact of sea level rise and coastal erosion in the future (Brundrit, 2009; Cartwright, 2009).

As the above discussion illustrates, careful consideration is necessary within this complex social-ecological system,[19] requiring a balance between promoting an ecosystem-based management approach while simultaneously addressing socioeconomic imperatives. Although this balance is achievable, addressing and shifting perceptions where such goals are perceived as being mutually exclusive and obstructive becomes equally important.

A key challenge at this stage is to achieve interdisciplinary solutions and to channel such solutions through an effective adaptation strategy. Because these issues are largely spatial in nature, the CCT is in the process of developing a coastal set-back line as a key spatial planning and urban design mechanism. The intention of the set-back line is essentially to guide city planning decisions relating to coastal development, with the aim of achieving three main outcomes. First, by determining a development-free zone along the coast, the functionality of ecosystems is retained, thereby improving the flow of ecosystem services to the city. Secondly, the retention of open spaces along the coast promotes the coast as a shared and common resource. This is important considering South Africa's history of racially determined exclusion. Thirdly, and as previously discussed, by retaining these remaining open spaces and coastal ecosystems, the CCT will prevent existing problems of infrastructure currently at risk from coastal erosion and storm surges from recurring and increasing in the future. The city realizes that, through protecting natural processes and the associated goods and services provided, the CCT has the potential to reduce risk over the long term.

Protecting coastal ecosystems requires that activities seaward of the set-back are regulated. The set-back is essentially represented by a line on a map, which is reflected in the city's Spatial Development Framework and Integrated Zoning Schemes. The position of this line effectively guides decisions for planning and regulation purposes both strategically and systematically.

The CCT has applied a transdisciplinary and broadly consultative approach towards better understanding the coastal "fabric". This approach has led to an enhanced understanding of the coastal space in that both its "hard" (physical) and its "soft" (socioeconomic) aspects and the connections between the two as coupled systems are understood. Knowledge of

Figure 7.12 The coastal set-back overlaid with the GIS Inundation Model
Source: CCT (2010a).

Please see page 484 for a colour version of this figure.

these issues and the nature of these connections is critical in determining the physical position of the set-back line and the associated zone it defines. Examples of "soft" aspects include the need to promote access to the coast and coastal resources for previously disadvantaged communities, to conserve the coastal aesthetics/sense of place and to retain the recreational and amenity value of the coast. Appropriate areas have been identified for future nodal development (Figure 7.12),[20] creating access to the coast for communities while also promoting a risk-averse approach to sea level rise and storm surge events. Examples of "hard" or more quantitative aspects include the threat that sea level rise and storm surge events pose to coastal communities and city infrastructure, the need to protect biodiversity and coastal ecological corridors and the need to reduce the exposure of coastal infrastructure to dynamic coastal processes (CCT, 2011a).

Although these aspects have been listed as separate "entities" for determining the position of the set-back, it is important to acknowledge the connectivity between these entities. For example, through the protection of coastal biodiversity, not only is the sense of place and coastal aesthetics retained, but the buffer potential that these natural systems provide is enhanced. This both reduces risk from an economic perspective and the transfer of risk to city ratepayers (it is ultimately the ratepayers who pay for the protection of city infrastructure against dynamic coastal processes)[21] and improves the recreational and amenity value of the coast.[22] The recognition that these systems are linked is critical in promoting an integrated and transdisciplinary approach to determining the CCT's coastal set-back. The end result is a variable zone that recognizes and accommodates both the "hard" and the "soft" issues and achieves a balance between socioeconomic imperatives while promoting an ecosystem-based management approach. This approach also departs from the conventional method of defining zones based on arbitrary and fixed distances from the high water mark. This zone is therefore defined within a more relative and holistic context.

Key challenges

The successful implementation of the CCT's coastal set-back line as a key planning intervention relies on a supporting legislative environment that will enable the realization of its intent. As such, the CCT is currently in the process of developing a Coastal Protection By-Law that aims to provide for the protection, regulation and integrated management of the space between the set-back and the sea (CCT, 2011a). Acceptance of the Coastal Protection By-Law by the city and the success of its implementation rest on the ability of the municipality to follow through with the necessary financial commitment and institutional support. However, such a commitment is evaluated against other priorities, including the need to connect previously disadvantaged communities to the coast.

Coastal regulations: Apartheid reinventing itself?

As indicated in previous sections, the legacy of the apartheid system has created a sense of mistrust on the part of the previously disenfranchised communities towards policies that appear to seek to restrict development in the coastal zone. Historically, separate development was imposed on the South African population. This often resulted in non-white communities being located in geographically undesirable areas of a town or city (such as the Cape Flats), with the desirable areas being reserved exclusively for white residents. This included access to beaches: most "nice" beaches were reserved for use by white people only.

Glaring examples of this environmental apartheid are the False Bay coastal recreational facilities, which were located in exposed and environmentally harsh areas. These areas are characterized by extremely windy

Figure 7.13 Infrastructure damaged by storm surge events at Monwabisi on the Cape Flats
Photo: City of Cape Town, 2007.

conditions and are subject to frequent large-scale cross-shore transport of wind-blown sand. Moreover, these recreational facilities are inappropriately located on exposed shorelines, rendering any infrastructure associated with these facilities vulnerable to storm surge events (Figure 7.13).

In some cases, the facilities have become so derelict because of their inappropriate location that they are no longer functional and have been abandoned (Figure 7.14). As representations of apartheid planning, these facilities not only absorb large proportions of municipal expenditure because of high maintenance costs but also attract and harbour anti-social behaviour.

To prevent inappropriate development and the associated problems from recurring and increasing in the future, coastal development needs to be more effectively regulated through mechanisms such as the CCT's setback. However, constraints imposed on development as a result of environmental concerns are often construed as anti-development where previously disadvantaged communities are now restricted from obtaining the same benefits that the privileged received in the past. According to Leck et al. (2011: 7) the injustice of the past "remains firmly entrenched

Figure 7.14 A derelict water slide at the Macassar recreational facility, Cape Flats
Photo: City of Cape Town, 2008.

in cultural memories and presents a possible formidable barrier to climate change adaptation, as poor and marginalized people often consider environmental protection to be about conserving nature for the benefit of the privileged few". As a consequence, many of the previously disadvantaged communities view attempts at restricting development within the remaining open spaces (a significant proportion of which occur along the coastline where poverty is rife) by means of a set-back as apartheid reinventing itself under the guise of "environmental risk management concerns" (Colenbrander et al., 2012).

In the process of developing the city's set-back line, and to address concerns about the environmental agenda, the CCT has undertaken a broad-scale public participatory process. This approach of deliberation and participation is critical for generating a better understanding, especially amongst the poor, of the negative and long-term implications of developing within areas of high environmental risk. Within this process, it is critical that conceptions of the environmental agenda are broadened so that a better understanding of the relationship between sound environmental management and poverty alleviation is achieved (Leck, 2011; Parnell et al., 2007).

Conflict between growing the city's rates base and retaining open spaces

As outlined in the Introduction to this chapter, the city's population is characterized by stark socioeconomic inequalities, necessitating the allocation of financial resources in a way that favours immediate service delivery imperatives over other priorities such as longer-term, less certain coastal climate change adaptability. This is illustrated by the escalation in the budget allocation for the period 2006–2013 for utility services – such as electricity, water, wastewater management and waste management – from approximately R5.5 billion to R16.0 billion. Moreover, budget allocations for infrastructure (roads, stormwater systems) and community services (clinics, libraries) more than doubled over the same period (CCT, 2011b). This is indicative of how measures to affect management seaward of the city's set-back line are likely to compete with these broader imperatives.

The set-back line is reflected as a boundary in the CCT's Spatial Development Framework. The demarcation of the set-back is inherently a highly contested issue, because it has implications not only for human settlement but also for commercial opportunities. From the city's economic development perspective, the development restrictions that apply seaward of the set-back line mean that the CCT is forgoing potential revenue, which would have been derived through the provision of utility services and the generation of rates. It would be a complicated exercise to estimate the potential revenue from unrestricted development in the coastal zone. However, considering that utility services generally provide approximately 58 per cent of the total income budget for the metropolis (CCT, 2011b), it is reasonable to assume that the missed potential revenue is significant. Moreover, the tourism, property and other commercial sectors would also lament the missed income opportunities available in the coastal zone.

Crime

The merits of preferring nodal development over strip development become diluted in the opposing arguments around what is perceived to be the continued constraining of historically disadvantaged communities from enjoying the benefits of the coastal space. Through the development restrictions associated with the set-back, the CCT intends to prevent this type of irresponsible development by advocating for nodal development as opposed to strip development (CCT, 2011c).

As much as nodal development is regarded as the solution for appropriate spatial planning, there are unintended negative consequences.

In ensuring the retention of open spaces, intermittently interrupted by pockets of developed areas, nodal development can inadvertently create opportunities for criminal activities. Cape Town, according to the United Nations, has one of the highest murder rates in the world, with a rate of over 40 per 100,000 people (United Nations Human Settlement Programme, 2007). As described in the Introduction, open coastal land along the northern shore of False Bay is characterized by vegetated or partially vegetated dunes. Because there is limited human activity in this area, it is often exploited by criminal elements, who take refuge here with the intention of actively participating in crime or evading law enforcement officers. This ensuing threat to public safety is thought to have the potential to compromise public support for nodal development and therefore for the retention of intact coastal ecosystems.

Conclusion

This case study has clearly indicated that climate change impacts, as manifested through sea level rise and increased storminess, pose a significant threat to the City of Cape Town. At an empirical level, this risk has been quantified and substantiated through the CCT's Sea-Level Rise Risk Assessment. This study has also shown that the city's racially divided past, socioeconomic attributes and physical characteristics all contribute significantly to the city's risk profile. Considering the variables that contribute to this risk profile, it is imperative that a transdisciplinary approach be adopted both to better understand these factors and to convert this knowledge into adaptation strategies that cope with this complexity.

This chapter has highlighted the importance of understanding and incorporating "hard" physical issues as well as the more conceptual, subtle or "soft" issues in developing practical and workable adaptation strategies. In developing the coastal set-back, the CCT has identified the coastal issues and used them as key factors in determining the position and placement of the set-back. The "hard" issues include vulnerability to inundation from sea level rise and storm surges, coastal dynamic processes and the presence of biodiversity networks. The more conceptual issues include social aspects such as the need to promote access to the coast as a shared and common resource, to retain the aesthetics and sense of place of the coastal landscape and to retain the recreational and amenity value of the coast. Although these issues have been listed in isolation, this chapter has shown that they are strongly interlinked and in effect function as a coupled system. This chapter has also shown that central to the resolution of the coastal issues experienced in Cape Town is the presence and preservation of healthy coastal ecosystems.

The coastal set-back, the CCT's most critical spatial planning and coastal adaptation tool, is based on the ability to retain and conserve the remaining coastal ecosystems. As this chapter has shown, however, this protectionist discourse is confronted by socioeconomic imperatives argued from an equally, if not more, emotive perspective that is entrenched in cultural memories and the subsequent need to address the injustices of the past.

In striving to find a balance between these similarly pressing needs and rights, dialogue becomes a critical tool in navigating a resolution. In this process, trade-offs are unavoidable. Although the development of the coastal set-back as a spatial planning and urban design adaptation mechanism is still work-in-progress, the CCT regards it as the most sustainable approach to addressing the coastal risks associated with climate change. The CCT's key challenge at this stage is taking decisions that are in the interests of the broader community and remaining objective and far-sighted in the process of weighing the trade-offs.

Notes

1. In terms of km^2, this equates to 0–500 persons/km^2 in high-income areas and 10,000–50,000 persons/km^2 in low-income areas.
2. The definition of vulnerability used throughout this chapter is taken from the United Nations International Strategy for Disaster Reduction's "Terminology on Disaster Risk Reduction", which defines vulnerability as "[t]he characteristics and circumstances of a community, system or asset that make it susceptible to the damaging effects of a hazard" (UNISDR, 2009: 30).
3. The coast in this context may be defined as the dynamic space between land and sea masses, where this transitional zone contributes either indirectly or directly to the livelihoods of people.
4. The definition of risk used in this chapter is "[t]he combination of the probability of an event and its negative consequences", as defined in UNISDR (2009: 25). In some instances in the chapter it refers more strongly to the probability of an event occurring, and in others the emphasis is placed on the consequences. However, when this is the case, the risk is usually referred to as "disaster risk", the UNISDR definition for disaster risk being "[t]he potential disaster losses, in lives, health status, livelihoods, assets and services, which could occur to a particular community or a society over some specified future time period" (2009: 9–10).
5. Ecosystem-based disaster risk reduction refers to an ecosystem management approach to reducing disaster risk. In this chapter, which focuses on risk reduction challenges posed primarily by climate change in the urban coastal zone, this approach shifts the need for ecosystem protection and management from a purely conservation argument to a critical green infrastructure perspective where ecosystems provide the regulatory, provision and cultural services necessary for human well-being.
6. "Strip development" means continuous mixed-use development along a road with in frequent access (CCT, 2010b).

7. For greater detail and explanation behind the model, refer to Phase 1 of the City of Cape Town's Sea-Level Rise Risk Assessment (Brundrit, 2008).

8. For greater detail and explanation behind derivations of values in Table 7.1, refer to Phase 3 of the City of Cape Town's Sea-Level Rise Risk Assessment (Cartwright, 2008).

9. There are many reasons for this, essentially revolving around the cost of such an approach and the lack of space in surrounding areas to relocate these buildings.

10. South Africa is governed by a three-tier system: national, provincial and local government.

11. Typically these would include seawalls, revetments, groynes, off-shore reefs and gabion structures.

12. Maladaptation is defined here as unintended negative consequences as a result of efforts to manage or adapt to climate change-related risks such as exposure of structures to storm surges and coastal erosion. In the case of Neptune Isle (see Figure 7.10), these ad hoc interventions have a significant negative impact on the tourism, recreational and amenity value of the area.

13. Determining the most appropriate course of action in respect of property at risk requires sensitive navigation through the multiple and often conflicting interests of the various stakeholders, from beach users, property owners, CCT officials to developers.

14. Phase 5 of the Sea-Level Rise Risk Assessment identified a total of 19 vulnerable locations along the coast of Cape Town (Cartwright, 2009: 13–14).

15. Functionality is defined as the ecosystem's ability to provide ecosystem services.

16. "Exposed" in this sense is defined in terms of physical exposure to storm surges. The determination of these vulnerable areas was a product of "fine-tuning" the GIS Inundation Model through more detailed and localized research into the following factors: wave set-up, wave run-up, coastal geology and the value and strategic nature of coastal development (Brundrit, 2009; Cartwright, 2009).

17. See <http://www.info.gov.za/asgisa/> (accessed 17 October 2012).

18. Five of the eight Spatial Development Initiatives identified by the South African government occur within coastal regions (Glazewski and Haward, 2005).

19. The theory of social-ecological systems is based on the notion that "social and ecological systems are in fact linked, and that delineation between social and natural systems is artificial and arbitrary" (Berkes et al., 1998: 4).

20. "Nodal development" means the significant and concentrated development in terms of scale, location, impact, diversity and agglomeration of function (facilities, services and economic activities) (CCT, 2010b).

21. Ratepayers pay fees to the CCT based on the value of the ratepayer's property. These fees are in turn used by the CCT to provide utility services to the property (e.g. electricity and water). Fees generally increase when more services are required. This includes the construction and maintenance of sea defence mechanisms in residential areas.

22. The nature of perceptions with regard to the retention and creation of open spaces differs according to a variety of factors including socioeconomic and cultural identities.

REFERENCES

Berkes, F., C. Folke and J. Colding (eds) (1998) *Linking Social and Ecological Systems: Management Practices and Social Mechanisms for Building Resilience.* Cambridge: Cambridge University Press.

Blaikie, P. et al. (1994) *At Risk: Natural Hazards, People's Vulnerability and Disasters.* London: Routledge.

Brundrit, G. (2008) *Global Climate Change and Adaption – A Sea-Level Rise Risk Assessment. Phase One: Sea Level Rise Model*. Report Prepared for the City of Cape Town Environmental Resource Management Department. Available at <http://www.capetown.gov.za/en/EnvironmentalResourceManagement/publications/Pages/Reportsand.aspx> (accessed 16 October 2012).

Brundrit, G. (2009) *Global Climate Change and Adaptation: City of Cape Town Sea-Level Rise Risk Assessment. Phase 5: Full Investigation of Alongshore Features of Vulnerability on the City of Cape Town Coastline, and Their Incorporation into the City of Cape Town Geographic Information System (GIS)*. Available at <http://www.capetown.gov.za/en/EnvironmentalResourceManagement/publications/Documents/Section_1_2_combined.pdf> (accessed 16 October 2012).

Cartwright, A. (2008) *Global Climate Change and Adaptation – A Sea-Level Rise Risk Assessment. Phase Three: Final Report. A Sea-Level Rise Risk Assessment for the City of Cape Town*. Report Prepared for the City of Cape Town Environmental Resource Management Department by Stockholm Environment Institute Cape Town. Available at <http://www.capetown.gov.za/en/EnvironmentalResourceManagement/publications/Pages/Reportsand.aspx> (accessed 16 October 2012).

Cartwright, A. (2009) *Global Climate Change and Adaptation: City of Cape Town Sea-level Rise Risk Assessment. Phase 5: Sea-Level Rise Vulnerability Assessment and Adaptation Options*. Available at <http://www.capetown.gov.za/en/EnvironmentalResourceManagement/publications/Documents/Section_1_2_combined.pdf> (accessed 16 October 2012).

CCT [City of Cape Town] (2005) "The Status of Cape Town: Development Overview". Presentation by K. Smith at "Cape Town 2025", Cape Town.

CCT (2009) "Cape Town Spatial Development Framework". Technical Report, Cape Town, South Africa.

CCT (2010a) "Enviroworks Special Edition: Marine and Coastal". Cape Town, South Africa.

CCT (2010b) "Draft Spatial Development Framework". Cape Town, South Africa.

CCT (2011a) "Coastal Protection Zone Management By-law: Draft for Comment". Cape Town, South Africa.

CCT (2011b) "City of Cape Town Budget 2010/11–2012/13", Cape Town, South Africa.

CCT (2011c) "Draft Cape Town Spatial Development Framework". Technical Report, Cape Town, South Africa.

Colenbrander, D. (2009) "Exploring Coastal Spaces: Towards Linking Social and Ecological Systems". Master's thesis, University of KwaZulu-Natal, Durban.

Colenbrander, D. et al. (2011) "Adaptation Strategies for the City of Cape Town: Finding the Balance within Social-Ecological Complexity". In K. Otto-Zimmermann (ed.), *Resilient Cities – Cities and Adaptation to Climate Change. Proceedings of the Global Forum 2010*. Dordrecht: Springer, pp. 311–318.

Colenbrander, D. et al. (2012) "Reducing the Pathology of Risk: Developing an Integrated Municipal Coastal Protection Zone for the City of Cape Town". In A. Cartwright, S. Parnell, G. Oelofse and S. Ward (eds), *Climate Change at the City Scale: Impacts, Mitigation and Adaptation in Cape Town*. London: Routledge.

CSIR [Council for Scientific and Industrial Research] (1989) "Woodbridge Island: Management of Coastal Dune Vegetation". CSIR, Stellenbosch.

Department of Environmental Affairs (2008) *Integrated Coastal Management Act.* Pretoria: Government Press.

Du Plessis, A. and J.G. Glass (1991) "The Geology of False Bay". In *Transactions of the Royal Society of South Africa* 47(4 & 5), *False Bay – An Environmental Assessment.* Cape Town: Royal Society of South Africa, pp. 495–518.

Glavovic, B.C. (2006) "The Evolution of Coastal Management in South Africa: Why Blood Is Thicker Than Water". *Ocean and Coastal Management* 49(12): 889–904.

Glazewski, J. and M. Haward (2005) "Towards Integrated Coastal Area Management: A Case Study in Co-operative Governance in South Africa". *International Journal of Marine and Coastal Law* 20(1): 66–84.

Illenberger, W. (2008) "Draft Revised Dune Management Plan for Dolphin Beach Complex, Cape Town".

Leck, H.J. (2011) "Rising to the Adaptation Challenge? Responding to Global Environmental Change in the Durban Metropolitan Region, South Africa" (working title). PhD thesis, work in prep.

Leck, H.J. et al. (2011) "Social and Cultural Barriers to Adaptation Implementation: The Case of South Africa". Paper produced for Institute of Global Dialogue, Johannesburg.

Parnell, S., D. Simon and C. Vogel (2007) "Global Environmental Change: Conceptualising the Growing Challenges for Cities in Poor Countries". *Area* 39(3): 357–369.

Rodriques, E., J. Gie and C. Haskins (2006) "Informal Dwelling Count (1993–2005) for Cape Town". Information and Knowledge Management Department, City of Cape Town.

Sen, A. (1986) "Food, Economics and Entitlements". *Lloyds Bank Review* 160: 1–20.

Turok, I., K. Sinclair-Smith and M. Shand (2010) "The Distribution of the Resident Population across the City of Cape Town, 2001". *Environment and Planning A* 42(10): 2295.

UNISDR [United Nations International Strategy for Disaster Reduction] (2009) "2009 UNISDR Terminology on Disaster Risk Reduction". United Nations, Geneva. Available at <http://www.unisdr.org/files/7817_UNISDRTerminologyEnglish.pdf> (accessed 16 October 2012).

United Nations Human Settlement Programme (2007) *Enhancing Urban Safety and Security: Global Report on Human Settlements 2007.* London: Earthscan.

8

Lessons from local initiatives on ecosystem-based climate change work in Tonga

Stavros Mavrogenis and Ilan Kelman

Introduction and background

Small Island Developing States

Small Island Developing States (SIDS), a group of 52 small countries and territories, have many vulnerabilities to anthropogenic climate change (for example, IPCC, 2007; Lewis, 1999; Pelling and Uitto, 2001). Impacts are likely to include sea level rise, changes to extreme weather regimes, sea water intrusion into freshwater supplies, ocean acidification and ecosystem changes affecting land- and sea-based food sources (for example, Byrne and Inniss, 2002; IPCC, 2007; Kelman and West, 2009; United Nations, 2005). Furthermore, SIDS are experiencing social challenges that interact with climate change, including rapid rural-to-urban migration, potential loss of languages and cultures through migration, and gender and ethnic inequalities (see a review by CICERO and UNEP/GRID-Arendal, 2008).

Despite the challenges, many SIDS communities display a long history of successful responses to social and environmental changes through sustainable livelihoods, although many other communities have been abandoned because they were unable to cope with change (see also discussion in Mercer, 2010; Nunn et al., 2007). The positive community experiences create hope for combining traditional and non-traditional practices to deal with disasters, including climate change, amongst other challenges

The role of ecosystems in disaster risk reduction, Renaud, Sudmeier-Rieux and Estrella (eds), United Nations University Press, 2013, ISBN 978-92-808-1221-3

faced by SIDS (for example, Mercer et al., 2009, 2010; Shaw et al., 2008, 2009).

One approach continually being developed and tested is community-based adaptation (CbA) to climate change. Reid et al. (2009: 13) define CbA for climate change as "a community-led process, based on communities' priorities, needs, knowledge, and capacities, which should empower people to plan for and cope with the impacts of climate change". A key element is "empowerment" – helping people to help themselves on their own terms (for example, for SIDS, see Mataki et al., 2007; Mercer et al., 2009, 2010; Warrick, 2009). To achieve this, Kelman et al. (2009) developed a CbA framework comprising a four-step process for establishing long-term cooperative partnerships between SIDS communities and external collaborators. As has long been established in the scientific literature (for example, Shaw et al., 2008, 2009; Wisner, 1995), the CbA framework emphasizes both local and external knowledge as complementary resources to be combined for successful CbA strategies.

Many CbA toolkits have been modified to improve how environmental aspects are factored in at the community level, aiming for ecosystem-based adaptation (EbA) to climate change (Marshall et al., 2009; Perez et al., 2010; Sudmeier-Rieux and Ash, 2009; Sudmeier-Rieux et al., 2006). Perez et al. (2010: 15–16) define EbA as "an approach that builds resilience and reduces the vulnerability of local communities to climate change ... EBA integrates sustainable use of biodiversity and ecosystem services in a comprehensive adaptation strategy". Combining EbA and CbA approaches links climate change adaptation, sound ecosystem management and livelihood development. Organizations such as the International Union for Conservation of Nature (IUCN) are developing CbA toolkits that focus on livelihoods adaptation, for example the Community-based Risk Screening Tool – Adaptation and Livelihoods (CRiSTAL) and the Mangrove Ecosystems for Climate Change Adaptation and Livelihoods (MESCAL).

The Many Strong Voices (MSV) programme has been exploring applications of EbA. MSV works with peoples from the Arctic and SIDS to help them deal with climate change (CICERO and UNEP/GRID-Arendal, 2008). This chapter reports work undertaken with MSV to understand more about ecosystem-based adaptation in SIDS. The aims are to examine how EbA is conducted in one SIDS, Tonga, and to extract lessons from local initiatives that seek to increase resilience to climate change impacts.

Following some background on Tonga's vulnerability context, we describe the fieldwork method. We then detail observations of several community-based and ecosystem-based projects around Tonga. Next, wider contexts and recommendations are provided, followed by brief conclusions, placing Tonga's experience in the context of similar work in other SIDS and reflecting on wider lessons. The focus is on examining actions on the ground, rather than on theoretical or policy framings regarding SIDS, climate change or disaster risk – which are amply discussed elsewhere.

Tonga

Tonga has a combined land and sea area of 720,000 km², of which 717 km² is the land area. The country comprises approximately 172 named islands, of which 36 (totalling 649 km²) are inhabited. The country's population is around 106,000, with almost 70 per cent living on the main island, Tongatapu. The main sources of livelihoods are agriculture and fishing, much of which is subsistence based. These two sectors account for a quarter of Tonga's annual gross domestic product (GDP) (De Fontenay and Utoikamanu, 2009; Jayaraman et al., 2010). Remittances from international sources can be up to 50 per cent of a village's income and rarely fall under 15 per cent for any village (Connell and Brown, 2005), with a country-wide average of about 39–40 per cent of annual GDP (De Fontenay and Utoikamanu, 2009; Jayaraman et al., 2010). Aid represents approximately 12 per cent of Tonga's annual GDP (Jayaraman et al., 2010). Tourism also generates revenue, with direct and indirect income from travel and tourism providing 11.6 per cent of Tonga's GDP and 11.9 per cent of Tonga's total employment in 2010 (WTTC, 2011).

Tonga has a long history of disasters such as volcanic eruptions, cyclones, earthquakes, floods and tsunamis (Lewis, 1979, 1981; Oliver and Reardon, 1982; Rogers, 1981). Tonga sits beside the Ring of Fire, where some of the world's most intense tectonic activity occurs. The country is about 200 km west of the active subduction zone of the Tonga Trench, a potential origin of tsunamis. Many of Tonga's islands, including the main island Tongatapu, are low and flat with an average altitude of 2–5 metres above sea level. Hence, they are highly vulnerable to storm surges and tsunami inundation (MECC, 2010). Cyclones further cause significant wind and rain damage (Reardon, 1992; Spennemann, 1987; Takau and Fungalei, 1987). A recent disaster was on 29 September 2009, when twin earthquakes were followed by tsunamis, killing almost 200 people in Tonga, Samoa and American Samoa (Beavan et al., 2010; Lay et al., 2010).

Tonga is also vulnerable to the El Niño Southern Oscillation, which causes droughts and floods and affects freshwater supplies – all influencing crops and livestock (for example, Van der Velde et al., 2006, 2007). At the same time, Tonga suffers from the impacts of environmental degradation owing to internal and external human pressures. Internally, rapid population growth and unsustainable harvesting and fishing are the main concerns (MECC, 2010). Externally, climate change is highlighted as potentially causing major problems for Tonga (MECC, 2010).

Climate change projections for the future do not exist that are accurate and precise enough for decision-making at the scale of specific Tongan islands. For tropical cyclones around the Pacific, models give varying results, and few specifics are available apart from noting that intensity is projected to increase, frequency is projected to change, and track patterns remain challenging to project (Knutson et al., 2010). For Tonga specifically, some analyses have been conducted in the context of coastal management under climate change impact scenarios, but they do not provide details on projections (for example, Mimura and Pelesikoti, 1997; Pelesikoti, 2003; Nunn and Wadell, 1992). Limited knowledge on climate change impacts is an ongoing challenge when undertaking climate change adaptation (CCA) in SIDS, unless adaptation is placed within wider contexts of disaster risk reduction (DRR) and development priorities (for example, CICERO and UNEP/GRID-Arendal, 2008).

Tongans have numerous indigenous ways of addressing their disaster vulnerability locally and nationally, from cultural attitudes (Quesada, 2005) to technical approaches utilizing local materials (Reardon, 1992). In the international arena, Tonga since 1998 has been a party to the United Nations Framework Convention on Climate Change (UNFCCC) and recently published a roadmap for 2010–2014 (MECC, 2010) in order to merge DRR and CCA, as is recommended by the scientific literature (for example, Shaw et al., 2010a, 2010b).

Mangroves have recently been gaining importance in Tonga as CCA and DRR measures, especially for addressing coastal erosion. Mangroves are viewed as appropriate because they slow incoming waves, preventing damage behind the mangroves while maintaining the shoreline as sediment is deposited (see also Ellison, 2003). Mangroves also support fishing livelihoods and traditional, medicinal plants. Although no solution can be perfect and controversies exist regarding some of mangroves' touted benefits, the Tongan view of the appropriateness of mangroves for DRR, including CCA, and for livelihoods is supported by a large body of scientific literature (for example, Badola and Hussain, 2005; Mazda et al., 1997). As such, mangroves are becoming an important, but not exclusive, strategy for CbA and EbA in coastal locations (for example, Nunn and Mimura, 1997; Sudmeier-Rieux and Ash, 2009). Planting of mangroves is linked to creating and supporting livelihoods, so that the community gains the benefits directly, as has been shown for Thailand and Ecuador (Hoanh et al., 2006) as well as for Tonga as reported here.

Fieldwork

Fieldwork was carried out to investigate community-based and ecosystem-based approaches for addressing Tonga's vulnerability, especially to the adverse impacts of climate change. The objective was to gather qualitative information on local understandings of, and actions with regard to, EbA for DRR and CCA in Tonga. No hypotheses were formulated, because this work was objective based to determine the examples of existing EbA activities and local residents' perspectives on those examples. The fieldwork comprised site visits, archival research and interviews.

The interviews were completed with members of Tongan non-governmental organizations (NGOs) involved in relevant projects, along with government officials participating in national and subnational processes as well as in international negotiations related to environmental issues, including climate change. For the interviews, a semi-structured interview guide was developed, listing several open-ended questions in order to guide the discussions with the interviewees, but permitting the interviewees to choose the main direction for the interview if they wished.

Out of the 21 interviewees, 15 were male and 6 were female. There were three male high school students in their teens and one female in her twenties, and the rest were above 30, with the oldest being three males and one female in their sixties. Aside from the students, six worked with NGOs, nine worked for the government and three were community members.

The field site visits were directed by local and national NGO partners. In consultation with local partners, the criteria to determine field visits were the following: (i) enough material was available to be gathered and analysed; (ii) a balance existed between positive examples and examples requiring improvements to permit comparison and contrast; and (iii) buy-in was available from those working at or with the sites. The amount of local buy-in was not always clear. Sometimes, local NGOs were staffed by local residents, but at other times the project appeared to be driven more by outsiders, generally from outside Tonga. Consequently, the balance of buy-in and project drivers between local NGOs and local residents who are not affiliated with the local NGO was not always clear.

Principal observations

The hazards, disasters and risk context, including climate change impacts and projections, are summarized above for Tonga. Little detailed information on these topics exists in the literature for the specific locations, but some references and overviews are given. Otherwise, the discussion is interpreted in the context of Tonga's overall profile.

Tongatapu island

Village of Kolovai

The village of Kolovai has a population of 584 and is located on the north-western peninsula of the main island of Tongatapu (Figure 8.1). On its eastern side, the village borders a shallow portion of the Pacific Ocean, dominated by far-reaching mudflats and seagrass beds. During extreme high tides and storms, sea water inundation has extended up to 80 metres inland. Climate change, in the form of sea level rise, is said by the villagers to be worsening this inundation, leading to flooding of low-lying properties along the eastern coastline of Kolovai. MECC (2010) corroborates this view, suggesting that the sea at Kolovai is penetrating inland to an average of 100 metres from the shoreline and raising concerns about sea level rise affecting numerous other villages around Tongatapu (see also

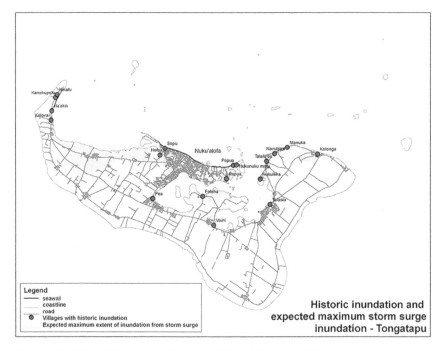

Figure 8.1 Map of Tongatapu showing Kolovai, Sopu and Popua
Source: MECC (2010).

Ellison, 2003; Mimura and Pelesikoti, 1997). Yet no time-series data are available for Kolovai, and the scientific references give general rather than localized figures. Satellite images are being piloted in two locations of Tonga to try to monitor sea level rise impacts.

Properties in Kolovai are also experiencing land degradation, in the form of soil erosion. Villagers reported a decrease in marine biodiversity following damage to the coastline after storms, most notably Cyclone Isaac in 1982. The villagers report these factors combining to cause a loss of livelihoods, especially in terms of loss of land for maintaining shelter, growing food and keeping livestock. Although peer-reviewed studies are not available for Kolovai to corroborate villagers' reports – despite the need (Nunn and Wadell, 1992) – other studies suggest a complex relationship between coastal ecosystems, storms and speed of recovery (for example, Harmelin-Vivien, 1994; Lugo et al., 2000). Nonetheless, the health and sanitation of many villages around Tonga were certainly at risk during and after inundation from Cyclone Isaac (Takau and Fungalei, 1987) and food security was threatened through the destruction of fishing equipment as well as storm-induced changes to coastal ecosystems (Latukefu, 1986).

To counter the challenges identified by people in Kolovai, a local NGO has (for just a few years) been planting mangroves as a response to land degradation, climate change impacts and the loss of marine biodiversity in Kolovai. All three aims can be achieved through planting and maintaining mangroves along the coastline (Figure 8.2), as supported by

Figure 8.2 The mangrove plantations in the Kolovai project area
Photo: Stavros Mavrogenis, 2010.

Figure 8.3 Rubbish in the Kolovai project area
Photo: Stavros Mavrogenis, 2010.

literature on other locations (for example, Hoanh et al., 2006; Mazda et al., 1997; Nunn and Mimura, 1997; Sudmeier-Rieux and Ash, 2009).

A key challenge experienced with planting and maintaining mangroves has been local residents dumping rubbish in the project area (Figure 8.3), a phenomenon witnessed in many other SIDS (Ellison, 2003). Community workshops are making some inroads into these destructive attitudes, especially when workshops achieve high local participation rates, during which elders communicate the importance of ecosystems.

Despite the community workshops and efforts to raise awareness, some people from Kolovai continue to dump their rubbish in the project area. The main reason is not opposition to the project. According to residents, most of them cannot afford to pay the monthly fee needed for the local authorities to come and pick up their trash (the fee is 5 pa'anga, approximately €2).

A wider factor influencing the dumping of rubbish is the changing nature of household waste in Tonga associated with changing lifestyles (Lal and Takau, 2006). Although the monthly rubbish collection fee was cited as an impediment to better waste disposal, recent trends in household purchases are clearly towards increased disposable and non-biodegradable items, especially plastics. Such purchases, mainly imported items, are assumed to be part of "modern" or "developed" lifestyles and livelihoods, and hence are viewed as attractive. As such, rubbish amounts are increasing, are more visible and are less degradable.

A longer-term question is evaluating the mangrove planting project. Baseline data do not exist and the local NGO does not have the time or the resources to take a detailed scientific approach to the project design or monitoring. For example, it used its own knowledge regarding the choice of mangrove species to plant and for selecting the locations, rather than seeking a full scientific assessment of the area's ecology and hydrology. For monitoring, the main concern has been maintaining fences to exclude roaming pigs and to prevent rubbish dumping. Yet the local NGO cannot even afford a laptop to regularly record and analyse its observations and the NGO's project officer must cover his own expenses when travelling to visit the Ministry of Environment and Climate Change and deliver handwritten evaluation reports.

The other principal option considered for coastal protection in Kolovai was building a seawall. Construction of a seawall made of earth had commenced in 2004, funded mainly by the Government of Canada. Some villagers preferred a seawall because they felt it would provide a more direct and tangible intervention measure to protect against coastal hazards. In contrast, mangroves were perceived by some villagers to be less of a proactive measure and would take time to demonstrate their effectiveness. However, according to the NGO, mangroves are cheaper and are easier for maintaining and supporting livelihoods, whereas a seawall would be focused on the single purpose of coastal "defence". These different perceptions strongly suggest the need for (i) continuing evidence regarding the effectiveness of EbA initiatives and (ii) continuing mechanisms for communicating that evidence to different audiences, especially people in communities where EbA initiatives are implemented.

Following construction of the seawall, little maintenance is evident but it has supported EbA around Kolovai (Figures 8.4, 8.5 and 8.6). Small lagoons surrounded by thick vegetation have been created, apparently as a result of the seawall, protecting inland areas from the ocean and providing a buffer for the village when coastal surges overtop or breach the wall. As such, the discussion should perhaps be framed not as "a seawall versus EbA" but instead as about selecting an appropriate portfolio of options in combination.

Tatakamotonga and Muinahafu villages

Tatakamotonga is located along the eastern side of Tongatapu's lagoon. It is one of the largest rural communities in Tonga, with 7,000 people. Around the village, indigenous vegetation has been cleared by modern developments and expanding settlements.

A project funded by the Global Environment Facility has restored an area where locals had previously dumped their metal trash, including old appliances and cars. Along the coastline, local residents planted mangroves together with local trees known for their medicinal uses, food

Figure 8.4 The Kolovai seawall
Photo: Stavros Mavrogenis, 2010.

Figure 8.5 New ecosystem behind the seawall
Photo: Stavros Mavrogenis, 2010.

Figure 8.6 Area not protected by the seawall
Photo: Stavros Mavrogenis, 2010.

value and cultural importance. In the near future, they plan to construct recreational areas for residents and a small wharf for tourists to dock their boats. The aim is to rehabilitate the area and improve livelihoods by allowing the local community to gain revenues from project activities. The project is framed as ecosystem restoration to support livelihoods, but it also contributes to standard CCA and DRR benefits associated with planting mangroves (see Chapter 4 in this volume).

Fonuatanu and Lapaha villages

Fonuatanu and Lapaha are situated on the eastern part of Tongatapu. Almost no baseline data or vulnerability studies exist for these areas.[1] The villages are experiencing soil erosion, which villagers attribute to sea level rise. In cases of strong wind, ocean surges have caused damage as far as 100 metres inland. The coastline is retreating towards people's homes, and villagers say that the speed of erosion is increasing. They state that some families' original land is substantially smaller than a generation ago, impinging on their livelihoods. No quantitative data exist to substantiate these statements; local comments are the only observations available.

In Lapaha, mangrove planting in the coastal areas has been completed by a local NGO since September 2010. Although the project was described as "mangrove reforestation", no studies have been published of previous ecosystems that might have existed in the area, and local knowledge could not provide details regarding past vegetation there.

The young mangroves planted recently are fenced in to prevent pigs and people from damaging or removing them. Workshops were conducted with community members to raise awareness about the importance and value of mangroves and other vegetation, connecting livelihood development, DRR and CCA. Similarly to Kolovai, Lapaha was also experiencing rubbish dumping in planted mangrove areas. To discourage such behaviour, project managers took photos before and after dumped rubbish was removed from the mangrove sites. They used the photos in community workshops, leading to some reduction in trash being dumped.

One possible difference from Kolovai is the more extensive and longer-term participation of elders in the workshops. The elders educated younger community members about the buffering role of mangroves against coastal hazards and about when mangroves should and should not be harvested. Mangrove bark is used as a raw material for dye for the common South Pacific tapa cloth (Rohorua and Lim, 2006). Tapa traditionally was manufactured for people's own use, for gifts to local chiefs and for donations to church-related institutions. Recently, demand has grown for selling tapa to tourists and tourist shops for cash income. Tapa's popularity has led to overharvesting of mangroves, as reported by locals in the interviews, along with cutting off branches and cutting down trunks to get the bark rather than just stripping the bark and leaving the tree intact (Murofushi and Hori, 1997). Mangrove harvesting for cash-based livelihoods has dramatically reduced mangrove coverage, resulting in increased coastal vulnerability as well as the loss of traditional knowledge concerning the sustainable growth, harvesting and use of mangroves (see also Murofushi and Hori, 1997).

Sopu and Popua villages

Sopu and Popua are located along Tongatapu's northern shore, just west and east respectively of Nuku'alofa. Cyclone Isaac severely affected Sopu, and many residents were resettled in Popua (Takau and Fungalei, 1987). In Sopu, the Government of Japan funded the construction of an earthen embankment (seawall) along the coast in order to prevent waves from washing inland. In places without a seawall, coastal erosion is evident, and there are no plans to tackle this problem (Figure 8.7), whereas coastlines with established mangroves display little coastal erosion (Figure 8.8). No definitive cause–effect linkages between mangroves and coastal erosion can be made because there are few comprehensive studies globally and none formally undertaken in Tonga that take into account other factors such as bathymetry, topography and wind/wave direction.

Figure 8.7 Coastal erosion in the Sopu area
Photo: Stavros Mavrogenis, 2010.

Figure 8.8 Mangroves and non-eroded coast in the Sopu area
Photo: Stavros Mavrogenis, 2010.

Figure 8.9 Remnants of Popua's mangrove swamp that protected the coastline
Photo: Stavros Mavrogenis, 2010.

Popua used to contain a rubbish dumping site for Tongatapu until a few years ago when the Government of Australia's Agency for International Development funded the relocation of the dump site and restored the area (Figure 8.9). Following this initiative, the Government of Tonga bulldozed the dense coastal mangroves in order to allocate plots for landless citizens, mainly Tongatapu settlers originating from outer islands. Popua is located at a lagoon entrance where high tides frequently inundate inhabited areas and leave the ground saturated (Figure 8.10), resulting in some residents placing their houses on stilts (Figure 8.11) – a strategy also used in other SIDS (Pelling, 1997).

Ha'apai islands

The Ha'apai group of islands (Figure 8.12) lies approximately 170 km north from Tongatapu. Many studies have examined Ha'apai's environmental data, especially regarding its ecology and geology (for example, Dickinson et al., 1994; Dickinson and Burley, 2007; Prescott, 1990; Steadman, 1998). Publications on the people tend to focus on anthropology,

Figure 8.10 Saturated ground in Popua
Photo: Stavros Mavrogenis, 2010.

Figure 8.11 House on stilts in Popua
Photo: Stavros Mavrogenis, 2010.

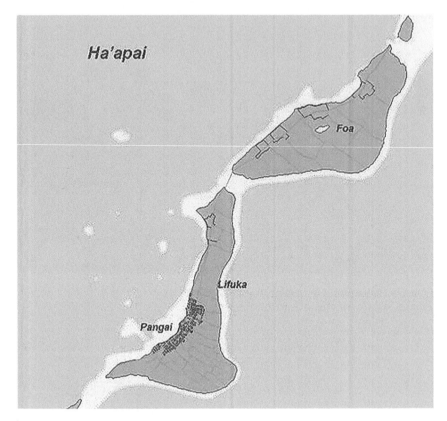

Figure 8.12 The Ha'apai group, Tonga
Source: Tonga Escapes Travel, <http://tonga-escapes.com/images/tonga-haapai-map.jpg> (accessed 18 October 2012).

although some environmental risk and community-based management studies exist (for example, Bender, 2001; Bender et al., 2002). Regarding disasters, the focus of previous studies is on hazards (for example, GVP, 2011, for volcanism).

Coastal management activities for Ha'apai aim to empower the communities on Lifuka and Foa islands to mitigate and adapt to climate change. Local residents state that sea level rise has resulted in significant beach erosion and affected the quality of groundwater. MECC (2010) agrees with this statement, but received most of its information from the communities through local consultations.

Following the 2009 tsunami, national and local NGOs implemented two coastal management projects on Lifuka. The first one, along Hihifo beach, involved building a seawall from sandbags to protect a community

Figure 8.13 Dying trees on Hihifo beach, Lifuka, with sandbags visible
Photo: Stavros Mavrogenis, 2010.

member's house that was severely damaged by the 2009 tsunami. Owing to lack of funding and knowledge, poor-quality sandbags were used, so the seawall soon eroded. Local residents suggested that either better-quality sandbags should be used or the sand should be mixed with cement. Planting trees was also attempted, but this failed because tree growth suffered as a result of waves and tides (Figure 8.13).

Also in Hihifo, local young people cultivate a community farm, using the revenues for their own benefit (for example, setting up an Internet café and acquiring further training to diversify their livelihood sources). On Foa island, a project focused on women's empowerment, supporting women in planting vegetables in home gardens using organic fertilizers and mixed cropping for their small, nearby farms. These agricultural projects have been more successful, especially in better connecting project objectives to livelihood priorities.

In addition to increasing food security, which has added DRR advantages (such as reducing the likelihood of famine and improving post-disaster self-sufficiency), the women's agricultural approach promotes environmental sustainability in land use, showing that agricultural practices can be integrated into ecosystem functions, a hallmark of EbA. The women recognize that adjustments in agricultural production might be needed in the context of climate change. As such, EbA projects that bolster food security contribute to reduced disaster vulnerability and increased resilience to climate change impacts. However, the women of Foa island indicate that they are doing it for themselves, to improve their community's health and environment and their own empowerment. This attitude further epitomizes EbA and sets the groundwork for future community-led EbA as part of DRR endeavours around Ha'apai and further afield.

The Ha'apai group does not have a dump site, yet the rubbish trends are similar to Kolovai in terms of increased use of imported goods, especially plastics. Local residents burn their rubbish or dump it in the forest.

The Hihifo youth and Foa women are active in continuing to seek better solutions, such as livelihood diversification, that generate income. Eco-tourism development is also being explored, but the tourist resorts across the Ha'apai island group are currently owned by New Zealanders and Germans – and the locals cannot afford to stay or eat in foreign-owned establishments. Local residents are therefore pursuing training on supporting tourism-based livelihoods – such as making handicrafts, setting up their own hotels and constructing a marina – in order to supplement their agricultural and fishing income. Again, the focus is on community-based approaches that build capacity for CbA and that reconnect with local environmental knowledge to support EbA. This approach matches with successful projects implemented in other SIDS such as Samoa (Daly et al., 2010) and Fiji (Chandra and Dalton, 2010).

Energy is another concern because electricity is generated from an old power plant on Lifuka that burns oil. Local residents are exploring solar and wind power. They are hoping to help themselves solve all their challenges, including preparing for environmental changes, in line with recommendations from case studies around the world (for example, Lewis, 1999; Shaw et al., 2009, 2010a, 2010b; Wisner et al., 2012).

Wider contexts and recommendations

The previous section has described the on-the-ground EbA projects in Tonga. A summary of the key messages is listed in Table 8.1. Placing the projects and the messages emerging from the fieldwork into wider national and global contexts helps illustrate how improvements to future DRR initiatives, including EbA, could be enacted. This section explores some of these wider contexts to indicate the challenges and ways of overcoming those challenges for improving on-the-ground action.

Table 8.1 illustrates lessons but does not indicate how these lessons could be implemented to overcome challenges such as funding, access to information, power relations, gender inequality and local interest in

Table 8.1 Key messages emerging from ecosystem-based approaches in Tonga

Key message	Locations	Justification
Successful community-based EbA means linking ecosystems and local livelihood benefits	All the locations visited	People are concerned about livelihoods. For instance, in Sopu and Popua, EbA was not feasible because giving people homes was the priority. In contrast, the examples from Ha'apai showed local buy-in when people understood how EbA would support their own livelihoods
Showing community benefits from EbA creates local buy-in, leading to behavioural change and sustainability	Lapaha Tatakamotonga and Muinahafu Lifuka: Hihifo beach	When community benefits from mangroves were shown (e.g. reduced storm damage and livelihood support), people dumped less rubbish there Locals saw that their livelihoods would gain from ecosystem restoration, so they did the work themselves The young people were motivated because the revenues from EbA helped them improve their own livelihoods
EbA requires tackling recent, negative perceptions and attitudes regarding ecosystems such as mangroves	Fonuatanu and Lapaha	Involving the elders in explaining indigenous knowledge and ecosystem values led to attitude and behavioural change (e.g. reduced rubbish dumping in mangroves)
Learning by doing can enhance local EbA initiatives	Lifuka: Hihifo beach	Locals tried some techniques which did not work, but they were motivated to continue trying
Traditional knowledge remains an important community asset, contributing to EbA	Lapaha Tatakamotonga and Muinahafu	Involving the elders in community awareness-raising was successful Local buy-in was increased by including traditional medicinal knowledge as part of the reason for selecting plants
Funding and capacity development are challenges for local NGOs, so further support in those areas is needed	Kolovai	The local NGO has neither the resources nor the capacity to use information technology to the fullest extent needed

Table 8.1 (cont.)

Key message	Locations	Justification
Gender empowerment and equality are both a means and a consequence of successful EbA	Foa island	EbA was supported through a women's empowerment project, which then motivated the women to continue EbA activities
Lack of baseline and monitoring data, including evidence demonstrating the effectiveness of EbA initiatives, along with lack of access to scientific information, such as appropriate selection of mangrove species, inhibits EbA decision-making with confidence	Kolovai Sopu and Popua Fonuatanu and Lapaha	Evaluating the effectiveness of the local work is not feasible owing to a lack of time-series data. Also, evidence demonstrating and comparing the effectiveness of ecosystems and engineered infrastructure (e.g. seawalls) is lacking. Setting specific goals and targets is difficult owing to the lack of time-series data.

supporting projects. Many of Tonga's EbA initiatives are linked to external funding, and success often depends on managing external funding processes. Additionally, the lack of information and information exchange is a major constraint on EbA implementation. These two factors – access to information and funding – emerged from interviews with government officials and local NGO members, and they need to be understood in more detail to determine how external interventions could best support EbA in Tonga and to translate lessons learned into improved practice. This section's recommendations provide some direction for maintaining and expanding EbA efforts.

Information and information exchange

Those interviewed from government and local NGOs suggested that donors and international NGOs could play a greater role in providing them with information and capacity development on CbA and EbA. Outside knowledge should be combined with traditional knowledge, especially from elders. As capacity is built and as young people learn from the elders, effecting two of the lessons from Table 8.1, more local groups could be mobilized to produce educational material and workshops for themselves – supported and evaluated, as needed, by national NGOs. For instance, local church institutions in Tonga are heavily involved in raising awareness about climate change. The interviewees felt that local church institutions should be engaged more actively in implementing and monitoring CbA and EbA initiatives.

As noted during interviews, local culture and limited local knowledge can inhibit EbA work. Many locals consider mangroves to be dirty and hence an appropriate place for disposing of household waste, but such negative perceptions are relatively recent and are linked to "modern" lifestyles, as discussed previously. National influences could also potentially play a role, such as national decisions regarding land use and housing development. Indigenous ecological knowledge also exists, often held by community elders, that recognizes the multiple benefits of mangroves. Consequently, although local residents blame climate change as a driver of many environmental changes, it is the combination of climate change, local behaviour and external (national and international) pressures that most likely leads to observed changes.

Climate change cannot be ignored, but it should not be assumed that any observed environmental change is the result of climate change (for example, Wisner et al., 2012). It would be particularly important to conduct research and comparatively assess the role of external and internal factors in influencing each observed environmental condition or trend. Baseline data would therefore be needed but, as noted in Table 8.1, the lack of such data impedes the selection and evaluation of EbA measures.

Funding

Challenges concerning the funding of EbA activities were a common theme raised during the interviews. Less than 1 per cent of the Tongan government's budget is allocated to activities related to climate change (see Fonua, 2011). With external assistance representing approximately 12 per cent of Tonga's annual GDP (Jayaraman et al., 2010), donors naturally have great influence over how funds are spent, which does not always include EbA.

Local and national NGOs work mostly on the basis of attracting grants from donors, but the NGOs tend to act as facilitators, not necessarily implementing all parts of a project but supporting the local communities in doing so while monitoring the implementation. Local buy-in for EbA requires trust amongst the implementing parties involved (see Table 8.1). NGOs often face budgetary constraints concerning the limited and slow release of funds, which can undermine their credibility with local residents and reduce overall community buy-in for EbA work.

Several recommendations emerged during the interviews on how to improve externally supported activities. Consultations between donors, local NGOs and communities can shape calls for proposals and project design, which would achieve a more locally driven and bottom-up process. Interviewees recognized the need for oversight and accountability, suggesting ways to improve wise use of funds without undue delay in disbursement. For example, funding should be given directly to credible groups with a clear plan on how to implement projects that support EbA work and apply the lessons listed in Table 8.1. Also, additional funding should be provided for capacity development of government officials and NGO staff to attend overseas training programmes, including for postgraduate degrees, provided that the recipients return to their current position upon completion. This would assist in building national and local capacity for designing and implementing EbA work informed by current international good practices. Hosting national as well as regional forums facilitating exchange of knowledge and experiences on EbA, DRR and CCA was also suggested. In this regard, issues related to funding and information access become directly linked; addressing these two concerns in Tonga would assist in translating the key messages in Table 8.1 into practice, as echoed by experiences in other locations (see Shaw et al., 2010a, 2010b; Wisner et al., 2012).

Conclusions

Many of the measures and approaches, in Tonga and in other case studies, are simple, straightforward and pragmatic – not revolutionary. The Tonga case study highlights what is taking place on the ground in isolated communities by local residents trying their best to deal with a changing society and environment. Their experience matches similar work in other SIDS.

In Samoa, Daly et al. (2010) detail a participatory process for CbA that was externally driven but involved coastal villagers on their own terms. Local knowledge was combined with external knowledge so that the village chiefs and national government could develop coastal management plans for the country's entire coast. The plans factored in CCA as well as other DRR considerations such as tsunamis and cyclones, seeking to preserve ecosystems to support livelihoods. Meanwhile, in Jamaica, UNEP (2010) consulted with community members and national government representatives to see how ecosystems could be better used for DRR, CCA and livelihood support. Many other examples exist from SIDS (Kelman et al., 2011, 2012) that should be investigated for their transferability to Tonga – as well as seeing how Tonga's experience could be transferred to other SIDS and elsewhere.

In most instances, ecosystems are interlinked with local livelihood sources, making it hard to differentiate between CbA and EbA. That also means not seeing CbA/EbA in opposition to other approaches, such as structural sea defences, but instead being aware of the wide portfolio of options available and seeing what combinations could be used for approaches to complement and support each other. Similarly, subtle distinctions between DRR and CCA within local contexts, which some scientists try to differentiate, make little difference on the ground (see also Gaillard, 2010; Mercer, 2010; Shaw et al., 2010a, 2010b). The interest is primarily in how to secure livelihoods and bring communities sufficient income over the long term.

Note

1. The available literature on these villages is mainly on anthropological and cultural views of the environment (for example, Kaeppler, 1967; Māhina, 1993), along with geological studies of the soil (for example, Cowie, 1980; Wiser et al., 2002).

REFERENCES

Badola, R. and S.A. Hussain (2005) "Valuing Ecosystem Functions: An Empirical Study on the Storm Protection Function of Bhitarkanika Mangrove Ecosystem, India". *Environmental Conservation* 32(1): 85–92.

Beavan, J. et al. (2010) "Near-simultaneous Great Earthquakes at Tongan Megathrust and Outer Rise in September 2009". *Nature* 466: 959–963.

Bender A. (2001) "God Will Send Us the Fish – Perception and Evaluation of an Environmental Risk in Ha'apai, Tonga". In G. Böm, J. Nerb, T. McDaniels and H. Spada (eds), *Environmental Risks: Perception, Evaluation and Management*. Bingley, UK: Emerald Group Publishing Limited, pp. 165–190.

Bender, A., W. Kägi and E. Mohr (2002) "Informal Insurance and Sustainable Management of Common-Pool Marine Resources in Ha'apai, Tonga". *Economic Development and Cultural Change* 50(2): 427–439.

Byrne, J. and V. Inniss (2002) "Island Sustainability and Sustainable Development in the Context of Climate Change". In H.-H.M. Hsiao, C.-H. Liu and H.-M. Tsai (eds), *Sustainable Development for Island Societies: Taiwan and the World*. Taipei: Asia-Pacific Research Program, pp. 2–29.

Chandra, A. and J. Dalton (2010) "Mainstreaming Adaptation within Integrated Water Resources Management (IWRM) in Small Island Developing States (SIDS). A Case Study of the Nadi River Basin, Fiji Islands". In A. Perez, H. Fernandez and C. Gatti (eds), *Building Resilience to Climate Change: Ecosystem-based Adaptation and Lessons from the Field*. Gland, Switzerland: International Union for Conservation of Nature, pp. 46–59.

CICERO [Center for International Climate and Environmental Research] and UNEP [United Nations Environment Programme] / GRID-Arendal (2008) *Many Strong Voices: Outline for an Assessment Project Design.* CICERO Report 2008:05. Oslo: CICERO.

Connell, J. and R.P.C. Brown (2005) *Remittances in the Pacific: An Overview.* Manila: Asian Development Bank.

Cowie, J.D. (1980) "Soils from Andesitic Tephra and their Variability, Tongatapu, Kingdom of Tonga". *Australian Journal of Soil Research* 18: 273–284.

Daly, M. et al. (2010) "Reducing the Climate Vulnerability of Coastal Communities in Samoa". *Journal for International Development* 22: 256–281.

De Fontenay, P. and S.T.T. Utoikamanu (2009) "Tonga: Economic Survey 2009". *Pacific Economic Bulletin* 24(3): 1–18.

Dickinson, W.R. and D.V. Burley (2007) "Geoarchaeology of Tonga: Geotectonic and Geomorphic Controls". *Geoarchaeology* 22: 229–259.

Dickinson, W.R., D.V. Burley and R. Shutler (1994) "Impact of Hydro-isostatic Holocene Sea-level Change on the Geologic Context of Island Archaeological Sites, Northern Ha'apai Group, Kingdom of Tonga". *Geoarchaeology* 9: 85–111.

Ellison, J. (2003) "How South Pacific Mangroves May Respond to Predicted Climate Change and Sea-Level Rise". *Advances in Global Change Research* 2: 289–300.

Fonua, P. (2011) "Tonga Lawmakers Loathe to Cut Bloated Payroll: 75 Percent of Operating Budget Goes to Salaries". *Pacific Island Report*, 10 June, <http://archives.pireport.org/archive/2011/june/06-13-07.htm> (accessed 18 October 2012).

Gaillard, J.C. (2010) "Vulnerability, Capacity and Resilience: Perspectives for Climate and Development Policy". *Journal of International Development* 22: 218–232.

GVP [Global Volcanism Program] (2011) "Tonga Islands", <http://www.volcano.si.edu/world/region.cfm?rnum=0403> (accessed 18 October 2012).

Harmelin-Vivien, M.L. (1994) "The Effects of Storms and Cyclones on Coral Reefs: A Review". *Journal of Coastal Research* 12: 211–231.

Hoanh, C.T., T.P. Tuong, J.W. Gowing and B. Hardy (2006) *Environment and Livelihoods in Tropical Coastal Zones: Managing Agriculture–Fishery–Aquaculture Conflicts.* Wallingford, UK: CABI.

IPCC [Intergovernmental Panel on Climate Change] (2007) *IPCC Fourth Assessment Report: Climate Change 2007.* Geneva: IPCC.

Jayaraman, T.K., C.-K. Choong and R. Kumar (2010) "Role of Remittances in Tongan Economy". *Migration Letters* 7(2): 224–230.

Kaeppler, A.L. (1967) "Folklore As Expressed in the Dance in Tonga". *Journal of American Folklore* 80(316): 160–168.

Kelman, I. and J. West (2009) "Climate Change and Small Island Developing States: A Critical Review". *Ecological and Environmental Anthropology* 5(1): 1–16.

Kelman, I. et al. (2011) "Participatory Action Research for Dealing with Disasters on Islands". *Island Studies Journal* 6(1): 59–86.

Kelman, I., J. Mercer and J.C. Gaillard (2012) "Indigenous Knowledge and Disaster Risk Reduction". *Geography* 97(1): 12–21.

Kelman, I., J. Mercer and J. West (2009) "Combining Different Knowledges: Community-based Climate Change Adaptation in Small Islands Developing States". *Participatory Learning and Action* 60: 41–53.

Knutson, T.R. et al. (2010) "Tropical Cyclones and Climate Change". *Nature Geoscience* 3: 157–163.

Lal, P. and L. Takau (2006) *Economic Costs of Waste in Tonga*. IWP Pacific Technical Report (International Waters Project) No. 33. Nuku'alofa, Tonga, Apia, Samoa, and Suva, Fiji: Government of Tonga, Secretariat of the Pacific Regional Environment Programme and the Pacific Islands Forum Secretariat.

Latukefu, T. (1986) "A Tongan Perspective on the Impact of Disaster Emergency Aid Following Cyclone Isaac". *Australian Overseas Disaster Response Organisation Newsletter* 4(3): 10–14.

Lay, T. et al. (2010) "The 2009 Samoa-Tonga Great Earthquake Triggered Doublet". *Nature* 466: 964–968.

Lewis, J. (1979) "Volcano in Tonga". *Journal of Administration Overseas* 18(2): 116–121.

Lewis, J. (1981) "Some Perspectives on Natural Disaster Vulnerability in Tonga". *Pacific Viewpoint* 22: 145–162.

Lewis, J. (1999) *Development in Disaster-prone Places: Studies of Vulnerability*. London: Intermediate Technology Publications.

Lugo, A.E., C.S. Rogers and S.W. Nixon (2000) "Hurricanes, Coral Reefs and Rainforests: Resistance, Ruin and Recovery in the Caribbean". *AMBIO: A Journal of the Human Environment* 29(2): 106–114.

Māhina, 'O. (1993) "The Poetics of Tongan Traditional History, 'Tala-ē-fonua': An Ecology-Centred Concept of Culture and History". *The Journal of Pacific History* 28(1): 109–121.

Marshall, N.A. et al. (2009) *A Framework for Social Adaptation to Climate Change: Sustaining Tropical Coastal Communities and Industries*. Gland, Switzerland: IUCN.

Mataki, M., K. Koshy and V. Nair (2007) "Top-down, Bottom-up: Mainstreaming Adaptation in Pacific Island Townships". In N. Leary, J. Adejuwon, V. Barros, I. Burton, J. Kulkarni and R. Lasco (eds), *Climate Change and Adaptation*. London: Earthscan, pp. 264–277.

Mazda, Y., M. Magi, M. Kogo and P.N. Hong (1997) "Mangroves as a Coastal Protection from Waves in the Tong Delta, Vietnam". *Mangroves and Salt Marshes* 1: 127–135.

MECC [Ministry of the Environment and Climate Change] (2010) *Joint National Action Plan on Climate Change Adaptation and Disaster Risk Management: 2010–2015*. Nuku'alofa, Tonga: MECC.

Mercer, J. (2010) "Disaster Risk Reduction or Climate Change Adaptation? Are We Reinventing the Wheel?" *Journal of International Development* 22: 247–264.

Mercer, J. et al. (2009) "Integrating Indigenous and Scientific Knowledge Bases for Disaster Risk Reduction in Papua New Guinea". *Geografiska Annaler: Series B, Human Geography* 91(2): 157–183.

Mercer, J. et al. (2010) "Framework for Integrating Indigenous and Scientific Knowledge for Disaster Risk Reduction". *Disasters* 34(1): 214–239.

Mimura, N. and N. Pelesikoti (1997) "Vulnerability of Tonga to Future Sea-Level Rise". *Journal of Coastal Research* 24: 117–132.

Murofushi, T. and N. Hori (1997) "Human Impact on Mangrove Habitats Maintenance against Sea-level Change: Case Study of Tongatapu Island, the Kingdom of Tonga, South Pacific". *Geographical Reports of Tokyo Metropolitan University* 32: 27–42.

Nunn, P.D. and N. Mimura (1997) "Vulnerability of South Pacific Island Nations to Sea-Level Rise". *Journal of Coastal Research* 24: 133–151.

Nunn, P.D. and E. Wadell (1992) *Implications of Climate Change and Sea Level Rise for the Kingdom of Tonga: Report of a Preparatory Mission*. Apia, Samoa: South Pacific Regional Environment Programme.

Nunn, P.D. et al. (2007) "Times of Plenty, Times of Less: Last-Millennium Societal Disruption in the Pacific Basin". *Human Ecology* 35: 385–401.

Oliver, J. and G.F. Reardon (1982) *Tropical Cyclone 'Isaac': Cyclonic Impact in the Context of the Society and Economy of the Kingdom of Tonga*. Townsville, Queensland: Centre for Disaster Studies, James Cook University of North Queensland.

Pelesikoti, N. (2003) "Sustainable Resource and Environmental Management in Tonga: Current Situation, Community Perceptions and a Proposed New Policy Framework". PhD thesis, University of Wollongong, New South Wales.

Pelling, M. (1997) "What Determines Vulnerability to Floods: A Case Study in Georgetown, Guyana". *Environment and Urbanization* 9: 203–226.

Pelling, M. and J.I. Uitto (2001) "Small Island Developing States: Natural Disaster Vulnerability and Global Change". *Environmental Hazards* 3: 49–62.

Perez, A., H. Fernandez and C. Gatti (eds) (2010) *Building Resilience to Climate Change: Ecosystem-based Adaptation and Lessons from the Field*. Ecosystem Management Series No. 9. Gland, Switzerland: IUCN.

Prescott, J. (1990) *A Survey of the Lobster Resources in the Ha'apai Group, Kingdom of Tonga*. FFA Report 90/93. Honiara, Solomon Islands: Pacific Islands Forum Fisheries Agency.

Quesada, C. (2005) "Les Hommes et leurs volcans: Représentations et gestion des phénomènes volcaniques en Polynésie (Hawaii et Royaume de Tonga)". *Journal de la Société des Océanistes* 1/2: 120–121.

Reardon, G. (1992) "Wind Effects on the Tongan 'Hurricane House'". In Y. Aysan and I. Davis (eds), *Disasters and the Small Dwelling: Perspectives for the UN IDNDR*. London: James & James, pp. 175–182.

Reid, H. et al. (2009) "Community-based Adaptation to Climate Change: An Overview". *Participatory Learning and Action* 60: 11–33.

Rogers, G. (1981) "The Evacuation of Niuafo'ou, an Outlier in the Kingdom of Tonga". *The Journal of Pacific History* 16(3): 149–163.

Rohorua, H. and S. Lim (2006) "An Inter-sectoral Economic Model for Optimal Sustainable Mangrove Use in the Small Island Economy of Tonga". Paper presented at the New Zealand Agricultural and Resource Economics Society Conference, 25–27 August, New Zealand.

Shaw, R., J.M. Pulhin and J.J. Pereira (eds) (2010a) *Climate Change Adaptation and Disaster Risk Reduction: An Asian Perspective*. Community, Environment and Disaster Risk Management, Vol. 5. Bingley, UK: Emerald Group Publishing Limited.

Shaw, R., J.M. Pulhin and J.J. Pereira (eds) (2010b) *Climate Change Adaptation and Disaster Risk Reduction: Issues and Challenges*. Community, Environment and Disaster Risk Management, Vol. 4. Bingley, UK: Emerald Group Publishing Limited.

Shaw, R., A. Sharma and Y. Takeuchi (eds) (2009) *Indigenous Knowledge and Disaster Risk Reduction: From Practice to Policy*. Hauppauge, NY: Nova Publishers.

Shaw, R., N. Uy and J. Baumwoll (eds) (2008) *Indigenous Knowledge for Disaster Risk Reduction: Good Practices and Lessons Learned from Experiences in the Asia-Pacific Region*. Bangkok: United Nations International Strategy for Disaster Reduction.

Spennemann, D.H.R. (1987) "The Impact of Cyclonic Surge on Archaeological Sites in Tonga". *Bulletin of the Indo-Pacific Prehistory Association* 7: 75–87.

Steadman, D.W. (1998) "Status of Land Birds on Selected Islands in the Ha'apai Group, Kingdom of Tonga". *Pacific Science* 52(1): 14–34.

Sudmeier-Rieux, K. and N. Ash (2009) *Environmental Guidance Note for Disaster Risk Reduction: Healthy Ecosystems for Human Security*. Ecosystem Management Series No. 8, Commission on Ecosystem Management, revised edition. Gland, Switzerland: IUCN.

Sudmeier-Rieux, K. et al. (eds) (2006) *Ecosystems, Livelihoods and Disasters: An Integrated Approach to Disaster Risk Management*. Gland, Switzerland: IUCN.

Takau, L. and L. Fungalei (1987) "Cyclone Devastation and Resettlement at Sopu, Nuku'alofa'". In L. Mason and P. Hereniko (eds), *In Search of a Home*. Suva, Fiji: Institute of Pacific Studies, University of South Pacific, pp. 118–122.

UNEP [United Nations Environment Programme] (2010) *Risk and Vulnerability Assessment Methodology Development Project (RiVAMP). Linking Ecosystems to Risk and Vulnerability Reduction: The Case of Jamaica. Results of the Pilot Assessment*. Geneva: UNEP.

United Nations (2005) *Draft Mauritius Strategy for the Further Implementation of the Programme of Action for the Sustainable Development of Small Island Developing States*. UN Doc. A/CONF.207/CRP.7, 13 January 2005. From the International Meeting to Review the Implementation of the Programme of Action for the Sustainable Development of Small Island Developing States, Port Louis, Mauritius, 10–14 January 2005. New York: United Nations.

Van der Velde, M. et al. (2006) "El Niño-Southern Oscillation Determines the Salinity of the Freshwater Lens under a Coral Atoll in the Pacific Ocean". *Geophysical Research Letters* 33: L21403.

Van der Velde, M. et al. (2007) "Sustainable Development in Small Island Developing States: Agricultural Intensification, Economic Development, and Freshwater Resources Management on the Coral Atoll of Tongatapu". *Ecological Economics* 61: 456–468.

Warrick, O. (2009) "Ethics and Methods in Research for Community-based Adaptation: Reflections from Rural Vanuatu". *Participatory Learning and Action* 60: 65–75.

Wiser, S.K. et al. (2002) "The Potential for Long-term Persistence of Forest Fragments on Tongatapu, a Large Island in Western Polynesia". *Journal of Biogeography* 29: 767–787.

Wisner, B. (1995) "Bridging 'Expert' and 'Local' Knowledge for Counter-disaster Planning in Urban South Africa". *GeoJournal* 37(3): 335–348.

Wisner, B., J.C. Gaillard and I. Kelman (eds) (2012) *Routledge Handbook of Hazards and Disaster Risk Reduction*. London: Routledge.

WTTC [World Travel & Tourism Council] (2011) *Travel & Tourism Economic Impact 2011: Tonga*. London: WTTC.

Part III

Water resources management for disaster risk reduction

9

Good flood, bad flood: Maintaining dynamic river basins for community resilience

Pieter van Eijk, Chris Baker, Romana Gaspirc and Ritesh Kumar

Introduction

Towards new concepts of risk and resilience?

The nature and scope of disaster risk reduction planning depend on the interpretation of concepts of risk and resilience. Often a narrow focus is adopted, where only short-term local socioeconomic vulnerabilities are addressed. Where this is the case, the occurrence of extreme events is considered a given; the socioeconomic and environmental root causes that inflict or exacerbate the hazards, and which become visible only at broader temporal and spatial scales, are not addressed. Some risk reduction professionals do incorporate such a broader "landscape approach". However, they often rely heavily on human-engineered solutions, such as the construction of dykes, dams and reservoirs. These infrastructure-based approaches generally aim to confine the variability of natural processes to manageable levels and thereby mitigate the impacts of extreme events.

These sectoral approaches have contributed to the common perception of floods as being hazardous events that need to be reduced at all costs. Too often they fail to acknowledge that the maintenance of dynamic river systems may represent a core component in risk reduction in itself.

The role of ecosystems in disaster risk reduction, Renaud, Sudmeier-Rieux and Estrella (eds), United Nations University Press, 2013, ISBN 978-92-808-1221-3

Box 9.1 Definition of terms

The following definitions have been adopted to explain the concepts that are dealt with in this chapter.

- *Exposure*: people, property, systems, or other elements present in hazard zones that are thereby subject to potential losses (UNISDR, 2009).
- *Flood:* the incidental or regular temporary submersion of land as part of the water cycle (this chapter).
- *Risk*: The combination of the probability of an event and its negative consequences (UNISDR, 2009).
- *Resilience:* The ability of a system, community or society exposed to hazards to resist, absorb, accommodate to and recover from the effects of a hazard in a timely and efficient manner, including through the preservation and restoration of its essential basic structures and functions (UNISDR, 2009).
- *Vulnerability*: The characteristics and circumstances of a community, system or asset that make it susceptible to the damaging effects of a hazard (UNISDR, 2009).
- *Wetland*: "areas of marsh, fen, peatland or water, whether natural or artificial, permanent or temporary, with water that is static or flowing, fresh, brackish or salt, including areas of marine water the depth of which at low tide does not exceed six metres" (Ramsar Convention, 1971: Article 1.1).

How dynamic river systems provide resilience

The regular advance and retreat of floodwaters is crucial to maintaining the diversity and health of wetlands across river basins, and thereby sustains a wealth of economically valuable goods and services: the provision of fishery resources, the creation of favourable conditions for agricultural production, water purification and many other services to a great extent depend on the "dynamic equilibrium" that floods provide over time (Junk and Wantzen, 2004; Junk et al., 1989; Nikula, 2008). Healthy networks of interconnected wetlands also play a role in the regulation of water flows, and may thereby mitigate hazardous extremes (Bullock and Acreman, 2003). Hundreds of millions of people depend on these services worldwide (McCartney and Acreman, 2009; MEA, 2005).

When floods become hazards

Communities in flood-prone areas have developed remarkable strategies to take advantage of, and cope with, the regular occurrence of floods. The construction of floating houses, flood recession agriculture and infrastructure development on constructed or natural elevations in low-lying areas are examples of ways in which people have managed to thrive in the dynamic environment of river-floodplain systems for thousands of years (Maltby, 2009; Plate, 2002). Floods turn into hazards if they have an impact on people who have not developed or who have abandoned necessary coping strategies, or, in the case of extreme events, where the duration, frequency or magnitude of floods reach beyond the range of circumstances to which people have developed adaptive capacity.

In recent years, the impact of water-related hazards on society has significantly increased. Between 1990 and 2000, approximately 320 million people were displaced by floods, and nearly 100,000 people were killed (Bradshaw et al., 2007). The number of flooding disasters and the related economic damage have doubled since 1980 (CRED, 2011; Jennings, 2011; see also Chapter 1 in this volume). The causes behind these increases are many. Population growth and rapid, poorly planned economic expansion in areas that are naturally prone to flooding have increased people's vulnerability and exposure (Plate, 2002). Additionally, projected climate change may aggravate the impacts of floods and droughts (IPCC, 2012).

Environmental degradation is another important yet underrated core driver of vulnerability. Large parts of Europe and North America have already lost over 50 per cent of their wetlands as a result of drainage and conversion during the last century (MEA, 2005). No less than 77 per cent of the discharge of the 139 largest river basins in this area is affected by channelization, fragmentation and regulation by dams, dykes and other infrastructure (Dynesius and Nilsson, 1994), and only 2 per cent of river-floodplain systems in Europe can be considered to be "natural" (Blackwell and Maltby, 2006). Developing countries are facing similar and rapidly increasing threats (Acreman et al., 2007). Loss of their natural resource base as a result of environmental degradation renders people who live in wetlands highly vulnerable. People outside wetland areas are affected as well; human disturbance has gravely influenced the way in which wetlands may store, regulate and release water flows (Acreman et al., 2003; Gore and Shields, 1995; Sparks, 1995). This has caused the aggravation of floods in some cases and resulted in their displacement to areas that did not face regular flooding before.

A new paradigm in disaster risk reduction?

The above trends indicate that conventional human-engineered solutions and local community-based approaches alone do not suffice to ensure maximum societal resilience against water-related hazards. In recent years, water managers have started to explore options that work alongside natural processes and integrate ecosystem-based approaches as a means to enhance resilience along river basins (Brouwer and van Ek, 2004; Fox, 2003; UNEP, 2009). This was the result of extensive dialogue with civil society organizations and following successful pilot projects in heavily modified river basins (Blackwell and Maltby, 2006; WWF, 2002). The core of this new risk reduction paradigm is to recognize the value of floods, to employ a combination of ecosystem-based and human-engineered solutions to avoid hazardous flooding and to integrate these approaches with conventional early warning, preparedness and response measures. It will be instrumental for such approaches to be fully integrated in risk reduction planning and for strategies to be tested in different environmental and social contexts.

This chapter provides the rationale for developing integrated ecosystem-inclusive risk reduction plans to address water-related hazards and identifies the steps towards accomplishing such integration.

Maintaining flooding regimes for healthy wetlands

The flood pulse

River basins are highly dynamic environments. They are characterized by a complex interaction of hydrological and geomorphological processes and conditions, which over time shape a diverse landscape of connected wetland ecosystems. The periodic rise and retreat of floodwaters is a dominating feature in this landscape. The duration, amplitude, frequency, predictability and rate of rise and retreat of this "flood pulse" are unique for each river basin and determine many of the ecological processes that occur. It is this dynamism and heterogeneity that drive the productivity of river-floodplain systems and determine its values for community livelihoods.

Junk et al. (1989) provided a detailed account of the ecological relevance of the flood pulse in river-floodplain systems. They described how the advance and retreat of floodwaters create an aquatic/terrestrial transition zone that drives primary productivity, decomposition processes and nutrient cycling. During the rise of floodwaters, nutrients are circulated throughout the system, boosting primary productivity in the transition zone. Periods of high water level and stagnation of flows are characterized by lower rates of production. Oxygenation during the recession of floods increases nutrient availability and causes a second boost of primary productivity. The flood pulse also plays a key role in maintaining the diversity of river-floodplain systems (Johnson et al., 1995; Robinson et al., 2002). The dynamic environment created by floods prevents productive generalist plant species from becoming dominant over specialist species that depend on the specific niches created by the flood pulse. Floods bring in sediment-bound nutrients (Tockner et al., 2000) and periodically connect habitats to each other, thereby allowing for the dispersal of biota (Johnson et al., 1995). Extreme floods reset ecosystems by flushing out soil and organic material. They thereby prevent ecological succession and maintain a heterogeneous environment (Hill et al., 1991; Tockner et al., 2000). This diversity is important because migratory fishes – representing a disproportionately large fraction of fish biomass in river-floodplain systems – and many other animal and plant species depend on a large range of habitats to complete their reproductive cycles (Grift, 2011; Van den Brink et al., 1996; Ward et al., 1999).

Bayley (1995) hypothesized that productivity is strongly linked to the rate of rise and fall of floodwaters, with a medium-speed pulse rendering optimal productivity. A slow pulse was predicted to result in relatively low productivity, owing to oxygen deprivation, and too-rapid pulsing prevents species making optimal use of the favourable conditions created in the aquatic/terrestrial transition zone. Similarly, the predictability of the flood pulse, as well as its interaction with climatic conditions, to a great extent determines the possibilities for biota to adapt to and take advantage of the niches that are created by the pulse (Junk et al., 1989; Tockner et al., 2000).

The economic relevance of pulsing systems

The economic advantages of pulsing ecosystems are significant. Various studies in tropical and temperate regions have found that fish harvests are higher per unit area in healthy river-floodplains compared with static deep reservoirs, representing an annual harvest that typically ranges from 200 to 2,000 kg per hectare and from 10 to 50 kg per hectare for the two systems, respectively (Bayley, 1995; Jackson and Marmulla, 2000; Marshall and Maes, 1994; Richter et al., 2010). The fertile soils of seasonally flooded agricultural land typically support high yields of staple crops such as rice, maize and sugar cane, and artificial fertilizer inputs and labour costs are often low compared with non-flooded areas (Wood and van Halsema, 2008). Additionally, recession agriculture enables the sustained harvest of other wetland products such as fish, which decrease or disappear in intensively managed agriculture systems (Sedara et al., 2002). The relevance of the flood pulse is clearly demonstrated in the lower Mekong Delta; Tonle Sap lake and its surrounding floodplains in Cambodia support one of the richest freshwater fisheries in the world, with annual fish production of over 400,000 tons, representing approximately 10 per cent of the country's gross domestic product (Fox, 2003; Hortle et al., 2004). With annual rice production of 2.5–2.7 tons per hectare, yields are more than two times higher compared with nearby rain-fed lowland areas (Vanhan, 2004).

Human impacts

Worldwide, the construction of dams, embankments and other infrastructure has contributed to the disturbance or loss of the flood pulse (Henry and Amoros, 1995; Richter et al., 2010; Simons et al., 2001). In some cases the costs resulting from the decline of valuable ecosystem services outweigh the economic benefits that are derived from such developments. This is, for example, the case in the Inner Niger Delta in Mali and the Hadejia-Nguru wetlands in Nigeria, where benefits from water use for various irrigation and hydropower developments were found to be smaller compared with scenarios in which water allocation to the wetlands is sustained (Barbier and Thompson, 1998; Zwarts et al., 2005). Where the net economic impacts of infrastructure development are positive, often some stakeholders dependent on natural resources, such as fisherfolk or pastoralists, lose out from a decrease in the natural resource base. As such, losses often take place hundreds of kilometres downstream and sometimes take several years before they become visible. The impact of changing flow regimes on disaster risk and the resilience of individual stakeholder groups or of society at large are often overlooked. Consequently, the maintenance of the flood pulse remains insufficiently accounted for in development and risk reduction plans.

The role of wetlands in flood and drought regulation

The regulating role of different wetland types

In recent years, the conservation community has widely promoted the role of wetlands in reducing water-related hazards. Their importance in regulating floods, recharging aquifers and supporting base flows during drought periods, for example, is often stressed (Emerton and Bos, 2004; Nellemann and Corcoran, 2010; WWF, 2011). Yet, although the current body of science confirms that wetlands indeed exert a major influence on hydrological processes, recent literature reviews indicate that their impact on the water cycle is far from universal.

Floodplains have been found in most cases to reduce downstream flooding, owing to their capacity to temporarily store large quantities of water and through soil infiltration and evaporation (for example, Nielsen et al., 1991; Sutcliffe and Parks, 1989). However, Bullock and Acreman (2003), in their review of 169 scientific papers on the regulating role of wetlands, concluded that, for other hydrological typologies, no single trend emerges on how wetlands affect hydrological features such as the gross water balance, the recharge of groundwater, the sustenance of flows, flood risk reduction and flow variability. Fewer than half of the studies on headwater wetlands covered in this analysis concluded that they contribute to a reduction or delay of flooding events, whereas a similar number found that they exacerbate flooding. Most wetlands have higher rates of evaporation compared with non-wetland ecosystems and thereby contribute to a decrease in overall annual flows. This reduction is mainly felt during dry periods: in two-thirds of the reviewed cases, wetlands were found to contribute to a reduction in base flows. Also, the role of wetlands in groundwater recharge differs: some studies reported a positive influence of wetlands on groundwater recharge, whereas in other areas wetlands were found to reduce recharge.

Different factors determine the water-regulating functions of wetlands

The diverse ways in which wetlands influence the water cycle indicate that their regulating role is dependent on a large number of factors, including biotic and abiotic circumstances, ecosystem health and local climate. Where local site conditions such as the topography and permeability of the soil result in high water saturation levels during most of the year, wetlands often generate floods because they have limited additional storage capacity during periods of high precipitation (Holden and Burt, 2003; Jansky and Kocum, 2008). Others might more easily absorb and store excess rainwater and thereby mitigate floods (Wilson et al., 2010).

Similarly, vegetation composition, which is highly site specific and often subject to inter- and intra-annual variation, has been found to be a key determinant of regulatory processes (Tabacchi et al., 2000). Trepel et al. (2003), for example, found that microphyte vegetation in a German floodplain contributed significantly to on-site water storage; they reported a drop in water level of 0.5–0.8 metres within several days after removal of this vegetation. Depending on the extent to which water flows are diverted, obstructed or facilitated, vegetation may contribute to both increases and decreases in flooding risk. Such impacts are generally largest during the dry season or at the beginning or end of a flooding period (Tabacchi et al., 2000).

This heterogeneity in hydrological functioning is also illustrated by the different responses of seemingly similar wetland types to degradation. Holden et al. (2004), for example, concluded, based on a literature review on the impact of drainage on peatland hydrology, that the direction of change is determined by a combination of often modest differences in local site characteristics such as topography, soil and vegetative conditions and the extent and type of drainage. For example, flooding risk might increase where runoff through drainage canals is more rapid, compared with natural surface and subsurface runoff processes; in other cases, peatland drainage may contribute to flood risk reduction, as dewatering of the soil resulted in greater water capturing capacity (for example, Archer, 2003; Robinson, 1980; Wilson et al., 2010).

There are indications that the hydrological response of wetlands following disturbance may change over time. Holden et al. (2006), for example, hypothesized that an initial increase in flooding risk following drainage may alternate with improved water regulation once the soil dewaters and becomes capable of storing excess water. They suggested a possible increase in flooding risk in the long term, following subsidence of the soil. Although such long-term relationships require more thorough investigation, the authors indeed recorded significant changes in stream flow processes over time, with increased runoff efficiency and higher levels of subsurface flow over a 50-year time-frame in four study sites in the United Kingdom.

Socioeconomic context

The extent to which wetlands reduce water-related hazards depends on the local hydro-geomorphological and environmental factors described above, but it is also dependent on the broader spatial socioeconomic context in which wetlands provide these functions: for example, a wetland that retains floodwaters may increase on-site or upstream flooding hazards, while reducing the risks downstream. The consumption of water by wetlands, particularly in drought-prone areas, might be perceived as a risk factor to downstream water users, whereas the sustained health of a wetland as a result of this water use provides resilience to wetland-dependent communities on-site. Thus, the contribution of wetlands to risk reduction needs to be judged on the basis of this heterogeneity. This requires consideration of wetlands' impacts on the water cycle in different parts of a river basin, together with an assessment of these functions for different stakeholder groups, whose needs may differ in space and time.

Towards wetland-integrated disaster risk reduction

Conventional risk reduction strategies remain largely biased towards socioeconomic and infrastructural solutions. However, as the impacts of environmental degradation on resilience against water-related hazards have become increasingly visible, risk reduction practitioners are confronted with the challenge of incorporating the sustainable management and restoration of wetlands and other ecosystems as a new dimension to their work. In this section, three key steps are outlined that facilitate implementation of an adaptive, ecosystem-inclusive disaster risk reduction approach.

Step 1. (E)valuate: Identify the root causes of risk and assess the costs and benefits of risk reduction approaches

Risk reduction planning often starts with the identification of existing hazards within a target area and an analysis of hazard impacts on people and economies. To date, however, most risk assessments fail to incorporate a *systemic* approach, where the way in which hazards occur is looked at across a wider physical landscape and where the root causes behind the occurrence of extreme events are identified. By integrating such a dimension, risk reduction experts gain critical insights into the way in which site-specific hydro-geomorphological and environmental conditions drive risk and how human interventions such as infrastructure development or land conversion have an influence on these interactions. By adopting a functional unit of land – a catchment or river basin in the case of water-related hazards – as a starting point of risk analysis, risk reduction experts are able to capture spatial and temporal dimensions, such as lag times in response to land management changes and upstream–downstream interactions. Adoption of such a landscape approach combined with local-level risk assessment allows for the identification of possible disaster risk reduction scenarios, which respond to both the hazard itself and its root causes at multiple scales and which employ multisectoral response strategies, including ecosystem-based solutions. Case Study 1 provides an example of a systemic approach to risk reduction analysis and planning (see Box 9.2).

Once different risk reduction scenarios are identified, in-depth analysis of the costs and benefits related to individual measures allows for the selection of the most appropriate response strategy to cope with or mitigate the identified hazards. Conventional cost–benefit analyses (CBAs) predominantly consider costs and benefits in the light of the directly visible market impacts of interventions. To ensure well-informed decision-making, CBAs should broaden their scope and also consider the indirect implications of risk reduction measures that are not directly visible or that do not have a market value (Aylward, 2000; Brouwer and van Ek, 2004). For example, in addition to assessing the on-site impacts of risk reduction measures, effects that take time to occur or reveal themselves

Box 9.2 Case Study 1: From beneficial floods to flood vulnerability in the
Mahanadi Delta, India

The Mahanadi Delta, located within the north-eastern region of Orissa
(India) at the confluence of the Mahanadi River with the Bay of Bengal, is of high ecological and socioeconomic importance. The region is
characterized by the presence of varied landforms such as distributary
channels, natural levees, channel bars and islands, floodplains, back-
water swamps, lakes, offshore bars and spits and lagoons. Spread over
9,000 km², the delta forms 5 per cent of the geographical area of the
state but is inhabited by over 30 per cent of its population. The biologically diverse ecosystems within the delta provide a range of ecosystem services that support the well-being of a large proportion of
the delta's inhabitants. Agriculture, supported by rich fertile soils and
abundant freshwater, represents the predominant livelihood option for
68 per cent of its population. Chilika Lake is an important fisheries
resource, accounting for 5–6 per cent of the total production in Orissa.
The lake is home to 46 economically important species of fish, prawns
and crabs, supporting the livelihoods of over 200,000 people (Orissa
Census, 2001). The Mahanadi River carries runoff from a huge catchment (132,000 km²), creating recurrent inundation within the deltaic
region. Similarly, tropical depressions of varying intensity are a common weather phenomenon. Consequently, the Mahanadi Delta is subject to multiple hazards, including floods, droughts and cyclones
(Mohanti, 2000).

Traditionally, the agrarian communities living within the delta developed farming systems that adequately distributed the risks of crop failure resulting from recurrent floods and droughts. Besides developing
flood- and drought-resistant rice strains, the cropping cycles were
spread across the year so that, even if one crop was affected, the others would provide sufficient production to compensate for the loss.
Farmers also distributed risk by cultivating in different soil types with
varying fertility and composition and located at different elevations.
Most importantly, the strategy recognized floods and resulting inundation patterns to be beneficial to the crops owing to their capacity for
natural fertilization of agricultural lands.

Developmental planning within the region has undermined the close
relationship between hydrological regimes and livelihoods, and focused on structural approaches to support agriculture by harnessing
hydrological regimes. The delta was subject to intensive hydrological
regulation primarily during colonial rule in the eighteenth century. The
dynamic fluvial environment of the delta was constrained by embankments and other hydraulic structures to provide a regulated water

Box 9.2 (cont.)

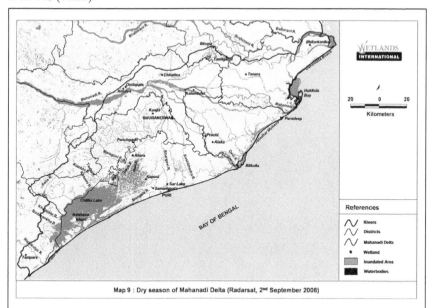

Map 9 : Dry season of Mahanadi Delta (Radarsat, 2ⁿᵈ September 2008)

(a) The delta in the dry season

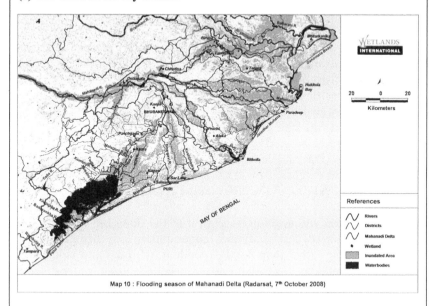

Map 10 : Flooding season of Mahanadi Delta (Radarsat, 7ᵗʰ October 2008)

(b) Floods within the delta

Figure 9.1 GIS maps illustrating the dynamic wetland regimes in the Mahanadi Delta, Orissa
Source: Wetlands International South Asia.

Box 9.2 (cont.)

Figure 9.2 Rice farming in the Mahanadi Delta (India), 2012
Photo: Pieter van Eijk.

supply to irrigated fields. In 1957, the Hirakud dam project was constructed on the Mahanadi River for hydropower generation and as a
major sediment trap for an intercepted catchment area of 83,500 km^2.
Weirs were constructed at the head of the Mahanadi Delta to capture
the downstream hydropower water release to irrigate 1.36 million hectares of land (CSE, 2003). Subsequently, the Bhargabi and Daya dis-
tributaries were embanked to Chilika as a flood preventive measure in
irrigated areas (Das and Jena, 2008). Later, development in the delta
emphasized the extension of these activities without reviewing their
long-term implications and without taking community perceptions into
consideration.

Because water resources management in the delta has failed to understand the role of fluvial regimes, communities have been rendered
flood vulnerable rather than flood dependent. With the flow connectivity severely impeded by embankments, the delta faces water-logging
and aggravated flooding damage. The water-logging leads to lower agricultural productivity as well as the increased incidence of diseases
attributed to stagnant waters. Assessments of remote sensing imageries
indicate that the extent of wetlands has declined considerably because

Box 9.2 (cont.)

of the loss of connectivity with the river regimes and changing land-use patterns in the delta, especially in the central deltaic region. During the period 1975–2010, nearly 30 per cent of wetland area was lost, along with associated natural resources. Small land holdings and limited opportunities for livelihood diversification have led to high poverty in the region, contributing to increased vulnerability to water-related hazards. In turn, increased vulnerability has resulted in the loss of lives and livelihoods and significantly constrains the long-term development opportunities of the local population. Women and low-caste communities have been most severely affected.

The role of floods and fluvial regimes is gradually becoming apparent; the traditional knowledge of farming communities on the role of floods was a key component of assessing environmental flows to Chilika Lake. When the Naraj weir at the head of the delta was replaced by the 940 metre Naraj barrage across the Kathjori tributary of the Mahanadi River, the state government commissioned an environmental flow assessment for Chilika Lake (Mohanti, 2003). Among the flow scenarios considered in the assessment, floodplain communities indicated a preference for scenarios that maintained water flows for their beneficial effects on agricultural productivity, which more than compensated for flood-induced damage to assets. Fishers in downstream Chilika Lake also expressed a preference for scenarios that maintained flows because they help keep the sea mouth open and ensure high productivity through the flushing of sediment and nutrients. Expressed in cost–benefit terms, floods of moderate intensity brought significant positive benefits both to floodplain agriculture and to downstream fisheries in the lagoon. Efforts to manage disaster risk in the delta now have an explicit focus on the ecosystem services of wetlands and have been aligned with existing approaches to community-based risk reduction. The government has adopted interventions to improve flow regimes and to implement ecosystem restoration measures such as the reforestation of hill slopes and nearby mangroves, the dredging of wetlands and the removal of invasive plants.

outside the area of intervention need to be documented. Differing impacts experienced across various stakeholder groups also need to be properly assessed and evaluated.

In light of these considerations, it is critical to identify the full range of ecosystem services that may be affected or restored under the different scenarios. As discussed above, ecosystems provide important, yet invisible, services to a large number of stakeholders across a wide geographical area and contribute to community resilience; failure to recognize these linkages may have far-reaching implications. The construction of a dam, for example, may well provide important water supplies during drought periods locally, but may affect ecosystem health downstream, causing a loss of valuable natural resources. Various ecosystem valuation studies have tried to untangle these complex interactions and have pioneered a variety of valuation methodologies (see, for example, Balmford et al., 2008; Costanza et al., 1997; and TEEB, 2010).

Step 2. Design ecosystem-based responses

Integrated risk reduction planning, as described in Step 1, will generally result in the identification of measures for improved land use, including approaches that aim to maintain or revitalize ecosystem services. Providing a description of the full range of ecosystem-based responses that could be adopted falls outside the scope of this chapter. However, two types of intervention stand out as critical for securing and enhancing the role of wetland ecosystems in reducing risk and providing resilience to water-related hazards: sustaining the water regimes required for maintaining ecosystem health and productivity; maintaining and restoring ecosystems and their services.

Sustain the water regimes required for maintaining ecosystem health and productivity

The ecological functions and processes that are driven by the flood pulse are key for maintaining ecosystem health across river basins. They ensure delivery of important provisioning and regulating services that contribute to flood and drought resilience. Thus, maintaining a minimum quality, quantity and timing (seasonality, variability) of water flows, also referred to as "environmental flows" (TNC, 2006), comes at the core of any programme targeted at the reduction of water-related disasters.

Consideration of such environmental flows is important for two reasons. First, risk reduction measures may alter water flows and sometimes inadvertently adversely affect ecosystem health downstream. Where possible, these impacts should be avoided, minimized or mitigated. For example, adverse impacts may become evident when construction of a dam results in a modified flow regime or when water harvesting structures reduce flow below a certain threshold (see Case Study 2 in Box. 9.3). The balance between locally derived improved resilience and increased vulnerability downstream as a result of ecosystem services loss should be identified early in the planning process. This could occur as part of the analysis of the costs and benefits of the identified scenarios. The assessment

Box 9.3 Case Study 2: Infrastructure developments and community resilience in the Inner Niger Delta

Fed by the Bani and Niger rivers, the Inner Niger Delta in Mali is a 3 million hectare wetland consisting of lush floodplains, lakes and river branches. The natural resources provided by this inland delta sustain the livelihoods of more than 1 million people. Each year, pastoralists migrate towards the delta, following the gradual retreat of the floods, to graze their cattle in the fields of floating *Bourgou* grass. Farmers use the floodplains for the production of floating varieties of rice, and the area produces 40,000–100,000 tonnes of fish each year. The annual floods are the engine behind these riches, and the extent of flooding determines the benefits derived: low floods and the failure of local rains cause widespread famine, whereas high floods deliver prosperity.

In recent decades, upstream developments have altered the rivers' flow regime significantly. The Selengue dam was created for hydropower generation and a barrage was built to divert water to the Office du Niger, a major rice production scheme; these developments resulted in a 20 per cent decrease of water flows towards the Inner Niger Delta and a change in the timing of the flood pulse. Plans exist to upscale hydropower generation through the construction of the Fomi dam, and concessions for a 100,000 hectare expansion of the Office du Niger scheme have been provided to Libyan, Saudi and Chinese investors. Such plans have raised concerns over the sustainability of these developments, because the environmental impacts may eventually undermine the economic benefits if too much water is withdrawn. Local communities in the Inner Niger Delta have already experienced significant decreases in the availability of natural resources, such as fish and floating grasses, increasing their vulnerability to drought years, and it is expected that new upstream developments may further exacerbate this risk.

An extended cost–benefit analysis was undertaken in 2005 to map the implications of existing and planned developments. This study not only identified direct operational and construction costs and benefits related to hydropower generation and rice production, but also assessed the indirect environmental costs related to decreases in water availability in the Inner Niger Delta. The study concluded that the Selengue dam and the current Office du Niger irrigation scheme represent a positive annual net economic value of respectively €2.7 million and €12.5 million, despite marked decreases in agricultural, livestock and fisheries production in the delta. Construction of the Fomi dam, however, was projected to result in the degradation of a significant part of the delta, leading to an annual net economic loss

Box 9.3 (cont.)

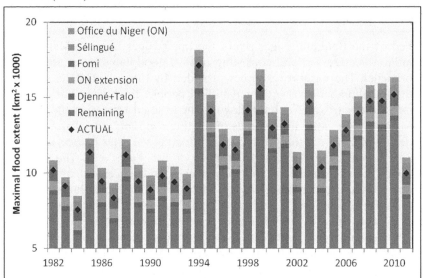

Figure 9.3 Measured and projected flooding extent in the Niger Delta, 1982–2010, under different scenarios: Without infrastructure (full bars) and if different existing and planned water infrastructures had been in place since 1982. The names in the key refer to schemes that have been put in place (above black dot) or that are currently under review (below black dot).
Notes: The names in the key refer to schemes that have been put in place (above black dot) or that are currently under review (below black dot). The decreases in flooding represent a massive increase in drought risk, because critical thresholds for maintaining ecosystem health have been passed.
Source: Leo Zwarts (Altenburg & Wymenga Ecologisch Onderzoek).

Please see page 485 for a colour version of this figure.

of over €20 million. Additionally, hydrological models predict that combined implementation of all planned irrigation and dam development schemes results in a seven-fold increase in the incidence of extremely low floods in the Inner Niger Delta. This means that a famine would strike once every two or three years, with disastrous consequences for the local population. Climate change might further aggravate water stress in the delta. For example, a moderate decrease in local rainfall of 10 per cent, combined with upstream water diversion, is projected to reduce water availability by an average of 70 per cent. This would cause the near-total collapse of the Inner Niger Delta.

These figures indicate that infrastructure developments along the Niger River may result in changing water flows beyond the thresholds required for the maintenance of ecosystems and thus the survival of rural communities dependent on these ecosystems. This in turn

Box 9.3 (cont.)

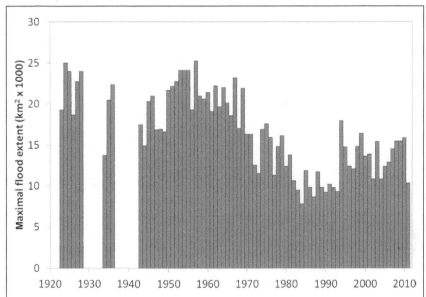

Figure 9.4 Decrease in flooding extent in the Niger Delta, 1920–2010
Note: Data are lacking for years without bars.
Source: Leo Zwarts (Altenburg & Wymenga ecologisch onderzoek).

Figure 9.5 Fishermen in the Inner Niger Delta (Mali), June 2008
Photo: Pieter van Eijk.

Box 9.3 (cont.)

Figure 9.6 Small-scale agriculture in the Inner Niger Delta (Mali), June 2008
Photo: Pieter van Eijk.

results in a massive increase in disaster risk and adversely affects the
Malian economy. Even where net benefits are positive, certain stakeholder groups will face increasing vulnerability as a result of declining
natural resources. Extensive dialogue between government agencies,
local communities and the private sector will be required to balance
stakeholder needs and address poverty and disaster vulnerability concerns. Moreover, adaptive water resources management approaches
are required to align water allocation schemes with changes in flow
regimes that occur as a result of climate change and variability. Such
an integrated approach to water management prevents river flows
from temporarily falling below critical sustainability thresholds as a result of water extraction.

Sources: Zwarts et al. (2005); Zwarts (2010).

may result in rejection or approval of the proposed water management
measures, or more commonly lead to their modification so that environmental flow requirements are met.

Second, risk reduction managers may increase resilience by restoring
flow regimes that have long been lost. A significant proportion of river
basins across the world have been heavily modified as a result of water

diversion, dam construction and canalization. The Millennium Ecosystem Assessment (MEA, 2005) estimates that to date no fewer than 45,000 large dams and 800,000 small dams have been constructed. Maintenance of the natural flow regime in the operations of many of these dams is either not considered or is insufficiently considered (Richter et al., 2010). Thus, reinstatement of environmental flows and optimization of flow regimes through adaptive water resources management is a cost-effective approach to ensuring the revival of important ecosystem services that contribute to enhanced resilience and risk reduction (for example, Richter and Thomas, 2007; Richter et al., 2010).

Environmental flow requirements for sustaining ecosystem services are highly site specific. Minimum flow regimes therefore need to be assessed on a case-by-case basis, in consultation with ecologists, hydrologists, dam operators and others. Various methodologies exist to identify environmental flows. For example, functional analysis identifies the key functions of the flow regime (for example, sediment flushing, habitat maintenance, reproduction of plants and animals) and the minimum requirements for sustaining each of these functions. Other approaches focus on the ecological requirements of habitats and species. Simple proxies are developed for these requirements, such as the extent of flooding or flooding duration, to aid identification of environmental flow requirements (Acreman and Dunbar, 2004; Richter and Thomas, 2007). Negotiation of ecologically sound water management regimes requires engagement of a multitude of stakeholders. Integrated water resources management therefore is a key element in the risk reduction planning process.

Maintain and restore ecosystems and their services

Although reinstatement of hydrological conditions is a key requirement in the restoration of ecosystem health, often additional structural wetland rehabilitation measures are needed to restore the provisioning and regulating services that contribute to resilience and risk reduction. The nature of such restoration measures is highly context specific and depends on ecological and hydro-geomorphological site conditions as well as the extent and nature of the degradation. Where watersheds have been heavily impounded following the establishment of embankments, channel normalization and dam construction, it is key to restore connectivity between rivers and associated (former) floodplain areas and increase their storage capacity. This functional restoration approach requires drastic engineering measures such as dyke relocation, depoldering, the lowering of floodplain areas and the creation of river bypasses. Such measures are currently implemented as part of the Room for the River Programme in the Netherlands, representing a total investment of €2.3 billion, as well as in other parts of Europe and the United States (Blackwell and Maltby, 2006; Room for the River, 2012; see Case Study 3 in Box 9.4). A strategic and broad-scale approach, in which options for restoration are assessed across the entire river basin, is imperative for such measures to deliver optimal results (Rohde et al., 2006).

In cases where the human impact on the hydro-geomorphological characteristics of a river basin is less profound, small-scale on-site restoration measures may be implemented that focus on the maintenance of environmental services provision. Examples include the blocking of erosion gullies in degraded peatlands to maintain water-regulating functions, removal of invasive vegetation to prevent siltation, and reforestation of upland areas to reduce sediment inflow. Parallel to the implementation of rehabilitation and water management interventions, it is important to establish regulatory frameworks to avoid future adverse environmental impacts of human interventions in the river-floodplain.

Step 3. Integrate and align approaches

Disaster risk reduction is usually tackled by different sectors, which in many cases implement activities separately. Humanitarian and development organizations have adopted a focus on community-managed risk reduction, where local-level preparedness, mitigation and response measures are identified and implemented by the local people themselves. Risk reduction measures at broader spatial scales (that is, using a landscape approach) are often underrepresented in their planning. On the other hand, water resources managers adopt a regional scope; they manage water-related hazards across river basins, but often rely heavily on infrastructure to store, allocate and regulate water. Local-level needs and possibilities for individual stakeholders to improve their resilience are sometimes overlooked or even constrained. The management and restoration of ecosystems in general and in relation to disaster risk reduction have traditionally been the realm of conservation organizations (for example, Nellemann and Corcoran, 2010; Sudmeier-Rieux and Ash, 2009).

The case for integrating disaster risk reduction approaches is clear: working in isolation or sectorally does not deliver a holistic solution that addresses all drivers of risk and vulnerability. Hence, it will be crucial for different sectors to bring together their skills and expertise and work towards integrated risk reduction planning. The best way to accomplish such integration is to establish national or regional risk reduction platforms in which each of these disciplines is represented and to ensure that all steps of the risk reduction cycle are implemented jointly. This requires joint local and regional risk assessments and identification and alignment of early warning, preparedness, prevention, mitigation and response measures. Engagement of local communities and private sector and government stakeholders is instrumental to ensure that risk reduction is

Box 9.4 Case Study 3: Flood risk reduction by providing Room for the River

Following centuries of floodplain reclamation, canalization and dyke construction, the Government of the Netherlands realized that the traditional approach of controlling rivers through infrastructure development no longer sufficed to cope with increasing flood risks. This became painfully clear in 1993 and 1995, when high water levels resulted in the relocation of 100,000 people along the Rhine and Meuse rivers. With projected increases in peak flows as a result of climate change and confronted with sea level rise and soil subsidence, an approach purely focused on further strengthening of the dykes was no longer an option; the costs and risks involved were considered too high.

Instead, inspired by a number of small-scale pilot projects, an alternative risk reduction approach was developed that focused on the reinstatement of the natural flow dynamics of the rivers and the revival of the capacity of the (former) floodplains to store and regulate water flows. This resulted in the formulation of the Room for the River Programme, and its approval by the Dutch government in 2007. Room for the River implements ecosystem restoration measures at 39 locations, such as the depoldering and lowering of former floodplain areas, dyke relocation, lowering of groynes and the construction of side channels. In urban and industrial centres or other areas where ecosystem-based

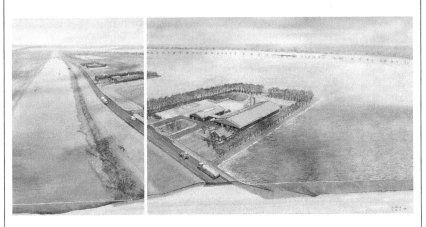

Figure 9.7 The "Room for the River" concept: Restoring former floodplains and using agricultural land for water retention, while protecting human settlements. Impression of the Overdiepse Polder during low and high flow periods
Source: Rudolf Das (Room for the River).

Box 9.4 (cont.)

responses are considered too costly or inappropriate, infrastructure solutions, such as strengthening of dykes, are adopted. The restoration
measures will be completed by 2015 and will result in reduced flood
risk for 4 million people along the Rhine, Meuse and IJssel rivers.

Sources: Room for the River (2012); Simons et al. (2001); Brouwer and van Ek (2004).

mainstreamed into development practice and to balance often contradict-
ing priorities and needs between target groups.

Conclusions

Current science and practice make a strong case for the adoption of
ecosystem-based solutions to disaster risk reduction. An increasing
number of development and conservation non-governmental organizations, government institutions and donor agencies have responded to this
evidence by exploring ecosystem-inclusive approaches. Yet some barriers
remain that may hinder such integration.

For some ecosystem types, more research is needed to gain full understanding of their contribution to resilience in different socioeconomic
and hydro-geomorphological settings. Once the heterogeneity in ecosystem services within different contexts is understood, it becomes much
easier to calculate the costs and benefits related to the management and
restoration of natural resources. This will help risk reduction planners to
make a strong case for adopting ecosystem-based approaches. Likewise,
restoration methodologies require further testing and intensive scientific
monitoring to ensure they are optimally adapted to a given context and
to provide maximum benefits at minimal cost.

Yet the biggest challenge is of a different nature: as long as global development remains geared towards achieving short-term economic gains
at the cost of long-term sustainability, the loss of nature's assets will continue to increase vulnerability. Although solving this lies beyond the
sphere of influence of the disaster risk reduction or environmental management community alone, the sectors involved can play a major role in
working towards a paradigm shift, whereby retaining ecosystem services
moves to the core of development planning. This demands political will
and innovation, and in some cases even a change in institutional mandates. It requires those who focus on community-based action to broaden

their views and engage in policy dialogue. Often this involves touching upon sensitive development and environmental issues where there are trade-offs to be made. It calls for a shift from an approach geared towards engineering towards one that is also built on environmental considerations. And, most importantly, it requires a broad vision where the different development sectors involved not only consider resilience from their own perspective but also acknowledge the perspectives of other sectors and seek greater inter-sectoral collaboration and integration in programme implementation. Implementing these changes is not easy, but successful embedding of environmental considerations in risk reduction planning will make a substantial contribution to improving the resilience of communities and society at large.

REFERENCES

Acreman, M. and M.J. Dunbar (2004) "Defining Environmental River Flow Requirements – Review". *Hydrology and Earth System Sciences* 8(5): 861–876.

Acreman, M.C., R. Riddington and D.J. Booker (2003) "Hydrological Impacts of Floodplain Restoration: A Case Study of the River Cherwell, UK". *Hydrology and Earth System Sciences* 7(1): 75–85.

Acreman, M.C. et al. (2007) "Hydrological Science and Wetland Restoration: Some Case Studies from Europe". *Hydrology and Earth System Sciences* 11(1): 158–169.

Archer, D. (2003) "Scale Effects on the Hydrological Impact of Upland Afforestation and Drainage Using Indices of Flow Variability: The River Irthing, England". *Hydrology and Earth System Sciences* 7: 325–338.

Aylward, B. (2000) "Economic Analysis of Land-use Change in a Watershed Context". Paper prepared for UNESCO Symposium/Workshop on Forest-Water-People in the Humid Tropics, Kuala Lumpur, August.

Balmford, A. et al. (2008) *The Economics of Biodiversity and Ecosystems: Scoping the Science.* Cambridge: European Commission (contract: ENV/070307/2007/486089/ETU/B2).

Barbier, E.B. and J.R. Thompson (1998) "The Value of Water: Floodplain versus Large-Scale Irrigation Benefits in Northern Nigeria". *Ambio* 6(27): 434–440.

Bayley, P.B. (1995) "Understanding Large River-Floodplain Ecosystems". *BioScience* 3(45): 153–158.

Blackwell, M.S.A. and E. Maltby (eds) (2006) *Ecoflood Guidelines: How to Use Floodplains for Flood Risk Reduction.* Directorate-General for Research, Sustainable Development, Global Change and Ecosystems. Luxembourg: Office for Official Publications of the European Communities.

Bradshaw, C.J.A. et al. (2007) "Global Evidence That Deforestation Amplifies Flood Risk and Severity in the Developing World". *Global Change Biology* 13: 2379–2395.

Brouwer, R. and R. van Ek (2004) "Integrated Ecological, Economic and Social Impact Assessment of Alternative Flood Control Policies in the Netherlands". *Ecological Economics* 50: 1–21.

Bullock, A. and M. Acreman (2003) "The Role of Wetlands in the Hydrological Cycle". *Hydrology and Earth System Sciences* 7(3): 358–389.

Costanza, R. et al. (1997) "The Value of the World's Ecosystem Services and Natural Capital". *Nature* 387: 253–260.

CRED [Centre for Research on the Epidemiology of Disasters] (2011) "EM-DAT: The OFDA/CRED International Disaster Database", <http://www.emdat.be/> – Université catholique de Louvain – Brussels – Belgium (accessed 2 October 2012).

CSE [Centre for Science and Environment] (2003) "Climate Change and Orissa, Factsheet". Global Environmental Negotiations. New Delhi: CSE.

Das, B.P. and J. Jena (2008) "Impact of Mahanadi Basin Development on Eco-hydrology of Chilika". In M. Sengupta and R. Dalwani (eds), *Proceedings of Taal 2007: The 12th World Lake Conference*, pp. 697–702.

Dynesius, M. and C. Nilsson (1994) "Fragmentation and Flow Regulation of River Systems in the Northern Third of the World". *Science* 266: 753–762.

Emerton, L. and E. Bos (2004) *Value: Counting Ecosystems as an Economic Part of Water Infrastructure*. Gland, Switzerland, and Cambridge, UK: IUCN.

Fox, I.B. (2003) "Floods and the Poor: Reducing the Vulnerability of the Poor to the Negative Impacts of Floods". Prepared for the 3rd World Water Forum held in Kyoto, Shiga, and Osaka, Japan, 16–23 March 2003. "Water for All series", Asian Development Bank.

Gore, J.A. and F.D. Shields (1995) "Can Large Rivers Be Restored?" *Ecology of Large Rivers* 3(45): 142–152.

Grift, R.E. (2011) "How Fish Benefit from Floodplain Restoration along the Lower River Rhine". PhD thesis, Wageningen University, The Netherlands.

Henry, C.P. and C. Amoros (1995) "Restoration Ecology of Riverine Wetlands: I. A Scientific Base". *Environmental Management* 6(19): 891–902.

Hill, M.T., W.S. Platts and R.L. Beschta (1991) "Ecological and Geomorphological Concepts for Instream and Out-of-Channel Flow Requirements". *Rivers* 2(3): 198–210.

Holden, J. and T.P. Burt (2003) "Hydrological Studies on Blanket Peat: The Significance of the Acrotelm-Catotelm Model". *Journal of Ecology* 91: 86–102.

Holden, J., P.J. Chapman and J.C. Labadz (2004) "Artificial Drainage of Peatlands: Hydrological and Hydrochemical Process and Wetland Restoration". *Progress in Physical Geography* 28(1): 95–123.

Holden, J. et al. (2006) "Impact of Land Drainage on Peatland Hydrology". *Journal of Environmental Quality* 35: 1764–1778.

Hortle, K.G., S. Lieng and J. Valbo-Jorgensen (2004) "An Introduction to Cambodia's Inland Fisheries". Mekong Development Series No. 4, Mekong River Commission, Phnom Penh, Cambodia.

IPCC [Intergovernmental Panel on Climate Change] (2012) "Summary for Policymakers". In *Managing the Risks of Extreme Events and Disasters to Advance Climate Change Adaptation* [Field, C.B., V. Barros, T.F. Stocker, D. Qin, D.J.

Dokken, K.L. Ebi, M.D. Mastrandrea, K.J. Mach, G.-K. Plattner, S.K. Allen, M. Tignor, and P.M. Midgley (eds.)] A Special Report of Working Groups I and II of the Intergovernmental Panel on Climate Change. Cambridge University Press, Cambridge, UK, and New York, USA, pp. 1–19.

Jackson, D. and G. Marmulla (2000) "The Influence of Dams on River Fisheries". In G. Marmulla (ed.), *Dams, Fish and Fisheries. Opportunities, Challenges and Conflict Resolution*. FAO Fisheries Technical Paper 419. Rome: Food and Agriculture Organization of the United Nations.

Jansky, B. and J. Kocum (2008) "Peat Bogs Influence on Runoff Process: Case Study of the Vydra Peat Bogs and Kremelna River Basins in the Sumava Mountains, Southwestern Czechia". *Geografie–Sbornik CGS* 113(4): 383–399.

Jennings, S. (2011) "Time's Bitter Flood: Trends in the Number of Reported Natural Disasters". Oxfam GB Research Report.

Johnson, B.L., W.B. Richardson and T.J. Naimo (1995) "Past, Present, and Future Concepts in Large River Ecology: How Rivers Function and How Human Activities Influence River Processes". *BioScience* 3(45): 134–141.

Junk, W.J. and K.M. Wantzen (2004) "The Flood Pulse Concept: New Aspects, Approaches and Applications - An Update". In R.L. Welcomme and T. Petr (eds), *Proceedings of the Second International Symposium on the Management of Large Rivers for Fisheries: Volume 2. Food and Agriculture Organization & Mekong River Commission*. RAP Publication 2004/16. Bangkok: FAO Regional Office for Asia and the Pacific, pp. 117–149.

Junk, W.J., P.B. Bayley and R.E. Sparks (1989) "The Flood Pulse Concept in River-Floodplain Systems". *Canadian Special Publication of Fisheries and Aquatic Science* 106: 110–127.

McCartney, M.P. and M.C. Acreman (2009) "Wetlands and Water Resources". In E. Maltby and T. Barker (eds), *The Wetlands Handbook*. Oxford: Wiley-Blackwell.

Maltby, E. (2009) "The Changing Wetland Paradigm". In E. Maltby and T. Barker (eds), *The Wetlands Handbook*. Oxford: Wiley-Blackwell.

Marshall, B. and M. Maes (1994) "Small Water Bodies and Their Fisheries in Southern Africa". CIFA Technical Paper No. 29, FAO, Rome.

MEA [Millennium Ecosystem Assessment] (2005) *Ecosystems and Human Wellbeing: Wetlands and Water Synthesis*. Washington, DC: World Resources Institute.

Mohanti, M. (2000) "Unprecedented Super Cyclone on the Orissa Coast of the Bay of Bengal, India". *Cogeoenvironment Newsletter* 16: 11–13 (IUGS-UNESCO, Torrens, Australia).

Mohanti M. (2003) "Mahanadi River Delta, East Coast of India: An Overview on Evolution and Dynamic Processes". Utkal University, Bhubaneswar, India.

Nellemann, C. and E. Corcoran (eds) (2010) *Dead Planet, Living Planet: Biodiversity and Ecosystem Restoration for Sustainable Development*. A Rapid Response Assessment. Nairobi, Kenya/Arendal, Norway: United Nations Environment Programme/GRID-Arendal.

Nielsen, S.A., J.C. Refsgaard and V.K. Mathur (1991) "Conceptual Modelling of Water Loss on Flood Plains and Its Application to River Yamuna Upstream of Delhi". *Nordic Hydrology* 22: 265–274.

Nikula, J. (2008) "Is Harm and Destruction All That Floods Bring?" In M. Kummu, M. Keskinen and O. Varis (eds), *Modern Myths of the Mekong: A Critical Review of Water and Development Concepts, Principles and Policies*. Water & Development Publications. Helsinki: Helsinki University of Technology, pp. 27–38.

Orissa Census (2001) *Primary Census Abstract, Census of India*. New Delhi, India: Office of the Registrar General.

Plate, E.J. (2002) "Flood Risk and Flood Management". *Journal of Hydrology* 267: 2–11.

Ramsar Convention (1971) "Convention on Wetlands of International Importance Especially as Waterfowl Habitat. Final Text Adopted by the International Conference on the Wetlands and Waterfowl at Ramsar, Iran, 2 February 1971". Gland, Switzerland: Ramsar Convention Secretariat.

Richter, B.D. and G.A. Thomas (2007) "Restoring Environmental Flows by Modifying Dam Operations". *Ecology and Society* 12(1): 12.

Richter, B.D. et al. (2010) "Lost in Development's Shadow: The Downstream Human Consequences of Dams". *Water Alternatives* 3(2): 14–42.

Robinson, C.T., K. Tockner and J.V. Ward (2002) "The Fauna of Dynamic Riverine Landscapes". *Freshwater Biology* 47: 661–677.

Robinson, M. (1980) "The Effect of Pre-Afforestation Drainage on the Streamflow and Water Quality of a Small Upland Catchment". Institute of Hydrology Report, 73, Institute of Hydrology, Wallingford, UK.

Rohde, S.M. et al. (2006) "Room for Rivers: An Integrated Search Strategy for Floodplain Restoration". *Landscape and Urban Planning* 78: 50–70.

Room for the River (2012) "Safety for Four Million People in the Dutch Delta". Room for the River, Utrecht, The Netherlands. Available at <http://www.ruimtevoorderivier.nl/media/88721/rvdr_corp_brochure_eng__def._.pdf> (accessed 19 October 2012).

Sedara, K., C. Sopal and S. Acharya (2002) "Land, Rural Livelihoods and Food Security in Cambodia: A Perspective from Field Reconnaissance". Working Paper 24, Cambodia Development Resource Institute, Phnom Penh.

Simons, J.H.E.J. et al. (2001) "Man-made Secondary Channels along the River Rhine (The Netherlands): Results of Post-project Monitoring". *Regulated Rivers: Research & Management* 17: 473–491.

Sparks, R.E. (1995) "Need for Ecosystem Management of Large Rivers and Their Floodplains". *BioScience* 45(3): 168–182.

Sudmeier-Rieux, K. and N. Ash (2009) *Environmental Guidance Note for Disaster Risk Reduction*. Gland, Switzerland: IUCN.

Sutcliffe, J.V. and Y.P. Parks (1989) "Comparative Water Balances of Selected African Wetlands". *Hydrological Sciences* 34: 49–62.

Tabacchi, E. et al. (2000) "Impacts of Riparian Vegetation on Hydrological Processes". *Hydrological Processes* 14: 2959–2976.

TEEB (2010) "The Economics of Ecosystems and Biodiversity: Mainstreaming the Economics of Nature: A Synthesis of the Approach, Conclusions and Recommendations of TEEB". Available at <http://www.teebtest.org/teeb-study-and-reports/main-reports/synthesis-report/> (accessed 22 October 2012).

TNC [The Nature Conservancy] (2006) "Environmental Flows: Water for People – Water for Nature". The Nature Conservancy, Boulder, CO.

Tockner, K., F. Malard and J.V. Ward (2000) "An Extension of the Flood Pulse Concept". *Hydrological Processes* 14: 2861–2883.

Trepel, M. et al. (2003) "Influence of Macrophytes on Water Level and Flood Dynamics in a Riverine Wetland in Northern Germany". International Conference "Towards Natural Flood Reduction Strategies", Warsaw, 6–13 September.

UNEP [United Nations Environment Programme] (2009) "The Role of Ecosystem Management in Climate Change Adaptation and Disaster Risk Reduction". UNEP Copenhagen Discussion Series 2.

UNISDR [United Nations International Strategy for Disaster Risk Reduction] (2009) "2009 UNISDR Terminology on Disaster Risk Reduction". United Nations, Geneva. Available at <http://www.unisdr.org/files/7817_UNISDRTerminologyEnglish.pdf> (accessed 9 October 2012).

Van den Brink, F.W.B. et al. (1996) "Biodiversity in the Lower Rhine and Meuse River-floodplains: Its Significance for Ecological River Management". *Netherlands Journal of Aquatic Ecology* 30(2–3): 129–149.

Vanhan, H. (2004) "Agriculture in the Wetlands of Cambodia". In M. Torell et al. (eds), *Wetlands Management in Cambodia: Socioeconomic, Ecological and Policy Perspectives*. Technical Report 64. Penang, Malaysia: World Fish Center, pp. 17–21.

Ward, J.V., K. Tockner and F. Schiemer (1999) "Biodiversity of Floodplain River Ecosystems: Ecotones and Connectivity". *Regulated Rivers: Research & Management* 15: 125–139.

Wilson, L. et al. (2010) "Recovery of Water Tables in Welsh Blanket Bog after Drain Blocking: Discharge Rates, Time Scales and the Influence of Local Conditions". *Journal of Hydrology* 391: 377–386.

Wood, A. and G.E. van Halsema (eds) (2008) *Scoping Agriculture–Wetland Interactions: Towards a Sustainable Multiple-Response Strategy*. FAO Water Report 33. Rome: Food and Agriculture Organization of the United Nations.

WWF (2002) "Managing Floods in Europe: The Answers Already Exist. More Intelligent Riverbasin Management Using Wetlands Can Alleviate Further Flooding Events". WWF Background Briefing Paper, Brussels. Available at <http://awsassets.panda.org/downloads/managingfloodingbriefingpaper.pdf> (accessed 22 October 2012).

WWF (2011) "The Value of Wetlands", <http://wwf.panda.org/about_our_earth/about_freshwater/intro/value/> (accessed 22 October 2012).

Zwarts, L. (2010) *Will the Inner Niger Delta Shrivel up Due to Climate Change and Water Use Upstream?* A&W Report 1537. Feanwâlden, The Netherlands: Altenburg & Wymenga ecologisch onderzoek.

Zwarts, L. et al. (eds) (2005) *The Niger, a Lifeline: Effective Water Management in the Upper Niger Basin*. Lelystad, The Netherlands: RIZA / Sévaré, Mali: Wetlands International / Amsterdam: Institute for Environmental Studies (IVM) / Veenwouden, The Netherlands: A&W ecological consultants.

10

Utilizing integrated water resources management approaches to support disaster risk reduction

James Dalton, Radhika Murti and Alvin Chandra

Introduction

Earthquakes, droughts, floods and other natural hazards continue to cause thousands of deaths and injuries and billions of dollars of economic losses each year. Disaster statistics demonstrate that flood events are becoming more frequent (World Bank, 2010). According to Guha-Sapir et al. (2011), flooding in 2010 affected 178 million people worldwide, representing over 56 per cent of all disasters and affecting 87 per cent of the globally reported population impacted by disasters. Between 2000 and 2006 there were 2,163 water-related disasters, costing US$422 billion in damages and affecting 1.5 billion people (Adikari and Yoshitani, 2009).

Floods, the most common hydrological hazard, affect both developed and developing nations. In 2010, the flooding in Pakistan was widely covered by the media, as was the flooding in Queensland, Australia, and the destructive floods and landslides in Brazil. However, floods often have a disproportionate impact on the poor and socially disadvantaged, who are most vulnerable to flooding events, least able to help themselves, or less able to cope with the far-reaching and long-term impacts of floods (ActionAid, 2006). Between 1900 and 2006, flooding represented 90 per cent of the "most-fatal" disasters (Adikari and Yoshitani, 2009), with infrastructure damage being a key component of total direct losses (World Bank, 1999). Global economic losses from floods alone average US$3 billion per year, equivalent to 20 per cent of new investment in the water sector in developing countries (WWDR, 2003).

The role of ecosystems in disaster risk reduction, Renaud, Sudmeier-Rieux and Estrella (eds), United Nations University Press, 2013, ISBN 978-92-808-1221-3

Many cities are already exposed to multiple hazards such as landslides, floods and coastal storm surges (IFRC, 2010). These hazards become disasters because of existing vulnerabilities and weakened capacity to prepare for, respond to and recover from disasters. Urban centres are growing: 70 per cent of the global population is predicted to live in cities by 2030 (WHO, 2010). Some of this urban growth takes place in informal settlements, where housing construction is often of poor quality and basic infrastructure (drainage, waste disposal, water supply) is lacking. These conditions multiply disaster vulnerability, especially for the poorest parts of the population, who tend to settle in cheaper, degraded and often more hazard-prone areas (Adikari et al., 2010). These vulnerabilities are further exacerbated by the lack of legal land entitlements, the lack of support to respond to disasters and limited means to recover from them (Gaillard et al., 2010; Noy, 2009).

The way we manage our environment has consequences for our safety, in both urban and rural areas. The complex pathways between rivers, urban drainage systems, coastal zones and agricultural drains, combined with changing cropping patterns, dam construction, building characteristics and paving, wetlands and forests, all interplay and affect each other (World Bank, 2010). In developing our river basins for economic growth, food security and energy needs, we have an impact on the hydrological properties of river basins, which in turn can lead to changes in, for example, flood peaks, flows and sediment loads (Opperman et al., 2009); other impacts on neighbouring habitats and ecosystem services are not yet properly understood. Ecosystem degradation affects our ability to protect ourselves and our livelihoods from disasters, especially when we choose to live in hazard-prone areas.

Integrated water resources management (IWRM) and disaster risk reduction (DRR) communities offer many lessons for implementing climate change adaptation approaches, given that adaptation is unlikely to work in practice unless sustainable water resources management is tackled (Pittock, 2009). Neither DRR nor climate change adaptation is a distinct "sector"; rather, they are competing policy objectives, requiring actions to be implemented through other sectors, which include water, agriculture, health, land use and planning, energy and environment (UNISDR, 2011a). Good risk reduction strategies, including adaptation to risks related to climate change, will depend on the balance between the ecological needs and development demands of communities.

This chapter is devoted to understanding the linkages between IWRM and DRR. It starts with a discussion on the two approaches, followed by a comparison. It further highlights the opportunities and challenges in capitalizing on the commonalities, especially in the context of ecosystem-based approaches for building resilience to disasters.[1]

Integrated water resources management

IWRM is a "process which promotes the co-ordinated development and management of water, land and related resources, in order to maximize the resultant economic and social welfare in an equitable manner without compromising the sustainability of vital ecosystems" (GWP-TAC, 2000: 22). At the Johannesburg World Summit on Sustainable Development (WSSD) in 2002, emphasis was on the need to manage water at the scale of the river basin, under the principles of good governance and public participation.[2] Furthermore, IWRM was included in the Johannesburg Plan of Implementation as a key component for achieving sustainable development.

IWRM is also based on the Dublin Principles agreed at the International Conference on Water and Environment in 1992 (ICWE, 1992). These state that (i) freshwater is a finite and vulnerable resource, essential to sustain life, development and the environment; (ii) water development and management should be based on a participatory approach, involving users, planners and policy-makers at all levels; (iii) women play a central part in the provision, management and safeguarding of water; and (iv) water has an economic value in all its competing uses and should be recognized as an economic good.

Organizing activities in a river basin requires coordinated, strategic interventions between water, environment, land, agriculture, disaster management and climate change communities-of-practice (Wenger et al., 2002). This is needed to maximize the knowledge, best practices and policy frameworks in order to address multiple and converging challenges simultaneously. Often, large river basins are scaled down to individual "catchments", such as individual valleys, so that efforts for land and water management can be coordinated at an appropriate scale following the principle of subsidiarity. This principle states that only through decentralization can participation, and therefore management, occur at the appropriate scale (Molle et al., 2007). This approach is designed to build capacity at catchment level and to scale this up to build wider river basin capacity and learning.

It can be argued that IWRM is the most internationally accepted water policy "tool" (Rahaman and Varis, 2005). However, integrated management of water and land is a challenging concept because it deals with resources that are subject to competing interests, degradation, economic values and highly complex legal and institutional environments – and yet they are fundamental to life and economic needs. IWRM has been criticized as a "nirvana" concept that lacks practical ways to link issues of water poverty with alternative livelihoods (Butterworth et al., 2010; Merrey et al., 2005; Wester et al., 2009). Although water management issues are fundamentally local in nature, they have the potential to disrupt national energy and food security (Grey and Sadoff, 2007). The concept of a single philosophical approach for sustainable water resources management that can encompass all countries seems almost impracticable, given the different cultures, social beliefs and values, climatic conditions, physical attributes, management and technical capacities, institutional and legal frameworks, and systems of governance (Muller, 2010). Consequently, there are criticisms of IWRM implementation (Biswas, 2004; Medema et al., 2008).

Disaster risk reduction and IWRM

Disasters are mainly social constructs: they are largely determined by how a society manages its environment, how prepared it is to face adversity and what resources are available for recovery from the hazard (Sudmeier-Rieux and Ash, 2009; see also Chapters 1 and 2 in this volume). DRR refers to the development and application of policies, strategies and practices that recognize and minimize vulnerabilities or underlying causal factors of disasters (UNISDR, 2009). The "Hyogo Framework for Action 2005–2015: Building the Resilience of Nations and Communities to Disasters" provides the international framework for guiding and prioritizing action on DRR and aims towards the substantial reduction of disaster losses in lives and in the social, economic and environmental assets of communities and countries (UNISDR, 2005).

Because of the variability in the location, quantity and quality of water and the role of extreme events (such as floods and droughts) in the natural hydrological cycle, managing risk and uncertainty has long been a key function in the development of water management capacity. Understanding disaster risk is critical to the implementation of IWRM, because water resources management requires decisions on levels of risk-bearing (that is, spreading the costs either financially or environmentally) or risk mitigation and is concerned with who will bear the costs or enjoy the benefits involved in water management decisions (Rees, 2002). Yet there are challenges to this approach. Water management often requires significant financial and human resources owing to the need for built infrastructure, and this can result in "risk-shifting" (Rees, 2002). For example, upstream abstraction for irrigation or for capturing and storing water to enhance water security leaves downstream users short of water, potentially increasing their risks during dry periods. Upstream decisions can therefore generate risks for downstream users.

Furthermore, decisions about which hazards to address, when and how have consequences for those outside this decision-making process. For example, built irrigation canals, embankments and land-grading provide benefits to agriculture, food security and economic activities, but can have huge implications during flood events, which can have an impact on wider society and the environment. Flooding in the Indus Basin in Pakistan in 2010 provides a case in point, when upstream decisions on dam operations were made that allowed some areas to flood in order to relieve other areas downstream from potentially devastating floodwaters (Mustafa and Wrathall, 2011). The Indus River Basin provides food and livelihoods for millions of people who depend on their land for subsistence. Upstream water management infrastructure, such as dams and diversion structures, have provided regular and controlled water for irrigation and this can in turn create a sense of security from floods in downstream populations. This sense of protection and water control can intensify development in floodplains, making it difficult to protect assets from flooding. Yet this sense of security often causes people to expect "back to normal" conditions as quickly as possible after flood events – disregarding the fact that the flood risk still remains.

The operating "frameworks" between IWRM and the Hyogo Framework for Action (HFA) have many similarities. Both are technocratic in nature, driven by science-based or technical assessments to underpin decision-making. Because many risks are water related, solutions therefore concern water management (Hoverman et al., 2011). In IWRM, water management is often taken down to local scale and can develop strong community-based institutions such as water user associations, drinking water unions, irrigation unions and watershed councils (Jaspers, 2003). These community governance structures should be seen as multi-sectoral development mechanisms, which can also contribute towards DRR. Bringing people together to participate collectively in solving problems is valuable because it can provide more efficient and cost-effective solutions. It can also deliver quicker action on the ground than top-down approaches (Pahl-Wostl et al., 2007).

Learning from water management communities-of-practice may also catalyse the action needed to address the cross-cutting issues of dealing with underlying risks identified in the HFA (priority 4), which are lagging behind in terms of implementation (UNISDR, 2011b). By bringing all sectors into the decision-making process (via governance actions and capacity-building), IWRM is able to contribute towards the objectives of DRR by means of planning for hydrological variability, the development of strong community agencies, providing technical support and tools, and understanding probability and impact (Ako et al., 2010).

At strategic levels, IWRM focuses on establishing an "enabling environment" in terms of new and improved policies, legislation and financial mechanisms, which could also support meeting HFA priorities. IWRM's focus on policy reform can help regulate stress on ecosystem services across different spatial dimensions of the hydrological cycle (that is, groundwater, surface water, watersheds, coastal and marine resources). IWRM is "designed" to be a contextual and tailored approach according to each country and river basin, operating as a philosophy in approach and not as a rigid framework. There is no prescription for the IWRM approach, despite many academic debates over the application, replicability and relevance of IWRM (IUCN, 2011). Although establishing an enabling policy environment is crucial for long-term sustainability and resourcing, action on the ground is needed to deliver on water-related priorities, including DRR.

Table 10.1 shows the IWRM framework advocated by the Global Water Partnership (GWP-TAC, 2000). The three "pillars" of IWRM – the enabling environment, the institutional framework and the management instruments required to implement IWRM – need to work together to deliver the maximum shared benefits from land and water resources. The right side of Table 10.1 shows our interpretation of the HFA, based on the outcome, strategic goals and priority action areas (UNISDR, 2005). Integrating both frameworks can provide an enabling environment to deal with multi-sectoral challenges, but it needs to be supported by the relevant institutions.

Table 10.1 shows that IWRM and DRR have common objectives and approaches. Both IWRM and DRR frameworks recognize the role of ecosystems in water management and DRR. IWRM and DRR both seek to strengthen policies and legislative frameworks and prioritize improving water and land management to maximize the benefits derived from these natural resources, through coordinated planning that takes into account water-related disaster risks. The two communities-of-practice also promote the need for strengthening institutional capacity in policy implementation and improving knowledge and social learning. IWRM and DRR approaches focus on assessment needs and technical capacity development – including conducting risk assessments, improving understanding of water resources and hydrological networks, and promoting new technologies (that is, space-based systems), early warning systems, data storage and information-sharing. Yet another shared feature between IWRM and DRR is the emphasis on cross-sectoral integration and multi-stakeholder participation to reduce transaction costs and improve awareness and efficiency.

The role of ecosystems in IWRM and DRR approaches

Operational water resources management generally assumes a level of natural climate *variability* (annually or over a decade/s), based on historical records of seasonal variation as a good indication of future hydrology (Matthews and Le Quesne, 2009; Milly et al., 2008). Yet, many regulated

Table 10.1 Integrated water resources management and the Hyogo Framework for Action

Integrated water resources management			**Disaster risk reduction** (adapted from the Hyogo Framework for Action)		
"A process which promotes the co-ordinated development and management of water, land and related resources, in order to maximize the resultant economic and social welfare in an equitable manner without compromising the sustainability of vital ecosystems."			"The substantial reduction of disaster losses, in lives and in the social, economic and environmental assets of communities and countries."		

Pillars of IWRM			Strategic goals of HFA		
Enabling environment	Institutional framework	Management instruments	Integration of disaster risk into sustainable development policies and planning	Development and strengthening of institutions, mechanisms and capacities to build resilience to hazards	Incorporation of risk reduction approaches into implementation of emergency preparedness, response and recovery programmes

IWRM components			DRR components		
Policies	Organizational set-up	Water resources assessments	Policy, legislative and institutional frameworks	Monitoring and evaluating progress	Planning and institutional coordination
Legislation	Institutional capacities	IWRM plans	Improved planning based on land-use, socioeconomic and environmental conditions	Improving early warning systems	Terminology standards
Financial incentives	Institutional roles and mandates	Water demand management	Recognition of geological and hydro-geological risks	Developing risk vulnerability and resource assessments	Training and learning on DRR
		Social change instruments		Data-sharing, forecasting	Awareness-raising
		Conflict resolution		Capacity development	Cross-sectoral integration
		Regulatory instruments			Sustainable ecosystems and environmental management
		Economic instruments			
		Information management			

Sources: IWRM – GWP-TAC (2000), DRR – UNISDR (2005), adapted by the authors.

river systems show a decline in environmental conditions as a result of efforts aimed at increasing hydrological *stability*, usually through engineered structures that make river flows more uniform in order to control water supplies, but which do not necessarily consider ecosystem requirements in relation to ensuring the temporal distribution and quality of water resources (for example, Nilsson and Malm Renöfält, 2008). As the climate is expected to become more variable, especially in areas where natural variability is more common, the planning, construction and design of built infrastructure solutions are expected to become more complicated, and probably more expensive (Bouwer, 2011). Well-built infrastructure normally lasts a long time but, with climate change impacts and increasing disaster risks, can built infrastructure offer "protection" in the context of future climate variability? Although such measures may initially work well for one or two decades, further changes in climate and the inflexible nature of built infrastructure may lead to challenging trade-offs in the future (Matthews et al., 2011).

With decreasing availability of financial resources, and in the context of future climate variability, ecosystem-based solutions are increasingly recognized as an invaluable tool for DRR (UNISDR, 2011a). Ecosystem management tools need to be promoted and implemented as part of disaster management strategies because they may provide cost-effective solutions for reducing disaster vulnerability, especially in local communities (discussed further in the next section). Moreover, ecosystem-based solutions often provide multiple livelihood benefits (for example, water, fuel, building materials, arable land) beyond risk reduction (Tallis et al., 2008; see also Chapter 2 in this volume). Not only are ecosystem management approaches cost-effective when compared with hard infrastructure investment plans (Emerton, 2006), they are also flexible and tried and tested, and they offer readily available lessons, allowing for quick start-up in implementation (Mainka and McNeely, 2011).

Owing to the more local and place-specific nature of ecosystems, local communities, especially those whose livelihoods are heavily dependent on natural resources, understand the value of the ecosystem services they use. Local communities and their natural resource base are also frequently affected by disasters, giving communities access to historical local knowledge and experience of past disaster events. Communities can therefore take an active role in water resources management for DRR.

The benefits of natural and built infrastructure

River basins may contain many different watersheds and ecosystems that are all hydraulically connected and are shaped by natural and anthropogenic processes and that cross administrative and even national boundaries (Cohen and Davidson, 2011). Ecosystems play an important part in water collection, purification and storage and in the water conveyance process. Ecosystem functions within the river basin, therefore, have implications for disaster risk, because too much or too little water can be destructive. Ecosystems in themselves can thus be considered as "natural infrastructure" (Smith and Barchiesi, 2009). Conventional built water infrastructure (for example, seawalls, dams, reservoirs, irrigation systems, levees, canals) relies on ecosystem services to function correctly, as do the livelihoods of poor people and the performance of key industry sectors.

However, ecosystem services, particularly their hazard regulatory functions, are usually overlooked in water and disaster risk investment decisions, which often entail large capital costs. The adverse impacts of built water infrastructure on local ecosystem services may thus go unrecognized. Ecosystem services therefore need to be linked more directly and clearly into water infrastructure development, as part of their broader integration into development and risk reduction interventions.

Many studies show the benefits of conserving and restoring ecosystems as infrastructure (Campbell et al., 2009; Ramsar Convention on Wetlands, 2010). Batker et al. (2010) provide evidence in their case study on the Mississippi Delta that ecosystem restoration options offer significant economic gains in addressing the problem of increasing flood risk in the delta. Increased flooding is the result of built infrastructure that has been constructed to provide a certain level of flood protection but that requires constant maintenance and has affected water flows along large stretches of the river system and delta. This can lead to risk transfer, where one area is protected from flooding while another is sacrificed. Hence, most modern flood management plans now include natural infrastructure solutions, such as the protection and/or restoration of wetlands and floodplains (Defra, 2008), as part of a portfolio of strategies, owing to their unique ability to regulate water and sediment flows. In the United States, Costanza et al. (2008) have valued wetlands at US$33,000 per hectare in their role of reducing the impacts of Caribbean hurricanes, and offshore coral reef systems have been valued at US$0.7–2.2 billion in total in terms of the protection they offer from coastal storms (Burke and Maidens, 2004).

Nonetheless, the relationship between hazard mitigation functions provided by ecosystems and built infrastructure is not linear (Koch et al., 2009). Built infrastructure solutions do not provide full protection against hazards; they deal with the uncertainty of future hydrology by using technical parameters and safety margins to reduce the risk of infrastructure failure. This requires the use of probability and statistical factors, such as planning flood protection measures based on the return period of floods with varying potential impacts. The science of probabilities and flood return periods is not communicated adequately to those living in areas of risk, and built solutions thus become the primary option selected to reduce risk. Communities living in floodplains often expect built infrastructure to provide the "protection" they need against water hazards (see Dickie, 2011; Murti and Dalton, 2010), and the general public demands action on risks without understanding or considering the full cost of providing protection (Margolis, 1996). Saalmueller (2009) further states that providing protection to "stop flooding through climate-proofing" can be counterproductive, and at worst fatal, in areas where people living in danger zones are not fully informed of the residual risks.[3]

Similarly, it must be recognized that ecosystems are themselves dynamic in their responses to changes in the climate, anthropogenic pressures and natural change, and determination of their responses to pressures is complex because they are non-linear and often unpredictable. As Feagin et al. (2010) point out, ecosystems are not a panacea, but ignoring the role of ecosystems in disaster risk management solutions may be both an economic mistake and a missed opportunity. Infrastructure planning and investment therefore need to consider alternative mixes or "portfolios" of built and natural infrastructures, based on their various social, economic and environmental costs and benefits.

If we are to include natural infrastructure in DRR approaches, then ecosystems themselves also need to be subjected to the same level of scrutiny that is applied to built infrastructure, in order to better understand risk, uncertainty and non-linearity in responding to disasters. In practice, it remains difficult to compare ecosystems with built infrastructure and to swap one for the other because of limited understanding of the responses of ecosystem options to disaster impacts and the difficulty in modelling these responses with any degree of certainty.

Nevertheless, there is a real opportunity to consider disaster risk options more clearly in water resources management. Given an increase in reported disasters (Emmanuel, 2005) and the potential additional risk of climate variability, we can no longer ignore disaster risk in natural resource management frameworks. Complementary approaches that learn from each other are required (Wågsæther and Ziervogel, 2011). Interdisciplinary thinking is critical for supporting the capacity-building of local administrations, for information exchange, for developing operational capabilities, for network development and for improving management skills. Cross-sectoral integration allows for consideration of stakeholder interests, as well as developing sectoral partnership strategies for the exchange of scientific data, facilitating the transfer of technology and linking with other development policy and planning processes. These are all critical "lag" items identified in the Mid-Term Review of the HFA (UNISDR, 2011b), which could be addressed and supported by experiences from IWRM communities-of-practice.

The opportunity of linking DRR with water resources management approaches can also bring benefits to more traditional approaches to water service provision. Following the 2007 earthquake in the Ica region of Peru, the cost of restoring the water supply and sewerage system to pre-earthquake levels was US$27.6 million (World Bank WSP, 2011: 6). This figure represented over six times the water and sanitation expenditure of municipalities in the region in 2007. The Water and Sanitation Program study (World Bank WSP, 2011) showed that proper maintenance work on the water systems could have led to the extent of damage being almost six times less, with savings totalling approximately US$23 million. The study concluded that proper risk management should be part of the on-going maintenance of water and sewerage systems. The study also recommended that different construction material should be used and that proper site selection and location of the piped and storage infrastructure networks in the landscape should be considered, including factors such as soil type and structure and slope gradients. This example provides a solid case for integrating improved risk assessment and forecasting into water resources management and water service delivery. More importantly, it also alerted engineers and planners to the need to harness the natural resilience of the landscape for locating built infrastructure, highlighting the crucial link between land and water management.

Applying IWRM for disaster risk reduction

Table 10.2 presents an ecosystem approach to water-related DRR based on lessons from Smith and Cartin (2011) and in relation to the summary recommendations from the Mid-Term Review of the HFA (UNISDR, 2011b). Application of the ecosystem-based approach (Shepherd, 2008) has been interpreted and tailored in the context of DRR, based on recommendations by Sudmeier-Rieux et al. (2006) and additional reflections from ourselves. The table elaborates on how IWRM approaches could be applied for water-related DRR (IUCN, 2011) and further emphasizes the similar and complementary goals and priorities for action advocated by the HFA and IWRM frameworks (as previously discussed; see also Table 10.1).

IWRM approaches take a strategic overview of water resources in river basins. Initiatives such as the Tacaná watersheds of Guatemala (see Box 10.1) have demonstrated that bottom-up and integrated approaches in highly degraded watersheds can help build cooperation, capacity and resilience for managing disaster risks. Disasters are most often location specific – and disaster events provide a useful entry point for introducing activities to reduce vulnerability and to rebuild using natural infrastructure, as also shown in the experience of Peru.

DRR approaches could be better included in water management planning and in supporting the delivery of the HFA strategic goals through improving the understanding of:

- the role of built infrastructure solutions in reducing risks, and the costs of providing this protection relative to the role and costs of natural infrastructure solutions for the same risks (including the cost of longer-term maintenance of ecosystem protection and function);
- complementary portfolios of natural and built infrastructure solutions (that is, "hybrid" solutions) to reduce risks and maintain ecosystem functions;
- entry points for DRR interventions in water management practices and processes at the river basin level, including in post-disaster contexts to facilitate the timely identification of natural infrastructure options for reconstruction and recovery.

Applying such integrated ecosystem-based DRR approaches will require moving beyond the mere documentation or understanding of the impacts on ecosystems following disasters. It will also require the application of engineering approaches to ecosystem solutions in order to reduce risk. At present, many of the tools and approaches available (PEDRR, 2010) have been developed by non-governmental and international organizations. Although this multiplicity of approaches, tools and methods may improve knowledge of practice, there is an urgent need to accelerate the learning processes required in establishing good practices, by convening cross-sectoral dialogues, documenting and disseminating good practices and scaling up quality interventions. Moreover, it is critical that traditional and more value-based knowledge is presented as part of the water management debate, in order to support more technocratic and purely scientific information.

Conclusion

The overall goals of IWRM can be complex to achieve over the short term, yet it provides a valuable framework already institutionalized by many countries. Given the increasing frequency of water-related disasters and the pressures on ecosystems, adopting an integrated risk management and IWRM approach is not only practical but cost-effective. More national IWRM plans are being formulated and implemented, providing better knowledge on best practices at the river basin and micro-watershed levels. This has provided the basis for national IWRM committees to refine programmes and adopt good practices and better technologies from

Table 10.2 Mobilizing practical IWRM approaches to water-related disaster risk reduction: Principles of the approach

Governance	Processes and approaches	Implementation
Institutions, policies and planning		Demonstration and learning
Identify and understand multi-stakeholder and institutional structures	Create discourse platforms for multi-stakeholder discussion, learning and data-sharing	Recognize that ecosystems are linked and better understand the cause–effect relationships between them
Operate at appropriate scale relative to multi-stakeholder and institutional needs and capacities (i.e. river basin spatial scale) and better understand temporal changes in ecosystems and hydrology	Operate at appropriate levels (i.e. community) and encourage social learning and use of local knowledge	Apply DRR approaches as demonstrations to learn and adapt across multi-sectoral environments – avoid getting caught in planning cycles with minimal implementation
Recognize that multi-stakeholder includes multiple sectors	Undertake HFA National Platform "reality check" discussions and provide evidence that the natural infrastructure offers appropriate protection based on rigorous testing and analysis	Capture evidence from demonstration practice and share experience
Understand and work with decision-making, technical and institutional capacity, and political realities	Ensure HFA National Platforms understand and work with water management agencies and vice versa – especially regarding data collection and sharing, early warning systems, etc.	Use cost–benefit analysis for evidence-based advocacy
Recognize, understand and harmonize where possible with frameworks for poverty reduction, sustainable development and climate change adaptation	Use IWRM platforms and approaches to replicate successes and support DRR activities (and vice versa with DRR)	During and after disaster events, capture evidence on the functioning of ecosystems in terms of protection offered and their role in recovery
	Mobilize investments to support natural infrastructure solutions to complement built infrastructure	Build strong and new partnerships across rural and urban contexts and sectoral divides

Take advantage of post-disaster and other sectoral policy windows to strengthen the enabling environment
Ensure flexibility in design of policies and regular feedback to avoid stagnant policies and practices (plan for uncertainty)

Reduce economic distortions and align incentives for conservation and sustainable use
Build on the subsidiarity principle of IWRM to inform decisions and use social learning techniques to strengthen self-organization

Stakeholder participation

Ensure natural infrastructure is included in analysis as a risk-reducing asset, subject to similar management controls as built infrastructure
Share all information – transparently

Note: Recall that IWRM represents "the co-ordinated development and management of water, land and related resources" (GWP-TAC, 2000).

261

Box 10.1 The Tacaná watersheds programme: Risk reduction through IWRM

The Tacaná watersheds of Guatemala on the Mexican border begin in the high-altitude watersheds of the Suchiate and Coatán rivers. These poor and fragile areas are heavily dependent on ecosystem services for livelihoods, but are very vulnerable in terms of ecological and political factors. Unregulated land-use change has damaged steep catchments and deforestation has reduced the capacity of the landscape to retain water, causing increases in rainfall runoff, a reduction in the soil's water storage capacity, and increases in flood risk after intense rainfall. Intensive animal farming and a relatively dense population associated with poor waste and wastewater management have contaminated rivers and affected fisheries along the Pacific coast.

In response to increased flood risk and landslides, community workshops were held to elaborate on the basic notions of disaster risk and to identify the main risks faced by the communities in the watersheds. During these capacity-building sessions, interactions between how human activities in the middle and upper zones of the catchment affected lower zones of the catchment were analysed and the importance of conservation and catchment management to reduce adverse impacts better understood. Knowledge around risks and vulnerability was generated predominantly at community levels.

Local government committees are now working together to be better prepared using tools such as Geographic Information Systems to identify and map areas more prone to landslides and the possible evacuation routes. Disaster preparedness is now a high priority for authorities when managing climatic variability and climate change adaptation in the region. Local communities have organized two micro-watershed councils around the Coatán River and another two around the Suchiate River.

Established in order to lead in watershed restoration and development that meet their priorities, the councils were recognized by local governments from the start, and mayors participated in their formation. Although participation in the upper watersheds was limited to municipal councils, the process has now started to incorporate the private sector in the mid-section of the Suchiate River.

Learning from these community-led initiatives, a National Micro-watershed Commission was established to recognize the watershed as a planning unit for institutions in Guatemala for environmental management and conservation. Capacity-building and empowerment played a major role in improving natural resource management in the catchment and reducing risk and vulnerability. The scaling-up of the micro-watershed approach and the creation of new institutions have

Box 10.1 (cont.)

improved social capital by developing and applying new skills in relation to risk awareness and risk reduction. By expanding learning from
the local to the national level, experiences in the Tacaná watersheds
have shown that it is possible to break through a "ceiling of impact"
by building up adaptive capacity through the creation of new national-
level coalitions. This experience has shown that, through linkages at
different levels, scaling-up of efforts has been achieved and communities have been able to push the limits of their influence and communicate their messages upwards.

Source: Adapted from Cartin et al. (2012).

other areas. The benefits of utilizing an IWRM approach to support DRR
include the ability to use adaptive strategies across multiple sectors to
deal with human insecurity resulting from disasters. Such investments require minimal financial maintenance, because they are largely based on
collaborative thinking, planning and decision-making and on adaptive
management approaches that are institutionalized by means of IWRM
programmes.

Natural infrastructure solutions may be politically and socioculturally
harder to implement than built infrastructure, but in some cases they may
be more cost-effective. Water managers cope with variability and changes
in hydrology, and decades of experience allows built solutions that reduce
disaster risk to be tried, tested and tested again. Although ecosystem
management approaches can also be regarded as tried and tested, further
applied research is required to understand ecosystem-based solutions
using natural infrastructure *in the context of disaster management*, in order
to better understand the role of ecosystems in DRR and post-disaster recovery (see Barbier, 2007; Feagin et al., 2010). Relying solely on ecosystems for DRR without understanding the probability or magnitude of
disasters and the vulnerability of people may result in substandard protection of at-risk populations and their assets and may raise the level of
"moral hazard" – in the sense that those who make the decision to rely
solely on ecosystems are not those in harm's way. Therefore, portfolios of
solutions need to be developed in the future, including early warning systems, contingency planning and hybrid solutions of both engineered and
natural infrastructure; but such an integrated approach challenges the
current institutional set-up in addressing both water management and
risk reduction.

Although combined engineered and ecosystem-based approaches are being tested, increases in water-related disasters have stimulated policy and behavioural changes in relation to disaster preparedness and risk reduction. It is imperative that political attention targets how to address institutional challenges, decentralization, participation and environmental stresses rather than developing new institutions to deal with the problems. Even if the capacity is there, it is often not interconnected across sectors. Because water and disasters have impacts across sectors and society, the opportunity is for both the water and the disaster risk management communities-of-practice to work more closely together through recognizing river basins and natural infrastructure as part of the solutions to reduce risk.

Notes

1. As defined by the Intergovernmental Panel on Climate Change (IPCC, 2012: 5), resilience is "[t]he ability of a system and its component parts to anticipate, absorb, accommodate, or recover from the effects of a hazardous event in a timely and efficient manner, including through ensuring the preservation, restoration, or improvement of its essential basic structures and functions".
2. Originally discussed at the United Nations Conference on Water in Mar del Plata (1977), IWRM was promoted as the framework to incorporate the multiple competing uses of water resources. This framework approach was further strengthened at the International Conference on Water and Environment in Dublin (1992), the Second World Water Forum in The Hague (2000), the Bonn International Conference on Freshwater (2001), WSSD in 2002, and the Third World Water Forum in Kyoto (2003).
3. The residual risks are risks that remain in unmanaged form (even when effective DRR measures are in place) and for which emergency response and recovery capacities must be maintained (UNISDR, 2009).

REFERENCES

ActionAid (2006) "Unjust Waters: Climate Change, Flooding and the Protection of Poor Urban Communities: Experiences from Six African Cities". ActionAid International, London.

Adikari, Y. and J. Yoshitani (2009) "Global Trends in Water-Related Disasters: An Insight for Policymakers". United Nations World Water Assessment Programme (UNESCO), INSIGHTS Side Publication series. Paris: UNESCO.

Adikari, Y., R. Osti and T. Noro (2010) "Flood-related Disaster Vulnerability: An Impending Crisis of Megacities in Asia". *Journal of Flood Risk Management* 3(3): 185–191.

Ako, A.A., G.E.T. Eyong and G.E. Nkeng (2010) "Water Resources Management and Integrated Water Resources Management (IWRM) in Cameroon". *Water Resources Management* 24: 871–888.

Barbier, E.B. (2007) "Valuing Ecosystem Services as Productive Inputs". *Economic Policy* 22: 177–229.

Batker, D. et al. (2010) *Gaining Ground. Wetlands, Hurricanes and the Economy: The Value of Restoring the Mississippi River Delta*. Washington, DC: Environmental Law Institute.

Biswas, A.K. (2004) "Integrated Water Resources Management: A Reassessment". *Water International* 29(2): 248–256.

Bouwer, L.M. (2011) "Have Disaster Losses Increased Due to Anthropogenic Climate Change?" *Bulletin of American Meteorological Society* 92: 39–46.

Burke, L. and J. Maidens (2004) *Reefs at Risk in the Caribbean*. Washington, DC: World Resources Institute.

Butterworth, J. et al. (2010) "Finding Practical Approaches to Integrated Water Resources Management". *Water Alternatives* 3(1): 68–81.

Campbell, A. et al. (2009) *Review of the Literature on the Links between Biodiversity and Climate Change: Impacts, Adaptation and Mitigation*. Technical series 42. Montreal: Secretariat of the Convention on Biological Diversity.

Cartin, M., R. Welling, R. Córdoba, O. Rivera, C. Rosal and F. Arrevillaga (2012) "Tacaná Watersheds: Guatemala & Mexico: Transboundary Water Governance and Implementation of IWRM through Local Community Action". IUCN Water & Nature Initiative Case Study, Gland, Switzerland.

Cohen, A. and S. Davidson (2011) "An Examination of the Watershed Approach: Challenges, Antecedents, and the Transition from Technical Tool to Governance Unit". *Water Alternatives* 4(1): 1–14.

Costanza, R. et al. (2008) "The Value of Wetlands for Hurricane Protection". *Ambio* 37(4): 241–248.

Defra [Department for Environment, Food and Rural Affairs] (2008) "Making Space for Water Urban Flood Risk and Integrated Drainage Pilots: Upper Rea Catchment Including Longbridge, Northfield and Rubery Districts of Birmingham. Volume Seven: Environment". Birmingham City Council, UK.

Dickie, M. (2011) "Failed Sea Walls Were Seen as Among the Best, Japan". *Financial Times*, 17 March. Available at <www.ft.com/intl/cms/s/0/12dc0ec0-50bf-11e0-9227-00144feab49a.html> (accessed 23 October 2012).

Emerton, L. (2006) *Counting Coastal Ecosystems as an Economic Part of Development Infrastructure*. Ecosystems and Livelihoods Group Asia, International Union for Conservation of Nature, Colombo, Sri Lanka.

Emmanuel, K. (2005) "Increasing Destructiveness of Tropical Cyclones over the Past 30 Years". *Nature* 436: 686–688.

Feagin R. et al. (2010) "Shelter from the Storm? Use and Misuse of Coastal Vegetation Bioshields for Managing Natural Disasters". *Conservation Letters* 3(1): 1–11.

Gaillard, J.C. et al. (2010) "Alternatives for Sustained Disaster Risk Reduction". *Human Geography* 3(1): 66–88.

Grey D. and C.W. Sadoff (2007) "Sink or Swim? Water Security for Growth and Development". *Water Policy* 19(6): 545–571.

Guha-Sapir D. et al. (2011) *Annual Disaster Statistical Review 2010: The Numbers and Trends*. Brussels: Centre for Research on the Epidemiology of Disasters.

GWP-TAC [Global Water Partnership Technical Advisory Committee] (2000) *Integrated Water Resources Management*. TAC Background Papers No. 4. Stockholm: Global Water Partnership.

Hoverman, S. et al. (2011) "Social Learning through Participatory Integrated Catchment Risk Assessment in the Solomon Islands". *Ecology and Society* 16(2): 17.

ICWE [International Conference on Water and the Environment] (1992) "The Dublin Statement on Water and Sustainable Development. Adopted January 31, 1992 in Dublin, Ireland". International Conference on Water and the Environment, Dublin, Ireland, 26–31 January.

IFRC [International Federation of Red Cross and Red Crescent Societies] (2010) *World Disasters Report 2010: Focus on Urban Risk*. Geneva: International Federation of Red Cross and Red Crescent Societies.

IPCC [Intergovernmental Panel on Climate Change] (2012) *Managing the Risks of Extreme Events and Disasters to Advance Climate Change Adaptation*. A Special Report of Working Groups I and II of the Intergovernmental Panel on Climate Change [Field, C.B., V. Barros, T.F. Stocker, D. Qin, D.J. Dokken, K.L. Ebi, M.D. Mastrandrea, K.J. Mach, G.-K. Plattner, S.K. Allen, M. Tignor, and P.M. Midgley (eds.)]. Cambridge and New York: Cambridge University Press.

IUCN [International Union for Conservation of Nature] (2011) "Achieving Implementation of Integrated Water Resource Management". Water Briefing series, Global Water Programme, IUCN, Gland, Switzerland.

Jaspers, F.G.W. (2003) "Institutional Arrangements for Integrated River Basin Management". *Water Policy* 5(1): 77–90.

Koch, E.W. et al. (2009) "Non-linearity in Ecosystem Services: Temporal and Spatial Variability in Coastal Protection". *Frontiers in Ecology and the Environment* 7(1): 29–37.

Mainka, S.A. and J. McNeely (2011) "Ecosystem Considerations for Postdisaster Recovery: Lessons from China, Pakistan and Elsewhere for Recovery Planning in Haiti". *Ecology and Society* 16(1): 13. Available at http://www.ecologyandsociety.org/vol16/iss1/art13/ (accessed 23 October 2012).

Margolis, H. (1996) *Dealing with Risk: Why the Public and the Experts Disagree on Environmental Issues*. Chicago: University of Chicago Press.

Matthews, J.H. and T. Le Quesne (2009) *Adapting Water Management: A Primer on Coping with Climate Change*. WWF Water Security Series 3. Godalming, Surrey: WWF-UK.

Matthews, J.H., B.A.J. Wickel and S. Freeman (2011) "Converging Currents in Climate-Relevant Conservation: Water, Infrastructure, and Institutions". *PLoS Biology* 9(9): e1001159.

Medema, W., B. McIntosh and P.J. Jeffrey (2008) "From Premise to Practice: A Critical Assessment of Integrated Water Resources Management and Adaptive Management Approaches in the Water Sector". *Ecology and Society* 13(2): 29.

Merrey, D.J. et al. (2005) "Integrating 'Livelihoods' into Integrated Water Resources Management: Taking the Integration Paradigm to Its Logical Next Step for Developing Countries". *Regional Environmental Change* 5(4): 197–204.

Milly, P.C. et al. (2008) "Stationarity Is Dead, Whither Water Management?" *Science* 318(5863): 573–574.

Molle, F., P. Wester and P. Hirsch (2007) "River Basin Development and Management". In D. Molden (ed.), *Water for Food, Water for Life: Comprehensive Assessment of Water Management in Agriculture*. London: Earthscan, pp. 585–625.

Muller, M. (2010) "Fit for Purpose: Taking Integrated Water Resource Management Back to Basics". *Irrigation and Drainage Systems* 24(3–4): 161–175.

Murti, R. and J.A. Dalton (2010) "Opportunities in IWRM: Recognizing the Role Ecosystems Play in Reducing Risk". Presentation at the International Disaster and Risk Conferences in Davos, Switzerland, 30 May – 3 June 2010.

Mustafa, D. and D. Wrathall (2011) "Indus Basin Floods of 2010: Souring of a Faustian Bargain?" *Water Alternatives* 4(1): 72–85.

Nilsson, C. and B. Malm Renöfält (2008) "Linking Flow Regime and Water Quality in Rivers: A Challenge to Adaptive Catchment Management". *Ecology and Society* 13(2): 18.

Noy, I. (2009) "The Macroeconomic Consequences of Disasters". *Journal of Development Economics* 88(2): 221–231.

Opperman, J.J. et al. (2009) "Sustainable Floodplains through Large-scale Reconnection to Rivers". *Science* 326: 1487–1488.

Pahl-Wostl, C. et al. (2007) "Social Learning and Water Resources Management". *Ecology and Society* 12(2): 5.

PEDRR [Partnership for Environment and Disaster Risk Reduction] (2010) "Demonstrating the Role of Ecosystems-based Management for Disaster Risk Reduction". Background paper to the *2011 Global Assessment Report on Disaster Risk Reduction*. Geneva: UNISDR.

Pittock, J. (2009) "Adaptation Lessons for Climate Change Adaptation from Better Management of Rivers". *Climate and Development* 1: 194–211.

Rahaman, M.M. and O. Varis (2005) "Integrated Water Resources Management: Evolution, Prospects and Future Challenges". *Sustainability: Science, Practice and Policy* 1(1): 15–21.

Ramsar Convention on Wetlands (2010) "Shoreline Stabilisation & Storm Protection". Wetland ecosystem services, Factsheet 3. Ramsar Convention Secretariat, Gland, Switzerland. Available at <http://www.ramsar.org/pdf/info/services_03_e.pdf> (accessed 23 October 2012).

Rees, J.A. (2002) *Risk and Integrated Water Management*. TEC Background Papers No. 6. Stockholm: Global Water Partnership (GWP).

Saalmueller, J. (2009) "Flood Management: Why It Matters for Development and Adaptation Policy". *Water Front Magazine* No. 3–4.

Shepherd, G. (ed.) (2008) *The Ecosystem Approach: Learning from Experience*. Gland, Switzerland: IUCN.

Smith, D.M. and S.B. Barchiesi (2009) "Environment as Infrastructure: Resilience to Climate Change Impacts on Water through Investments in Nature". Perspective Document – Water & Climate Change Adaptation, Adapting to Climate

Change in Water Resources and Water Services: Understanding the Impacts of Climate Change, Vulnerability Assessments and Adaptation Measures. World Water Forum, Istanbul.

Smith, D.M. and Cartin, M. (2011) *Water Vision to Action: Catalysing Change through the IUCN Water & Nature Initiative.* Gland, Switzerland: IUCN.

Sudmeier-Rieux, K. and N. Ash (2009) *Environmental Guidance Note for Disaster Risk Reduction: Healthy Ecosystems for Human Security.* Ecosystem Management Series No. 8, Commission on Ecosystem Management, revised edition. Gland, Switzerland: IUCN.

Sudmeier-Rieux, K. et al. (eds) (2006) *Ecosystems, Livelihoods and Disasters – An Integrated Approach to Disaster Risk Management.* Ecosystem Management Series No. 4. Gland, Switzerland: IUCN.

Tallis, H. et al. (2008) "An Ecosystem Services Framework to Support Both Practical Conservation and Economic Development". *Proceedings of the National Academy of Sciences of the United States of America* 105(28): 9457–9464.

UNISDR [United Nations International Strategy for Disaster Reduction] (2005) "Hyogo Framework for Action 2005–2015: Building the Resilience of Nations and Communities to Disasters". United Nations International Strategy for Disaster Reduction, Geneva.

UNISDR (2009) "2009 UNISDR Terminology on Disaster Risk Reduction". United Nations International Strategy for Disaster Reduction, Geneva. Available at <http://www.unisdr.org/files/7817_UNISDRTerminologyEnglish.pdf> (accessed 9 October 2012).

UNISDR (2011a) *2011 Global Assessment Report on Disaster Risk Reduction: Revealing Risk, Redefining Development.* Geneva: United Nations.

UNISDR (2011b) *Hyogo Framework for Action 2005–2015: Building the Resilience of Nations and Communities to Disasters. Mid-Term Review, 2010–2011.* Geneva: United Nations.

United Nations (2002) *Report of the World Summit on Sustainable Development. Johannesburg, South Africa, 26 August–4 September 2002.* UN Doc. A/CONF.199/20. New York: United Nations. Available at <http://www.unmillenniumproject.org/documents/131302_wssd_report_reissued.pdf> (accessed 22 October 2012).

Wågsæther, K. and G. Ziervogel (2011) "Bridging the Communication Gap: An Exploration of the Climate Science–Water Management Interface". *Environment – Science and Policy for Sustainable Development* 53(3): 32–44.

Wenger, E., R. McDermott and W.M. Snyder (2002) *Cultivating Communities of Practice: A Guide to Managing Knowledge.* Boston, MA: Harvard Business School Press.

Wester, P., J. Hoogesteger and L. Vincent (2009) "Local IWRM Organizations for Groundwater Regulation: The Experiences of the Aquifer Management Councils (COTAS) in Guanajuato, Mexico". *Natural Resources Forum* 33(1): 29–38.

WHO [World Health Organization] (2010) "Urbanization and Health". *Bulletin of the World Health Organization* 88(4): 245–246.

World Bank (1999) *World Bank Development Indicators.* Washington, DC: World Bank.

World Bank (2010) *Convenient Solutions to an Inconvenient Truth: Ecosystem-based Approaches to Climate Change*. Washington, DC: Environment Department, World Bank.

World Bank WSP [Water and Sanitation Program] (2011) "Economic Impact of the 2007 Earthquake in the Water and Sanitation Sector in Four Provinces of Peru. What Did Unpreparedness Cost the Country?" Disaster Risk Management in Water and Sanitation, Technical Paper 63267. Washington, DC: World Bank.

WWDR [World Water Development Report] (2003) *Water for People, Water for Life*. Paris: UNESCO World Water Assessment Programme and Berghahn Books.

11

The matter is not if, but when and where. The role of capacity development in disaster risk reduction aiming for a sustainable water supply and sanitation

Madeleine Fogde, Luis Macario and Kirsten Carey

Introduction

The geographical location of Mozambique makes it highly prone to disasters. According to a national government report on climate change impacts, the country has experienced 53 disasters in the last 45 years, which has led to a common understanding that it is not a matter of if, but rather when and where, the next hazard event will strike (MICOA, 2007).

The extreme floods of 2000, which resulted in 700 deaths and displaced approximately 500,000 people, caused huge material damage and slowed annual growth in gross domestic product (GDP) from roughly 10 per cent to about 2 per cent (Christie and Hanlon, 2001). The scale and impact of the disaster prompted the Government of Mozambique to review national disaster preparedness within existing policy frameworks, develop institutional capacities and assume a more proactive role in mitigating disaster risk by improving collaboration with partners. Since 2000, several major national and regional institutional changes have been made to incorporate disaster risk reduction and secure the human and financial resources needed for effective coordination of disaster mitigation and disaster response.

Mozambique's first National Adaptation Programme of Action to address the impacts of climate change was only produced in 2007. Meanwhile, local initiatives and different models for disaster preparedness had been tested in provinces prone to hazards. In a place where local communities experience disasters repeatedly, even annually, it is also crucial to

The role of ecosystems in disaster risk reduction, Renaud, Sudmeier-Rieux and Estrella (eds), United Nations University Press, 2013, ISBN 978-92-808-1221-3

incorporate both resilience thinking and disaster plans in development programmes to ensure targets can be met.

The province of Sofala was severely affected by the floods in 2000. At that time, the Government of Austria had initiated bilateral cooperation with the provincial government. One of the subsector programmes within the cooperation agreement was a Programme for Rural Water Supply and Sanitation (Projecto de Abastecimento de Água Rural e Saneamento em Sofala, PAARSS). The goal was to provide sustainable water and sanitation services by implementing the National Water Policy (Política Nacional de Águas, adopted in 1995) in the districts of Dondo on the Pungwe River, Búzi and Chibabava on the Búzi River, Marromeu on the Zambezi River, and Cheringoma nearby (see the map in Figure 11.1). Over a period of 10 years, PAARSS worked with the provincial and local authorities to improve access to water and sanitation for the rural population.

Problems arose in the first year of operation, as most of the districts included in the programme were flooded and vehicular access was restricted (Borowczak and Parkinson, 2005; Manndorff et al., 2004). It became apparent early on that planning for sustainable water and sanitation needed to minimize the risks from frequent extreme floods, droughts and cyclones. Even normal rainfall would periodically block road access. It was decided that the best solution was to increase community resilience and self-sufficiency. Eventually, PAARSS planning and capacity-building efforts in disaster risk reduction at the local level were linked up and coordinated with provincial disaster management contingency plans and actions (Borowczak and Parkinson, 2005).

In order to respond to the rural communities' demand for improved water supplies and access to sanitation, it was important to establish efficient communication mechanisms and strengthen local technical capacities. High illiteracy rates, an inadequate road network and a lack of public transportation hindered communication and the spread of information to rural communities. Radio and mobile phone networks were easily destroyed or compromised by extreme weather such as cyclones and floods. Planning tools were also found to be ineffective owing to irregular data collection, updates and storage. A reality such as this made it necessary to proceed with caution in order to improve, rather than worsen, the situation.

The long-term implementation of PAARSS, from 1999 to 2007, offers important lessons on how a development programme can incorporate resilience and disaster risk reduction measures and achieve its goals. This chapter focuses specifically on addressing the lack of access to potable water and sanitation, which can weaken a population's defences during and after an extreme event. These are what the United Nations' Hyogo

SOFALA Province

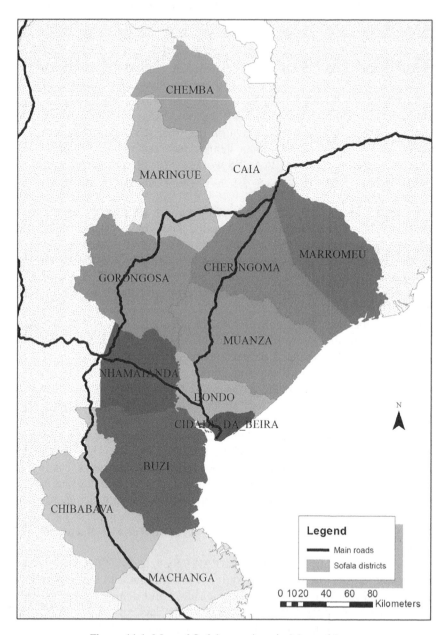

Figure 11.1 Map of Sofala province in Mozambique

Framework for Action defines as "underlying risk factors" under its Priority 4, which are part of the everyday lives of vulnerable populations. In this case, the solution is to ensure a safe water supply and minimize the sources of water contamination. Ecosystem management is also important for water quality, and one of the aims of PAARSS was to raise awareness of the importance of ecosystem services, especially through integrated water management.

Background

Living with disasters

Mozambique is one of the poorest countries in Africa. Agriculture is the main economic sector, contributing 40 per cent of the nation's GDP. Approximately 80 per cent of the labour force is employed in the agriculture, livestock and fishery sectors. Nearly three-quarters of population (73 per cent) resides in rural areas. Mozambique ranks near the top of the United Nations Development Programme's Disaster Risk Index, at 8 out of 173 (Kring, 2011).[1]

Sofala province is in the central part of the country, between the Zambezi and Save rivers. In roughly 4 out of every 10 years, it experiences droughts that cause acute food shortages. Floods, on the other hand, occur annually, because five major transboundary rivers reach the Indian Ocean through the province. In addition to flooding caused by the region's location on a major floodplain and its proximity to the shores of the Mozambique Canal, the province is also prone to tropical cyclones. Official records indicate that the frequency of disasters has also increased over the last decade – see Figure 11.2 (INGC, 2009; Queface, 2004).

The province's vulnerability to natural hazards is exacerbated by the fact that most of the infrastructure was destroyed in a prolonged civil war that ended in 1992. Sofala had the highest poverty rates in Mozambique in the 1997 census, with 88 per cent of the population under the absolute poverty line. In the province's rural areas, 92 per cent of the population was classified as poor (INE, 1999). The illiteracy rate was also high, especially among women, reaching 95 per cent in some rural districts (INE, 1999).

Human health and other quality-of-life indicators reflect the poverty in the region, with an infant mortality rate of 135 per 1,000 live births, for example (ADA, 2007). Lack of access to safe, clean water and sanitation exacerbates these health risks: in 2007, only 26 per cent of the rural population had access to an improved water source and only 19 per cent had access to improved sanitation facilities. The most common diseases in the

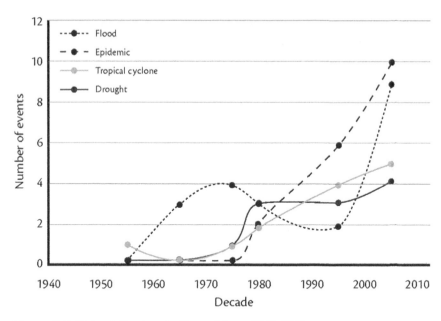

Figure 11.2 Natural disasters in Mozambique, 1956–2008
Sources: INGC and UEM (2009); INGC (2009).

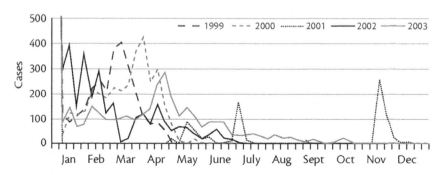

Figure 11.3 Number of cholera cases per month in Sofala province, 1999–2003
Source: WHO (2006).

region are diarrhoea, malaria and endemic cholera (see Figure 11.3 for cholera cases).

Institutional developments

In February 2000, Cyclone Eline, a category 4 cyclone, struck Mozambique's shores south of Beira, the capital of Sofala. More than

300,000 people had already been displaced, and hundreds killed, by floods related to Cyclone Connie a few days earlier; Eline disrupted relief efforts and pushed total casualties in five provinces, including Sofala, up to 700. The response of the Mozambican government was piecemeal and disorganized, especially in relation to partner organizations. The recovery took so long that its flood response could not be significantly improved before another devastating flood, in 2001 on the Zambezi River.

The inadequate response to two major floods in the same province highlighted the need not only to strengthen coordination and operations but also to incorporate disaster prevention within local development plans. The National Disaster Management Institute (Instituto Nacional de Gestão das Calamidades, INGC) was reorganized, disaster management was delegated to different sectors and the National Emergency Operations Centre (Centro Nacional Operativo de Emergência, CENOE) rescue operation units were decentralized. The units are now mobile, with coordination centres located in the regions most likely to be affected by specific disasters. The CENOE operation unit for floods is in Caia, on the Zambezi River in Sofala province.

The 2000 floods also showed how devastating natural disasters can be for a country's social and economic development. In order to obtain donor support for disaster risk reduction efforts, however, the government first had to revise a number of policies. In a short period, national development plans and sectoral policies were amended to incorporate actions to mitigate disaster risks and adverse impacts on development caused by extreme weather variability.

The Government of Mozambique's Five Year Plan for 2005–2009 reflected a heightened awareness of disaster risks, as well as the recognition that disasters could exacerbate poverty. Similarly, the National Poverty Reduction Strategy (Plano de Acção para a Redução da Pobreza Absoluta, PARPA), a set of macroeconomic, structural and social policies aimed at promoting growth and reducing poverty, explicitly addressed disaster preparedness and responses, as did PARPA II, for the period 2006–2009 (Republic of Mozambique, 2006). PARPA defines priorities for each sector and seeks to maximize synergies. For water and sanitation, PARPA stresses how the sector can help reduce deaths caused by diseases related to poor sanitary conditions.

The National Water Policy had defined water supply and sanitation as a decentralized and demand-driven process (Republic of Mozambique, 1995). The policy aimed to educate and mobilize users to contribute towards the infrastructure they chose to build in their communities, and to commit themselves to its future operation and maintenance. After 2000, the policy was amended to incorporate disaster prevention in order to decrease human losses and to minimize the negative social and economic impacts of floods. In relation to drought mitigation, the aim of the policy is to reduce the shortage of drinking water in rural areas (Republic of Mozambique, 2007).

In 2007, Mozambique developed its National Adaptation Programme of Action, which outlines the most urgent needs with regard to climate change and includes a national action plan for climate change adaptation and for social and economic capacity development in sectors such as agriculture, fisheries and energy (MICOA, 2007).

Using information, maps and plans to boost resilience: PAARSS

The PAARSS water and sanitation programme was designed to operate in five districts in Sofala province. The main aim was to guarantee a sustainable water supply to rural communities by implementing the National Water Policy. One of the first steps was to map out the existing infrastructure. In 1999, local university students, working with water technicians, established district-level inventories of the infrastructure based on Geographic Information Systems (GIS). This provided valuable information to the provincial government and the INGC technical emergency units to use in their disaster response (Borowczak and Parkinson, 2005). The collected data also allowed for strategic planning of the water supply, targeting the vulnerable and least-served communities.

Basic water and sanitation infrastructures were planned in elevated safe zones to which people are relocated during floods, and deep boreholes were strategically located to guarantee a secure water supply in semi-arid areas throughout prolonged droughts. To ensure that the data would be safely stored and kept up to date, local administrative staff were trained on how to use GIS, and all district administrations received global positioning system (GPS) units to facilitate local data collection. The availability of GPS technology in the districts allowed civil servants to locate all infrastructure, store data and produce maps.

The importance of communications

In order to engage rural communities and increase their awareness of their right to improved access to water and sanitation under the National Water Policy, a paradigm shift was needed, from a system based on supplying services towards a system oriented by demand from informed end-users. Accordingly, PAARSS encouraged communities to get organized, express their needs and be prepared to assume responsibility for the maintenance of infrastructure. However, high levels of illiteracy, a poor road network and insufficient means of public communication made this difficult. A communication strategy adapted to the local, rural context was needed. It also became clear that a gender strategy was needed, because women were responsible for meeting their household's water and hygiene needs. The National Water Policy envisioned increased female participation, but PAARSS went further, developing a strategy to ensure the active participation of women in the activities. The aim of both the communication strategy and the gender strategy was to create a network of informed actors within a particular geographical area who would be able to support isolated rural communities and enable them to get organized, request needed infrastructure and maintain that infrastructure (see Figure 11.4). These local networks became known as Community Education Programme (Programa de Educação Comunitária) zones, a concept that was later integrated into national implementation plans for rural water supply and sanitation (Borowczak and Parkinson, 2005; Cumbana et al., 2007).

Figure 11.4 Illustration of a communication strategy to establish a local web of information-sharing
Source: The author.

Building resilience through a web of capacities

In Sofala, the realities of water and sanitation provisioning are quite stark. The previously war-stricken province had a team of just 10 professional water technicians tasked with servicing the water and sanitation needs of more than 1.5 million consumers within a geographical area larger than Denmark (ADA, 2007). With this constraint, it was necessary to be creative in the planning and development of provincial and district capacities. An extensive and inclusive capacity development programme made it possible to increase and sustain the coverage of infrastructure and improve the level of services.

The provincial technicians were trained to provide technical support to district planners and to monitor the development and implementation of district and community plans for water supply and sanitation. The National Water Policy also linked this effort to disaster risk reduction. In the event of an emergency, the same technicians were called upon to provide the expertise needed to supervise water and sanitation provision in the temporary camps and post-emergency resettlement zones (Cumbana et al., 2007). Provincial seminars and regular coordination meetings were organized to give district-level civil servants the capacity to analyse district plans and discuss how to increase the coverage of infrastructure, to mitigate disaster risks and, equally important, to improve the level of service to guarantee infrastructure maintenance (Borowczak and Parkinson, 2005). The training of personnel from local organizations, non-governmental organizations (NGOs) and community-based organizations under the National Water Policy focused mainly on techniques useful for engaging the rural communities (Cumbana et al., 2007).

Implementation of the National Water Policy at district level

In order to promote acceptance and increase understanding of the policy in rural areas, it was crucial to involve all local actors. One important way to accomplish this, and to reduce the rural population's vulnerability, was to incorporate water and sanitation activities in local action plans. Those plans included the establishment of emergency committees, early warning systems, identification of areas suitable for temporary camps and local measures for mitigating outbreaks of waterborne diseases during weather extremes. Political, religious, economic and traditional leaders within local communities were organized to prepare them to mobilize and support their communities to keep water and sanitation infrastructure operational during the seasons of high risk of epidemics. Given the risk of disease in the absence of safe water supplies and sanitation, this was an important measure to reduce vulnerability to disasters.

Civil servants in the local administrative posts were also trained to collect and update data on the status of existing water and sanitation infrastructure (Cumbana et al., 2007). Weekly educational radio programmes relevant to community water and sanitation supply were produced and transmitted in local languages. During flood seasons, these programmes also reinforced official alerts and health messages aimed at reducing the risks from outbreaks of waterborne diseases (Cumbana et al., 2007).

Street theatre was also used to educate the community. PAARSS supported the creation of district-based theatre groups that trained unemployed youths in theatre techniques and then travelled around and brought water safety messages to rural communities at times of heightened risk. Theatre is a powerful and very useful medium to convey health messages during emergencies, when the otherwise scattered rural population is concentrated in temporary shelters (Macario and Fogde, 2005).

Around every hand pump, water committees were established to collect contributions from water users and to ensure that the pumps remained operational. During rainy seasons, the committees transmitted alerts to water consumers about the importance of drinking only potable water and of maintaining household-level hygiene (Cumbana et al., 2007). In addition, local actors engaged in the private sector, such as mechanics and rural shopkeepers, were trained to keep stocks of necessary spare parts for water and sanitation systems. Vendors were encouraged to stock up prior to the rainy season, ensuring that spare parts would be available locally and enabling committees to keep infrastructure operational year-round (Cumbana et al., 2007). Local access to spare parts contributed significantly to increasing the resilience of rural communities during seasons of extreme weather, when those communities often become isolated.

In addition, local mechanics were trained to help maintain hand pumps, which was particularly valuable in semi-arid areas with deep boreholes. Malfunctioning and inadequate water infrastructure – such as when a single pump serves more than 1,000 people – causes water stress and leads to easily damaged hand pumps. Water committees and the districts signed contracts with local mechanics to manage the deep boreholes and keep them operational. This delegated management system turned out to be a rather lucrative business model for the mechanics and stimulated further private investment in both the repair of abandoned boreholes and the construction of new boreholes, expanding the local infrastructure network and improving the water supply (Fogde et al., 2007).

Another educational strategy was to engage schools and communities in the celebration of World Water Day, which roughly coincides with the end of the rainy season in Mozambique. Given the close links between rainy-season floods and water contamination, this was an important opportunity to reinforce messages about the links between water safety and

sanitation and human health. It was also a chance to teach about contaminated stormwater as a breeding ground for disease vectors and how
to mitigate this risk, and about the importance of responding to early
warning systems when the water is rising. To raise the profile of World
Water Day and strengthen the messages in schools and communities, the
provincial celebrations were decentralized to the districts, which organized events and art and sports competitions. Local theatre groups presented key messages related to water and health (see Figure 11.5). The
local celebrations were covered by the media and provided a high-profile
annual reminder of the importance of local water resources management
for human health and survival (Cumbana et al., 2007).

After the 2000 floods, local emergency committees were set up in all
districts, with representatives of the local government, the Red Cross, the
private sector, extension workers and NGOs. Many committee members
benefited from training organized by PAARSS and brought knowledge about water and sanitation into local emergency activities. The local
committees collaborated with INGC in the development of district-level

Figure 11.5 Local theatre performance as part of World Water Day celebrations
in Búzi, 2003
Source: PAARSS archives.

contingency plans and the establishment of early warning systems (Corneliusson, 2011).

Demarcation and preparation of safe zones

Another key aspect of local disaster preparedness is to find short-term solutions for water and sanitation provisioning during emergencies. To better target resources, the elevated land areas used to accommodate the evacuated population during the 2000 and 2001 floods were formally established as "recognized safe zones" (Corneliusson, 2011). These zones were prioritized in the provision of basic water and sanitation facilities, to ensure they would have the capacity to serve the evacuated population until the emergency technical teams arrived and installed emergency water and sanitation supplies. They could accommodate 5,000–8,000 people during an emergency.

It was not long before the safe zones became organized centres for local development, with administration, water supply and sanitation, hospitals, schools and a market in place (ADA, 2007; Corneliusson, 2011). To gain regular access to these services, families chose to move out of high-risk areas and resettle within safe zones. However, the elevated areas usually lack arable land, so many farming families opted to have both a permanent home in the safe zone and a temporary home in the fertile farming areas on the floodplains. During flood alerts, farmers have to evacuate production areas in high-risk zones. Most families move out of farming areas and into temporary camps when the messages from the emergency committees and the radio broadcasts go out. However, many others are reluctant to leave, because the emergency response is slow and farmers lack alternative livelihood opportunities in the safe zones (Corneliusson, 2011).

Protecting drinking water in the safe zones

In the initial phase of the 2000 flood emergency, thousands of people in the district of Búzi were placed in temporary camps in what was deemed a safe zone, which in time was transformed into the resettlement area of Guara Guara. In the camp, families identified an immediate risk from the construction of pit latrines because the groundwater level was less than 0.5 metres under the surface. The construction of normal pit latrines would contaminate the groundwater, the main source of drinking water in the camps, thus aggravating the risks of outbreaks of severe diarrhoea or even cholera in the densely populated camps (Macario and Fogde, 2005).

One way that PAARSS helped address this risk was to provide 210 litre metallic drums to 300 families to hold human waste. However, a more sustainable and permanent solution was needed. PAARSS thus introduced the urine-diverting dry toilet (UDDT) with a closed chamber system to prevent groundwater contamination. The application of this technology complemented post-emergency planning for the resettlement area, which was aimed at improving the livelihoods of resettled families through the provision of adequate infrastructure. The UDDTs provided not only for sanitation needs but also for bathing needs because they were designed with an attached bathing compartment. This new technology was quickly accepted by the inhabitants of the resettlement area, local officials and the line ministries of health, environment and infrastructure. In a short period of time, the UDDT technology was included in the national guidelines as a technical choice for domestic and public sanitation systems suitable for densely populated areas with high groundwater tables. The introduction of UDDTs also opened up choices for sanitation technologies that take ecosystem services into consideration. It is of vital interest to protect shallow groundwater, since it is interlinked with the surrounding wetlands and nearby river ecosystems (Macario and Fogde, 2005).

Risk reduction innovations in areas with deep groundwater tables

Other parts of the Búzi district are characterized by deep aquifers, sterile aquifers (which do not produce water) and aquifers that produce saline water. If the hydrostatic level is more than 50 metres, the installation of hand pumps is not normally recommended. In semi-arid areas with deep aquifers (>50 metres), normal hand pumps frequently break down, increasing vulnerability in rural communities, which are left without drinking water, and causing conflicts (Fogde et al., 2007). One strategy to secure the water supply was to engage private mechanics to maintain the pumps, as described above. The delegated management system and financial incentives made it possible to operate strategically placed community pumps for deep boreholes, which would constitute an indispensable water supply in periods of prolonged drought (Fogde et al., 2007). When PAARSS started the intervention in 1999, water was captured at a distance of 50 km directly from the Búzi River and sold in drinking cups in Mexuenge town (Fogde, 1998). By the end of 2007, families were able to consume 20 litres or more of potable water per day, and commercial activities were thriving (Fogde et al., 2007).

A similar approach was taken with solar power systems, which PAARSS began to introduce in 1999. By 2007, four out of five small water-pumping systems were driven by solar energy (see Figure 11.6).

Figure 11.6 Solar pumps in Búzi district, 2007
Photo: M. Fogde.

Use of solar energy helped to capture water in deep boreholes, which proved to be more environmentally and financially sustainable in remote areas than the diesel pumps previously used. Operating costs were minimal owing to the reliable and near-constant renewable energy source (ADA, 2007; Borowczak and Parkinson, 2005).

A test of disaster preparedness

In the rainy season of 2006–2007, after seven years of PAARSS implementation, the early onset of torrential rains in Mozambique and persistent rains in neighbouring countries led to increased water flow in the Zambezi River. The rapidly rising water levels led the INGC to signal a red alert in early February and to enforce the contingency plan for the Zambezi Valley. People were evacuated from their homes and some were even airlifted from areas in danger to safe zones such as Chupanga in Marromeu district. The INGC mobilized pre-positioned resources at the national, provincial and district levels and, by the end of February, 120,000 people were residing in temporary shelters in accommodation camps (ADA, 2007).

Since the 2001 floods, the Chupanga safe zone had developed into a vibrant centre for local economic growth. Chupanga was one of the administrative posts that benefited from infrastructure and capacity development support from PAARSS. The PAARSS intervention there entailed the training of local civil servants, traditional leaders, and health and local activists in the principles of the National Water Policy. Perhaps the most important contribution to capacity development was the extensive transmission of hygiene messages that helped communities reduce their exposure to health risks associated with water contamination during floods and heavy rains. The infrastructure network for water and sanitation in the area had expanded considerably and was kept operational by the community with support from local activists. During the height of the floods in March 2007, it was reported that 49 of 53 hand pumps were operational, a major achievement given that many of these pumps were now inaccessible owing to flooded transport links. Although the 2007 floods were as severe as those in 2001, the capacity and preparedness in terms of the physical and social infrastructure in Chupanga were much improved, with clear results (ADA, 2007).

João Jonas, administrative chief of the Chupanga Resettlement Centre, was interviewed in March 2007, when the impacts of flooding were most palpable. He said the centre had received 1,902 families, with a total of 7,697 people, during the floods. Even though flooding had not subsided, some families had already returned to their fields, eager to make the most of the humidity and fertile lands. The Chupanga school was able to start the school year on time, with the classrooms housed in three large tents provided by UNICEF. With regard to public health, malaria is one of the most serious post-flood diseases, as stagnant rainwater provides a perfect breeding ground for mosquitoes. Malaria cases did arise in Chupanga, but they were effectively diagnosed and treated in the Chupanga health clinic (ADA, 2007). The emergency water sanitation units also provided an ample water supply (see Figure 11.7) – 300,000 litres of potable water each day – enough for all the displaced families (ADA, 2007). The operations supervisor of the water and sanitation facilities in the camp was a water technician from the Sofala Department for Water and Sanitation at Public Works and Housing, who had been sent to the camp on the first days of flooding. During her time at the camp, she mobilized camp inhabitants to construct emergency latrines (see Figure 11.8) and dig trenches to extend the network of water pipes. Her main task, however, was to monitor water quality on a daily basis and supervise hygiene practices in the camp (ADA, 2007). This was typical of Sofala's response to the 2007 floods: the provincial government sent water technicians to all the camps, and they stayed there and supported the daily provisioning of water supply and sanitation services. The benefits of improved

Figure 11.7 Administrative chief João Jonas and provincial technician Bernadette Manga in front of the emergency water supply in Chupanga, 2007
Photo: M. Fogde.

disaster response and increased local awareness and organization were dramatic: for the first time in 10 years, there was a severe flood but no cholera outbreak in the province's temporary accommodation camps.

The floods of 2007 also had no casualties. Water and sanitation services and infrastructure were well organized and supervised, and health messages were conveyed regularly in the camps, preventing the outbreak of any severe diarrhoeal diseases. The government's effort was even more notable given that it was also dealing with the destruction caused by a tropical cyclone that had hit the same region (ADA, 2007).

The effective and comprehensive response to the disaster did carry a cost: because most of the provincial budget for water and sanitation infrastructure in 2007 was spent during the floods, scheduled development activities had to be postponed. Nonetheless, the 2007 Zambezi floods illustrated how a government can develop adequate contingency plans, train staff and local communities in disaster management, and link up with regional operation centres to maximize coordination. Unlike in 2000,

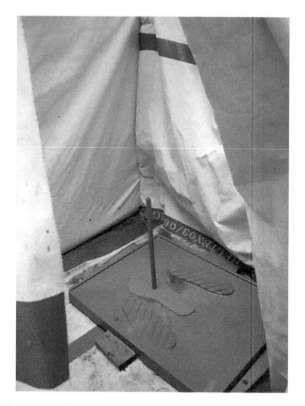

Figure 11.8 A clean, well-maintained emergency latrine in Chupanga, 2007
Photo: M. Fogde.

the government did not make an official appeal for aid, although it welcomed support from interested parties for both the emergency response and the subsequent resettlement.

Lessons learned from Sofala province, 2000–2007

Early in the implementation of PAARSS, it became clear that, if the goals for a sustainable rural water supply and sanitation were to be achieved in districts affected by annual disasters, vulnerability and risk reduction would have to be taken into consideration. A decade later, it is possible to look back and draw lessons on how planning and implementation activities focused on safe water and sanitation could also strengthen the local capacity to mitigate and respond to disasters.

A strategic communication plan made it possible to reach out with important messages from the province level to the rural communities, and vice versa. By creating a network of local people with the capacity to support communities in maintaining water and sanitation infrastructure, the programme helped improve health conditions and reduce the vulnerability of isolated rural communities to serious hazards. The use of integrated approaches and empowered local actors resulted in the efficient planning and implementation of sustainable water and sanitation infrastructure, which, in turn, reduced the incidence of serious waterborne diseases such as cholera.

The initial baseline analysis and mapping of infrastructures at district level using GIS were also valuable, because they created local databases and maps that were used as an important tool in district-wide planning. The gathered and updated information was found to be very useful for disaster response.

Rural communities also learned how to address risks from contaminated ground or surface water, using innovative approaches such as the delegated management system for water pump maintenance and the introduction of technologies such as UDDTs and solar-powered pumps. Delegating responsibilities to private actors offered financial incentives

Figure 11.9 Safe resettlement area in Guara Guara with UDDT toilets, 2003
Source: PAARSS archives.

and made it possible to provide local water supply services and to operate hand pumps on a continuous basis. This also inspired the private sector to invest and expand the services in rural communities.

Thanks to the increased provincial and local capacities and preparedness, it was possible to efficiently provide temporary camps with water and sanitation services and avoid a cholera outbreak (see Figure 11.9). Community engagement was also bolstered through improved communication and local networks that helped change the paradigm from a supply-driven water and sanitation provision system to a demand-driven one in which users take ownership of the infrastructure. This also helped make rural communities more resilient and more aware of water safety issues and of the importance of protecting ecosystem services in a disaster-prone environment.

Note

1. The Disaster Risk Index is used to identify countries in highest need of prevention and development. It takes into account a country's economic, political and ecological factors in determining its capacity to respond to disasters.

REFERENCES

ADA [Austrian Development Agency] (2007) "Project for Rural Water Supply and Sanitation in Sofala – PAARSS, Phase III 2007–2010". Project document draft, ADA, Vienna.
Borowczak, W. and J. Parkinson (2005) *Project for Rural Water Supply and Sanitation in the Province of Sofala / Mozambique – PAARSS (2003-01/03): Mid-term Review*. Final Report Version 2.1, 10.10.2005. Austrian Development Agency.
Christie, F. and J. Hanlon (2001) *Mozambique and the Great Flood of 2000*. African Issues series. Bloomington, IN: Indiana University Press.
Corneliusson, E. (2011) "A Tamed River and Flooded Farms? An Examination of Responsive Behaviour in the Face of Floods along the Zambezi River in Central Mozambique". Department of Government, MFS Report 176.
Cumbana, A., L. Macario and M. Fogde (2007) "When Communication Counts". *Waterlines* 1: 23–26.
Fogde, M. (1998) "Preparatory Report for 1999–2001 Sector Program, Rural Water Supply and Sanitation". Austrian Development Cooperation.
Fogde, M. et al. (2007) "Sustainable Rural Water Supply in Mozambique – Technological Choices or Adequate Management Model?", <http://www.bscw.ihe.nl/pub/bscw.cgi/d2607348/Fodge.pdf> (accessed 24 October 2012).
INE [Instituto Nacional de Estatística] (1999) *Recenseamento Geral da População e Habitação 1997: Resultados Definitivos, Provincia de Sofala*. Maputo: National Institute of Statistics, April.

INGC [Instituto Nacional de Gestão das Calamidades] (2009) *Study on the Impact of Climate Change on Disaster Risk in Mozambique. Synthesis Report – First Draft.* National Institute for Disaster Management, February. Available at <http://www.irinnews.org/pdf/Synthesis_Report_Final_Draft_March09.pdf> (accessed 24 October 2012).

INGC and UEM [University of Eduardo Mondlane] (2009) "Abordagem Geral Sobre Desasters Naturais e Mudancas Climaticas em Mozambique", <http://www.desastres-moz.org/desastres-naturais.pdf> (accessed 24 October 2012).

Kring, T. (2011) "The Global Human Development Report (HDR) 2011: Sustainability and Equity". Brief: Economic and Policy Analysis Unit, UNDP Mozambique, No. 02/2011, Maputo.

Macario, L. and M. Fogde (2005) "Ecological Sanitation in Guara Guara". Conference paper, Third International Conference on Ecological Sanitation, Durban, South Africa, 23–26 May, <http://conference2005.ecosan.org/papers/macario_et_al.pdf> (accessed 24 October 2012).

Manndorff, H. et al. (2004) *Evaluation of the Country Programme Mozambique of the Austrian Development Cooperation: Final Report.* Vienna, Austria: L&R Sozialforschung. Available at <http://www.oecd.org/dataoecd/56/26/35125045.pdf> (accessed 24 October 2012).

MICOA [Ministry for the Coordination of Environmental Affairs] (2007) *National Adaptation Programme of Action (NAPA).* Approved by the Council of Ministers at its 32nd Session, 4 December 2007, Maputo. Available at <http://unfccc.int/resource/docs/napa/moz01.pdf> (accessed 24 October 2012).

Queface, A. (2004) "Mozambique and Its Vulnerability to the Effects of Extreme Weather Events". Presentation at United Nations Framework Convention on Climate Change, Bonn, 18 June. Available at <http://unfccc.int/files/meetings/workshops/other_meetings/application/pdf/queface.pdf> (accessed 24 October 2012).

Republic of Mozambique (1995) "Política Nacional de Águas". *Boletim da Republíca* I Série, No. 34, 23 August. Available at <http://www.portaldogoverno.gov.mz/docs_gov/fold_politicas/outrasPol/politica_aguas.pdf> (accessed 24 October 2012).

Republic of Mozambique (2006) *Plano de Accão Para a Redução da Pobreza Absoluta 2006–2009 (PARPA II). Versão Final Aprovada pelo Conselho de Ministros aos 02 de Maio de 2006.* Maputo: Council of Ministers. Available at <http://www.pap.org.mz/downloads/parpa_ii_aprovado_pt.pdf> (accessed 24 October 2012).

Republic of Mozambique (2007) "Politica Nacional de Águas". Revised policy approved by the Council of Ministers, Resolution No. 46/2007, 30 October.

WHO [World Health Organization] (2006) "Cholera Country Profile: Mozambique". Global Task Force on Cholera Control, 15 December. Available at <http://www.who.int/cholera/countries/Mozambique%20country%20profile.pdf> (accessed 24 October 2012).

Part IV

Sustainable land management for disaster risk reduction

12

The role of vegetation cover change in landslide hazard and risk

Maria Papathoma-Koehle and Thomas Glade

Introduction

Landslides cause economic losses as well as considerable loss of life worldwide. They are commonly triggered either by hydro-meteorological events or by earthquakes. However, preconditioning factors such as topography, geology, soils, hydrological conditions, landslide history and vegetation cover determine the response of a landslide-prone catchment to a specific trigger. In this chapter, the focus is on the role of vegetation within the preconditioning factors and how a change might influence the consequent landslide risk. Also, aspects of climate change are addressed.

According to the Intergovernmental Panel on Climate Change (IPCC) Working Group I (2007), the type, frequency and intensity of extreme events such as heatwaves, droughts and floods are expected to change as a result of climate variations. Moreover, in a recent IPCC report (2012) it is suggested that there is high confidence that changes in heavy precipitation will affect landslides in some regions. Moreover, landslide occurrence in terms of magnitude, intensity, temporal pattern and spatial extent might be affected by this change. For example, increasing precipitation frequency and intensity as well as changes in soil temperature leading to a changed soil moisture regime can reduce slope stability (UNU, 2006). At large scales, higher temperature and mild winters will cause permafrost melting and saturation of soils, which might affect slope stability and eventually the occurrence of landslides (Bärring and Persson, 2006). Bo et al. (2008) also point out that climate change will affect

The role of ecosystems in disaster risk reduction, Renaud, Sudmeier-Rieux and Estrella (eds), United Nations University Press, 2013, ISBN 978-92-808-1221-3

the stability of slopes owing to changes in vegetation and in ground and surface water levels and they list the types of slopes that are most vulnerable to such change. Indeed, not all landslide types are expected to have the same reaction to these climatic changes. According to Geertsema et al. (2007), landslide types such as debris slides, debris flows and rock fall respond rapidly to these hydro-meteorological variations, whereas other types, such as earth slides and flows, have a delayed response. Responses are also heavily dependent on the magnitude of the triggering event.

Not only might climate change directly affect landslide occurrence but it can also influence the preconditioning factors of landslide initiation. For example, vegetation transformation driven by climate change might lead to changed slope stability and consequent landslide occurrence. However, such changes occur at different scales. Whereas direct interventions such as deforestation are occurring in rather smaller regions over short periods, climate change is affecting larger regions and principally at longer time scales. Thus, changes in vegetation cover as the result of climate change may be two-fold (see Figure 12.1): (1) climate change might slowly but constantly develop vegetation cover (for example, a slow shift in the tree line), and (2) extreme events might result in rapid changes (for example, fires remove forests or wind destroys forest cover). In addition to climatic stresses, anthropogenic forces often result in dramatic vegetation changes. Such forces might be related to (3) the logging of

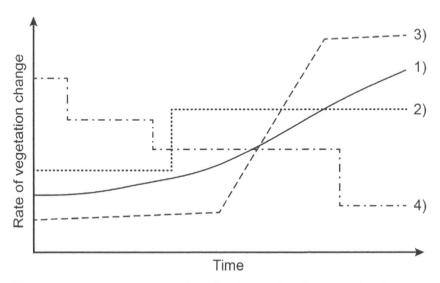

Figure 12.1 Schematic representation of various options for vegetation change in a given catchment/region with (1) continuous climate change; (2) extreme hydro-meteorological events; (3) forest logging; and (4) changes in agricultural practices

forests in large areas or (4) changes in agricultural practices owing to policy decisions or farmers' economic motives.

Numerous studies have investigated the role of vegetation in relation to the occurrence of hazardous phenomena such as landslides, rock falls and debris flows (Alcántara-Ayala et al., 2006; Bathurst et al., 2009; Dorren et al., 2004, 2006; Gerrard and Gardner, 2002; Glade, 2003a; Greenway, 1987; Kuriakose et al., 2006; Masuya et al., 2009; Schmidt et al., 2001; Steinacher et al., 2009; Sudmeier-Rieux et al., 2011; Wasowski et al., 2007; Woltjer et al., 2008). They all regard vegetation as an important factor that influences slope stability.

Changes in vegetation as a result of climate change or anthropogenic factors may affect landslide occurrence but they may also play an important role in increasing or decreasing the physical vulnerability of individual elements at risk. Since vulnerability is of major importance to risk assessments and risk reduction strategies, as emphasized in the Hyogo Framework for Action 2005–2015, its role has to be closely examined and taken into consideration by decision-makers. Vulnerability is affected by people moving into previously forested areas with consequent impacts on landscapes because of the construction of critical infrastructure, the building of urban areas, a change in land use in regions cleared of forests, etc. Thus, the elements at risk and vulnerability are increasing concurrently with a reduction in vegetation cover. In addition, removal of "protection forests" in already developed regions might increase the vulnerability of existing critical infrastructure or houses (see below on protection forests).

Hence, the effects of climate change should not be overestimated. It is very difficult to assess the impact of climate change on slope stability owing to a lack of data on historical landslide activity and to other factors that also affect slope stability (Alcántara-Ayala et al., 2006). These other factors range from anthropogenic slope modifications, such as levelling, to a changed hydrological regime through drainage and also water supply to the slopes. According to Winter et al. (2010), these factors might have a positive or a negative influence on slope stability that even exceeds that of climatic changes. For example, Wasowski et al. (2007) concluded for their investigated catchment in Italy that changed slope stability is related not to climate change but to land-use change. Nevertheless, all authors dealing with the effects of climate change on natural hazards point out that it is urgent for decision-makers to consider climate change and put mitigation and adaptation strategies high on their agenda.

This chapter examines the ways in which changes in vegetation cover can affect the spatio-temporal pattern of landslide occurrences, its related consequences and the implications that these changes might have in decision-making and disaster management. We review the trends in vegetation change resulting from climate change and anthropogenic factors and the possible consequences for landslide occurrence and overall landslide risk. We present recent strategies of using land cover and vegetation for landslide risk reduction and emphasize the possible gaps and needs for future research.

Landslide hazard, vulnerability and risk

Landslides can be defined as the downslope movement of soil, rock or debris as the result of gravitational forces, which can be triggered by heavy rainfall, rapid snow melting, slope undercutting, etc. (see, for example, Crozier, 1999; Glade and Crozier, 2005b). The term "landslide" is used in this chapter for shallow landslides (defined by BRP, BWW and BUWAL, 1997, as less than 2 metres deep), debris flow (solid material with a high water content) and rock fall (loose stones and boulders) according to the internationally widely accepted definitions of Cruden and Varnes (1996) and Dikau et al. (1996). These types of landslides are mainly affected by vegetation cover and human activity, in contrast to deep-seated landslides, which are less likely to be stabilized by vegetation cover and are more affected by geological and hydrological conditions. The impact of landslides on buildings and infrastructure ranges from zero (if no buildings are exposed) or minimum (if landslide magnitude is minor and only negligible damage can be expected) to maximum (collapse or burial of buildings and infrastructure, loss of life and loss of agricultural land; refer to Glade and Crozier, 2005b, for more details). As far as debris flows and soil flows are concerned, not only do they influence the stability of buildings, but also, during low-magnitude events, material can enter buildings through doors or windows and damage building interiors (Holub and Fuchs, 2009). In contrast, large-magnitude events damage or even destroy the building structure such as walls (see Figure 12.2). On the other hand, rock falls usually affect individual buildings rather than large areas and they may also damage building interiors. Although, in Europe, large-magnitude landslides have a low probability of claiming lives, the concentration of assets on steep slopes, high standards of living and high population densities have rendered European households vulnerable to even small-magnitude landslide events (Blöchl and Braun, 2005).

The majority of studies concerning landslide hazards focus on hazard assessments (mapping and zoning), landslide modelling and landslide risk management. Although hazard assessments are very important for disaster risk reduction, understanding the vulnerability of the built environment, the natural environment and society is equally important.

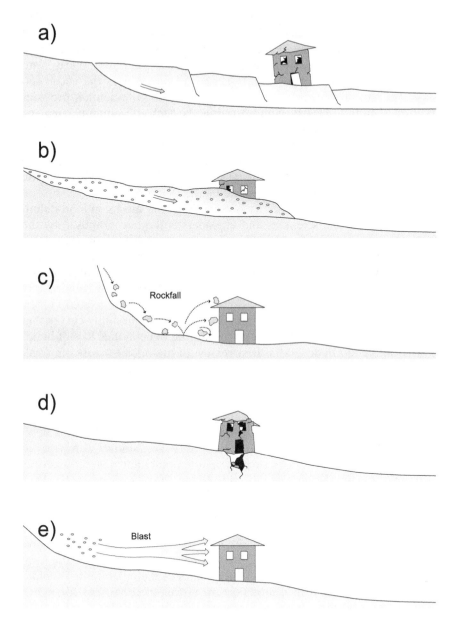

Figure 12.2 Examples of the consequences of landslide occurrence for different event magnitudes: (a) shallow translational or rotational landslide; (b) debris flow; (c) rock fall; (d) subsidence and (e) rock avalanche
Source: Based on Glade and Crozier (2005b).

Vulnerability assessment of elements at risk of landslide-related phenomena is a relatively new field of research (Glade, 2003b; Hufschmidt and Glade, 2010; Zhihong et al., 2010), which additionally brings together scientists from different disciplines (Fuchs, 2009). Because there is no common definition of vulnerability across all disciplines (the social sciences, the natural sciences, engineering), each group of scientists provides its own definition, clearly demonstrating the lack of common language and hindering vulnerability research from moving forwards (Brooks, 2003). In the social sciences, vulnerability is related only to the social context, whereas engineers and natural scientists try to define thresholds in order to determine acceptable risk and at what point risk reduction measures should be taken (Bohle and Glade, 2007).

As far as physical vulnerability is concerned, the most common definition used by natural scientists and engineers is the one proposed by the Office of the United Nations Disaster Relief Coordinator (UNDRO, 1984: 3): "Vulnerability is the degree of loss to a given element, or set of elements, within the area affected by a hazard. It is expressed on a scale of 0 (no loss) to 1 (total loss)." On this basis, the majority of vulnerability assessment methods for landslides either estimate the associated vulnerability (Glade, 2003b) or concentrate on creating vulnerability curves that connect the intensity of a process to the degree of economic loss of buildings (Bohle and Glade, 2007). In a review of methods for assessing vulnerability to alpine hazards, Papathoma-Köhle et al. (2011b) suggest that nearly half of the methods apply vulnerability curves. However, that means that in most cases only one characteristic of the element at risk (usually the building type) and of the phenomenon (intensity expressed as, for example, the thickness of the deposit in the case of debris flow) is taken into consideration. However, there are studies referring to other vulnerability indicators, such as demographics and vegetation cover near buildings (for example, Bell and Glade, 2004; Kappes et al., 2012; Papathoma-Köhle et al., 2007).

Papathoma-Köhle et al. (2007) introduced a framework to undertake an assessment of the vulnerability of buildings to landslides, based on the development of an "elements at risk database". It takes into consideration the characteristics and use of buildings, their importance for the local economy and the demographic characteristics of the inhabitants (population density, age, etc.). In a modification of this methodology for multi-hazards, the type of vegetation surrounding a building is also taken into consideration (Papathoma-Köhle et al., 2011a; Kappes et al., 2012) in assessing its overall physical vulnerability. Four categories of vegetation surrounding buildings are presented: no trees, few trees, closed tree line and buildings located within the forest. However, the role of different vegetation types in protecting an element at risk has yet to be further explored.

The role of vegetation cover in landslide risk

Vegetation can reduce the probability of a landslide through the reduction of the soil pore-water pressure and can reduce the possibility of soil erosion through reinforcement of soil properties through the root system. In Figure 12.3, the destabilized slopes on the unforested part of the hills in East Cape, North Island, New Zealand, are shown. Alternatively, vegetation can increase the hazard by overloading the slope with weight and by weakening the regolith strength through movement of the roots, for example during strong wind storms (Popescu, 2002; Sidle et al., 1985; Steinacher et al., 2009). Another observed effect is that the vegetation cover indeed stabilizes the slope through root reinforcement; however, if the slope fails, the root weight could actually increase the size of the

Figure 12.3 Destabilized slopes on the unforested part of the hills, East Cape, North Island, New Zealand
Photo: Michael Crozier.

landslide. In the case of shallow landslides, rock fall or debris flows, vegetation can also reduce the vulnerability of elements at risk. Here, vegetation not only prevents the initiation of the landslide process but also acts as a protective barrier. In this section, the role of vegetation in landslide hazard, the vulnerability of the elements at risk and, finally, landslide risk are discussed through some examples for shallow landslides, debris flows and rock fall.

Different land uses and corresponding vegetation cover can have a significant influence on slope stability. During a rainstorm event in 2004 in the East Cape region of North Island, New Zealand, large areas were affected by landslides. As other studies have shown, the region has undergone significant land-use changes over the past century owing to the conversion of hillsides into farm pastures (for example, DeRose et al., 1995). Areas affected by landslides recover very slowly, often never returning to pre-landslide conditions (Smale et al., 1997). The landslide process often starts as shallow translational soil slides, which develop within the channels into mud and debris flows. As soon as the displacement of the regolith has been initiated, the transported materials turn into very liquefied matter. Once the drainage line or channel has been reached, these flow types can travel for very long distances, from tens to hundreds of metres downslope, causing damage to buildings and infrastructure that lie in their way. In contrast, forested slopes remain stable (Figure 12.3). Obviously, the magnitude of this triggering event was not large enough to destabilize the areas covered by forests to a similar extent. In the case of this specific event, the forest functioned as a protection against regolith destabilization and subsequent landsliding. However, this does not imply that the forested region and the exposed elements at risk located further downstream in the valleys are completely safe. It can be expected that, with an increasing triggering magnitude, even forested areas and elements at risk near the destabilized slopes will be affected. For events with a magnitude lower than or similar to that of 2004, forest cover can clearly be regarded as a protection against shallow landslides and consequent mud and debris flows.

Also in terms of landslide risk, the consequences are heavily dependent on the vegetation cover in the source areas of the catchment. In the case of 2004, regions below the forests were safe and did not experience any significant damage from landslides. In contrast, exposed elements at risk located in the non-forested regions experienced significant damage ranging from extensive mud cover (see Figure 12.4) to completely damaged houses and infrastructure. Therefore, management of vegetation cover can extensively influence landslide occurrence and consequent landslide risk.

In other regions outside New Zealand, a considerable number of studies have investigated the role of vegetation (in most cases forests) in

Figure 12.4 Extensive mud and debris deposits behind a fence following extensive landsliding in the catchment, East Cape, North Island, New Zealand
Photo: Michael Crozier.

slope stability and landslide occurrence. Peduzzi (2010) investigated the role of vegetation in slope stability in North Pakistan and concludes that the "presence of denser vegetation has a mitigation effect on landslide susceptibility" (Peduzzi, 2010: 633). He supports this argument with the results of landslide modelling with and without considering vegetation density, determined through the Normalized Difference Vegetation Index. The susceptibility of the area to landslides rose by 15.1 per cent when the presence of vegetation was not taken into consideration (Peduzzi, 2010). On the other hand, Popescu (2002) suggests that, although vegetation often reduces the occurrence of landslides through water content reduction and root anchoring, it may also have the opposite effect. He lists some negative effects of vegetation on slope stability, such as the fact that trees may destabilize slopes owing to their weight and their exposure to wind forces. Additionally, Popescu suggests that the roots of trees and plants can penetrate and expand the joints of rock, thus destabilizing the slope. However, he emphasizes that these effects are minor and that the positive effects of the vegetation on slope stability are the dominant ones.

Table 12.1 The influence of woody vegetation on slope stability

Mechanisms	Influences on types of landslides	
	Shallow, rapid	Deep-seated
Hydrological mechanisms		
Interception of rainfall and snow by canopies of vegetation, promoting evaporation and reducing water available for infiltration	B	B
Root systems extract water from the soil for physiological purposes (via transpiration), leading to lower soil moisture levels	B	B
Roots, stems and organic litter increase ground surface roughness and soil's infiltration capacity	MA	MA
Depletion of soil moisture may cause desiccation cracks, resulting in higher infiltration capacity of water to a deeper failure plane	MA	MA
Mechanical mechanisms		
Individual strong woody roots anchor the lower soil mantle into the more stable substrate	B	MB
Strong roots tie across planes of weakness along the flanks of potential landslides	B	B
Roots provide a membrane of reinforcement to the soil mantle, increasing soil shear strength	B	B
Roots of woody vegetation anchor into firm strata, providing support to the upslope soil mantle through buttressing and arching	B	MB
The weight of trees (surcharge) increases the normal and downhill force components	MA/MB	MA/MB
Wind transmits dynamic forces to the soil mantle via the tree bole	A	MA

Source: Marston (2010).
Note: A = mechanism adverse to stability; MA = marginally adverse mechanism; MB = marginally beneficial mechanism; B = beneficial mechanism.

The role of woody vegetation (trees and plants with hard stems) in slope stability is discussed extensively by Marston (2010). The mechanisms that influence slope stability are divided into two categories: hydrological and mechanical (see Table 12.1, which is modified from Greenway, 1987, and Sidle and Ochiai, 2006).

As far as rock fall is concerned, Corominas et al. (2005) suggest that falling rocks often lose their kinetic energy as the result of the presence of trees and never make it to the lowest part of the slope. However, Bigot et al. (2009) suggest that forests can offer protection to buildings only if the forest structure is adapted to this function. They also consider forests to be not only aesthetically more appealing in comparison with other protective measures such as nets and dams, but also cheaper to maintain. Numerous research studies have been carried out, and there is still ongoing investigation in order to determine the effect of protection forests on rock falls (Dorren et al., 2004, 2006; Masuya et al., 2009; Woltjer et al., 2008; see also below on protection forests).

The effect of vegetation on debris flow initiation and propagation has often been investigated in the past (Pabst and Spies, 2001). Kuriakose et al. (2006) quantify the effect of vegetation on the initiation of debris flow by using numerical simulation. The results revealed that, although during high-intensity rainfall the mitigating role of vegetation might be reduced, vegetation remains crucial to slope stability. Kuriakose et al. also point out that the mechanical effect (that is, root cohesion) rather than the hydrological effect of vegetation seems to play the most important role.

Rickli and Graf (2009) investigate the differences in shallow landslide occurrence between open land and areas covered with forests. By looking at six different landslide areas in Switzerland, they conclude that landslide density in open land is clearly higher than landslide density in forested areas. As far as landslide dimensions are concerned, there are no significant differences, with the exception that landslide depth is greater in forested terrain. Finally, Rickli and Graf (2009) suggest that shallow landslides in forested terrain are triggered in areas with steeper slope inclination.

Furthermore, the role of vegetation in maintaining slope stability has been investigated globally by numerous scientists in several case studies. Despite these efforts, there is still the need for more research on the role of vegetation in relation to the occurrence of rock fall. The vast majority of studies conclude that the role of vegetation in slope stability is positive but its significance varies depending on specific local characteristics such as topography, lithology and hydrology.

Change in vegetation cover and its effect on slope stability

Changes in vegetation cover can result from climate change and from anthropogenic activity (for example, deforestation, land-use change, logging, arson).

Climate change

With respect to climate change, plants may respond in three ways: persistence, migration and extinction (Theurillat and Guisan, 2001).

According to Theurillat and Guisan, possible changes in vegetation in the Alps owing to climate change may include altitudinal shifts of vegetation, changes in its composition and changes in the growth and productivity of grasslands. More specifically, as far as Switzerland is concerned, an increase of 3.3°C in mean air temperature would cause an upward altitudinal shift of 600 metres, which would reduce the area of alpine vegetation belt by 63 per cent (Theurillat and Guisan, 2001). However, the response of tree species in the Alps may vary. For example, a rise in temperature might increase the radial growth of the larch pine (*Larix decidua*), but at the same time it will reduce the radial growth of the Scots pine (*Pinus sylvestris*) because of the lack of water (Theurillat and Guisan, 2001).

In a wider study of the Euro-Mediterranean area, it is suggested that vegetation in Southern and Eastern Europe as well as in North Africa will be most affected by climate change. In more detail, in coastal northern Africa and Spain, grass will be replaced by temperate trees, whereas in non-coastal northern Africa there might be a transition to bare ground conditions as a result of severe drought (Anav and Mariotti, 2011). According to the same study, in Eastern Europe boreal vegetation and grass will be replaced by temperate deciduous trees owing to higher temperatures and increased rainfall.

In the United States, the impact of climate change on vegetation has already been observed, although it varies throughout the country. Modelling of vegetation change under different climatic scenarios for the United States has shown that, for moderate climate change scenarios, vegetation density will increase, but that, under more severe climate change scenarios, there will be a decrease in vegetation density. Especially in the eastern United States, catastrophic fires may cause a transition from forest to savanna (Bachelet et al., 2001). In addition, existing land-use practices (for example, timber harvesting, vegetation conversion, fire, road construction, residential development, mining activities) may accelerate or counteract the response of vegetation to climate change (Sidle et al., 1985; Wasowski et al., 2007). For this reason, land-use planning that takes into account climate change effects on vegetation is crucial (Theurillat and Guisan, 2001).

Deforestation

According to the Food and Agriculture Organization of the United Nations (FAO, 2010), deforestation is decreasing worldwide, although the rate of deforestation is still alarmingly high. Every year in the last decade, 13 million hectares of forest were converted to agriculture or were lost from natural causes. Furthermore, the deforestation rate varies significantly from country to country. For example, countries such as Brazil or Indonesia managed to reduce the rate of forest loss, whereas in Australia the rate increased as a result of forest fires (FAO, 2010). Moreover, forest areas managed for the protection of soil and water increased by 59 million hectares worldwide, mainly because of extensive forest planting in China (FAO, 2010).

Despite these general trends, deforestation is of major importance on hilly or mountainous slopes with regard to landslide occurrence. Although there are numerous, detailed studies on the effects of deforestation on slopes and adjacent landslide occurrence (for example, Gerrard and Gardner, 2002; Wang, 2004), no overall and global information is currently available on this topic.

Forest fires

Forest fires are often the result of a combination of factors, which may include ignition agents, fuel condition, topography, climate, wind velocity and direction, precipitation and humidity. Many studies suggest that an increase in forest fires should be expected as a result of climate change (for example, Flannigan et al., 2000). In particular, studies show that there has been an increase in forest fires in North America and Europe. Intensive forest fires strip slopes of vegetation, which could also have a significant impact on the occurrence of landslides (Cannon et al., 1998, 2001; Gabet, 2003). According to Rice (1977) the immediate effect of wild fires is similar to the effect of clear-cuts and may not immediately affect landslide occurrence. At a later stage, however, the remaining roots of the old vegetation will disappear, the macro-pores in the regolith will increase and the landslide hazard may increase. Moreover, Johansen et al. (2001) suggest that, following a fire, the amount of mineral soil exposed may increase by 60–70 per cent. By applying rainfall simulation and comparing the results with rainfall simulation on unburned plots, they conclude that burned plots produced 25 per cent more sediment yield than the unburned plots.

Cannon et al. (2003) suggest that burned plots of land are very susceptible to debris flow events. Following a fire, the soil is dry and incapable of absorbing rainwater. As a consequence there is increased overland flow. The increased runoff may lead not only to extensive soil erosion but also to the transport and deposition of this material in the lower areas of the catchment, for example by channelized debris flows (Cannon et al., 2003). The effect of vegetation change on slope stability may be greater from logging, which is short lived (5–20 years, the period between residual root decay and subsequent regeneration), compared with forest fires (Sidle et al., 1985).

Land-use change

In order to assess the impact of land-use change on landslide occurrence, many scientists have developed models that consider land-use scenarios in order to assess this impact. For example, Vanacker et al. (2003) modelled the impact of land-use change on landslide occurrence in the Andes, and Van Beek (2002) and Van Beek and Van Asch (2004) have developed several scenarios of land-use change in order to assess changes in landslide-susceptible areas in the Mediterranean.

In Mediterranean environments in Europe, the abandonment of cultivated agricultural land is increasing as a result of globalization, mechanization and intensification (Van Beek, 2002). Van Beek and Van Asch (2004) use a physically based model in order to assess the spatial and temporal landslide activity for two scenarios of land-use change involving land abandonment. The results demonstrate that landslide activity is likely to decrease and consequently the areal extent of landslides will hardly change. These results might have implications for perceived hazard levels and for the landslide hazard zonation of the area. Vanacker et al. (2003) modelled landslide susceptibility with a model that suggested that land-use change would continue in the same way that it had over the preceding 37 years in the Ecuadorian Andes. The modelling results clearly indicate that the conversion of secondary forest to grassland or cropland is likely to increase shallow landslide activity.

Meusburger and Alewell (2008) investigated the ways that land-use and climate changes are influencing the occurrence of landslides by investigating spatial landslide distributions in the Urseren Valley in Switzerland between 1959 and 2004. In this period, the area affected by landslides increased by 92 per cent. This can be explained only by the increase in extreme rainfall events and by land-use change. Specifically, goat pastures and spring pastures had disappeared and remote and less productive areas had been abandoned, being replaced by uncontrolled grazing within confined areas. Moreover, the abandonment of traditional farming practices, in combination with the mechanization of local agriculture, might have contributed to increased soil erosion and consequently to the occurrence of landslides. On the other hand, areas colonized by shrubs show low landslide density (Meusburger and Alewell, 2008).

Glade (2003a) focuses on geomorphic responses to anthropogenic land-use and land-cover changes in New Zealand. By analysing sedimentation rates in swamp, lake, coastal and marine environments, Glade

(2003a) concludes that the deforestation that took place after the arrival of the European settlers was connected with increased landslide activity, which was reflected in the sedimentation rates in these environments.

Common to all these studies is the strong interlinkage between landslide occurrence and changes in vegetation cover. Indeed, the link can work both ways. As argued above, forest cover can protect regions against landsliding for lower-magnitude triggering events but may also expand the landslide regions for large triggering events despite root reinforcement of the ground. Nevertheless, the focus of this chapter so far has been on the role of vegetation in preventing the initiation of landslides; the possible change in landslide risk and relevant disaster reduction strategies have yet to be addressed in detail.

Disaster reduction strategies

Vegetation has often been used by planners for hazard reduction and to protect exposed elements against various hazard types such as tsunamis (Forbes and Broadhead, 2007; Ohira et al., 2012; Tanaka et al., 2006) and snow avalanches (Brang et al., 2006; Clouet and Berger, 2010; Schönenberger et al., 2005). In many cases, restoration of vegetation coverage can serve as a cost-effective mitigation measure (Peduzzi, 2010). For example, in the case of tropical cyclones in Viet Nam, planting and protecting mangrove forests as a protection measure not only proved to be seven times cheaper than dyke maintenance but also offered secondary benefits to society such as exploitation of mangrove products by locals in order to increase their income (IFRC, 2002).

In the case of landslides, Popescu (2002) suggests that, although in the post-war period landslides were seen as "engineering problems" that would require "engineered solutions" such as the construction of walls and fences or the use of nets for rock fall, in recent decades there has been a clear shift towards non-structural solutions and environmental consideration. This shift is related to a number of reasons. Not only are civil engineering solutions such as slope flattening, tied-back retaining walls or sheet piles very expensive but they may not justify direct short-term economic investments (Bo et al., 2008). On the other hand, measures such as reforestation schemes to manage landslide hazards may have additional benefits to society, for example employment in forestry and the export of forest products (Phillips and Marden, 2005). As a side-effect, forests might also be used for recreational purposes. Most recently, the aesthetic aspect of landscapes, including forested landscapes, has been expressed as an important added value to society (Taboroff, 2003).

Within disaster reduction strategies, spatial landslide hazard analysis is of major importance for landslide risk assessments. The types of methods range from heuristic assessments to statistical and physically based modelling. Here, the type and spatial distribution of vegetation are some of the main factors determining, respectively, landslide distribution and hazards. Consequently, vegetation is commonly taken into account in spatial landslide hazard analysis and in the delimitation of landslide hazard zones (Van Beek and Van Ash, 2004; Wilkinson et al., 2002).

Besides its consideration within spatial analysis, vegetation is also used to assist risk reduction strategies worldwide (for example in France – Berger and Rey, 2004) in order to enhance slope stability (O'Loughlin, 1984). In particular, protection forests have regularly been used for slope stabilization in many countries in the world for many decades and even centuries (Stoffel et al., 2005). Here, the steep landslide-prone terrain is of particular importance. According to the FAO (2010), approximately 330 million hectares of forest (about 8 per cent of the world's forests) have as their objective the conservation of soil and water, avalanche control, sand dune stabilization, desertification control or coastal protection. The protective functions of the forest are summarized by Sakals et al. (2006) under the following two categories: retaining material in upslope conditions; containing, confining and resisting material during transport and deposition.

Of course, a forest's ability to protect an area from landslides depends also on its position in relation to the hazard. Clouet and Berger (2010) summarize the ability of forests to control different hazards in the departure and deposition zones (Table 12.2).

Berger and Rey (2004) recognize the role of forests in protecting against natural hazards in mountainous areas; however, they suggest that their role also depends on the position of the forest, the type of vegetation, its age and the spatial scale of the hazard. They stress that the protection of the forest can be active (when it is located in the hazard

Table 12.2 The ability of forests to control natural hazards

Natural hazard	Location	Forest control implemented
Avalanches	Departure zone	Yes
	Transit and stopping zone	No
Rock falls	Departure zone	Yes
	Transit and stopping zone	Yes
Landslides	Departure zone	No
	Transit and stopping zone	No

Source: Clouet and Berger (2010).

departure zone) or passive (when it is located in the departure and stop-ping zones). Yet the role of forests is rarely taken into account in risk mapping (Berger and Rey, 2004). Clouet and Berger (2010) suggest that the age of the forest can significantly decrease its protective efficiency. Although they recognize that forest management is very important, they suggest that silvicultural interventions may be very expensive. For this reason, Clouet and Berger (2010) have developed an analysis tool based on Geographic Information Systems that can assist in the prioritization and identification of areas within the forest where intervention is needed.

Berger and Rey (2004) stress that there is a need for a common guide as a tool for decision-making in the management of forests that offer protection against natural hazards in countries such as Austria, France and Switzerland. They present an example from France and make recom-mendations for better forest management for controlling natural hazards in mountainous areas. They discuss the methodological steps for protec-tive forest delimitation. In France, the delimitation of protective forest areas is used in risk prevention plans. In 2006, a set of guidelines for pro-tection forest maintenance was published (Wehrli et al., 2007).

In Austria, the role of the protective forests was understood as early as 1870 when the lack of forests in torrential catchments and the poor state of existing mountainous forests were considered to have contributed to the catastrophic consequences of floods (Austrian Federal Forests, 2009). Since then, protective forests have been used to mitigate the impact of natural hazards such as avalanches and landslides and, according to the Austrian Forest Act, are divided into three categories (FMAFEWM, 2009):

- site-protection forests: they protect themselves;
- protective forests: they provide protection from natural hazards or they enhance and maintain positive environmental effects such as cli-mate or water balance;
- object-protection forests: they protect human settlements and agricul-tural areas.

Based on information provided by the Austrian Federal Ministry of Agri-culture, Forestry, Environment and Water (Bundesministerium für Land- und Forstwirtschaft, Umwelt und Wasserwirtschaft), at least 29 per cent of Austrian forests are protection forests and there are at least 83 current protection forest projects in the country. According to the Ministry, the ideal protection forest is a typical mixed forest with several types of old trees. As far as tree types are concerned, larch (*Larix decidua*) is ideal for use against rock fall, whereas spruce (*Picea*) forests are good against snow avalanches owing to their density. The Austrian authorities recog-nize that protection forests are a cheap alternative to structural protec-tion measures but they also stress that sustainable forest management is required (Austrian Federal Forests, 2009). The necessary actions for the protection and management of protection forests in Austria are implemented through the "Protection Forest Platforms" of every federal state (FMAFEWM, 2009).

Finally, since the early 1980s there have been measures for the management of protection forests in Switzerland. A large amount of money is invested every year for their protection and management.

Phillips and Marden (2005) review the use of protection forests in New Zealand, where the importance of erosion control was already understood in the early 1940s. The first reforestation project using a variety of tree species started in 1948 and continued in 1953 with the purchase of eroded land by the government for the establishment of dual-purpose exotic forest, for protection against erosion and for timber production. In 1968 the East Coast Project (1968–1987) was approved so that unforested parts of the critical headwaters could be planted with protection forests. In 1988, the project was reviewed following Cyclone Bola, which caused widespread landslides in the country (Marden and Rowan, 1993). Following this event, it was obvious that mature native forest and pine forest offered significant protection (Hicks, 1991). In 1992, the East Coast Project was replaced by the East Coast Forestry Project, which aimed to plant 200,000 hectares in 28 years (Phillips and Marden, 2005).

In Australia, the Australian Geomechanics Society suggested that changes in vegetation can clearly increase the landslide risk and, for this reason, it includes retention of natural vegetation wherever practicable in the guidelines for hillside construction (AGS, 2000). In other countries, such as South Korea, Taiwan and Japan, forests are also used for erosion control and landslide risk reduction (Phillips and Marden, 2005). In South Korea, although erosion control projects started as early as 1907 and the forest area now occupies almost 65 per cent of the entire country, the majority of the forests consist of very young trees as a result of forest management (Phillips and Marden, 2005).

However, although vegetation can be, and often is, used as a non-structural protection measure against landslides, Peduzzi (2010) stresses that, depending on the slope, increasing vegetation density may not be the only solution since other factors contribute to landslide susceptibility, such as slope characteristics. For example, a common practice for slope stabilization is "bio-engineering", a combination of techniques to protect slopes against erosion, reduce the probability of planar sliding and improve surface drainage (Florineth et al., 2002). Bio-engineering uses vegetation in combination with other methods in order to stabilize a slope and reduce landslide hazard. According to Singh (2010: 385), bio-engineering is "the successful use of vegetation (both live and dead plants as well as use of raw materials derived from plants like jute and coir) together with engineering structures to increase slope stability. These include the use of vegetation and horticultural practices, coir and jute netting, asphalt mulch solution, retards, wattling etc. in combination with slope modification and improved agronomic practices." According to Singh, the most economical and simple method for slope stabilization is vegetation turfing. Florineth et al. (2002) suggest that the plants used in bio-engineering are selected on the basis of pioneer plant character, a dense and deep rooting system, potential and adventitious rooting system and fast and simple propagation.

In most cases, vegetation has been used mainly to enhance slope stabilization and avoid the occurrence of landslides rather than for mitigating the vulnerability of individual elements at risk. A review of studies concerning alpine hazards has shown that there are a limited number of vulnerability assessment methodologies dealing with the physical vulnerability of elements at risk of landslides (Papathoma-Köhle et al., 2011b). The review highlights that most methods do not take into account the presence of vegetation (for example forests, single trees, hedges) surrounding the exposed elements at risk (especially buildings). However, there are exceptions, such as the methods presented by Papathoma-Köhle et al. (2011a) and Kappes et al. (2012), who have included the presence of trees surrounding buildings in a database of physical vulnerability indicators for elements at risk.

It is evident that landslide occurrence and consequently landslide risk owing to climate change and anthropogenic factors will change significantly in the future. It is expected that vegetation change will have an effect on slope stability, contributing to an increase in landslide risk. The following recommendations might be beneficial for societies dealing with landslide hazard and risk in the face of climate and vegetation change:

1. Decision-making and planning for mitigation and adaptation should be based on an integrated observation and information system. Thus, systematic monitoring and robust modelling of landslide occurrence and also changes in the factors that affect slope stability (for example vegetation change) are very important (Watson and Haeberli, 2004). For this reason, a further refinement of models linking climate, slope hydrology, vegetation cover and stability is essential (as started by Brooks et al., 2004). Robust monitoring will contribute to determining the sensitivity of different landslide types to changing boundary conditions such as climate change (Glade and Crozier, 2005a).

2. Legislation should strengthen and expand existing restrictions on development in landslide-prone terrain, taking into consideration possible changes resulting from climate change (Bo et al., 2008). For example, in Seattle in the United States, municipal codes forbid the removal or clearing of vegetation or trees within landslide-prone areas

or any action detrimental to the habitat (Kazmierczak and Carter, 2010). In exceptional cases where vegetation removal has to take place, a reforestation plan should be ensured (Kazmierczak and Carter, 2010).

3. More research on the effects of vegetation on the different landslide types should be carried out. Currently, there is some research on the functions of different vegetation types in slope stability, but it is not commonly detailed by landslide type (for example, debris flows, shallow translational landslides, deep-seated rotational landslides).

4. The consequences of vegetation changes for landslide occurrence, and thus the landslide risk, have to be further explored. Here, the physical vulnerability of elements at risk, such as buildings and infrastructure, might be reduced by the presence of vegetation. Notwithstanding studies on rock fall, there is sparse research on how landslide risk reduction can be achieved and which characteristics of the vegetation could enhance its protective role. This could be done by extensive investigation of past event damage reports but also by establishing post-event damage recording protocols (Glade and Crozier, 2005a; Hübl et al., 2002).

5. There should be a shift from civil engineering measures to sustainable silvicultural actions that might also benefit the local economy and community, given that the maintenance costs are not as high as for engineering measures.

6. Climate change should be further taken into consideration in land-use planning, for example by allocating land susceptible to increased landslide activity because of climate change in a way that lowers hazard exposure. Examples of good practice are using land for open public space and sports fields rather than for housing development. In some cases, site abandonment may also be an option (Lee and Jones, 2004).

7. Climate change should be considered in the design of measures for slope stabilization and erosion control. For example, the specification of structural measures should allow for climate uncertainty or variability in the design parameters (Lee and Jones, 2004).

8. Finally, landslide risk assessments should take into account changes in climate and vegetation cover – in addition to socioeconomic changes (for example, the extension of urbanized regions or the development of new critical infrastructure such as transport networks and power lines).

Conclusions

The role of vegetation in landslide occurrence has been investigated for many decades. However, its influence on elements at risk (houses, critical infrastructure), their vulnerability and overall landslide risk is still an open question. This is even more so considering the short- and long-term effects of climate change. Climate and environmental change are expected to modify vegetation patterns, in particular in sensitive mountain areas. Land-cover changes in combination with increased precipitation may increase the probability of landslide occurrence. More research is needed in order to fully understand the relationship between vegetation and geomorphology (Marston, 2010), especially in landslide research. Although most studies suggest that the existence of vegetation increases slope stability and reduces the occurrence of landslides, many scientists point out that this is not always the case (Marston, 2010; Rickli and Graf, 2009). There are not sufficient studies quantifying the effects of vegetation change on landslide occurrence in both time and space and defining the thresholds of forests or other vegetation types for stabilizing and destabilizing slopes.

Moreover, the change in both landslide magnitude and intensity is still a challenging field of research. The use of protection forests is a common practice in many countries (for example in Austria, China, France, Japan, New Zealand and Switzerland). In most cases, vegetation cover and land use are taken into account in landslide hazard assessments and hazard zonations. However, the protective role of vegetation as far as reducing the physical vulnerability of buildings and infrastructure is concerned is usually not considered. More research is needed focusing on the role of the vegetation surrounding an element at risk and how this element reacts when it is affected by a particular landslide such as a rock fall or debris flow. Last but not least, vegetation and land-use changes caused by climate change should be taken into consideration in decision-making and planning processes.

REFERENCES

AGS [Australian Geomechanics Society] (2000) *Landslide Risk Management Concepts and Guidelines*. Sub-Committee on Landslide Risk Management. Available at <http://australiangeomechanics.org/admin/wp-content/uploads/2010/11/LRM2000-Concepts.pdf> (accessed 26 October 2012).

Alcántara-Ayala, I., O. Esteban-Chávez and J.F. Parrot (2006) "Landsliding Related to Land-cover Change: A Diachronic Analysis of Hillslope Instability Distribution in the Sierra Norte, Puebla, Mexico". *Catena* 65: 152–165.

Anav, A. and A. Mariotti (2011) "Sensitivity of Natural Vegetation to Climate Change in the Euro-Mediterranean Area". *Climate Research* 46: 277–292.

Austrian Federal Forests (2009) "Presseaussendung: Bundesforste-Schutzwälder: Grüner Wall gegen Lawinen, Muren und Steinschlag". Österreichische Bundesforste, <http://www.bundesforste.at/index.php?id=54&no_cache=1&tx_ttnews[tt_news]=398> (accessed 26 October 2012).

Bachelet, D. et al. (2001) "Climate Change Effects on Vegetation Distribution and Carbon Budget in the United States". *Ecosystems* 4: 164–185.

Bärring, L. and G. Persson (2006) "Influence of Climate Change on Natural Hazards in Europe: Natural and Technological Hazards and Risks Affecting the Spatial Development of European Regions". *Geological Survey of Finland, Special Paper* 42: 93–107.

Bathurst, J.J., C.I. Bovolo and F. Cisneros (2009) "Modelling the Effect of Forest Cover on Shallow Landslides at the River Basin Scale". *Ecological Engineering* 36: 317–327.

Bell, R. and T. Glade (2004) "Quantitative Risk Analysis for Landslides: Examples from Bildudalur, NW-Iceland". *Natural Hazards and Earth System Sciences* 4(1): 117–131.

Berger, F. and F. Rey (2004) "Mountain Protection Forests against Natural Hazards and Risks: New French Developments by Integrating Forests in Risk Zoning". *Natural Hazards* 33(3): 395–404.

Bigot, C., L.K.A. Dorren and F. Berger (2009) "Quantifying the Protective Function of a Forest against Rockfall for Past, Present and Future Scenarios Using Two Modelling Approaches". *Natural Hazards* 49: 99–111.

Blöchl, A. and B. Braun (2005) "Economic Assessment of Landslide Risks in the Schwabian Alb, Germany: Research Framework and First Results of Homeowners and Experts Surveys". *Natural Hazards and Earth System Science* 5: 389–396.

Bo, M.W., M. Fabius and K. Fabius (2008) "Impact of Global Warming on Stability of Natural Slopes". In J. Locat, D. Perret, D. Turmel, D. Demers and S. Leroueil (eds), *Proceedings of the 4th Canadian Conference on Geohazards: From Causes to Management*. Quebec: Presse de l'Université Laval.

Bohle, H.-G. and T. Glade (2007) "Vulnerabilitätskonzepte in Sozial- und Naturwissenschaften". In C. Felgentreff and T. Glade (eds), *Naturrisiken und Sozialkatastrophen*. Heidelberg: Spektrum Akademischer Verlag, pp. 99–119.

Brang, P. et al. (2006) "Management of Protection Forests in the European Alps: An Overview". *Forest, Snow and Landscape Research* 80(1): 23–44.

Brooks, N. (2003) "Vulnerability Risk and Adaptation: A Conceptual Framework". Tyndall Centre for Climate Change Research, Working Paper 38.

Brooks, S.M., M.J. Crozier, T. Glade and M.G. Anderson (2004) "Towards Establishing Climatic Thresholds for Slope Instability: Use of a Physically-based Combined Soil Hydrology–Slope Stability Model". *Pure and Applied Geophysics* 161: 881–905.

BRP [Bundesamt für Raumplanung], BWW [Bundesamt für Wasserwirtschaft] and BUWAL [Bundesamt für Umwelt, Wald und Landschaft] (1997) "Berücksichtigung der Massenbewegungsgefahren bei raumwirksamen Tätigkeiten: Empfehlung", <http://www.planat.ch/de/infomaterial-detailansicht/datum/2011/06/29/beruecksichtigung-der-massenbewegungsgefahren-bei-raumwirksamen-taetigkeiten/> (accessed 26 October 2012).

Cannon, S.H., R.M. Kirkham and M. Parise (2001) "Wildfire-related Debris-flow Initiation Processes, Storm King Mountain, Colorado". *Geomorphology* 39(3–4): 171–188.

Cannon, S.H., P.S. Powers and W.Z. Savage (1998) "Fire-related Hyperconcentrated Debris Flows on Storm King Mountain, Glenwood Springs, Colorado, USA". *Environmental Geology* 35: 2–3.

Cannon, S.H. et al. (2003) "Debris-Flow Response of Basins Burned by the 2002 Coal Seam and Missionary Ridge Fires, Colorado". In D.D. Boyer, P.M. Santi and W.P. Rogers (eds), *Engineering Geology in Colorado: Contributions, Trends, and Case Histories*. Association of Engineering Geologists Special Publication 14, Colorado Geological Survey Special Publication 55, CD-ROM.

Clouet, N and F. Berger (2010) "New GIS Developments in Mountain Protection Forests Zoning against Snow Avalanches and Rockfalls". In *Proceedings of the International Symposium Interpraevent 2010*, 26–30 April 2010, Taipei, Taiwan, pp. 382–390.

Corominas, J. et al. (2005) "Quantitative Assessment of the Residual Risk in a Rockfall Protected Area". *Landslides* 2: 343–357.

Crozier, M.J. (1999) "Slope Instability: Landslides". In D. Alexander and R.W. Fairbridge (eds), *Encyclopedia of Environmental Science*. Dordrecht: Kluwer, pp. 561–562.

Cruden, D.M. and D.J. Varnes (1996) "Landslide Types and Processes". In A.K. Turner and R.L. Schuster (eds), *Landslides: Investigation and Mitigation*. Special Report. Washington, DC: National Academy Press, pp. 36–75.

DeRose, R.C. et al. (1995) "Effect of Landslide Erosion on Taranaki Hill Pasture Production and Composition". *New Zealand Journal of Agricultural Research* 38: 457–471.

Dikau, R. et al. (eds) (1996) *Landslide Recognition: Identification, Movement and Causes*. Chichester: John Wiley & Sons.

Dorren, L.K.A., F. Berger and U.S. Putters (2006) "Real-size Experiments and 3-D Simulation of Rockfall on Forested and Non-forested Slopes". *Natural Hazards and Earth System Sciences* 6: 145–153.

Dorren, L.K.A. et al. (2004) "Combining Field and Modelling Techniques to Assess Rockfall Dynamics on a Protection Forest Hillslope in the European Alps". *Geomorphology* 57(3–4): 151–167.

FAO [Food and Agriculture Organization of the United Nations] (2010) *Global Forest Resources Assessment 2010: Main Report*. FAO Forestry Paper 163. Rome: FAO.

Flannigan, M.D., B.J. Stocks and B.M. Wotton (2000) "Climate Change and Forest Fires". *The Science of the Total Environment* 262: 221–229.

Florineth F., H.P. Rauch and H. Staffler (2002) "Stabilization of Landslides with Bio-engineering Measures in South Tyrol/Italy and Thankot/Nepal". In *Proceedings of the International Congress INTERPRAEVENT 2002 in the Pacific Rim, 14–18 October 2002, Matsumoto, Japan*. Congress publication, Vol. 2, pp. 827–837.

FMAFEWM [Federal Ministry of Agriculture, Forestry, Environment and Water Management, Austria] (2009) "Der österreichische Wald". Available at <http://www.lebensministerium.at/publikationen/forst/der_oesterreichische_wald.html> (accessed 26 October 2012).

Forbes, K. and J. Broadhead (2007) "The Role of Coastal Forests in the Mitigation of Tsunami Impacts". Food and Agriculture Organization of the United Nations.

Fuchs, S. (2009) "Susceptibility versus Resilience to Mountain Hazards in Austria: Paradigms of Vulnerability Revisited". *Natural Hazard and Earth System Sciences* 9: 337–352.

Gabet, E. (2003) "Post-fire Thin Debris Flows: Sediment Transport and Numerical Modelling". *Earth Surface Processes and Landforms* 28: 1341–1348.

Geertsema, M., V.N. Egginton, J.W. Schwab and J.J. Clague (2007) "Landslides and Historic Climate in Northern British Columbia". In R. McInnes, J. Jakeways, M. Fairbank and R. Methie (eds), *Landslides and Climate Change: Challenges and Solutions*. London: Taylor & Francis, pp. 9–16.

Gerrard, J. and R. Gardner (2002) "Relationships between Landsliding and Land Use in the Likhu Khola Drainage Basin, Middle Hills, Nepal". *Mountain Research and Development* 22(1): 48–55.

Glade, T. (2003a) "Landslide Occurrence as a Response to Land Use Change: A Review of Evidence from New Zealand". *Catena* 51: 297–314.

Glade, T. (2003b) "Vulnerability Assessment in Landslide Risk Analysis". *Die Erde* 134(2): 121–138.

Glade, T. and M.J. Crozier (2005a) "Landslide Hazard and Risk: Concluding Comment and Perspectives". In T. Glade, M.G. Anderson and M.J. Crozier (eds), *Landslide Hazard and Risk*. Chichester: Wiley, pp. 767–774.

Glade, T. and M.J. Crozier (2005b) "The Nature of Landslide Hazard Impact". In T. Glade, M.G. Anderson and M.J. Crozier (eds), *Landslide Hazard and Risk*. Chichester: Wiley, pp. 43–74.

Greenway, D.R. (1987) "Vegetation and Slope Stability". In M.G. Anderson and K.S. Richards (eds), *Slope Stability: Geotechnical Engineering and Geomorphology*. Chichester: Wiley, pp. 187–230.

Hicks, D.L. (1991) "Erosion under Pasture, Pine Plantations, Scrub and Indigenous Forest: A Comparison from Cyclone Bola". *New Zealand Forestry* 36(3): 21–22.

Holub, M. and S. Fuchs (2009) "Mitigating Mountain Hazards in Austria: Legislation, Risk Transfer, and Awareness Building". *Natural Hazard and Earth Systems Science* 9: 523–537.

Hübl, J., H. Kienholz and A. Loipersberger (eds) (2002) "DOMODIS – Documentation of Mountain Disasters: State of Discussion in the European Mountain Areas". Journal Series 1, Manual 1, International Research Society INTERPRAEVENT, Klagenfurt, Austria.

Hufschmidt, G. and T. Glade (2010) "Vulnerability Analysis in Geomorphic Risk Assessment". In I. Alcántara-Ayala and S. Goudie (eds), *Geomorphological Hazards and Disaster Prevention*. Cambridge: Cambridge University Press, pp. 233–243.

IFRC [International Federation of Red Cross and Red Crescent Societies] (2002) "Mangrove Planting Saves Lives in Vietnam". Press release, June, <http://www.grida.no/publications/et/ep3/page/2610.aspx> (accessed 26 October 2012).

IPCC [Intergovernmental Panel on Climate Change] (2007) *Climate Change 2007: The Physical Science Basis*. Contribution of Working Group I to the

Fourth Assessment Report of the Intergovernmental Panel on Climate Change [Solomon, S., D. Qin, M. Manning, Z. Chen, M. Marquis, K.B. Averyt, M. Tignor and H.L. Miller (eds.)]. Cambridge UK, and New York, NY, USA: Cambridge University Press.

IPCC (2012) "Summary for Policymakers". In *Managing the Risk of Extreme Events and Disasters to Advance Climate Change Adaptation* [Field, C.B., V. Barros, T.F. Stocker, D. Qin, D.J. Dokken, K.L. Ebi, M.D. Mastrandrea, K.J. Mach, G.-K. Plattner, S.K. Allen, M. Tignor, and P.M. Midgley (eds.)]. A Special Report of Working Groups I and II of the Intergovernmental Panel on Climate Change. Cambridge, UK, and New York, NY, USA: Cambridge University Press, pp. 1–19.

Johansen, M.P., T.E. Hakonson and D.D. Breshears (2001) "Post-fire Runoff and Erosion from Rainfall Simulation: Contrasting Forests with Shrublands and Grasslands". *Hydrological Processes* 15: 2953–2965.

Kappes, M., M. Papathoma-Köhle and M. Keiler (2012) "Assessing Physical Vulnerability for Multi-hazards Using an Indicator-based Methodology". *Applied Geography* 32(2): 577–590.

Kazmierczak, A. and J. Carter (2010) *Adaptation to Climate Change Using Green and Blue Infrastructure: A Database of Case Studies*. Manchester: University of Manchester Press.

Kuriakose, S.L. et al. (2006) "Effect of Vegetation on Debris Flow Initiation: Conceptualization and Parameterization of a Dynamic Model for Debris Flow Initiation in Tikovil River Basin, Kerala, India, Using PCRASTER". In *2nd International Symposium on Geo-information for Disaster Management (Gi4DM) – Remote Sensing and GIS Techniques for Monitoring and Prediction of Disasters*, 25–26 September 2006, Goa, India.

Lee, E.M. and D.K.C. Jones (2004) *Landslide Risk Assessment*. London: Thomas Telford.

Marden, M. and D. Rowan (1993) "Protective Value of Vegetation on Tertiary Terrain before and during Cyclone Bola, East Coast, North Island, New Zealand". *New Zealand Journal of Forestry Science* 23(3): 255–263.

Marston, R.A. (2010) "Geomorphology and Vegetation on Hillslopes: Interactions, Dependencies and Feedback Loops". *Geomorphology* 116: 206–217.

Masuya H. et al. (2009) "Basic Rockfall Simulation with Consideration of Vegetation and Application to Protection Measure". *Natural Hazards and Earth System Sciences* 9: 1835–1843.

Meusburger, K. and K. Alewell (2008) "Impacts of Anthropogenic and Environmental Factors on the Occurrence of Shallow Landslides in an Alpine Catchment (Urseren Valley, Switzerland)". *Natural Hazards and Earth System Sciences* 8: 509–520.

Ohira, W., K. Honda K. and K. Harada (2012) "Reduction of Tsunami Inundation by Coastal Forests in Yogyakarta, Indonesia: A Numerical Study". *Natural Hazards and Earth System Sciences* 12: 85–95.

O'Loughlin, C.L. (1984) "Effectiveness of Introduced Forest Vegetation for Protection against Landslides and Erosion in New Zealand's Steeplands". In C.L. O'Loughlin and A.J. Pearce (eds), *Symposium on Effects of Forest Land Use on*

Erosion and Slope Stability. Honolulu, Hawaii: New Zealand Forest Service, pp. 275–280.

Pabst, R.J. and T.A. Spies (2001) "Ten Years of Vegetation Succession on a Debris-flow Deposit in Oregon". *Journal of the American Water Resources Association* 37(6): 1693–1708.

Papathoma-Köhle, M. et al. (2007) "Elements at Risk as a Framework for Assessing the Vulnerability of Communities to Landslides". *Natural Hazards and Earth System Sciences* 7: 765–777.

Papathoma-Köhle, M., M. Kappes and M. Keiler (2011a) "An Indicator-based Methodology for Vulnerability Assessment in Alpine Areas". Geophysical Research Abstracts, Vol. 13, EGU2011-4942, EGU General Assembly.

Papathoma-Köhle M., et al. (2011b) "Physical Vulnerability Assessment for Alpine Hazards: State of the Art and Future Needs". *Natural Hazards* 58(2): 645–680.

Peduzzi, P. (2010) "Landslides and Vegetation Cover in the 2005 North Pakistan Earthquake: A GIS and Statistical Quantitative Approach". *Natural Hazards and Earth System Sciences* 10: 623–640.

Phillips, C.J. and M. Marden (2005) "Reforestation Schemes to Manage Regional Landslide Risk". In T. Glade, M.G. Anderson and M.J. Crozier (eds), *Landslide Hazard and Risk*. Chichester: Wiley & Sons., pp. 517–546.

Popescu, M.E. (2002) "Landslide Causal Factors and Landslide Remediatial Options". Keynote Lecture, Proceedings 3rd International Conference on Landslides, Slope Stability and Safety of Infra-Structures, Singapore, pp. 61–81. Available at Online Geoengineering Library, <http://www.geoengineer.org/Lanslides-Popescu.pdf> (accessed 25 October 2012).

Rice, R.M. (1977) "Forest Management to Minimize Landslide Risk". In *Guidelines for Watershed Management*. FAO Conservation Guide No. 1. Rome: Food and Agriculture Organization of the United Nations, pp. 271–287.

Rickli, C. and F. Graf (2009) "Effects of Forests on Shallow Landslides: Case Studies in Switzerland". *Forest, Snow and Landscape Research* 82(1): 33–44.

Sakals, M.E. et al. (2006) "The Role of Forests in Reducing Hydrogeomorphologic Hazards". *Forest, Snow and Landscape Research* 80(1): 11–22.

Schmidt, K.M. et al. (2001) "The Variability of Root Cohesion as an Influence on Shallow Landslide Susceptibility in the Oregon Coast Range". *Canadian Geotechnical Journal* 38(5): 995–1024.

Schönenberger, W., A. Noack and P. Thee (2005) "Effect of Timber Removal from Windthrow Slopes on the Risk of Snow Avalanches and Rockfall". *Forest Ecology and Management* 213(1–3): 197–208.

Sidle, R.C. and H. Ochiai (2006) *Landslides: Processes, Prediction, and Land Use*. Water Resources Monograph Series, Vol. 18. Washington, DC: American Geophysical Union.

Sidle, R.C., A. Pearce and C.L. O'Loughlin (1985) *Hillslope Stability and Land Use*. Water Resources Monograph Series Vol. 11. Washington, DC: American Geophysical Union.

Singh, A.K. (2010) "Bioengineering Techniques of Slope Stabilization and Landslide Mitigation". *Disaster Prevention and Management* 19(3): 384–397.

Smale, M.C., M. McLeod and P.N. Smale (1997) "Vegetation and Soil Recovery on Shallow Landslide Scars in Tertiary Hill Country, East Cape Region, New Zealand". *New Zealand Journal of Ecology* 21(1): 31–41.

Steinacher, R. et al. (2009) "The Influence of Deforestation on Slope Instability". *Austrian Journal of Earth Sciences* 102(2): 90–99.

Stoffel, M.D. et al. (2005) "Analyzing Rockfall Activity (1600–2002) in a Protection Forest: A Case Study Using Dendrogeomorphology". *Geomorphology* 68(3–4): 224–241.

Sudmeier-Rieux, R. et al. (2011) "The 2005 Pakistan Earthquake Revisited: Methods for Integrated Landslide Assessment". *Mountain Research and Development* 31(2): 112–121.

Taboroff, J. (2003) "Natural Disasters and Urban Cultural Heritage: A Reassessment". In A. Kreimer, M. Arnold and A. Carlin (eds), *Building Safer Cities: The Future of Disaster Risk*, Vol. 3. Washington, DC: World Bank, pp. 233–272.

Tanaka, N. et al. (2006) "Coastal Vegetation Structures and Their Functions in Tsunami Protection: Experience of the Recent Indian Ocean Tsunami". *Landscape and Ecological Engineering* 3(1): 33–45.

Theurillat, J.-P. and A. Guisan (2001) "Potential Impact of Climate Change on Vegetation in the European Alps: A Review". *Climatic Change* 50: 77–109.

UNDRO [Office of the United Nations Disaster Relief Coordinator] (1984) *Disaster Prevention and Mitigation: A Compendium of Current Knowledge. Vol. 11: Preparedness Aspects*. New York: United Nations.

UNU [United Nations University] (2006) "Landslides". News Release, MR/E01/06, 17 January.

Van Beek, L.P.H. and T.W.J. Van Asch (2004) "Regional Assessment of the Effects of Land-Use Change on Landslide Hazard by Means of Physically Based Modelling". *Natural Hazards* 31: 289–304.

Van Beek, R. (2002) *Assessment of the Influence of Changes in Land Use and Climate on Landslide Activity in a Mediterranean Environment*. Netherlands Geographical Studies NGS 294, Utrecht.

Vanacker, V. et al. (2003) "Linking Hydrological, Infinite Slope Stability and Land-use Change Models through GIS for Assessing the Impact of Deforestation on Slope Stability in High Andean Watersheds". *Geomorphology* 52: 299–315.

Wang, Y. (2004) "Environmental Degradation and Environmental Threats in China". *Environmental Monitoring and Assessment* 90(1): 161–169.

Wasowski, J., D. Casarano and C. Lamanna (2007) "Is the Current Landslide Activity in the Daunia Region (Italy) Controlled by Climate or Land Use Change?" In R. McInnes, J. Jakeways, H. Fairbank and E. Mathie (eds), *Landslides and Climate Change – Challenges and Solutions. Proceedings of the International Conference on Landslides and Climate Change, Ventnor, Isle of Wight, UK, 21–24 May 2007*. London: Taylor & Francis, pp. 41–49.

Watson R.T. and W. Haeberli (2004) "Environmental Threats, Mitigation Strategies and High-mountain Areas". *Ambio Special Report* 13: 2–10.

Wehrli, A. et al. (2007) "Schutzwald management in den Alpen: Eine Übersicht". *Schweizerische Zeitschrift für Forstwesen* 158(6): 142–156.

Wilkinson, P.L. et al. (2002) "Landslide Hazard and Bioengineering: Towards Providing Improved Decision Support through Integrated Numerical Model Development". *Environmental Modelling & Software* 17(4): 333–344.

Winter, M.G. et al. (2010) "Introduction to Land-use and Climate Change Impacts on Landslides". *Quarterly Journal of Engineering Geology and Hydrogeology* 43: 367–370.

Woltjer M. et al. (2008) "Coupling a 3D Patch Model and a Rockfall Module to Assess Rockfall Protection in Mountain Forests". *Journal for Environmental Management* 87(3): 373–388.

Zhihong, L. et al. (2010) "Quantitative Vulnerability Estimation for Scenario-based Landslide Hazards". *Landslides* 7: 125–134.

13

Protection forests: A key factor in integrated risk management in the Alps

André Wehrli and Luuk Dorren

This article is dedicated to our colleague and friend Philippe Duc, who lost his life in a tragic accident.

Introduction

In the twentieth century, as we entered the era of technology, problems caused by natural hazards were thought to be controllable by engineering solutions. The disasters of the past 10 years (for example, large-scale flooding and landslides in the Alps in 2005 – FOEN, 2008) have demonstrated that hazard management based on technical measures alone does not solve the problem. In addition, higher population density, increasing traffic, the various needs for work and leisure time will continuously increase the risk posed by natural hazards in the coming decades. It is and will be impossible to guarantee 100 per cent safety and, therefore, a transition towards a culture of risk acceptance is required. The Government of Switzerland has started implementing integrated and holistic risk management, which considers all types of measures for natural disaster reduction: measures of prevention and preparedness, response and recovery (reconstruction) are applied equally. Prevention and preparedness consist of measures that aim to minimize the vulnerability of people and material assets to natural hazards (PLANALP, 2010).

Forests and the protection they provide against natural hazards play a key role in prevention as part of Switzerland's integrated risk management strategy (Figure 13.1). In this concept of integrated management,

The role of ecosystems in disaster risk reduction, Renaud, Sudmeier-Rieux and Estrella (eds), United Nations University Press, 2013, ISBN 978-92-808-1221-3

the so-called protection forests are considered equal to engineered measures. Forests in the Alps protect people and their assets against rock fall, snow avalanches, erosion, landslides, debris flows and flooding (Brang et al., 2001). These hazardous processes are relatively frequent in the Alps (EEA, 2010), which is the reason many alpine regions have a comparatively high proportion of protection forests: according to the third Swiss National Forest Inventory, approximately 43 per cent of the Swiss forest has a direct or indirect protective function against natural hazards (Duc and Brändli, 2010). This is consistent with estimates based on the nation-wide protection forest delimitation project SilvaProtect-CH (Giamboni and Wehrli, 2008), which reports a slightly higher proportion (around 50 per cent) of protection forests (personal communication from Stéphane Losey, FOEN, 2011). In France, about 65 per cent of the mountain forests protect against riverbed erosion, 14 per cent against snow avalanches, 10 per cent against rock fall and 11 per cent against landslides (see Sonnier, 1991).

In the Bavarian Alps in south-eastern Germany, approximately 60 per cent of the forests are considered to be protection forests according to

Figure 13.1 Avalanche protection forest in Andermatt, Switzerland
Photo: WSL Institute for Snow and Avalanche Research SLF.
Note: Where forest is absent, expensive snow rakes had to be built.

the Bavarian Forest Act (Brosinger, 2004). In the Bavarian high mountains, covering some 5,300 km^2, about 63 per cent of the forests protect from erosion and debris flow, 42 per cent from snow avalanches and 64 per cent from flooding (Plochmann, 1985). In Austria, approximately 31 per cent of the entire forest area has a protective function (BMLFUW, 2006). In the alpine areas, the proportion of protection forests is considerably larger, as evidenced in Tyrol, where the proportion rises to more than 66 per cent (about 330,000 hectares; AdTL, 2005). In the autonomous region of the Aosta Valley in Italy, about 80 per cent of the forests have a protective function (Meloni et al., 2006). Despite obvious differences in methodology, these figures clearly reveal the importance of protection forests in the Alps.

During the past five decades, the importance of protection forests has increased. Remote mountainous areas that were formerly avoided in winter time are now expected to be permanently accessible for tourists, settlements have been spreading into areas that were previously considered unsafe, and transportation infrastructure crossing the Alps (roads, railways and power lines) has increased (BUWAL, 2001). Some figures from different regions clearly illustrate this trend. In the Bavarian Alps, population has quadrupled in the last 150 years, now reaching a density of 400 inhabitants per km^2 inhabitable land (BayStMELF, 2000). Additionally, the region is visited by more than 4.5 million tourists per year (Bayerischer Landtag, 2006). In Tyrol, some 8 million guests enjoy summer or winter holidays there, which increases the population density to 800 inhabitants per km^2 during the high season.

Given these figures, it is evident that the total assets exposed to hazards in mountainous regions have been increasing. Therefore, large investments in protective measures have become necessary. For example, the Government of Switzerland has spent 120–150 million Swiss francs per year on protective measures in the forests ("Schutzaktivitäten im Waldbereich"; see Schärer, 2004), including engineering measures (avalanche barriers, flexible rock fall nets, etc.), during the past decade. Approximately 60 per cent of this amount (that is, 70–94 million Swiss francs) was spent on measures to maintain or enhance the protective effect of forests (Schärer, 2004). In Austria, some €120 million per year is invested in technical protection measures for torrent and avalanche control as well as the management of protection forests. In the Austrian Bundesland Vorarlberg, investments for the management of protection forests totalled about €2.5 million in 2006, which equals, if divided by the total area of protection forests, approximately €48 per hectare (ha). In Tyrol, this annual reference value is even higher, around €80 per ha (AdTL, 2005). In the Italian region of Piedmont, up to €80 per ha was invested in protection forests during 2006–2008 to maintain or increase

the ecological and physical stability of these forests and to partially compensate forest owners for the disadvantages related to protection forest
management (measure I action 7 of the "Piano di Sviluppo Rurale" –
D.G.R. 26-3081 following Council regulation (EC) No. 1257/1999). In
Bavaria, approximately €60 million has been invested since the start of
the protection forest rehabilitation programme in 1986 (BayStMELF,
2006). This equals an average annual amount of some €250 per ha for the
last 20 years. In France, structural financial means for the management of
protection forests have been available since 2011 and comprise financial
aid of around €5,000 per ha, which is meant to cover the financial deficits
of silvicultural interventions in protection forests. This aid is provided
only if the forest is managed by using a cable crane, which reduces forest
damage.

As is evident from the examples above, protection forests play an important role in risk management in the Alps. In the following sections, we
will provide a short overview of the current state of knowledge related to
protection forests and their management in the Alps. We start with a definition of a protection forest and then elaborate on the management of
such forests, providing an example of how the protective function of forests could be evaluated. We end with conclusions.

Definition of protection forests and their protective effects against natural hazards

The main components of the protection forest system

The main function of a protection forest is the protection of people, their
assets and infrastructure against natural hazards (Brang et al., 2006). The
protection forest system consists of three main components: (1) the hazard potential (for example, an unstable rock cliff), (2) the endangered or
exposed assets, and (3) the forest in between (Brang et al., 2001). The
third element is considered a protection forest if it is able to reduce or
prevent the impact of a natural hazard at a given site (see Figure 13.2).

Protection forests can be divided into forests with a direct protective
effect and those with an indirect protective effect (Brang et al., 2006). A
protection forest has a direct protective effect if its functioning is directly
related to its particular location, normally right above the exposed assets.
This is the case, for example, with an avalanche protection forest, which
usually is located above a village or a road. In contrast, the indirect protective effect is related not to the particular location of a forest but rather
to the presence of this forest on a broader scale (for example the landscape), which makes it rather difficult to link the protective effect of a

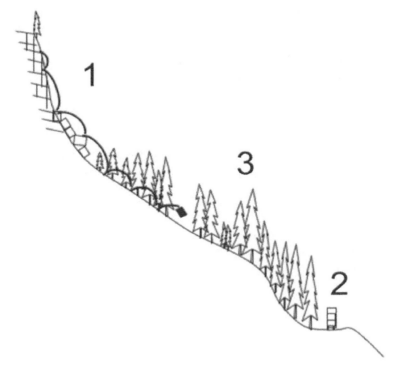

Figure 13.2 The protection forest system with its three main components: (1) the hazard potential, (2) the exposed assets, and (3) the forest in between
Source: Brang et al. (2001).

forest to exposed assets. Examples of protection forests with indirect protective effects are often found in river catchments, where they can prevent or at least contribute to the mitigation of erosive processes or flooding (Hamilton, 1992).

Forests can have a protective effect against several natural hazards such as snow avalanches, rock fall, landslides, debris flows, erosive processes and flooding (see Brang et al., 2006). The protection benefits that a forest can provide depend on the hazard type and could have different results, that is, prevention or mitigation. For snow avalanches, for instance, the protective effect of a forest is merely preventive. This is because the large volumes and high energies involved in snow avalanches make the deceleration of snow avalanches almost impossible (Bartelt and Stöckli, 2001; Berger, 1996; Margreth, 2004). However, trees, and in particular coniferous species, can impede the building up of a homogeneous snow layer, thereby avoiding the slide-off of such a compact layer (In der

Gand, 1979) and preventing the release of a snow avalanche (Margreth, 2004).

On the other hand, protection forests can provide a significant mitigating effect against rock fall, up to a volume of 5 m^3 (Berger et al., 2002; Dorren et al., 2007). Trees, trunks lying on the ground and root plates may act as barriers, which effectively reduce the energy of falling rocks or even stop them (Couvreur, 1982; Dorren et al., 2005; Gsteiger, 1993; Jahn, 1988; Lafortune et al., 1997). The mitigating effect of a forest thereby depends on two main factors: (1) the size and kinetic energy of a falling rock, and (2) the combination of obstacles in the transit route, for example, trees, root plates, lying tree trunks or rocks (Schönenberger et al., 2005). An optimal rock fall protection forest does not, however, necessarily consist only of large trees. As shown by Dorren et al. (2007), a well-structured forest with a broad distribution of tree diameters (and thus tree size) might provide much more effective rock fall protection in some cases.

Tree roots can prevent or at least reduce shallow landslides by mechanistic reinforcement of the soil (Coppin and Richards, 1990; Hamilton, 1992; Rickli et al., 2001; Schwarz, 2011). In addition, they may increase water storage capacity, particularly in soils with limited permeability (Hegg et al., 2005), and can positively influence erosive and hydrological processes by, for example, reducing superficial erosion through permanent provision of litter (Hamilton, 1992). Last but not least, trees may positively influence the interception of precipitation as well as the balance of evapotranspiration, which in turn can lead to an improved water balance of the soil (Frehner et al., 2005, 2007).

The protective effect of a forest thus depends on the type of hazard, in particular on the probability and the intensity of the hazard, as well as on the state of the forest itself. Protection forests cannot provide complete protection, but they can considerably reduce the intensity (mitigating effect) and also the probability (preventive effect) of a hazardous process. The residual risk may, if needed, be further reduced by additional engineered measures such as rock fall nets or snow avalanche barriers (see Figure 13.3). Even if additional measures are necessary in certain cases, protection forests are in general a very effective and efficient protective measure within the concept of integrated risk management (Ammann and Schneider, 2005). They provide their protective effect over large areas (for example, an entire slope) and against different types of natural hazards at the same time. They thus have clear advantages when compared with technical measures, which are often spatially restricted and normally provide protection against only one type of hazard (for example against snow avalanches or rock fall, but not both; Wehrli et al., 2007). Additionally, the management of protection forests is 5–10 times less

Figure 13.3 Photo of a local road in Austria threatened by rock fall with three commonly used protective measures in the Alps: A rock fall net, a rock fall dam and a protection forest
Photo: Luuk Dorren, 2004.

expensive than the construction and maintenance of technical or engineered measures (Sandri, 2006).

The location and delimitation of protection forests

Protection forests are often located on mountainous slopes because many relevant types of hazard are gravity-driven processes. However, protection forests can also be located at the bottom of a valley or on an alluvial/debris fan, providing similar protective effects against flooding and superficial erosion (Wilford et al., 2003). So far, there is no standardized method for delineating protection forests in the alpine space. This is because the definition of what constitutes a protection forest is far from straightforward. On the one hand, the protective effect of a forest is often difficult to assess owing to a limited understanding of the hazardous process or to a lack of information on hazard frequency or intensity. On the other hand, the definition is determined by the exposed assets. These assets are, however, addressed in different ways from region to region. As a result, the definition and delimitation of protection forests differ across the alpine space (see Box 13.1).

Box 13.1 Differing definitions and delimitations of protection forests across the alpine space

- In Italy, no delimitation of protection forests exists at the national level. Delimitation has been applied only for single valleys or communities, often based on very different methods (Lingua et al., 2003; Zampa et al., 2004).
- In Germany and France, the situation is similar: there is no delimitation of protection forests at the national level, but there are at least approaches at a regional level:
- The Forest Act in Bavaria (Germany) requires the registration of protection forests, and the criteria for the delimitation of protection forests are specified in a publication by the Bavarian Ministry for Food, Agriculture and Forests (Zerle et al., 2006), which covers different aspects related to natural hazards and the terrain (slope, location, etc.). The delimitation itself is made by specialists, which leads to a rather precise delimitation of these forests.
- In France, the National Research Institute of Science and Technology for Environment and Agriculture (IRSTEA) is currently delimiting rock fall and avalanche protection forests for the entire region of Rhône-Alpes.
- In Austria, the Forest Act defines multiple categories of protection forests and consequently defines criteria for each category. An "object protection forest", for instance, protects settlements, traffic routes and other infrastructure, as well as arable land, against natural hazards. Both the Forest Act and the delimitation of the protection forests are the responsibility of the various local authorities (province and county). Together, these authorities designate different forest functions, including their protective services, and put them in forest development plans.
- In Switzerland, criteria for a nationwide standardized delimitation of protection forests have recently been developed, based on a harmonized data set of natural hazards, exposed assets and forested area. Using these criteria, specialist units of the cantons have established officially designated protection forest areas. On the basis of these, the Government of Switzerland will produce a national overview (see also <http://www.bafu.admin.ch/silvaprotect>).

The sustainable management of protection forests

Forest dynamics and protective effect

A forest is a dynamic system, which cannot be maintained in a particular state over a long period of time (Brang, 2001). The stand structure is constantly changing, which likewise influences and continuously changes the protective effect of a forest. For instance, stands with high stem density, which are very effective at preventing rock fall (Cattiau et al., 1995; Omura and Marumo, 1988), cannot be maintained in the long term. One scenario in such forests is that only the more vital trees become dominant, while the others die off, subsequently reducing the stem density with time. Another scenario could be that such high-density stands become susceptible to storm damage (Rottmann, 1985) and snow break (Oliver and Larsen, 1990; Rottmann, 1986). In many cases, these high-density stands do not allow sufficient tree regeneration. In protection forests, however, sufficient tree regeneration is crucial, because it ensures continuous forest cover in the long term, which in turn provides a long-term protective effect. In mountain forests, a lack of renewal is particularly serious; because of slow tree growth at high altitudes (Ott et al., 1997), it will impair the protective effect only after decades and may therefore be noticed too late (Wehrli, 2005).

Heterogeneous forest stands with a mixture of trees of different sizes and ages are generally considered to provide the best protective effect against natural hazards (Dorren et al., 2004; Motta and Haudemand, 2000; O'Hara, 2006; Ott et al., 1997). Such heterogeneous stands also have the potential to protect against multiple hazards. In addition, they seem to be more resistant to natural disturbances and have better resilience after disturbances such as windthrow by storms (Brang et al., 2006). However, many forest stands in the alpine space are at present generally homogeneous. Such stands often suffer from a lack of tree regeneration, which challenges their long-term protective effect. In Switzerland, for instance, many mountain forests are dominated by Norway spruce (*Picea abies* (L.) Karst.); they represent a large fraction of the protection forests in the country and are currently experiencing sparse tree regeneration (Brang and Duc, 2002). The same is true in Austria, where the national forest inventory shows evidence of a significant lack of tree regeneration, with only 30 per cent of the forest area showing a sufficient level of regeneration (BMLFUW, 2006).

The long-term protective effect of protection forests may be threatened by other factors, including gaps, stand age, windthrow, bark beetle infestations or browsing by herbivores. Such factors can have a significant influence on the protective effect of forests. In recent years, the protective function of more than 12,000 ha of protection forest in Bavaria (BayStMELF, 2005) and of approximately 85,000 ha in Tyrol (AdTL, 2006) was considered to be inadequate.

The management of protection forests in the Alps

Protection forest management is based on the assumption that there is a direct link between the level of risk and the state of a forest. The goal of protection forest management is to ensure that a forest is as effective as possible in reducing potential damage from hazards. The sustainable long-term protective effect of a forest can often be achieved only with the support of silvicultural measures such as thinning or the cutting of regeneration gaps. Through such measures, the dynamics of mountain forests and their protective effect can be influenced (Schönenberger and Brang, 2004). Silvicultural measures often aim at generating a small-scale patchwork of trees of all ages and development stages, with only small areas devoid of trees. To achieve such a mosaic, the homogeneous stand has to be split up into smaller patches by means of strip cutting. Once regeneration in an initially felled strip has reached a secure stage, the mosaic-creating process needs to be continued by additional strip felling. This process should be carried out during the whole development cycle of a stand in order to obtain phase-shifted mosaic structures (Dorren et al., 2004). Such silvicultural measures are often successful but they are relatively expensive.

It can be difficult to assess the need for silvicultural measures in protection forests, and some recent studies indicate that in certain circumstances forests can provide a protective effect for a limited time without silvicultural measures (see, for example, Frey and Thee, 2002; Kupferschmid Albisetti, 2003, 2004; Schönenberger et al., 2005). In general, however, it is still advised to manage protection forests actively by using silvicultural measures according to scientifically based guidelines.

In many alpine countries, the management of protection forests has been optimized through the elaboration and implementation of specific guidelines. In Bavaria, for instance, silvicultural guidelines for mountain forests have existed since 1982 (BayStMELF, 1982). In addition, a handbook on the remediation of protection forests was elaborated in 1997 (BayStMELF, 1997). The aim of both guidelines is to maintain or create mixed and heterogeneous forest stands, that is, stands that are as close as possible to their original and most natural state.

In Italy, most silvicultural measures were prohibited in key protection forests, but proactive management of these forests has recently been allowed. As a support to the foresters, workshops on the sustainable management of protection forests were organized in several regions. Additionally, a network of permanent forest plots was set up in 2001, which allows for the study of the long-term effect of silvicultural measures on the forest and its protective effect. On these plots, the current protective effect against natural hazards and the need for silvicultural measures were assessed based on the handbook by Berretti et al. (2006).

In France, very detailed guidelines were published in 2006, providing a sound basis for the management of protection forests (Gauquelin et al., 2006). Similar to the Italian guidelines, the French guidelines are partly based on the 2005 Swiss guide, *Sustainability and Success Monitoring in Protection Forests* (Nachhaltigkeit im Schutzwald, or NaiS guidelines; Frehner et al., 2005). The NaiS guidelines list seven guiding principles for the efficient management of protection forests:

1. With a focus on the protective target
Silvicultural interventions in protection forests serve exclusively to reduce natural hazards.
2. In the right place
Silvicultural interventions are carried out in areas where the forest can prevent or reduce the effects of natural hazards on people and material assets.
3. At the right time
Silvicultural interventions are carried out at that point in time when an optimal effect can be attained with minimal effort.
4. Consistent with natural life processes
Silvicultural interventions are tailored to site conditions, to make use of the forces of natural forest dynamics.
5. Tailored to each stand, transparent, replicable and controllable
Silvicultural interventions are determined by experts on the spot. This makes it possible to adapt them to small-scale variation in site factors. A standard decision-making procedure is followed and documented. This makes it transparent, replicable and controllable.
6. Effective
The silvicultural interventions are very likely to lead to the targets.
7. With reasonable effort
The silvicultural interventions have a reasonable cost–benefit ratio.

The concept of NaiS is based on a comparison of the current state of a forest, with target profiles for natural hazards and site types taking into consideration the natural forest dynamics (see Frehner et al., 2005). The hazard-related targets specify targets to prevent or reduce the effects of hazardous processes to a sufficient degree. They mainly concern structural elements such as stem numbers, the size of openings in the stand and canopy density. The site-related targets focus on the provision of a long-term protective effect. The most stable states of a forest are assumed to be represented by the range in variation of development of a natural forest. Thus, the stand structure should be diverse, with single trees or clusters able to resist disturbances, and regeneration should be continuous. Moreover, the site-related targets should include all important tree species of the climax stand. To provide a sustainable, long-term protective effect, both targets need to be fulfilled. Examples of the target profiles can be found in Figure 13.4.

Deciding which silvicultural measures are required in a given protection forest complex takes place at a local level, using a standardized procedure. To do this, a planning area is subdivided into areas with identical target profiles for natural hazards and site types – the target types. This

Natural hazard:	Site type:
Rockfall in the transit zone *Relevant rock size about 50 cm* *Target profile see Appendix 1*	Typical Silver fir-Beech forest on carbonatic bedrock Target profile see Appendix 2B (unavailable in English)

Stand and tree characteristics	Minimum profile	Ideal profile
Mixture Type and degree	Beech　　　　30–80 % Silver fir　　　10–60 % Norway spruce　0–30 % Sycamore maple　Seed trees	Beech　　　　　40–60 % Silver fir　　　30–50 % Norway spruce　0–20 % Sycamore maple, ash 10–30 %
Structure dbh variation	Sufficient number of trees with development potential in at least 2 different dbh classes per ha	Sufficient number of trees with development potential in at least 3 different dbh classes per ha
horizontal structure	Individual trees, possibly clusters	Individual trees, possibly clusters, canopy closure open
	At least 300 trees/ha with dbh > 24 cm	*At least 400 trees/ha with dbh > 24cm*
	In the case of openings in the fall line, distance between stems < 20 m *Lying logs and high stumps to supplement standing trees,* *if they are not in danger of falling*	
Stability carriers Crowns	Crown length of silver fir at least 2/3, of Norway spruce at least 1/2	Crown length at least 2/3
Coefficient of slenderness	< 80	< 70
Stand/anchoring	Upright stems, well anchored, few trees leaning at extreme angles	Upright stems, well anchored, no trees leaning at extreme angles
Regeneration Seedbed	Area with strongly competing vegetation < 1/3	Area with strongly competing vegetation < 1/4
Small saplings (10 cm to 40 cm tall)	At canopy closure < 0.6 at least 10 beech/silver fir per 0.01 ha (on average one sapling every 3 m). In openings maple present	At canopy closure < 0.6 at least 50 beech/silver fir per 0.01 ha (on average one sapling every 1.5 m). In openings maple present
Large saplings (40 cm tall to 12 cm dbh)	On each ha, at least 1 group (0.02 - 0.05 ha), on average 1 group every 100 m) or canopy cover at least 4 % Mixture in line with target profile	On each ha, at least 3 groups (0.02–0.05 ha), on average 1 group every 60 m) or canopy cover at least 7 % Mixture in line with target profile

Figure 13.4 Example of target profiles from the NaiS guidelines
Source: Frehner et al. (2005: Fig. 3).

division is based on information on relevant hazardous processes as well as a map of site types. Within one target type, forest stands with similar stand structures are then grouped into different treatment types. For each treatment type, the need for action, including the type of silvicultural measure, is then determined on a representative indicator plot of approximately 1 ha. This is done by comparing the current stand structure and its projected development in 10 and 50 years with the target profiles in a checklist (see Figure 13.5).

If the projected forest state in 50 years does not fulfil the target profiles, but certain silvicultural measures could influence the forest dynamics towards the profiles, then these silvicultural measures should be applied. In some cases, however, no measures are needed to reach the target profiles in the long term. Such cases can also be clearly identified by this standardized procedure.

A standardized decision-making process is key for successful monitoring, which in turn is very important for the further development and improvement of protection forests. The goal in monitoring protection forests is to achieve a high protective effect as efficiently as possible. It comprises four stages:

1. Implementation assessment – were the planned interventions completed at the correct location and were they executed professionally?
2. Analysis of effectiveness – did the executed interventions have the desired effect on the state of the forest?
3. Silvicultural monitoring – to what extent does the forest's state correspond to the target profiles?
4. Target review – are the target profiles adequate and appropriate?

Stages 1 and 2 are monitored at a micro level (within the forest stand), whereas stages 3 and 4 are monitored at a more macro level (that is, local and regional).

Protection forests and risk analysis

The protective effect of a protection forest can also be assessed quantitatively, as is currently being done in the Swiss project Protect-BIO, in which the effect of the forest on gravitational hazard processes is evaluated in three steps. It starts with a general assessment, followed by an assessment of the protection forest characteristics, and finally a quantitative assessment of the protective effect. The hazards accounted for are snow avalanches, rock fall, shallow landsliding and local flooding/debris flows. The ultimate goal of the quantitative assessment is to be able to carry out cost–benefit analyses of protection forests in a similar manner as is being done for technical protective measures, such as, for example, rock fall nets, rock fall and avalanche dams, and sediment retention basins.

NaiS / Form 2

Decision-making table

| Locality: | Pfäfers | Plot no: 1 | Date: 02.10.2006 | Author: | N.N. |

1. Site type: Fir - Beech forest (18M) / 18°

2. Natural hazard and effectiveness: Avalanches, inclination 60 - 70 %, 1370 m above see level

3. State of the forest, trend analysis and interventions

Stand and single tree characteristics	Minimum profile (including natural hazards)	Current state of the forest Year 1997	Current state, trend in 10 & in 50 years	Effective interventions	6. Stage targets with check values To be checked in 10 years (year 2007)	appropriate
● **Species mixture** (type and degree)	Beech: 30 - 70 % Fir 10 - 60 % / Spruce 0 - 30 % Sycamore seedtrees Conifers 30 - 70 % (avalanches)	Beech 4 % Fir 20 % / Spruce 70 % Sycamore 1 % Larch 5 %			Beech, Fir, Sycamore, Larch increased Spruce reduced	☐
● **Vertikal structure** (dbh variation)	viable trees in minimum 2 different diamter classes	viable trees: 0 - 12 cm sufficient 12 - 30 cm sufficient 30 - 50 cm sufficient < 50 cm single trees			viable trees: 0 - 12 cm sufficient 12 - 30 cm sufficient 30 - 50 cm sufficient < 50 cm single trees	☐
● **Horizontal structure** (% cover, gap length, stem density)	Single trees or small groups; openings in the fall line < 50 m; canopy density > 50 %	Single trees and small groups; openings in the fall line < 20 m; canopy density approx. 80 %			Single trees and small groups with green edges; openings approx. 20 x 30 m; canopy density approx. 70 %	☐
● **State of the stability carriers** (crown develop., slenderness, target dbh)	Crown develop. Fir min. 2/3, Spruce min. 1/2; slenderness <80; straight trunks, single leaning trees only	Crown develop. 1/3 - 2/3; slenderness < 80; some leaning trees (Säbelwuchs)	■	Promotion of selected beech, sycamore, fir	Crown develop. of promoted trees: Fir 2/3, Spruce 1/2; slenderness < 80; single leaning trees only	☑
● **Regeneration - seedbed**	Area covered with vegetation competition < 1/3	Area covered with vegetation competition < 1/3			Area covered with vegetation competition < 1/3	☐
● **Regeneration - small saplings** (10 - 40 cm tall)	When crown density < 0.6, min 10 pieces of Beech/Fir per are (approx. every 3m); there is Sycamore in the openings	When crown density < 0.6, many saplings of Fir (< 10 cm), some Spruce, Beech, Sycamore; (influence of game)			When crown density < 0.6, min 10 pieces of Beech/Fir per are (approx. every 3m); there is Sycamore in the openings	☐
● **Regeneration - large saplings** (40 cm tall to 12 cm dbh)	Min. 1 group (size 2 - 5 are) per ha or groups of planted spruce, some singel fir, beech, sycamore canopy density > 4 %; species composition corresponding target	groups of planted spruce, some singel fir, beech, sycamore		To help existing saplings - create openings; reduce game influence	in the openings Fir, Spruce, Sycamore, Beech 40 to 100 cm tall	☑

Current state, trend in 10 & in 50 years scale: very bad — minimum — ideal

| **4. Need for action** | ☑ yes | ☐ no | Next intervention: in 15 to 20 years | **5. Urgency** | ☐ small | ☑ medium | ☐ high |

Figure 13.5 Checklist from the NaiS guidelines for comparing the current protection forest stand structure and its projected development in 10 and 50 years

Sources: Frehner et al. (2005; 2007: Fig. 5).

Notes: The second column (indicated under 3.) of the form includes the minimal target profile derived from site type (indicated under 1.) and natural hazard (indicated under 2.). The third column reflects the current state of the forest. In the fourth column, the forester has to assess the development of the current forest state without intervention for the coming 10 (vertical bars) and 50 years (horizontal bars). This is done with arrows indicating the estimated development of each single indicator.

In step 1, a simple decision tree is applied to reveal if the forest has a protective effect, a worsening effect or no effect at all on the natural hazard. This step allows one to calculate in an affordable way whether or not the subsequent steps for assessment are needed. Step 2 evaluates characteristics of the protection forest with regard to the hazard, which allows for the reliability of the protection forest to be assessed. The relevant criteria, that is structural safety, usability and durability, are assessed by using different scenarios. Step 3 finally quantifies the influence of the measures on the hazardous process, taking into account the relevant criteria mentioned above. This is done per scenario and results in values for magnitudes and frequencies, which can be plotted on intensity maps. The latter then serve as a basis for establishing a quantitative risk analysis and hazard maps.

Based on the risk analysis, the potential yearly damage caused by natural hazards can be expressed in monetary terms. As an input variable, a hazard scenario (its magnitude and frequency) can be used for an analysis with and without the mitigation effect of a given forest. The difference between the two scenarios in the value of the potential yearly damage provides the risk reduction due to the forest, expressed in monetary terms. Figure 13.6 shows an example of the evaluation of the protective effect of a mountain forest against rock fall in the Swiss Alps. In this particular case, the rock fall risk was evaluated for those driving on the roads downslope from the forest-covered, active rock fall slope, using 3D rock fall simulations with and without the mitigation effect of the existing forest. It shows that the forest reduces the risk for road users at this particular site by 91 per cent. In monetary terms, this risk reduction corresponds to approximately 1,000 Swiss francs per ha per year. The same approach applied at six other sites, in the framework of the French/Italian/Swiss Interreg Innovative Foresight Planning project, resulted in risk reductions of 50–1,000 Swiss francs per ha per year. Another approach was used to quantitatively evaluate the protective role of a forest against rock fall based on the replacement cost. To replace a forest by a technical structure providing the same degree of protection was calculated at 18,000–53,000 Swiss francs per ha.

Conclusions

The examples from several alpine countries provide evidence of the importance of protection forests in the Alps. Protection forests are a highly effective and efficient measure against natural hazards, playing a key role in integrated risk management in the Alps.

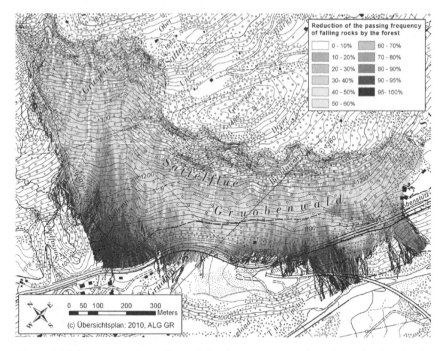

Figure 13.6 The protective effect of the forest expressed as the reduction in the number of passing rocks
Source: tur GmbH, Switzerland.
Note: To create this map, the current forested situation was compared with non-forested conditions.

Please see page 486 for a colour version of this figure.

Over many decades, the management of protection forests has been improved in many countries. Modern management of protection forests is mainly based on harnessing the protection potential of natural ecosystems (structures and processes) and can thus also contribute to the restoration of such ecosystems. By making use of natural structures and processes, the whole management of protection forests becomes more effective and also more efficient. Some countries therefore provide subsidies to forest owners in order to promote the use of the management concepts as described in the mentioned guidelines. The success of this approach is to a large extent based on the quality of the guidelines, but, in addition, workshops for foresters and forest owners need to be provided to guarantee the proper implementation of these guidelines.

The present guidelines are based on the current state of knowledge and are conceptually sound. Still, there is some room for improvement.

There are knowledge gaps regarding the effect of naturally or anthropogenically influenced forest dynamics on stand structure and their protective effect against certain natural hazards. In addition, our knowledge about the entire forest protection system is still patchy, but the successful management of protection forests is strongly interdisciplinary, requiring biological, silvicultural, technical and economic challenges to be addressed (Brang et al., 2006; Wehrli, 2005). At a time when the financial means for protection forest management are limited but the demand for the protective effect of such forests is high (owing to more assets being exposed to natural hazards), science should additionally clarify the possibilities and risks that are linked to a reduction in or omission of proactive forest management.

Protection forests are complex systems where, over very long time periods, slow processes such as tree regeneration or tree growth may be faced with sudden and brutal natural forces such as snow avalanches or storms. To get a better insight into these protection forest systems, combined natural hazard–protection forest simulation models are increasingly being applied (see Brang and Hallenbarter, 2007; Dorren et al., 2004; Wehrli, 2005; Wehrli et al., 2006; Woltjer et al., 2008). These models are useful for further improving existing guidelines or for investigating the effects of forest dynamics on the long-term protective effect of forests (Wehrli, 2005).

Last but not least, there is still a need for a reinforcement of interregional and international cooperation related to the management of protection forests. Some successful examples of such cooperation exist, such as the INTERREG project "Network Mountain Forest", in which nine countries (Austria, Italy, Slovenia, Switzerland, Germany, Liechtenstein, Bulgaria, Slovakia and Greece) have developed the basis for a common strategy for managing mountain forests. One long-term goal would be to raise political awareness about these protection forests and their management within the European Union and beyond. To do this, it would be useful to establish a system of international cooperation for the ongoing exchange of experiences and knowledge in the management of protection forests.

REFERENCES

AdTL [Amt der Tiroler Landesregierung] (2005) *Tiroler Waldbericht 2005.*
AdTL (2006) *Tiroler Waldbericht 2006.*
Ammann, W. and T. Schneider (2005) *Strategie Naturgefahren Schweiz. Synthesebericht.* PLANAT – Die Nationale Plattform Naturgefahren. Available at <http://www.planat.ch/fileadmin/PLANAT/planat_pdf/alle/R0543d.pdf>.

Bartelt, P. and V. Stöckli (2001) "The Influence of Tree and Branch Fracture, Overturning and Debris Entrainment on Snow Avalanche Flow". *Annals of Glaciology* 32: 209–216.

Bayerischer Landtag (ed.) (2006) "Interpellation. Umsetzung der Alpenkonvention in Bayern". *Drucksache* 15/5263.

BayStMELF [Bayerisches Staatsministerium für Ernährung, Landwirtschaft und Forsten] (ed.) (1982) *Grundsätze für die Waldbehandlung im bayerischen Hochgebirge.*

BayStMELF (ed.) (1997) *Handbuch zur Sanierung von Schutzwäldern im bayerischen Alpenraum.*

BayStMELF (ed.) (2000) *Der Schutzwald in den bayerischen Alpen. Funktionen – Zustand – Sanierung.*

BayStMELF (ed.) (2005) "Pressemitteilung. Fitnessprogramm für den Bergwald. Miller setzt auf Sanierung, Pflege und Jagd".

BayStMELF (ed.) (2006) *Waldzustandsbericht 2006.*

Berger, F. (1996) "Mapping of the Protective Functions of the Mountain's Forest". In *Proceedings of the International Congress Interpraevent 1996, Garmisch-Partenkirchen (Germany)*, Vol. 1, pp. 171–180.

Berger, F., C. Quetel and L.K.A. Dorren (2002) "Forest: A Natural Protection Mean against Rockfalls, But with Which Efficiency? The Objectives and Methodology of the Rockfor Project". In *Proceedings of the International Congress Interpraevent 2002 in the Pacific Rim (Matsumoto, Japan)*, Vol. 2, pp. 815–826.

Berretti, R. et al. (2006) *Selvicoltura nelle foreste di protezione: Esperienze ed indirizzi gestionali in Piemonte e Valle d'Aosta.* Arezzo, Italy: Compagnia delle Foreste.

BMLFUW [Bundesministerium für Land- und Forstwirtschaft, Umwelt und Wasserwirtschaft] (2006) *Waldentwicklungsplan. Richtlinie über Inhalt und Ausgestaltung – Fassung 2006.* Vienna.

Brang, P. (2001) "Resistance and Elasticity: Promising Concepts for the Management of Protection Forests in the European Alps". *Forest Ecology and Management* 145: 107–119.

Brang, P. and P. Duc (2002) "Zu wenig Verjüngung im Schweizer Gebirgs-Fichtenwald: Nachweis mit einem neuen Modellansatz". *Schweizerische Zeitschrift für Forstwesen* 153: 219–227.

Brang, P. and D. Hallenbarter (2007) "Bewertung von Handlungsstrategien in Schutzwäldern: Ein integraler Modellansatz". *Schweizerische Zeitschrift für Forstwesen* 158: 176–193.

Brang, P. et al. (2001) "Forests as Protection from Natural Hazards". In J. Evans (ed.), *The Forests Handbook.* Oxford: Blackwell Science Ltd.

Brang, P. et al. (2006) "Management of Protection Forests in the European Alps: An Overview". *Forest, Snow and Landscape Research* 80(1): 23–44.

Brosinger, F. (2004) "Integriertes Schutzwaldmanagement im Bayerischen Alpenraum. Konzept und Umsetzung". In *Proceedings of the 10°Congresso/Kongress/Congress/Congrès INTERPRAEVENT 2004 Riva del Garda (Italy)*, Vol. 3, pp. 23–33.

BUWAL [Bundesamt für Umwelt, Wald und Landschaft] (2001) *Lawinenwinter 1998/1999.* Bern, Switzerland: Bundesamt für Umwelt, Wald und Landschaft.

Cattiau, V., E. Mari and J.P. Renaud (1995) "Forêt et protection contre les chutes de rochers". *Ingéneries – EAI* 3: 45–54.

Coppin, N.J. and I.G. Richards (1990) *Use of Vegetation in Civil Engineering*. London: Butterworth.

Couvreur, S. (1982) *Les forêts de protection contre les risques naturels*. Nancy, France: École Nationale du Génie Rural des Eaux et Forêts (ENGREF).

Dorren, L.K.A. et al. (2004) "Integrity, Stability and Management of Protection Forests in the European Alps". *Forest Ecology and Management* 195: 165–176.

Dorren, L.K.A. et al. (2005) "Mechanisms, Effects and Management Implications of Rockfall in Forests". *Forest Ecology and Management* 215(3): 183–195.

Dorren, L.K.A. et al. (2007) "State of the Art in Rockfall–Forest Interactions". *Schweizerische Zeitschrift für Forstwesen* 158(6): 128–141.

Duc, P. and U.-B. Brändli (2010) "Der Schutzwald hat sich verbessert: Ergebnisse des dritten Landesforstinventars LFI3". *Wald und Holz* 1/10: 25–28.

EEA [European Environment Agency] (2010) *Mapping the Impacts of Natural Hazards and Technological Accidents in Europe: An Overview of the Last Decade*. EEA Technical Report 13/2010. Luxembourg: Publications Office of the European Union. Available at <http://www.eea.europa.eu/publications/mapping-the-impacts-of-natural> (accessed 29 October 2012).

FOEN [Federal Office for the Environment] (2008) "The Floods of 2005 in Switzerland – Synthesis Report on the Event Analysis", Bern, Switzerland. Available at <http://www.bafu.admin.ch/publikationen/publikation/00819/index.html?lang=en> (accessed 29 October 2012).

Frehner, M., B. Wasser and R. Schwitter (2005) *Nachhaltigkeit und Erfolgskontrolle im Schutzwald: Wegleitung für Pflegemassnahmen in Wäldern mit Schutzfunktion*. Bern, Switzerland: BUWAL (Bundesamt für Umwelt, Wald und Landschaft).

Frehner, M., B. Wasser and R. Schwitter (2007) *Sustainability and Success Monitoring in Protection Forests: Guidelines for Silvicultural Interventions in Forests with Protective Functions*. Partial translation by P. Brang and C. Matter. Environmental Studies No. 27/07. Bern, Switzerland: Federal Office for the Environment (FOEN). Available at <http://www.bafu.admin.ch/publikationen/publikation/00064/index.html?lang=en> (accessed 29 October 2012).

Frey, W. and P. Thee (2002) "Avalanche Protection of Windthrow Areas: A Ten Year Comparison of Cleared and Uncleared Starting Zones". *Forest, Snow and Landscape Research* 77: 89–107.

Gauquelin, X. et al. (2006) *Guide des sylvicultures de montagne*. Cemagref/CRPF Rhône-Alpes/ONF, France.

Giamboni, M. and A. Wehrli (2008) "Improving the Management of Protection Forests in Switzerland. The Project SilvaProtect-CH". In *INTERPRAEVENT 2008 – Conference Proceedings*, Vol. 2, pp. 469–480. Available at <http://www.interpraevent.at/palm-cms/upload_files/Publikationen/Tagungsbeitraege/2008_2_469.pdf> (accessed 29 October 2012).

Gsteiger, P. (1993) "Steinschlagschutzwald: Ein Beitrag zur Abgrenzung, Beurteilung und Bewirtschaftung". *Schweizerische Zeitschrift für Forstwesen* 144: 115–132.

Hamilton, L.S. (1992) "The Protective Role of Mountain Forests". *GeoJournal* 27: 13–22.

Hegg, C. et al. (2005) "Forest Influence on Runoff Generation". In B. Commarmot and F. Hamor (eds), *Natural Forests in the Temperate Zone of Europe – Values and Utilization. Conference, 13–17 October 2003, Mukachevo, Ukraine. Proceedings.* Birmensdorf: Swiss Federal Research Institute WSL; Rakhiv, Ukraine: Carpathian Biosphere Reserve, pp. 72–79.

In der Gand, H. (1979) "Verteilung und Struktur der Schneedecke unter Waldbäumen und im Hochwald". In International Union of Forestry Research Organizations, Working Party Snow and Avalanches, *Mountain Forests and Avalanches: Proceedings of the Davos Seminar September 1978.* Davos: Swiss Institute for Snow and Avalanche Research, pp. 97–122.

Jahn, J. (1988) "Entwaldung und Steinschlag". *Proceedings of the International Congress Interpraevent 1988, Graz (Austria)*, Vol. 1, pp. 185–198.

Kupferschmid Albisetti, A.D. (2003) "Succession in a Protection Forest after Picea abies Die-back". PhD thesis, ETH Zürich, Zurich.

Kupferschmid Albisetti, A.D. (2004) "Wie gut schützen Totholzbestände vor Naturgefahren? Schutzwirkung von Gebirgsfichtenwäldern nach Buchdruckerbefall". *Wald und Holz* 1/04: 33–36.

Lafortune, M., L. Filion and B. Hétu (1997) "Dynamique d'un front forestier sur un talus d'éboulis actif en climat tempéré froid (Gaspésie, Québec)". *Geographie Physique et Quaternaire* 51: 1–15.

Lingua, E., A. Collatin and J.C. Haudemand (2003) "Individuazione ed analisi delle foreste di protezione diretta (FPD) nel comune di Cogne (Valle d'Aosta)". In *Proceedings of the 7th Conferenza Nazionale ASITA. L'informazione territoriale e la dimensione tempo, Verona, 28–31 Ottobre 2003*, pp. 1325–1330.

Margreth, S. (2004) "Die Wirkung des Waldes bei Lawinen". In Eidgenössische Forschungsanstalt WSL (ed.), *Schutzwald und Naturgefahren.* Forum für Wissen 2004. Birmensdorf: Eidgenössische Forschungsanstalt für Wald, Schnee und Landschaft WSL, pp. 21–26.

Meloni, F., E. Lingua and R. Motta (2006) "Analysis of the Protective Function of Forests: A Study Case in the Aosta Valley (Italy)". *Forest@* 3(3): 420–425. Available at <http://www.sisef.it/forest@/show.php?action=&id=388&lang=en> (accessed 29 October 2012).

Motta, R. and J.C. Haudemand (2000) "Silvicultural Planning in Protection Forests in the European Alps: An Example of Planning in the Aosta Valley". *Mountain Research and Development* 20: 74–81.

O'Hara, K.L. (2006) "Multiaged Forest Stands for Protection Forests: Concepts and Applications". *Forest, Snow and Landscape Research* 80(1): 45–56.

Oliver, C.D. and B.C. Larsen (1990) *Forest Stand Dynamics.* New York: McGraw-Hill.

Omura, H. and Y. Marumo (1988) "An Experimental Study of the Fence Effects of Protection Forests on the Interception of Shallow Mass Movement". *Mitteilungen der Forstlichen Bundes-Versuchsanstalt Mariabrunn* 159: 139–147.

Ott, E. et al. (1997) *Gebirgsnadelwälder: Ein praxisorientierter Leitfaden für eine standortgerechte Waldbehandlung.* Bern, Switzerland: Verlag Paul Haupt.

PLANALP [Platform on Natural Hazards of the Alpine Convention] (2010) "Integral Natural Hazard Risk Management: Recommendations". Bern, Switzerland: PLANAT. Available at <http://www.alpconv.org/en/organization/groups/WGHazards/Documents/PLANALP_Hotspot_Paper.pdf> (accessed 29 October 2012).

Plochmann, R. (1985) "Der Bergwald in Bayern als Problemfeld der Forstpolitik". *Allgemeine Forst- und Jagdzeitung* 156: 138–142.

Rickli, C., P. Zimmerli and A. Böll (2001) "Effects of Vegetation on Shallow Landslides: An Analysis of the Events of August 1997 in Sachseln, Switzerland". In M. Kühne et al. (eds), *International Conference on Landslides. Causes, Impacts and Countermeasures, 17–21 June 2001, Davos, Switzerland.* Essen: Verlag Glückauf, pp. 575–584.

Rottmann, M. (1985) *Wind- und Sturmschäden im Wald: Beiträge zur Beurteilung der Bruchgefährdung, zur Schadensvorbeugung und zur Behandlung sturmgeschädigter Nadelholzbestände.* Frankfurt a.M.: Sauerländer.

Rottmann, M. (1986) *Schneebruchschäden in Nadelholzbeständen: Beiträge zur Beurteilung der Schneebruchgefährdung, zur Schadensvorbeugung und zur Behandlung schneegeschädigter Nadelholzbestände.* Frankfurt a.M.: Sauerländer.

Sandri, A. (2006) "Vom Nutzen des Waldes". *Referat Fachtagung 200 Jahre Bergsturz von Goldau, 1. September 2006.*

Schärer, W. (2004) "Der Schutzwald und seine Bedeutung in der Waldpolitik des Bundes". In Eidgenössische Forschungsanstalt WSL (ed.), *Schutzwald und Naturgefahren.* Forum für Wissen 2004. Birmensdorf: Eidgenössische Forschungsanstalt für Wald, Schnee und Landschaft WSL, pp. 87–90.

Schönenberger, W. and P. Brang (2004) "Silviculture in Mountain Forests". In J. Burley, J. Evans and J.A. Youngquist (eds), *Encyclopedia of Forest Sciences.* Amsterdam: Elsevier, pp. 1085–1094.

Schönenberger, W., A. Noack and P. Thee (2005) "Effect of Timber Removal from Windthrow Slopes on the Risk of Snow Avalanches and Rockfall". *Forest Ecology and Management* 213: 197–208.

Schwarz, M. (2011) "Hydro-mechanical Characterization of Rooted Hillslope Failure: From Field Investigations to Fiber Bundle Modeling". PhD thesis, ETH Zürich.

Sonnier, J. (1991) "Analyse du rôle de protection des forêts domaniales de montagne". *Revue forestière française* 43: 131–145.

Wehrli, A. (2005) "Mountain Forest Dynamics and Their Impacts on the Long-term Protective Effect against Rockfall: A Modelling Approach". PhD thesis, ETH Zürich.

Wehrli, A. et al. (2006) "Modelling the Long-term Effects of Forest Dynamics on the Protective Effect against Rockfall". *Forest, Snow and Landscape Research* 80(1): 57–76.

Wehrli, A. et al. (2007) "Schutzwaldmanagement in den Alpen: Eine Übersicht". *Schweizerische Zeitschrift für Forstwesen* 158(6): 142–156.

Wilford, D.J., M.E. Sakals and J.L. Innes (2003) "Forestry on Fans: A Problem Analysis". *Forest Chronicle* 79(2): 291–296.

Woltjer, M. et al. (2008) "Coupling a 3-D Patch Model and a Rockfall Module to Assess Rockfall Protection in Mountain Forests". *Environmental Management* 87: 373–388.

Zampa F., M. Ciolli and M.G. Cantiani (2004) "A GIS Procedure to Map Forests with a Particular Protective Function". In *Geomatics Workbooks*, Vol. 3, pp. 1–23. Available at <http://geomatica.como.polimi.it/workbooks/n3/> (accessed 29 October 2012).

Zerle, A. et al. (2006) *Forstrecht in Bayern, Kommentar*. Stuttgart: Deutscher Gemeindeverlag.

14

Forest cover and landslide trends: A case study from Dolakha District in central-eastern Nepal, 1992–2009

Stéphanie Jaquet, Karen Sudmeier-Rieux, Marc-Henri Derron and Michel Jaboyedoff

Introduction

Forests are essential for livelihoods in Nepal, providing fodder, timber and fuel. Decades of forest degradation led the country to find new ways for reducing this negative trend. Community forests (CFs) began developing in Nepal in 1978, following the Panchayat forest rules (Forestry Nepal, 2011a). By the end of the 1970s, 29 districts were chosen for establishing Community Forest User Groups (CFUGs), aimed at reducing forest degradation (Forestry Nepal, 2011b). By 2009, over 1,229,669 hectares (ha) of forests were managed by CFs, or 25 per cent of the total forest cover, with 1,659,775 households belonging to 14,439 CFUGs (Ojha et al., 2009). After the forest cover declined from 51 per cent in the 1950s to 29 per cent in 2001 (CBS, 2008; Singh and Chapagain, 2006), the transition to community forestry resulted in local increases in forest cover and the rate of forest loss in Nepal slowed to −1.35 per cent annually in 2005 (Petley et al., 2007), compared with −3.4 per cent annually between 1970 and 2000 (Tse-ring et al., 2010). Forest cover is therefore increasing substantially in many localities where community forests have been established, significantly reducing denuded mountain landscapes (Acharya and Dangi, 2009). In spite of significant differences in management, the CF programme overall has brought about positive environmental change and improved livelihood opportunities for a majority of community forest users (Pokharel et al., 2005; Singh and Chapagain, 2006). Another potential outcome of improved forest management is a reduction in soil erosion

The role of ecosystems in disaster risk reduction, Renaud, Sudmeier-Rieux and Estrella (eds), United Nations University Press, 2013, ISBN 978-92-808-1221-3

and the occurrence of shallow landslides (<2–5 metres deep), an increasing yet neglected phenomenon in Nepal's Middle Hills (Sudmeier-Rieux et al., 2011). However, the potentially positive effect of Nepal's CFs on slope stability has received little to no attention in the literature.

According to official statistics for the period 1979–2009, landslides directly caused over 100 casualties annually, compared with 70 casualties caused by flooding (Ministry of Home Affairs, 2009). Yet, owing to the remoteness and dispersed nature of landslides, it is likely that casualty figures are significantly underestimated. In addition, these statistics do not take into account the considerable impact that shallow landslides have on rural livelihoods, sweeping away terraces, blocking roads or damaging houses and irrigation canals, which requires expensive repairs and reconstruction. Stabilizing landslides can be extremely costly and technically challenging, depending on the local topography and intense monsoonal precipitation. Vegetation cover, especially with deep-rooted species, is one of the most cost-effective means of stabilizing slopes and often the most readily available bio-engineering technique (Lammeraner et al., 2007; Morgan, 2007; Phillips and Marden, 2005; Chapters 12 and 13 in this volume). The questions guiding this interdisciplinary research were: what were the trends in forest cover in selected Village Development Committees (VDCs)[1] in Dolakha District of central-eastern Nepal and what effect did these trends have on landslide occurrence during the period 1992–2009?

Background

The geographical and political context

Several dominant characteristics determine Nepal's unique land-use patterns: topography, monsoonal climate, a largely rural population living on steep terrain, rural development marked by outmigration, political instability and decentralization of power and budgets to local government. The country (147,181 km^2) covers a range of altitudes from 70 metres above sea level (m.a.s.l.) (Kanchan Kalan in the Terai plain) to 8,848 m.a.s.l. (Everest) over a width of about 200 km (NNE to SSW) and length of about 825 km. Although narrow, Nepal covers five different physiographical areas, from south to north: the Terai (17 per cent, lowland plains), the Siwaliks (foothills), the Middle Hills, the Middle Mountains and the High Mountains (83 per cent combined) (Upreti and Dhital, 1996) (see Figure 14.1). The monsoon winds and the orographic conditions of the Himalayan Range control Nepal's climate. The monsoon

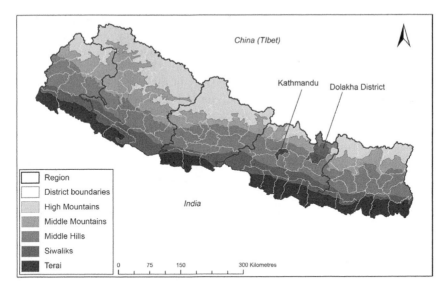

Figure 14.1 Physiographical map of Nepal
Sources: Based on data from the Mountain Environment and Natural Resources'
Information System of the International Centre for Integrated Mountain Development (<http://geoportal.icimod.org/>).

season starts in mid-June and ends in mid-September, during which time up to 80 per cent of annual precipitation occurs (Upreti and Dhital, 1996).

In 2010, 28 million people lived in Nepal, of whom 80 per cent lived in rural areas (CBS, 2009). Despite its rugged topography, the population density of Nepal was projected to be 194 people per km^2 for 2011 and the growth rate projected for 2011 was 2.13 per cent per annum (CBS, 2009). Nepal is ranked among the world's poorest countries – 138 out of 169 countries in the 2009 Human Development Index of the United Nations Development Programme (UNDP, 2009), even though recent advances in poverty reduction are being made thanks to large in-flows of remittance income (CBS, 2011). The main causal factors of Nepal's poverty are a proneness to physical hazards, the unequal distribution of land, a lack of access to education and health facilities, low levels of infrastructure development, low employment opportunities and political instability (UNDP, 2009). In 2001, Nepal's land use was divided as follows: forest (29 per cent), agricultural land (21 per cent), grass/pastureland (12 per cent), shrub (11 per cent), non-cultivated land (7 per cent), water/lakes (2 per cent) and "other" (18 per cent), which included snow areas, barren land, rocky areas and eroded areas (CBS, 2008).

Rural development is characterized by high outmigration framed by various push factors – poor food security, poor access to health care, frequent disasters, a decade of conflict – and pull factors – better economic opportunities elsewhere, especially in the Gulf states owing to a construction boom. The most common destinations of migration are Kathmandu, India, Qatar, Saudi Arabia and Malaysia (CBS, 2009). In parallel, the increased decentralization that has taken place since the Maoist government was formed in 2008 has given new unprecedented powers and budgets to district and village-level authorities. The number of local roads being built by communities, districts and VDCs has increased exponentially, resulting in a doubling of the road network between 1998 and 2007, from 4,740 to 9,399 km (DoR, 2012). Very frequently, these roads are bulldozed in the dry season and washed out in the rainy season, most often without oversight by the Nepal Department of Roads and with a high risk of increased landslides and loss of land. The emphasis placed on road-building reflects popular demand for increased connectivity and access to the economic opportunities and amenities that roads and urban centres bring.

Forest cover and land degradation in Nepal

Forest cover decline, increasing numbers of landslides and flooding, owing to more intense monsoon rains, are some of the major environmental issues facing Nepal (Baidya et al., 2008; Sudmeier-Rieux et al., 2012). The cause of landslides in Nepal, whether they are the result of human agency or whether they are naturally occurring, has been subject to debate over past decades since Eckholm (1975) popularized the "Theory of Himalayan Environmental Degradation", claiming that deforestation by Nepali farmers was the main cause of erosion and flooding in the Ganges Basin. Subsequent studies by Ives and Messerli (1989) disclaimed Eckholm's theory, stating that, on the contrary, landslides and erosion are mainly naturally occurring events. Other authors, notably Laban (1979), Zurick and Karan (1999) and, more recently, Petley et al. (2007), provide a more balanced view: human agency, mainly road-building and land degradation, are most likely responsible as "preparatory factors" for approximately half of all landslides, especially shallow landslides, which are also the most common type of landslides both worldwide and in Nepal. Preparatory factors refer to human or natural factors that may weaken slope stability, such as grazing, excavation for road-building or rainfall (Crozier, 1986; Chapter 12 in this volume). Rainfall can be both a preparatory and a triggering factor and one of the most common factors leading to shallow landslides, especially on slopes that have been weakened by any of

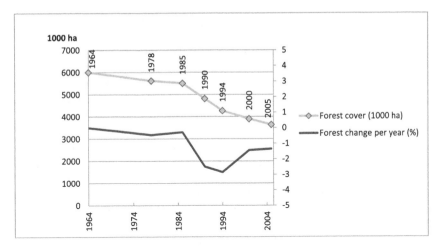

Figure 14.2 Trends in Nepal's forest cover, 1964–2004
Sources: Data from FAO (1999 and 2005).

the above-mentioned factors (Crozier, 1986). The Middle Hills in Nepal
are especially susceptible to landslides, a consequence of geological predisposition, rainfall and human activities. The steady increase in fatalities
is the result of a greater occurrence of roads being built and more intense
monsoon rainfall patterns (Petley et al., 2007).

In parallel, the forest cover has generally decreased in most of Nepal,
especially during the 1970s and 1980s, from 5.6 million ha in 1978 to 4.2
million ha in 1994 (the last reliable data from the Nepal Forest Inventory) because of rapid population growth and poor forest management
(Acharya and Dangi, 2009) (see Figure 14.2). Related to this trend, erosion rates have increased in areas without vegetation cover (Petley et al.,
2007).

Vegetation is known to have an overall positive impact on slope stability, with some exceptions depending on the depth of the soil and the type
of vegetation (Greenway, 1987). The absence of vegetation cover is a
common preparatory condition for shallow landslides, making a slope
more susceptible to rainfall (Glade, 2002; Chapter 12 in this volume).
Furthermore, grassy hill slopes are generally more prone to landslides
than forests (Marden and Rowan, 1993). Glade (2002) demonstrated that
the arrival of Europeans in New Zealand led to the conversion of forests
for agriculture, a sharp increase in erosion and greater susceptibility to
landslides. Before the change in land use, landslide occurrence in forest-
covered hill slopes was rare, demonstrating the protective effects of the
forest on slope stability.

The role of community forests in protection and livelihoods

The reasons for land degradation can be traced back through Nepal's history of land use and rapid population growth (Pokharel et al., 2005). Hobley (1996), cited in Pokharel et al. (2005: 2), has divided the history of Nepal's forests into three periods: privatization (before 1951), nationalization (1951–1987) and populism (participative) (1987 to the present). The periods after 1951 were marked by a series of forest and land reforms in an attempt to curb forest decline and promote greater decentralization (for example, the 1961 Forest Act, the 1967 Forest Protection Act and the 1976 National Forest Policy Act). These Acts had little effect on forest decline, and forest cover continued to drop from 51.0 per cent in 1950 to 35.7 per cent in 1977 (Singh and Chapagain, 2006). In 1978, the concept of community-based forestry began to emerge gradually through the establishment of CFUGs as part of forest management plans. Between 1978 and 1993, the concept of CFs was institutionalized in the Forest Act of 1993 (Singh and Chapagain, 2006), giving CFUGs a legal status.

Community forest principles and benefits

There are well-defined principles and rules that guide how CFs are to be managed, the first requirement being the establishment of a CFUG, with the coordination of the Federation of Community Forest Users, Nepal (FECOFUN) and the Nepal Department of Forests (DoF). Significant overseas development assistance by agencies has been invested in the organizational and leadership training of CFUGs, establishing guidelines and monitoring progress (for example, AusAID, the UK Department for International Development, Swiss Development Cooperation and German Development Cooperation). CFUG members are elected by their communities to reflect different ethnic groups and gender, deliberately including marginalized groups in the CFUG committees. They must prepare a plan with the assistance of DoF rangers and define ways to "protect, manage and utilize the forest, fix the price of, sell or dispose of its products, and punish violators. An operational plan is valid for five years and renewable after termination" (Singh and Chapagain, 2006: 125). CFUGs gain access to previous state forests in order to ensure sufficient household supplies of firewood, fodder and timber for house construction and limited amounts for sale. Households generally pay small fees to become CFUG members; they must participate in meetings and they are usually responsible for guarding their CF, depending on which type of management they choose. Proceeds from CFs can be used to hire a forest guard, buy seedlings, create plantations, or for community projects, such as a local access road.

Although forests are now overall better managed, and on paper all groups are purportedly represented, higher-status (caste) members often dominate CFUG committees, reflecting existing societal inequalities (Pokharel, 2008). Yet, according to Pokharel et al. (2005), there are two major benefits of CFs linked to the Forest Act of 1993: improvements in forest quality and landscape; and institution-building. By following CFUG rules, farmers are supposed to improve forest quality to generate better timber, fuel and fodder (Pokharel et al., 2005). A combination of better-established CF boundaries and greater local ownership has significantly reduced encroachment and poaching (Koirala et al., 2008). Strict rules on grazing have resulted in most livestock being stall fed instead of freely grazing along stream beds and steep hillsides. Because many CFUG leaders have received training in organizational skills (for example from FECOFUN), people have also become more aware about how to manage forests and forest products (Pokharel et al., 2005). These organizational skills are transferable to other situations, such as emergency preparedness. Another positive outcome of CFs that has not been addressed in the literature is the impact of CFs on slope stability, which is the research goal of this study.

Methodology

After an initial field visit in April 2010 to a number of CFs and landslides in Dolakha District, one of the first districts to develop CFs, 10 VDCs in Dolakha District were selected for a more in-depth study of forest cover and land degradation. This study consists of a comparison of aerial photographs (Survey Department, Nepal) taken in 1992 and satellite images of Dolakha District taken in 2009 (IKONOS satellite). Other data were obtained from Google Earth to complete the data set.

Aerial photographs were geo-referenced using ERDAS IMAGINE remote sensing software, from which Geographic Information System shape files were created; forest delineation was performed using ArcMap (Esri GIS software). Forest boundary data in the form of shape files from aerial photographs of 1992 and from the 1992 topographic survey maps were obtained from the Nepal Survey Department. Owing to the inconsistent forest classification used by the 1992 topographic maps, both dense and sparse forest were classified as "forest". Supervised classification, a simple method of remote sensing (using ERDAS) could have been used to classify land use with purchased IKONOS satellite images from 2009. However, for 2009 Google Earth images, a manual classification method was used to ensure a homogeneous comparison for the area covered. Thus, a detection change method (the union tool in ArcMap) was used to

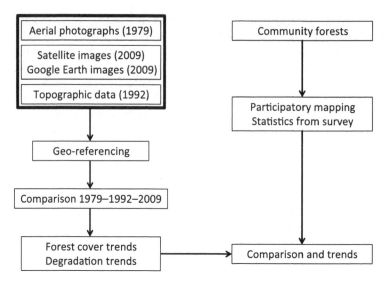

Figure 14.3 Methodology scheme for forest cover, degradation and community forest trends.

define changes in forest cover in 1992 and 2009. This method calculated each pixel classification and any classification changes. There were some difficulties in clearly distinguishing between shadows and forests and in defining the exact boundaries of the forest areas, because of the poor image quality of some of the aerial images from 1992, but overall it was possible to map forest cover changes between 1992 and 2009 (see Figure 14.3).

Degraded areas were defined as those areas visibly degraded on the satellite images and the aerial photographs: these included mainly shallow landslides, gullies and mud and debris flows. Field verification was carried out for a majority of these areas. Degraded areas were then separated into three categories: shallow landslides along gullies; shallow landslides along roads; other shallow landslide locations. Surface areas were calculated and compared with forest cover trends between 1992 and 2009 as detected on the satellite images. To explore the influence of CFs on forest trends, the final step was to compare forest cover trends with CF boundaries. The main challenge was a lack of geo-referenced, GIS-mapped CF boundaries. The CF boundaries are known by the local population and the DoF authorities but, other than simple sketches, in most cases accurate maps do not exist (Yadav et al., 2003). Thus, the CF boundaries in this study were determined from different sources, mainly participatory mapping using topographic maps and with field verification with the District Soil and Conservation Office of Dolakha District and the Nepal Swiss Community Forestry Project, Kathmandu (NSCFP).[2]

Results

Study area background

The selected area of study was located in the Janakpur zone in Dolakha District, north-east of Kathmandu in Central Nepal. It covers 10 of the 51 VDCs in Dolakha District, or 9.6 per cent of the district surface area (Figure 14.4, Table 14.1). Because of the difficulty in obtaining reliable

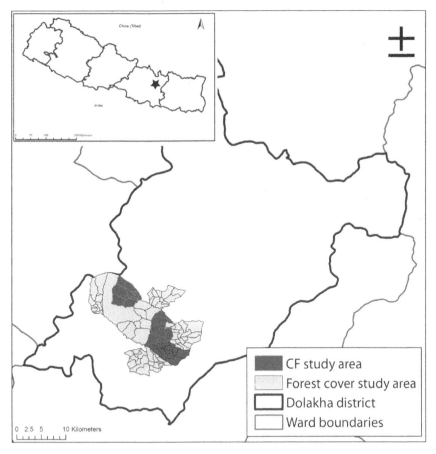

Figure 14.4 Map showing Dolakha District, the forest cover study area and the community forest study area.

Table 14.1 Surface of different areas of Dolakha District, Nepal, in 2009 based on most recent data sources

Area	Surface area (ha)	Per cent of total district
CF study area	4,812[1]	2.2
Forest cover study area	20,840[1]	9.6
Community forest in Dolakha District	29,901[2]	13.8
District forest cover	78,111[3]	36.0
Dolakha District	216,413[3]	100.0

Data sources: [1] Current study data; [2] District Soil and Conservation Office (2006); [3] CBS (2008).

data on CF boundaries, the CF area covered by this study is 4,812 ha, or 2.2 per cent of the district area (see Figure 14.5). CFs in total are believed to cover 13.8 per cent of the district area (District Soil and Conservation Office, 2006).

Dolakha District lies in Nepal's Middle Hills/Middle Mountains and is crossed north to south by the Tamakoshi River (Upreti and Dhital, 1996). The district headquarters is Charikot, an important market place, transportation hub and government centre. The area is also crossed by the east–west Lamosangu–Jiri road, built between 1974 and 1985 by the Swiss Development Cooperation agency. The road network, as for all of Nepal, has expanded considerably, from a road density of 6 km per 100 km^2 in 2001, or from 137 km of roads in the district to an anticipated doubling of this figure in 2012, especially of small earthen roads, although precise and current figures are not available (DoR, 2012). The land use of the district is diverse: it is mainly agricultural, with one-third of the total surface forested (District Soil and Conservation Office, 2006). In 2006, Dolakha District counted 204,744 inhabitants with an average of 4.7 inhabitants per household and a population density of 93.5 inhabitants/km^2 (District Soil and Conservation Office, 2006).

The range of precipitation in the area is 1,000 to 3,000 mm per year, with a mean of 2,039 mm in Charikot (1,940 m.a.s.l.) according to the Nepal Department of Meteorology and Hydrology (personal communication, 2008). July is the month with the highest precipitation, followed by August, June and September. It is important to note the possibility of so-called "cloudbursts", when it is not unusual to receive 300 mm of precipitation in one locality in one day. Geologically, Dolakha District is located in the Lesser Himalaya Zone with predominantly weakly metamorphosed sediments and rocks of higher metamorphic grade. The weathering is deep and the soil depth is important (Stöcklin, 1980). The main types of geology in the area are phyllite, quartzite and orthogneiss,

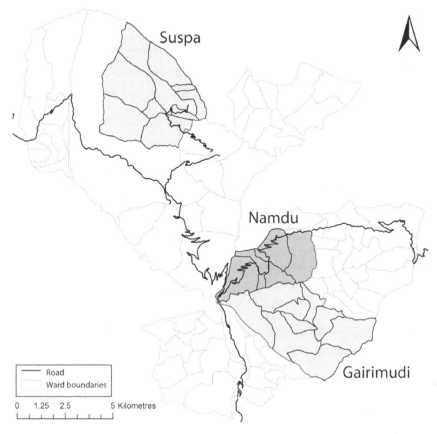

Figure 14.5 Community forests studied in Dolakha District: Gairimudi, Namdu and Suspa VDCs.

although in the Gairimudi area talc is also found, a mineral that becomes extremely slippery in the presence of water but is highly valued for painting houses in the traditional white.

Results: Forest cover and landslide trends, 1992–2009

Forest cover trends

According to our findings, 27.9 per cent of the total study area was covered by dense and sparse forests in 1992; this increased to 46.3 per cent in 2009. Thus, over 17 years, the forest cover of the study area increased by 21.3 per cent, in contrast to the national forest cover trend, which continued to decline (−1.35 per cent), although at a lower rate than in the 1980s. The forest expansion occurred especially around older forests and along

Table 14.2 Land-use change in the study area (10 VDCs), 1992–2009

	Per cent of total study area	
Land use	1992	2009
Forests	27.9	46.3
Shallow landslides (gullies, along roads, other)	0.5	0.2
Agriculture, built-up areas, water bodies	71.5	53.5

rivers and streams, and it replaced some terraced areas. In 1992, the study area's north-west section had more significant forest cover because it had the steepest areas where agriculture was scarce. In 2009, the forest cover increase had mainly occurred in the centre of the study area. By contrast, agricultural areas in the eastern part of the study area have high soil fertility; consequently, the forest increase was lower there.

Thus the forest cover increased visibly for the entire study area (Table 14.2, Figure 14.6), with some exceptions owing to differences in land use between the VDCs. Forests are found especially in the upper part of the mountainside where slopes are steeper, whereas on gentler slopes mainly fields and cultivated areas are dominant (Figure 14.7). Some areas that were not forested in 1992 showed a significant increase in forest cover in 2009. This is probably as a result of forests expanding onto previously degraded bare soils and grazing areas, which were not suitable for agriculture and grazing. Small forest decreases were observed along ridges in the north-west where forests were already present in 1992. The reasons for this decline are probably management differences because most of the ridge areas in 2010 were still under State Forest ownership (District Forest Officer, personal communication, 2010). These areas are still open to communities for firewood collection and therefore are often highly degraded.

The presence of CFs is believed to contribute to the increase in Dolakha District's forest cover. According to 2008 statistics, CFs covered 13.8 per cent (29,901 ha) of Dolakha District (216,413 ha) (CBS, 2008; DoF, 2008). Data on CFs from three VDCs were obtained, showing interesting results. In 2009, CFs accounted for an above-average 44 per cent of the total forest cover in Gairimudi, 89 per cent in Namdu and 86 per cent in Suspa (Table 14.3). In the latter two VDCs, we can assume that CFs have contributed significantly to the area's reforestation.

These findings are consistent with data collected by other studies on forest trends and CFs (Fort and Cossart, 2011; Gautam et al., 2002; Nagendra, 2007; Nagendra et al., 2005; Niraula and Maharjan, 2011; Petley et al., 2007), in addition to local observations about forest quality

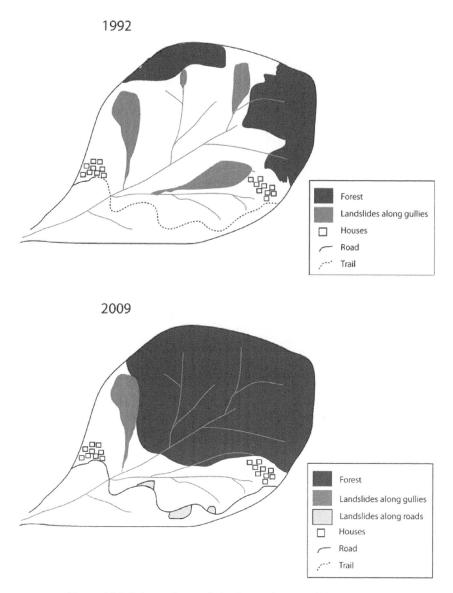

Figure 14.6 Schematic trends in the study area, 1992 and 2009.

improvements (Sudmeier-Rieux et al., 2011). These study results are also confirmed by a study conducted by Niraula and Maharjan (2011), which demonstrated similar trends in Dolakha District between 1990 and 2010. This study used similar remote sensing methods, but it covered 111 CFs,

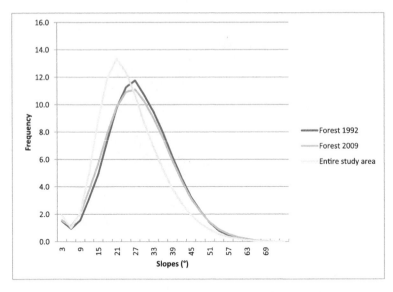

Figure 14.7   Forest cover linked to slope angle for study area

Table 14.3 Results: Community forests and forest cover changes in the study area, 1992–2009

	CF area (ha)	Total forest area in 2009 (ha)	CF as per cent of total forest area	Forest cover increase 1992–2009 (per cent)
Gairimudi VDC	359.0	823.4	44.0	+28.6
Namdu VDC	313.0	351.7	89.0	+20.2
Suspa VDC	1,134.8	1,312.9	86.0	+6.2
Dolakha District total	29,901.0	78,111.0	14.0	n/a

or 11,117 ha, in Dolakha District, where dense forest cover was found to increase by 10–30 per cent (Niraula and Maharjan, 2011).

Figure 14.8 illustrates the locations of old landslides present in 1992 but no longer present in 2009, which are represented by circles; landslides present in 1992 and still visible are represented by squares; new landslides since 2009 are represented by triangles.

Landslide trends

Three different types of land degradation (gully erosion, shallow landslides along roads) were found in the study areas. Before 1992, these

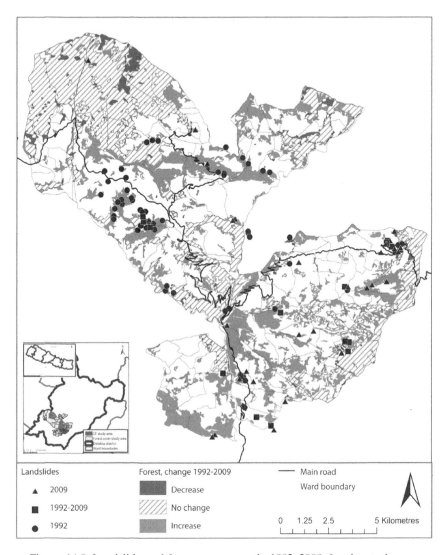

Figure 14.8 Landslide and forest cover trends, 1992–2009, for the study area

landslides occurred mainly along gullies (68.0 ha), whereas "other shal-low landslides" (39.8 ha) most likely occurred on previously degraded slopes and ridges owing to human activity such as grazing and unsustain-able forest harvesting, or occurred along roads (5.8 ha) (Table 14.4). The most important finding is that, between 1992 and 2009, the total surface area of landslides decreased by 78.6 ha. By 2009, degraded areas were

Table 14.4 Landslide areas in 1992 and 2009

Landslide type	Surface (ha)		Difference 1992–2009	
	1992	2009	Hectares	Per cent
Gullies	68.0	9.1	−58.9	−86.6
Other	39.8	18.1	−21.7	−54.5
Along roads	5.8	7.8	+2.0	+34.4
Total	113.6	35.0	−78.6	−69.2

Table 14.5 Landslide areas in 1992 covered by forests in the study area in 2009

Landslide type	1992 landslide area covered by forest in 2009	
	Area (ha)	Per cent
Gullies	34.9	30.7
Other	15.2	13.4
Along roads	0	0
Total	50.1	44.1

more commonly found in "other shallow landslides" areas (18.1 ha) and along roads (7.8 ha, an increase of 2 ha) compared with 1992. Thus, landslides related to gullies decreased but landslides along roads increased (see also Figure 14.6).

Of the total number of landslide areas in 1992, 44.1 per cent were covered by forests in 2009 (Table 14.5). In these reforested landslide areas, 30.7 per cent of landslides related to gullies were covered by forests. Roads were obviously not covered by forest but 13.4 per cent of other shallow landslides were. As discussed above, in most cases forests are an important factor in reducing shallow landslide occurrence (see also Chapter 12 in this volume). Based on our case-study data from Dolakha District, Nepal, this study further documents the positive function of forests in reducing shallow landslides and gullying.

Two examples are presented to illustrate this trend (see Figure 14.9 for their location). The first example shows highly degraded areas along river channels and gullies in 1992. In 2009, these areas were mainly covered by forests and only a few degraded patches remained (Figure 14.10).

As mentioned above, roads have a considerable effect on slope stability. The second example (Figure 14.11) is located along a road that was built between 1974 and 1985, whose impacts remain today. Old landslides present in 1992 and still visible are shown by squares and new landslides are shown by triangles. This is an inhabited area and the impacts of the road are negatively affecting households both upslope and downslope

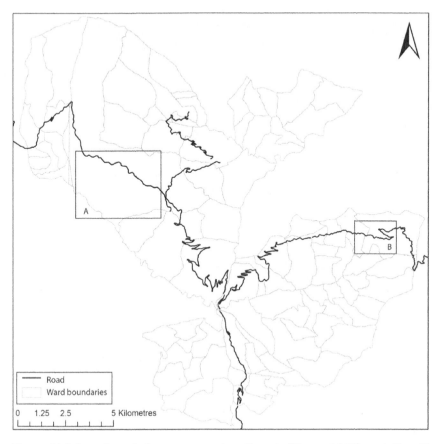

Figure 14.9 Location of the two examples: Case A (Figure 14.10) and Case B (Figure 14.11).

owing to soil removal and modification of the slope, which induce land-slides, even though the road is an asset to them.

Discussion of the results

As mentioned in the introduction, the main research questions guiding this study were: what were the trends in forest cover in selected areas in Dolakha District of central-eastern Nepal and what effects did these trends have on landslide occurrence over the period 1992–2009? The study results have demonstrated a trend towards improved forest cover and reduced land degradation and shallow landslide occurrence. The

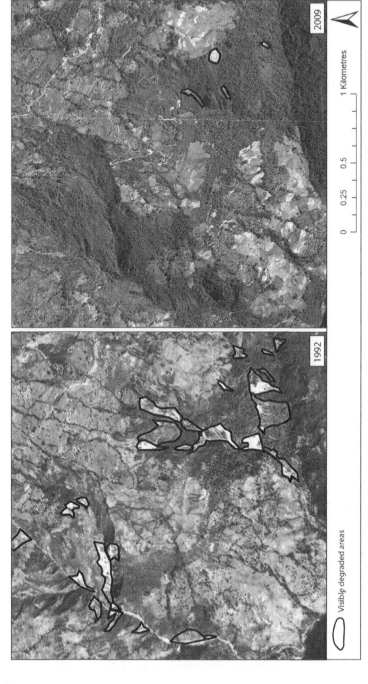

Figure 14.10 Case A: Degradation along the rivers in Bimeshwar municipality, 1992 and 2009
Sources: Aerial photograph 1992 – Survey Department, Kathmandu; satellite image 2009 – Google Earth.

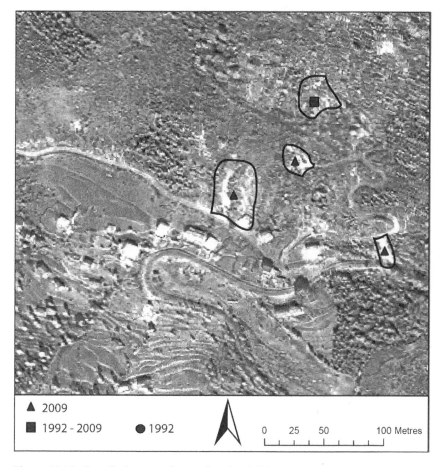

Figure 14.11 Case B: Impact of a road on landslide occurrence
Source: Satellite image 2009 – Google Earth.
Note: Squares indicate landslides already present in 1992 and triangles indicate new landslides.

study has also demonstrated the mitigating effects of the forest on shallow landslide occurrence.

Three major trends can be underlined:

• a clear significant increase in forest cover between 1992 and 2009 that is most likely the result of improved forestry management through the establishment of CFs, although few data were available;

• an increase in the road network between 1992 and 2009, which can be linked to the increase in landslide occurrence along the roads (DoR, 2012; Fort and Cossart, 2011; Petley et al., 2007);

Table 14.6 Effects of forests on slopes

Degradation type	Forest effects
Deep-seated landslides	No effect on slope stability; can provide income to population; increase evapotranspiration
Landslides on steep slopes	No effect; harsh vegetative conditions
Gullies	Stabilizing effect; can significantly reduce erosion; can provide income to population
Shallow landslides	Stabilizing effect; can significantly reduce soil losses; slows slope movements; can provide income to population
Erosion	Stabilizing effect; can significantly reduce erosion; can provide income to population

- a decrease in landslides along gullies, which can be linked to the increase in forest cover between 1992 and 2009.

However, there were insufficient data on CFs to be able to statistically correlate their development with a reduction in landslide occurrence. The major obstacle to determining such a correlation is the lack of accurately mapped CF boundaries and different definitions of what constitutes a forest between the 1992 topographic maps from the Nepal Survey Department and our study's definitions in 2010. The limited accuracy of the 1992 maps and very broad definitions of what constitutes a forest may have skewed CF boundaries. Nonetheless, our case-study results reveal trends towards a positive role for CFs in improving forest cover and, indirectly, slope stability. Table 14.6 summarizes different forest effects on various types of degradation. Consistent with other studies (for example, Chapter 12 in this volume), vegetation cover is linked to fewer shallow landslides and less gully erosion. Certainly the role of forests is less important in terms of deep-seated landslides and on steep slopes where tree roots have little impact on slope stability. However, if forests can be grown in degraded areas that are largely unsuitable for agriculture, they can provide essential fuel, timber and fodder for populations.

Recommendations

Forest cover as observed in the study is an excellent, cost-effective way of reducing shallow landslide risk and of stabilizing degraded areas as compared with the cost of installing expensive physical stabilization measures (Howell, 1999; Upreti and Dhital, 1996). The benefits of CFs in Nepal are well known, as demonstrated by numerous studies (Acharya, 2005; Joshi, 1998; Pokharel et al., 2005), for carbon storage (for example, Reducing

Emissions from Deforestation and Forest Degradation projects) (Dhital, 2009), biodiversity (Koirala et al., 2008), forest products for local communities (Pokharel et al., 2005) and social organizations (Singh and Chapagain, 2006), in addition to halting forest degradation as demonstrated by this current study and others (Pokharel et al., 2005). However, in order to see the real benefit of the CFs in Nepal, the lack of geo-referenced data on CF boundaries needs to be addressed (J. Carter, HELVETAS Swiss Intercooperation, personal communication, 2011; M. Kshetri, UNDP, personal communication, 2010). Future research is required to quantify and correlate landslide trends in relation to community forestry with geo-referenced maps for crosschecking with complete landslide inventories.

Conclusions

Our results have shown that firm links between CF cover trends and shallow landslide occurrence are difficult to establish owing to the lack of reliable data on CF boundaries in Nepal's data-poor environment, in addition to few or outdated data on forest cover, road network trends, etc. However, the main finding of this case study was a trend towards less gully erosion and fewer shallow landslides in the areas studied in Dolakha District in 1992–2009, in parallel with a large increase in forest cover, most likely the result of the development of CFs. This finding is consistent with other studies in the same area or other districts of Nepal on forest cover trends (Gautam et al., 2002; Nagendra, 2007; Niraula and Maharjan, 2011). However, this study is one of the few empirical studies linking landslide and CF cover trends in Nepal.

There are certainly differences between the VDCs in CF cover and forest quality, most likely owing to variations in forest management. There are some areas where forest cover is still decreasing slightly, mainly along ridges and in some areas by rivers. Most areas along the ridges are under state ownership, often considered open for firewood collection and other uses by the local population. Areas where there are increasing numbers of landslides are mainly along roads because of poorly managed road construction practices. This study has demonstrated the value of longitudinal remote sensing studies for detecting trends in forest cover and land degradation, as well as the high potential to work with CFUGs to enhance locally adapted practices for erosion and landslide reduction. This study has also confirmed that the supposed "Himalayan dilemma" of the 1980s (Ives and Messerli, 1989), that is, forest degradation and erosion, is being replaced by another looming dilemma for Nepal's rural development: rural road construction is leading to unprecedented roadside landslides, increased fatalities and lost agricultural land. Addressing this dilemma cost-effectively through bio-engineering practices is the next big challenge facing rural Nepal.

Acknowledgements

We would like to thank staff of the Nepal Swiss Community Forestry Project and Sushma Shrestha, who helped us during the field trip and during data and information researches. We are grateful to the inhabitants of Suspa VDC who created the participatory map of the community forest boundaries. And, lastly, thanks are due to University of Lausanne/ Institute of Geomatics and Risk Analysis (UNIL-IGAR) for financial, technical and moral support. This study was funded by the Swiss National Fund for Interdisciplinary Research 2009–2011 (No. 26083591), for which we are very grateful.

Notes

1. Each district is divided into Village Development Committees, and then into wards, the lowest administrative unit.
2. NSCFP was a Swiss Development Cooperation project, 1990–2011.

REFERENCES

Acharya, K.P. (2005) "Private, Collective, and Centralized Institutional Arrangements for Managing Forest 'Commons' in Nepal". *Mountain Research and Development* 25(3): 269–277.

Acharya, K.P. and R.B. Dangi (2009) "Forest Degradation in Nepal: Review of Data and Methods". Case Studies on Measuring and Assessing Forest Degradation, Forest Resources Assessment Working Paper 163. Rome: Food and Agriculture Organization of the United Nations, Forestry Department.

Baidya, S.K., M.L. Shrestha and M.M. Sheikh (2008) "Trends in Daily Climatic Extremes of Temperature and Precipitation in Nepal". *Journal of Hydrology and Meteorology* 5(8): 38–51.

CBS [Central Bureau of Statistics] (2008) *Environmental Statistics of Nepal 2008*. Kathmandu: Central Bureau of Statistics, Government of Nepal National Planning Commission Secretariat.

CBS (2009) *Statistical Year Book of Nepal 2009*. Kathmandu: Central Bureau of Statistics, Government of Nepal National Planning Commission Secretariat.

CBS (2011) "Nepal Living Standards Survey III". Press release, 8 August.

Crozier, M.J. (1986) *Landslides: Causes, Consequences, and Environment*. London: Croom Helm.

Dhital, N. (2009) "Reducing Emissions from Deforestation and Forest Degradation (REDD) in Nepal: Exploring the Possibilities". *Journal of Forest and Livelihood* 8: 56–62.

District Soil and Conservation Office (2006) *Sub Watershed Management Plan of
Khani–Gopi Khola Sub Watershed*. Charikot, Nepal: DSCO.

DoF [Department of Forests] (2008) "CFUG Database Record". Community
Forestry Division, Department of Forests, Kathmandu, Nepal.

DoR [Department of Roads] (2012) "Road Statistics", <http://www.dor.gov.np/
road_statistics.php> (accessed 30 October 2012).

Eckholm, E. (1975) "The Deterioration of Mountain Environments: Ecological
Stress in the Highlands of Asia, Latin America and Africa Takes a Mounting
Social Toll". *Science* 189(5): 764–770.

FAO [Food and Agriculture Organization of the United Nations] (1999) *Forest
Resources of Nepal: Country Report*. Forest Resources Assessment Working
Paper 16. Rome: FAO.

FAO (2005) *Global Forest Resources Assessment 2005: Progress towards Sustainable Forest Management*. FAO Forestry Paper 147. Rome: FAO.

Forestry Nepal (2011a) "Community Forestry", <http://www.forestrynepal.org/
wiki/137> (accessed 30 October 2012).

Forestry Nepal (2011b) "Land Use of Nepal According to MPFS", <http://www.
forestrynepal.org/wiki/322> (accessed 30 October 2012).

Fort M. and E. Cossart (2011) "Aléas naturels et menaces sur les axes de communication en Himalaya du Népal: La vallée de la moyenne Kali Gandaki". *Bulletin de l'association de géographes français* 88(1): 35–45.

Gautam, A.P., E.L. Webb and A. Eiumnoh (2002) "GIS Assessment of Land Use/
Land Cover Changes Associated with Community Forestry Implementation in
the Middle Hills of Nepal". *Mountain Research and Development* 22(1): 63–69.

Glade, T. (2002) "Landslide Occurrence as a Response to Land Use Change: A
Review of Evidence from New Zealand". *CATENA* 51: 297–314.

Greenway, D. (1987) "Vegetation and Slope Stability". In M. Andersen and
K. Richards (eds), *Slope Stability*. New York: Wiley.

Hobley, M. (1996) *Participatory Forestry: The Process of Change in India and
Nepal*. London: ODI.

Howell, J. (1999) *Roadside Bio-engineering: Site Handbook*. Kathmandu: Government of Nepal, Department of Roads.

Ives, J.D. and B. Messerli (1989) *The Himalayan Dilemma*. New York: Routledge.

Joshi, A.L. (1998) "Underlying Causes of Deforestation and Participatory Forest
Management Policy in Nepal". IGES International Workshop, Japan, 21–23
July. Available at <http://enviroscope.iges.or.jp/modules/envirolib/upload/1508/
attach/1ws-8-Joshi.pdf> (accessed 8 November 2012).

Koirala, R., K. Giri and B.K. Pokharel (2008) "Development and Status of Community Forestry Governance in Nepal". Paper presented at the National Convention of the Society of American Foresters, Reno-Tahoe, Nevada, USA, 5–9
November.

Laban, P. (1979) "Landslide Occurrence in Nepal". Integrated Watershed Management project, Working Paper No. 13. Department of Soil Conservation and
Watershed Management, Ministry of Forests, Kathmandu.

Lammeranner, W., H.P. Rauch and G. Laaha (2007) "Implementation and Monitoring of Soil Bioengineering Measures at a Landslide in the Middle Mountains of Nepal". In A. Stokes, I. Spanos, J. Norris and E. Cammeraat (eds), *Eco- and Ground Bio-Engineering: The Use of Vegetation to Improve Slope Stability*. Dordrecht: Springer.

Marden, M. and D. Rowan (1993) "Protective Value of Vegetation on Tertiary Terrain before and during Cyclone Bola, East Coast, North Island, New Zealand". *New Zealand Journal of Forest Science* 23: 255–263.

Ministry of Home Affairs (2009) *Nepal Disaster Report 2009: The Hazardscape and Vulnerability*. Kathmandu: Government of Nepal.

Morgan, R. (2007) "Vegetative-based Technologies for Erosion Control". In *Proceedings of the First International Conference on Eco-Engineering, Dordrecht, 13–17 September 2004*, pp. 265–272.

Nagendra, H. (2007) "Drivers of Reforestation in Human-dominated Forests". *PNAS* 104(39): 15218–15223.

Nagendra, H., M. Karmacharya and B. Karna (2005) "Evaluating Forest Management in Nepal: Views across Space and Time". *Ecology and Society* 10(1): 24.

Niraula, R.R. and S.K. Maharjan (2011) "Forest Cover Change Analysis in Dolakha District (1990–2010)". Nepal Swiss Community Forestry Project, Kathmandu.

Ojha, H., L. Persha and A. Chhatre (2009) *Community Forestry in Nepal: A Policy Innovation for Local Livelihoods*. IFPRI Discussion Paper 00913. Washington, DC: International Food Policy Research Institute.

Petley, D.N. et al. (2007) "Trends in Landslide Occurrence in Nepal". *Natural Hazards* 43: 23–44.

Phillips, C. and M. Marden (2005) "Reforestation Schemes to Manage Regional Landslide Risk". In T. Glade, M. Anderson and M. Crozier (eds), *Landslide Hazard and Risk*. London: John Wiley, pp. 517–548.

Pokharel, B.K., T. Stadtmüller and J.-L. Pfund (2005) *From Degradation to Restoration: An Assessment of the Enabling Conditions for Community Forestry in Nepal*. Bern: Intercooperation.

Pokharel, R.K. (2008) "Nepal's Community Forestry Funds: Do They Benefit the Poor?" Working Paper No. 31-08, SANDEE, Kathmandu.

Singh, B.K. and D.P. Chapagain (2006) "Trends in Forest Ownership, Forest Resources Tenure and Institutional Arrangements: Are They Contributing to Better Forest Management and Poverty Reduction? Community and Leasehold Forestry for the Poor: Nepal Case Study". In FAO, *Understanding Forest Tenure in South and Southeast Asia*, Forestry Policy and Institutions Working Paper 14, pp. 115–152.

Stöcklin, J. (1980) "Geology of Nepal and Its Regional Frame". *Journal of Geological Society of London* 137: 1–34.

Sudmeier-Rieux, K. et al. (2011) "A Case Study of Coping Strategies and Landslides in Two Villages of Central-Eastern Nepal". *Applied Geography* 32(2): 680–690.

Sudmeier-Rieux, K. et al. (2012) "Floods, Landslides, and Adapting to Climate Change in Nepal". In A. Lamadrid and I. Kelman (eds), *Climate Change Modeling for Local Adaptation in the Hindu Kush-Himalayan Region*. Bingley, UK: Emerald Group Publishing, pp. 119–140.

Tse-ring, K. et al. (2010) *Climate Change Vulnerability of Mountain Ecosystems in the Eastern Himalayas*. Kathmandu: International Centre for Integrated Mountain Development.

UNDP [United Nations Development Programme] (2009) *Nepal Human Development Report 2009*. New York: United Nations Development Programme.

Upreti, B.N. and M.R. Dhital (1996) *Landslide Studies and Management in Nepal*. Kathmandu: International Centre for Integrated Mountain Development.

Yadav, N.P. et al. (2003) "Forest Management and Utilization under Community Forestry". *Journal of Forest and Livelihood* 3: 37–50.

Zurick, D. and P.P. Karan (1999) *Himalaya: Life on the Edge of the World*. Baltimore, MD: Johns Hopkins University Press.

Part V

Policy, planning and future perspectives

15

Reducing vulnerability: The role of protected areas in mitigating natural disasters

Nigel Dudley, Kathy MacKinnon and Sue Stolton

Introduction

The protection and restoration of ecosystem services can be an important step towards enhancing disaster mitigation. Protected areas provide an effective mechanism for maintaining natural habitats and ecosystem function. After decades in which engineering solutions were automatically the first choice for minimizing the risk of disasters such as flooding and avalanches, the importance of protecting ecosystems is increasingly being recognized, although still by no means universally incorporated, in disaster risk reduction strategies. The Inter-Agency Secretariat of the United Nations International Strategy for Disaster Reduction (UNISDR) noted in its *Global Review of Disaster Reduction Initiatives* (2004: 298): "Although the links between disaster reduction and environmental management are recognized, little research and policy work has been undertaken on the subject. The concept of using environmental tools for disaster reduction has not yet been widely applied by practitioners." There is now greater recognition of the links between environmental management and disaster risk management (DRM), but gaps in capacity and implementation still remain, as noted by UNISDR in its *2011 Global Assessment Report* (2011: 128): "the monetary undervaluation of ecosystem services remains an important obstacle to the adoption of ecosystem-based DRM. As a consequence, relatively few countries are taking advantage of tools such as 'payments for ecosystem services'."

The role of ecosystems in disaster risk reduction, Renaud, Sudmeier-Rieux and Estrella (eds),
United Nations University Press, 2013, ISBN 978-92-808-1221-3

By far the most extensive application of deliberate management of ecosystems is the global protected area network, encompassing national parks, wilderness preserves, nature reserves and marine protected areas, already covering over 12.7 per cent of the world's land surface outside Antarctica, 7.2 per cent of coastal waters and 3.5 per cent of territorial waters. Although protected areas were originally set up primarily to protect natural landscapes, wildlife and, more recently, biodiversity, their wider societal benefits are increasingly being recognized, including their role in disaster mitigation (Dudley et al., 2010; Stolton and Dudley, 2010; World Bank, 2010a).The examples collected together in this book show that there is already a growing body of knowledge about utilizing natural habitats and ecosystem services within disaster reduction strategies. We argue in this chapter that protected areas provide a critical and often undervalued tool for disaster reduction.

Current losses of ecosystem services

Unfortunately, although the "protective" role of natural ecosystems against hazards is finally receiving the attention it deserves, the ecosystems themselves are continuing to decline: forests are still being cleared throughout the tropics, deserts are expanding, grasslands are degrading, coastal mangroves and coral reefs are being destroyed by pollution and overexploitation and wetlands are being drained (UNEP, 2007). This is not just a threat to biodiversity. Environmental degradation increases the risk that extreme weather events and geological events will lead to disaster for vulnerable communities. Many of the deaths stemming from earthquakes in mountainous areas, for instance, come from subsequent landslides, and disaster risks increase dramatically when deforestation has taken place on steep slopes (EERI, 2006). Preventing further environmental degradation and restoring degraded ecosystems are thus important components in both local and national disaster reduction strategies.

Climate change is exacerbating the problems generated by degradation of natural ecosystems, both by increasing the frequency and variability of extreme weather events (Bates et al., 2008; Dore, 2005) and by reducing ecosystem resilience and capacity to protect human communities from natural hazards such as flooding, tidal surges, landslides and drought (Helmer and Hilhorst, 2006; Huq et al., 2007; Van Aalst, 2006). Where environmental degradation is coupled with inequality in land ownership, poverty, poor infrastructure and inadequate disaster warning, human vulnerability to disasters is even greater. The Intergovernmental Panel on Climate Change notes that "[c]limate change will interact at all scales with other trends in global environmental and natural resource concerns

... Their combined impacts may be compounded in future in the absence of integrated mitigation and adaptation measures" (Pachauri and Reisinger, 2007: 70). Although the protection of ecosystems alone cannot halt the impacts of climate change, there is increasing evidence that large, healthy and functioning ecosystems are likely to be more resistant to the impacts of climate change when it occurs (for example, Maestre et al., 2012; Noss, 2001).

Protected areas reducing vulnerability to disasters

In fact, the concept of protecting ecosystems for disaster mitigation is not new. Some of the earliest "protected areas" were established explicitly to buffer human communities against extremes of climate and associated hazards (that is, to reduce their vulnerability to disaster), rather than for the biodiversity conservation values we associate with national parks and nature reserves today. In Japan, for instance, forest protection was introduced in the fifteenth and sixteenth centuries to counter landslides (Kumazaki et al., 1991). Today, Japan has almost 9 million hectares (ha) of protection forests, with 17 uses including 13 relevant to reducing the impacts of extreme climate events (Government of Japan, n.d.). In Switzerland, similar measures were taken in the nineteenth century (see Box 15.1).

Box 15.1 Protecting and restoring forests for avalanche and landslide control

In Switzerland, the government recognized 150 years ago that deforestation was contributing to avalanches, landslides and flooding and introduced a system of protection and restoration (McShane and McShane-Caluzi, 1997). Following a serious flood in 1987, further steps were taken to use forests as protection against natural hazards, through Federal Ordinances on Flood and Forest Protection. Stands are managed to help protect against rock fall, landslides and avalanches (Brändli and Gerold, 2001), with actions embedded within a comprehensive strategy focusing on four key elements: hazard assessment, definition of protection requirements, planning of measures and emergency planning (Lateltin et al., 2005). Forests are recognized as a major component of disaster prevention; nowadays, 17 per cent of the total area of Swiss forests is managed mainly for its protective function, providing a range of environmental services estimated to be worth US$1,000/hectare/year (Chapter 13 in this volume).

The role of protected ecosystems in preventing or mitigating disasters is not confined to forests. In the Middle East, protected areas called *hima* were established well over 1,000 years ago to prevent deforestation and grassland erosion through over-grazing (Bagader et al., 1994). The Prophet Muhammad adopted the existing system and abolished private *hima* belonging to powerful individuals in favour of the "common welfare", including rangelands, forests, woods, watersheds and wildlife. Although at one time largely abandoned, *hima* are now being used as the basis for establishing new protected areas (Sulayem and Joubert, 1994). Throughout the tropics, many traditionally managed indigenous and community conserved areas and sacred natural sites recognize the value of natural vegetation to protect against floods and landslides caused by extreme weather events (Pathak et al., 2005). Such traditional experience is increasingly being adopted and in some cases updated within protected area strategies so that places set aside for conservation perform a dual function of protecting human communities from extreme weather events. The design of the protected area system plan for Indonesia, for example, recognizes the environmental as well as the biodiversity benefits of protected areas (MacKinnon and Budi Artha, 1981; MacKinnon et al., 1996); China stopped logging in mountain forests after devastating downstream floods and re-designated those forests as protected areas for their watershed and biodiversity values (World Bank, 2010a).

The most immediate role of protected areas in disaster risk reduction is to buffer against the effects of a natural hazard, by physically stabilizing the movement of water, earth, rocks and snow or by providing space for the energy generated by disasters to dissipate harmlessly. In this regard, protected areas provide three main benefits:

1. maintaining predominantly natural ecosystems that buffer against sudden natural hazards such as tidal surge (coastal mangroves, coral reefs), flash floods (wetlands, floodplains) and landslides (forests and other native vegetation) (see references collected in Stolton et al., 2008, and Box 15.2);
2. maintaining traditional cultural ecosystems and crops that have an important role in mitigating extreme weather events, such as agroforestry systems, terraced crop-growing and fruit tree forests in arid lands that can protect against the impacts of drought and desertification (Amend et al., 2008);
3. providing an opportunity for active or natural restoration of such systems where they are degraded or lost, such as reforesting steep slopes or restoring floodplains (Dobson et al., 1997).

In practice, protected areas sometimes also provide emergency sources of food, freshwater, building materials and living space following disasters. If such uses are planned and agreed with the protected area management

Box 15.2 Wetland protection for regulating floods

The Whangamarino Ramsar site in New Zealand is the second-largest bog and swamp complex remaining in North Island and is a good example of the value of protecting floodplains. The wetland has a significant role in flood control (the value of which has been estimated at US$601,037 per annum at 2003 values) and sediment trapping (Schuyt and Brander, 2004). Values rise in years when there is flooding and it is estimated that flood prevention in 1998 was worth US$4 million alone. There have been 11 occasions since 1995 when the wetlands were needed to absorb floods (DoC, 2007). The site is also of considerable biodiversity value and more botanically diverse than any other large low-lying peatland in North Island.

(whether these be government, communities or private individuals and trusts), such benefits can often be supplied without long-term losses. Conversely, if unplanned and without due care they can conflict with conservation priorities and lead to long-term degradation such that the area becomes less resilient against disaster in the future. Table 15.1 demonstrates the range of ways in which protected areas can address a variety of hazards.

Investing in protected areas versus infrastructure?

The UNISDR *2011 Global Assessment Report* estimates that 69.4 million people are affected by flooding every year. This number has increased by 114 per cent since 1970, in contrast to the world's population, which increased by 87 per cent during this period. This average can be exceeded in a bad year: in 2008 at least 36 million people were displaced by natural disasters, including over 20 million displaced by climate-related disasters (OCHA, 2009). Despite global efforts at disaster mitigation, economic losses from weather and floods have increased 10-fold in 50 years (Stolton et al., 2008) and over half the world's population are now exposed to hazards with the potential to become disasters (Dilley et al., 2005). There is general recognition at a global level that actions to date have been inadequate, with too much effort placed on responses and not enough on taking steps to minimize the risk of a disaster developing. The World Bank's influential report *Natural Hazards, Unnatural Disasters: The Economics of Effective Prevention* notes that, "[f]or environmental buffers, it is cheaper to protect than to restore them" (World Bank, 2010b: 106) and concludes that, for major prevention measures by national, state and

Table 15.1 Examples of the role of protected areas in preventing or mitigating against natural disasters

Hazard	Role of protected area	Protected area habitat type	Examples
Flooding	Providing space for overspill of water/ flood attenuation	Marshes, coastal wetlands, peat bogs, natural lakes	The two reserves that form the Muthurajawela Marsh in Sri Lanka, cover an area of 3,068 ha near Colombo. The economic value of flood attenuation (converted to 2003 values) has been estimated at US$5,033,800 per year (Costanza et al., 2008).
	Absorbing and reducing water flow	Riparian and mountain forests	Natural forests in the Paraná river basin, Argentina, have been established as protected areas as part of flood control strategies to protect downstream communities (World Bank, 2010a). Benefits from forest protection in the upper watersheds of Mantadia National Park in Madagascar, in terms of reduced flood damage to crops, were estimated at US$126,700 (in 1991 Madagascar had per capita GNP of US$207) (Kramer et al., 1997). Floods that had affected the coastal city of Malaga in Spain for 500 years were eliminated through reforestation and protection of an area of the watershed (Dudley and Aldrich, 2007).
Landslide, rock fall and avalanche	Stabilizing soil, loose rock and snow	Forests on steep slopes	Floods and landslides are frequent hazards in Nepal, claiming around 200 lives a year (Government of Nepal, 2004). Shivapuri National Park is the main source of water for domestic consumption in Kathmandu. Landslide protection measures have been implemented in 12 localities in the protected area (Chapter 14 in this volume).
	Buffering against earth and snow movement	Forests on and beneath slopes	Swiss forests (see example in Box 15.1); similar policies exist throughout the European Alps (Chapters 12 and 13 in this volume).
Tidal waves and storm surges	Creating a physical barrier against ocean incursion	Mangroves, barrier islands, coral reefs, sand dunes	The indigenous communities living in the Río Plátano Biosphere Reserve in Honduras are reforesting the shore of the Ibans Lagoon with mangrove and other species to improve fish habitats and to counter erosion of the narrow coastal strip (Simms et al., 2004).
	Providing overspill space for tidal surges	Coastal marshes	The Black River Lower Morass is the largest freshwater wetland ecosystem in Jamaica. The marsh acts as a natural buffer against river flood waters and incursions by the sea and is an important economic resource for 20,000 people.

Hazard	Ecosystem service / role	Habitats	Examples
Drought and desertification	Reducing grazing and trampling	Particularly grasslands but also dry forest	Protection and re-establishment of salt marshes form part of coastal defence strategies in the UK (Stolton et al., 2008). In Djibouti, the Day Forest National Park is a protected area, with regeneration projects initiated to prevent further loss of this important forest area and further encroachment by deserts (UNCCD, 2006).
	Maintaining drought-resistant plants	All dryland habitats	In Mali, the role of national parks in desertification control is recognized, and protected areas are seen as an important reservoir of drought-resistant species (Berthe, 1997).
Fire	Maintaining management systems that control fire	Savannah, dry and temperate forests and scrub	In Mount Kitanglad Range Natural Park, Philippines, volunteers from different ethnic communities in the area undertake fire-watching duties. Being members of volunteer guard initiatives fits well with traditional ideas of land stewardship and a council of tribe elders endorses their appointment (Karki, 2002).
	Maintaining natural fire resistance	Fire refugia in forests, wetlands	Studies in and around Kutai National Park, Indonesia, found that the 1982–3 forest fires killed more trees in secondary forest than in protected primary forests (MacKinnon et al., 1996). Similarly, recent studies in the Amazon found the incidence of fire to be lower in protected areas relative to surrounding areas (Adeney et al., 2009). Forest fragmentation also leads to desiccation of ground cover, increasing the fire hazard.
Hurricanes and storms	Buffering against immediate storm damage	Forests, coral reefs, mangroves, barrier islands	The protected mangrove system of the Sundarbans in Bangladesh and India helps to stabilize wetland and coastlines and contributes to buffering inland areas from cyclones. Mangroves can break up storm waves, which can exceed 4 metres in height during cyclones, and result in the coastal areas protected by these forests suffering less from wind and wave surges than those areas with little or no mangrove cover (Stolton et al., 2008).

Source: Adapted from Dudley et al. (2010).

local governments, "[t]hree spending items generally have high returns. The first is more funding for weather forecasting with accompanying oversight to prevent careless spending.... The second is ensuring that certain critical infrastructure remains functional after a disaster. And the third is protecting environmental buffers, sensible but difficult to translate into action: better institutions will help" (World Bank, 2010b: 133).

There is a growing body of evidence about the economic benefits of maintaining natural ecosystems to protect against disasters. An analysis of the role of wetlands in reducing flooding associated with hurricanes in the United States calculated an average value of US$8,240/ha/year, with coastal wetlands in the United States estimated to provide US$23.2 billion per year in storm protection services (Costanza et al., 2008). A global assessment of the value of wetlands estimates that the median economic value of wetland (at year 2000 values) for flood control is US$464/ha/year (Schuyt and Brander, 2004). A study of the value of mangroves in Thailand found that replacement costs in terms of shoreline protection were conservatively estimated at US$3,679/ha based on a 20-year timeline (Sathirathai and Barbier, 2001) and that a 1 km^2 decline in mangrove area will increase the expected number of disasters by 0.36 per cent (Barbier, 2007). Similar studies have been carried out in Sarawak, Malaysia (Bennett and Reynolds, 1992). The various reports of the recent The Economics of Ecosystems and Biodiversity (TEEB) study have elaborated many other examples.

Direct comparisons between the costs of investing in built infrastructure and protected area designation and management are scarce and remain an important area for research. In most cases, disaster mitigation benefits are *in addition* to the existing benefits in terms of biodiversity conservation, recreation and cultural value. Nevertheless, the disaster mitigation benefits from protected areas provide powerful additional social and economic arguments in support of conservation action.

Ecologists, engineers and disaster relief specialists are starting to look for an optimal balance between development, conservation and disaster preparedness, especially a better balance between engineered solutions and "natural solutions" such as habitat protection or restoration. In Argentina and Ecuador, for instance, flood control projects use the natural storage and recharge properties of critical forests and wetlands by integrating them into "living with floods" strategies that incorporate forest protected areas and riparian corridors (see Box 15.3).

Despite some exceptions (such as the examples cited above), exploiting the link between protected areas and disaster mitigation is still far from general practice amongst governments, where disaster preparedness is still often linked narrowly with engineered solutions. Adaptation to climate change is likely to involve more investment in infrastructure such as

Box 15.3 Protecting natural forests for flood control

The irregular rainfall patterns prevailing in Argentina cause floods and droughts. Under all climate change scenarios, these boom-and-bust cycles will be exaggerated. Currently, about one-fourth of the country is repeatedly flooded. This is particularly true for north-eastern Argentina, which has three major rivers – Paraná, Paraguay and Uruguay – and extensive, low-lying plains, which make up almost 30 per cent of the country and include more than half of Argentina's population. The first phase of a two-stage flood protection programme provided cost-effective flood protection for the most important economic and ecological areas and developed a strategy to cope with recurrent floods. Activities included the development and enforcement of flood defence strategies, the construction and maintenance of flood defence installations, early flood warning systems, environmental guidelines for flood-prone areas, and flood emergency plans. Extensive areas of natural forest were also protected as part of the flood defence system. This incorporation of natural habitats into flood defences provided a low-cost alternative and supplement to more costly infrastructure, with the added benefit of high biodiversity gains through protection of 60 per cent of Argentina's birds and more than 50 per cent of its amphibians, reptiles and mammal species. The small investment in environmental protection (including wetland protection and management) – US$3.6 million compared with the total investment of US$488 million in the river basin flood defences – has led to significant changes in state and municipal regulations in four provinces, including the establishment of protected areas as part of flood protection schemes. As changing climate makes extreme weather events and flooding more likely, the experience of Argentina provides some useful lessons on how best to harness natural habitats to reduce the vulnerability of downstream communities.

Source: Quintero (2007).

dams and levees for water storage and flood control and more investment in coastal defences against rising sea levels and storm surges (see Box 15.4). Such traditional engineered solutions may work against nature, especially when they lead to loss of habitat, are poorly planned, designed or operated, or cause problems for downstream communities or ecosystems through changes in volumes, patterns and quality of water flows. Careful design and planning to protect natural ecosystems in, and

Box 15.4 Investing in mangroves

The maintenance or restoration of mangroves, where ecologically appropriate, can reduce the vulnerability of coastal areas and communities to sea level rise and extreme weather events, while also contributing to food security by protecting local fisheries. Often such ecosystem-based approaches are highly cost-effective.

- Mangrove forests have an estimated economic value of US$300,000 per km as coastal defences in Malaysia (Stolton et al., 2008).
- Since 1994, communities have been planting and protecting mangrove forests in Viet Nam as a way to buffer against storms. An initial investment of US$1.1 million saved an estimated US$7.3 million a year in sea dyke maintenance and significantly reduced the loss of life and property from Typhoon Wukong in 2000 in comparison with other areas (Brown et al., 2006).
- Loss of mangrove area has been estimated to increase storm damage on the coast of Thailand by US$585,000, or US$187,898 per km^2 (total economic value in 1996 US dollars) (Stolton et al., 2008).
- In Surat Thani, Thailand, the sum of all measured goods and services of intact mangroves (US$60,400 total economic value, including coastal protection) exceeds the economic benefits of shrimp farming from aquaculture by around 70 per cent (Balmford et al., 2002).

around, the new facilities can benefit both biodiversity and the efficiency and effectiveness of the infrastructure investment (World Bank, 2010a).

There are several reasons why implementation of disaster reduction strategies has not made more conscious use of protected areas. Budgets are limited and governments and donors alike may have a bias towards investing in hard infrastructure, which is easy to understand, see and report on. The companies involved in such projects often have significant and sophisticated lobbying systems in place to push decisions towards engineering solutions, adding to existing political pressure from governments that want to be seen to take firm action. There is also probably still a lack of awareness about the potential of both natural ecosystems and the associated role of protected areas. The civil servants making decisions about disaster mitigation are likely to be in a different ministry from those who are addressing biodiversity conservation. Other pressures for development are often simultaneously acting against efforts to conserve natural ecosystems. After the devastating effects of Hurricane Katrina in New Orleans in 2005, the need for the restoration of floodplain forests and wetlands was widely recognized, but still had to compete with pressures to develop the bayous (Stolton et al., 2008).

Do protected areas work as part of disaster mitigation strategies?

Although their role is often unrecognized, protected areas are already mitigating natural disasters. How well protected areas can continue to deliver such ecosystem services depends on how effectively they are managed, how well they are integrated with surrounding landscapes and land-use strategies and supported by local communities, and the extent to which they are accepted by, and integrated into, national, regional, community and commercial disaster mitigation strategies.

Unlike other forms of land use, protected areas already have many important management elements in place that are specifically designed to protect and maintain natural habitats and their functions. Investments in protected areas globally (from both national and international funds) are difficult to calculate but have been conservatively estimated at US$6 billion annually, with US$750 million spent annually in tropical countries (Balmford and Whitten, 2003). This works out to US$453/km^2 globally, though just US$93/km^2 is spent in the tropical countries. A more detailed recent estimate for tiger reserves assesses funds currently spent at 42 source sites for tiger conservation as US$47 million (almost US$500/km^2/year or US$365/km^2/year outside India). Because of the substantial international support for this charismatic species, these figures are some of the highest conservation expenditures in developing countries (Walston et al., 2010).

Recent estimates suggest that establishing and managing a comprehensive global network of protected areas would cost roughly US$23 billion per year. This is more than four times the current expenditure, but low- to middle-income countries would require less than one-tenth of this sum, just double what is currently spent (Butchart et al., 2012). Nevertheless, even if global figures are quadrupled to US$23 billion a year, it would seem that this investment is remarkably good value given the multiple benefits that protected areas provide (Dudley et al., 2010).[1] Indeed, many protected areas can probably be justified on socioeconomic values alone, including their role in disaster risk reduction.

Most protected areas have agreed borders, usually legally defined and physically marked, and they operate under legal or equivalent cultural frameworks that provide stable mechanisms for maintaining ecosystem services. Protected areas also usually have systems for establishing and codifying land tenure agreements and have agreed governance structures, ranging from state-managed parks and wildlife areas to indigenous reserves and areas established and managed by local groups. Indeed, recent studies show that indigenous reserves are some of the most effective in maintaining natural forests (Nelson and Chomitz, 2009). To an increasing extent, private, communal or co-management options are being developed the better to engage local stakeholders and expand the conservation estate. They are backed by a range of supportive conventions and agreements, including the Convention on Biological Diversity (CBD), which has an agreed Programme of Work on Protected Areas, UNESCO's Man and the Biosphere programme and World Heritage Convention, and the Ramsar Convention on Wetlands, plus regional agreements such as the European Union's Natura 2000. Protected areas are supported by associated government departments, policies, guidelines and established management procedures. As society expectations change, many managers of protected areas are implementing mechanisms to engage local people in management, which is essential for sustaining protection efforts for multiple benefits.

Protected areas also have management processes that will be useful or essential for managing ecosystem services, including data sources to set baselines, monitoring systems, staff and equipment that can provide management expertise and existing infrastructure. Many will already have invested in start-up costs and will be able to draw upon existing funding from governments or trusts. Efforts towards disaster mitigation using protected areas can sometimes complement those from other funding sources. Protected areas exist in a culture in which management planning is expected and new plans can focus on maintaining ecosystem services, as well as the more traditional issues relating to biodiversity, landscape and visitor requirements. Protected areas also usually have disciplined and trained staff and management structures, often in remote situations, that can be useful in early responses to disasters. In Pakistan, for example, protected area staff in mountain areas responded quickly to provide earthquake disaster relief (Stolton et al., 2008). Finally, protected areas are backed by global networks of experts prepared to provide advice and assistance, including particularly the International Union for Conservation of Nature World Commission on Protected Areas, development agencies and non-governmental organizations. A series of research studies suggest that this combination of strengths is resulting in effective habitat conservation, as illustrated in Table 15.2. Research shows that protected areas are effective in maintaining natural ecosystems, even in places where they have otherwise been degraded or have disappeared.

Many protected areas already have the necessary policies, infrastructure, capacity and proven track record in maintaining natural ecosystems for disaster mitigation. What they are lacking, in most cases, are the policies, organizational framework and in-house skills to facilitate such integration. Developing closer links between the protected area and disaster relief communities should be an urgent priority.

Table 15.2 Results from studies on the effectiveness of protected areas in maintaining vegetation cover

Organization	Results
Conservation International	A study on threats facing 92 protected areas in 22 tropical countries concluded that most protected areas are successful in protecting ecosystems (Bruner et al., 2001).
WWF and World Bank	A survey of 330 protected areas around the world using a consistent methodology found biodiversity condition consistently scoring high (Dudley et al., 2007).
University of Queensland	A global meta-study assessed management effectiveness evaluations from over 4,000 protected areas and found that 87 per cent met their own criteria for good management (Leverington et al., 2010).
Indiana University and Ashoka Trust	Research found lower rates of land-clearing in protected areas compared with surrounding areas (Nagendra, 2008).
Duke University	Research across four tropical areas assessed natural vegetation changes. Overall, protected areas were effective; forest cover was often "strikingly higher" than in surrounding areas (Joppa et al., 2008).
World Bank	Tropical protected areas, especially those conserved by indigenous peoples, lose less forest than other management systems (Nelson and Chomitz, 2009).
UNEP World Conservation Monitoring Centre	Forests in protected areas accounted for just 3 per cent of tropical forest losses in 2000–2005 in the countries studied, which is far better than average (Campbell et al., 2008).
Stanford University and partners	Studies in the Amazon found that protected areas, indigenous reserves and national forests generally, but not invariably, afforded protection against logging (Asner et al., 2005).

Conclusions

Protected areas can provide cost-effective and sustainable solutions to maintain ecosystem services that reduce the impact of natural hazards and disasters. As illustrated above, they can, and do, complement, and sometimes substitute for, more costly infrastructure interventions designed to protect vulnerable communities as part of comprehensive disaster prevention and mitigation strategies. Although they do not provide total protection – the largest disasters will usually overwhelm both natural defence systems and human-engineered systems – they can, and do, play a role in reducing the number of lives lost and the economic costs of disasters. This is especially true in the increasingly frequent medium-scale disasters that escape international attention but continually erode development gains (UNISDR, 2009).

At the 10th Conference of the Parties of the CBD in 2010, countries agreed to expand the overall coverage of protected areas to 17 per cent of land area. Generating support for this expansion will require stronger social and economic arguments to engender the necessary political backing and acceptance by communities, governments and industry. Bringing disaster mitigation benefits into the overall discussion about protected areas is an important step in this process, which offers benefits to both conservation and hazard management. Such a move will require much closer cooperation between those in government responsible for disaster relief and those responsible for conservation management. This support can be created only by increasing awareness of the multiple benefits that protected areas provide, including their role in reducing disaster risk and mitigating the impacts of natural hazards and their aftermath. Emphasizing this role also implies some responsibilities for protected area managers – whether they be state employees or communities – and for protected area agencies, users and other stakeholders. Five issues are worth mentioning:

1. **Rigorous economic, engineering and environmental analyses:** Government institutions, universities and the private sector should be encouraged to invest in rigorous economic, engineering and environmental analysis of proposed infrastructure projects to determine when and where there are benefits of incorporating green infrastructure versus hard infrastructure (or some combination of both) into disaster reduction plans.

2. **Broad-scale spatial planning:** At a national and regional/transboundary scale, disaster relief agencies should cooperate with partners to identify places where natural ecosystems could prevent and mitigate disasters and to develop associated ecosystem protection strategies. This should include, where appropriate, the establishment of new protected areas in vulnerable regions to safeguard vital ecosystem services that buffer communities. This should be undertaken in the context of broader disaster risk management plans and systems. National and regional economic development plans and disaster preparedness plans should be revised to reflect the value of protected areas for mitigating disaster risk. It could also be an added layer in the types of national protected area gap analyses requested by the CBD.

3. **Management plans:** Some protected area authorities may consider revising management objectives and management plans in order to better reflect and maintain the contribution of protected areas in miti-

gating disasters and to increase awareness of these values among the general public.

4. **Payments for ecosystem services and financing strategies:** Disaster risk reduction institutions should work with managers of protected areas to develop innovative financing strategies for these areas that recognize payments for ecosystem services. These could include additional government budgets and support that acknowledge the role that protected areas play in reducing disaster risk as well as potential investments from communities and businesses that are benefiting from the extra protection afforded by effectively managed protected areas.

5. **Restoration:** In some cases it may be useful to protect and restore degraded ecosystems specifically to improve their role in disaster mitigation; in such situations some level of active management may be required, for example the removal of invasive alien species to allow natural regeneration or the planting of native species to restore natural processes.

The critical role of protected areas in reducing vulnerability and disaster mitigation is already well documented. What is now needed is greater appreciation of the multiple benefits that protected areas provide as well as innovative financing mechanisms and institutional arrangements that can protect and promote green infrastructure as part of national and local strategies to ensure the safety of citizens as well as meet long-term recovery and livelihood needs. Enhanced protection of natural habitats, especially through the designation of protected areas, can provide a cost-effective third pillar to disaster strategies that also include better planning and early warning systems as well as hard infrastructure.

Note

1. Compare this with the fact that developed countries alone spend US$17 billion annually on pet food and US$34 billion each year on slimming products (Balmford and Whitten, 2003).

REFERENCES

Adeney, J.M., N.L. Christensen Jr and S.L. Pimm (2009) "Reserves Protect against Deforestation Fires in the Amazon". *PLoS One* 4: 3–12.

Amend, T. et al. (eds) (2008) *Protected Landscapes and Agrobiodiversity Values.* Volume 1 in the series Values of Protected Landscapes and Seascapes, IUCN and GTZ. Heidelberg: Kasparek Verlag.

Asner, G.P., D.E. Knapp, E.B. Broadbent et al. (2005) "Selective Logging in the Amazon". *Science* 310: 480–482.

Bagader, A.A. et al. (1994) *Environmental Protection in Islam*. IUCN Environmental Policy and Law Paper No. 20. Rev. 1994. Gland, Switzerland: International Union for Conservation of Nature.

Balmford, A. and T. Whitten (2003) "Who Should Pay for Tropical Conservation, and How Could the Costs Be Met?" *Oryx* 37: 238–250.

Balmford, A. et al. (2002) "Economic Reasons for Conserving Wild Nature". *Science* 297(5583): 950–53.

Barbier, E.B. (2007) "Valuing Ecosystem Services as Productive Inputs". *Economic Policy* 1: 177–229.

Bates, B. et al. (eds) (2008) *Climate Change and Water*. Geneva: Intergovernmental Panel on Climate Change, WMO and UNEP.

Bennett, E.L. and C.J. Reynolds (1992) "The Value of a Mangrove Area in Sarawak". *Biodiversity and Conservation* 2(4): 359–375.

Berthe, Y. (1997) "The Role of Forestry in Combating Desertification". World Forestry Congress, Antalya, Turkey.

Brändli, U.-B. and A. Gerold (2001) "Protection against Natural Hazards". In P. Brassel and H. Lischke (eds), *Swiss National Forest Inventory: Methods and Models of the Second Assessment*. Birmensdorf: WSL Swiss Federal Research Institute.

Brown, O., A. Crawford and A. Hammill (2006) *Natural Disasters and Resource Rights: Building Resilience, Rebuilding Lives*. Manitoba, Canada: International Institute for Sustainable Development.

Bruner, A.G. et al. (2001) "Effectiveness of Parks in Protecting Tropical Biodiversity". *Science* 291: 125–129.

Butchart, S. et al. (2012) "Protecting Important Sites for Biodiversity Contributes to Meeting Global Conservation Targets". *PLoS One* 7(3): e32529.

Campbell, A. et al. (2008) *Carbon Emissions from Forest Loss in Protected Areas*. Cambridge: UNEP-WCMC.

Costanza, R. et al. (2008) "The Value of Coastal Wetlands to Hurricane Prevention". *Ambio* 37: 241–248.

Dilley, M. et al. (2005) *Natural Disaster Hotspots: A Global Risk Analysis*. Washington, DC: World Bank.

Dobson, A.P., A.D. Bradshaw and A.J.M. Baker (1997) "Hopes for the Future: Restoration Ecology and Conservation Biology". *Science* 277: 515–522.

DoC [Department of Conservation] (2007) "The Economic Values of Whangamarino Wetland". Auckland, New Zealand.

Dore, M.H.I. (2005) "Climate Change and Changes in Global Precipitation Patterns: What Do We Know?" *Environment International* 31(8): 1167–1181.

Dudley, N. and M. Aldrich (2007) *Five Years of Implementing Forest Landscape Restoration: Lessons to Date*. Gland, Switzerland: WWF International.

Dudley, N. et al. (2007) *Tracking Progress in Managing Protected Areas*. Gland, Switzerland: WWF International.

Dudley, N., S. Stolton, A. Belokurov, L. Krueger, N. Lopoukhine, K. MacKinnon, T. Sandwith and N. Sekhran (2010) *Natural Solutions: Protected Areas Helping People Cope with Climate Change*. Gland, Switzerland: WWF International.

EERI [Earthquake Engineering Research Institute] (2006) "The Kashmir Earthquake of October 8, 2005: Impacts in Pakistan". EERI Special Earthquake

Report – February, California, USA. Available at <https://www.eeri.org/lfe/pdf/ kashmir_eeri_2nd_report.pdf> (accessed 31 October 2012).

Government of Japan (n.d.) *Forest Conservation in Japan.* Tokyo: Government of Japan.

Government of Nepal (2004) "Strengthening Disaster Preparedness Capacities in Kathmandu Valley". Draft report for United Nations Development Programme. Available at <http://saarc-sdmc.nic.in/pdf/nepal/file9.pdf> (accessed 31 October 2012).

Helmer, M. and D. Hilhorst (2006) "Editorial: Natural Disasters and Climate Change". *Disasters* 30: 1–4.

Huq, S. et al. (2007) "Editorial: Reducing Risks to Cities from Disasters and Climate Change". *Environment and Urbanization* 19(3).

Joppa, L.N., S.R. Loarie and S.L. Pimm (2008) "On the Protection of 'Protected Areas'". *Proceedings of the National Academy of Sciences* 105: 6673–6678.

Karki, S. (2002) *Community Involvement in and Management of Forest Fires in Southeast Asia.* Jakarta, Indonesia: Project FireFight Southeast Asia.

Kramer, R. et al. (1997) "Ecological and Economic Analysis of Watershed Protection in Eastern Madagascar". *Journal of Environmental Management* 49: 277–295.

Kumazaki, M. et al. (eds) (1991) *Green Forever: Forests and People in Japan.* Tokyo: National Land Afforestation Promotion Organisation.

Lateltin, O. et al. (2005) "Landslide Risk Management in Switzerland". *Landslides* 2: 313–320.

Leverington, F. et al. (2010) "A Global Analysis of Protected Area Management Effectiveness". *Environmental Management* 46(5): 685–698.

MacKinnon, J. and M. Budi Artha (1981) *National Conservation Plan for Indonesia.* Field report of UNDP/FAO national parks development project. Rome: Food and Agriculture Organization of the United Nations.

MacKinnon, K.S. et al. (1996) *The Ecology of Kalimantan.* Oxford: Oxford University Press.

McShane, T.O. and E. McShane-Caluzi (1997) "Swiss Forest Use and Biodiversity Conservation". In C.H. Freese (ed.), *Harvesting Wild Species: Implications for Biodiversity Conservation.* Baltimore, MD: Johns Hopkins University Press.

Maestre, F.T. et al. (2012) "Plant Species Richness and Ecosystem Multifunctionality in Global Drylands". *Science* 335: 214.

Nagendra, H. (2008) "Do Parks Work? Impact of Protected Areas on Land Cover Clearing". *Ambio* 37: 330–337.

Nelson, A. and K. Chomitz (2009) *Protected Area Effectiveness in Reducing Tropical Deforestation.* Washington, DC: World Bank.

Noss, R.F. (2001) "Beyond Kyoto: Forest Management in a Time of Rapid Climate Change". *Conservation Biology* 15: 578–591.

OCHA [Office for the Coordination of Humanitarian Affairs] (2009) *Monitoring Disaster Displacement in the Context of Climate Change: Findings of a Study by the United Nations Office for the Coordination of Humanitarian Affairs and the Internal Displacement Monitoring Centre.* Geneva: United Nations Office for the Coordination of Humanitarian Affairs and Norwegian Refugee Council Internal Displacement Monitoring Centre.

Pachauri, R.K. and A. Reisinger (eds) (2007) *Climate Change 2007: Synthesis Report*. Contribution of Working Groups I, II and III to the Fourth Assessment Report of the Intergovernmental Panel on Climate Change. Geneva: IPCC.

Pathak, N., T. Balasinorwala and A. Kothari (2005) "Community Conserved Areas: Lessons from India". For the CBD Programme of Work, Kalpavriksh, Pune, India.

Quintero, J.D. (2007) *Mainstreaming Conservation in Infrastructure Projects: Case Studies from Latin America*. Washington, DC: World Bank.

Sathirathai, S. and E.B. Barbier (2001) "Valuing Mangrove Conservation in Southern Thailand". *Contemporary Economic Policy* 19(2): 109–122.

Schuyt, K. and L. Brander (2004) *The Economic Values of the World's Wetlands*. Gland, Switzerland: WWF.

Simms, A., J. Magrath and H. Reid (2004) *Up in Smoke? Threats from, and Responses to, the Impact of Global Warming on Human Development*. London: New Economics Foundation.

Stolton, S. and N. Dudley (eds) (2010) *Arguments for Protected Areas: Multiple Benefits for Conservation and Use*. London: Earthscan.

Stolton, S., N. Dudley and J. Randall (2008) *Natural Security: Protected Areas and Hazard Mitigation*. Gland, Switzerland: WWF.

Sulayem, M. and E. Joubert (1994) "Management of Protected Areas in the Kingdom of Saudi Arabia". *Unasylva* 45: 35–41.

UNCCD [United Nations Convention to Combat Desertification] (2006) *Ten African Experiences: Implementing the United Nations Convention to Combat Desertification in Africa*. Bonn, Germany: Secretariat of the UNCCD.

UNEP [United Nations Environment Programme] (2007) *Global Environmental Outlook 4: Environment for Development*. Nairobi: UNEP.

UNISDR [United Nations International Strategy for Disaster Reduction] (2004) *Living with Risk: A Global Review of Disaster Reduction Initiatives*. Geneva: United Nations Office for Disaster Risk Reduction.

UNISDR (2009) *2009 Global Assessment Report on Disaster Risk Reduction: Risk and Poverty in a Changing Climate*. Geneva: United Nations Office for Disaster Risk Reduction.

UNISDR (2011) *2011 Global Assessment Report on Disaster Risk Reduction: Revealing Risk, Redefining Development*. Geneva: UNISDR.

Van Aalst, M.K. (2006) "The Impacts of Climate Change on the Risk of Natural Disasters". *Disasters* 30(1): 5–18.

Walston, J. et al. (2010) "Bringing the Tiger Back from the Brink: The Six Percent Solution". *PLoS Biol* 8(9): e1000485.

World Bank (2010a) *Convenient Solutions to an Inconvenient Truth: Ecosystem-based Approaches to Climate Change*. Washington, DC: World Bank.

World Bank (2010b) *Natural Hazards, Unnatural Disasters: The Economics of Effective Prevention*. Washington, DC: World Bank.

16

Urban disaster risk reduction and ecosystem services

Lorenzo Guadagno, Yaella Depietri and Urbano Fra Paleo

The process of urbanization

Cities have been defined as "humankind's most durable artifacts" (Vale and Campanella, 2005). For, threatened, damaged or destroyed as they have been throughout history by wars, epidemics, economic and political crises, and disasters, they have seldom been abandoned (notable exceptions include ancient cities such as Mohenjo-daro in Pakistan and Troy in Turkey, and, more recently, Prypiat in Ukraine). Cities such as Baghdad, Istanbul, Athens and Rome still stand as enduring footprints of human history.

Despite the existence of urban settlements as early as 4,000 years BCE, urban dwellers never represented more than 10 per cent of the global population until the second half of the nineteenth century, when their numbers started growing rapidly (UN-HABITAT, 2003). Urban population reached 1 billion in the early 1960s and 2 billion in the late 1980s, and is now estimated at around 3.5 billion, accounting for 50.1 per cent of the total population and outnumbering, for the first time in human history, the total of rural settlers. According to projections, urban growth will continue during the coming decades, accounting for at least 90 per cent of the global demographic increase. Cities and towns will be home to 6 billion people by the first half of this century, about 68 per cent of the total human population (UNDESA, 2010).

This unprecedented concentration of people has led 21 urban areas to grow to over 10 million inhabitants during the last six decades (UNESCAP,

The role of ecosystems in disaster risk reduction, Renaud, Sudmeier-Rieux and Estrella (eds), United Nations University Press, 2013, ISBN 978-92-808-1221-3

2005) and is expected to translate into regional megalopolises of up to 50 million inhabitants, such as the Hong Kong–Guandong or the Rio de Janeiro–São Paulo areas (Borja and Castells, 1997; Davis, 2004). But expansion is mostly taking place in small and middle-size urban centres, while the largest seem to stagnate. In 2007, 62 per cent of the world's urban population resided in cities with fewer than 1 million inhabitants, and just 15 per cent in agglomerations of more than 5 million (UNDESA, 2007).

Small towns, cities, megacities and complex metropolitan areas are different forms of urban areas. They are – and have been – the locus of innovation and modernization, where secondary and tertiary sectors dominate over the primary sector (Albala-Bertrand, 2003). Although these characteristics are progressively extending to rural areas, in particular in developed countries, urbanization allows individuals and social groups to interact, as an organismic whole, in order to give spatial expression to the flow of time, defining symbols, culture and the future of an increasingly cosmopolitan humanity (Mumford, 1938).

There is a close link between urbanization and the economic performance of modern nations: the Making Cities Resilient campaign of the United Nations International Strategy for Disaster Reduction (UNISDR) has defined urban settlements as "the lifelines of today's society" (UNISDR, 2010). Services, which are by definition urban activities, generate 63.2 per cent of the global gross domestic product (CIA, 2010). The most urbanized countries tend to have higher per capita income (UNISDR, 2009), higher average life expectancy, a higher literacy rate and stronger cultural and democratic institutions (Johnson et al., 2010). For the city dweller and the rural migrant, urban life represents the opportunity for better medical care and education, a richer cultural life, higher incomes and economic stability.

The urbanization of disaster risk

Historically, cities have also offered an opportunity for human communities to reduce their livelihood dependency on local natural resources, which characterizes the rural way of life. They allow for the development of collective coping strategies, by providing centralized, more reliable services and diversification of productive activities, sources of income and markets that can continue to provide food and shelter in times of hardship. Nonetheless, urban societies do not necessarily manage to make their environment completely safe. In fact, urbanization processes redefine the interactions between humans and ecosystems, transforming physical landscapes as well as building new forms and structures of social aggregation. They reshape, but do not necessarily reduce, the environmental risks that communities face, including those related to natural hazards (Mitchell, 1999).

Table 16.1 reports data on some notable urban disasters. It is interesting to note how hazards traditionally associated with rural contexts, such as floods and droughts, are increasingly affecting cities all over the world, becoming more prevalent in rapidly urbanizing and developing countries (Blaikie et al., 1994), but also in highly developed urban settings.

As vulnerable populations and unprotected physical capital increasingly concentrate in cities, disaster risk patterns follow urban development (UNISDR, 2009). For economic and military purposes, many urban centres have been founded in fertile floodplains, on hilltops and volcanic slopes, and on river crossings and coastlines, and have grown significantly exposed to dangerous natural events (UN-HABITAT, 2010). Hazard events, even small ones, threaten large numbers of people, because urban areas tend to be densely populated. By 2050, 870 million people worldwide are expected to be living in cities in areas of high seismic activity and 680 million in urban areas affected by severe storms (Lall and Deichmann, 2009).

The rise in human exposure is accompanied by a concentration of economic activities, livelihoods and infrastructures. Urban habitats are hotspots of wealth prone to suffering huge economic losses when a hazardous event strikes (see Table 16.1, which includes all the costliest events ever recorded). In addition, the concentration and diversity of activities, buildings and land uses magnify the risk of cascading effects, when an initial natural disturbance triggers another or multiple technological hazards (also known as "Natech" events), which often have catastrophic, long-lasting effects in and around urban areas. Such was the case of the 1999 earthquake in Izmit, Turkey, which triggered a fire in an oil refinery, causing the release of toxic gases and widespread environmental damage (Vatsa, 2005), or the urban fire after the 1906 San Francisco earthquake, or the 2011 Tōhoku tsunami, which caused the Fukushima nuclear disaster in Japan.

Cities have always relied on a peripheral hinterland for essential functions such as food, water and raw material production or waste disposal. Globalization has expanded the urban areas' influence to a global scale, to include any region, no matter how remote or disconnected, that participates in its production and consumption processes. Such interconnections mean that a city will both influence and be influenced by any hazard event hitting any area providing its inputs or absorbing its outputs (Showers, 2002). On the other hand, because cities are crucial joints in increasingly global economic and political processes, the damage they suffer will clearly affect activities well beyond their geographical limits (Munich Re, 2004; Surjan and Shaw, 2009).

Table 16.1 Some notable disasters in cities and metropolitan areas

Year	Event	City	Country	Fatalities	Economic losses (US$m, 2011 value)	Physical environment
2011	Tornado	Joplin, Missouri	USA	142[1]	7,000[1]	Great Plains
2011	Tohoku earthquake and tsunami	Sendai	Japan	20,319[1]	210,000[1]	Pacific coast
2011	Earthquake	Christchurch	New Zealand	181[1]	20,000[2]	Port Hills fault
2011	Landslides	Five cities in Rio de Janeiro state	Brazil	904[3]		Serra dos Órgãos reliefs
2010	Earthquake	Port-au-Prince	Haiti	222,570[1]	8,130[4]	Enriquillo–Plantain Garden fault system
2008	Cyclone Nargis	Labutta Township	Myanmar	84,454[5]		Irrawaddy delta
2008	Earthquake	Wenchuan	China	87,476[1]	88,681[1]	Longmen Shan fault system
2005	Hurricane Katrina	New Orleans	USA	1,577[6]	93,539[7]	River delta
2004	Tsunami	Urban areas in Aceh	Indonesia	165,357[8]	5,081[8]	Malacca Straits coast
2003	Heat wave	Urban areas	France	>14,800[9]	5,332[9]	Mid-latitude temperate
2000	Flood	Johannesburg	South Africa	80[9]	208[9]	Highveld plateau
1999	Earthquake	Istanbul, Izmit	Turkey	17,127[1]	26,807[1]	North Anatolian fault
1999	Tornado	Oklahoma City	USA	50[9]	2,680[9]	Oklahoma river basin
1998	Flood	Dhaka	Bangladesh	1,050[9]	5,859[9]	Ganges floodplain and delta
1995	Great Hanshin earthquake	Kobe	Japan	5,297[1]	145,000[1]	Suma and Suwayama faults
1994	Earthquake	Northridge, California	USA	60[9]	45,189[9]	San Fernando Valley
1993	Flood	Cologne	Germany	5[9]	926[9]	Rhine river basin
1992	Hurricane Andrew	Greater Miami	USA	62[9]	42,258[9]	Wetlands, Biscayne bay
1992	Winter storm	New York	USA	20[9]	4,783[9]	Atlantic coast
1991	Wildfire	Oakland, California	USA	25[10]	3,276 buildings[10]	Pacific coast

Year	Event	City	Country			Location
1989	Loma Prieta earthquake	San Francisco	USA	68[9]	18,185[9]	Pacific coast
1987	Heat wave	Athens	Greece	1,000[1]		Attica basin
1985	Earthquake	Mexico City	Mexico	9,500[1]	8,566[1]	Plateau, bed of the historic Lake Texcoco
1984	Hailstorm	Munich	Germany	0[9]	2,035[9]	Elevated plains of Upper Bavaria
1976	Earthquake	Tangshan	China	242,000[1]	22,180[1]	North China plain
1972	Earthquake	Managua	Nicaragua	10,000[1]	4,527[1]	Central American volcanic chain
1967	Flood	São Paulo, Rio de Janeiro	Brazil	>600[9]	66[9]	Plateau, Atlantic coast
1962	Storm surge	Hamburg	Germany	347[9]	4,404[9]	River Elbe basin
1962	Flood	Barcelona	Spain	1,000[9]	734[9]	Mediterranean coast
1959	Typhoon Vera (Isewan)	Nagoya	Japan	5,089[1]		Low-level plateau, Kiso and Shōnai river basins
1954	Flood	Wuhan	China	30,000[1]		Yangze and Han river basins
1937	Typhoon	Hong Kong	China	11,000[11]		
1926	Miami hurricane	Miami	USA	373[10]	161,100[7]	Wetlands, Biscayne bay
1923	Great Kantō earthquake	Tokyo	Japan	143,000[9]	36,703[9]	Tokyo bay
1908	Earthquake and tsunami	Messina	Italy	75,000[1]		Mediterranean coast
1906	Earthquake and fire	San Francisco	USA	3,000[9]	13,627[9]	San Andreas fault
1902	Volcanic eruption	St. Pierre	Martinique	>30,000[12]	Entire city destroyed	Slopes of Pelée, Caribbean coast
1900	Galveston hurricane	Galveston	USA	est. 8,000[13]	105,780[7]	Galveston Island
1882	Tropical storm	Mumbai	India	100,000[9]		Konkan coast
1871	Fire	Chicago	USA	250[10]	17,420 buildings destroyed, 100,000\ homeless[10]	Lake Michigan

Table 16.1 (cont.)

Year	Event	City	Country	Fatalities	Economic losses (US$m, 2011 value)	Physical environment
1864	Tropical storm	Kolkata	India	50,000[9]		Ganges floodplain and delta
1755	Earthquake and tsunami	Lisbon	Portugal	>30,000[14]	85 per cent of buildings destroyed[14]	Tagus River estuary
1746	Lima-Callao earthquake and tsunami	Lima	Peru	18,000[9]		Peruvian coastal plain, mountain slopes
1737	Tropical storm	Kolkata	India	300,000[9]		Ganges floodplain and delta
1731	Earthquake	Beijing	China	100,000[9]		Hai river system
1666	Fire	London	UK	8[15]	13,200 buildings destroyed, 100,000 homeless[15]	Thames River Basin
1657	Meireki fire	Edo (Tokyo)	Japan	100,000[10]		Tokyo Bay
526	Earthquake	Antioch (Antakya)	Turkey	250,000[10]		Dead Sea rift
79	Volcanic eruption	Four cities on the Gulf of Naples	Italy	18,000[9]	Four cities buried	Slopes of Vesuvius, Gulf of Naples
430 BCE	Epidemic	Athens	Greece	30,000[10]		Attica basin

Sources: [1] CRED (n.d.); [2] Daniell and Vervaeck (2012); [3] *O Globo* (2011); [4] Cavallo et al. (2010); [5] OCHA (2009); [6] Knabb et al. (2011); [7] Pielke et al. (2008); [8] Desinventar Indonesia, <http://www.desinventar.net/>; [9] Munich Re (2004); [10] Bradford and Charmichael (2007); [11] Strzepek and Smith (1995); [12] Tilling (1985); [13] Weems (n.d.); [14] Pereira (2006); [15] Porter (1994).

Note: The table lists exclusively urban disasters as well as preponderantly urban events (as in the case with the aggregated data from "EM-DAT: The OFDA/CRED International Disaster Database").

Despite these factors, living in a city does not necessarily mean being at great risk. Urban dwellers might enjoy a safe living location, good-quality housing and widespread access to education, health care, employment and income opportunities. Nevertheless, in many cities and towns, urbanization translates into higher deaths and damages where the local institutions are not able to provide their citizens with access to resources that reduce their exposure and vulnerability: a sufficient and sustainable income and asset base, safe shelter, adequate access to essential services, safety nets, political and civil representation, or appropriate disaster and emergency management systems (Satterthwaite, 2010). The urban poor, who are deprived of adequate access to these essential goods and services and are induced to live in unsafe conditions – such as flood zones or degraded industrial areas – are more vulnerable, especially in developing countries (Global Forum on Local Development, 2010). Yet it is precisely in the cities of developing countries where demographic growth over the coming decades is expected to take place (UNDESA, 2010) and where the bulk of future disaster risk is expected to accumulate.

Urban centres and ecosystem services

In this chapter, we argue that disaster risk is increasingly a manifestation of urban growth and its depleting effects on the capacity of ecosystems to support life and biodiversity, purify air and water, and mitigate extreme natural events such as floods, landslides, coastal storms and wildfires. Because most of the production, consumption and distribution of wealth takes place in urban areas or depends on the lifestyle of their dwellers (GDRC, n.d.), cities ultimately determine global-scale processes such as deforestation, modification of the composition of the atmosphere and oceans, and alteration of the world's biogeochemical cycles, which leaves no ecosystem completely devoid of direct or indirect human influence (Vitousek et al., 1997).

Nonetheless, much like any other ecosystem, cities are functional units in which dynamic complexes of micro-organism, plant, animal and human communities interact with a non-living environment (CBD, 1992). What differentiates urban landscapes is that they are predominantly characterized by elements that have been created or modified by human beings (Wilkie and Roach, 2004). They are socio-natural landscapes defined by the interplay of a community with its specific biophysical environment (Srinivas et al., 2009), and they can be analysed through ecological models in order to better understand them as a system of relations (Pickett et al., 1997; also see Figure 16.1). Urban dwellers depend on both the built environment and natural capital for their well-being. In particular,

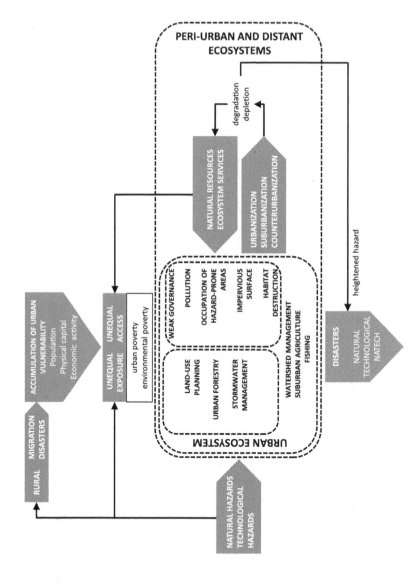

Figure 16.1 Interactions between the social and ecological systems in urban areas in the production of urban risk and disasters

Source: authors' own elaboration.

they rely on biologically productive ecosystems, located in both local and remote or peri-urban areas, for the whole array of fundamental services that ecosystems provide.

Local ecosystems

An urban landscape can encompass extremely diverse natural features, including coastal zones, forests and vegetated areas, reliefs, water bodies and streams. Such components, no matter how small in size, play a multifold role in supporting a safe and satisfying living environment for the urban dwellers (Bolund and Hunhammar, 1999). Because cities are usually dominated by built infrastructure, the benefits provided by local ecosystems are easily overlooked in planning processes. Urban nature is often regarded only as an amenity and therefore fragmented and depleted.

In reality, urban ecosystems also provide food, fuel and fibre and, even though most urban dwellers do not directly rely on local ecosystems for food and raw materials, urban and suburban agriculture practices have proved a valuable coping strategy in times of hardship (Altieri et al., 1999). Urban vegetation allows for improved water drainage, by providing permeable areas that absorb excess runoff in the event of precipitation (see Boxes 16.1 and 16.2), and filters water-borne sediments and pollutants (Guglielmino, 1997). By providing shade, absorbing heat, improving air circulation and consuming solar energy, green areas and water bodies also help to control temperatures and counter the heat island effect, described as the difference between urban and rural temperatures in the same region (Pickett et al., 2001; see also Box 16.3). This will increasingly be relevant in the future when heat waves are expected to be more frequent and longer lasting (Meehl and Tebaldi, 2004). An extensive review of the potential role of local ecosystems in mitigating the impacts of heat waves in urban areas is presented in Depietri et al. (2012). Vegetation can also act as a windbreak during winter storms (McPherson, 1994).

Urban green spaces, in particular urban trees, also generate tangible benefits for the health of urban dwellers. They help reduce noise, a major cause of stress, hypertension, hearing loss and sleep disturbance, and they enhance air quality by removing air pollutants, which are positively related to respiratory and cardiovascular illnesses (Nowak, 1994; see also Coombes et al., 2010; Ulrich, 1984). In addition, urban green areas contribute to making cities diversified landscapes that can be favourable habitats for a varied flora and fauna (Donnelly and Marzluff, 2006; Kühn et al., 2004). Finally, they play an essential role in defining the cultural identity of a city, by characterizing its physical landscape and providing spaces where its cultural and social life can take place. Nature thus is

Box 16.1   Urban flood reduction in New York, USA

In New York, the capacity of the obsolete sewerage system is systematically exceeded during intense storm events, which has led to flooding in New York City streets. A significant amount of polluted water flows directly into local water streams without being processed in the water treatment plants. Instead of spending an expected US$6.8 billion to improve the system, the city has decided to finance green infrastructure for US$5.3 billion (New York City, 2010). Trees, lawns and gardens will be planted on roofs, streets and sidewalks. They will absorb and percolate more rainwater to the ground and reduce the burden on the city's sewerage system, while improving air and water quality and potentially reducing water and energy requirements.

An ecosystem-based strategy has also been envisaged to ensure a clean water supply. In 1997, the city committed to invest around US$1.5 billion over 10 years to restore and protect the surrounding watersheds, as well as to promote measures that improve the local economies of watershed residents (Postel and Thompson, 2005). A comprehensive study by the National Research Council has highlighted a whole range of non-structural measures that have been established for water quality protection, such as land acquisition, buffer zone designations, conservation agreements with landowners, and zoning ordinances (Pires, 2004). It noted how the establishment of protected natural reserves, national parks and wilderness areas allows for both the conservation of local biodiversity and the enhancement of the water resources on which the city depends (Postel and Thompson, 2005).

Source: UNISDR (2011).

"essential to achieving the quality of life that creates a great city and that makes it possible for people to live a reasonable life within an urban environment" (Botkin and Beveridge, 1997: 18).

Peri-urban and regional ecosystems

Despite their multiple functions, local ecosystems alone do not suffice in supporting the life of large, dense communities of urban dwellers. Cities have been defined as parasites on the biosphere (Odum, 1971), which underscores how the net flow of ecosystem services is invariably into urban centres rather than out of them (McGranahan et al., 2005). Their ecological footprint steadily grows well beyond their boundaries, as they

Box 16.2 Chicago, USA: Green Permit Program

Chicago's Department of Buildings has developed an incentive pro-gramme that encourages developers to incorporate green design ele-ments, including green roofs, in new buildings. The initiative is known as the Green Permit Program. It is part of a larger portfolio of initia-tives aimed at making Chicago's built environment more sustainable and better at managing stormwater and mitigating urban floods. The incentive is an expedited permit process, through which developers can save both time and money. Additional benefits of the programme include mitigation of greenhouse gas emissions through reduced need for heating and cooling in buildings with green roofs. The programme is enhancing the city's image and the emergence of businesses special-izing in green roof installation.

Source: Kazmierczak and Carter (2010: 110–118).

Box 16.3 Stuttgart, Germany: Combating the heat island effect and poor air quality with green aeration corridors

Stuttgart, home to more than 2 million people, is a highly industrial-ized area located in a valley with a mild climate and low-intensity winds. Since the 1970s it has experienced a steady decline in air qual-ity. The situation has worsened as the valley slopes underwent growing urbanization, which increasingly prevented natural air circulation from taking place around and through the urban centre. As a consequence, the urban heat island effect became more pronounced, and it is ex-pected to worsen as heat waves become more frequent and intense owing to climate change.

In order to control overheating, the Stuttgart city government planned a series of ecosystem-based measures that may contribute to reactivating air flow and restoring wind patterns. New land-use and zoning regulations were passed based on data and evidence collected in a Climate Atlas, which maps temperature patterns and air flows throughout the city. Urban plans have prioritized open green spaces and vegetation cover, especially in the more densely built-up areas.

Source: Kazmierczak and Carter (2010: 26–35).

rely on an increasingly global hinterland as a source of inputs and a sink of outputs (Tarr, 1997), but it is particularly at the peri-urban and regional scales that ecosystems play a direct role in reducing the levels of risk in urban communities. For instance, cities are part of a watershed,[1] which usually includes a variety of different ecosystems, such as forests, savannas, grasslands, shrublands or wetlands. At the watershed or river basin scale, the interplay among its natural components allows for the delivery of ecosystem services, such as the supply of freshwater, the treatment of wastewater and regulation of the hydrological cycle, that are essential to the life of urban communities.

Forests and vegetation cover around urban areas allow more water to percolate into the ground, reduce runoff and ultimately mitigate the impact of stormwater. They account for improvements in the recharge of groundwater, guaranteeing better access to water resources during dry periods, while also enhancing water quality by filtrating and absorbing nutrients and contaminants (Pickett et al., 2001). Figuerola and Pasten (2008), basing their analysis on a previous study by Núñez et al. (2006), estimated the economic value of temperate forests located in the Llancahue watershed in Chile to be US$937.9 per hectare for the summer period and US$355.3 per hectare for the rest of the year, with respect to their role in contributing to freshwater supplies in southern Chilean cities. Peri-urban forests also provide wood and non-timber products that can play an important role in sustaining people's livelihoods and guaranteeing open recreational spaces for the city's inhabitants.

Vegetation helps, to a certain extent, to regulate the flow of rainwater into water streams, which is a crucial variable in the functioning of agricultural systems, industrial activities and energy production facilities. It also mitigates the action of wind and rain, especially on slopes and riverbanks, thereby protecting against soil erosion, conserving soil fertility and avoiding associated downstream costs (Morrow et al., 1995). It contributes to stabilizing soil, by creating a root system that helps reduce the frequency and magnitude of mass movements such as landslides, avalanches and mudflows (Stolten et al., 2008; Teich and Bebi, 2009; see also Box 16.4; Chapter 12 in this volume).

Wetlands in the urban periphery improve water quality through the removal of nitrogen and phosphorous. Wetlands and peatlands also provide storage space for floodwater (see Box 16.5), groundwater recharge and maintenance of dry season flows (see Chapter 9 in this volume). Coastal forests and mangroves, seagrass and coral reefs, dunes and saltmarshes effectively mitigate small- and medium-scale coastal hazards such as wind waves and coastal floods caused by storm surges, and have proved effective to some extent in protecting people from sea level rise (UNEP-WCMC, 2006; see also Chapters 5 and 6 in this volume).

Box 16.4 Reforestation in the Rokko Mountain Range, Japan

The Rokko Mountain Range is a series of elevations surrounded by a population of 2.3 million, living in the cities of Kobe, Ashiya, Nishinomiya and Takarazuka. Following urban growth and deforestation of the mountains' vegetation cover, frequent floods and landslides affected human settlements in the area as early as the seventeenth century, and reached a catastrophic peak during the second half of the nineteenth century, when deforestation culminated. In the last decade of the nineteenth century, the government enacted the River Law, the Erosion Control Law and the Forest Law in order to enforce some basic concepts of conservation and restoration of natural landscapes around the country. In 1895, the Hyogo Prefecture began planting trees in order to stabilize slopes and prevent soil erosion. Tree species with high fertilizing effects were introduced to achieve complete reforestation as quickly as possible on land where parent rock had been exposed.

In recent years, in response to the public demand for landslide protection generated by the 1995 Kobe earthquake and the increasing value of Mount Rokko as a recreational area and as a source of potable water for the city, the Prefecture developed the Rokko Mountain Range Green Belt Development Project, aimed at improved forest quality, soil stability, water runoff and water availability, through planting deep-rooting trees and developing undergrowth vegetation. Between 1996 and 2005, by allocating approximately 1,300 hectares for public land and forest reserves, the project, at a total cost of ¥690.5 billion, has resulted in saving an estimated ¥4,598.4 billion by preventing damage from hydro-geological hazards, while providing additional cultural and recreational benefits to the urban population.

Source: Ministry of the Environment, Government of Japan (2011).

Urbanization, environmental degradation and disaster risk

Evidence from UNISDR's 2009 and 2011 Global Assessment Reports points to ecosystem degradation induced by poorly managed urbanization processes as a main driver of disaster risk at the global scale. As deforestation, wetland reclamation, land development and alterations of water flows degrade ecosystems within and around urban centres, their capacity to deliver services, including those that reduce people's exposure and vulnerability to natural hazards, is compromised (Abramovitz, 2001).

Box 16.5 Flood reduction in Boston's Charles River Basin, USA

Boston's history has always been closely connected to the Charles River, which has allowed the city to serve as a port and marketplace for the entire inland region. More than 10 per cent of the river's watershed area (about 8,000 hectares) consists of freshwater wetlands (Platt, 2006).

In the 1950s and 1960s, as urban and industrial development reclaimed large parts of the floodplain, disastrous flood events became a major threat to the low-lying settlements. In the 1970s, a flood management project was designed jointly by the Charles River Watershed Association (CRWA) and the Army Corps of Engineers based on a set of hard engineering and ecosystem conservation solutions, including: "acquisition and protection of several thousand acres of wetlands for water storage; promotion of floodplain and wetland regulation by local administrative authorities; construction of a new dam at the river's mouth to alleviate overflow of the basin in Boston and Cambridge" (PEDRR, 2011: 8).

By 1983, about 8,100 natural wetlands were acquired from private owners by the Corps and transferred to administrative authorities for management as natural flood storage and ecological restoration sites. The economic value of wetlands in the Charles River Basin was estimated back in 1981 at US$153,535 to $190,009 per acre (Thibodeau and Ostro, 1981). Concurrently, several municipalities in the watershed began to regulate wetland use, which has helped to preserve natural water storage, reduce development in the floodplains and reduce pollution of wetlands and streams. Efforts towards rehabilitation, especially with respect to monitoring and improving the status of river water quality, have continued throughout the 1990s and 2000s, with endorsement from the United States federal government (PEDRR, 2011: 8). After four decades, the CRWA has achieved measurable improvement in flood mitigation, water quality and public recreation.

Source: Platt (2006).

The scarcity of permeable surfaces such as soft soils and green areas in and around cities can multiply, by up to a factor of 10, the amount of water that runs off the ground, increasing peak discharge in a watershed (Gholami et al., 2010), lag time (Espey et al., 1965) and flooding (Nirupama and Simonovic, 2006).The amount of water and debris transported during heavy rainfalls easily exceeds the capacity of the city's sewerage system, particularly in the absence of drains or a separate storm

sewer system, typically leading to urban floods. These are a recurrent feature in cities as diverse as Mumbai (Gandy, 2008) and New York (New
York City, 2010) and can reach staggering proportions, as in Bangkok in
2011 (*The Guardian*, 2011). Increases in flood risk as a result of intense
urbanization have been measured in the watershed of the Upper Thames
River, around the City of London, in Canada (Nirupama and Simonovic,
2006) and in coastal areas of Galicia in north-western Spain after forest
fires burned land cover in watersheds and heavy rains occurred upstream
(Fra Paleo, 2010). In Taiwan, the clearing of forests to increase land availability for productive activities has led to reduced slope stability, increased sediment and pollutant delivery downstream, and increased peak
flows in a region that is highly exposed to typhoons and other meteorological hazards (Lu et al., 2001).

The substitution of original land cover with highly impervious surfaces
(asphalt, concrete) and the high level of thermal emissions related to
concentrated, high-intensity energy and fossil fuel consumption are directly responsible for the heat island effect, which can reach maxima of
+10°C (Pickett et al., 2001). These conditions drastically amplify the incidence of heat waves and, together with higher concentrations of air pollutants, pose a serious threat to the life of urban dwellers, as demonstrated
by the 70,000 deaths caused by the 2003 summer in Europe (CRED, n.d.).
Hence, human-driven land-use changes in urbanized environments serve
as triggers of potentially dangerous events, increasingly regarded as
"socio-natural hazards" (Garatwa and Bollin, 2001).

Urban poverty and disaster risk

The incidence of environmental problems in urban areas and urban risk
is closely associated with poverty (Balk et al., 2009). In cities all around
the world, the poor tend to live in less safe locations and conditions, and
have limited coping mechanisms to enable them to recover from shocks.
This is particularly true for individuals who belong to vulnerable groups
owing to age, gender, ethnicity or income (Anderson, 2003; see Box 16.6).

The mismatch between the demand for essential services, such as safe
shelter, health care and employment, and the limited capacities of national and local administrations to actually provide them pushes poor
people to adopt "future eroding" strategies to cope with their daily needs,
and translates spatially into the development of the slums that characterize cities in many parts of the world. These settlements are usually located on marginal, unsafe land, prone to hydro-geological hazards, and
are rarely served by networks of communication, transportation, water
and energy or healthcare services. In slums, constructions are often

Box 16.6 Urban flood risk in Mozambique

It has been estimated that about 70 per cent of the victims of the February 2000 floods in Mozambique were urban residents, a death toll
largely caused by extensive urbanization and deforestation processes
and a lack of enforcement of land-use plans. In particular, it was the
urban poor who suffered the most, especially those recently arrived in
the country's cities following the civil war and the debt crisis and who
were forced to occupy buildings made of locally retrievable materials
in undesirable locations such as hill slopes and ravines.

Source: Chege et al. (2007).

substandard, highly vulnerable to flood, earthquake, fire and disease and
inhabited by people with very limited resources and capacity to recover
from disasters (UNISDR, 2009). Lack of access to the formal housing
market pushes slum dwellers to environmentally unsafe locations, on land
where it is either not desirable or not legally permissible to build – a
phenomenon especially demonstrated in developing areas such as the
Payatas landfill in Manila in the Philippines or the riverine settlements in
Santo Domingo in the Dominican Republic (Pelling, 2003), but also in
developed urban settings, such as Los Angeles, where Latinos tend to live
in housing built before the introduction of anti-seismic building codes
(Wisner, 1999).

Moreover, the urban poor continue to rely on local natural resources
to secure access to food, fuelwood and building materials, and therefore
can create additional risk through destructive livelihood practices. For instance, in the Rocinha favela in Rio de Janeiro, a steady urbanization
process has taken place over recent decades, progressively improving the
living conditions of the *favelados*, in particular at its bottom fringe, which
is closest to the formal city. Its upper fringe, however, still hosts communities of newcomers and poorer inhabitants who increasingly put pressure
on the surrounding vegetation cover for their daily fuelwood and for further land reclamation. This results in frequent mudslides and rock falls
that seriously threaten the lives of the most vulnerable *favelados* (World-
Watch Institute, 2004).

Ecosystem management for urban risk reduction

Urban governments are increasingly considering conservation and enhancement of natural infrastructure as key measures to protect people

Box 16.7 The Netherlands: "Room for the River"

In the Netherlands, a complex solution for flood mitigation, based on a network of canals, dykes and pumping systems, has traditionally and until recently been regarded as a model of technological innovation. The Dutch model is now arousing concerns about its environmental and economic unsustainability, and hard infrastructure is being replaced by ecosystem-based measures that take into account natural processes of periodic flooding. This new approach has been formalized through the "Room for the River" Project (see Chapter 9 in this volume).

Source: Corvers (2009).

and investments in the face of natural hazards (see Box 16.7). UNISDR's Making Cities Resilient campaign has as one of its 10 priorities the protection of ecosystems and natural buffers to mitigate floods, storm surges and other hazards as well as adapt to climate change (UNISDR, 2010).

Cities can be in a favourable position to achieve risk reduction through sustainable environmental management, because local governments are increasingly responsible for land-use and development planning, infrastructure development and maintenance, zoning and building codes, and social services provision. Unlike national governments, which operate along clear sectoral lines, city governments often are better placed to work in a cross-sectoral manner, making it easier to adopt an integrated approach in tackling local issues. The proximity and density of urban population, businesses, structures and infrastructures allow for economies of scale when undertaking measures to mitigate natural hazards and reduce the community's vulnerability. By influencing a city's resource consumption pattern, urban governments also play a key role in determining the levels of pressure on local and global ecosystems, one of the main drivers of disaster risk at both the local and the global scale (UNISDR, 2011).

At the local level, effective action can range from small-scale measures, such as green roofing or green windbreaks, to city-wide initiatives that preserve or restore green areas and water bodies to improve air quality and to retain soil or stormwater, to integrated watershed management plans that require coordination between upstream and downstream communities and across administrative units. However, a strong integration with regional and national government agencies, as well as international

Table 16.2 Policy measures dealing with various natural hazards and their relationship with the local ecosystem in various geographical areas

Region/country	City/urban area	Ecosystem	Hazard	Anthropogenic impact	Policy issues
Rokko Mountain Range, Japan	Kobe, Ashiya, Nishinomiya and Takarazuka	Mountain region	Floods and landslides	Urban expansion and deforestation	Measure: • Rokko Mountain Green Belt Development Project (1995): restoration of about 1,300 hectares to public land and conserving it as healthy forest Aims: • cost-effective solution for hydro-geological hazard mitigation • provision of additional cultural and recreational benefits to the urban population
Germany	Stuttgart	Valley	Heat waves	Highly industrialized region with increasing urbanization	Measure: • new land-use and zoning regulations based on data and evidence collected by the Climate Atlas Aims: • prioritize green spaces and vegetation cover, especially in more densely urbanized areas

Boston's Charles River, USA	Boston	River basin, freshwater wetlands	Floods	Industrial development (1950s–1960s)	Measure: • in the 1970s, a flood management project based on a set of hard engineering and ecosystem conservation solutions Aims: • measurably improve flood mitigation, water quality and public recreation
New York, USA	New York	Urban green areas	Local intense storm events	Obsolete sewerage system	Measure: • trees, lawns and gardens will be planted on roofs, streets and sidewalks Aims: • absorb and percolate more rainwater to the ground • reduce the burden on the city's sewerage system • improve air and water quality • potentially reduce water and energy requirements
Chicago, USA	Chicago	Urban green area	Storms and floods		Measure: • Green Permit Program: encourages developers to incorporate green design elements, including green roofs on new buildings Aims: • better manage stormwater and mitigate urban floods

407

institutions, is fundamental in risk governance; it is only at a wider scale that many drivers of risk can be tackled (for example, at the watershed scale in the case of floods and droughts).

A series of case studies that address disaster risk reduction through ecosystem restoration and enhancement have been presented in the previous sections. The key features of these cases are summarized in Table 16.2. They all demonstrate how ecosystem conservation and enhancement can be long-term cost-effective measures to reduce disaster risk in urban areas. Ideally, ecosystem-based urban risk reduction should be integrated into a broader framework of sustainable urban development.

Experience has shown that the reduction of disaster risk through ecosystem management is most effective when policy and legal frameworks are in place to support the actions of urban governments. The participation and involvement of community stakeholders should be promoted to better evaluate existing ecosystem services as well as to ensure effective communication and ownership of planned interventions. Environmental department staff are usually most directly responsible for ecosystem management, but mainstreaming such approaches into urban planning is essential (PEDRR, 2011).

Budgeting processes can be extremely relevant entry points for the integration of ecosystems into public management processes. Budgeting decisions express a system's political priorities between conflicting interests over limited resources. An ecosystem approach can expose the full value of services that urban and peri-urban ecosystems provide. This can allow public authorities and private investors to anticipate the social and economic costs and benefits of their future actions for present and future generations, which are easily neglected in urban management. By considering the value of natural capital alongside economic and human resources, local authorities can better compare and identify different management options, take more informed decisions and communicate these more clearly to the public (TEEB, 2011).

Urban and regional planning is another critical instrument for promoting proactive strategies to prevent hazard exposure and to reduce disaster risk through the avoidance of conflicting land uses and the integration of multiple stakeholder interests (Fra Paleo, 2009). Identifying the areas that contribute most to the personal and material security of urban dwellers and those that are most threatened by urbanization is a fundamental step towards establishing spatial development policies that control and reduce the levels of risk (TEEB, 2011). The integration of an ecosystem management-based approach into urban planning can help reconcile environmental and developmental priorities of local authorities, and can contribute to creating safer, more sustainable cities.

Conclusions

Despite evidence of their multiple benefits, including their cost-effectiveness, ecosystem-based risk reduction measures have not been widely implemented in urban areas. Historically, cities have been situated in strategic locations, such as floodplains, coastal flats, deltas or hill slopes, which allowed for easy trade access, defensibility in case of war, and the availability of natural resources, but have generally been exposed to natural hazards. Therefore, urbanization frequently results in increasing exposure of unprotected populations and assets to hazardous events, and is currently a significant factor shaping risk at the global level. Disasters have thus increasingly gained an urban dimension.

Urban areas in developed countries have pursued safety through structural measures and "hard" engineering solutions. A few alternative examples of city administrations promoting improved ecosystem management in and around urban areas have been featured in this chapter. Many initiatives respond foremost to the need to reduce costs, although they recognize their added social and environmental benefits. For instance, the adoption of green building construction, particularly with respect to green roofing, as in New York and Chicago in the United States, illustrates how the high financial costs of complying with the Federal Clean Water Act and building separate storm sewer systems have driven the transition towards a more cost-efficient, environment-friendly, storm-water management system in these cities (Tian, 2011). Given that financial issues are even more of a priority for developing countries and cities, and given the high costs often associated with engineered measures, ecosystem-based solutions for risk reduction might provide more cost-effective options.

Successful implementation of sustainable ecosystem management for urban disaster reduction can be achieved only through changes in urban governance and decision-making processes, by adopting more integrated approaches through cross-sectoral and multi-stakeholder dialogue. This further requires taking into account ecosystems in peri-urban and regional areas and the essential services they provide to urban centres.

Note

1. A watershed is defined as the topographical unit from which rain or melting snow drains into a given body of water.

REFERENCES

Abramovitz, J. (2001) "Unnatural Disasters". Worldwatch Paper #158. Washington, DC: Worldwatch Institute.

Albala-Bertrand, J.M. (2003) "Urban Disasters and Globalization". In A. Kreimer, M. Arnold and A. Carlin (eds), *Building Safer Cities: The Future of Disaster Risk*. Washington, DC: World Bank, pp. 75–82.

Altieri, M.A. et al. (1999) "The Greening of the 'Barrios': Urban Agriculture for Food Security in Cuba". *Agriculture and Human Values* 16(2): 131–140.

Anderson, W.A. (2003) "Women and Children Facing Disaster". In A. Kreimer et al. (eds), *Building Safer Cities: The Future of Disaster Risk*. Washington, DC: World Bank, pp. 57–74.

Balk, D. et al. (2009) *Spatial Distribution and Risk for Urban Populations: An International Overview*. New York: Population Council.

Blaikie, P. et al. (1994) *At Risk: Natural Hazards, People's Vulnerability, and Disasters*. New York: Routledge.

Bolund, P. and S. Hunhammar (1999) "Ecosystem Services in Urban Areas". *Ecological Economics* 19: 293–301.

Borja, J. and M. Castells (1997) *Local and Global: Management of Cities in the Information Age*. London: Earthscan.

Botkin, D.B. and C.E. Beveridge (1997) "Cities as Environments". *Urban Ecosystems* 1: 3–19.

Bradford, M. and R.S. Charmichael (eds) (2007) *Notable Natural Disasters*. Pasadena: Salem Press.

Cavallo, E., A. Powell and O. Becerra (2010) "Estimating the Direct Economic Damages of the Earthquake in Haiti". *The Economic Journal* 120(546): F292–F312.

CBD [Convention on Biological Diversity] (1992) "Convention on Biological Diversity". Available at <http://www.cbd.int/convention/text/> (accessed 1 November 2012).

Chege, L.W. et al. (2007) "Living with Floods in Mozambique: Urban Impact in a Context of Chronic Disaster". Unpublished case study prepared for UN-HABITAT, *Global Report on Human Settlements 2007*. United Nations Human Settlements Programme.

CIA [Central Intelligence Agency] (2010) "The World Factbook", <https://www.cia.gov/library/publications/the-world-factbook/fields/2012.html> (accessed 1 November 2012).

Coombes, E., A.P. Jones and M. Hillsdon (2010) "The Relationship of Physical Activity and Overweight to Objectively Measured Green Space Accessibility and Use". *Social Science & Medicine* 70: 816–822.

Corvers, R. (2009) "Vulnerable to Flooding? Nature Development and 'Room for the River': A Governance Perspective". In U. Fra Paleo (ed.), *Building Safer Communities: Risk Governance, Spatial Planning and Responses to Natural Hazards*. Amsterdam: IOS Press, pp. 125–136.

CRED [Centre for Research on the Epidemiology of Disasters] (n.d.) "EM-DAT: The OFDA/CRED International Disaster Database", <http://www.emdat.be>

– Université catholique de Louvain – Brussels – Belgium (accessed 1 November 2012).

Daniell, J. and A. Vervaeck (2012) "Damaging Earthquakes Database 2011: The Year in Review". CEDIM Earthquake Loss Estimation Series Research Report 2012-01. Karlsruhe: Center for Disaster Management and Risk Reduction Technology. Available at <http://earthquake-report.com/2012/01/09/catdat-damaging-earthquakes-database-2011-annual-review/ (accessed 1 November 2012).

Davis, M. (2004) "Planet of Slums, Urban Involution and the Informal Proletariat". *New Left Review* 26: 5–34.

Depietri, Y., F.G. Renaud and G. Kallis (2012) "Heat Waves and Floods in Urban Areas: A Policy-oriented Review of Ecosystem Services". *Sustainability Science* 7: 95–107.

Donnelly, R. and J.M. Marzluff (2006) "Relative Importance of Habitat Quantity, Structure, and Spatial Pattern to Birds in Urbanizing Environments". *Urban Ecosystems* 9: 99–117.

Espey, W.H., Jr, C.W. Morgan and F.D. Masch (1965) "A Study of Some Effects of Urbanization on Storm Runoff from a Small Watershed". Technical Report 44D 07-6501 CRWR-2, Center for Research in Water Resources, University of Texas, Austin.

Figuerola, E. and R. Pasten (2008) "Forest and Water: The Value of Native Temperate Forests in Supplying Water for Human Consumption: A Comment". *Ecological Economics* 67(2): 153–156.

Fra Paleo, U. (2009) "On Exposure to Natural Hazards: Revisiting a Neglected Primal Action". In U. Fra Paleo (ed.), *Building Safer Communities: Risk Governance, Spatial Planning and Responses to Natural Hazards*. Amsterdam: IOS Press, pp. 61–78.

Fra Paleo, U. (2010) "Las dimensiones de las inundaciones históricas en Galicia en la comunicación del riesgo". In U. Fra Paleo (ed.), *Riesgos naturales en Galicia*. Santiago de Compostela: University of Santiago de Compostela Press, pp. 47–63.

Gandy, M. (2008) "Landscapes of Disaster: Water, Modernity and Urban Fragmentation in Mumbai". *Environment and Planning A* 40(1): 108–140.

Garatwa, W. and C. Bollin (2001) *Disaster Risk Management: A Working Concept*. Eschborn: Deutsche Gesellschaft für technische Zusammenarbeit.

GDRC [Global Development Research Center] (n.d.) "Introduction: Urban Environmental Management", <http://www.gdrc.org/uem/doc-intro.html> (accessed 1 November 2012).

Gholami, V., M. Mohseni and H. Ahmadi (2010) "Effects of Impervious Surfaces and Urban Development on Runoff Generation and Flood Hazard in the Hajighoshan Watershed". *Caspian Journal of Environmental Sciences* 8: 1–12.

Global Forum on Local Development (2010) "Localizing the MDGs: What Role for Local Governments?" In *Global Forum on Local Development Report: Pursuing the MDGs through Local Government*. New York: UN Capital Development Fund, pp 17–29.

Guglielmino, J. (1997) "Greenways: Paths to the Future". *American Forests* 103(3): 26–27.

Johnson, C. et al. (2010) "Urban Disaster Trends". In IFRC, *World Disasters Report 2010: Focus on Urban Risk*. Geneva: International Federation of Red Cross and Red Crescent Societies, pp. 10–29.

Kazmierczak, A. and J. Carter (2010) *Adaptation to Climate Change Using Green and Blue Infrastructure: A Database of Case Studies*. Manchester: University of Manchester.

Knabb, R.D., J.R. Rhome and D.P. Brown (2011) *Tropical Cyclone Report, Hurricane Katrina, 23-30 August 2005*. Miami: National Hurricane Center.

Kühn, I., R. Brandl and S. Klotz (2004) "The Flora of German Cities Is Naturally Species Rich". *Evolutionary Ecology Research* 6: 749–764.

Lall, S.V. and U. Deichmann (2009) *Density and Disasters: Economics of Urban Hazard Risk*. Washington, DC: World Bank.

Lu, S.-Y., J.D. Cheng and K.N. Brooks (2001) "Managing Forests for Watershed Protection in Taiwan". *Forest Ecology and Management* 143: 77–85.

McGranahan, G., P. Marcotullio, X.M. Bai, D. Balk, T. Braga, I. Douglas, T. Elmqvist, W. Rees, D. Satterthwaite, J. Songsore, H. Zlotnick, J. Eades, E. Ezcurra and A. Whyte (2005) "Urban Systems". In R. Hassan, R. Scholes and N. Ash (eds), *Ecosystems and Human Well-Being: Current State and Trends*. Millennium Ecosystem Assessment Series. Washington, DC: Island Press, pp. 795–825.

McPherson, E.G. (1994) "Energy-saving Potential of Trees in Chicago". In E.G. McPherson et al. (eds), *Chicago's Urban Forest Ecosystem: Results of the Chicago Urban Forest Climate Project*. USDA, Forest Service General Technical Report NE-186, pp. 95–114.

Meehl, G.A. and C. Tebaldi (2004) "More Intense, More Frequent, and Longer Lasting Heat Waves in the 21st Century". *Science* 305: 994–997.

Ministry of the Environment, Government of Japan (2011) "Reforestation by Public Works for the Purpose of Restoring Ecosystem Service in the Rokko Mountain Range, Hyogo Prefecture, Japan", <http://www.env.go.jp/nature/satoyama/syuhourei/pdf/cje_4.pdf> (accessed 1 November 2012).

Mitchell, J.K. (1999) *Crucibles of Hazard: Mega-Cities and Disasters in Transition*. Tokyo: United Nations University Press.

Morrow, S. et al. (1995) "Using Vegetation for Erosion Control on Construction Sites". Oklahoma State University, BAE-1514.

Mumford, L. (1938) *The Culture of Cities*. New York: Harcourt Brace & Company.

Munich Re (2004) *Megacities – Megarisks: Trends and Challenges for Insurance and Risk Management*. Munich: Münchener Rückversicherungs Gesellschaft.

New York City (2010) "NYC Green Infrastructure Plan: A Sustainable Strategy for Clean Waterways". City of New York.

Nirupama, N. and S.P. Simonovic (2006) "Increase of Flood Risk Due to Urbanisation: A Canadian Example". *Natural Hazards* 40: 25–41.

Nowak, D.J. (1994) "Air Pollution Removal by Chicago's Urban Forest". In E.G. McPherson et al. (eds), *Chicago's Urban Forest Ecosystem: Results of the Chicago Urban Forest Climate Project*. USDA Forest Service General Technical Report NE-186, pp. 63–81.

Núñez, D. et al. (2006) "Forests and Water: The Value of Native Temperate Forests in Supplying Water for Human Consumption". *Ecological Economics* 58: 606–616.

OCHA [Office for the Coordination of Humanitarian Affairs] (2009) "Labutta Township Profile, March 2009", <http://www.themimu.info/docs/Profile_Labutta%20Township_March%2009.pdf> (accessed 1 November 2012).

Odum, E.P. (1971) *Fundamentals of Ecology*. Philadelphia: Saunders.

O Globo (2011) "Número de mortos na Região Serrana já passa de 900 após chuvas de janeiro", 16 February, <http://oglobo.globo.com/rio/numero-de-mortos-na-regiao-serrana-ja-passa-de-900-apos-chuvas-de-janeiro-2822331#ixzz10MKQaJxi> (accessed 1 November 2012).

PEDRR [Partnership for Environment and Disaster Risk Reduction] (2011) "Managing Watersheds for Urban Resilience". Policy Brief presented at the Global Platform for Disaster Risk Reduction, Roundtable on "Managing Watersheds for Resilience", 12 May 2011, Geneva, Switzerland. Available at <http://pedrr.net/portals/0/PEDRR_policy_brief.pdf> (accessed 1 November 2012).

Pelling, M. (2003) *The Vulnerability of Cities*. London: Earthscan.

Pereira, A.S. (2006) "The Opportunity of a Disaster: The Economic Impact of the 1755 Lisbon Earthquake". Discussion Paper 06/03, Centre for Historical Economics and Related Research at York, York University.

Pickett, S.T.A. et al. (1997) "A Conceptual Framework for the Study of Human Ecosystems in Urban Areas". *Urban Ecosystems* 1: 185–199.

Pickett, S.T.A. et al. (2001) "Urban Ecological Systems: Linking Terrestrial Ecological, Physical, and Socioeconomic Components of Metropolitan Areas". *Annual Review of Ecological Systems* 32: 127–157.

Pielke, R.A., Jr. et al. (2008) "Normalized Hurricane Damages in the United States: 1900–2005". *Natural Hazards Review* 9(1): 29–42.

Pires, M. (2004) "Watershed Protection for a World City: The Case of New York". *Land Use Policy* 21(2): 161–175.

Platt, R.H. (2006) "Urban Watershed Management. Sustainability, One Stream at a Time". *Environment* 48(4): 26–42.

Porter, R. (1994) *London: A Social History*. London: Hamish Hamilton.

Postel, S.L. and B.H. Thompson (2005) "Watershed Protection: Capturing the Benefits of Nature's Water Supply Services". *Natural Resources Forum* 29: 98–108.

Satterthwaite, D. (2010) "Avoiding the Urbanization of Disasters". In IFRC, *World Disasters Report 2010: Focus on Urban Risk*. Geneva: International Federation of Red Cross and Red Crescent Societies, pp. 10–29.

Showers, K.B. (2002) "Water Scarcity and Urban Africa: An Overview of Urban–Rural Water Linkages". *World Development* 30(4): 621–648.

Srinivas, H., R. Shaw and A. Sharma (2009) "Future Perspective of Urban Risk Reduction". In R. Shaw, H. Srinivas and A. Sharma (eds), *Urban Risk Reduction: An Asian Perspective*. Bingley, UK: Emerald, pp. 105–116.

Stolten, S., N. Dudley and J. Randall (2008) *Natural Security, Protected Areas and Hazard Mitigation*. Gland, Switzerland: WWF and Equilibrium.

Strzepek, K.M. and J.B. Smith (1995) *As Climate Changes: International Impacts and Implications*. New York: Cambridge University Press.

Surjan, A.K. and R. Shaw (2009) "Essentials of Urban Disaster Risk Reduction". In R. Shaw and R.R. Krishnamurthy (eds), *Disaster Management: Global Challenges and Local Solutions*. Chennai: Universities Press, pp. 543–555.

Tarr, J.A. (1997) "The City and the Natural Environment", Global Development Research Center, <http://www.gdrc.org/uem/doc-tarr.html> (accessed 1 November 2012).

TEEB – The Economics of Ecosystems and Biodiversity (2011) *TEEB Manual for Cities: Ecosystem Services in Urban Management*. Available at <http://www.teebweb.org> (accessed 1 November 2012).

Teich, M. and P. Bebi (2009) "Evaluating the Benefit of Avalanche Protection Forest with GIS-based Risk Analyses – A Case Study in Switzerland". *Forest Ecology and Management* 257: 1910–1919.

The Guardian (2011) "Trash, Sewage Boost Disease Risk in Bangkok Floods", 3 November.

Thibodeau, F.R. and B.D. Ostro (1981) "An Economic Analysis of Wetland Protection". *Journal of Environmental Management* 12: 19–30.

Tian, S. (2011) "Managing Stormwater Runoff with Green Infrastructure: Exploring Practical Strategies to Overcome Barriers in Citywide Implementation". Community and Regional Planning Program: Student Projects and Theses, Paper 7, University of Nebraska-Lincoln, <http://digitalcommons.unl.edu/arch_crp_theses/7>.

Tilling, R.I. (1985) "Volcanoes". USGS General Interest Publication.

Ulrich, R. (1984) "View through a Window May Influence Recovery from Surgery". *Science* 224: 420–421.

UNDESA [United Nations Department of Economic and Social Affairs] (2007) *World Urbanization Prospects: The 2007 Revision*. New York: United Nations.

UNDESA (2010) *World Urbanization Prospects: The 2009 Revision*. New York: United Nations.

UNEP-WCMC [United Nations Environment Programme World Conservation Monitoring Centre] (2006) *In the Front Line: Shoreline Protection and Other Ecosystems Services from Mangroves and Coral Reefs*. Cambridge: UNEP-WCMC.

UNESCAP [United Nations Economic and Social Commission for Asia and the Pacific] (2005) *Urban Environmental Governance for Sustainable Development in Asia and the Pacific: A Regional Overview*. Bangkok: United Nations Economic and Social Commission for Asia and the Pacific..

UN-HABITAT (2003) *Slums of the World: The Face of Urban Poverty in the New Millennium?* Nairobi: UN-HABITAT.

UN-HABITAT (2010) *State of the World's Cities 2008/2009: Harmonious Cities*. London: Earthscan.

UNISDR [United Nations International Strategy for Disaster Reduction] (2009) *Global Assessment Report 2009: Risk and Poverty in a Changing Climate*. Geneva: United Nations International Strategy for Disaster Reduction.

UNISDR (2010) "Strategy Outline for the 2010–2011 World Disaster Reduction Campaign on Making Cities Resilient, Addressing Urban Risk". Geneva: United Nations International Strategy for Disaster Reduction.

UNISDR (2011) *2011 Global Assessment Report on Disaster Risk Reduction: Revealing Risk, Redefining Development.* Geneva: United Nations International Strategy for Disaster Reduction.

Vale, L.J. and T.J. Campanella (eds) (2005) *The Resilient City.* New York: Oxford University Press.

Vatsa, K.S. (2005) "Home for Almost Half the World". In T. Jeggle (ed.), *Know Risk.* Geneva: United Nations International Strategy for Disaster Reduction, pp. 282–285.

Vitousek, P.M. et al. (1997) "Human Domination of Earth's Ecosystems". *Science* 277(5325): 494–499.

Weems, J.E. (n.d.) "Galveston Hurricane of 1900". *Handbook of Texas Online,* <http://www.tshaonline.org/handbook/online/articles/ydg02> (accessed 1 November 2012).

Wilkie, K. and R. Roach (2004) *Green among the Concrete: The Benefits of Urban Natural Capital.* Calgary: Canada West Foundation.

Wisner, B. (1999) "There Are Worse Things Than Earthquakes: Hazard Vulnerability and Mitigation Capacity in Greater Los Angeles". In J.K. Mitchell (ed.), *Crucibles of Hazard: Mega-Cities and Disasters in Transition.* Tokyo: United Nations University Press, pp. 375–427.

WorldWatch Institute (2004) "Residents of Rio's Favelas Face Diverse Risks", <http://www.worldwatch.org/node/4756> (accessed 1 November 2012).

17

Applying environmental impact assessments and strategic environmental assessments in disaster management

Anil Kumar Gupta and Sreeja S. Nair

Rationale: Paradigm shift to ecosystem-based disaster risk reduction

The first paradigm shift in disaster management that took place over the past two decades moved "response- and relief-centric approaches" towards "mitigation- and preparedness-centric approaches", but this resulted in a key emphasis on hard engineering solutions, early warning and response preparedness. However, the growing focus on vulnerabilities and exposure has shifted attention towards environment-based approaches. This new emphasis is widely advocated as a second paradigm shift in disaster risk management (Figure 17.1; Gupta and Nair, 2010), which also links with people's livelihoods and the sustainability of their natural resource base. Sustainable natural resource management is recognized as a key element in vulnerability reduction (IADB, 1999; UNISDR, 2011).

The current priorities of the Hyogo Framework for Action (HFA) (UNISDR, 2005) offer environmental opportunities for disaster risk reduction (DRR) through the following provisions (see also Chapter 1 in this volume):

1. Policy, legislative and institutional frameworks for environmental planning and action to mainstream DRR (HFA Priority 1).
2. Knowledge of the hazards and analysis of the environmental dimensions of physical, social and economic vulnerabilities (HFA Priority 2).
3. Risks related to changing environmental conditions and land use, and the impact of hazards associated with geological events, weather,

The role of ecosystems in disaster risk reduction, Renaud, Sudmeier-Rieux and Estrella (eds), United Nations University Press, 2013, ISBN 978-92-808-1221-3

water, climate variability and climate change, to be addressed in sector development planning and programmes as well as in post-disaster situations (HFA Priority 4).

Major environmental changes generating or exacerbating hazards and increasing vulnerabilities to disasters are: climate change, land-use changes and natural resource degradation (Gupta and Nair, 2011).

> Human societies cannot be dissociated from the environment that they shape and which in turn influence their development and livelihoods. Together they form a comprehensive system with intrinsic levels of vulnerability and inherent coping mechanisms. The less degraded the environmental component of this system, the lower its overall vulnerability and the higher its coping capacity. (OECD, 2010: 7)

Recognition of the potential role of environmental management in DRR begins with the recognition of disasters as human processes interacting with the physical environment (see Box 17.1 for a classification of disasters based on the origin of the hazard). Environmental assessments, therefore, can be utilized to provide scientific and strategic insights into the risks and vulnerabilities that are associated with the implementation of policies, programmes and projects and move towards a culture of safety and prevention.

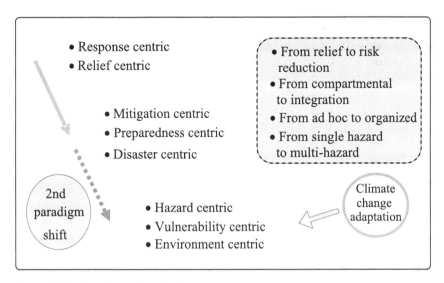

Figure 17.1 Paradigm shifts in disaster management
Source: Gupta and Nair (2010).

Box 17.1 Classification of disasters based on origin of hazards

1. *Natural hazards*
   Hydro-meteorological, vegetation fire, geophysical, geo-chemical, biological, epidemics, etc.
2. *Technological hazards*
   Industrial (chemical), electrical, mechanical, nuclear/radiological, aviation, dam break, mining, structural collapse, etc.
3. *Civil disasters and conflicts*
   Civil unrest, strike, war, sabotage, mass poisoning, bomb blast, stampede, transport accidents, etc.

Disasters may be induced by natural hazards, which could also trigger technological or human-induced (i.e. civil conflicts) disasters. On the other hand, a technological or civil disaster may exacerbate the impacts of natural hazards.

Incorporating DRR in environmental impact assessments

The frequency of disasters experienced by some countries should certainly place disaster risk at the forefront of development planners' minds. For example, Mozambique faces a regular cycle of droughts (1981–1984, 1991–1993) and floods (1976–1978, 1996–1998, 1999–2000). It is now well recognized that it is not only nature that generates disaster risk but developmental processes that aggravate hazards and shape human vulnerability, which in turn paves the way for disasters. Human activities can alter the magnitude and frequency of natural hazards (for example, flooding, landslides and desertification) by changing natural hydrological processes and land-use patterns.

Environmental degradation is contributing to increasing disaster losses. For instance, in many countries deforestation has disrupted watersheds and resulted in siltation of riverbeds, leading to more severe droughts and floods (Benson and Twigg, 2007). The influence of past development on present disaster risk therefore underlines the significance of contemporary decision-making that might have an impact on disasters experienced by future generations. Environmental impact assessments (EIAs) offer to bring together both disaster risk reduction and development concerns within an environmental management framework.

Every anthropogenic activity has some impact on the environment. However, a society's development is dependent on utilizing environmental goods and services for its food, security and other needs and cannot survive without these socio-ecological interactions (see also

Chapter 1 in this volume). Consequently, there is a need to harmonize developmental activities with environmental concerns. The EIA is one of the tools available to development planners. The objective of an EIA is to foresee and address potential environmental problems or concerns at an early stage of project planning and design. An EIA should assist planners and government authorities in the decision-making process by identifying the key potential environmental impacts and formulating mitigation measures.

EIAs produce targeted environmental analyses by reporting on current and anticipated future environmental conditions and identifying drivers of change. There are many types and forms of traditional and innovative EIA options, for example:

- EIAs of projects (for example, development projects such as water resources, highways, airports, tourism, housing complexes, railways or industrial projects in manufacturing, mining, food, dairy, etc.);
- strategic environmental assessments (SEAs);
- regional EIAs (also known as country EIAs or cumulative impact assessments);
- developmental planning process based on a carrying capacity assessment (Gupta et al., 2002a);
- developmental planning based on environmental risk mapping (Gupta et al., 2002b);
- health impact assessments (as part of an EIA or risk analysis) (Gupta et al., 1999).

Early EIAs focused primarily on the impacts of a project on the natural or biophysical environment (such as effects on air and water quality, flora and fauna, noise levels, climate and hydrological systems). Over time, increased consideration has been given to the social, health and economic aspects of environmental consequences. This trend has been driven partly by public involvement in the EIA process and is reflected in the evolving definition of "environment" in EIA legislation, guidance and practice, which include effects on the following (Bhatt and Khanal, 2009):

- human health and safety,
- flora, fauna, ecosystems and biological diversity,
- soil, water, air, climate and landscape,
- use of land, natural resources and raw materials,
- protected areas and designated sites of scientific, historical and cultural significance,
- heritage, recreation and amenity assets, and
- livelihood, lifestyle and well-being of those affected by a proposal.

More recently, greater emphasis has been placed on incorporating hazards and disaster risk analysis into the environmental assessment process itself. ProVention Consortium and the Caribbean Development Bank published *Tools for Mainstreaming Disaster Risk Reduction*, which included a Guidance Note on "Environmental Assessments" (Benson and Twigg, 2007). This important publication focused on environmental assessment as the natural starting point in the design of a project to address natural hazards and related risk. It provides guidance on analysing disaster risk-related consequences of developmental activities as a result of their environmental impacts, as well as the potential threat posed by natural hazards to the projects. Environmental assessments are now expected to measure the risk reduction benefits of proposed environmental impact mitigation measures within the proposed development project (CDB and CARICOM Secretariat, 2004). Environmental assessments provide opportunities to collate data on natural hazards (that is, hazard types, magnitudes and probabilities of occurrence) as part of the project appraisal stage, and these inform project design and identify risk-sensitive environmental mitigation measures.

Examples

A number of examples may be cited to illustrate how DRR can be mainstreamed in EIAs.

India

In India, environmental concerns in relation to major developmental projects were considered in the Fourth Five-Year Plan (1969–1974), which marked the beginning of EIA policy and practice in India. Even then, concerns related to catastrophic disaster risks and displacement as well as mitigation requirements were already flagged for certain megadams and river valley projects. In 1985, the Department of Environment and Forests issued guidelines for environmental assessment of river valley projects. "These guidelines require various studies, such as impacts on forests and wildlife in the submergence zone, water logging potential, upstream and downstream aquatic ecosystems and fisheries, water related diseases, climatic changes and seismicity" (ECT, 2005: 3). "Site clearance" from the state government, including a "no objection" certificate from the district administration, is the first step towards an "environmental clearance" procedure (ECT, 2005) and is expected to take into account the disaster risks associated with the site and the region.

Germany

Environmental Impact Assessment Act 2001 (Article 2) of the Federal Republic of Germany envisages the identification, description and assessment of the direct and indirect impacts of a project on: (1) human beings, animals and plants, (2) soil, water, air, climate and landscape and (3) cultural heritage and other material assets, and it also incorporates the identification and assessment of associated natural hazards. Understanding of the environmental impacts of project activities on various social components offers information on vulnerability to natural hazards. The broad range of projects and activities (such as construction of a dam or dredging in rivers or lakes to obtain minerals) covered under Germany's EIA Act indicates the extent to which disaster risk and vulnerability factors could be addressed in EIAs.

China

China's new Law on Environmental Impact Assessment (2003) focuses on the assessment of potential impacts from development or industrial projects. In addition to assessing impacts on all aspects of the environment, including public safety, health and livelihoods, the EIAs are required to incorporate information on natural hazards as well as technological and chemical risks.

Nepal

In Nepal, the EIA system addresses the risk of flooding, erosion and landslides that may be aggravated by land-use and landscape changes, and recognizes that the sustainability of a project or proposed development is linked to risks associated with natural hazards (Bhatt and Khanal, 2009).

Botswana

The Republic of Botswana's "Guidelines for Preparing Environmental Impact Assessment Reports for Mining Projects" envisage an efficient information system for risk management decisions, in addition to addressing the underlying factors of vulnerability (see Box 17.2). The guidelines call for the assessment of almost all aspects of land, land use, water resources and water bodies as well as the socioeconomic setting of the project site. Data incorporated into the EIA are similar to the data requirements for risk and vulnerability assessments related to natural hazards. The EIA process takes into account issues related to water scarcity, flooding sites, eroded slopes, among others.

The Philippines

In the Philippines, the Environmental Management Bureau, through a special memorandum dated 11 November 2011, produced *EIA Technical Guidelines Incorporating Disaster Risk Reduction (DRR) and Climate*

Box 17.2 EIA of mining projects

The Republic of Botswana's "Guidelines for Preparing Environmental Impact Assessment Reports for Mining Projects" (2003) offer opportunities for incorporating disaster risk concerns throughout the EIA process.

The project description requires information regarding adjacent land-use and river catchment systems, and the section on "Consideration of project alternatives" incorporates the following information:

- sources of water
- mine infrastructure sites
- mine residue disposal sites
- domestic and industrial waste disposal sites
- housing sites
- land-use options after rehabilitation
- alternatives to river diversions

The EIA procedure applicable to mining projects in Botswana takes into account the hazards in the area as well as physical, social and economic conditions that can interact with hazards during mining-related activities. For example, the EIA assesses pre-mining conditions, including the incidence of extreme weather conditions such as frost, hail, drought and high winds, as well as topography, soil types, and existing and potential land-use patterns (such as for agriculture, forestry, fisheries, recreation, archaeological and cultural sites). In addition, the state of the water environment is assessed, including water courses (streams, rivers, dams, etc.), water use rights in the affected area, flood peaks and volumes, and drainage density. A rehabilitation plan, along with measures of prevention and mitigation, is required under the Environmental Management Programme.

Hence, the EIA aims to recognize disaster-prone or vulnerable sites by taking into account the hazards, socioeconomic conditions and state of natural resources during the EIA process, and thus helps to identify underlying vulnerabilities and to mitigate or prevent adverse impacts from mining.

Change Adaptation (CCA) Concerns (Environmental Management Bureau, 2011).

As illustrated in these examples, disaster risk analyses can be incorporated into the EIA process by utilizing the data generated through the EIA process itself. A procedural framework for an EIA is given in Figure 17.2, which incorporates risk analysis and a Disaster Management Plan

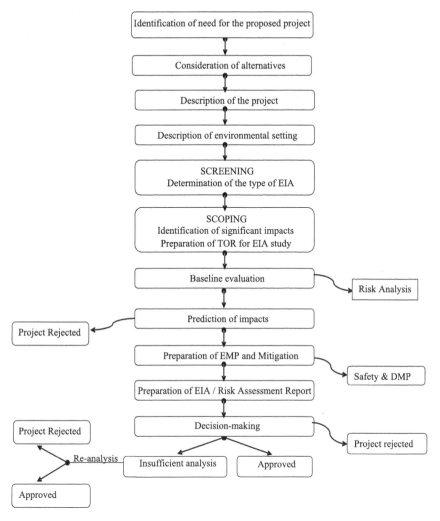

Figure 17.2 Basic components of an EIA study in India
Source: Bureau of Indian Standards (2011: 6).
Note: TOR = Terms of Reference; EMP = Environmental Management Plan;
DMP = Disaster Management Plan.

(DMP) as EIA outputs. Environmental regulations provide for the application of environmental assessment and evaluation tools that help reduce the risk of disasters by generating knowledge about the hazards and underlying causes of vulnerability within the process of planning itself. Environmental clearance of major developmental and industrial projects in India through EIA notification (1994, 2006) under the Environmental Protection Act of 1986 specifically requires that the Environmental Management Plan includes a DMP and, when necessary, a rehabilitation plan. Germany's Environmental Impact Assessment Act 2001 envisages that the planning procedure will include environmental assessment pursuant to the provisions of the applicable Building Codes, which in turn include provisions related to disaster-resistant housing and infrastructure.

Incorporating DRR in strategic environmental assessment

The SEA is the "formalized, systematic and comprehensive process of identifying and evaluating the environmental consequences of proposed policies, plans or programmes to ensure that they are fully included and appropriately addressed at the earliest possible stage of decision-making on a par with economic and social considerations" (Dalal-Clayton and Sadler, 1999: 2). SEAs are like EIAs because they also assess and mitigate potential environmental impacts. The main difference is that SEAs may be applied to a national policy for an entire sector (for example, energy policy) or to programmes covering a geographical area (for example, a national, state or regional development scheme). The SEA aims at environmental sustainability over the long term and assesses the impacts of developmental activities across broader spatial extents. It is an important tool for mainstreaming DRR in development policies, plans and programmes at national and sectoral levels (OECD, 2008).

The basic steps of SEAs are similar to the steps in environmental impact assessment. Figure 17.3 illustrates a conceptual framework for an SEA process, using the example of an SEA in the context of agricultural policy. The SEA helps analyse a policy, plan or decision for its direct and indirect impacts on environmental components, given that decisions made on the ground are often influenced by policies (Urban et al., 2010). The impacts and consequences of a policy decision, such as an agricultural policy, on the environment and natural resource settings may also alter hazard patterns and modify local vulnerability to the impact of disasters when they occur. SEAs can also help analyse changes in socioeconomic conditions that create and influence vulnerability at local levels (Benson and Twigg, 2007). Simultaneously, SEAs can assess the potential qualitative and quantitative changes in natural resource systems and the subsequent potential impacts on the level of hazards and social, economic and ecological resilience to absorb the shocks.

The OECD published an Advisory Note on "Strategic Environmental Assessment and Disaster Risk Reduction" and identified the following considerations for undertaking SEAs (2010: 4):

- particular situations or circumstances that will require unique sensitivity and awareness (e.g. post-conflict environments);
- providing further perspectives, information and guidance on emerging issues that may need to be more adequately integrated into an SEA (e.g. climate risk or status of ecosystem services); and/or
- a key emerging issue or policy area that was not sufficiently addressed within previous SEA guidance.

Country environmental analysis (CEA) is a variation of SEA and a relatively new analytical tool applied by international agencies in a regional or country context. The CEA provides systematic analysis of key environmental issues most critical to the sustained development of a country and opportunities for overcoming constraints in reference to the environmental impact of a development policy. The CEA aims to focus on mainstreaming environmental issues into development planning and provides an important opportunity to highlight disaster risks, especially those linked to environmental issues, and helps ensure that they are adequately addressed during planning stages.

The Asian Development Bank's CEA for Tajikistan, for instance, identifies natural hazards, including drought, landslides and earthquakes, as some of the country's key environmental problems and promotes improved environmental management in reducing poverty and vulnerability to disasters. In order to enhance disaster resilience, it recommends investment in activities that contribute to greater physical stability (for example, prevention of soil erosion); reduced vulnerability and improved support for livelihoods (for example, drainage of land prone to mudslides

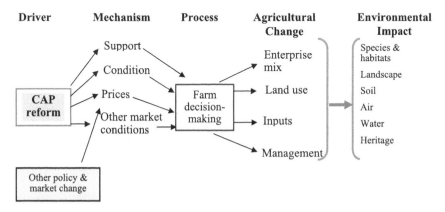

Figure 17.3 Sample SEA framework for agricultural policy
Source: After EEAC Working Group Governance (2009).
Note: CAP = Common Agricultural Policy.

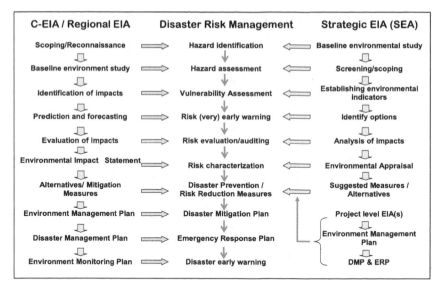

Figure 17.4 Inputs of EIA and SEA to DRR
Source: Gupta and Nair (2012: Figure 4).
Notes: C-EIA = Cumulative EIA; DMP = Disaster Management Plan; ERP = Emergency Response Plan.

and use of the collected water for irrigation); and enhanced attention to zoning of economic activities. More generally, the CEA promotes a development policy that favours DRR over emergency response and reconstruction (ADB, 2004).

All CEAs are expected to include collation of basic hazard data and background information on past disaster losses to give a preliminary overview of the significance of disaster risk in a country and to provide baseline information that informs future environmental assessments of individual projects and country programming. The United Nations Development Programme's environmental guidelines (UNDP, 1992), for instance, already indicate that country environmental reviews should include baseline data on rainfall, climate, temperatures and hazards, such as seismic faults, cyclones and droughts. Figure 17.4 illustrates how different forms of EIAs can have a direct input into various aspects of disaster risk management.

Applying EIAs in disaster management

The EIA as a decision-support system and information tool can help in planning throughout all stages of disaster risk management (see Figure 17.5).

EIA methodology utilizes a range of tools such as matrices, weighted ranking and computer-aided modelling, which help in comparing and determining the relationship between different actions, environmental changes and their primary and secondary impacts (Gupta, 2010). Information generated by EIAs can help improve early warning because the EIA process can provide data for risk-mapping and scenario-building in relation to the potential impacts of projects. Hence, EIAs can be applied to help assess the conditions of hazards and patterns of vulnerability in the context of the developmental planning process. EIA reports also include an environmental monitoring plan. Monitoring parameters usually can cover early signals of potential disasters.

EIAs applied in the disaster prevention and mitigation phase can help inform planning for DRR, for instance by providing guidance on choices of mitigation methods (Gupta and Yunus, 2004), technology investments and site locations for activities. In a post-disaster context, conducting a rapid environmental impact assessment (REA) helps to ensure that sustainability concerns are factored into the relief, reconstruction and recovery planning stages (Gupta et al., 2002c). The REA does not replace an EIA, but fills a gap in an emergency context until an EIA can be appropriately conducted (discussed further in the next section).

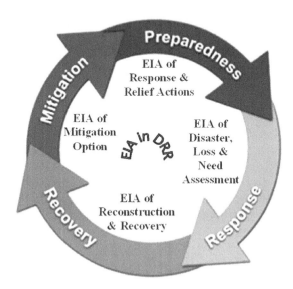

Figure 17.5 EIA applications in DRR phases
Source: Gupta and Nair (2012).

EIAs in post-disaster relief and recovery

Disasters have significant impacts on ecology, infrastructure, people, livelihoods and properties. People and their assets are affected either directly in the form of casualties, injuries or damage, or indirectly through the impacts of a disaster on ecosystem productivity, environmental services and the natural resource base. Disaster impacts may be categorized into the following:

(a) physical (effects on infrastructure, buildings, physical property, industry, roads, bridges, monuments, etc.);
(b) environmental (effects on water, land/soil, land use, landscape, crops, lakes/rivers/estuaries, aquaculture, forests, animals/livestock, wildlife, atmosphere/climate, energy, etc.);
(c) social (effects on life, health, livelihoods, employment, relations, security, peace, etc.);
(d) economic (effects on assets, deposits, reserves, income, commerce, production, guarantee/insurance, etc.);
(e) ecological (effects on ecosystem integrity and ecosystem health, structure and functions, productivity, succession, carrying capacity, etc.).

However, environmental impacts are rarely given consideration in damage (and loss) assessments conducted following a disaster, although some consideration is given to environmental components with direct economic values, for example agricultural production. In the aftermath of the Indian Ocean tsunami, Blaikie et al. (2005) suggested that effective recovery and reduction in future vulnerability for local people depended on:

• recognizing that ecosystem services provide the basis for sustainable reconstruction and reduction in future vulnerability;
• long-term monitoring of both ecological and socioeconomic parameters and a management strategy that encourages adaptation to changing circumstances;
• providing a clear articulation of the rationale for including biodiversity conservation concerns in reconstruction planning.

An REA applied in a disaster context is a tool to identify, define and prioritize potential environmental impacts in disaster situations (Benfield Hazard Research Centre–CARE International, 2005: iv). A simple, consensus-based qualitative assessment process, involving narratives and rating tables, is used to identify and rank environmental issues and follow up actions during a disaster. The REA is designed for natural, technological or political disasters, and is viewed as a best practice tool for effective disaster assessment and management. REAs can be used shortly before a disaster and up to 120 days after a disaster, or for any major change in an extended crisis. The REA does not provide answers on how to resolve environmental problems, but it does provide sufficient information to allow those responding to a disaster to address key issues raised in the REA.

In recent years, there have been innovative applications of EIAs in the context of recovery and reconstruction. For example, WWF and the American Red Cross developed the Green Recovery and Reconstruction Toolkit (GRRT, 2010), which contains a dedicated module on the role of EIA in recovery (see Box 17.3). Moreover, Benfield Hazard Research Centre and CARE International (2005) have developed more detailed and comprehensive guidelines on REA in the context of disaster response. These guidelines focus analyses in the following areas (2005: v):

• assessment of the general context of a disaster;
• immediate impacts on the environment;
• unmet basic needs of disaster survivors (for example, for fuelwood and building materials) that could lead to adverse impacts on the environment; and
• potential negative environmental consequences of relief and recovery operations.

The methodology is based on qualitative assessments, drawing heavily on people's perceptions and often based on incomplete data, but it provides sufficient information in difficult circumstances to facilitate rapid assessment of needs and priorities.

Post-disaster environmental assessments need to explore whether proposed relief, reconstruction and rehabilitation efforts will have acceptable environmental impacts (for example, environmentally sound selection of

Box 17.3 Humanitarian response and EIA

WWF and the American Red Cross developed a toolkit to equip field staff to integrate environmental sustainability into international disaster recovery and reconstruction. The Green Recovery and Reconstruction Toolkit (GRRT) aims to make communities more resilient by integrating environmental concerns as part of the recovery process. Environmental assessment tools are provided to determine the environmental impacts of humanitarian projects regardless of project type or sector. Module 3 explains the value of conducting EIAs and answers the questions of how, when and why an assessment should be conducted.

Source: <http://green-recovery.org/?page_id=278> (accessed 2 November 2012).

sites for refugee camps and sourcing of reconstruction materials) and whether they will strengthen resilience as well as reduce vulnerabilities to future natural hazards. In addition, they need to ensure that the response and recovery process addresses environmental problems caused by the disaster (for example, contamination of water and soil).

The UN High Commissioner for Refugees developed *Environmental Guidelines* (UNHCR, 2005) to incorporate a framework for identifying and addressing environmental issues associated with refugees, returnees and disaster relief activities. The Guidelines focus on natural resource deterioration and ecosystem services impairment and their consequences for the health and socioeconomic well-being of the people. Several donor organizations have established their own guidelines, which include checklists on environmental assessment of disaster relief and humanitarian assistance operations – see, for example, the Asian Development Bank (ADB, 2003); the Swedish International Development Cooperation Agency (Sida, 2002); and the UK Department for International Development (DFID, 2003).

The Joint UNEP/OCHA Environment Unit is the United Nations mechanism for mobilizing and coordinating emergency assistance to countries affected by environmental emergencies and natural disasters with significant environmental impacts. The Joint Environment Unit has developed "Guidelines for Environmental Assessment Following Chemical Emergencies" (Bishop, 1999), with the purpose of deploying environmental experts to undertake rapid identification of environment-related problems following an industrial emergency.

Key challenges and recommendations

Despite the improved understanding of the potential benefits of applying ecosystem management approaches for DRR, the gap between the two sectors is wide, especially at the level of policy planning and governance. There is seldom integration in a real sense, except in academic forums. EIAs are often viewed with suspicion, because they are known to simply "rubber stamp" the environmental clearances required from the authorities to gain approval of development projects.

Current EIA and SEA practices do not adequately reflect or incorporate disaster risk and disaster mitigation concerns, even though environmental legislation and policy frameworks may already support such integration (for example, in the case of India). Moreover, despite increasing cooperation between DRR and climate change communities-of-practice, there remains a wide divide across the two communities between practitioners, their approaches and also the vocabulary used. For example, terms such as "vulnerability", "mitigation" and "risk" are understood very differently within each community and terms such as "no-regrets measures" and "adaptation", which are frequently used by climate change experts, are less common in DRR parlance. However, this may be changing as there is increased global recognition for integrating DRR and CCA and the Intergovernmental Panel on Climate Change (IPCC) Special Report on Extreme Events (IPCC, 2012) adopts terminology that is closer to that of the international DRR community.

In order to overcome these challenges, several recommendations may be presented, drawing from the context in India:

1. The presence of environmental policy and EIA/SEA experts is needed at the highest levels of decision-making authority and institutions on disaster management (for example, the National Disaster Management Authority in India). Conversely, representation of DRR expertise is warranted at the highest institutional levels of the environment and natural resource management sectors (for example, the Ministry of Environment Planning Commission's Environment Division). This would ensure increased integration of environment and DRR concerns in their respective policies, programmes and plans.

2. Integrating DRR and environmental management policy and practice will require adapting and customizing both the disaster management and environmental management systems and governance. DRR and environment agencies need to work together and develop common guidelines for integrating DRR within the EIA process as well as applying EIA in the context of disaster management (for example, conducting rapid EIAs in post-disaster response). Further work is needed in interpreting environmental law and policies, including for EIAs and SEAs, towards achieving DRR outcomes.

3. Given that SEAs and EIAs are important tools for anticipating the potential environmental impacts of development activities, there is a need to apply SEAs and EIAs that are sensitive to disaster risks in the context of local (regional) and national development planning. A requirement for regional EIAs (at district level) should be made a prerequisite to planning. For example, five-year planning cycles are common in India, and a regional EIA can facilitate an "Environmental Action Plan" that is also sensitive to disaster risks at district or state level. A suggested framework of convergence between DRR and environmental planning is shown in Figure 17.6.

The district is an administrative unit in India and the evolution of an integrated planning approach across sectors rather than "isolated" sectoral plans is under way. On the other hand, a Disaster Management Plan at district level is required by the Disaster Management Act of India (2005), which would include hazard, risk and vulnerability

Figure 17.6 Integration of environmental and natural disaster management at district level

analyses and plans for disaster mitigation, preparedness and emergency response. It has been suggested that a regional EIA and/or an SEA of proposed development in the district during the designated plan period (five years in India) should result in the provision of an Environmental Management Plan that incorporates the components of habitat and ecological protection, natural resources management and DRR and requires the integration of various sectoral plans. This is useful because the data needed to develop these plans are common to a great extent, a part from information related to search and rescue. An Environmental Action Plan at the district level needs to integrate with the DMP to facilitate environment-based risk reduction and mainstreaming towards an integrated development planning process.

4. One recent development towards EIA application in disaster management is a disaster impact assessment (DIA) component within the environmental clearance procedure of development projects. Such an initiative was started by a joint proposal by Pakistan's National Disaster Management Authority (NDMA) and its Ministry of Environment. However, the anticipatory assessment methodology framework for a DIA of a project's implications in terms of increasing or decreasing disaster risks and vulnerability in the geographical area of concern is lacking. India's National Institute of Disaster Management and Pakistan's NDMA have recently proposed a collaboration to fill this meth-

odological gap by jointly working on establishing an EIA system that takes into account the project's impact on natural disaster risk.

5. Finally, there is a need to update environment-related academic curriculums and training courses to recognize the added value of improved environmental management for DRR. Leading universities in India and the region have already incorporated "disaster management" as a specialization in the environmental sciences, but such efforts still need to be strengthened with case studies of successes and failures, the use of interdisciplinary knowledge and modern tools such as geoinformatics and space technology, and the promotion of research.

Acknowledgements

A range of international and national literature and other documents from published, unpublished and Web resources have been utilized and interpreted in developing the contents of the present chapter, and their original sources are gratefully acknowledged.

REFERENCES

ADB [Asian Development Bank] (2003) *Environmental Assessment Guidelines*. Available at <http://www.adb.org/sites/default/files/pub/2003/Environmental_Assessment_Guidelines.pdf> (accessed 2 November 2012).

ADB [Asian Development Bank] (2004) *Tajikistan: Country Environmental Analysis*. Manila: Asian Development Bank. Available at <http://www.adb.org/documents/country-environmental-analysis-tajikistan> (accessed 2 November 2012).

Benfield Hazard Research Centre–CARE International (2005) *Guidelines for Rapid Environmental Impact Assessment in Disasters*. Version 4.4, April. Available at <http://transition.usaid.gov/our_work/humanitarian_assistance/ffp/rea_guidelines.pdf> (accessed 2 November 2012).

Benson, C. and J. Twigg (2007) "Guidance Note 7". In *Tools for Mainstreaming Disaster Risk Reduction: Guidance Notes for Development Organisations*. Geneva: International Federation of Red Cross and Red Crescent Societies/ ProVention Consortium, pp. 79–89.

Bhatt, R.P. and S.K. Khanal (2009) "Environmental Impact Assessment System in Nepal – An Overview of Policy, Legal Instruments and Process". *Kathmandu University Journal of Science, Engineering and Technology* 5(2): 160–170.

Bishop, J.A. (1999) "Guidelines for Environmental Assessment Following Chemical Emergencies". Joint UNEP/OCHA Environment Unit. Available at <http://ochanet.unocha.org/p/Documents/Guidelines%20for%20Environmental%20Assessment%20following%20Chemical%20Emergencies.pdf> (accessed 2 November 2012).

Blaikie, P., S. Mainka and J. McNeely (2005) "The Indian Ocean Tsunami: Reducing Risk and Vulnerability to Future Natural Disasters and Loss of Ecosystems
Services". International Union for Conservation of Nature Information Paper,
February. Available at <http://data.iucn.org/dbtw-wpd/edocs/Rep-2005-006.pdf>
(accessed 2 November 2012).

Bureau of Indian Standards (2011) "Preliminary Draft: Guidelines for Environmental Impact Assessment of River Valley Projects", Doc. WRD 24(596), September 2011. Available at <http://www.bis.org.in/sf/WRD_24%28596%29.pdf>
(accessed 2 November 2012).

CDB [Caribbean Development Bank] and CARICOM [Caribbean Community]
Secretariat (2004) *Sourcebook on the Integration of Natural Hazards into the
Environmental Impact Assessment (EIA) Process: NHIA-EIA Sourcebook.*
Bridgetown, Barbados: Caribbean Development Bank. Available at <http://
www.caribank.org/uploads/projects-programmes/disastersclimate-change/
reports-and-publications/Source%20Book5.pdf> (accessed 2 November 2012).

Dalal-Clayton, B. and B. Sadler (1999) "Strategic Environmental Assessment: A
Rapidly Evolving Approach". Environmental Planning Issues No. 18, International Institute for Environment and Development, London.

DFID [Department for International Development] (2003) *Environment Guide:
A Guide to Environmental Screening.* London: DFID. Available at <http://www.
dfid.gov.uk/Documents/publications/environment-guide-2003.pdf> (accessed 2
November 2012).

ECT [Environment Conservation Team] (2005) "Environment Impact Assessment
Process in India and the Drawbacks". Vasundhara, Bhubaneshwar. Available at
<http://www.freewebs.com/epgorissa/ENVIRONMENT%20IMPACT%20
ASSESSMENT%20PROCESS%20IN%20INDIA%20AND%20THE%20
DRAWBACKS-1.pdf> (accessed 2 November 2012).

EEAC [European Environmental and Sustainable Development Advisory Coun-
cils] Working Group Governance (2009) *Sustainable Development and the Governance of Long-term Decisions.* RMNO-series Preliminary studies and
background studies no. V.17. The Hague: RMNO (Advisory Council for Research on Spatial Planning, Nature and the Environment). Available at <http://
www.eeac.eu/download/EEAC_WG_GOV_SDGovernanceLong-termDecisions_
1009_final.pdf> (accessed 2 November 2012).

Environmental Management Bureau (2011) *EIA Technical Guidelines Incorpo-
rating Disaster Risk Reduction (DRR) and Climate Change Adaptation (CCA)
Concerns.* Memorandum Circular 2011-005, Department of Environment and
Natural Resources, Republic of the Philippines. Available at <http://www.emb.
gov.ph/eia-new/MC-2011-005/PDF%20Copy/PDF%20Files.pdf> (accessed 2
November 2012).

GRRT [Green Recovery and Reconstruction Toolkit] (2010) "Green Recovery
& Reconstruction: Training Toolkit for Humanitarian Aid", <http://green-
recovery.org/?page_id=2> (accessed 2 November 2012).

Gupta, A.K. (2010) "Policies, Strategies and Options for Disaster Risk Reduction
Interventions in India". In A.K. Gupta et al. (eds), *Risk to Resilience: Strategic
Tools for Disaster Risk Management. Proceedings of the International Work-*

shop, 3–4 February 2009. New Delhi: National Institute of Disaster Management; Boulder, CO: ISET.

Gupta, A.K. and S.S. Nair (2010) "Policies, Strategies and Options for Disaster Risk Reduction in India". In A.K. Gupta et al. (eds), *Risk to Resilience: Strategic Tools for Disaster Risk Management. Proceedings of the International Workshop, 3–4 February 2009*. New Delhi: National Institute of Disaster Management; Boulder, CO: ISET, pp. 87–91.

Gupta, A.K. and S.S. Nair (eds) (2011) "Environmental Knowledge for Disaster Risk Management – Concept Note". In National Institute of Disaster Management, New Delhi, and GIZ, Germany (eds), *Abstract Book of the International Conference, 9–10 May 2011, New Delhi*.

Gupta, A.K. and S.S. Nair (eds) (2012) *Ecosystem Approach to Disaster Risk Reduction*. New Delhi: National Institute of Disaster Management.

Gupta, A.K. and M. Yunus (2004) "India and WSSD (Rio+10) Johannesburg: Issues of National Concern and International Strategies". *Current Science* 87(1): 37–43.

Gupta, A.K. et al. (1999) "Environmental-Health Assessment of Thermal Power Project within the Scope of EIA and Risk Analysis: Guideview". In *Proceedings of National Seminar on Energy & Environment, Lucknow, July 1999*, pp. 86–95.

Gupta, A.K., A. Kumar, J. Misra and M. Yunus (2002a) "EIA and Disaster Management: Principles, Methodological Approach and Application". In Y.C. Tripathi and G. Tripathi (eds), *Bioresources and Environment*. New Delhi: Campus Books International, pp. 150–177.

Gupta, A.K. et al. (2002b) "Environmental Risk Mapping Approach – Risk Minimizing Tool in Developing Countries". *Journal of Cleaner Production* 10: 271–281.

Gupta, A.K. et al. (2002c) "Environmental Impact Assessment and Disaster Management: Emerging Disciplines of Higher Education and Practice". In P. Srivastava and D.P. Singh (eds), *Environmental Education*. New Delhi: Anmol Publishers, pp. 7–23.

IADB [Inter-American Development Bank] (1999) *Reducing Vulnerability to Natural Hazards: Lessons Learned from Hurricane Mitch. A Strategy Paper on Environmental Management*. Working Paper, Stockholm, Sweden.

IPCC [Intergovernmental Panel on Climate Change] (2012) *Special Report: Managing the Risks of Extreme Events and Disasters to Advance Climate Change Adaptation (SREX)*. [Field, C.B., V. Barros, T.F. Stocker, D. Qin, D.J. Dokken, K.L. Ebi, M.D. Mastrandrea, K.J. Mach, G.-K. Plattner, S.K. Allen, M. Tignor, and P.M. Midgley (eds.)]. A Special Report of Working Groups I and II of the Intergovernmental Panel on Climate Change. Cambridge, UK, and New York, NY, USA: Cambridge University Press. Available at <http://www.ipcc-wg2.gov/SREX/> (accessed 16 November 2012).

OECD [Organisation for Economic Co-operation and Development] (2008) "Strategic Environmental Assessment and Adaptation to Climate Change". Endorsed by Members of the DAC Network on Environment and Development Co-operation (ENVIRONET) at their 8th Meeting on 30 October 2008.

OECD (2010) "Strategic Environmental Assessment (SEA) and Disaster Risk Reduction (DRR)". DAC Network on Environment and Development Co-operation (ENVIRONET), Advisory Note. Paris: Organisation for Economic Co-operation and Development. Available at <http://www.oecd.org/dac/environmentanddevelopment/42201482.pdf> (accessed 2 November 2012).

Republic of Botswana, Department of Mines (2003) "Guidelines for Preparing Environmental Impact Assessment Reports for Mining Projects", Volume No. 1, September. Available at <http://www.mines.gov.bw/eia%20guidelines%20 for%20mining%20projects%20vol1.pdf> (accessed 2 November 2012).

Sida [Swedish International Development Cooperation Agency] (2002) *Indicators for Environmental Monitoring in International Development Cooperation*. Stockholm: Sida. Available at <http://www.unpei.org/PDF/PEMonitoring/Indicators-Env-Monitoring-IDC.pdf> (accessed 2 November 2012).

UNDP [United Nations Development Programme] (1992) *Handbook and Guidelines for Environmental Management and Sustainable Development*. New York: United Nations Development Programme, Sustainable Energy and Environment Division.

UNHCR [UN High Commissioner for Refugees] (2005) *UNHCR Environmental Guidelines*. Geneva: UNHCR. Available at <http://www.unhcr.org/protect/PROTECTION/3b03b2a04.pdf> (accessed 2 November 2012).

UNISDR [United Nations International Strategy for Disaster Reduction] (2005) "Hyogo Framework for Action 2005–2015: Building the Resilience of Nations and Communities to Disasters". United Nations International Strategy for Disaster Reduction, Geneva.

UNISDR (2011) *2011 Global Assessment Report on Disaster Risk Reduction: Revealing Risk, Redefining Development*. Geneva: United Nations International Strategy for Disaster Reduction.

Urban, F., T. Mitchell and P. Silva Villanueva (2010) "Greening Disaster Risk Management: Issues at the Interface of Disaster Risk Management and Low Carbon Development". Strengthening Climate Resilience Discussion Paper 3, Institute of Development Studies, Brighton, UK.

18

Opportunities, challenges and future perspectives for ecosystem-based disaster risk reduction

Marisol Estrella, Fabrice G. Renaud and Karen Sudmeier-Rieux

Introduction

In a world with many competing interests and multiple development priorities, the benefits of disaster prevention remain difficult to measure and sell politically in spite of some progress in early warning and preparedness (UNISDR, 2011a). Benefits may take years to become tangible and may need other intervening factors to bring about results. Assessing disaster risk reduction (DRR) deals with less tangible outcomes, for instance avoided losses; in some cases, disaster risk is never actualized, or will be but in some distant future. According to the World Bank and the United Nations, investments in disaster prevention versus relief are highly influenced by "politicians, voters, and the media on one hand; and foreign donors on the other, especially in poor countries where they may have some influence" (World Bank and United Nations, 2010: 111). Investing in ecosystem management for DRR is subject to the same constraints as other disaster prevention measures, but, in addition, suffers from a common preference for technological or engineered infrastructure over ecological buffers (World Bank and United Nations, 2010).

Although a number of influential policy documents[1] have recommended investing in ecosystem management and restoration for DRR, in practice ecosystem management has yet to be mainstreamed into DRR policies and practices, and these in turn into development plans and programmes. Policy-makers are still questioning the value-added of ecosystem management for reducing risks related to disasters and climate

The role of ecosystems in disaster risk reduction, Renaud, Sudmeier-Rieux and Estrella (eds), United Nations University Press, 2013, ISBN 978-92-808-1221-3

change (PEDRR, 2010). This book is therefore an initiative to fill this gap between policy and action by highlighting good practices for ecosystem-based disaster risk reduction and climate change adaptation (CCA). It includes discussions on a number of natural hazards, namely storm surges, flooding, landslides, drought and water scarcity, snow avalanches, rock fall and sea level rise linked to climate change; along coasts, mountains, wetlands and river basins; in rural and urban contexts; as well as in developed, emerging and developing countries in South and Southeast Asia, the Pacific islands, North and Central America, the Caribbean, southern and west Africa, and Europe. It describes research efforts by scientists as well as initiatives undertaken by national and local governments, communities, international organizations and civil society.

Although this volume does not claim to provide exhaustive coverage of ecosystem-based DRR (for instance, research and case studies on drylands and integrated fire management have not been covered), it contributes to the ongoing discussions by focusing analysis specifically on the role of ecosystems in DRR. This concluding chapter distils the key lessons, the challenges and opportunities, and the future outlook for ecosystem-based DRR, based on this volume's 17 chapters written by 57 professionals from around the world.

Key lessons

Sustainable livelihoods are at the core of ecosystem-based DRR

As elaborated in Chapters 1 and 2, improved ecosystem management has the potential to influence all three elements of the disaster risk equation, in terms of regulating and mitigating hazards, controlling exposure and reducing vulnerability. Subsequent chapters demonstrated how healthy and well-managed ecosystems can function as natural infrastructure that can regulate, mitigate and prevent the hazards themselves, as well as reduce the exposure of people and assets to hazard impacts (see, for instance, Chapters 3, 4, 5, 9, 12, 13, 15 and 16).

However, an equally important – though arguably less tangible – aspect of ecosystem-based DRR is its contribution to vulnerability reduction. Given the multiple causes of vulnerability (Birkmann, 2006), it is often not easy to measure the direct contribution of ecosystems to reducing vulnerability to disasters. Nonetheless, there is recognition by scientists and practitioners that sustainable ecosystem management supports basic needs and local livelihoods and, in this regard, helps reduce socio-economic vulnerability to hazard impacts (Chapters 4, 5, 8, 9 and 11). For example, in western Jamaica, one coastal community must often rely on groundwater from springs for potable water, because storm surges and flooding can cut off the one main road and water delivery for several weeks at a time, emphasizing the importance of protecting watersheds (Chapter 5).

For Tonga, Mavrogenis and Kelman (Chapter 8) emphasize the importance of linking ecosystem-based DRR and adaptation with meeting local livelihood priorities, in order to reduce local vulnerability as well as achieve greater local buy-in and ownership of ecosystem restoration activities. Van Eijk et al. (Chapter 9) stress that not all floods are necessarily "bad" and describe efforts in the Mahanadi Delta, India, whereby the state government and agrarian communities are working together to better manage flooding regimes in order to maximize crop production and flood regulation services provided by wetlands. In this regard, the benefits of ecosystems often go beyond DRR concerns. Sustainable ecosystem management provides multiple social, economic and environmental benefits – regardless of whether a disaster occurs – and is therefore considered a no-regret investment (Chapters 1 and 2).

Ecosystem management contributes to an integrated, cross-sectoral approach to DRR and CCA

From the viewpoint of local communities, disaster and climate change impacts are very much linked, if not often one and the same. Hence, efforts to better manage and reduce disaster risk are now being undertaken in reference to CCA, and vice versa. There is a clear trend towards greater coherence and convergence between DRR and CCA policy and practice.

Similarly, integrating ecosystem management in both DRR and CCA is increasingly emphasized. Beck et al. (Chapter 6) analyse increasing vulnerabilities to coastal hazards, including both storm surges and accelerated sea level rise (induced by climate change), in New York and Connecticut, United States, and formulate development planning tools that facilitate decision-making on ecosystem-based DRR and adaptation options, for example the protection and restoration of coastal marshes. Similar efforts were undertaken in western Jamaica (Chapter 5) and South Africa (Chapter 7) to incorporate ecological systems and sea level rise in the analysis of risk and vulnerability in order to identify ecosystem-based DRR and CCA options. In Tonga, community-based ecosystem management approaches are being implemented to promote both DRR and adaptation (Chapter 8).

A key feature of such integrated ecosystem-based DRR-CCA efforts is the need to work across development sectors and academic disciplines. Ecosystem management, DRR and CCA have traditionally been tackled by separate sectors and communities-of-practice (see also Chapter 2).

Gupta and Nair (Chapter 17), for instance, note the wide gap that remains in India between the environment and DRR sectors at the level of policy planning, governance and institutional mechanisms, which constrains efforts to adequately incorporate DRR in environmental impact assessments (EIAs) and strategic environmental assessments (SEAs). Common terms, such as "vulnerability", "mitigation" and "risk", are understood differently within the DRR and climate change communities.

Several chapters stress the importance of promoting cross-sectoral and interdisciplinary thinking and practice. Gupta and Nair (Chapter 17) recommend having environmental policy and EIA/SEA experts present at the highest levels of decision-making authority and institutions in disaster management, and, conversely, DRR specialists at the highest institutional levels in the environmental and natural resource management sectors. In order to work towards integrated DRR planning, van Eijk et al. (Chapter 9) suggest establishing national or regional risk reduction platforms that adequately represent the different sectors and jointly involve environmental and disaster management actors in all steps of the risk reduction cycle (see also Chapter 15).

Dalton et al. (Chapter 10) argue that natural resource management frameworks can no longer ignore disaster risk and they call for integrated risk assessments and forecasting, for instance in water resources management and water service delivery. The authors point out the major opportunities from bringing together the water and DRR communities-of-practice through recognizing the role of river basins and natural infrastructure as part of the solutions to reduce disaster risk.

Ecosystem-based and engineered measures may be combined as hybrid solutions

Another important insight gained from this volume is that ecosystem-based and engineered measures are not mutually exclusive, and, in many cases, combined approaches or so-called "hybrid" solutions are necessary and possibly even more effective. Van Eijk et al. (Chapter 9) discuss how a new DRR paradigm is emerging that employs a combination of ecosystem-based and engineered solutions to prevent hazardous flooding and integrates such measures with conventional early warning, preparedness and response measures. The authors point out, however, that the key priority when applying hybrid solutions is still to maintain and restore ecosystems and their services. Ecosystem restoration measures could entail engineered interventions such as dyke relocation, depoldering, lowering floodplain areas and the creation of river bypasses, as used in the Netherlands.

Dalton et al. (Chapter 10) also note that most modern flood management plans now include natural infrastructure solutions, such as protection or restoration of wetlands and floodplains, as part of a portfolio of strategies, owing to their unique ability to regulate water and sediment flows. Papathoma-Koehle and Glade (Chapter 12) further point out that a common practice for slope stabilization against landslides is bio-engineering, which combines the use of vegetation and engineering structures, for example improved vegetation and horticultural practices, coir and jute netting, or asphalt mulch solutions. Guadagno et al. (Chapter 16) discuss the successful experience of urban flood management in Boston, United States, where both engineering and ecosystem conservation measures were utilized.

Applying the "right" alternative mixes or portfolios of built and natural infrastructure should be based on rigorous analyses of their various social, economic and environmental costs and benefits (Dalton et al., Chapter 10; see also Chapter 15). Papathoma-Koehle and Glade suggest that the maintenance costs of silvicultural measures for slope stabilization are often lower than engineering measures. The costs and benefits of applying ecosystem-based DRR are discussed further in the next section.

Involving local communities in decision-making is key

As discussed throughout this volume, applying ecosystem-based DRR entails overcoming sectoral divides and calls for behavioural and institutional changes at different levels. One major enabling factor in successful ecosystem-based DRR is working with local communities and obtaining local buy-in and ownership. Lacambra et al. (Chapter 4) discuss the importance of involving local populations when considering options of mangrove reforestation, bioshield programmes or physical engineering solutions, so they can be more effectively integrated into local land-use planning strategies. Beck et al. (Chapter 6) describe their successful experiences of working with local decision-makers and community residents in developing environmentally sustainable and risk-sensitive solutions to coastal zone development.

Colenbrander et al. (Chapter 7) also stress the importance of engaging local communities, especially poorer segments of the population, in order to raise awareness of the negative implications of developing within areas of high risk and to jointly identify solutions that meet development priorities as well as reduce disaster risk. Mavrogenis and Kelman (Chapter 8) discuss the role of women as well as elders in gaining local support for ecosystem-based DRR and adaptation initiatives.

Ecosystem-based DRR is not a panacea

Both scientists and practitioners who have contributed to this volume fully acknowledge that ecosystems do not provide a stand-alone solution to DRR. Rather, ecosystem-based measures should be part of a larger disaster risk management strategy and viewed as complementary to other essential risk management measures, such as early warning systems and contingency plans (Chapter 2; see also Sudmeier-Rieux and Ash, 2009).

As with engineered infrastructure, ecosystems also have their own thresholds and limits for protecting against hazards. Ecosystem composition (size, density, species) and health status, the type and intensity of the hazard event, and other geomorphological and topographical features in specific locations all affect the effectiveness of ecosystems in hazard regulation, mitigation and prevention (discussed in Chapters 2, 3, 4, 9, 12, 13 and 15). Dalton et al. (Chapter 10) stress that ecosystems themselves are dynamic in their response to changes in the climate, to human pressures and to natural changes, and their responses are complex. Although studies in this field are still at preliminary stages (discussed further in the next section), there is growing evidence supported by scientists, researchers and practitioners, as demonstrated in this volume, that ecosystems provide DRR services, functioning as buffers against natural hazards and reducing socioeconomic vulnerability. Ignoring the role of ecosystems in the range of DRR options would result in missing opportunities for sustainable, cost-effective solutions.

Challenges and opportunities

There are several reasons why ecosystem solutions to DRR have not yet gained full acceptance. There is often greater confidence in engineered solutions and technology in spite of the high cost and physical shortcomings. This section will discuss what we consider to be the main challenges to ecosystem-based DRR as well as the opportunities in mainstreaming ecosystem-based DRR in development programming and planning.

DRR as a fundamental development issue: Land-use planning and ecosystem investments

We begin by highlighting the challenges inherent in ecosystem management as part of land-use planning for DRR. Because this issue is about where people live and the type of livelihood they have, most of the chapters have addressed land-use planning and DRR directly, indirectly or implicitly. A majority of the chapters describe various ways in which risk is created, because most human settlements develop in naturally hazard-ous areas such as coastlines, riverbeds, mountains or volcanic slopes. The various types of trade-offs or conflicting decisions that are taken over time, space and scale influence how risk is generated. Trade-offs and con-flicts frequently occur between, on the one hand, people seeking eco-nomic opportunities in productive yet dangerous places (such as coasts and river beds) and, on the other hand, governments' responsibility to keep people safe and ensure the sustainable use of natural resources (see also Chapter 7). Oftentimes, conflicts arise when private economic pressures for development are not compatible with public safety and eco-system management goals. Actors vary from organized real estate devel-opers to women and men migrating to informal settlements in economic hubs, to government agencies mandated to ensure public safety, to envir-onmental managers entrusted with natural resources management to planners involved in regulating urban development and land-use plan-ning. In the best of worlds, land-use planning should be considered the master plan under which all competing goals are negotiated and consoli-dated. Yet these goals may be considered mutually exclusive and need to be negotiated to achieve beneficial outcomes over time, space and scale.

Time

Land-use planning and DRR bring to light conflicting priorities between long-term disaster reduction and ecosystem management and short-term livelihood needs. In Tonga (Chapter 8), community priorities were clearly focused on short-term human security and livelihoods, which were at odds with the longer-term ecological and climate risk objectives proposed by national non-governmental organizations (NGOs). Community con-sultations enabled the NGOs to negotiate objectives to achieve accept-able outcomes that included both short and longer time-scales. Chapter 11 also illustrated the need to satisfy short-term human security needs while protecting long-term groundwater resources. Time and long-term plan-ning are also required for restoring and protecting ecosystems for DRR, because ecosystems need time to recover and mature, which may be dif-ficult when political mandates follow shorter time-scales. On the other hand, as ecological infrastructure matures, benefits accrue, whereas engi-neered infrastructure decays, requiring more maintenance over time.

Space

Trade-offs might have to be considered when it comes to the use of eco-systems in DRR in places where land is scarce. Setting up "green" spaces or vegetative buffers requires space and, in some circumstances, the lack of space might be a limiting factor, especially in densely populated areas where engineering measures may be the main option. In Cape Town, South Africa (Chapter 7), conflict over coastal space becomes more complex as urban growth pressures increase disaster risks and inequalities, and remaining green spaces need to be managed as natural buffers for disaster risks and also to reduce social inequities. Achieving positive outcomes will require strong institutions, regulations, incentives and community involvement in defining the importance of green spaces for DRR. The critical role of community involvement in negotiating conflicting interests over space was highlighted by several chapters. In Chapter 6, a community-based approach in the US east coast was employed to manage competing economic, public safety and ecological goals, the last goal being considered crucial for buffering against coastal hazards and protecting human settlements. Here, positive outcomes over a limited area were established through a "Coastal Resilience" framework, which provided the means for negotiating future development towards areas that are less ecologically and climate sensitive.

Scale

Land-use exemplifies the need for planning at both micro and macro scales. Examples of how such conflicts can be addressed are highlighted in Chapter 10, where integrated water resources management (IWRM) is used to manage and plan for immediate land-use needs and long-term risk prevention and ecological objectives. The Tacaná watersheds project in Mexico is a good example of how the issue of scale was addressed by the creation of micro-watershed committees, yet linked at the macro level through stakeholder consultations at the river basin scale. The project managed to improve DRR, land-use and ecological objectives by decreasing deforestation, reducing flash floods and landslides and improving early warning systems. Further examples of the need for macro-scale planning were given in Chapters 15 and 16; regional-level land-use planning is often critical to protecting watersheds for the provision of clean drinking water for many of the world's cities. Thus, land-use planning to reduce disaster risks can include ecosystem management through various tools, whether IWRM or integrated coastal zone management, EIAs/SEAs or community-level planning, which can be an extremely powerful approach to addressing multiple and conflicting needs, over both the short and the long term and at multiple scales.

Based on the many examples given in this volume's chapters, key success factors include strong institutions and regulations that provide incentives for multiple private and public stakeholders to negotiate conflicting objectives, and a political willingness to find common ground. Given the strong demographic, financial and political pressures behind urban growth, land-use planning and DRR, finding common ground may not always be possible. Unfortunately, it often takes a disaster to create windows of opportunity for collaboration, new thinking and a political swing, such as the trend towards "green versus grey infrastructure" exemplified by the shift towards ecosystem solutions for flood management in several states in the United States and in European countries (Sudmeier-Rieux, 2012). Ecosystem solutions mainstreamed into land-use planning for DRR will require considerable political commitment and resource allocations from donors and public institutions that create platforms for negotiating diverse land-use planning goals.

The economics gap: Valuing ecosystem services for DRR

It is well known that investing in preventive measures, including the protection of ecosystems, is more cost-effective than rebuilding after a disaster (World Bank and United Nations, 2010). Decisions on public spending for DRR are often based on cost–benefit analyses of various risk reduction options, including whether to invest in ecological or engineering solutions (or a combination of both). One of the explanations for the limited investment in ecosystem solutions for DRR is the lack of quantitative figures on the value of ecosystem services, especially in relation to their regulating functions and other non-use values, and estimations of returns on investment for ecosystem protection and restoration. The main challenge in valuations is that ecosystems provide a number of "free services" that are often overlooked or undervalued, such as clean water and hazard regulation, although the Millennium Ecosystem Assessment contributed significantly towards our understanding of all types of ecosystem values. Yet there are no standards for measuring ecosystem services and many studies are context specific, making it difficult to compare valuation studies. As a result, the economic benefits of ecosystems to DRR are often under-appreciated by policy-makers and planners. In order to enable prioritization of integrated ecosystem management and risk reduction strategies, cost–benefit analyses need to take account of ecosystem values, including the "invisible" ecosystem services.

Nonetheless, the tide is turning, and there is now an increasing number of monetized hazard mitigation analyses of ecosystem services (Chapter 2). For example, The Economics of Ecosystems and Biodiversity (TEEB) and similar initiatives to incorporate the value of natural capital into national accounting systems – such as Wealth Accounting and Valuation of Ecosystem Services facilitated by the World Bank together with several UN agencies, national governments, NGOs and academic institutions – are bringing more attention to the economic valuation of ecosystem services, including hazard mitigation values, and their subsequent incorporation into national planning and public investments. Even approximate estimates can be useful to guide resource management decisions.

Chapter 2 provides a number of well-documented examples of values of ecosystem services for DRR for all different types of ecosystems. For example, the economic valuation of coastal wetlands for hurricane protection in the United States was estimated at US$8,240 per hectare per year (Costanza et al., 2008), compared with US$77,420 per hectare per year in Spain (Brenner et al., 2010). It is true that discrepancies in valuing coastal ecosystems are likely depending on the elements at risk and the frequency and magnitude of expected hurricanes. This demonstrates how each estimate is highly context specific. Dudley et al. (Chapter 15) also quote a number of very specific ecosystem values for DRR, for example the Whangamarino wetlands in New Zealand with an estimated flood prevention value in 1998 of US$4 million alone (Schuyt and Brander, 2004). Lacambra et al. (Chapter 4) quote Rönnbäck's (1999) estimate for the global annual market value of capture fisheries supported by mangroves to be between US$750 and US$16,750 per hectare, whereas Aburto-Oropeza et al. (2007) calculated the annual value of fisheries associated with mangroves in the Gulf of California to be US$37,500 per hectare. Estimates for a specific location thus appear much more useful for decision-making than more general global economic estimates of ecosystem services.

To be of further use to decision-makers, future ecosystem valuation studies could strive to differentiate between ecosystem services that have an impact on the different components of disaster risk, for instance with regard to direct hazard mitigation or prevention, exposure reduction and the reduction of social and economic vulnerabilities, as measures of an ecosystem's overall contribution to risk reduction. In addition, valuation studies should capture the cost incurred in replacing ecosystem services should they be damaged or completely removed. For example, in Chapter 13, Wehrli and Dorren estimated that the value of protection forests in Switzerland along roads subject to rock fall and avalanches was US$1,000 per hectare per year, compared with a cost of US$18,000–53,000 per hectare for replacement by artificial structures. The first value does not take into account the additional benefits gained from tourism, wildlife or agroforestry; thus, this figure could be even higher. Chapter 15 quotes the estimated value of a flood defence scheme in north-eastern Argentina based on environmental protection, including wetland protection and management, at US$3.6 million, compared with a total investment of US$488 million in river basin flood defences, which led to significant changes in state and municipal regulations in four provinces (Quintero, 2007).

More innovative financial and regulatory incentives are needed to further promote ecosystem solutions to DRR. As highlighted in Chapter 15, the monetary undervaluation of ecosystem services remains an important obstacle to the adoption of ecosystem-based DRR, with few countries taking advantage of tools such as "payments for ecosystem services" (UNISDR, 2011a). Examples include payments for protecting watersheds for drinking water as well as downstream flooding, which could attract both public and private investments (PEDRR, 2011). Local governments can create innovative financial and regulatory incentives, such as through "green permitting schemes", for promoting more "green" infrastructure and technology not only to provide cooler and healthier cities but also to reduce flood risks (Chapter 16). New infrastructure projects at local and national levels can be given financial and regulatory incentives to comply with both DRR and ecological requirements through EIAs and SEAs (Chapter 17).

From the many valuation studies quoted throughout this volume, we can also conclude that, in spite of the challenges in estimating values, ecosystems provide multiple direct and indirect benefits for DRR (for example, enhancing human well-being through cultural, aesthetic and recreation services that cannot easily be valued or provided by man-made structures). A word of caution, therefore, is also warranted with regard to over-monetizing all values related to ecosystem services. For example, van Eijk et al. (Chapter 9) illustrate the value of naturally dynamic rivers for fishery resources, the well-known creation of favourable conditions for agricultural production and water purification without necessarily attributing specific economic figures. It is also possible to quantify ecosystem services for DRR based on scientific analytical tools (Chapters 3, 4, 5, 12, 13 and 14) without necessarily attaching monetary figures, which may be disputed. Nonetheless, economic valuations will remain important in order to estimate the costs of damaging or destroying ecosystems, which need to be compensated through the public or private sector, and to influence policy decisions in support of the protection, restoration and management of ecosystems as part of DRR strategies.

Bridging the policy and institutional gap

Estrella and Saalismaa (Chapter 2), Beck et al. (Chapter 6) and Papathoma-Koehle and Glade (Chapter 12) note that, in order for the role of ecosystems to be integrated in DRR, two conditions need to be fulfilled. First, an enabling policy environment is needed, including putting in place integrated policies and legislation that will encourage ecosystem-based DRR. Second, when in place, these policies and legislation need to be acted upon and enforced.

Although addressing the policy gap on DRR has improved over the years, as documented in the *Mid-term Review* of the Hyogo Framework for Action (HFA) 2005–2015 (UNISDR, 2011b), many countries still have inadequate or no policies that address both environmental management and DRR under the same policy or legislative framework. Good progress has been achieved in Europe through the Water Framework Directive and the Flood Directive, which countries such as the United Kingdom, France and the Netherlands have translated into integrated flood management and water resources management strategies (Sudmeier-Rieux, 2012). Ecosystem-based DRR can be achieved only if natural resources are restored to optimal levels of functionality. This requires a shift in policy priorities and institutional mandates.

Significant progress can be achieved in promoting ecosystem-based DRR approaches by ensuring that disaster risks and disaster risk reduction are addressed explicitly in environmental policies and legislative frameworks and that environmental management institutions integrate DRR fully into their mandates. In Mozambique, the National Water Policy in 2000 was amended to incorporate flood and drought risk management through improving water service delivery. This facilitated the establishment of an institutional support network for water and sanitation services, including in the context of emergencies (Chapter 11). Papathoma-Koehle and Glade (Chapter 12) and Wehrli and Dorren (Chapter 13) cite forest legislation in several alpine countries (such as Austria and Switzerland) that recognizes the hazard protection functions of forests, for instance against landslides, snow avalanches and rock fall. Gupta and Nair (Chapter 17) discuss how DRR is being integrated into EIA legislation in different countries and argue for enhanced implementation of such integrated EIA practices. See also Dudley et al. (Chapter 15) for the specific case of protected areas.

Recognizing the environmental drivers of risk and the role of environmental management in DRR policies and legislation is equally critical in facilitating increased cooperation between environmental and disaster management agencies and in lending support to ecosystem-based DRR solutions, such as the Philippines' National Disaster Risk Reduction and Management Framework (Republic Act No. 10121). Beck et al. (Chapter 6) discuss mismatching and conflicting mandates between institutions working on environmental management, DRR and climate change, which constrain efforts to address problems jointly. In some instances, new DRR policy and legislative frameworks are needed that would clearly articulate the roles and mandates of the various government institutions in delivering their specific DRR-related priorities.

There are several sectors where the integration of ecosystem management and DRR concerns could be better maximized in the respective policies and operating frameworks, for instance in water resources management (Chapter 10), coastal zone management (Chapters 5, 6 and 7), protected area management (Chapter 15), forest management (Chapters 12, 13 and 14) and urban and land-use planning (Chapter 16). Sustainable drylands management for effective drought management is another important cross-cutting sector requiring better-integrated planning (United Nations Environment Management Group, 2011).

Developing capacities for ecosystem-based DRR

At the heart of the institutional challenges for mainstreaming ecosystem management with DRR is the limited extent or lack of institutional and human capacities. As outlined by Estrella and Saalismaa (Chapter 2), it is important to integrate the role of ecosystem management in DRR training programmes and to continue developing specific ecosystem-based DRR training modules and courses. These courses are required at every level: in primary and secondary schools, in training programmes targeting both professionals (including NGO staff) and public officials, and in tertiary education systems (Chapters 2, 8 and 17). Hosting national and regional forums that facilitate the exchange of knowledge and experiences of ecosystem-based DRR and CCA is another way to support capacity development (Chapter 8).

Capacity development means enhancing awareness and skills at the country level and in communities and mainstreaming such integrated approaches into national and local development planning. Fogde et al. (Chapter 11) and Mavrogenis and Kelman (Chapter 8) stress the importance of strengthening capacities in communities and "learning by doing", so that ecosystem-based DRR initiatives build local self-reliance in the face of emergencies and harness traditional ecological knowledge and local experience. However, in order to support community capacity development, an enabling national policy environment is needed to facilitate local empowerment and community participation in decision-making processes.

Another critical aspect of capacity development is improving access to information to guide and inform decision-making. More decision-making support tools are needed, such as those being developed and tested by Beck et al. in the United States (Chapter 6) and Colenbrander et al. in South Africa (Chapter 7). These are based on establishing robust and reasonable scenarios of impacts and alternatives, which become critical in facilitating dialogue among stakeholders and handling conflicting interests. Wehrli and Dorren (Chapter 13) discuss establishing standardized decision-making processes to support the management of protection forests, for instance through the use of a checklist, forest simulation models and stringent monitoring. Gupta and Nair (Chapter 17) propose using EIAs as a decision support system and information tool to inform planning through all stages of disaster risk management.

Integrating the role of ecosystems into risk assessments can also help improve decision-making. Risk assessments often fail to incorporate the regulatory and protection functions of ecosystems – for example, analysing the role of coastal ecosystems in shoreline protection (Chapter 5) or the presence of vegetation surrounding the exposed elements at risk (Chapter 12). By integrating ecosystem services in disaster risk assessments, risk reduction experts can gain critical insights into the way in which specific environmental conditions drive or reduce risk.

Scientific knowledge gaps: The need for more research

There is already solid empirical evidence that ecosystem-based DRR works in many contexts, as highlighted in preceding chapters. This approach allows for the exposure and vulnerability of social and ecological systems to hazards to be reduced and also contributes to CCA. This is particularly true when we consider healthy and functioning ecosystems. However, ecosystem management alone will not lead to the achievement of all DRR and CCA goals (see Dudley et al., Chapter 15).

Despite the wealth of knowledge available on the role of ecosystems in DRR, many gaps still need to be addressed by the scientific community, some of which were mentioned in Chapter 1. We identify here two general areas where further research is required.

First, although there is good empirical evidence that healthy ecosystems reduce risks for some hazards (in particular, hydro-meteorological hazards), we have limited understanding of their role when these hazards become more frequent or more extreme or when ecosystems are degraded. For example, there is evidence that healthy mangroves and other coastal vegetation types can effectively buffer populations against many types of coastal hazards such as storm surges (Chapters 3 and 4). However, their role in high-magnitude and, in some regions, low-frequency events, such as tsunamis, still needs further investigation and can be very locally specific. Similar conclusions can be drawn for other hazard types such as floods, droughts or landslides. Linked to this, we need to move from a focus on single hazards to consideration of multiple hazards. This is not easy to achieve because the role of ecosystems can vary greatly between locations and for different hazard types. Further efforts are required in understanding better and characterizing more systematically the role of ecosystems in exposure and vulnerability reduction as well as in increasing the coping capacities of systems (that is, local communities) affected by these hazards.

Second, there is a need for broader-scale research, which would complement localized investigations that typically focus on a narrower set of research questions. The research objectives should be designed to include criteria for upscaling approaches and/or replicability through, for example, the provision of clear guidelines to steer implementation. Similarly, research needs to address the complexity of coupled social and ecological systems, as described by Colenbrander et al. (Chapter 7) and others in this volume. This type of research needs to be both multidisciplinary and interdisciplinary. In many cases, research is still piecemeal, and so-called interdisciplinary projects may still work by discipline rather than being fully integrated.

Beyond these broader questions, more hazard-specific research gaps have been identified throughout this book. As highlighted by Lacambra et al. (Chapter 4), we still need to find out much more about the biophysical performance of mangroves during natural disturbances and about other factors that may reduce coastal populations' vulnerability to these disturbances. Research on ecosystems for tsunami protection, as reported by Hettiarachchi et al. (Chapter 3) and other groups around the world, constitutes a step in the right direction. Yet, to be of practical value to decision-makers, it could be enhanced with broader socioeconomic considerations of ecosystem-based DRR. Van Eijk et al. (Chapter 9) note that more research is needed to understand the role of wetlands and other ecosystems in terms of flood risk reduction, since what works in one socioeconomic and hydro-geomorphological setting might not work in another. Furthermore, ecosystem restoration methodologies require further testing and intensive scientific monitoring to ensure they are optimally adapted to a given context and provide maximum benefits at minimal cost (Chapter 9). More generally speaking, further applied research is required to understand ecosystem-based solutions in the context of both DRR and post-disaster recovery (Chapter 10).

With respect to landslide mitigation, Papathoma-Koehle and Glade (Chapter 12), Wehrli and Dorren (Chapter 13) and Jaquet et al. (Chapter 14) demonstrate the critical role played by vegetation in slope stabilization. They point to a few key areas of research that still need to be addressed: further refinement of models linking climate, slope hydrology, vegetation cover and slope stability; better understanding of the effects of vegetation on the different landslide types; the role of the vegetation surrounding an element at risk and how this element reacts when it is affected by a particular landslide such as a rock fall or debris flow; and the incorporation of not only changes in climate and vegetation cover but also socioeconomic changes in landslide risk assessments. In addition, Wehrli and Dorren (Chapter 13) consider that there are knowledge gaps regarding the effects of natural or anthropogenic-influenced forest dynamics on stand structure and their protective role against certain natural hazards.

Another key research priority is to bring together different schools of thought on vulnerability and risk assessments between the DRR and CCA communities. Fortunately, the need for this is being increasingly recognized by scientists and policy-makers (for example, Birkmann and von Teichman, 2010; IPCC, 2012; Shaw et al., 2010). Perhaps the best recent example is the consolidation of terminology in the IPCC Special Report on Managing the Risks of Extreme Events and Disasters to Advance Climate Change Adaptation (SREX), which was written by scientists from both the CCA and DRR fields of research. One of the outcomes is that the IPCC SREX report clearly links DRR and CCA within a sustainable development context (IPCC, 2012). Reconciling the two schools of thought could have many practical implications for linking actors, policy-making and practices that have often operated in separated spheres yet should be working closely together. This is important so that policies, practices and research can concentrate more effectively on finding solutions to saving people and assets as opposed to redefining terms or assessment frameworks. As highlighted by Mavrogenis and Kelman (Chapter 8), communities in particular are more interested in solutions to secure livelihoods than in distinctions between DRR and CCA.

One of the most critical areas for future work and research is developing more solid methodologies for including ecosystem services in cost–benefit analyses for DRR measures (discussed in the section in this chapter on "Bridging the policy and institutional gap"). Research on the effectiveness of ecosystems for DRR thus needs to be complemented by research on econometrics, that is, how best to capture the economic benefits of ecosystem services for disaster risk reduction (Chapter 2). Economic analysis and detailed studies at various geographical scales are two of several criteria that have to be considered to determine whether to invest in ecosystem-based infrastructure, in engineered infrastructure or in a combination of the two (see Chapters 4 and 15).

Some of the recommendations made above are not necessarily new and are valid in other contexts too, yet research on ecosystem-based DRR continues to be localized, to address single hazards and to be oriented to a single discipline. This is not for a lack of recognition by the research community of the necessity for interdisciplinary and larger-scale empirical research. However, there are limitations with respect to research funding, which still largely favours typically short-term, case-study-oriented research. There needs to be a shift away from this, with funding agencies considering larger-scale, multi-year and interdisciplinary projects that address both basic and applied research.

Monitoring and evaluating ecosystem-based DRR

Although implementation of DRR projects and initiatives has increased over the years, the monitoring and evaluation of DRR interventions have always posed a major challenge. There are several reasons for this. DRR is usually about measuring what does not happen or take place (for example, damage avoided). Also, because of the multiple drivers of disaster risk, single interventions can usually tackle only some of these root causes over limited geographical areas and time-scales. DRR benefits, especially in relation to vulnerability reduction, may become tangible only over the long term and may require many years of sustained investment. For example, the success of the MERET (Managing Environmental Resources to Enable Transitions to More Sustainable Livelihoods) programme in Ethiopia on sustainable land and water management to mitigate drought risks was based on over 30 years of intervention (Nedessa and Wickrema, 2010; see also Chapter 1). As a consequence, continuous monitoring and the establishment of baselines and targets are frequently not undertaken. Mavrogenis and Kelman (Chapter 8) discuss how the lack of baseline and monitoring data, which could demonstrate the effectiveness of ecosystem-based initiatives, inhibits confident decision-making and careful weighing of options.

In cases where monitoring has been undertaken, examples emerge of successful utilization of the monitored data. For example, Fogde et al. (Chapter 11) describe how monitoring was used to measure improved access to water and the reduction of outbreaks of water-borne diseases in the context of flooding conditions between 1999 and 2007, demonstrating the effectiveness of investing in local capacities in water service delivery. Such experiences show the importance of monitoring and evaluating ecosystem-based DRR interventions to provide evidence-based advocacy and to support making choices between alternative DRR options. Monitoring and evaluation will need to be incorporated as part of implementation and adjusted according to scale depending on the level of intervention (for example, community project versus national programme), types of stakeholders involved and the ecosystem services being monitored for DRR.

Future outlook

The year 2012 fixed DRR firmly in the international development policy agenda. At the Rio+20 United Nations Conference on Sustainable Development (20–22 June 2012), DRR was endorsed by the international community as an integral component of sustainable development and poverty eradication (United Nations General Assembly, 2012: paras 186–189). The G20 Leaders' Declaration following the Los Cabos Summit in Mexico (18–19 June 2012) and the ongoing climate change negotiations have affirmed the importance of DRR in meeting the challenges of development. In Durban, South Africa, in December 2011, countries committed to negotiate a new, legally binding climate change treaty by 2015, which would include measures to reduce and transfer disaster risk. Formal consultations have begun to reflect on what will follow the Millennium Development Goals when they expire in 2015 and how DRR might be incorporated into the new sustainable development framework. At the same time, formal discussions have begun to negotiate a new global agreement on DRR when the HFA expires in 2015.

This unique alignment of international policy processes presents a crucial opportunity to make a strong case for adopting ecosystem-based approaches in efforts to promote both disaster-resilient *and* sustainable development. Ecosystem management provides the "missing bridge" between DRR and development, in so far as ecosystems are able to mitigate or prevent hazards, control exposure and reduce socioeconomic vulnerabilities through sustainable livelihoods and poverty reduction. As the term "resilience" becomes much more mainstream in both DRR and climate change communities-of-practice, an ecosystem-based approach puts the spotlight on uncovering environmental drivers of risk and reducing underlying vulnerabilities as a keystone for building resilience to disasters.

The role of ecosystems in DRR is already captured by the HFA (UNISDR, 2005) under "Priority for Action 4: Reduce the Underlying Risk Factors" (see Chapter 1), but it is formulated in fairly generic terms. Future discussions on the post-HFA agreement should consider the role of ecosystems in DRR but in relation to development policy planning, integrated risk and vulnerability assessments, sectoral and land-use planning, capacity development, knowledge and technology transfer, the economic valuation of DRR actions in general, and addressing scientific and information gaps. In addition, greater attention and investment are needed to support national and subnational (local) efforts to mainstream and institutionalize DRR and ecosystem-based DRR in sectoral development planning, especially in agriculture, water, tourism, forestry, urban development and land-use planning. Finally, although increased attention is being paid to involving the private sector in DRR, its role needs to be better defined in relation to the various actors (for example, private business in key sectors such as tourism, insurance companies, large industries) and how it can best support more environmentally sustainable practices with risk reduction outcomes while ensuring their own business continuity.

Note

1. See Chapter 1; see also IPCC (2012), World Bank and United Nations (2010), UNISDR (2009 and 2011a).

REFERENCES

Aburto-Oropeza, O. et al. (2007) "Mangroves in the Gulf of California Increase Fishery Yields". *Proceedings of the National Academy of Sciences* 105: 10456–10459.

Birkmann, J. (ed.) (2006) *Measuring Vulnerability to Natural Hazards: Towards Disaster Resilient Societies*. Tokyo: United Nations University Press.

Birkmann, J. and K. von Teichman (2010) "Integrating Disaster Risk Reduction and Climate Change Adaptation: Key Challenges – Scales, Knowledge, and Norms". *Sustainability Science* 5: 171–184.

Brenner, J. et al. (2010) "An Assessment of the Non-market Value of the Ecosystem Services Provided by the Catalan Coastal Zone, Spain". *Ocean & Coastal Management* 53: 27–38.

Costanza, R. et al. (2008) "The Value of Coastal Wetlands for Hurricane Protection". *Ambio* 37: 241–248.

IPCC [Intergovernmental Panel on Climate Change] (2012) *Managing the Risks of Extreme Events and Disasters to Advance Climate Change Adaptation*. A Special Report of Working Groups I and II of the Intergovernmental Panel on Climate Change [Field, C.B., V. Barros, T.F. Stocker, D. Qin, D.J. Dokken, K.L. Ebi, M.D. Mastrandrea, K.J. Mach, G.-K. Plattner, S.K. Allen, M. Tignor, and P.M. Midgley (eds.)]. Cambridge: Cambridge University Press.

Nedessa, B. and S. Wickrema (2010) "Disaster Risk Reduction: Experience from the MERET Project in Ethiopia". In S.W. Omamo, U. Gentillini and S. Sandström (eds), *Revolution: From Food Aid to Food Assistance*. Rome: World Food Programme, pp. 139–156.

PEDRR [Partnership for Environment and Disaster Risk Reduction] (2010) "Demonstrating the Role of Ecosystems-based Management for Disaster Risk Reduction". Background paper to the *2011 Global Assessment Report on Disaster Risk Reduction*. Available at <http://www.preventionweb.net/english/hyogo/gar/2011/en/bgdocs/PEDRR_2010.pdf> (accessed 5 November 2012).

PEDRR (2011) "Managing Watersheds for Urban Resilience". Policy Brief presented at the Global Platform for Disaster Risk Reduction Roundtable "Managing Watersheds for Urban Resilience", Geneva, Switzerland, 12 May.

Available at <http://pedrr.net/portals/0/PEDRR_policy_brief.pdf> (accessed 5 November 2012).

Quintero, J.D. (2007) *Mainstreaming Conservation in Infrastructure Projects. Case Studies from Latin America.* Washington, DC: World Bank.

Rönnbäck, P. (1999) "The Ecological Basis for Economic Value of Seafood Production Supported by Mangrove Ecosystems". *Ecological Economics* 29: 235–252.

Schuyt, K. and L. Brander (2004) *The Economic Values of the World's Wetlands.* Gland, Switzerland: WWF.

Shaw, R., J.M. Pulhin and J.J. Pereira (eds) (2010) *Climate Change Adaptation and Disaster Risk Reduction: An Asian Perspective.* Community, Environment and Disaster Risk Management, Vol. 5. Bingley, UK: Emerald Group Publishing Limited.

Sudmeier-Rieux, K. (2012) "Ecosystem Approach to DRR: Basic Concepts and Recommendations to Governments, with a Special Focus on Europe". A special publication for the Council of Europe, European and Mediterranean Major Hazards Agreement (EUR-OPA), Strasbourg.

Sudmeier-Rieux, K. and N. Ash (2009) *Environmental Guidance Note for Disaster Risk Reduction: Healthy Ecosystems for Human Security.* Ecosystem Management Series No. 8, Commission on Ecosystem Management, revised edition. Gland, Switzerland: IUCN.

UNISDR [United Nations International Strategy for Disaster Reduction] (2005) "Hyogo Framework for Action 2005–2015: Building the Resilience of Nations and Communities to Disasters". United Nations International Strategy for Disaster Reduction, Geneva.

UNISDR (2009) *2009 Global Assessment Report on Disaster Risk Reduction.* Geneva: United Nations.

UNISDR (2011a) *2011 Global Assessment Report on Disaster Risk Reduction: Revealing Risk, Redefining Development.* Geneva: United Nations.

UNISDR (2011b) *Hyogo Framework for Action 2005–2015. Building the Resilience of Nations and Communities to Disasters: Mid-Term Review 2010–2011.* Geneva: United Nations.

United Nations Environment Management Group (2011) *Global Drylands: A UN System-wide Response.* United Nations.

United Nations General Assembly (2012) *The Future We Want.* Resolution adopted by the General Assembly, 66th Session, 27 July, UN Doc. A/RES/66/288, 11 September. Available at <http://www.un.org/ga/search/view_doc.asp?symbol=A/RES/66/288> (accessed 5 November 2012).

World Bank and United Nations (2010) *Natural Hazards, UnNatural Disasters: The Economics of Effective Prevention.* Washington, DC: World Bank.

Index

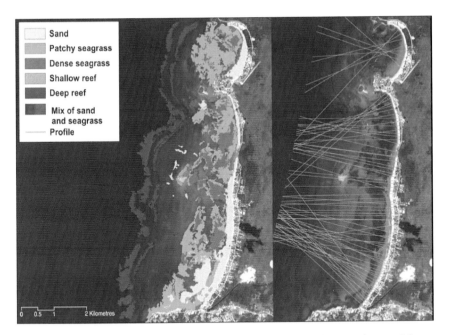

Figure 5.1 Distribution of the coastal ecosystems of Negril, Jamaica, and locations of the 74 beach profiles used in the study

Sources: Key ecosystem features derived from analysis of a QuickBird high-resolution satellite image (0.6 m, multispectral) obtained on 16 January 2008; beach profiles collated from SWI (2007).

Note: The fringing reef is found at about 20–25 metres depth (UNEP, 2010).

Please see page 113 for this figure's placement in the text.

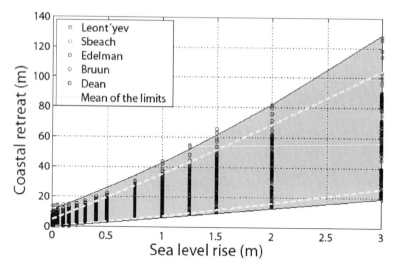

Figure 5.6 The means of the lower and upper limits of the beach retreats estimated by the ensemble models

Please see page 126 for this figure's placement in the text.

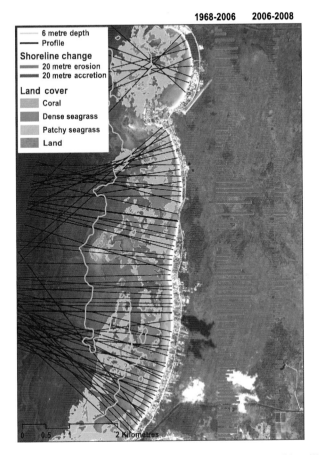

Figure 5.7 Near-shore bed cover and shoreline changes along Negril's beaches, also showing the location of the 74 beach profiles used
Note: Note the decreased rates of erosion at the beach sections fronted by either the shallow coral reef and/or extensive seagrass meadows.

Please see page 127 for this figure's placement in the text.

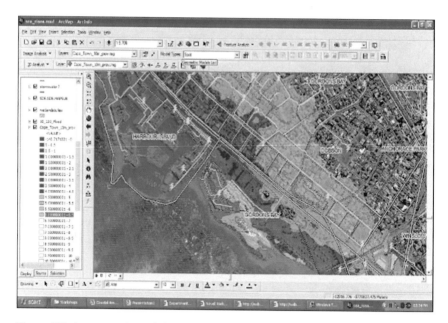

Figure 7.7 A screen-shot of the GIS Inundation Model depicting three temporary inundation scenarios, overlaid with the city's service infrastructure
Source: City of Cape Town (Environmental Resource Management Department).

Please see page 173 for this figure's placement in the text.

Figure 7.8 Examples of highly vulnerable areas in Cape Town
Source: City of Cape Town (Environmental Resource Management Department).

Please see page 175 for this figure's placement in the text.

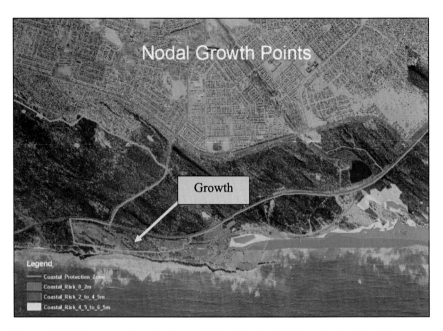

Figure 7.12 The coastal set-back overlaid with the GIS Inundation Model
Source: CCT (2010a).

Please see page 181 for this figure's placement in the text.

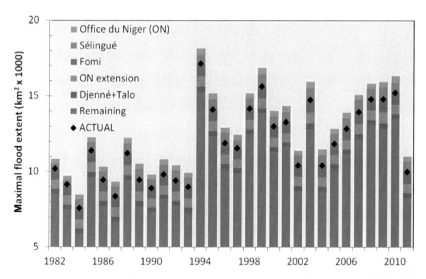

Figure 9.3 Measured and projected flooding extent in the Niger Delta, 1982–2010, under different scenarios: Without infrastructure (full bars) and if different existing and planned water infrastructures had been in place since 1982. The names in the key refer to schemes that have been put in place (above black dot) or that are currently under review (below black dot).

Notes: The names in the key refer to schemes that have been put in place (above black dot) or that are currently under review (below black dot). The decreases in flooding represent a massive increase in drought risk, because critical thresholds for maintaining ecosystem health have been passed.

Source: Leo Zwarts (Altenburg & Wymenga Ecologisch Onderzoek).

Please see page 236 for this figure's placement in the text.

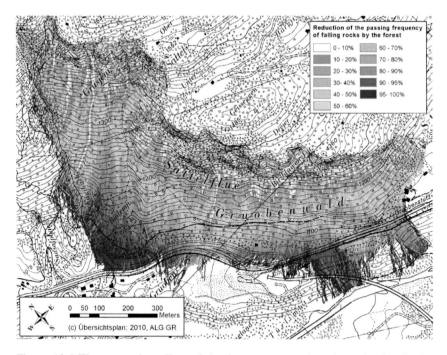

Figure 13.6 The protective effect of the forest expressed as the reduction in the number of passing rocks

Source: tur GmbH, Switzerland.

Note: To create this map, the current forested situation was compared with non-forested conditions.

Please see page 336 for this figure's placement in the text.